# Verdict According to Conscience

Thomas Andrew Green

# Verdict According to Conscience

*Perspectives on the*
*English Criminal Trial Jury*
*1200–1800*

**University of Chicago Press**

**Chicago and London**

The University of Chicago Press, Chicago 60637
The University of Chicago Press, Ltd., London

**Library of Congress Cataloging in Publication Data**

Green, Thomas Andrew.
  Verdict according to conscience.

  Includes bibliographical references and index.
  1. Jury—England—History.  2. Criminal law—
England—History.  I. Title.
KD8400.G73   1985      345.42'075      84-16227
ISBN 0-226-30610-0      344.20575

THOMAS ANDREW GREEN is professor of
history and law at the University of Michigan.

For Ruth
and for my mother,
Gladys B. Green
In memory of my father,
Alan B. Green

# Contents

# Acknowledgments

The essays that are brought together here to form a book on one aspect of the English criminal trial jury, 1200–1800, have evolved over a period of twenty years

That period includes: the years (1964–69) during which I researched (at Harvard and in England) and wrote (while teaching at Bard College) my dissertation on medieval English criminal liability; my Harvard Law School student years (1969–72), when I developed part of my dissertation into the article now revised as Chapter 2; the decade or so that I have been at the University of Michigan (1972–present), during which I wrote the remainder of this book, including the articles now revised as Chapters 3 and 8.

All these years, at all these places, I have been the beneficiary of helpful teachers, colleagues, and students. At the outset of a book that has in some sense been a collective effort, I would like to thank those who have contributed to its coming into being. Many who lent a hand (especially student research assistants) toiled along by-ways—*culs de sac*—that I left unmarked on the terrain mapped by the essays published here. But what has been included has inevitably been influenced by my consideration of matters I have not taken up. Save for those most appropriately mentioned in the preface of my book on the American criminal trial jury (still years—decades?—in the future), I include all of my students who played a part in my ongoing research on the jury: Bruce Howell, Jeffrey Liss, Margaret Mahoney, Neil Mann, Patricia Katzman, Jean Prchlik, Rosalind Rettman, John Dickey, Diana Pratt, Andrew Walkover, Robert Jerry, Janet Parker, Victoria List, Anne Sutherland, Lael Sorensen, Patricia McCune, Ruth Milkman, Karl Kensinger, Susan Tukel, Peter Tjapkes, Nancy Rosenberg, Audrey Krasnow, Lee Wandel, Ann Moyer, and Valerie Sax. Two students played an especially important role: Elizabeth Clark and Alexander Scherr.

Many colleagues read and criticized drafts of the articles mentioned above; my thanks to them are recorded in those articles. I also owe a great debt to those who read a part of the draft of this book: Professors Marvin Becker, Mark Kishlansky, Richard Lempert, Howard Nenner, Robert Palmer, Robert Seaberg and Stephen White; Drs. Francis Boersma and Edward Powell; and Kate Gilbert. Several colleagues deserve mention for their criticism of a draft of the full manuscript: Professors John Beattie, James Cockburn, Charles Donahue, Jr., DeLloyd Guth, Cynthia Herrup, Jonathan Marwil, and William Nelson, all of whom devoted more time and attention to my scholarly life than required by even the most generous interpretation of the "call of duty." But even they were let off easy when one compares their fate to that of John Langbein, whose faithful labors on my behalf over the last decade are beyond reckoning or repayment.

Among the many who have facilitated my research in England are: Professors Geoffrey Elton, Edmund Fryde, Brian Manning and the late Ralph Pugh; Drs. John Baker, John Guy, Sheila Lambert, and David Yale; Susan Reynolds; and Roy Hunnisett, David Clark, and Christina Cook of the Public Record Office, London.

I want to thank also the staff of the Beinecke Library of Yale University and Dean Harry H. Wellington and the faculty of the Yale Law School, where I spent the winter of 1976 as a Visiting Fellow. Two Yale law students served me as research assistants: Sherry Bellamy and Lois Raff.

My work in legal history began under the supervision of Professor Samuel E. Thorne of Harvard University, ever friend, mentor, and source of inspiration. This book is ultimately a product of my association with the University of Michigan, where I have taught, among other subjects, the history of criminal law in the Law School and History Department. Many Michigan students and colleagues have, over the years, listened patiently and responded thoughtfully to my musings about the English criminal trial jury. To the Michigan Law School community I owe a particular debt of gratitude, both for encouraging me to write the kind of history I have wanted to write and for supporting my work, with unexampled generosity, through the resources of the William W. Cook Endowment Fund.

I would like also to give special thanks to Dorothy Blair, who typed my drafts as fast as I could change them, and blessed me when others would have cursed.

My wife, Ruth Brownell Green, has, over the years, read and improved this book; it is she who provided the understanding and encouragement that made its completion possible.

I gratefully acknowledge permission to reprint revised versions of the following: Green, "Societal Concepts of Criminal Liability for Homicide in Mediaeval England," *Speculum*, vol. 47 (October 1972), pp. 669–94 (published by the Medieval Academy of America) (Chapter 2 in this volume); Green, "The Jury and the English Law of Homicide, 1200–1600," *Michigan Law Review*, vol. 74 (January 1976), pp. 413–99 (Chapter 3 in this volume); Green, "Juries, Seditious Libel, and the

Criminal Law,'' in Green and Richard H. Helmholz, *Juries, Libel, and Justice: The Role of English Juries in Seventeenth- and Eighteenth-Century Trials for Libel and Slander* (Los Angeles: William Andrews Clark Memorial Library, University of California, 1984) (Chapter 8 in this volume).

# Introduction

## I

This book treats the history of the English criminal trial jury from its origins to the eve of the Victorian reforms in the criminal law. It consists of eight free-standing essays on important aspects of that history and a conclusion. Each chapter addresses the phenomenon that has come to be known as "jury nullification," the exercise of jury discretion in favor of a defendant whom the jury nonetheless believes to have committed the act with which he is charged. Historically, some instances of nullification reflect the jury's view that the act in question is not unlawful, while in other cases the jury does not quarrel with the law but believes that the prescribed sanction is too severe. Order is imposed on the book not by time but by a unity of concern. This approach trades the continuity of a comprehensive narrative for a more detailed treatment of issues and events of particular significance.

With one exception, these essays are not concerned with establishing the fact of nullification. No one who has studied the history of criminal law doubts that on occasion this practice occurs. (Indeed, the practice is a central topic in many of the important studies of the social history of crime that have appeared in recent years.) What interests me most is not the persistence of nullification but its impact through time on the substantive law, on the administration of the law, and on the ways in which Englishmen—officials, jurists, and laymen—thought about both the jury and the law. It is on these aspects that I focus, and it is that focus that makes the book (at least in the author's mind) a general social and intellectual history of an important element of English criminal law.

In writing this book I have been aided by scholarship on the history of criminal law, and at times I draw heavily on such work. Some of my most important intellectual debts are to those with whom I disagree. This will be clear at a number of points where I state how my own view of the criminal law—of its administration and place in English culture—differs from that of those who have gone before. I hope that the reader will be stimulated by these disagreements and will find my citations to the recent scholarship that relates to each chapter useful. More generally, I am aware that the story I am telling cannot be told fully without a great deal more attention to many matters that, given the particular focus of each chapter, I barely touch. If this book provides a framework within which broader discussion of the subjects I treat can be placed, or if it stimulates scholars interested in those subjects to test the plausibility of the framework I advance, it will have served its purpose.

The separate chapters in this volume represent different styles of historical writing. The problem I examine is best approached through the study of official and lay commentary on the jury specifically, and on the criminal law in general. That literature is, of course, very sparse before the sixteenth century. Thus, early chapters draw upon medieval trial records, in the traditional mode of legal history, whereas the later chapters depend on texts of a kind familiar to readers of political and intellectual history. Moreover, parts of both early and late chapters are best described as historical sociology of the kind that characterizes much recent writing on the history of crime. By and large, I have not sought to minimize these differences in approach and tone.

Some readers may find the transitions both in subject matter and approach more than a little jarring. We are used to such differences between books, not between chapters in one book by a single author. My own view is that the analysis of most historical problems requires a variety of approaches and that historians may fail to exploit their subjects fully if they insist on a single approach or a satisfyingly consistent voice. This is particularly true with regard to legal history; for the development of legal doctrines and institutions is in part a matter of internal logic, in part a matter of the relationship between institutions and society, and in part a matter of pervasive cultural attitudes. But there is, I concede, another, more personal point. Simply put, I enjoy trying my hand at different kinds of historical scholarship. The justification I have given stands, but it is a fair criticism that, where there may be conflict between my readers' sensibilities and my own, I have consistently erred on the side of self-indulgence.

The essentially hybrid nature of this book is revealed in yet another way. I have tried to present a unified (if tentative and partial) account of the history of the criminal trial jury that will profit specialists and lay readers alike. The former will find some of the bridge material unnecessary; the latter will not wish to pursue some specific subjects quite so far as the text and copious footnotes pursue them. It is hoped that readers will make the use of this book that their personal interests dictate without feeling it necessary to focus on material presented for the convenience of other readers.

A final note: The history of the criminal law, long (and I sometimes think, mercifully) neglected, now boasts nearly as many scholars as there ever have been justices of the peace. Even criminals undetected in their own day, long since dead and resting peacefully, are hunted down, classified, quantified, and correlated—treated less respectfully, all in all, than those caught, convicted, hanged, and dissected. In the next several years, scores of articles and upward of a dozen books will be published dealing with the English criminal law before 1850. The present study makes reference to many recent and forthcoming works, but it attempts no definitive listing of the literature in this rapidly changing field. Instead, I have been guided throughout by an effort to make use of, and to cite, those very recent works that bear most importantly on the episodes in the history of the criminal trial jury that I treat in greatest detail.

# II

Most of the chapters in this volume are self-contained and can be read on their own. To aid the reader whose interests are selective I have tried to place each essay within the context of the unfolding story that the book relates. This necessarily entails some repetition for those who read the story straight through.

A brief summary of contents may serve to guide those whose concerns lie in a specific period or aspect of legal history, or whose curiosity about the jury, though more general, falls short of an obsession. Chapter 1 is an introduction to the institutional setting of the medieval criminal trial jury. Resting almost exclusively on secondary writings, it offers an interpretation of how changing institutional arrangements paved the way for the jury to play an active, albeit de facto, discretionary role. Jury discretion was most common in cases of sudden, unplanned homicides and in thefts that did not involve physical violence or housebreaking. In these cases, which had been settled by "composition" in pre-Angevin times, juries frequently manipulated the fact-finding process to prevent the imposition of capital punishment. They thus blunted the impact of the Angevin reforms, accommodating those reforms to long-held social concepts of liability and just deserts. Chapter 2 further explores this subject through an extensive empirical analysis of jury behavior in homicide cases. The law of homicide is the focus partly because of the relative richness of the extant evidence and partly because in homicide cases, unlike theft, jury discretion reflected opposition not merely to the level of sanction but also to the rules of the substantive law itself. Although homicides decreased over the centuries covered in this study, in the medieval period they were common and made up a very large percentage of the court agenda. As I shall show, the jury's role in homicide cases shaped the way people thought about what the jury was supposed to do. The influence of the jury's role in homicide long outlived the period of frequent homicide prosecutions and was felt in other areas of the law.

The impact of jury behavior on the evolution of the substantive law in the medieval period is the subject of Chapter 3. This important aspect of the relationship between law and society is one to which historians have seldom attended and one which readers not trained in law understandably find very difficult. I have tried to minimize the difficulties while giving the history of homicide doctrine its due. My hypothesis is that the relationship between law and society was one of constant interaction: the evolution of jury discretion reflected the influence of legal institutions and ideas that were themselves at least in part the by-product of jury-based discretion. Moreover, one of the few indices of the societal reaction to jury behavior in the medieval period is the approach that officials who were aware of that behavior took in the elaboration and application of the law. Although the central subject matter of Chapters 2 and 3 is the law of homicide, I have drawn inferences from developments in that sphere to elucidate similar developments in theft, the other common felony where jury discretion was frequent. I also discuss the relationship between the particular kind of jury behavior that I am describing in Part I and the administration of the medieval criminal law generally. Jury nullification of the law of sanctions, I suggest, was accommodated by authorities who did not foresee the long-run implications of their acquiescence in this relatively benign form of jury-based intervention.

Chapter 4 deals with changes both in procedure and in substantive law in the sixteenth and early seventeenth centuries. These changes involved the decline of the self-informing jury, the rise of the prosecution, and the development, for the first time in English history, of effective means for controlling the criminal trial jury. The question I am concerned with is how these developments affected the role and impact of jury-based discretion. The chapter argues that authorities used their new powers selectively and, having to some extent tamed the jury, continued to acquiesce in a substantial amount of jury discretion which the bench saw as harmless. The result was that while authorities provoked a reaction to their attempts at jury control in some kinds of cases, for the most part they further sanctified the ancient tradition of jury "law-finding." This argument requires me to establish the relationships among many early modern developments in the administration of the criminal law. Thus, Chapter 4, like Chapter 1, may be read as an interpretive overview and introduction to the two chapters that follow it.

Those chapters (5 and 6) deal with the emergence and maturation of the claim that the jury has the right to "find law." These matters require an understanding of how seventeenth-century writers viewed both the history of the jury and the place of the criminal trial jury in the English constitution. Chapter 5 focuses on Interregnum (mainly Leveller) ideas concerning law-finding. I discuss those ideas against the background of

the 1649 and 1653 trials of John Lilburne, and in the light of the tracts that
those trials provoked. Although some pamphleteers argued against the
legitimacy of the judiciary and for comprehensive jury law-finding, by the
mid-1650s the dominant pro-jury position accepted the judiciary as the
ordinary interpreters of the law. The jury's law-finding role was to nullify
judicial instructions in those (presumably rare) cases where the instructions, in the eyes of the jury, clashed with the "true" English common
law. Chapter 6 deals with Restoration thought regarding the right of the
jury to be free from judicial coercion. The centerpiece of the chapter's
lengthy narrative is Chief Justice Vaughan's famous opinion in *Bushel's
Case* (1670–71), in which Vaughan held such coercion to be unlawful. I
attempt to establish the relationship between the law-finding tradition and
Vaughan's opinion. To put it simply, Vaughan steered clear of that
tradition, but his opinion was subsequently glossed and appropriated by
late-Restoration proponents of the law-finding jury. These two chapters
introduce a major focus of the second half of the book, the ideological
relationship between the jury's "merciful" role in routine felonies, where
the community's quarrel was rather more with the capital sanction than
with the definition of crimes, and the jury's more dramatic nullifying role
in some political cases, where elements in the community viewed the law
itself as an aspect of governmental tyranny.

The last part of this book carries the story down to the early nineteenth
century. Chapter 7 begins with another overview, a brief discussion of
changes in the administration of the criminal law in the century following
the Glorious Revolution. There is now a substantial literature dealing with
the criminal trial and the administration of the criminal law in the
eighteenth century, and my own work ought to be read in conjunction
with that literature. The emphasis in Chapter 7 is on the way in which
some contemporaries viewed the role of the jury in routine felonies. As is
well known, many English jurists and lay writers who were influenced by
the Continental movement for law reform became critics of jury-based
mitigation. Yet, if I am correct, these critics, reflecting certain distinctively English ideas about the criminal law, lent some support to jury-
based mitigation even as they argued for a criminal justice system in
which such jury behavior would be unnecessary.

In Chapter 8, the last of the essay chapters, I address the political and
legal struggle in the eighteenth century surrounding the law of seditious
libel. The celebrated criminal libel trials of this period became the
occasion for a wide-ranging debate over the jury's right to find law as well
as fact. Passions ran high, and both official and lay commentators were
involved. I pay particular attention to the impact on this debate of the jury
nullification in more routine cases that authorities countenanced with
relative equanimity. The chapter concludes with an assessment of the

manner in which the centuries-long tradition of jury nullification influenced the development of what might be called the constitutional role of the criminal trial jury. I attempt to bring together two problems that are too often kept separate in historical scholarship: the daily administration of the law in routine cases, and the more episodic, and epiphenomenal, "political" trials that generated far-reaching claims about the rights of Englishmen.

Chapter 9 concludes this history with a brief commentary on the relationship between the role of the jury and the partial reform of the law of sanctions in mid-nineteenth-century England. I link this commentary to my concluding discussion and summary of the main themes of this book on the relationship between social attitudes, legal institutions, and legal doctrine. Here, as at earlier points, I assess the influence of the history of the jury on contemporary views regarding criminal justice and discuss the unity implicit in the centuries-long dialectic that I have traced.

# III

Jury nullification, the concept that lies at the heart of the various essays in this book, may take on a variety of meanings or shades of meaning. In some of its senses, the jury's war with the law and the judges who represent the law is a strong conflict, and in other senses it is much less so. Although I try to keep the different meanings clear as I write, I believe the reader will find that a general discussion of the term is a helpful prelude to the substantive chapters.

Jury nullification in its strongest sense occurs when the jury recognizes that a defendant's act is proscribed by the law but acquits because it does not believe the act should be proscribed. The behavior, in other words, is not criminal in the eyes of the jury, and the jury is willing to assert its view in the face of what it is told by the judge. An intermediate form of nullification reflects the jury's view that although the act proved is properly classified as criminal, it is within a class of acts that do not deserve the punishment prescribed for them. Such nullification serves to protect defendants from punishments that are regarded as excessive. A relatively weak form of nullification reflects the jury's view that although the act proved is criminal and falls in a class of acts that may well deserve the prescribed punishment, such punishment is inappropriate in the case at hand. When nullification is in this way ad hoc, a defendant, because of personal characteristics or the particular features of the case at hand, will escape the generally fair sanctions that a concededly just law prescribes.

Nullification begins in the medieval period with jury mitigation in routine felonies. It appears that the jury was in part disagreeing with substantive legal rules and in part merely mitigating the sanction provided by law. Because of the available data, I pay most attention to the subset of legally nonpardonable homicides that juries characterized as pardonable self defense. The cases in which jurors so characterized killings, and thereby preserved defendants from death, fall primarily into the intermediate category of systemic nullification of the law of sanctions but also, no doubt, contain instances of the other two types. It appears that the typical situation was one in which death was thought too severe a penalty for a wrongful, but victim-provoked, killing. In other cases of victim provocation the act was probably viewed as blameless in the first instance, and in still other cases there was an ad hoc quality since the defendant apparently benefited from his good reputation. Nullification in the case of theft, the other common capital felony, appears almost always to be systemic rejection of the capital sanction or an ad hoc merciful acquittal. The jurors had no quarrel with the laws protecting property, but they apparently believed that some kinds of theft should not be punished capitally and that specific defendants or those thieving in certain, special circumstances did not deserve to die. While the data permit us to identify such law-evading leniency, they do not always allow us to be certain of the jurors' motives. It is also probably the case that in some instances in which the jury appears to have been conforming, despite their sentiments, to the law, they were in fact engaging in ad hoc harshness. Thus, the refusal to return a life-sparing verdict for the kind of crime that usually elicited one may reflect disapproval of the defendant rather than the fortuitous assembly of twelve men who approved of the law or who, while disapproving, believed they should defer to it.

Later chapters of the book analyze jury nullification in political cases, and so engage true, or "strong" nullification. The state's problem is not that the jury disbelieves the proof offered in support of an indictment; rather, it is that the jury does not believe that the behavior the indictment alleges should be a crime. One major theme of these later chapters is the interrelationship between, on the one hand, systemic and ad hoc nullification of capital sanctions (merciful acquittals) in common-run felonies and, on the other, strong nullification (repudiation of the law) in political offenses.

The judicial perspective on the jury's behavior is significant, because our characterization of the jury's behavior must be made in the light of the bench's stance toward the law. Strong nullification, as I am using the term, assumes that the judge adheres to the legal rule and believes the jury ought to adhere to it. Thus the strongest form of jury nullification represents a repudiation of the rules set forth by the bench, and it is not surprising that it led to official attempts to restrain or redefine the role of the jury. This contrasts with the systemic or ad hoc nullification in common felonies, which frequently met with the acquiescence or en-

couragement of the bench. Indeed, where judges encouraged or acquiesced in merciful verdicts, we might wonder whether there was nullification at all. From one perspective, we might say that the bench was, in
effect, suspending the law, or interpreting the law in such a way that the
jury's action was consistent with it. Where the bench disagreed with the
jury, it might have viewed what was for the jury an ad hoc nullification as
an instance of systemic nullification, or it might have appreciated the ad
hoc nature of the verdict but believed it inappropriate in the given case.
In either instance, the jury's leniency might be regarded as a serious
abuse of the jury's de facto power. Political conflict has never been
essential to judicial criticism of what juries do.

It must also be noted that juries nullified the law in many instances not
out of mercy but out of fear of the defendant's friends or relatives, or for
political favor, or even, perhaps, for monetary gain. The bench could not
always be certain whether the jury's motives were mercenary or merciful,
and such doubts must have influenced their response to life-sparing
verdicts. Although this book concerns the phenomenon of "conscientious" verdicts, it will be necessary to keep in mind that some verdicts
were corrupt and that the bench had to guard against them.

Verdicts that reflect systemic and ad hoc mercy have, once we take
account of the bench's perspective, two histories: as quasi-legitimate
responses permitted by the bench and as illegitimate, law-flouting responses. As we shall see, some lay writers extrapolated from judicial
acquiescence in cases involving quasi-legitimate "nullification" to a right
of juries to nullify even when the bench objected. The bench, on the other
hand, sometimes viewed what were in fact ad hoc nullifications of the
weakest form as true repudiations of substantive legal standards. The
several strands of nullificatory behavior that I have tried to separate in
theory were in practice intimately intertwined, and, as we shall see, were
often confounded by those in the thick of the debates concerning the
jury's role.

Note.—Unless otherwise indicated, quotations from antiquarian English sources have
been modernized throughout this volume. Titles of antiquarian English sources have been
left in their original form. Original foreign language quotations have been extended;
punctuation and capitalization remain as in the original. All unpublished archival material
not otherwise identified in the footnotes is from the Public Record Office, London, England.

# Part I　　　　　　Origins

# 1    The Criminal Trial Jury: Origins and Early Development— an Interpretive Overview

From about 1220, trial by jury has been the primary means for determining guilt or innocence in prosecutions for felony. Trial by jury, as is well known, replaced trial by ordeal after the Church in 1215 proscribed clerical participation in that "barbaric" practice.[1] Although regular use of the jury represented a significant transformation in the administration of the criminal law, juries had from time to time been employed in this particular setting for at least a generation. The historian has more reason to ask why it took so long for trial by jury to become the general rule than why it ultimately replaced the ordeal, for by the third decade of the thirteenth century juries were in common use in a variety of other closely related settings. Trial by something other than a jury had become virtually an anomaly.

It may be that as long as the ordeal was thought to reflect God's will it was thought necessary to invoke its powers before putting to death an alleged felon. Men might on oath make determinations that affected the disposal of property or the payment of fines, but God alone could mandate the taking of a human life. And even if belief in the divine nature of proof by ordeal had begun to wane long before the decree of 1215 brought its use to an abrupt end, tradition may have sustained its use in the late twelfth and early thirteenth centuries—tradition and the lack of a divinely endowed alternative. Even after 1215, recourse to the verdict of men sworn to say the truth could not be had without the suspect's consent.[2]

The decision to employ a trial jury in criminal cases appears to have been an act of administrative expediency. The justices in eyre in 1218 had raised the issue of an appropriate substitute for the ordeal; they were ordered (in the absence of a formal trial mechanism) to imprison or to banish those accused by a jury of presentment of having committed a serious

---

1. Lateran IV (1215) c. 18, in J. Alberigo et al., eds., *Conciliorum oecumenicorum decreta* (3rd ed., Bologna, 1972), p. 220. See e.g. R. C. van Caenegem, "La Preuve dans le droit du moyen age occidental: rapport de synthese," *La Preuve*, Receuils de la Société Jean Bodin, vol. 17 (Brussels, 1965), pp. 715–18; John Baldwin, "The Intellectual Preparation for the Canon of 1215 against Ordeals," *Speculum*, vol. 36 (1961), p. 613.

2. See generally P. R. Hyams, "Trial by Ordeal: The Key to Proof in the Early Common Law," in Morris S. Arnold et al., eds., *On the Laws and Customs of England* (Chapel Hill, N.C., 1981), pp. 90–126.

offense.[3] It seems more than a little odd that the question had not been settled before the justices reached the provinces. The solution seems only slightly less so. It is likely that the order to imprison or banish confirmed an existing plan and that the decision to punish mere suspects hardly imposed upon the presenters a new responsibility. Having named all those suspected of having committed a felony, the presenters probably indicated which suspects they considered guilty. This may not have been a departure from earlier practice: it does not seem plausible that before 1215 all whom the presenters had named had gone forward to the ordeal. The presenters had probably always determined who the "true" suspects were; the ordeal may well have been managed to confirm the presenters' determinations. From the 1218 procedure to the trial jury was, according to this theory, a relatively short step: a number of the original presenters, afforced perhaps by others, were sworn to give a verdict on those whom they and the other presenters had named as suspects. It was not so much that the trial jury was adopted as that the ordeal was dispensed with.[4]

The resort to a trial jury in criminal cases was the final stage of a century-long evolution in the administration of the criminal law. Because that evolution involved the steady increase of royal control over the criminal process, it might seem paradoxical that this almost final stage placed the defendant in the hands of the local community. But, as we shall see, this was a natural development, one that at once expanded and defined the limits of royal power. It was a development that allowed the new form of criminal process to work. The interpretive overview presented here can hardly do justice to the complex legal and social origins of the criminal trial jury, a subject that has only recently received the attention it deserves. I shall piece together a story that, in its details, is both partial and tentative. Subsequent chapters shed further light, at least by way of inference, on the question of early jury behavior. The present discussion is intended to introduce an institution, its early institutional setting, and the problems involved in assessing its behavior and influence in the resolution of felony cases.

# I

The roots of a royal system of criminal justice run deep into the English past. Long before the Conquest, perhaps even from the outset of the

3. F.W. Maitland, ed., *Pleas of the Crown for the County of Gloucester, 1221* (London, 1884), pp. xxxviii–xxxix; T. F. T. Plucknett, *A Concise History of the Common Law* (5th ed., Boston, 1956), p. 119.

4. See generally Roger D. Groot, "The Jury of Presentment before 1215," *American Journal of Legal History*, vol. 26 (1982), pp. 1–24. I shall at several points draw upon Groot's important conclusions. See also Catherine Hamilton Kappauf, "The Early Development of the Petty Jury in England: 1194–1221," doctoral dissertation (University of Illinois, 1973), *passim*. For Kappauf's discussion of the procedure followed in 1218 see pp. 169–74.

Anglo-Saxon period, some offenses were prosecuted on behalf of the Crown, and those persons found to have perpetrated the most heinous of them were at the Crown's mercy. Unless the king chose to commute their sentence, they were executed at the king's hand.[5] These offenses—pleas of the Crown—may be contrasted to all other pleas, which were prosecuted by the aggrieved or his kin, though typically in a public court, and which usually led to composition or monetary compensation by the convicted wrongdoer.[6] At the core of the theory of royal pleas lay those enormities perpetrated against the Crown that amounted to treason. From very early the king also exercised sole jurisdiction over the most heinous offenses, such as murder—that is, homicide by stealth, in circumstances where the offender not only took his victim offguard but also concealed his identity from third parties.[7] During the several centuries between the reigns of Alfred (871–99) and Henry II (1154–89), the list of royal pleas gradually lengthened so that the number of "private" criminal prosecutions leading to composition between private parties was steadily reduced.[8] Nonetheless, until the twelfth century most prosecutions remained private; simple homicide and larceny, the two most common offenses, were still both privately prosecuted and emendable.

The expansion of the scope of royal pleas left its mark on even those offenses over which the Crown did not take sole jurisdiction. Offenders were required to pay a fine to the king in addition to the composition they rendered to the injured party.[9] Yet there were limits at this stage to the practical effects of the growth of the theory of Crown law. Even where the king took sole jurisdiction, prosecution was commenced privately, either in the traditional Anglo-Saxon manner, wherein proof was achieved by compurgation or by ordeal, or through the Norman institution of the appeal, which led to trial by battle.[10] Because punishment in Crown pleas

---

5. Naomi D. Hurnard, *The King's Pardon for Homicide before A.D. 1307* (Oxford, 1969), pp. 1–3. On Crown pleas generally see Frederick Pollock and Frederic William Maitland, *The History of English Law*, 2 vols. (2nd ed., reissued with an introduction by S. F. C. Milsom, Cambridge, 1968), vol. 2, pp. 453–56; Frederick Pollock, "The King's Peace in the Middle Ages," *Harvard Law Review*, vol. 13 (1900), pp. 177 *et seq.*, reprinted in *Select Essays in Anglo-American Legal History*, 3 vols. (Boston, 1907–9), vol. 2 (1908), pp. 403 *et seq.*

6. See e.g. Dorothy Whitelock, *The Beginnings of English Society* (2nd ed., Middlesex, 1965), pp. 137–46.

7. Thomas A. Green, "Societal Concepts of Criminal Liability for Homicide in Mediaeval England," *Speculum*, vol. 47 (1972), pp. 686, 689; Thomas A. Green, "The Jury and the English Law of Homicide, 1200–1600," *Michigan Law Review*, vol. 74 (1976), p. 416.

8. See generally Pollock, "The King's Peace in the Middle Ages."

9. On this fine, the *wite,* see e.g. Pollock and Maitland, *History of English Law*, 2:458–60.

10. On early modes of trial see James Bradley Thayer, *A Preliminary Treatise on*

was at the hands of the Crown, society may have viewed prosecution and trial in such cases as in the name of the Crown. Procedure, however, with its heavy dependence upon private initiative, remained largely the same as before.

The Crown's interest in prosecutions for crime was represented by the sheriff and the hundred official, who presided, respectively, in the courts of the county and of the hundred, a division of the county or "shire," where trials were traditionally held.[11] Central justices at times joined or replaced these county-based officials, although how often they had come to do so by the early decades of the twelfth century remains unknown.[12] Yet even the sporadic appearance of royal justices must have reinforced the increasingly royal aspect of the administration of the criminal law and eroded the once firm distinction between Crown pleas and private prosecutions. Possibly a significant percentage of simple homicides and larcenies led to execution rather than composition as early as the reign of Henry I (1100–1135). Even so, the reforms effected in the later twelfth century by Henry II were hardly less dramatic than historians have commonly assumed them to be.[13]

The Angevin reforms, whether they amounted to the creation of new procedures or the regularizing of preexisting ones, were embodied in the famous Assize of Clarendon of 1166.[14] The Assize is a complex document registering the Crown's concern not only with felony but also with the

---

*Evidence at the Common Law* (New York, 1969), ch. 1; Whitelock, *Beginnings of English Society*, pp. 137–46.

11. W. A. Morris, *The Medieval English Sheriff to 1300* (Manchester, 1927), esp. ch. 7. See also Hyams, "Trial by Ordeal," p. 93; A. Harding, *The Law Courts of Medieval England* (London, 1973), pp. 18, 28–29.

12. See H. G. Richardson and G. O. Sayles, *The Governance of Mediaeval England from the Conquest to Magna Carta* (Edinburgh, 1963), ch. 9.

13. Hurnard (*King's Pardon For Homicide*, pp. 8–9) suggests that many felonies had become unemendable as early as the reign of Henry I (1100–35). The king's peace was extended to cover slayings that occurred at specified places or on certain occasions. Thus, in Hurnard's view, the reforms effected by Henry II (1154–89) represented a coalescence of earlier, piecemeal extensions of the king's peace. On the impact of Henry II's legal reforms see generally Julius Goebel, *Felony and Misdemeanor* (1937; reprinted, Philadelphia, 1976), pp. 423–40; Richardson and Sayles, *Governance of Mediaeval England*, 173–215; Doris M. Stenton, *English Justice between the Norman Conquest and the Great Charter, 1066–1215* (London, 1965), pp. 65–82; Naomi D. Hurnard, "The Jury of Presentment and the Assize of Clarendon," *English Historical Review*, vol. 56 (1941), pp. 374 *et seq.*; Harding, *Law Courts of Medieval England*, pp. 49–57; W. L. Warren, *Henry II* (London, 1973), pp. 317–61.

14. Assize of Clarendon, in C. Stephenson and F. Marcham, trans. and eds., *Sources of English Constitutional History* (New York, 1937), pp. 76–80. The Assize of Northampton (1176) developed the program set in motion by the earlier assize, increasing the range of felonies to be prosecuted. The presentment procedure was not altered. For the Assize of Northampton, see ibid., pp. 80–83, esp. c. 1.

political, religious, and social matters that interfered with effective policing of the realm.[15] Henry II's government was moving decisively to assert its jurisdiction over trial and execution for all felony at the expense of existing, competing jurisdictions[16] and to ensure that local officials were actively associated with the royal program of law enforcement. The key to the new program was the procedure of presentment, or lay accusation made on oath in the presence of royal officials. The presenters were bound by their oath to report all those suspected of the commission of felony; all those thus accused were ipso facto within the Crown's jurisdiction. No interference with the prosecution of the accused would be brooked, whether that interference stemmed from lawfully held liberties or the exercise by the Church of legitimate privileges.

According to the terms of the Assize, twelve lawful men of each hundred were to be chosen to take the oath. No doubt these were to be men of substantial stature, men whose word would not be doubted and whose role in the process would strengthen the royal position. Although their accusations were supposed to be made before the royal justices, it appears that more often than not they testified before the sheriff in county court. The presentments and the process those presentments set in motion were monitored, mostly after the fact, by royal justices, whose regular circuits commenced as a result of the Assize.[17] The sheriff or justices ordered the accused persons to be taken and held for trial; those already in hand were tried immediately. Trial was typically by the ordeal of cold water. In this second stage of the transformation of criminal process the procedure of accusation was radically altered; the method of proof, however, remained unchanged.[18]

15. *Ibid.*, c. 7 (pp. 77–78): mandates construction of gaols; c. 8 (p. 78): requires holders of liberties to participate in presentment procedure; c. 9 (p. 78): states that no one may forbid the sheriff to enter land for view of frankpledge; c. 15 (p. 78): forbids giving lodging to strangers; c. 20 (p. 79): requires religious orders to examine reputation of prospective entrants.

16. The royal program was not so comprehensive as this suggests. For an excellent account of competing jurisdictions that lasted in some cases down to the fifteenth century see J. B. Post, "Local Jurisdictions and Judgment of Death in Later Medieval England," *Criminal Justice History*, vol. 4 (1983), pp. 1–22.

17. See Richardson and Sayles, *Governance of Mediaeval England*, pp. 198–202. The authors conjecture that the presentment jurors were to make their oath before local justices and sheriffs; they state that royal justices were deployed to "oversee the activities of the sheriffs and local justices" (p. 200). The account I give in the text should be taken as a model for succeeding accusations and visitations; the procedure under the Assize of Clarendon may have been almost entirely local. For discussion of the mechanics of late-twelfth-century presentment, see Kappauf, "Early Development of the Petty Jury," pp. 77 *et seq.* Kappauf concludes that presentments were often made in written form as well as recited orally.

18. Assize of Clarendon, c. 2 (p. 77). I use "proof" in the technical sense; in fact, the accusation process seems to have included a weighing of evidence that must be considered

The new, public procedure of accusation was mandated by the Assize, but it is by no means clear exactly what the presenting juries were supposed to do—or did. The Assize bound the lawful men to present *all* persons who had been accused of having committed theft, homicide, or another serious offense.[19] The words seem very inclusive; there is little in them to suggest that the presenting jury was supposed to employ a significant degree of discretion. Nonetheless, we have good reasons for inferring that they did employ some discretion. At the very least, the presenting jury was to determine which persons had been "accused" or were "publicly known" to be felons. If the presenters were indeed required to pass along the names of all those who had been accused, no matter how casually, we cannot imagine that all those named were supposed in fact to undergo the ordeal. The most recent scholarship argues that the presenters were not merely conduits for private accusations but that they also played an adjudicatory or a screening role. Presentment by the twelve lawful men leading to the ordeal involved a broader-based accusation, one that carried greater force—a greater presumption of truthfulness—than the bare accusation of an aggrieved party.[20]

Not everyone named by the hundredmen on oath could "make his law" by oath and ordeal. Not only those who had been caught red-handed or had confessed but also those of very low reputation were to be treated summarily.[21] It appears even on the face of the Assize, therefore, that the presenting jury was in some cases to make a finding of its own regarding the character of the accused. There is one other point worth making. Although we have very little evidence regarding the manner in which the ordeal itself was administered, there are reasons for supposing it was not

part of the method of proof. See below, nn. 20, 26, 35, and accompanying text. The ordeal of cold water involved submerging the suspect in water to determine whether God accepted him (in which case the suspect sank) or rejected him (in which case the suspect bobbed to the surface). The other common ordeal, reserved typically for freemen, involved carrying a bar of hot iron for a certain distance. If after several days one's hands were still deeply scarred, one was adjudged guilty.

19. *Ibid.*, c. 1 (p. 77): the "lawful men" were put on oath "to tell the truth, whether in their hundred or in their vill there is any man accused or publicly known as a robber or murderer or thief."

20. See Groot, "Jury of Presentment." Groot argues convincingly (pp. 5 *et seq.*) that the presenters were first to name all who were suspected but then to specify whom they truly suspected; only the latter were forced to undergo the ordeal. Groot's evidence does not allow the conclusion that the presentment jury's true suspicion always amounted to the kind of certainty later trial juries were expected to have before they convicted, or, for that matter, to the certainty the presenters would have insisted upon if their unfavorable "verdicts" were final ones. In this sense, the presenting jury was not a trial jury but was closer to our grand jury. I use the phrase "screening role" to signal this.

21. Assize of Clarendon, cc. 12–13 (p. 78).

imposed upon everyone who was, in theory, liable to undergo it. Moreover, many who were subjected to the ordeal must have experienced only a very mitigated version of it. It is, then, reasonable to suppose that the presenting juries were instrumental in the sorting out of the accused. So long as the method of proof remained brutal and blunt, the process of accusation was probably sensitive and subtle.[22]

The Assize and subsequent commissions to justices to hear and determine hundred-jury presentments constituted a significant advance where the Crown took control over the law of felony. All homicide and all theft were subject to presentment by the hundredmen. Private accusations leading to private composition, in the Anglo-Saxon manner, had come virtually to an end. Only the appeal remained, and, as we shall see, even this private suit was about to be turned into a means of generating accusations for presenting juries to consider.

It is difficult to escape the conclusion that Henry II's reforms, by substantially widening the reach of monarchical power, created new tensions in the criminal process. Private parties were stripped of their traditional remedy; royal jurisdiction and royal remedies dominated. The injured or his kin sometimes attempted settlement out of court, using the threat of appeal or public accusation leading to presentment for leverage.[23] The Crown, seeking to vindicate its jurisdiction, imposed fines upon defaulting appellors and upon presenting juries that concealed felonies, thereby limiting their discretionary role.[24] Although in some cases the king or his justices allowed concords between the defendant and the aggrieved,[25] most convicted defendants now faced mutilation or death rather than payment of monetary compensation. Inevitably, the presenting jury was being employed to undermine the interests of private parties in obtaining compensation for themselves. Perhaps more significantly, the

22. See generally Hyams, "Trial by Ordeal," pp. 93–94 and *passim*. I am treating very briskly a complex subject that has recently received excellent scholarly attention. Groot ("Jury of Presentment") and Hyams have revolutionized scholarship on accusation and proof before the Lateran Council of 1215. See also Peter Brown, "Society and the Supernatural: A Medieval Change," *Daedalus*, vol. 104 (1975), pp. 133–51. For an interesting discussion of the implications of some of the new anthropological and historical scholarship on the ordeal see Lawrence Rosen, "Intentionality and the Concept of the Person," in *The Theory of Criminal Justice, NOMOS*, vol. 27 (1984).

23. Hurnard, *King's Pardon for Homicide*, pp. 8–12.

24. Ibid., pp. 10, 24–25. Hurnard is concerned mainly with royal efforts to prevent concealment of felony by those seeking extrajudicial settlement. See also Pollock and Maitland, *History of English Law*, 2:648.

25. *Ibid.*, p. 22. See also Roger Groot, "The Jury in Private Criminal Prosecutions before 1215," *American Journal of Legal History*, vol. 27 (1983), pp. 132–40, for an extensive discussion of judicially allowed concords where appellors retracted their appeals in return for reparations by the appellees.

hundred jurors were constrained to set in motion a procedure that led to the mutilation or execution of many who, under the traditional system of dispute settlement, had been allowed a chance to make peace, to restore harmony through payment of fines.

We are not in a position to say how the presenting jury functioned in these straits. Our best guess is that the hundredmen made presentments—thus avoiding being fined for concealment of pleas—and then exercised discretionary power in the subsequent task of stating whom they truly suspected. If suspects of particularly bad reputation were not allowed to exculpate themselves entirely by making their law, it seems likely that the same discretion might be exercised to spare persons of particularly good reputation the pain and ignominy that accompanied the ordeal.[26]

The Angevin transformation of the criminal law was largely a jurisdictional revolution. By harnessing the prestige and knowledge of the most respected members of local communities, the Crown was able to assert its sole jurisdiction over virtually all those suspected of felony. Surely the Crown's first priority was to shore up the enforcement of law against those over whom the Crown already had sole power of punishment—traitors, murderers, and robbers—but who escaped all punishment unless a private accusation were made and sustained through the traditional Anglo-Saxon trial procedure. Prudence may have suggested that the Crown hear presentments of all felons; otherwise, injured parties seeking compensation might pass off the most heinous offenses as lesser felonies that were still emendable.[27] The extension of mutilation or (as soon came to be the general sanction) capital punishment to lesser felonies was a clear result of Angevin policy; it was probably not its raison d'être. Why lesser punishments for simple homicide and larceny were not established is difficult to explain unless we assume that the Crown either believed such offenses merited execution or, realizing the nature of the presenting and ordeal practice, expected such offenders would not in fact be subjected to capital punishment. As we shall see, the little evidence that sheds light on this problem is ambiguous. Probably we shall never know why all felony was made capital or how much discretion the Crown

26. Groot does not discuss the problem of presentment jury "discretion," or the refusal, on grounds of mercy, to send to the ordeal persons whom the presenters truly suspected. The evidence he has adduced—and no one has yet dug deeper—does not make clear whether presenters exercised such discretion. My account encourages the speculation that presenters played such a role; any excess in this regard should be blamed on me, not on Groot.

27. Hurnard, *King's Pardon for Homicide*, pp. 23–27. Hurnard thus explains the requirement for reporting all homicides and the need for a royal pardon even in excusable homicides. It seems likely that the logic of her argument extends also to cases of theft.

intended for the presenting jury.[28]

The half century that followed the Assize of Clarendon was the foundation period of the English common law. Henry II put the ancient practice of sworn lay testimony to work in a variety of contexts. In private law the grand and petty assize juries came to dominate;[29] on the criminal side, the jury of presentment was in frequent use. All of these juries, save for the presenting jury, rendered verdicts on the question of guilt or innocence, or on some other dispositive question of fact. In theory the purpose of the presenting jury was solely to name persons who were suspected of having committed a felony. In practice, it then stated whether it believed there was a credible basis for the suspicion. The suspects it exonerated went free; those it truly suspected were held to undergo the ordeal. By and large, dispositive verdicts leading to the severe sanctions of the criminal law were left to the ordeal and to God.

There was, nevertheless, sufficient leeway for other embryonic forms of the criminal trial jury to make their way into the workings of the law around the year 1200. The difficulties and dangers that beset the highly formal Norman institution of private accusation by the victim of a felony or by the victim's close kin—the accusation and process known as the appeal—proved fruitful in this regard. Persons who had been appealed and imprisoned could secure an inquest into the merits of the appeal before being subjected to the forms of physical proof available in such actions—combat or ordeal.[30] These early jury trials usually involved soliciting a verdict from the presenters who had presented the appeal (in effect, noted the existence of the private accusation) or from an inquest composed of similar persons.[31] In theory, the jurors usually were to respond to the question whether the appeal had been made out of "hatred and malice" (*de odio et atia*),[32] but, in fact, from early on the jurors

28. I shall return to this matter of the "original assumptions" in Chapters 2, 3, and 9.

29. See Plucknett, *Concise History*, pp. 357–62; S. F. C. Milsom, *Historical Foundations of the Common Law* (2nd ed., Toronto, 1981), pp. 130–43; Harding, *Law Courts of Medieval England*, pp. 58–63; see also Kappauf, "Early Development of the Petty Jury," pp. 69–71, 132–35.

30. See Roger Groot, "Jury in Private Criminal Prosecutions," pp. 113–41. Because Groot's recent article appeared as the present work was going to press, I have only partially incorporated his findings. Groot's work is central: it lays bare the workings of proceedings set in motion by appeals and relates those workings to the interests (often financial reparations rather than "punishment" of the accused) of the private parties involved. Taken together, Groot's articles on presentments and appeals constitute the foundation for the prehistory of the criminal trial jury.

31. Groot (*ibid.*, p. 126) points out that appeals in the central courts at Westminster could result in referral of an inquest to a local jury. At the eyre, the jury that presented the appeal was immediately available.

32. Hurnard, *King's Pardon for Homicide*, Appendix I, pp. 339–74.

looked to the more general question of the appellee's guilt or innocence.[33] It is not always easy to tell whether such inquests undertook full-scale resolutions of guilt or innocence or, instead, rendered a more modest assessment of the credibility of the private accusation (the screening process undertaken by presenting juries in public prosecutions). If merely the latter, we should not be surprised, for the appellee who received an unfavorable verdict had still to be tried by a form of physical proof.[34] Recent research suggests, however, that many early inquests pursuant to appeals were indeed comprehensive determinations.[35] If presentment-process jury determinations were limited in nature—and even that remains unclear—at least many appeals inquest determinations were not.[36]

There is some evidence that suggests defendants incarcerated pursuant to a hundred-jury presentment also availed themselves of writs ordering special inquisitions. In such cases the need for screening private accusations likely was not involved; that step had already been undertaken by the presenting jury. It is probable that defendants claiming to have slain through accident or self-defense were among those who secured the writs. Like many who had been appealed, they were not asserting noninvolvement or that they had been accused out of malice. They were claiming, rather, that they had not acted feloniously. Ultimately, they would seek and obtain a royal pardon; pending the eyre, they would establish their bona fides and secure bail. Others, too, obtained the writ, either to secure

33. Groot, "Jury in Private Criminal Prosecutions," pp. 118–24. See also Hurnard, *King's Pardon for Homicide*, p. 340.

34. Groot, "Jury in Private Criminal Prosecutions," p. 125. See also Hurnard, *King's Pardon for Homicide*, p. 343.

35. Groot, "Jury in Private Criminal Prosecutions," pp. 127–28. The use of the word "guilty" (as opposed to "suspected") is probably significant. In this regard, see Groot's remarks, pp. 129–30. He rightly points out that the same persons served sometimes as presenters of presentments, sometimes as presenters of appeals, and sometimes as inquest jurors in appeals. In practice, presenters may have done much the same thing in their screening and their inquest roles, whatever the difference may have been in theory between the two roles.

36. Groot's approach complements the earlier research on the appeal of J. M. Kaye, trans. and ed., *Placita Corone* (London, 1966), pp. xxiv–xxviii. Kaye argues that the appeal remained in use throughout the thirteenth century and that judges were not opposed to it as a means of accusation. Rather, the bench sought to avoid delays involved both in the appellee's various defenses to the appeal and in trial by battle. Thus the bench induced appellees to make a general denial and to opt for trial by jury. The groundwork for this approach to the use of the appeal had, evidently, been well established in the pre–trial-jury period. Kaye is probably correct in the view that Holdsworth overstated judicial opposition to the appeal. See William Holdsworth, *A History of English Law*, 17 vols. (London, 1903–72), vol. 2 (3rd ed., London, 1923), pp. 256–57, 360 *et seq.* For a recent study of the use of the appeal in medieval and early modern England see Daniel R. Ernst, "The Moribund Appeal of Death: Compensating Survivors and Controlling Jurors in Early Modern England," *American Journal of Legal History*, vol. 28 (1984), pp. 164–85.

bail pending trial or to avoid trial by ordeal altogether. Typically, these last persons paid a substantial sum for the privilege of what amounted to jury trial at the eyre.[37]

By 1215, when the use of the ordeal in England came suddenly to an end, there was ample precedent for putting substantial laymen on oath to say whether or not a suspect was guilty of felony. The prototype trial juries were very similar to their descendants, although the student of the history of jury discretion must recognize that the unfavorable verdicts of the pre-1215 prototypes were rarely final and thus may not have been rendered by jurors who went through the same psychological process as the later true trial jurors.[38] The institution of the trial jury had developed largely, though not entirely, as a remedy for the defects of the appeal that the evolving procedure of presentment threw into relief. It may in some few cases have been employed as a true alternative to the ordeal. But that step, which was momentous if not unprecedented, was not commonly taken until the ordeal was formally abolished.[39]

# II

It is well known that the institutions of presenting jury and trial jury were from the outset closely related. It would be too much to say, however, that, as of 1220, they were usually identical in composition. That was sometimes the case, but more often the presenters made up one part of the trial jury, which might be a larger body. This was a time for experiment, and it appears that the Crown was anxious that the trial jury carry real authority.[40] The trial jury undertook one facet of the parent institution's earlier role. Before 1215, that "screening" aspect of the

37. See e.g. Hurnard, *King's Pardon for Homicide*, p. 345; Kappauf, "Early Development of the Petty Jury," pp. 143, 164, 165. It is possible that had these suspects been "found guilty" by the inquests they procured they would have had to go to the ordeal.

38. A suspect who was purged by the ordeal might be required to abjure the realm. Groot, "Jury in Private Criminal Prosecutions," pp. 118, 140. How this prospect affected jury behavior we cannot say. The risk that the "suspected" person would not be purged and would be put to death would probably have sufficed to induce presenting juries to render merciful verdicts in at least some cases, if anything would have made them do so. See Kappauf, however, who reports that most suspects were purged by the ordeal ("Early Development of the Petty Jury," p. 167).

39. See Hurnard's comments (*King's Pardon for Homicide*, pp. 345–46) on Magna Carta, c. 36, which stipulated that "the writ of inquisition concerning life and limbs . . . shall be issued gratis and shall not be denied" (Stephenson and Marcham, trans. and eds., *Sources of English Constitutional History*, pp. 120–21). Hurnard contends that this clause referred not only to the writ *de odio* but to writs for inquisitions in cases begun by indictment. The framers of Magna Carta, Hurnard suggests, were anxious to create the right to jury trial in place of the ordeal for all who preferred it.

40. Kappauf, "Early Development of the Petty Jury," pp. 188–96.

presenting jury's role had been nearly incidental and never well-defined. It had been, I have suggested, largely a by-product of the traditional method of proof, the ordeal. The ordeal may have been seen as a ritual that confirmed the judgment of the lawful men of the hundred; in a certain sense, it may have been "rational" precisely because it was implemented in accordance with the presenters' own belief about a defendant's guilt. The ultimate verdict was seen to be God's; He demonstrated the innocence or guilt of the accused who, presumed guilty by men, was made to endure the ultimate test.[41] When the ritual was dispensed with, the two functions of the jury were separated and, thus, more clearly defined. The presenting jury proper now named *all* those for whom there was a soundly based accusation. If the defendant consented to a verdict by the "country," untempered by God's confirming judgment, he put himself upon the judgment of his countrymen, who were sworn to give a truly dispositive verdict on the basis of what they had learned about the suspect's guilt.

The trial jury's role in part corresponded to the earlier screening function and possibly in practice to the discretionary role of the presenting jury—but only in part. For one thing, it must have made some difference to the hundredmen that the ordeal stood between their verdict and the defendant's fate. The trial jury was, in contrast, formally charged with finding the guilt or innocence of the accused. Moreover, the trial jurors gave their verdict in open court, not only upon their prior knowledge but also upon their viewing of the confrontation between the accused and the bench. Thus, the history of the trial jury can only be understood in terms of the history of the trial. Since we shall return to specific aspects of the medieval trial in Chapters 2 and 3, a brief overview of its history will suffice.

The judicial eyres of the thirteenth and early fourteenth centuries were undertaken in a given county at six- or seven-year intervals.[42] They were administrative as well as purely legal undertakings. The king's justices in eyre were empowered not only to hear civil and criminal pleas but also to scrutinize coroners' rolls and other official records for notations of fines owed to the Crown. It is well known that these visitations inspired a

---

41. This remains unclear. Much depends upon what the presenters actually did, or were thought to have done. The more the screening process involved a full assessment of the defendant's guilt or innocence, the more the ordeal may have been accepted as mere confirmation.

42. On the judicial eyres see e.g. Meekings, ed., *Wiltshire Eyre*, pp. 1–9; C. A. F. Meekings and David Crook, eds., *The 1235 Surrey Eyre* (Guildford, 1979), pp. 4–26, and Appendix I: A Bibliography of the Common Pleas Eyre; Harding, *Law Courts of Medieval England*, pp. 63–80, 86–88; Milsom, *Historical Foundations*, pp. 27–31.

mixture of awe, fear, and hatred.[43] The judicial business of the eyre was routine and tedious. This must have been especially true on the criminal side, for the justices apparently heard an interminable series of presentments involving defendants who had not been taken or who had been bailed but did not appear at the eyre. The records contain many more judicial orders that suspects be taken than judgments upon verdicts of trial juries. Process in all of these cases was carefully noted; communities, frankpledges, and officials were amerced, the fines being inscribed on the eyre rolls by the busy clerks. The tedium was relieved from time to time by the trial of a suspect who had appeared and put himself, for good or ill, upon the country.[44]

Most of those persons who were tried at the eyre were brought forward after they had been named by the presenting jury and were asked how they pleaded. Virtually all pleaded not guilty and put themselves on the country. A few refused to plead, exercising a right that was by the later decades of the thirteenth century a bare fiction. They were subjected to the infamous *peine forte et dure*, wherein weights were laid upon them until they pleaded or expired; the recalcitrant perished, but, not having been convicted, they avoided forfeiture.[45] To go on the country meant, at first, to be tried by a body of persons that included some or all of the hundredmen who had comprised the jury of presentment.[46] From the outset, however, there were exceptions to this, and over the course of the century the two juries became increasingly distinct. Some defendants requested an entirely different jury, or challenged at least some of those trial jurors who had been part of the presenting jury, but it appears that defendants could not yet demand such a jury as a matter of right.[47] The

43. Pollock and Maitland, *History of English Law*, 1:202; Kappauf, "Early Development of the Petty Jury," p. 58.

44. Pollock and Maitland, *History of English Law*, 1:201, 2:644 *et seq.*; Harding, *Law Courts of Medieval England*, pp. 63–68; Meekings, ed., *Wiltshire Eyre*, pp. 16–23.

45. Plucknett, *Concise History*, p. 126; Harding, *Law Courts of Medieval England*, p. 67. See also Groot, "Jury in Private Criminal Prosecutions," pp. 137–41. Groot has found pre–trial-jury-period cases in which the bench ordered inquests (leading potentially to trial by ordeal) where neither presentment nor continued appeal was forthcoming. This, he conjectures, suggests ancient roots of later royal attitudes about subjecting defendants to trial on the Crown's own order.

46. Pollock and Maitland, *History of English Law*, 2:648–49; Harding, *Law Courts of Medieval England*, p. 67; Plucknett, *Concise History*, p. 120; Kappauf, "Early Development of the Petty Jury," pp. 188–96.

47. Plucknett, *Concise History*, p. 127. For an interesting case involving a knight who successfully challenged prospective trial jurors who had served on the jury of presentment that accused him (of rape) see Henry Summerson, "Plea Roll and Year Book: The Yorkshire Eyre of 1293–94" (paper presented at the Fifth British Legal History Conference, Bristol, July, 1981). I am grateful to Dr. Summerson for allowing me to see his important study based

real break between presenting and trial juries came in the last decades of the century, however, and accompanied the expansion of the system of gaol delivery.

We know very little about what transpired after the jury was sworn, whether at the eyre or at gaol delivery. The defendant stood at the bar, in the sight of both judge and jury; he stood alone, unaccompanied by counsel or friend. The sheriff or other official repeated the charges, then fell back, leaving the defendant to face the bench. No witness could come forward either for or against him, the self-informed jurors were the witnesses for good or ill.[48] Two voices only were to be heard: the justice questioned, the defendant answered. Presumably the defendant was asked what he had to say for himself and in most cases replied he had not committed the act with which he had been charged. We do not know how often he supplied an alibi.[49] Occasionally, a defendant who had pleaded not guilty to a charge of homicide admitted he had slain the deceased but claimed to have done so accidentally or in self-defense.[50] In such a case the bench had some leeway to test the defendant's story, at least with respect to its internal consistency, and even to attempt to trick the defendant into an assertion that fell short of what the law required for pardonable homicide.[51] In most cases, however, the exchange between the bench and the defendant must have been brief and productive of little hard evidence beyond that which the jury had in hand at the moment they were sworn to serve.

It is commonplace that the medieval jury was "self-informing." But just how jurors came to be informed remains largely a matter of conjecture. The problem is less intractable with regard to the early period. So long as trial jurors were drawn, at least in large number, from the

upon his comparison of a plea roll with the yearbook version of several cases on the plea roll. See below, n. 58.

48. This may be an exaggeration of the situation at the eyre. Witnesses as well as others were attached to appear at the eyre, either as witnesses or as potential suspects. It is not clear that they gave information at the trial itself rather than before the trial to presentment and trial juries. When the suspect did not appear they may have given evidence that was instrumental to his being exacted and outlawed.

49. See Kaye, ed., *Placita Corone*, pp. 1–31. This mid-thirteenth-century pleading manual provides the best extant descriptions of medieval trials. It must be used with care, however, for it was compiled with the purposes of instruction in mind. It is not always clear whether a particular procedure or colloquy was included because it was typical or because it was unusual. Most of the "cases" involve appeals (this was above all a form book for pleaders); the accusations and denials are therefore highly formal. In one case which has the ring of the commonplace, the defendant, indicted for theft of farm animals, claimed he had purchased the animals at a certain fair on a certain day (*ibid.*, p. 18).

50. See below, Chapter 2.

51. See below, Chapter 3, text at nn. 3–7.

presenting jury, the appropriate question to ask is how the presenters learned the facts of individual cases. The answer, at least in general, is not difficult to imagine. The presenters were established figures in the hundred. Although they were not likely to have firsthand knowledge of slayings and thefts, they were well positioned to make inquiries. They soon learned of complaints made to local officials, who were bound to keep track of the raising of the hue and cry.[52] In the case of homicide, the coroner's inquest provided a context for the gathering of testimony, little of which was taken down by the coroner or his clerk but much of which must have come to the attention of the village elites.[53]

Formal presentments were made in hundred and county courts in the years between judicial visitations. The rumors and suspicions that circulated in the wake of a felony became the governing perceptions of the truth of the matter; the early stages of criminal procedure gave shape to the facts of individual cases. By the time of the eyre, much had been sorted out, though many cases must have remained tentative for lack of solid evidence. The eyre and the imminence of trial must have given focus to those cases where the suspect was likely to be present. The defendant's reputation, his bearing since the time of the felony in question, the response of those into whose midst he would be returned if acquitted—these and other considerations must have been central to the men who would present and try him. This is not to say that these matters were unknown before the coming of the justices. In many cases, this complex process of community judgment had been completed long before the eyre, and its results were well enough known that they conditioned the willingness or unwillingness of those suspects who were not under secure guard to come forward after presentment to be tried.[54]

So far as we can tell, juries rendered their verdicts in simple and conclusory terms, stating that the defendant was guilty or not guilty, or that, in some cases of homicide, he had slain the deceased but had done so accidentally or in self-defense.[55] In these last cases, the jury repeated

---

52. Pollock and Maitland, *History of English Law*, 1:578–79; R. F. Hunnisett, *The Medieval Coroner*, (Cambridge, 1961), pp. 55–58; Alan Harding, "The Origins and Early History of the Keeper of the Peace," *Transactions of the Royal Historical Society*, 5th ser., vol. 10 (1960), p. 90; Barbara A. Hanawalt, *Crime and Conflict in English Communities, 1300–1348* (Cambridge, Mass., 1979), pp. 33–35.

53. See Hunnisett, *The Medieval Coroner*, esp. chs. 2 and 6. See also below, Chapter 2.

54. See F. W. Maitland et al., eds., *Eyre of Kent, 6 and 7 Edward II*, 3 vols. (London, 1909–14), vol. 1, p. xlii.

55. The extant trial rolls record the jury's verdict: *est culpabilis; non est culpabilis*, except in cases of excusable homicide, for which see below, Chapter 2. *Placita Corone* is no more helpful. It is possible that juries said a great deal more, especially at the eyre where,

the story the defendant had told, perhaps embellishing it to meet the rules of law. The fact that the jury had in many cases decided upon its verdict even before it was sworn does not mean that it was not in many others influenced by the defendant's statements and bearing in court or by the tone or substance of the questions that the justices asked. The trial often may have constituted an important part of the process by which the jury informed itself or confirmed its earlier impressions.[56]

The jury may have retired to discuss their verdict among themselves; the evidence on this point is far from clear. In some instances, juries were unable to reach unanimous agreement and reported a divided verdict to the court. In the early decades of recourse to trial jury verdicts, the bench did not always require unanimity. Later on, when unanimity became the rule, the justices pushed juries to reach agreement, as was already the practice in civil cases, and even applied some degree of coercion to help the process along.[57] Only rarely, it seems, did the bench question a jury's verdict. In cases of pardonable homicide they sometimes did so, but only because jury verdicts in such cases were not entirely conclusory and left the bench some measure of freedom to test the jurors' report.[58] In the great majority of cases, the verdict was conclusory and conclusive. Only the defendant's demeanor provided the bench with grounds for doubting an acquittal in a particular case, though the steady flow of not guilty verdicts doubtless made the bench suspicious of acquittals in general. The pretrial and trial procedure left the jury in almost total control of the outcome of cases. The bench might doubt the veracity of a defendant's story or of the jury's verdict, but lacking an independent source of evidence, the bench was not in a position to challenge either one effectively.[59]

if they found the defendant not guilty, they often said whom they did suspect. See Kappauf, "Early Development of the Petty Jury," pp. 196–201.

56. This is largely conjecture. It is borne out, however, by sixteenth-, seventeenth-, and eighteenth-century trial procedure and writings on the criminal trial, and there is no reason to believe that jury practice had changed in this respect. See below, Chapters 4 and 7.

57. Plucknett, *Concise History*, p. 129.

58. See below, Chapter 2. See also Summerson, "Plea Roll and Year Book." Dr. Summerson demonstrates that judges frequently put questions to juries. His study does not suggest that judges frequently questioned juries on their verdicts; what is most striking about the evidence he has uncovered—it seems to me—is that judicial questioning (and even badgering) of juries on specific aspects of given cases did not seem to prevent those juries from returning an acquittal.

59. In the two chapters that follow, I shall develop this theme in some detail. I have perhaps overstated the point here. It is possible that witnesses attached to appear at the eyre in the thirteenth century made representations before the justices; victims of theft, especially those who had been robbed by persons they could subsequently recognize, may have played a role. It would appear, however, that such testimony was taken into account by presentment juries. The justices might choose to weigh all indictments heavily, but from

The jury's power to determine the defendant's fate was virtually absolute. Those acquitted were with only rare exceptions released sine die; a few of them were released upon pledges of an official or other person of importance for their good behavior.[60] The guilty were hanged almost immediately. There was no time for appeal or pardon. In a very few cases the bench refused to accept a verdict, but those cases involved special verdicts of self-defense where the original verdict left some doubts. It does not appear that a second trial jury ever reversed the verdict given by the trial jury it superseded.[61]

Although jurors might be held liable to punishment for what amounted to perjury—giving false verdicts under oath—that liability extended in criminal cases only to outright corruption. Jurors proven to have been bribed or who admitted they had lied might be fined or imprisoned. The more general liability to attaint, and to the extreme form of punishment it involved, was never extended to the criminal trial jury.[62] The closest the bench came to application of the dreaded process of attaint was the impaneling of a second jury to test the first jury's special verdict of self-defense, and there is no evidence to suggest that the first jury would have been punished had its verdict been repudiated.

The trial jury's immunity to punishment for an honest but mistaken verdict has never been easy to explain. It may be that the divine aspect of the ordeal, which at first delayed the adoption of the trial jury, attached to the latter institution when it replaced the ordeal after 1215. The verdict of the criminal trial jury, unlike that of the civil trial jury, was thus not open to challenge, for its judgment reflected a will greater than that of humans, a will to which all humans were bound. But this traditional explanation seems entirely too mechanistic. It is more plausible that the immunity of the criminal trial jury was owing to the presumption of lawfulness accorded its members in the institution's early years, when presenters made up a large percentage of many, perhaps most, juries. Nothing short

the records it does not appear that they were in a position to determine which indictments were particularly well grounded. So many indictments were ultimately repudiated by juries on which at least some of the indictors sat, that the justices must have been stymied in their efforts to get at the truth. At gaol delivery (see below, text at n. 79) their job was doubly difficult.

60. See e.g. C. A. F. Meekings, "Introduction" to Meekings and Crook, eds., *The 1235 Surrey Eyre*, p. 126.

61. See below, Chapter 3 text at nn. 3–7 and *passim*.

62. Plucknett, *Concise History*, p. 132; Milsom, *Historical Foundations*, p. 411. On attaint see Thayer, *Preliminary Treatise*, pp. 137 *et seq.* The matter of fining jurors in the sixteenth and seventeenth centuries is discussed at length below, Chapters 4, text at nn. 149–58, and 6, *passim*. Seventeenth- and eighteenth-century commentary on attaint in criminal cases is discussed below, Chapters 6, text at nn. 138–46, and 8, nn. 95–96 and accompanying text.

of proof of gross abuse of office sufficed to refute the word of the substantial hundredmen who served as presenters. Moreover, that the defendant's life was at stake must have counted for something. The power of the jury may have reflected more than its institutional setting and role: it may have reflected a social understanding about the appropriate circumstances under which a person's life might be surrendered to the Crown. On this view, jury discretion was from the outset a given of the administration of the criminal law. Abuse of discretion involved conscious subversion of the trial process, the rendering of a verdict in bad faith. A verdict rendered according to conscience and reflecting the jury's conception of just deserts was divine in the sense that it was beyond judicial reproach.[63]

# III

The adoption of the trial jury as a regular means of proof effected the first major transition in the post-Angevin administration of the criminal law—a natural, though profound, step. Less dramatic but perhaps not less important was the second transition, one that occurred over several decades: the decline of the eyre and the recourse to regular commissions of gaol delivery.[64] There were frequent gaol deliveries in the mid- and late-thirteenth century; by the early fourteenth century, deliveries were held at least twice yearly.[65] The eyre was infrequently held by that time.[66]

---

63. Maitland's classic explanation of the finality of the criminal trial jury's verdict stressed the fact that the defendant "had put himself upon the oath of the jurors; a professedly unanimous verdict would satisfy the justices; it was the test that the prisoner had chosen. On the whole, trial by jury must have been in the main a trial by general repute." Pollock and Maitland, *History of English Law*, 2:655. Milsom gives a similar explanation: "Because a jury was the defendant's own proof, chosen by himself, attaint was in principle not available in criminal cases. This process, by which a verdict could be challenged before a larger jury, was appropriate to such procedures as the petty assizes, where the defendant had no choice either in the question or the means by which it was to be answered." *Historical Foundations*, p. 411.

64. For discussion of the transition from eyre to gaol delivery and other, related proceedings (and of the relevant literature on the subject) see Bernard McLane, "The Royal Courts and the Problem of Disorder in Lincolnshire, 1290–1341," doctoral dissertation (University of Rochester, 1979), ch. I.

65. See R. B. Pugh, *Imprisonment in Medieval England* (Cambridge, 1968), chs. 12 and 13. See also M. Gollancz, "The System of Gaol Delivery," M. A. dissertation (University of London, 1936); M. Taylor, "The Justices of Assize," in J. F. Willard and William A. Morris, eds., *The English Government at Work, 1327–1336*, 3 vols. (Cambridge, 1940–50), vol. 3, pp. 219–47.

66. See Hunnisett, *Medieval Coroner*, pp. 114–15; Richard W. Kaeuper, "Law and Order in Fourteenth-Century England; The Evidence of Special Commissions of Oyer and Terminer," *Speculum*, vol. 54 (1979), p. 738.

The decline of that cumbersome and unpopular administrative and judicial institution was also signaled by the Crown's increasing use of special commissions of trailbaston and of oyer and terminer to hear presentments and to try those taken pursuant to them.[67] These special commissions had broader authority than did justices of gaol delivery, whose jurisdiction extended only to persons already gaoled upon an indictment for felony.[68]

Our own interest lies mainly with felony trials at gaol delivery. But we shall have to keep in mind the contemporaneous proceedings, in the main for trespasses,[69] before justices upon commission of oyer and terminer, and we must remember that the transition from eyre to gaol delivery involved a major readjustment in the Crown's administration of criminal justice.[70] This readjustment, which reflected new and sometimes contradictory attitudes, involved changes—though perhaps unintended ones—in the institution of the trial jury in felony cases. The commissions to justices to deliver England's gaols ordered the justices to make certain that jurors from each hundred in the counties they were to visit would be present at the proceedings.[71] The justices in turn notified the sheriffs of those counties, and the sheriffs sent appropriate orders to the hundred bailiffs.[72] Typically, a hundred was represented by a panel of eighteen persons from whom the twelve triers would be chosen for each felony committed in the hundred.[73] Those who were tried had been presented earlier in the county court; because they were not re-presented before the justices of gaol delivery, the attendance of the presenters was not required. There was nothing to prevent a bailiff from returning persons

---

67. See R. B. Pugh, "Some Reflections of a Medieval Criminologist," *Proceedings of the British Academy*, vol. 59 (1973), pp. 83–84; Alan Harding, "Early Trailbaston Proceedings from the Lincoln Roll of 1305," in R. F. Hunnisett and J. B. Post, eds., *Medieval Legal Records edited in memory of C. A. F. Meekings* (London, 1978), pp. 130–38.

68. See generally Kaeuper, "Law and Order," pp. 734–84.

69. See McLane, "Royal Courts and the Problem of Disorder," pp. ll–12, 24.

70. *Ibid.*, ch. I. The increase in actions for trespass contributed to the need for frequent local sessions; the strain thus placed on the central justices contributed to the use as judges (for oyer and terminer; not for gaol delivery, where felony was the principal business) of local magnates and gentry and to the development of the offices of keeper of the peace and, by the 1330s, of justice of the peace. By then, if not long before, the easy availability of such actions drew cases away from the gaol delivery and other sessions that heard felonies. Especially important was the prosecution of much relatively minor theft that might have been prosecuted as felony, as mere, indictable trespass, or indeed as private suits of trespass for money damages. On the origins of trespass see Alan Harding, *The Roll of the Shropshire Eyre of 1256* (London, 1981), pp. xxxii–lviii, and sources cited therein.

71. Thomas A. Green, "Pardonable Homicide in Medieval England," doctoral dissertation (Harvard University, 1970), p. 167.

72. *Idem.*

73. See e.g. C 260/4, no. 19 (1288); C 260/6, no. 7 (1292); C 260/16, no. 12 (1306).

who had served in the county court on the presenting jury.[74] In some instances there must have been substantial overlap between the original presenters and those sent to the county town for proceedings before justices of gaol delivery. But more often than not these frequent proceedings saw men of lesser status, men less able to avoid the onerous service of the trial juror. The separation of the juries was not, however, merely the result of the transition from eyre to delivery. During the late thirteenth and early fourteenth centuries it had come to be thought that the defendant ought to be tried mainly by persons who had not presented him. Thus administrative development and nascent concepts of due process worked together to produce the virtual separation of the two juries long before 1352, when statute allowed challenge of a prospective juror on grounds he had served as an indictor.[75]

The decline in the status of trial jurors was not dramatic in the early decades of the fourteenth century. But gradually thereafter its impact was felt as exemptions from service reduced the base of substantial jurors. This apparent "democratizing" of the trial jury may have weakened the institution, as its members were now more often susceptible to pressure from powerful friends or foes of defendants.[76] Legislative attention to jury malpractices grew more intense, and in the fifteenth century there were attempts to set property qualifications for jury service.[77] By then, the resistance to serving was great enough to doom any meaningful reform.

This is not to suggest that, at least in the fourteenth century, the system of gaol delivery was unworkable. In fact, it represented in some respects a great improvement over the eyre in the administration of criminal law with regard to felonies. The system's most significant virtue was the frequency of judicial visitations. Suspects who had been taken were tried within a matter of weeks or months, not years; bail was less important and less universally resorted to. In homicide, special commissions were very rarely held after the late thirteenth century, for the denial of bail worked far less hardship.[78]

The conviction rate at gaol deliveries was roughly what it had been for homicide at the eyre, and double what it had been for theft. Juries condemned about 15 percent of homicide suspects and nearly one third of those indicted for theft.[79] One might have expected higher rates of

74. Pugh, "Reflections of a Medieval Criminologist," pp. 92–93.

75. Stat. 25 Edw. 3, stat. 5. c. 3. See Plucknett, *Concise History*, p. 127.

76. See e.g. J. H. Bellamy, *Crime and Public Order in England in the Later Middle Ages* (London, 1973), p. 149.

77. See below, Chapter 4, n. 25 and accompanying text.

78. Green, "Pardonable Homicide in Medieval England," p. 148.

79. Given found that 17.4 percent of those charged with homicide alone at eyres in the thirteenth century were "executed." This may include cases actually tried at gaol delivery

conviction at gaol delivery than at the eyre: relatively few suspects appeared at the eyre, and many of those who did had reason to be confident that they would be exonerated. At gaol deliveries, all those who were being held pending trial had to come forward to face the bench and a trial jury. Far fewer suspects had been bailed; certainly those held for the most heinous offenses and possibly those who were most suspect had not. If the conviction rates are surprisingly low by the standards of the eyre, they are even more strikingly low by modern standards. The reasons for this are complex and require further consideration of the administration of criminal justice in the period that began with the decline of the general eyre.

The maturation of gaol delivery belongs to the period of late medieval criminal administration about which we know least. The attention of modern scholars has fallen mostly on the mid-thirteenth-century eyres and on the fourteenth-century system of gaol delivery. It is conventional to treat the late thirteenth century as the beginning of a long period of social decline and disruption and to treat the transition from eyre to delivery as in part a symptom of that decline and in part an attempt to remedy the disruption.[80] All ages think themselves the victims of increasing criminal activity. In some, people are especially articulate about their perceptions, and we must not uncritically equate oft-stated fears with realities.[81] The attention which Edward I's legislation pays to the problem of crime may say more about such fears[82] and about the impulse to legislate than about relative rates of criminal activity. Edward's legislation and the creation of new procedures to deal with crime may have represented (amateurish) attempts to deal with longstanding problems for which the eyre was too irregular and too cumbersome.[83]

but reported and recorded at a subsequent eyre; it does not include many tried by special commissions and found to have slain in self-defense. James B. Given, *Society and Homicide in Thirteenth Century England* (Stanford, 1977), p. 133. Hanawalt gives 12.4 percent as the conviction rate for homicide at early fourteenth-century gaol deliveries and about 30 percent as the conviction rate for theft. *Crime and Conflict*, p. 59. Pugh examined the Newgate (London and Middlesex) gaol delivery rolls for the decade 1281–90; he found a condemnation rate of 21 percent for homicide (where no other charge was involved) and 31 percent for all forms of theft (excluding only cases where an additional charge of homicide, forgery, or prison breach accompanied the charge, or charges, of theft). "Reflections of a Medieval Criminologist," pp. 6–7.

80. On the literature regarding the "crisis in order and justice" in this period see Kaeuper, "Law and Order," p. 735, n. 4, and works cited therein.

81. See Kaeuper's excellent treatment of this problem at *ibid.*, pp. 735 *et seq.* See also McLane, "Royal Courts and the Problem of Disorder," pp. 60, 115. McLane concludes that there was an increase.

82. Pugh, "Reflections of a Medieval Criminologist," p. 84. See Statute of Winchester, preamble (Stat. 13 Edw. 1, c. 1; *Statutes of the Realm*, 1:96).

83. See T. F. T. Plucknett, *Edward I and Criminal Law* (Cambridge, 1960), ch. 4.

The late thirteenth and early fourteenth centuries saw the use of special commissions of trailbaston and oyer and terminer, increased reliance on keepers of the peace, and an attempt to tighten the bail system.[84] By the middle of the fourteenth century the keepers had attained the status of justices, adding the capacity to try misdemeanants and (sometimes) felons to their traditional power to hear presentments.[85] The quarter sessions of the justices of the peace soon absorbed most of the criminal business that had earlier been handled by the less flexible commissions of trailbaston and oyer and terminer. Local law enforcement capacities had been greatly enhanced during the period of transition from eyre to quarter sessions and regular delivery of gaols.[86] Frequent gaol deliveries, therefore, were only one aspect of a major overhaul of the system of criminal administration. Conviction rates at gaol delivery must be read in the light of these reforms: the results must have been disappointing.

The statistics must also be read in light of the disasters that beset England in the fourteenth century. Famine, plague, and war brought on social dislocation, hurrying the disintegration of older forms of social structure and increasing the numbers of dispossessed.[87] The Crown sought to establish means to deal with these problems and with the criminal activity they brought in their wake, but it may have intensified them through, among other things, the granting of pardons "of grace" to those who would serve in foreign wars.[88] Pardons of grace, which absolved the most hardened criminals of all their felonies by making them immune to prosecution,[89] were issued in large numbers in the 1290s and

84. Kaeuper, "Law and Order," pp. 735 *et seq*; Alan Harding, "The Origin and Early History of the Keeper of the Peace," *Transactions of the Royal Historical Society*, 5th ser., no. 10 (1950), pp. 85–109.

85. Bertha Haven Putnam, *Proceedings before the Justices of the Peace in the Fourteenth and Fifteenth Centuries* (London, 1938), pp. xix–xxxii; "The Transformation of the Keepers of the Peace into the Justices of the Peace, 1327–80," *Transactions of the Royal Historical Society*, 4th ser., no. 12 (1929), pp. 19–48; "Shire Officials: Keepers of the Peace and Justices of the Peace," in Willard et al., eds., *English Government at Work*, 3:182–217; Plucknett, *Concise History*, pp. 167–69.

86. See McLane, "Royal Courts and the Problem of Disorder," pp. 37–43, for discussion of the reforms effected and the problems they brought in their wake. See also Post, "Local Jurisdictions and Judgment of Death," pp. 12–15, for the impact of royal commissions of the peace on residual private jurisdiction over felony.

87. See below, Chapter 3, text at nn. 8–10.

88. Pardons of grace are to be distinguished from pardons of course. All pardons were emanations of the royal prerogative. Those pardons that came to be granted automatically, for slaying in self-defense, through accident or through insanity, as though the defendant had done no wrong, were pardons "of course." All other pardons were granted by "grace" of the king, who—usually for a price—"mercifully" absolved a person of a wrongdoing, or at least insured the person against prosecution.

89. See e.g. Hurnard, *King's Pardon for Homicide*, pp. 311–23; H. J. Hewitt, *The*

throughout the fourteenth century. Assumptions of contemporaries about the destructive impact of this policy are reflected in parliamentary petitions and statutes seeking to limit the royal pardoning power. Periodically the Crown consented to limit the sale of pardons but then soon breached its promise; not until the last decade of the fourteenth century was even a mildly effective brake placed on the flow of pardons of grace.[90]

How, then, does one begin to account for the vast number of acquittals even of those accused and held for commission of felony? And what pressures were brought to bear upon the juries that were forced to respond in individual cases to the question of capital liability? These are among the questions that the following chapters explore. By way of conclusion to this introductory essay we may suggest the direction that our explorations will take.

Some, perhaps many, of those tried at gaol delivery were not guilty of the acts with which they had been charged. The system of presentment, including the supporting scheme of amercements for failure to name a suspect, produced some false accusations. This had been true from the beginning of the presentment process.[91] It is possible that the replacement of the ordeal by the jury actually increased the amount of false charging, for the latter institution provided a more trustworthy and less painful means of exoneration. By the fifteenth century, the modern indictment process was emerging out of the older system of presentment.[92] This process, wherein officials investigated complaints and put the evidence they had gathered before the grand jury, must have placed a check on unsubstantiated accusations, but for most of the medieval period the margin of error at the presentment stage was very great.[93] In addition, many of those accused were guilty in fact but not proven to be so. Jurors

*Organization of War under Edward III, 1338–62* (Manchester, 1966), pp. 173–75; Hanawalt, *Crime and Conflict*, pp. 235–37. Hanawalt cautions that the gaol delivery rolls do not provide clear evidence that the pardoning policy resulted in a dramatic increase in crime.

90. See below, Chapter 3, nn. 12–30 and accompanying text.

91. Not all "false" accusations resulted from bad faith. Perhaps the better phrase is "wrong accusations." Presentment, we have seen, was deemed an improvement upon the appeal, which produced a substantial amount of truly false ("malicious") prosecution.

92. See below, Chapter 4, text preceding n. 19. For the thirteenth-century origins of indictment by bill see Alan Harding, "The Origins of the Crime of Conspiracy," *Transactions of the Royal Historical Society*, 5th ser., vol. 33 (1983), pp. 94–95.

93. The crime of "conspiracy" in its original meaning: an agreement falsely to indict of crime, was statutorily defined in 1300. *Statutes of the Realm*, vol. 1, p. 139. See also Pugh, "Reflections of a Medieval Criminologist," p. 97. For a recent important account of conspiracy see Harding, "Origins of the Crime of Conspiracy." Harding marshals the evidence for a near-crisis in the administration of the criminal law owing to the practice of false accusation (pp. 97–99). It remains unclear how much such false accusation was responsible for trials at gaol delivery of persons held for homicide or theft (as opposed to trials at eyres or before justices of trailbaston for assaults and like offenses).

were sworn to state the truth, not to confirm suspicions. They were supposed to acquit those against whom a firm case had not been made, and probably they generally did.[94]

At the other extreme were cases where the jury believed the defendant to be guilty but acquitted him nonetheless out of fear of retribution or out of partisanship. This latter category included the simple favor shown to friends and neighbors as well as the more serious instances where the jury had been bribed to save the guilty suspect's life. Authorities believed that coercion and bribery were common and that the truly corrupt verdicts that resulted forestalled attempts to bring very grave offenders to justice. Concern with this kind of corruption lay behind parliamentary attempts to secure more qualified jurors and might have been reflected in the increasing investigative activity of the justices of the peace.[95]

There were, of course, many other defendants who were guilty under the strict rules of the law whom juries refused to convict. These were persons whose acts, whether theft, homicide, or rape, were not considered sufficiently serious to merit capital punishment. The jury was reacting to the reputation of the accused,[96] the nature of his offense, and—perhaps most important—the punishment he would incur. Thefts of a relatively trivial amount perpetrated by persons in dire straits, slayings born of sudden anger by persons long of good standing, these were offenses for which the law prescribed death but for which the community frequently refused to convict. Juries in these cases simply nullified the law of felony.[97]

The jury's power to render verdicts against the evidence was perhaps the most distinctive aspect of medieval criminal law. Whether such verdicts resulted from mercy, fear, or outright corruption, they evidenced the trial jury's domination of the system of justice. In part, the jury's power flowed from its institutional setting. From its inception, and perhaps until Tudor times, the jury was the source of practically all of the

94. See Pugh, "Reflections of a Medieval Criminologist," pp. 97–98. Jurors were sworn to tell the truth "to the best of their knowledge. If, however, they did not know it or possessed imperfect knowledge they could not then support the prosecution, for they must not reach their verdict on the basis of mere 'thoughts.'" See also Thayer, *Preliminary Treatise*, pp. 100–101, n. 2.

95. See Bellamy, *Crime and Public Order*, pp. 149–50. On statutes setting qualifications for jurors see below, Chapter 4, n. 25. On investigation by justices of the peace see below, Chapter 4, text at nn. 15–21.

96. Pugh, "Reflections of a Medieval Criminologist," p. 98: "When acquitting [jurors] often said no more than that a suspect's character was good. He who had the reputation of *Fidelitas* must have had a flying start toward liberation." The role played by reputation is difficult to assess. Jurors might have been using it as evidence and inferring innocence from good reputation or taking it into account in extending mercy to one they believed guilty.

97. See below, Chapter 2.

evidence put before the court. Typically, jury verdicts were conclusions based on assessment of facts gathered before the defendant went on trial. Although juries were probably influenced by the defendant's bearing in court, their reactions to that drama must have been played back against what they had already learned about him and the circumstances of the act with which he had been charged.

In part, too, the jury's power reflected deep-seated assumptions about justice, assumptions which—as may increasingly have become the case— authorities shared with those they ruled. The verdict was a verdict "of the country," made by persons on oath before God to tell the truth according to their consciences. It was an inscrutable verdict, though it is by no means clear to us why that was so. We may try to understand the various aspects of the inscrutability of verdicts: they were, it was thought, divinely inspired; if the defendant so chose, the matter of life and death was for his countrymen to determine. Nevertheless, the trial jury's power also reflected incapacities of central government that could not be confronted openly and that may have induced authorities to conceive of jury verdicts as presumptively legitimate. Only clear corruption was open to correction; the notion of truth according to conscience was sufficiently broad to cover misreadings of evidence and verdicts rendered knowingly against the evidence but inspired by mercy.

The problem of merciful or otherwise principled nullification—the subject of this study—is extremely complex. In the medieval period, for one thing, specific instances of nullification were largely hidden from view. Such verdicts were usually indistinguishable, from the perspective of the bench, from acquittals based on the belief that the defendant had not been involved. Moreover, if the justices did in a given case suspect nullification, they might have thought it of the unprincipled sort, the product of bribery, extortion, or abject fear. Those were more serious and perhaps more common problems. Simple merciful nullification, especially in close cases, was often sheltered from view and frequently protected by the jury's duty to acquit where the evidence was uncertain. It was also a relatively trivial matter, given the perception of a substantial increase in truly serious crimes. Nullification, in this particular sense, was probably an unintended by-product of the medieval system of criminal justice. But its importance should not for that reason be underestimated. Although it was a relatively insignificant form of jury lawlessness, it involved serious long-term implications for the relationship between rulers and ruled. In the ensuing chapters we shall search out the evidence for jury nullification of the rules of capital felony, and we shall attempt to assess the judicial reaction to this kind of jury behavior. We shall, in short, inventory a lost part of the legacy of the medieval criminal trial jury that the modern world inherited and took over for its own.

# 2 Societal Concepts of Criminal Liability and Jury Nullification of the Law in the Thirteenth and Fourteenth Centuries

We move in this chapter from an overview of the institutional setting of the criminal trial jury to consideration of one very important aspect of the jury's social role: the jury as law finder. I shall show that the medieval criminal trial jury imposed upon the courts the community's—or the communities'—concepts of liability for felony. In doing so, the jury exercised a de facto power, since its legal role was to find and declare fact and to leave to the bench judgment according to law. This extended role is one of the two main themes of this book. The second theme—the effect of such jury behavior on the development of the law and on the way official and lay Englishmen viewed the jury—is introduced in Chapter 3.

Early juries obviously nullified at least to some degree the reach of the capital laws. It would be more extraordinary, and possibly more interesting, had they not done so. But it is not easy to show juries playing this role in specific cases. Moreover, it is not obvious that this aspect of jury behavior mattered very much; from the perspective of the bench, other aspects of jury behavior must have mattered a great deal more.

The great majority of defendants in felony trials were acquitted. Many of these acquittals were deserved, for the system of presentment often resulted in prosecutions of the truly innocent, and the means for gathering evidence were so rudimentary that in many instances a case simply could not be made. Many acquittals were, on the other hand, undeserved, arising not from defects in pretrial procedures but from corruption of the trial process itself. Juries were sometimes bribed and often fear-stricken; moreover, they might lie out of dishonest partisanship that did not rise to the level of conscientious nullification. These problems plagued the bench, and the fact that the judges were at pains to discover whether an acquittal was of the former, deserved kind, or of the latter, undeserved kind, only worsened their predicament. Because the jury produced the evidence, it prevented the bench from seeing exactly what was occurring in individual cases. The bench, and officialdom in general, lashed out blindly against the major forms of corruption—the bribing and intimidation of jurors—which it knew played a role in a substantial number of cases that ended in acquittal.

Somewhere in between the deserved and undeserved acquittals lay the presumably large number of acquittals based on jury repudiation of the death sanction. These jury responses were only partly visible to the bench. Many of them were indistinguishable from the other, more or less serious, forms of jury behavior. To speak of them as isolable even in theory is, of course, to engage in oversimplification, for in any given case feelings of simple mercy might have been mixed either with doubts about the evidence or with a purely partisan attitude, or even with fear of retaliation by the defendant's kin or associates.

What follows in this chapter is a tentative exploration of one relatively hidden phenomenon that characterized trial by jury: jury assessment of the nature of the defendant's act. Given the nature of the extant evidence, the greatest amount of attention shall be paid to jury behavior in homicide. I mean to accomplish several things: to demonstrate that in homicide cases juries systematically imposed upon the courts a distinction the formal legal rules did not draw; to establish the presumption that juries played a similar nullifying role in other kinds of cases, especially in theft, the other main felony reflected on the trial rolls; to make possible the drawing of inferences regarding the kinds of nullification in which juries engaged in felonies other than homicide, again mainly in theft; and to suggest that the Angevin revolution in procedure and sanctions had less impact on the actual resolution of cases than is sometimes supposed, and thereby to raise questions (to be addressed in Chapter 3) regarding the reasons for using the jury in the way it was used.[1]

# I

The early history of English criminal law lies hidden within the laconic formulas of the rolls and law books. The rules of the law, as expounded by the judges, have been the subject of many studies; but their practical application in the courts, where the jury of the community was the final and unbridled arbiter, largely remains a mystery. Only now are we coming to know something about the social mores regarding crime and criminals.[2]

1. See below, Chapter 3, section IV.
2. Among the recent works that address these latter concerns are Given, *Society and Homicide*; Hanawalt, *Crime and Conflict*; McLane, "Royal Courts and the Problem of Disorder"; Carl I. Hammer, "Patterns of Homicide in Fourteenth-Century Oxford," *Past and Present*, vol. 78 (1978), pp. 1–23. Given's book represents the most detailed analysis to date of the "sociology" of homicide. Its strengths lie in its data on perpetrators and victims, their geographical and social background, and their relationship to each other. Given may overstate the degree to which violence was accepted (see p. 213) rather than the capital sanction repudiated. His sources did not give him much room to investigate the behavior of juries regarding their assessment of the defendant's act. Probably juries reacted to both act and person, their view of one influencing their view of the other. Given's book, as well as the other works cited in this note, should be read alongside this chapter.

The following study attempts to demonstrate that from late Anglo-Saxon times to the end of the Middle Ages there existed a widespread societal distinction between "murder," i.e., homicide perpetrated through stealth, and "simple" homicide, roughly what a later legal age termed "manslaughter." This distinction, which was imposed upon the courts through the instrument of the trial jury, was fundamentally at odds with the letter of the law. It is therefore necessary to state briefly what the rules of law were.

In the early twelfth century, the Crown took exclusive jurisdiction over all homicides and defined them as (1) culpable and thereby capital, (2) excusable and thereby pardonable, (3) justifiable and thereby deserving of acquittal.[3] The last class at first incorporated the slaying of manifest felons (e.g., "hand-having thieves") and outlaws who resisted capture. By the middle of the fourteenth century it came to include the killing of housebreakers and robbers caught in the act, though it was not until the sixteenth century that a statute turned this policy into firm law.[4] Pardonable homicides were those committed by the insane, those committed in self-defense, and those committed unintentionally. The rules of self-defense were rigorous throughout the entire medieval period. The slayer had to have made every possible attempt to escape his attacker, must have reached a point beyond which he could not retreat, and must have retaliated out of literally vital necessity.[5] All other intentional homicides, those deliberate but of a sudden, as well as those planned and stealthily perpetrated, fell into the large category of culpable homicide. According to the rules of the law, there were to be no distinctions made among them. This classification remained intact until the late sixteenth century, when the judicial distinction between murder and manslaughter finally emerged.[6] Originally, of those meriting pardons for excusable homicide, only persons who had tried to flee suffered forfeiture of goods; after 1343, all pardonable slayers were supposed to lose their goods.[7]

We have seen that the king might as a special favor grant a pardon to a felonious slayer, usually for a considerable fee, or as a reward for service abroad in the royal army. These pardons "of grace" (de gratia) were emanations of the royal prerogative. Pardons for self-defense, accident, and insanity were, by the late thirteenth century, pardons "of course" (de cursu): all who deserved them according to the rules of the law were

---

3. Hurnard, *King's Pardon for Homicide*, pp. 1 *et seq.*
4. 24 Hen. 8, c. 15 (1532).
5. See below, text at n. 22.
6. J. M. Kaye, "The Early History of Murder and Manslaughter," *Law Quarterly Review*, vol. lxxxiii (July and Oct., 1967), pp. 365–95, 569–601.
7. For discussion of the rule of automatic forfeiture see below, Chapter 3, n. 105.

to receive them.[8] After 1294, due mainly to the needs of military
recruitment, pardons of grace issued in far greater numbers than ever
before to perpetrators of felonious slayings of all sorts.

Because of the evidence on which this chapter is based, it has seemed
best to proceed in reverse chronological order, to move backward from
late-fourteenth-century evidence to a consideration of the rules of criminal liability in the Anglo-Saxon period. Subsection 1 examines jury
behavior in the decades immediately following 1390 when some coroners
and justices of the peace distinguished in their indictments between
"murder" and simple homicide. Although both types of homicide remained felonious, juries appear to have been loath to convict for the
latter, while they frequently condemned perpetrators of the former.
Before 1390, terms of indictment in all felonious homicides were uniform
and no such correlation can be made. Subsection 2, therefore, utilizes
another source of evidence: a correlation of fourteenth-century coroners'
indictments with their corresponding verdicts for self-defense. It will be
shown that many of those who received pardons for self-defense had in
fact committed a felonious, simple homicide. The area of pardonable
homicide, it appears, served as a possible way out in cases where the
community did not believe the defendant deserved to be hanged.

Because coroners' rolls are very sparse in the period before 1300, there
exists no trustworthy method of proving that the societal attitudes traced
here precede the fourteenth century. In fact, an important study of
pardonable homicide in the thirteenth century argues that jurors were
fairly scrupulous in giving evidence and that their determinations did not
vary substantially from at least the spirit of the law.[9] Nevertheless, in
subsection 3 I shall contend that there is reason to believe verdicts were
fabricated before the fourteenth century. Moreover, I shall argue that the
early history of criminal liability, especially for the period just preceding
the imposition of royal jurisdiction in all homicides, suggests that from
their very inception the official rules ran counter to and never really
became a part of social practice. This argument, admittedly speculative,
takes the following form. During the Anglo-Saxon period only those who
committed homicide through secrecy or stealth—murder—had to pay for
their act with their life. The new, twelfth-century practice subjected to the
death penalty not only "murderers" but the large class of open slayers
formerly allowed to compensate for their act by payment of the wergeld.
The community resisted this harsh extension of capital punishment and
subsequently found means—acquittals and verdicts of self-defense—to
impose upon the courts their long-held notions of justice, a process that

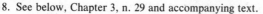

8. See below, Chapter 3, n. 29 and accompanying text.
9. Hurnard, *King's Pardon for Homicide*, pp. 267–68.

becomes visible to us only in the fourteenth century. Thus the societal distinction between murder and simple homicide had its source deep in the English past. The introduction of novel and strict official rules of liability did away with the traditional means of dispute settlement in simple homicide, but it did not erase traditional social attitudes about liability. Nor did the imposition of a new scheme of criminal administration prevent society from acting, within the context of that scheme, in accordance with its traditional attitudes.

Finally, in subsection 4, I shall elaborate upon the nature of the medieval societal concept of "murder" and the place of that concept within the process of dispute settlement.

I

Throughout the medieval period for which written records are extant, the great majority of defendants who stood trial for homicide were acquitted. While today many are acquitted, one must take into account the fact that most suspects do not now stand trial; the vast majority of them plead guilty. In the Middle Ages few pleaded guilty to any felony since the penalty was invariably capital.[10]

Many defendants doubtless deserved acquittal, for many charges were poorly supported. The coroner's report might reflect the testimony of only a few neighbors and might present only the most serious charges that circulated in the wake of a homicide.[11] Although coroners were required to list all those present at a homicide, they often failed to do so. In many cases they recorded the details of a slaying, yet maintained that no one had been present except the slain man, who had died immediately, and the slayer, who had thereupon fled.[12] What, or who, then, was the source of those details? There had probably been witnesses who were not anxious to become involved, who did not wish to risk coming under suspicion themselves. To come forward later was to risk a fine for not

---

10. Convictions were particularly rare at the eyre, for few would appear who had neither a pardon nor assurance of acquittal by the country. At gaol delivery, where nearly all the defendants had been arrested against their will, the record of conviction was not much better. The roll of Thomas Ingelby and his associates, e.g., compiled at deliveries of Derbyshire, Leicestershire, Lincolnshire, Northamptonshire, Nottinghamshire, and Warwickshire, 40–45 Edward III, contains the trials of 160 individuals accused of homicide (twenty-four were cited as accessories or receivers). Only fifteen were found guilty; seventy-four were acquitted, fifty-nine were given special verdicts of self-defense. The remainder came with pardons or were released for other reasons. Of the principals who denied the charges against them 80 percent were acquitted outright. JUST 3/142, mm.3 ff.

11. Hunnisett, *Medieval Coroner*, p. 24.

12. E.g. R. R. Sharpe, ed., *Calendar of Coroners' Rolls of the City of London, A.D. 1300–1378*, (London, 1913), Roll B, no. 36; Roll D, no. 5.

having raised the hue.[13] On the other hand, what they had seen must soon have become the common knowledge of the countryside, and, allowing for the usual exaggerations or alterations of the true story, may have appeared in the coroner's enrollment as a fairly accurate account of the event. But it is difficult to separate the accurate descriptions from the cases of mere guesswork. The trial jurors probably took a more reasonable view, rejecting unsubstantiated testimony.[14]

Though malicious prosecution and honestly moved but mistaken indictments may account in part for the high rate of acquittals, other factors must also have been at work. It is contended here that, for the most part, those few who were condemned had especially offended against the standards of the community. By discriminating between them and the many who committed homicides of a less serious nature, the jurors were creating a de facto classification roughly similar to the later legal distinction between murder and manslaughter.

The clearest evidence of juries discriminating on the basis of the nature of the slaying dates from the end of the fourteenth century and the first decades of the fifteenth. In 1390 century-long protests against the royal pardoning policy culminated in a statute that restricted the king's power to grant pardons of grace to those who had committed murder.[15] "Murder," as a term of art, referred to the most heinous forms of homicide, those perpetrated through stealth, at night, or by ambush. The statute appears to have been directed especially at murderous assaults committed by professional highwaymen and burglars for monetary gain. The king agreed not to use his pardon powers casually; moreover, no pardon for murder would be valid unless it made specific mention of "murder." Significantly, culpable homicide continued to include both murder and simple homicide. Both were capital; no judicial distinction was made between them. The term "murder" was employed, where relevant, solely for the purpose of administering the Statute of 1390, i.e., for regulating the granting of pardons of grace to felonious slayers. Though the statute's effectiveness was short-lived, for several decades "murder" found its way into some homicide indictments.

Analysis of several trial rolls that include indictments by coroners and justices of the peace who, despite the courts' failure to apply the 1390

13. Hunnisett, *Medieval Coroner*, pp. 10, 25.

14. See Hurnard, *King's Pardon for Homicide*, pp. 361 *et seq.* for an analysis of inquisitions, held on a writ *de odio et atia*, to ascertain the veracity of appeals and indictments.

15. The background to the statute of 1390 is given in Kaye, "Early History," Part I. My interpretation of the statute itself differs from that of Kaye, who argued that it limited pardons in all types of felonious homicides. See Green, "Jury and the Law of Homicide," pp. 462–69.

statute, bothered to discriminate between murder and simple homicide, reveals that juries acquitted the great majority of nonmurderers and sent murderers to the gallows about 50 percent of the time.[16] A gaol delivery roll covering the first eight years of the reign of Henry VI demonstrates the point quite clearly.[17] The roll was compiled for James Strangways and his fellows, who visited the gaols of Lincoln, Nottingham, Northampton, Warwick, and Leicester. A total of 114 defendants came before them to answer indictments for homicide in seventy-seven different cases. Of these, excluding those excused for faulty indictments and those for whom the jury returned special verdicts, eighty-four persons were acquitted and twenty were condemned to death. The latter group, with one exception, had been indicted for murder. Acquittals, on the other hand, were registered for thirty-seven indicted for simple homicide and for forty-seven held for murder. Taking only principals into account, eighteen of the nineteen hanged had been charged with murder, and of the forty-five acquitted only seventeen were murder suspects. Thus, while an indictment for simple homicide practically assured the principal defendant of exculpation (one of twenty-nine was hanged), an allegation of murder put his chances at about fifty-fifty (eighteen of thirty-five were hanged).[18]

Similarly, John Cokayn's roll, compiled over the years of Henry V's reign from deliveries of the gaols in Derbyshire, Leicestershire, Lincolnshire, Northamptonshire, Nottinghamshire, Rutland, and Warwickshire, records fifteen convictions based on murder indictments and only four based on simple homicide, despite the fact that there are substantially more simple homicides on the roll.[19] The enrollments for Leicester gaol, based on several deliveries during the reign of Henry IV, show only four convictions, all based on murder allegations. Of the thirteen acquittals, seven of the original indictments were for murder, six for simple homicide.[20] John Martyn's roll for the far western circuit (1424–30) presents ten simple homicides, nine of which ended in acquittal, and five murders, four of which led to convictions.[21]

16. I have chosen those rolls, or sections of rolls, that contain a substantial number of indictments for homicide and where it seems clear that coroners and justices of the peace inserted, when relevant, *murdravit* or its statutory equivalent: *insidiavit*. On many other rolls, of course, where no distinction was made, indictments not including these terms of art often ended in convictions.

17. JUST 3/203.

18. Two of the seventeen had been indicted for murder by one inquest and for simple homicide by the other: coroners' indictments often differed from those of the justices of the peace.

19. JUST 3/195.

20. JUST 3/188.

21. JUST 3/205. The "simple homicide" resulting in conviction was the slaying of a man by his wife, an act the community frequently construed as murder.

Despite the lack of evidence on the point, we might speculate that the judges sometimes urged juries to convict in cases brought on murder indictments. But it is not safe to conclude that the judges encouraged juries to acquit those indicted for simple homicide. Only the grounds of self-defense justified the deliberate slaying of a person who was neither a convicted nor a manifest felon, and the test for self-defense remained quite rigorous. As late as 1454 Prisot, J., stated the test for merely threatening to kill in self defense:

> . . . if a man assaults you in order to beat you it is not lawful for you to say you will kill him and to menace his life and limb: but if the case is such that he has you at such advantage that it may be understood that he is going to kill you as if you seek to flee and he is swifter than you and pursues you so that you are unable to escape; or if you are on the ground under him; or if he chases you to a wall or hedge or dike, so that you cannot escape, then it is lawful for you to say that if he won't desist, you want to slay him to save your own life, and thus you may menace him for such special cause.[22]

## 2

Our demonstration that juries acted upon their own extralegal notion of culpable homicide based on the distinction between serious and simple homicide is limited thus far to the post-1390 period. It is likely that juries made this distinction earlier, but it is not easy to prove. Before 1390 gaol delivery enrollments, in recording the indictment made before the coroner or justice of the peace, almost invariably used only the unenlightening phrase *felonice interfecit* ("feloniously slew"). Thus it is impossible to show from them that juries distinguished between types of felonious homicides. If we work backward from the trial roll to the indictment as it appeared on the original coroner's roll, two nearly insuperable problems are presented: the greater part of the original inquests are no longer extant; those that do survive generally contain only the operative phrase, *felonice interfecit*, with few details from which the nature of the act can be deduced. One of the few coroners' rolls that does supply such details

22. *Year Books, 1422–1461* (Henry VI) (London, 1556–74), 33 Hen. 6, Easter, pl. 10: ". . . *quar si un home vous assaute de vou batre n'e loial pour vous adire que vous voiles luy tuer, et de luy menasser de vie et de membre: mes si l'cas soit tiel, q'il ad vous a tiel advantage que par entendment il voilloit vous tuer come si voiles fuir, et il est plus courrant que vous estes, et alla apres vous, issint que ne vous poies luy escaper; ou autrement que vous estes desouh luy al'terre; ou s'il ad enchace vous a un mure ou un hedge ou dike, issint que vous ne poies luy escape, donq's est loial pour vous adire que s'il ne veut departir de vous, q'vous en salvatio de vostre vie luy voiles tuer, et issint vous poies luy menasser pour tiel special cause.*"

is the roll of Edmund de Ovyng.[23] It is also the longest (sixty-nine membranes) of the extant coroners' rolls. Of the twenty-five cases on Ovyng's roll that present homicides identifiable on the trial rolls, only two ended in convictions.[24] Both show the characteristics of murder, but in one the defendant confessed and turned approver.[25] This sort of piecemeal evidence, drawn from isolated cases on many different rolls over a century or more, does not afford convincing proof.

The only feasible approach to our problem is to compare the coroner's indictment with the trial enrollment in cases ending in a verdict of self-defense. As we have seen, the law of self-defense was very strict. The slayer had to have acted as a last resort, which meant, in effect, that the jury had to detail the defendant's attempts to escape his assailant. Verdicts of self-defense appear on the trial rolls as a series of formulas that put the defendant's actions in the best possible light. The slain man was usually said to have provoked the fight and dealt the first blow; the defendant then had attempted to escape, only to find himself cornered or thrown down and held to the ground; gravely wounded, the defendant as a last resort drew a weapon and saved his life in the only way possible. Often, it was specified that the defendant had retaliated with a single blow.[26] Some of these details doubtless represented embellishments of the truth; some even went beyond the rigorous requirements of the law. It would have been sufficient, for purposes of eligibility for royal pardon, to allege that the defendant had retreated as far as possible and had struck

23. JUST 2/18 (Cambridgeshire, 14–39 Edw. III).
24. Nine ended in acquittals, eleven in findings of self-defense, one defendant came forward with a pardon, one died in gaol, and one was remanded to gaol pending further proceedings.
25. JUST 2/18, m.21/4 (1349): "... *noctanter felonice interfecit R. B. et M. uxorem eius* ..." The gaol delivery roll (JUST 3/134, m.38/5) used the form, "*felonice et sediciose interfecit . . . noctanter.*" In the second case, testimony was recorded at the coroner's inquest [JUST 2/18, m.5d/4 (1346)] that "... *post horam cubitus* [A] *surexit extra cubitum suum . . . insultum fecit eidem W. . . . W. surexit a lecto suo*" and raised the hue, at which point the defendant stabbed him to death. The accused turned approver [i.e., confessed and then appealed others in hope of obtaining their convictions and, in return, of gaining pardon for his own offense. See Pugh, "Reflections of a Medieval Criminologist," pp. 16–17; F. C. Hamil, "The King's Approver," *Speculum*, vol. ll, p. 238; Jens Roehrkasten, "The King's Approver in the Fourteenth Century" (paper delivered at the British Legal History Conference, Norwich, July, 1983)]. For the gaol delivery enrollment, see JUST 3/134, m.34/4 (1346). Although little can be made of such rare cases, they deserve some comment. They are the only cases that led to conviction. Both have elements of "murder." The first was secretly done, at night; the second was an attack on a man in his own bed. Though the defendant confessed, it is unlikely he would have done so had the jury not been about to declare him guilty. This is precisely what we would expect to find if a more extensive comparison were possible.
26. E.g. JUST 3/142, m.6d/2 (1367); JUST 3/142, m.10d/2 (1371).

back as a last resort; had he not yet been wounded or had he needed to retaliate with multiple blows, he would still have been eligible.

It thus becomes critical to determine just how much the jury embellished the defendant's true case. If juries used the category of pardonable homicide to exculpate manslaughterers, they would have fabricated stories of retreat and last resort where in fact there had been neither. They would have cast fights willingly entered by the defendant, possibly ones wherein he had struck the first blow, as struggles in which the defendant was an unwilling participant. If the juries perpetrated such fabrications, it would be visible to us only through a comparison of the trial enrollments with the corresponding coroners' enrollments. The coroner's enrollment was often far less formulistic and represented a more candid response from the jury. It was a record that could be contradicted or embellished in court without reprimand to the jury or detriment to the defendant's case.[27]

Admittedly, several methodological difficulties arise in employing the coroners' rolls. In the first place, the coroner's inquest was held very soon after the homicide occurred, and in some cases additional evidence must have come to light after the inquest had been held. Moreover, the coroners' enrollments nearly always name only one suspect and set forth only one set of facts as to the circumstances of the homicide. The process by which these unanimous inquest verdicts were reached is unknown. They probably represented the belief of the majority of the jurors. Many inquest votes may have been close, and their outcome may have resulted from the prestige or power of one or two persons. Many coroners (or their clerks) were erratic in the enrollment of details; that only a few facts were set down in a given case does not mean that others were not stated at the inquest. Finally, some enrollments were malicious indictments. This is more likely to have been the case where there had been only one witness, or where there had not been a witness but merely a "first finder." The witness or finder would have been in a strong position to place the blame where he pleased.

Several steps have been taken in order to mitigate the above problem. Coroners' inquest juries often stated that a homicide had been committed in self-defense although the evidence they presented did not meet the legal requirements for a pardon. These cases are the best source of evidence of community attitudes, and I have relied heavily upon them. I

---

27. Some coroners' enrollments were highly formulistic, the local inquest apparently having already "embellished" a suspect's defense. Although the coroner's enrollment could be (implicitly) repudiated, it probably caused the bench in some cases to examine the defendant or the trial jury closely. The testimony given at the inquest must have had *some* influence; it was not evidence "of record," however.

have excluded from my study coroners' rolls which include very few details. It is clear that the clerks compiling these rolls did not bother to enroll evidence of self-defense but merely characterized all homicides as felonious. Therefore, it is unsafe to assume that any corresponding trial verdict of self-defense represented an alteration of the facts. Instead, I have relied upon rolls that include a great deal of detail in most cases. This allowed the assumption that where the coroner's inquest did produce testimony of self-defense it was duly enrolled.

In order to justify killing in self-defense, it will be recalled, the man attacked had to retreat until retreat was no longer possible. At the trial the jurors always alleged such a predicament, and though it was sometimes true,[28] a comparison of the coroners' rolls and the trial rolls reveal that it often was not and that a petty jury had so altered the facts as to make pardonable what the law considered nonpardonable. Thus from the community's point of view, a violent attack could be met by a violent response. A man whose life was threatened did not have to seek some means of escape; indeed, he need not do so though he was in no danger of losing his life. The court's concern with last resort indicates a concept of criminal liability clearly at odds with prevailing social norms.

A case from a Norfolk coroner's roll indicates the looseness of the social concept of self-defense:

> William put his hand to his knife in order to draw it and strike Robert. Robert, fearing that William wanted to kill him, in self-defense struck William on the head with a hatchet.[29]

Edmund de Ovyng, the Cambridge coroner, was usually very careful to report inquest findings in detail.[30] He recorded a case of homicide, described by the inquest jurors as homicide *se defendendo*, in which the

---

28. For various examples on coroners' rolls of clearly stated last resort see JUST 2/102, m.9d/2: "*fugit usque ad quoddam angulum domus*" (1363); JUST 2/18, m.5/4: "*iacuit super ipsum*" (1345); JUST 2/102, m.11d/2 (1364); JUST 2/67, m.5/3: "*quandam ripam ubi voluit transisse et non potuit pro profunditate et largitudine dicte aque*" (1354); JUST 2/18, m.52d/2: "*cessidit ad terram . . . A. fuit in proposito interfecisse . . . B.*" (1361); JUST 2/18, m.61/l: "*supersit predictum J. in ulnas suas*" (1364); JUST 2/23, m.2/2: "*non potuit evadere propter multitudinem inimicorum suorum*" (1373). The fact that the coroner's inquest produced such testimony does not mean that the facts were true; they might have been altered at this early stage. But in such cases the trial jury was not adducing facts contrary to those of the indictment.

29. JUST 2/102, m.9/2: "*Willelmus misit manum suum ad cultellum suum abtrahendum et ad percuciendum dictum Robertum. Idemque Robertus timens quod idem W. voluit occidisse eum in defensione vite sue percussit eundem W. in capite super cervicem eiusdem cum quadam hachia*" (1363). The trial record (Oyer and Terminer) has not been located, but the slayer was pardoned for self-defense: *Calendar of the Patent Rolls, 1232–1422* (London, 1906), May 6, 1367, p. 395. Hereafter cited as *C.P.R.* See also JUST 2/58, m.2/2 (1379).

30. E.g. JUST 2/18 (14–39 Edw. III); JUST 2/256, mm.1–4 (44–48 Edw. III).

assailant had seized the defendant's beard. Walter Clerk and Thomas Clerk argued until Thomas, threatening to kill Walter,

> suddenly jumped from the cart and took up an iron fork, intending to run at Walter, but Walter immediately grabbed the fork in his own hand and threw it from Thomas lest he do further damage with it; for which Thomas took Walter by the beard; Walter, because of this, drew his knife and in self-defense struck Thomas in the left arm so that he died.[31]

Thomas's attack and intentions, rather than the imminence of danger to Walter's life, were, apparently, the basis for the community's view that Walter had acted in self-defense. In a similar instance, Hugh Harpour, chaplain, took John atte Lane, also a chaplain, in his hands and

> threw him down feloniously at his feet and wanted to kill him . . . because of this, John, fearing death and getting up, drew his knife and stabbed Hugh in the chest.[32]

Hugh seems to have been weaponless, so that John was not in imminent danger of death. Nevertheless, he was repelling an attack and, thus, defending himself. The resistance was excessive, but the community did not scruple as to the nature of the retaliation. The trial jury provided an elaborate story of self-defense.[33]

Jurors at a Leicestershire coroner's inquest in 1365 told a complicated story with respect to the death of Richard de Sydenfen.[34] Richard Ruskin and his son William came to the door of William de Assheby's house in Melton and the elder Ruskin brought Assheby outside with sword drawn

---

31. JUST 2/18, m.45d/5: "*W. C. et T. C. . . . simul cum una caretta pro garbis querendo . . . et contencio mota inter ipsos T. . . . stetit super carettam querandam et minavit ipsum Walterum de vita et membra et festinans descendens de caretta cepit unum furcum ferratum et voluit concurasse super dictum W. et incontinenti dictus W. cepit furcum in manu sua et illud iactavit ab ipso ne dampnum ulterius cum illo faceret quo facto dictus T. cepit ipsum W. per barbam suam quo facto dictus W. traxit cultellum suum et in defensione sua percussit predictum T. in brachio sinistro*" (1357). The trial enrollment has not been located.

32. JUST 2/18, m.47d/4: "*cepit in manibus suis et iactavit ipsum feloniter humo sub pedibus suis et ipsum voluit interfecisse . . . quo facto predictus Johannes atte Lane timens mortem suam et in resurgendo de pedibus ipsius Hugonis traxit cultellum suum . . . et percussit predictum Hugonem in pectore*" (1358).

33. The trial enrollment (C 47, Cambridge, 6/87) is partly blind, but the legible parts indicate a classic form of self-defense. See also JUST 2/58, m.4/2 (1380), where the accused had been thrown to the ground before slaying his assailant. There is no mention of any weapon used by the assailant, but the jury maintained the homicide was committed in self-defense. No trial enrollment located. In some cases, the self-defender seems to have stood his ground and waited for his assailant to reach him despite the fact that there was no apparent obstacle to retreat. E.g. JUST 2/18, m.16/3 (1351); trial enrollment at JUST 3/134, m.41/l. JUST 2/58, m.3d/l (1379); trial enrollment not located.

34. JUST 2/53, m.3d/4.

by calling him a liar. After a struggle, Assheby chased his enemies to the door of their house where the elder Ruskin's servant, Sydenfen, seeing that his master was in grave danger, felled Assheby with a blow of a club. The latter revived and, drawing a small knife, slew the servant "in self-defense." Assheby did not retreat once he had risen to his feet, but that was of no consequence. Nor did it matter that he had entered the fray of his own choosing. When he killed Sydenfen he was acting in "self-defense."[35]

Jurors at the inquest in Aldgate Ward, London, in 1325, described a somewhat one-sided fight which grew out of a sudden quarrel:

> John le Marche, "*pottere*," and Agnes de Wycoumbe after the hour of curfew, were quarreling in the High Street opposite the house of John . . . when the said Agnes taking a staff . . . out of the hand of John . . . therewith struck the said John on the back and sides; that thereupon came Geoffrey de Caxtone . . . and Andrew de Wynton, "*pottere*," with staves in their hands to assist the said Agnes and struck the said John on the head and body, so that he died a week later.[36]

A trial enrollment is extant only in the case of Andrew.[37] The petty jurors testified that John met Andrew some distance from the place of the slaying and struck him on the head with a staff.[38] Andrew fled until he was up against a wall and forced to retaliate.[39] There was no mention of other principals to the homicide.

Testimony of a more unusual sort was given by inquest jurors at an Aldersgate viewing of a dead man, a certain John de Chiggewell:

> John Pentyn would have hanged himself in his solar, and on that account his wife Clemencia raised the cry so that the said John de Chiggewell, John atte Adam de Mersshe, Wykham and other neighbors, names unknown, came to her assistance, and that when the said John de Chiggewell would have entered the solar before the others, . . . Pentyn feloniously struck him on the head . . . inflicting a mortal wound.[40]

At Pentyn's trial the petty jury alleged that he had argued with his wife and, after she had left the house, had locked the door and gone up to his

---

35. When Assheby came to trial he already had a pardon. JUST 3/142, m.18/1; *C.P.R.*, Dec. 6, 1366, p. 345.

36. *London Coroners' Rolls*, Roll E, no. 35, pp. 162–63.

37. According to the coroner's roll, Andrew and a certain Robert le Raykere, who had "aided and abetted" the felony, were immediately captured; Agnes and Geoffrey fled.

38. C 260/37, no. 7 (1326). See also JUST 3/43/3, m.2/1 (1326) for the original trial enrollment.

39. Pardon: *C.P.R.*, Feb. 22, 1327, p. 24.

40. *London Coroners' Rolls*, Roll B, no. 42, pp. 65–66.

bed in the solar. Clemencia returned in the evening and finding herself locked out raised the hue, at which point Chiggewell arrived, ascended the stairs to the solar, and tried to kill Pentyn with a hatchet. Pentyn, unable to escape, grabbed an iron window bar and in self-defense gave his assailant one blow from which he died fifteen days later.[41]

Finally, a simple homicide led to a special verdict of self-defense in the case of John Counte, who, after quarreling with Robert Paunchard in Bishopsgate Ward, London, drew a knife and stabbed Paunchard to death.[42] The trial jury maintained that Paunchard had thrown rocks at Counte and driven him to a wall.[43]

By the middle of the fourteenth century, a defendant who had slain a housebreaker might be acquitted by judgment of the court.[44] The same applied where he had slain someone who came to rob him. But the courts were not consistent in their treatment of such cases, and it appears that at least until late into the century acquittal might depend upon clear evidence of self-defense.[45] In this area, the community was ahead of the courts. Trial juries supplied evidence of self-defense where, on the basis of coroner's inquest testimony, there had been neither true self-defense nor even clear evidence of housebreaking or attempted theft.

In one instance, where self-defense may in fact have been involved, though the jurors at the inquest made no mention of last resort, the deceased had entered the close of William Childerle

> at the hour of Prime [about one o'clock, a.m.] without the license of William and against the latter's will.[46]

William returned home from the fields and met Richard on the stairs of his solar where a struggle ensued and the intruder was slain. At the trial, the petty jury assured the court that William had fled to a wall near the door of the house where he was finally cornered and forced to strike back in self defense.[47] Thomas Randolph of Braunston, Leicestershire, saw someone standing outside his window at night and demanded to know who it was.[48] Receiving no answer, he took up a club and went outside

---

41. C 260/32, no. 15 (1322). Order to bail Pentyn: *Calendar of the Close Rolls, 1272-1447* (London, 1900–1937), April 13, 1323, p. 636. Hereafter cited as *C.C.R.*

42. *London Coroners' Rolls*, Roll H, no. 9, pp. 242–43.

43. C 260/50, no. 61 (1339). It is possible that the jury was influenced by the location of the slaying. The fight had taken place in the close of the Earl of Warwick where Robert Artoys, by whom Counte was employed as a cook, resided.

44. See below, Chapter 3, nn. 53–54 and accompanying text.

45. *Ibid.*, text at n. 55.

46. JUST 2/18, m.41d/2: "*circa horam prima sine licencia ipsius Willelmi et contra voluntate ipsius Willelmi*" (1356).

47. C 260/68, no. 20 (1357); Pardon: *C.P.R.*, May 3, 1357, p. 530.

48. JUST 2/58, m.1/l (1379).

where the trespasser, John Sherman, attacked him. Standing his ground, Thomas dealt Sherman a fatal blow, which the inquest jurors said was done in self-defense.[49] Similarly, Henry Priour, attacked by William, son of John Paryn, who came one evening to the door of Henry's house, retaliated immediately with a club.[50] At Priour's trial, the petty jury asserted that William attacked Henry *"ad domum ipsius Henrici"* and drove him to a wall where he, Henry, happened to find the club he used; he thus had slain in self-defense.[51]

In a more extreme case, it was considered self-defense where the defendant on his master's property slew a man who had hurled insults at him.[52] William de Walynford, *"brewere,"* quarreled with Simon de Parys in Cheap and the latter followed William home, threatening him as they went. The coroner recorded that William forbade Simon to insult him in his master's house and then immediately William fetched a knife and plunged it into Simon's chest. In the petty jury's account, however, the facts were altered to show that Simon had attacked William with a knife as they stood in the king's highway. William fled to his master's house, where, being cornered by his assailant, he had slain him as a last resort.[53]

One related and extraordinary case, for which coroner's indictment and trial enrollment are both extant, shows how the community sanctioned the slaying of an adulterer. An aggrieved husband was not permitted to take the adulterer's life,[54] but, as in the case of a trespasser upon his land, he would have been able to drive him away. Robert Bousserman returned home at midday, an inquest jury testified, to find John Doughty having sexual intercourse with his wife (*"ad fornicandum cum illa"*).[55] Bousserman forthwith dispatched Doughty with a blow of his hatchet. The petty jury altered the facts to make Robert a self-defender who could not escape and to emphasize the aspect of trespass:

> John Doughty came at night to the house of Robert in the village of Laghscale as Robert and his wife lay asleep in bed in the peace of the King, and he entered Robert's house; seeing this, Robert's wife secretly arose from her husband and went to John and John went to bed with Robert's wife; in the meantime Robert awakened and hearing noise in his house and seeing that his wife had left his bed rose and

49. No trial enrollment has been located for this case. Possibly, the defendant was acquitted as a slayer of a thief.

50. JUST 2/18, m.44d/3 (1354).

51. JUST 3/139, m.13d/1 (1356). Priour was remanded to await a pardon.

52. *London Coroners' Rolls*, Roll C, no. 13, p. 80.

53. JUST 3/43/1, m.21/1 (1324).

54. Pollock and Maitland, *History of English Law*, 2:484. Referring to an earlier period, the authors suggest that the right to slay the adulterer was already doubtful.

55. JUST 2/211, m.1d/1 (1341).

sought her in his house and found her with John; immediately John attacked Robert with a knife . . . and wounded him and stood between him and the door of Robert's house continually stabbing and wounding him and Robert seeing that his life was in danger and that he could in no way flee further, in order to save his life he took up a hatchet and gave John one blow in the head.[56]

The allegation that the slain man had secretly entered a house at night while the master of the house slept was one of the common elements of later indictments for "murder."[57] In this case it was unnecessary; the jurors needed to do no more than provide the usual allegations of homicide *se defendendo*. Possibly, the elaborations by the trial jury indicate an especially strong sense of outrage.

The community was also ready to excuse homicide that occurred in defense of a kinsman though the slayer was not himself in mortal danger. The petty jury had to alter the true facts by asserting that the accused himself had come under attack and had slain his assailant as a last resort.[58] This may be seen in a number of cases. A Buckinghamshire coroner, John atte Broke, recorded that John Colles, senior, and his son John stood talking to William Shepherde when an argument broke out. Shepherde struck Colles senior with a staff.

> Seeing this, John Colles junior drew his knife and struck Shepherde in the right part of the neck wounding him mortally.[59]

Broke concluded his enrollment with the phrase, "and thus he slew him feloniously," and indeed the younger Colles had clearly not been attacked. At the trial, however, the petty jury asserted that after Shepherde

56. JUST 3/78 m.2d/l: "*infra nocte predictus Johannes Doughty venit ad domum ipsius Roberti in predicta villa de Laghscales prefato R. cum uxore sua in lecto suo in pace Regis iacente et sompniente et domum ipsius R. intravit quod percipiens uxor ipsius R. secrete a viro suo surexit et ad ipsum J. ivit et predictus J. uxorem ipsius R. ibidem concubiit . . . medio tempore predictus R. vigilavit et audiens tumultum in domo sua et percipiens uxorem suam a lecto suo abesse surexit et querendo eam in domo sua invenit eam cum predicto J. et statim predictus J. in ipsum R. cum quodam cultello vocato* [tear in membrane] *ibidem insultum fecit et ipsum verberavit vulneravit et inter ipsum et hostium eiusdem domus stetit semper cum cultello predicto ipsum percuciendo et vulnerando ipsum ibidem ad interficiendum et predictus R. videns periculum mortis sibi iminere et se ulterius nullo modo posse diffugere causa mortem suam propriam evitandi sumpsit quoddam polhachet et inde percussit predictum J. solo ictu in capite usque cerebrum unde statim obiit.*" (1342).

57. Green, "Societal Concepts of Criminal Liability," p. 692.

58. Hurnard states the common law rule as restricting self-defense to defense of one's own life. She appears to have found no cases where defense solely of one's kin was alleged.

59. C 260/105, no.13: "*. . . hoc videns extraxit cultellum suum . . . et percussit prefatum Willelmum in dextera parte colli faciens ei plagam mortalem et sic ipsum felonice interfecit*" (1393). The coroner's indictment is enrolled on the King's Bench transcript of the trial proceedings.

had begun the quarrel, and had struck Colles senior, Colles junior intervened to part them. Shepherde then turned on Colles junior, who fled as far as a wall between two houses where he was forced to slay his attacker in self-defense.[60]

According to a London coroner's roll, Simon Chaucer and Robert de Uptone quarreled on the street in Cordwainer Street Ward; Simon struck Robert, wounding him on the upper lip (there is no mention of a weapon). John, Robert's son, who was present and saw the incident, seized a "dorbarre" with which he beat Simon on the hands, side, and head, killing him.[61] The petty jury told an elaborate story that made John eligible for a royal pardon:

> A quarrel broke out between Simon and Robert over certain pennies which Simon owed the latter. Simon took up a staff and wanted to strike Robert, but Robert grasped it firmly in his hands. . . . Simon drew his knife and stabbed Robert in the mouth so that blood flowed. John, sitting in a shop [*shopa*], saw the fight and rising and taking up a dorbarre ran to the fight to pacify the two if he could. When Simon saw John coming he left Robert and went after John with the knife . . . he chased John as far as a wall in *Aldermannescherche* and held him tightly against the wall so that John could not escape.[62]

Similarly, Alice, the wife of James Almand, "*Pipere*," who slew John Langetolft in London, was said at her trial to have entered a fray to save James, only to end by slaying in self-defense. The petty jury added, however, that she slew John in order to save not only her own life but that of her husband.[63] The coroner's indictment copied onto the gaol delivery

---

60. *Idem*. Colles junior was released, pending his pardon, in the hands of four men, one of whom was his father.

61. *London Coroners' Rolls*, Roll F, no. 4, pp. 175–76.

62. C 260/50, no. 60: ". . . *contencio oriebatur inter Simonem et Robertum de Uptone patrem predicti Johannis pro certis denariis eidem Roberto per prefatum Simonem debitis. Ita quod predictus Simon cepit in manu sua quendam baculum . . . et inde percussisse voluit predictum Robertum quem baculum predictus Robertus in manibus suis ita firmiter tenuit. . . . Simon . . . extraxit quendam cultellum suum qui vocatur "Bideu" et inde percussit predictum Robertum in ore ita quod sanguis inde exivit. Predictus Johannes sedens ibidem in quadam shopa et videns dictum patrem suum et prefatum Simonem sic fore in contumelia surrexit et cepit quendam Dorebarre in manu sua et cucurrit eis ad contumeliam illam pacificandam si potuisset. Et cum predictus Simon vidit ipsum Johannem sic venientem reliquit predictum Robertum et se dedit eidem Johanni cum prefato Bideu in manu sua extracto et ipsum inde fugavit ad quandam parietem de Aldermannescherche contra quem parietem predictus Simon ipsum Johannem cum manu sua sinistra ita strite tenuit quod ex nulla parte evadere potuit*" (1340). Despite his immediate capture, John did not appear at gaol delivery until 1339, some three years thereafter. John was pardoned in Jan., 1340 (*C.P.R.*, p. 351).

63. C 260/72, no. 15. (1361).

roll states that she slew John feloniously, no mention being made of self-defense.

A Cambridge jury converted a more serious manslaughter into pardonable homicide when it altered the facts of Richard Godmancester's slaying at the hands of William Holdy. Edmund de Ovyng's coroner's roll states that William came upon his brother Thomas and Richard as they quarreled. William drew his knife and stabbed Richard in the back.[64] Ovyng termed the homicide a felony. The trial jury's reworking of the facts provided ample evidence of last resort and asserted that Godmancester had died of a wound in the stomach, a rather more reasonable place for a self-defender to stab his adversary.[65]

In none of the above cases had the defendant acted out of true premeditation. Where the defendant had supplied the initial provocation, it appears to have been a less than homicidal attack, which then escalated with fatal results. Certainly, these slayings were not "murders" in the sense that term was used by the late fourteenth century. The defendant had not ambushed the deceased or employed other means of stealth. But in none of them would the defendant have merited a royal pardon under the terms of the law. Had the true story come out in court, as the statement of Prisot indicates, the defendant would have been sentenced to death.[66]

One final and difficult question: Are we dealing here with an expanded notion of self-defense, or with a broader attitude that only murderers ought to be hanged? The answer must be that there is evidence of both. In many, perhaps most, of the above cases the community surely believed the slaying was justified even though the official rules of self-defense had not been met. But in others there had been little or no element of

---

64. JUST 2/18, m.15d/3 (1351).

65. JUST 3/134, m.41/4 (1348). The accused was thrown to the ground and lay "*subtus quandam parietem . . . insurgendo versus dictum parietem se defendendo percussit predictum Willelmum* [sic] *in ventre.*" For a case in which self-defense involved striking a man in the back see *Calendar of Inquisitions Miscellaneous (Chancery), 1219–1377* (London, 1916–37), vol. l, pp. 568–69, no. 2126.

66. This study remains tentative. The great majority of cases for which I located both an indictment and a trial enrollment could not be used. In hundreds of cases, indictments for felonious homicide led to trial verdicts of self-defense, but it is unclear that the coroner bothered to record details of self-defense. In many others where both indictment and verdict agreed on self-defense the former was so formulistic as to raise suspicion that fact alteration had already taken place. Another possible approach to the problem of demonstrating fact alteration is to analyze the formulistic verdicts of self-defense and to infer alteration from the frequent use of a limited number of excuses. My approach draws attention to the plausibility of such an inference but goes a step further by showing that the formulas were not merely convenient summaries for what were in fact instances of pardonable homicide.

*why?*

self-defense, and the trial verdict appears to be an entire fiction devised for purposes of saving the defendant's neck.

Perhaps all that can be said is that, given the nature of medieval life, the rules of both self-defense and felonious homicide were unrealistically strict. If firmly applied, they would have meant the condemnation of persons of pride who, when under attack, did not turn tail and flee until cornered beyond all hope of further escape. They would also have meant the hanging of men who, in sudden anger, struck a blow not in itself mortal but which, due to infection or careless treatment, resulted in death. These are different cases, occasioning different motives for leniency. Many homicides must have combined elements of both cases. It is, however, impossible to determine where society drew the line between homicides it viewed as justifiable self-defense and homicides it viewed as unjustifiable but still not deserving capital punishment. Nor, for that matter, is it possible to determine which slayings in the latter class were considered so impetuous as to be akin to accidental homicides. It is likely that some simple homicides were recast by trial jurors as misadventures, and hence made pardonable, but there are too few such special verdicts on the fourteenth-century rolls to make comparison with the coroner's enrollment profitable. The subgroups within the area of simple homicide must have shaded into one another, and distinctions among them probably differed over time and locale. Moreover, as I shall suggest in subsection 4, many social and psychological factors must have played a role in the formation of the community's attitude toward individual defendants and its perception of their deeds.

3

The foregoing suggests that in the fourteenth century trial jurors were not above characterizing as pardonable "simple" homicide, roughly what we would call manslaughter. The present section of this study seeks to assess whether thirteenth-century trial jurors' verdicts closely represented the truth. Naomi D. Hurnard concluded her pioneering and learned study of royal pardons for homicide with the end of the reign of Edward I, but she hinted that jury behavior might have changed in the ensuing period.[67] She pointed out that the sudden increase of pardons *de gratia* after 1294 caused a fundamental break with earlier practice. The implication of her remarks is that conclusions arrived at on the basis of fourteenth-century evidence cannot be carried back into the earlier

67. Hurnard, *King's Pardon for Homicide*, p. 268: "[T]he jurors were not yet falling back on one or other of a set of prefabricated tales which could be borrowed, disguised only with minor variants, to substantiate their declaration that slayings had been in self-defense."

period. The specific argument here would be that, after 1294, jurors, with knowledge of the indiscriminate dispensing of pardons to slayers, altered their outlook toward homicide defendants—especially toward those who had committed a simple homicide—and found pardonable circumstances where there had been none. The jury would have reasoned, in effect, that a man who by acting with more dispatch might have made himself invulnerable to prosecution should not be hanged unless he was of the most disreputable sort. In my view, while the new pardoning policy might have increased the jury's willingness to alter the facts in favor of the defendant, that policy was not the real source of jury attitudes. Jury behavior did not change radically after 1294; from the very outset of the common law period, juries were inclined to structure the evidence in such a way as to save the life of the manslaughterer.

In her chapter on trial jury verdicts Hurnard examined the extent to which juries fabricated facts in order to ensure that the defendant would receive a pardon for excusable homicide. She compared the allegations made by jurors at special inquisitions held for the purpose of deciding whether bail ought to be granted with those set forth at the actual trial before justices in eyre. Her findings support her conclusion that

> on the whole, discrepancies between two or more verdicts were over details of location and the sequence of events, the sort of thing on which independent witnesses could easily differ. . . . The impression which these comparisons give is of pretty general agreement on the issue of self-defense or accident.[68]

In one case of "serious discrepancy," the eyre jury suppressed the fact that the defendant had retaliated against blows of a staff with a relatively more lethal weapon, a small ax, alleging instead that he had used a staff in self-defense. The inquisition had alleged that the defendant had been struck on the head and cornered and that he had employed his ax because he could not otherwise have escaped death.[69] The alteration "may have been literally vital" to the defendant, as Hurnard argues, but this would be true only because of the overly strict rules of self-defense, not because the trial jurors were coming to the aid of a person who had not in fact slain in self-defense.

How much weight ought we to accord to the "pretty general agreement" between special inquisitions and trial enrollments? The former were indeed less formal than the latter; they were not necessarily final and sometimes less attention was paid to the stringent rules of pardonable self-defense. But special inquisitions were directed to the issue of

68. Hurnard, *King's Pardon for Homicide*, p. 265.
69. *Ibid.*, p. 261.

excusable circumstances and were held at the "request of the accused or his friends, who probably had some reason for confidence in their outcome."[70] They represented a point in the procedure at which the community view of the homicide had become known, and they probably were held only when it was fairly clear that community sympathy lay with the suspect. This may help to explain why Hurnard was able to find only one such commission that determined the defendant had slain feloniously.[71] In fact, the partiality of jurors at special inquisitions sometimes resulted in favorable verdicts that trial jurors later overturned.[72] Hurnard's comparison, therefore, is of limited usefulness. Having set alongside the trial verdicts a body of evidence overwhelmingly favorable to the defendants, i.e., special inquisitions, she concluded that the trial verdicts were relatively scrupulous; where they disagreed with the special inquisitions, they took a more critical, and probably a more objective, view of the circumstances. But Hurnard was unable to establish the relationship between a random selection of indictments and the trial verdicts. That relationship can be established, if at all, only by comparing the coroners' enrollments with the verdicts given at trial. Hurnard recognized the potential value of such a correlation, but rightly concluded that too few thirteenth-century coroners' rolls exist to carry it out.

There exists one important piece of evidence that sheds some light on contemporary practice. A thirteenth-century precedent book, *Placita Corone*, describes the case of a man indicted for homicide. The defendant, a certain Thomas, came before the court and told his story as follows:

> And because I refused him [the deceased] the loan of my horse he ran at me in my own house with a Welsh knife, horn handled, in his right hand and inflicted several wounds on my head, shoulders, feet, and elsewhere on my body wherever he could reach. I did not at first return his blows; but when I realized that he was set on killing me I started to defend myself: that is to say I wounded him in the right arm with a little pointed knife which I carried, making no further onslaught and acting in this way to save my own life.[73]

One justice put the court's impatience with such formulistic defenses quite succinctly:

> Thomas, you have greatly embroidered your tale and coloured your defense: for you are telling us only what you think will be to your advantage, and suppressing whatever you think may damage you, and

70. *Ibid.*, p. 110.
71. *Ibid.*, p. 254.
72. *Ibid.*, p. 110.
73. Kaye, trans. and ed., *Placita Corone*, pp. 19–20.

I do not believe you have told the whole truth.[74]

Nevertheless, the defendant stood his ground, putting himself upon the country. When the petty jury testified under oath that Thomas's story was true, the court could only remand him to await his pardon.

Thomas's case is perhaps an exaggerated example,[75] but it is not very different from a great many thirteenth-century enrollments. Moreover, it strongly suggests that the justices were aware that coloration in cases of self-defense was common but that doubts expressed from the Bench would not intimidate juries. Hurnard recognized that formulistic descriptions of self-defense raise "suspicion that some of these circumstances were borrowed from other cases." She admitted:

> It may be judged that too many slayers in self-defense pulled stakes from fences and poles from carts, bolted into *culs de sac* or tried and failed to climb walls, were brought up against dykes or rivers, found swords unexpectedly but conveniently to hand or made random knife thrusts that just happened to hit vital spots.[76]

Hurnard concluded that victims of assault "naturally reacted in a similar manner"; that the "paucity of many of the clerks' Latin vocabulary" led them to fall back on the same terminology. Before 1307, she maintained,

> the jurors were not yet falling back on one or other set of prefabricated tales which could be borrowed, disguised only with minor variants, to substantiate their declaration that slayings had been in self-defense.[77]

Perhaps she is correct, but there appears to be little evidence to support her view.[78] One must still explain the high number of acquittals on the medieval rolls, rather than view pardonable homicides in isolation from other elements of the administration of criminal law. This is so because

74. *"Thomas, vous avez mut enbeli vostre parole et vostre defens enflori: kar vous pronunciez quant ke vous quidez ke vous poet valer et conceler ce ke grever vos poet, kar je ne quid pas ke vos eiez tote la verite conte"* (idem).

75. See above, Chapter 1, n. 49, for cautionary remarks regarding the use of this source.

76. Hurnard, *King's Pardon for Homicide*, p. 267.

77. *Ibid.*, p. 268.

78. In her analysis of the king's role in the pardoning process, Hurnard argues that "in a sample of well over 500 cases identified on the plea rolls pardon is very unlikely to have been granted to felonious killers in more than twenty percent, and even ten percent may be considerably above the mark" (p. 245). This assumes, of course, that the evidence on the plea rolls is trustworthy. What the author has proved is that the king did not often grant pardons to persons for whom there was not some favorable testimony, not that those who in fact slew feloniously were seldom able to obtain pardons. Hurnard also shows that presenting juries often used the phrase *"mota contencione"* to describe "fatal free fights"; they did not adduce testimony of pardonable circumstances in all such free fights. This does not prove the *trial* jury would not have done so had the suspect appeared and put his life in their hands.

the possibility that the acquittals resulted from jurors' failure to tell the truth threatens to undermine the notion that jurors were particularly scrupulous in cases of excusable homicide. There are, in fact, good reasons to believe that fourteenth-century social attitudes were not radically different from those of the preceding period. To explore these reasons, we must turn from the narrow confines of pardonable homicide to the general contours of the early history of liability for homicide.

We have seen that in the Anglo-Saxon period, and for perhaps a century after the Norman Conquest, some homicides were unemendable, leading to punishment—usually capital—at the hands of the Crown.[79] These homicides, secret homicides known as "murders," were considered particularly heinous and, as outrages against society as a whole, were exclusively royal pleas. It cannot be determined how closely the Anglo-Saxon "murder" corresponded to the "murder" of the late fourteenth century.[80] Probably the term always had connoted stealth; the slayer acted when his victim was off guard. But it appears that any homicide committed in the absence of a witness was presumed to have been committed through stealth. It was in secret and, hence, a murder.[81] Open homicide, on the other hand, remained until the outset of the twelfth century an emendable act.[82] The guilty party or his kin paid wer, bot, and wite. Failure to pay the wer could result in liability to the feud; after the tenth century, only the slayer could be subjected to the vengeance of the slain man's kin.[83] Although there is no evidence as to the frequency of such feuds, it is likely that settlement in money or in kind was the usual result of sudden and open acts of homicide. If the slaying resulted from a mutual quarrel and involved fighting on both sides, some elements of self-defense probably lay side by side with elements of excessive retaliation. Settlements probably took these elements into account, though in an impressionistic way. The extension of royal jurisdiction in the twelfth century to encompass the entire area of homicide had two revolutionary

79. See above, Chapter 1, text at nn. 5–8.

80. See Pollock and Maitland, *History of English Law*, 2:486; Kaye, "Early History," Part I, pp. 366 *et seq*. Kaye argues that "murder" retained its ancient meaning of "secret or stealthy killing" during the twelfth through fourteenth centuries, despite the fact that it was also used as a synonym for the general term "kill" and a fine for an unexplained homicide. It seems clear that the concept was deeply embedded in social attitudes during the entire period. Possibly, the social view of "murder" changed, due to the growth of professional crime, from certain specific acts, e.g., poisoning, to all planned homicides.

81. See below, nn. 100, 102–3, and accompanying text.

82. Hurnard, *King's Pardon for Homicide*, p. 8. Hurnard ventures the judgment that "the process may have been completed by the end of the reign of Henry I" (1135). But she cautions: "The date when this occurs is not known."

83. II Edmund, 1, in A. J. Robertson, trans. and ed., *The Laws of the Kings of England from Edmund to Henry I* (Cambridge, 1925), p. 9.

effects: many homicides that formerly had not resulted in capital punishment were now made capital under the law; strict and largely unenforceable requirements were introduced into a law of self-defense.

The evidence as to jury attitudes in the fourteenth century may aid in understanding social attitudes toward criminal liability in the entire period from late Anglo-Saxon times to the end of the Middle Ages. If so, the argument would run as follows. Originally, the Anglo-Saxons practiced the feud in homicide cases. The kin of the slain took vengeance upon the slayer or one of his kin, who were jointly liable for their kinsman's act.[84] Whether the mental element was taken into account is unknown. Secret homicide was a matter for the king, but all other homicides were emendable; failure to pay the wergild rendered the slayer and his kin liable to vendetta, though reduction of the amount of compensation by agreement was probably common. By the tenth century, the laws restricted liability to vendetta to the actual slayer. They also mandated a reduction of wergild compensation where there had been mitigating circumstances.[85] In such cases, where the slayer had acted in self-defense or through accident, the king relinquished the *wite*.[86] While the kin of the slain may have taken a narrow view of such mitigating circumstances, society at large took a broader view of the matter, having nothing to gain from feud or compensation, and in a day when fights began easily and led often to death due to sepsis or other results of poor medical techniques. In its eyes, secret homicide or especially malicious attacks justified punishment by death. Simple homicides were seen as requiring compensation, with mitigation if the act was unintentional or to some extent provoked. When all homicides were drawn within the sphere of royal jurisdiction and made, unless excusable, punishable by death, the community was forced to choose between presentment of the slayer and payment of the *murdrum*, a fine imposed for an unexplained homicide.[87] Before 1215, persons presented for homicide were forced to undergo the ordeal, so that if the community desired to absolve a slayer it had to fail to present him in the first place.[88] The records do not permit us to observe

84. Whitelock, *Beginnings of English Society*, p. 39.

85. III Edgar, 1, 2: "[T]here is to be such remission in the compensation as is justifiable before God and supportable in the State." Quoted by Hurnard, *King's Pardon for Homicide*, p. 5; VI Ethelred, 52, l: "[H]e who is an involuntary agent in his misdeeds should always be entitled to clemency and to better terms." *Idem.*

86. Francis Sayre, "Mens Rea," *Harvard Law Review*, vol. 45 (1932), p. 982.

87. Hurnard has traced the use of presentment from the late tenth century to the Assize of Clarendon. "The Jury of Presentment and the Assize of Clarendon," *English Historical Review*, vol. 56 (1941), pp. 374–410. On the *murdrum* fine see *ibid.*, pp. 385 *et seq.*; Richardson and Sayles, *Governance of Mediaeval England*, pp. 195–96. Pollock and Maitland, *History of English Law*, 2:487.

88. Groot ("Jury of Presentment," *passim*; above, Chapter 1, n. 20 and accompanying

the resulting tension between the bonds of friendship and the demands of the pocketbook. By the third decade of the thirteenth century, however, this tension had been relieved: once the slayer had been presented, it was left to the trial jury to state whether he was guilty or not.[89] This provided them with an opportunity to acquit or to adduce circumstances of pardonable homicide. The compromise that resulted is illustrated in *Placita Corone*, where a defendant who successfully pleaded self-defense was asked who put him in prison. He replied:

> Sire, my neighbors: for they were afraid of being involved in the affair and suffering loss thereby.[90]

Thus, from the outset of the common law period, trial juries were prepared to voice a sense of justice fundamentally at odds with the letter of the law. They persisted throughout the thirteenth and fourteenth centuries in using their role as submitters of evidence to condemn many murderers and to acquit or render pardonable those whom a later legal age would term "manslaughterers." Trial juries remained free to say the "truth" as they knew it, to reject the conclusions of both juries of presentment and coroners' inquest juries. Of course, in many cases the process of fact alteration began before the trial jury gave its verdict: it was not uncommon for a coroner's jury to use elaborate formulas to describe a case of self-defense.[91] The trial jurors, drawn from the hundred where the homicide was committed, but not necessarily from the immediate vicinage, probably reflected already settled attitudes of the countryside toward individual defendants.[92] It remains to suggest, by way of conclusion to this preliminary study, what the significant determinants of these societal attitudes were.

text) has shown that the presenters screened suspects before formally presenting them to make their law. They screened out suspects who they believed had not committed the felony of which the suspects had been accused by someone in the hundred. Presumably, they were obliged to present all whom they suspected of committing homicide; if they failed to present those whom they suspected of having committed simple homicide or even true self-defense, they were nullifying the law and subject to being amerced.

89. Doris M. Stenton, ed., *Rolls of the Justices in Eyre, being the Rolls of Pleas and Assizes for Lincolnshire, 1218–1219, and Worcestershire, 1221*, (London, 1934), pp. lxviii–lxxi. As Lady Stenton points out, judges had never been partial to the ordeal and had, before 1215, tried to persuade defendants to put themselves upon the country.

90. Kaye, trans. and ed., *Placita Corone*, p. 19.

91. E.g. JUST 2/58, m.4/2 (1380).

92. From the 1280s at least, the sheriff, in preparing for a gaol delivery, ordered the hundred bailiffs of his county to supply a panel of sixteen or twenty knights and freeholders for use as jurors. See C 260/4 no. 19 (1288); C 260/5 no. 14 (1289). Trial juries at the eyre were not always drawn from the hundred of the homicide. Meekings, ed., *Wiltshire Eyre*, p. 52.

4

We have seen that in the Anglo-Saxon period murder meant homicide through secrecy or stealth. Originally, murder was secret in the narrow sense that the slayer hid his victim's body to conceal the deed,[93] but it probably was soon used more broadly to refer to any homicide whose perpetrator was unknown. It is with this aspect of murder that the *murdrum* fine was associated, for the hundred was amerced in all cases of unexplained homicide.[94] It is likely, however, that already in Anglo-Saxon times murder sometimes implies that the slayer's identity was concealed from his victim, so that the latter was taken off guard.[95] Both Glanvill[96] and Bracton[97] refer to murder as homicide wherein the conceal- ment was relative to third parties, but this may be because by the time they wrote the sole function of the allegation of murder was to relieve the appellor from the requirement that he claimed to have seen the deed with his own eyes. For our purposes, of course, the important question is not which acts the official concept of murder encompassed, but which acts society considered so heinous that it believed the perpetrator deserved to be hanged. The answer to this question for the twelfth century will probably never be known.

By the fourteenth century, society's concept of serious homicide was far broader than that corresponding to the original technical meaning of murder. Evidence shedding light on the notion of serious homicide is sparse and difficult to interpret. The principal sources of such evidence are trial enrollments in verdicts of self-defense. In several cases, all dating from the first half of the fourteenth century, the jurors included elaborate allegations as to the nature of the attack by the deceased upon the defendant:

*A. M. was staying at the house of S. . . . and R., knowing M. was staying there, through murder and malice aforethought came to the house of S. and sought M. in order to kill him . . . R. immediately broke the door of the room and entered it and . . . ferociously attacked . . .* [98]

93. Pollock and Maitland, *History of English Law*, 2:485.
94. See above, n. 87.
95. Hurnard assumes too much when she defines murder as "secret and so presumably premediated killing." *King's Pardon for Homicide*, p. 1.
96. G. D. G. Hall, trans. and ed., *Glanvill* (London, 1965), p. 174.
97. Bracton, *De Legibus*, 2:378–79 (fol. 134b).
98. C 260/15, no. 38 (1305): "*M. hospitatus ad domum cuiusdam Sarre F. . . . et R. sciens predictum M. ibidem hospitatum esse per murdram et maliciam precogitatam venit ad domum predicte Sarre et quesivit predictum M. ad ipsum interficiendum . . . R. ostium eiusdem camere statim fregit et cameram intravit et . . . ferociter insultavit . . .*"

*B.* M. . . . about noon of that day maliciously entered and afterward, maliciously abusing the said W. and committing hamsoken against him, of his malice aforethought, . . . attacked him there in the house [and] threw him to the ground.[99]

*C.* R. left the aforesaid house and stood outside the door of the house of the aforesaid W. beneath the wall of that house lying in wait for A. in order to slay him because of an old quarrel between them, A. knowing nothing at all about R.'s lying in wait.[100]

*D.* W. was in his house and W. B. knew this. W. B. entered the close of W. at night and hid there during the night through malice aforethought, and maliciously lay in wait for the said W. in order to kill him, W. being ignorant of this; and when W. arose at dawn and left his house closing the door behind him thinking no evil, W. B. with malice aforethought suddenly and feloniously . . .[101]

*E.* H. and S. fought together in a mill . . . and S. attacked H. with a hatchet and wanted to strike him, but they were separated from one another by certain bystanders and S. was expelled from the mill. . . . S., nevertheless his furious intention continuing, maliciously devised deceitful plans against H., hiding himself outside of the mill. And [when] H., believing that the argument between them had been settled, left a little later thinking he was leaving safely and in peace . . . [102]

*F.* J. [was] lying hidden in ambush with two strangers in the house of H. They saw H. coming along the way and immediately, feloniously and in a deliberate assault, they attacked H. from all sides.[103]

99. C 262/l/l, no. 6 (1318): "*M. . . . circa horam nonam eius diei maliciose intravit ac postmodum maliciose ipsum W. insultando et hamsoken super ipsum faciendo ex malicia sua precogitata . . . ipsum W. ibidem in domum ad terram prostravit.*"

100. C 260/20, no. 26 (1310): "*R. exivit domum predictam et stetit extra ostium domus predicti W. subtus murum dicte domus insidiando predictum A. ad ipsum interficiendum ratione antiqui odii inter eos perhabiti et ipso A. insidiacionem illam omnino nesciente.*"

101. C 47, Bedfordshire, File 4/86 (1314): "*W. in domo sua propria extitisset et predictus W. B. hoc scivisset. W. B. clausum ipsius W. noctanter intravit et ibidem pernoctavit latitando* (sic) *per maliciam excogitatam et predicto W. maliciose insidiabatur ad ipsum W. interficiendum ipso W. hoc omnino ignorante et cum W. in aurora diei surrexisset et domum suam exivisset et hostium post se clausisset nulli malum cogitans predictus W. B. malicia precogitata in ipsum W. subito felonice prosiliit et cum quodam baculo ipsum insultavit . . .*"

102. C 260/15, no. 9 (1304): "*H. et S. contenderunt adinvicem infra molendinum . . . et idem S. cum quadam hachia que vocatur hache a Pyke ipsum H. insultavit et ipsum H. percussisse voluit set per quosdam circumstantes seperati fuerunt abinvicem et predictus S. a molendino illo fuit expulsus. . . .* [S]*et tamen idem S. animo furioso et perseveranti insidias excogitatas adversus ipsum H. maliciose machinabatur abscondendo se extra molendinum predictum. Et predictus H. credens contencionem illam inter eos pacificari post pauca exivit a molendino illo credens secure et pacifice recessisse . . .*"

103. C 260/54, no. 40. (1343): "*J. cum duobus hominibus extraneis latitanter insidiando*

The chief purpose of the testimony in the above cases was to support a verdict of self-defense. Housebreaking immediately puts those residing within on the defensive. Stealth on the part of the assailant, whose presence was until the last moment unknown to the eventual slayer, is strong evidence that the latter lacked malice (cases *C, D, E*). It might be argued that the second part of the testimony, the formal allegation of last resort (which I have omitted from the above excerpts), was alone insufficient in proving that the defendant had not provoked the fight. But it should have been enough merely to assert, as most juries did, that A attacked B, wounded B, and drove B to the wall. Whatever additional strength the above details lent to a special verdict, whether they represented the truth or were mere fabrications, the jury was describing what society took to be the most repugnant form of attack.

There can be no doubt that the jurors were alleging that the deceased had attempted to commit what was considered to be serious homicide— what we may call the community's concept of murder. Cases *A, C, D, E,* and *F* involved stealth; housebreaking occurs in *A* and *B*; and in all these cases there was some measure of planning: malice aforethought was specified in *A, B,* and *D,* and seems implicit in *C* and *F*; in *E*, though his mind was in a fury, the assailant "devised deceitful plans." The difficulty lies in discerning whether stealth, housebreaking, or malice aforethought were critical to the societal concept of murder or were merely incidental.

The use of *"per murdram"* in case *A*, which was recorded in 1305, is extremely rare.[104] *Murdrum* at this time was used almost exclusively to refer to the fine for an unexplained homicide; it almost never describes the slayer's act.[105] It would appear, then, that the phrase meant "through stealth" in the sense that the slayer acted in such a way as to conceal his identity from third parties. But stealth in *C, D, E,* and *F* involves the intended victims knowing nothing of the presence of their ambusher. Murder was no longer conceived, if indeed it ever had been, solely as the concealment of the slayer's identity from third parties.

The only case that does not involve stealth is *B*. Here the jurors alleged that the would-be slayer committed housebreaking, presumably with intent to kill, an act which in Anglo-Saxon times had been regarded by the law as particularly heinous.[106] It may well be that such acts had always been included in the societal view of murder. *[handwritten: before Norman conquest]*

... *in domo cuiusdam H. predictum H. transeuntem per viam videbant et statim felonice et insultu premeditato ipsum H. . . . incircuiter insultaverunt."*

104. Kaye found a "Latinised form of the English 'to murder,' synonymous with 'to kill' " in a 1281 eyre roll (JUST I/147, m.13a). "Early History," Part I, p. 371.

105. The *murdrum* fine was effectively abolished in 1340. 14 Edw. 3, stat. l, c. 4.

106. Pollock and Maitland, *History of English Law*, 2:457.

The phrase *malicia precogitata* and its variants, which I have translated as "malice aforethought," was used commonly in indictments of homicide throughout the Middle Ages to denote the threshold degree of *mens rea* for felonious homicide: mere deliberateness.[107] As I have demonstrated elsewhere,[108] the phrase could also be used in the fourteenth century to refer to true premeditation. Everything depended upon the context. In case *A*, the assailant came to the defendant's house with malice aforethought, not mere deliberateness; "*ex malicia sua precogitata*" in case *B* seems contextually to represent more than the formulistic "*malicia precogitata*"; the ambusher in *D*, who lay in wait throughout the night "*per maliciam excogitatam*," exhibited more than mere deliberateness.[109] In case *C*, the assailant carried an old grudge; like the assailants in *E* and *F*, he lay in wait for the defendant. Only the assailant in *E* appears to have acted in hot blood.

Clearly, the jurors were attentive to the mental state of the assailant. It might be argued, however, that this resulted from their concern to blame the fight on the deceased; or, that planning was merely incidental to most acts of stealth and that premeditation was a common, but not an essential, aspect of murder. The foregoing evidence from the early decades of the fourteenth century is unclear on this point, and, as we shall see, there is reason to believe that even by the end of the century premeditation had not yet become a necessary element in the societal concept of murder.

The Statute of 1390 equated murder with ambush and malice aforethought.[110] Its drafters were undoubtedly concerned mainly with highwaymen and housebreakers who robbed and slew their victims.[111] The official term, "murder," operative only in the administration of pardons, now clearly embraced homicide perpetrated through stealth with respect to the victim. Moreover, true premeditation had come to be conceived officially as at least a common incident of murderous intent. But most murder indictments contain only the operative phrase "*murdravit*" or "*insidiavit*" (ambushed), and are thus insufficiently detailed to provide insight into the social, as opposed to the official, concept of murder.

There is nevertheless some indication that the short lived statute cast murder in terms too narrow for the community. If murder was, *stricto sensu*, homicide through stealth where the victim was taken off guard, it was in its broadest societal use a particularly repugnant homicide. A case from the roll of John Fovyll, coroner in Leicester and one of the first to

---

107. Kaye, "Early History," Part I, pp. 371 *et seq.*
108. Green, "Jury and the Law of Homicide," pp. 462–69.
109. Later on in the indictment, "*malicia precogitata*" is used in its formulistic sense.
110. "*Murdre, Mort d'ome occis par agait, assaut, ou malice purpense.*" Stat. 13 Richard 2, stat. 2, c. 1.
111. See below, Chapter 3, nn. 26–30 and accompanying text.

employ the word "murder" systematically in his indictments, lays to rest the notion that the societal concept of a murderous act was dependent upon secrecy or stealth. John Howetson came upon two boys, Roger and Richard Malynson, working near the road and wanted to strike them because of a long-held grudge. Seeing this, a certain Robert Malesherbe interceded, saying he would take whatever punishment was coming to the boys. Their sister Maud arrived at this point and similarly offered to make amends, but Howetson, calling her a whore, tried to strike her with a hatchet, pursuing her as she fled to her house. Malesherbe followed, imploring Howetson not to strike the woman, at which point Howetson turned upon him, swinging the hatchet "with great force." Malesherbe,

> thinking no evil, neither having a knife with him nor seeing any other weapon to prevent a blow upon his head, sprang from him and ran into Maud's house to get some weapon for defending himself.

Malesherbe grabbed a stake, but Howetson broke this and then, aided it seems by his son and another relative, proceeded to finish the job. While the two held Malesherbe down, the other struck him, and when the victim could no longer struggle, all dealt mortal blows so that "they slew and murdered Robert without any cause."[112]

In another case, admittedly a rare one, there was stealth but not premeditation. It was alleged that after a vigorous argument, one of the disputants, B,

> turned his back to [A] in the field and A ran to B and suddenly drew the dagger of B and feloniously stabbed him twice in the side. . . . The jurors say he slew him feloniously and murdered him.[113]

The allegation of murder seems to have turned on the deviousness of the act, which was apparently not premeditated but committed in hot blood. The word "*felonia*," rather than "*murdrum*," was later marginated, perhaps indicating that the coroner took a different view of the requisite *mens rea*.

There is one final point to be made about the late-fourteenth-century murder indictments. The slaying of master by servant and of husband by

112. JUST 2/61, m.12/l (1409): ". . . *nullum malum cogitans nec super se habens cultellum nec aliqua alia arma videns ictum illum supra caput suum eminere saltavit ab eo et cucurrit in domum ipsius Matillidis ad aliqua arma sibi assumenda pro defensione et salvacione vite sue . . . absque aliqua causa dictum R. M. interfecerunt et murdraverunt.*" See also JUST 2/61, m.92/2 (1406), where the slayer's dog attacked the victim, bringing him to the ground, whereupon the slayer "murdered" him.

113. JUST 2/63, m.3/2 (1400): ". . . *vertebat dorsum suum ad eundem in campum, predictus A. cucurrit ad predictum B., subito extraxit daggarium ipsius B. et felonice percussit . . . bis in latere. . . . [J]urati dicunt felonice interfecit et murdravit.*"

wife, two forms of statutory petty treason,[114] had for centuries counted among the most reprehensible homicides. Such slayings figured prominently in the indictments for murder, and all too frequently the jurors alleged that the victim had been slain while he slept in his bed or taken at night by ambush.[115] And, what is more revealing, occasionally it was said in such cases that the slayer had attempted to hide the deceased to conceal the act.[116] Thus, murder had not entirely lost its most ancient meaning, and its stigma, one suspects, could be attached to any homicide that society found particularly repugnant.

The process by which the community determined that a given slayer was a murderer was undoubtedly complex and by no means solely a function of the act itself. Coroners' juries and trial jurors were swayed in many cases by the status and reputations of the combatants and by what was known about past relations between them. Such considerations may have been critical to the determination that the defendant had acted through stealth, that he had caught his victim off guard. Conversely, these factors must sometimes have contributed to the conclusion that the parties had fought together on equal terms, out of sudden and mutual anger. There is, in fact, evidence that in some cases jurors perceived simple homicides as "accidental" ones because the parties were known to have been "friends."[117] It may be, too, that an informal, extrajudicial system of monetary compensation long outlived the demise of formal wergild settlement.[118] If so, the relations between the slayer and his victim's kin may have determined the community's perception of the homicide or, at least, of the slayer's just deserts.

We must be careful not to assume too much precision in medieval evidence-gathering techniques. The coroners' rolls leave the impression one would expect: in many cases the inquest jurors were imprecise, confessed lack of knowledge or made little effort to assess blame for a

114. Stat. 25 Edw. 3, stat. 5, c. 2 (1352).

115. E.g. JUST 3/180, m.23d/6 (Gloucester, 1393); JUST 3/180, m.31/l (Hereford, 1390); JUST 3/203, m.11d/3 (Lincoln, 1429); JUST 2/190, m.4/3 (Warwickshire, ca. 1390); JUST 2/242, m.5d/6 (Yorkshire, 1388). This last case, recorded by a coroner before the Statute of 1390, was one of many indictments reflecting the use of "murder" in a commission to justices of the peace in 1380. *Rotuli Parliamentorum*, 3, 84b. For discussion of justice of the peace indictments based on the commission of 1380, see Kaye, "Early History," Part I, pp. 379 *et seq.* The Statute of 1390, with slight modification, repeated the categories represented in the commission. I have based my discussion upon the Statute to avoid confusion, but it should be noted that indictments began to employ the term "murder" a decade before the Statute. See Green, "Jury and the Law of Homicide," pp. 461–62.

116. JUST 2/163, m.1/6 (1389) and m.2/ll (1393).

117. E.g. JUST l/1185, m.3; C 145, File 59/46.

118. Hurnard stated that out of court settlement was common during the twelfth century, but it is unclear how long this continued. Hurnard, *King's Pardon for Homicide*, p. 9.

fight ending in homicide. Many homicides must have been viewed from a distance or not all. To the extent that facts were unknown, poorly documented, or in conflict with other testimony, social and psychological assessments unrelated to the actual homicide but related instead to the parties involved must have been used.[119] It may be true that in the fourteenth century trial jurors were more lenient in some cases than they had been before the change in the Crown's pardoning policy.[120] But it is also possible that with the increase in social mobility and the rise of professional crime trial jurors were called upon more frequently to pass judgment on strangers to the neighborhood and dealt with them more harshly.[121] In any case, these would be merely two more examples of foreign elements creeping into the verdict process. The essential nature of that process had not suddenly changed. Due to the nature of the extant evidence, it suddenly becomes visible to us, but the available evidence suggests that it had for centuries been integral to the phenomenon of dispute settlement.

# II

Theft, in its various forms, was the most common capital offense committed by medieval Englishmen.[122] To judge from presentments on the thirteenth-century eyre and fourteenth-century gaol delivery rolls, thieving was endemic; and these sources reflect only a fraction of the offenses actually committed. In theft, even more dramatically than in homicide, the formal legal rules prescribed the death sanction for what was commonplace social behavior. It comes as no surprise that most defendants were acquitted—typically two-thirds to three-quarters at gaol

---

119. For extensive discussion of this and related issues, see the important work of Given, McLane, Hanawalt and Hammer, cited above, n. 2.

120. Pugh ("Reflections of a Medieval Criminologist," pp. 102–3) suggests that the "additional impediments" of the later period may have made some difference but cautions against assuming that juries acquitted significantly less in the 1280s.

121. See Hanawalt, *Crime and Conflict*, p. 54.

122. Hanawalt (*ibid.*, p. 66) found that in the eight counties she studied (1300–48) larceny (38.7 percent), burglary (24.3 percent) and robbery (10.5 percent) accounted for 73.5 percent of all felony indictments. These exclude, of course, thefts not reported as well as thefts prosecuted as criminal or as civil trespasses. See below, n. 135 and accompanying text. Homicide, though less common, accounted for a substantial minority of those felonies actually tried. Hanawalt (*idem*) found 18 percent. Pugh ("Reflections of a Medieval Criminologist," pp. 86–87) found 22 percent for London gaol deliveries of the 1280s. McLane ("Royal Courts and the Problem of Disorder") noted a very high percentage of homicide indictments (more than half of all felony indictments) but suggests this does not reflect the true rate of occurrence of this felony.

deliveries.[123]

Roughly stated, the forms of theft ranged from violent taking from the person (robbery) to taking upon a housebreaking, often under cover of night (burglary), to a simple taking and carrying off (larceny).[124] Each was practiced by all kinds of persons. Nonetheless, robbers frequently were or were viewed as outsiders and professionals who operated as highwaymen through ambush.[125] They often physically overpowered, injured, or even slew their victims. Compared with robbers, burglars were more often "local," less often professional, and they less frequently assaulted their victims. They were, however, more likely to be professional or to act in consort than larcenists. Larcenists stole goods of less value than did those who committed the more professionally oriented offenses.[126] Nearly all theft involved stealth or surprise attack. Burglary was frequently nocturnal and its perpetrator had entered, often unseen, the victim's private domain. Larceny was the act of the pickpocket or casual sneakthief. Ambush characterized much robbery. Although actually committed openly, it usually involved actions that gave its perpetrator an unfair advantage over his victim. Few thefts were responses to what society recognized as provocation on the part of the victim. Some, perhaps many, however, were understood as responses to the hardships of life.[127] As Hanawalt has demonstrated, the juries' treatment of theft suspects in the royal courts involved a complex of factors having to do with the nature of the actor and his act, the relationship between defendant and victim, and—to put it bluntly—the temper of the times.[128]

Analysis of jury verdicts in cases of felonious theft is doubly complicated by the fact that many thefts were not prosecuted at all and many others were prosecuted as other than felonies. Many minor unlawful takings were settled informally or privately prosecuted as trespass, even though an indictment would have been appropriate. Many other unlawful takings of goods worth 12 pence or more (that were thus felonies) were presented as mere criminal trespasses. At both the private and the

123. Hanawalt, *Crime and Conflict*, p. 59. See above, Chapter 1, n. 79.

124. See T. F. T. Plucknett, "A Commentary on the Indictments," in Putnam, ed., *Proceedings before Justices of the Peace*, pp. cxxxix–cxlvi. The questions of the carrying-off requirement in burglary and of the intent requirement in larceny are problematic. See Pollock and Maitland, *History of English Law*, 2:492–93; Plucknett, *Concise History*, pp. 446–47.

125. See Hanawalt, *Crime and Conflict*, p. 83.

126. *Ibid.*, p. 75.

127. *Ibid.*, p. 253. See Pugh, "Reflections of a Medieval Criminologist," p. 88. Pugh observes that most thefts tried at late-thirteenth-century Newgate gaol deliveries involved goods of "comparatively small value . . . taken for immediate use by ordinary citizens out of houses, often because of poverty or instant temptation."

128. Hanawalt, *Crime and Conflict*, pp. 52–54 and chs. 4 and 5.

community level, there was a preindictment sorting process that we can discern but not always closely examine.[129]

Theft and homicide presented different problems for trial juries and for those responsible for the administration of the criminal law. They do as well for historians who seek to understand the behavior both of juries and administrators. Nearly all homicides were reported, and most of them led to indictments. Although many suspects were not taken, virtually all who were taken were tried at the felony level. Some significant distortion is produced by the fact that the least culpable slayers were the most likely to surrender themselves for trial—or to remain where they might easily be taken. But while that distortion affected the acquittal and conviction rates, it does not conceal from us the attitudes of juries toward the least culpable. Quite the opposite: prosecution of homicide at the capital level tended to fall disproportionately on the least culpable. In theft such prosecution fell on the most serious cases, the ones least likely to be handled as lesser offenses.[130] Moreover, there was no category of excusable, i.e., pardonable, theft. Juries had either to convict and thus condemn (before the expansion of benefit of clergy in the fifteenth century), or acquit the defendants whom they tried. In homicide, not only was there an intermediate, pardonable category, but juries were required to state the facts in cases falling within that category.[131] Finally, coroners were required to hold inquests in homicide, and their records often were far more detailed than the summary indictments recorded by the clerks or sheriffs and justices of the peace.

Thus, conviction and acquittal rates in prosecutions for capital theft tell us far less than the historian of social attitudes would like to know. They confirm the most obvious fact: juries sent relatively few defendants to the gallows. Only about a third of those tried were convicted. More were sentenced to die than in homicide,[132] but that may have been due as much to the screening out of "lesser" offenders as to anything else. If we may draw any conclusion it is that with regard to capital sanction, theft, while typically involving stealth, was treated little differently by society at large than was homicide. One ought not make too much of the difference in conviction rates at gaol delivery; certainly there is no evidence that

129. See the important work of McLane, "Royal Courts and the Problem of Disorder," esp. pp. 84–86, 93–95. McLane has carried analysis of this sorting process further than any other student of medieval criminal administration. See also Barbara Hanawalt, "Community Conflict and Social Control," *Mediaeval Studies*, vol. 28 (1976), pp. 402–3.

130. McLane, "Royal Courts and the Problem of Disorder," p. 85.

131. Even after 1300 when pardons for homicide in self-defense and through accident were granted *de cursu*, the verdict had to be sent by the presiding judge to Chancery for consideration. See below, Chapter 3, text at n. 20.

132. Hanawalt, *Crime and Conflict*, p. 59. See above, Chapter 1, n. 79.

property was more highly prized than life.[133] Theft was common social behavior, reprehensible but not generally viewed as deserving the ultimate penalty.

Some evidence confirms the commonsense guess that juries distinguished between the professional and the amateur thief, between the truly premeditated and the opportunistic theft, between the most aggravated and the simplest forms of stealthy behavior. The most serious cases were those where the law of theft and the law of homicide converged. Excluding treason, conviction rates in capital cases were highest in trials on indictments for slaying by ambush by professional thieves.[134] We have seen also that the pardon statutes ostensibly relating to murder were aimed mainly at thieves (i.e., robbers), not at slayers who acted without the motive of pecuniary gain. Once again, there was a substantial overlap between the interests of the administrators of the criminal law and the attitudes of trial juries. Nonetheless, not all such defendants were convicted: frequently fearful juries could be managed by them or their powerful patrons. This, presumably, posed a serious problem for legal officials and the classes that sought to reduce the disorder that plagued the land. We shall return to this issue in the next chapter.

Jury behavior in the less serious forms of theft is difficult to analyze. There is little to relate beyond the bare record of massive acquittals, a record that, as we shall see, in slightly different form extends down to modern times. As in the case of homicide, juries were influenced as much by the defendant's reputation and social position as by the act with which he had been charged. Indeed, it is likely that in theft, even more than in homicide, who the defendant was counted for more than what he had done, for even the lesser forms of theft were regarded as very wrongful, insidious behavior that might reflect a disposition to engage in more serious forms of theft.[135] In homicide, by contrast, many defendants were considered to have acted justifiably, in defense of their honor, their family, or their friends. We have seen how difficult it is to determine in a given case whether the jury approved of the defendant's behavior, merely "accepted" it, or disapproved of it but nonetheless thought it did not merit the defendant's execution. Whereas some acquittals or self-defense verdicts in homicide cases reflected the view that, despite the official rules, the defendant had acted "lawfully" (true rule nullification), perhaps

133. See the remarks of McLane, "Royal Courts and the Problem of Disorder," pp. 109–10.

134. See Given, *Society and Homicide*, p. 133: 42.6 percent of those who were accused of both robbery and homicide and who appeared for trial were condemned.

135. See the remarks of C. M. Radding, "Evolution of Medieval Mentalities: A Cognitive Structural Approach," *American Historical Review*, vol. 83 (1978), p. 586.

virtually all nullification in theft occurred in cases involving socially disapproved behavior. Acquittals in theft cases typically represented what we may term systemic nullification of the prescribed sanction, the phenomenon of the purely "merciful acquittal."

Because theft was by definition both insidious and wrongful behavior, juries were bound to pay close attention to the defendant's social standing. The stranger who committed casual theft was perhaps necessarily more vulnerable to conviction than the one who committed simple homicide. Local communities with some justice believed they were constantly under threat from roving brigands. Moreover, within the community, status differences between jurors and the defendant probably counted for more in theft than in homicide. And this fact must be kept in mind also when one assesses the conviction and acquittal rates in the more highly stratified urban areas.

There are, then, few concrete conclusions to be drawn about jury nullification in theft. We are left for the most part to draw inferences from our study of jury behavior in homicide and to test them against what we do know regarding the prevalence of theft and the outcome of trials of thieves.

First, as noted above, the most serious forms of homicide, from the perspective of the Crown, legal officials, Parliament, and trial juries, involved slayings by professional thieves, mainly highway robbers and burglars. It is reasonable to suppose that jurors convicted a substantial number of such thieves even when the offenders did not slay their victims and that such convictions represent a fair percentage of the total number of convictions for theft. Second, jurors probably came down hard on strangers and others whose ties to the local community were attenuated for one reason or another. The leniency accorded villagers by their neighbors may be put down to favoritism, but given what jury behavior in homicide suggests, that may be just another way of saying that jurors thought the rules too harsh when forced to apply them to persons whom they knew well enough to identify with.[136]

I have earlier suggested that social mores reflected in traditional, private forms of dispute resolution in homicide influenced the handling of cases at common law. A similar hypothesis probably ought to be put forward in the case of theft. In pre-Angevin times, many forms of theft had been emendable. There is every reason to suppose that in theft the revolution in sanctions was as out of step with social attitudes as it was in homicide. The nearly blanket rule mandating capital punishment never

---

136. Hanawalt's preliminary study of indictment and conviction patterns in Ramsey Abbey is of great interest. *Crime and Conflict*, esp. pp. 53–54. I have drawn heavily upon her conclusions regarding the importance of status and residence to the outcome of theft cases.

truly took hold within the community, which imposed its own standards both outside of and within the formal legal system. The hypothesis is strengthened by what we know about the substantial amount of down-grading of felony to trespass, and what we might expect to result from such a potentially arbitrary process. Very likely, many whom the indictment jury left to be tried by authorities for the capital offense were viewed by the community at large as perhaps less savory but as no more deserving of death than many who were prosecuted merely for trespass.

Finally, the acquittal rate speaks for itself. It is of course possible that most acquittals were the product of bribery, fear, and belief in the defendant's innocence. But it is likely that just as many sprang from mercy and from deeply ingrained notions of how social harmony was to be maintained through composition with, rather than ultimate rejection of, the offender. Much thieving was opportunistic and committed against one's neighbor. Much of it was committed by the desperate and destitute of the local community,[137] and it was these locals who were the most likely to be apprehended and made to stand trial. Some of them, no doubt, suffered as a result of the community's frustration at not being able to bring all of the truly evil persons to justice. Many others of them, however, must have been spared simply because they were not among the truly evil in the eyes of their neighbors.

137. *Ibid.*, p. 253.

# 3 Judge, Jury, and the Evolution of the Criminal Law in Medieval England

We shall never know a great deal about the official response to the law-finding role of the medieval criminal trial jury. Most of what we do know we understand by way of inference from records that do not speak directly to this problem. Our lack of hard evidence, however, should not discourage speculation. In the present essay I shall attempt to put the problem of the law-finding jury into perspective. I shall suggest that the jury behavior described above influenced the bench in its interpretation and development of the substantive law of homicide. I shall also suggest the way authorities might have viewed the place of merciful verdicts in the less serious felonies as they considered the problems of the administration of the criminal law generally.

The difficulties in determining how the Crown, bench, and other officials viewed jury nullification are compounded by the fact that nullification was only one pattern of jury behavior that caused concern.[1] Nor was it likely to have been viewed as the most worrisome. Corruption, though not necessarily determinative in a great number of cases, was undoubtedly perceived as a greater problem. Jury timidity was less serious but perhaps more common, and likely to be present in just those cases in which officials were most anxious to secure convictions. Verdicts resulting from partisanship that did not involve outright graft were serious enough and might have seemed more akin to corrupt verdicts than to merciful ones. By comparison, rule or sanction nullification, whether systemic or ad hoc, may have been—especially in close cases—relatively easy for officials to tolerate.

Two other factors require our constant attention. Pretrial procedures resulted in a substantial amount of overindictment; there could hardly be a presumption against individual defendants in most cases. Even where indictments were justified, the trial jury might not be able to obtain dispositive evidence. Honest acquittals of guilty suspects were probably very common. On the other hand, simple rule or sanction nullification, when it did occur, was not easily distinguished from corrupt, timid, or purely partisan verdicts, and it may not have even captured the bench's

---

1. For a related discussion of the points raised in these introductory paragraphs see above, Chapter 1, text at nn. 87–97.

attention. If so, from the perspective of the bench the universe of exculpatory verdicts was divided mainly between rightful acquittals of the innocent—or those not proven guilty—and corrupt acquittals of true offenders. By the same token, however, the bench might have over-estimated the instances of nullification in close cases. Attention to this form of jury behavior might have blinded the bench to much of the corruption that plagued the system. The procedures that concealed so much from the bench conceal just as much—or more—from us. In reconstructing the perspective of the bench, we come to understand how little insight the judges were allowed into the actual workings of the system they administered. In the end, we cannot be certain whether they hesitated to draw any general conclusions, given their actual position of ignorance, or whether, without real justification, they drew such conclusions. A fortiori, we cannot know whether the bench thought it was more commonly confronting outright jury corruption, or well-intentioned jury nullification, or something in between.

# I

The Crown and royal officials were of course aware of the many problems that beset the administration of criminal justice. They sought in a variety of ways to combat the bribing and intimidation of juries, which were among the most serious of those problems. So far as one can tell, however, the official response rarely included either the refusal to enter a verdict or the punishment of a particular trial jury. Grand juries could be fined for intentional concealment when they failed to present a felony, but trial juries were, by and large, immune to penalties for acquittals or verdicts of pardonable homicide.[2] Why should this have been so?

The nature of criminal procedure shielded jurors against judicial monitoring of their behavior. In most cases the bench was dependent upon the jury and the defendant for information concerning the defendant's guilt or innocence. The judges might have suspected some mode of corruption, but they could not prove that it existed in individual cases. The judges at gaol delivery could invoke the strictest standards of the law but could not impose them upon the jury. They could relieve their frustration only by getting on to the next case, the next county town. Evidence of false testimony lay all about them, but pursuing it would have been very time consuming. Testimony at coroners' inquests and before sheriffs and justices of the peace could not have been as systematically wrong as the verdicts of petty juries made it appear. Yet if questioned, the jurors would simply have continued to swear on their oaths that the

2. See above, Chapter 1, text at n. 62.

defendant was not guilty. The court could have done little, short of undertaking a full-scale investigation of the homicide or theft, and lacking a police force or any sophisticated evidence-gathering techniques, even that seldom would have made the matter any clearer.

Ironically, our best evidence of judicial attempts to get at the truth in individual cases comes from cases about which the bench possibly cared least—cases involving verdicts of self-defense. Here the judges had some leeway in testing verdicts, for the jury had to state the evidence that justified the special verdict; a simple "not guilty" or "self-defense" would not do. There can be little doubt that the bench was aware that in many cases involving verdicts of self-defense the strict rules of the law had not in fact been met. The numbers of such verdicts were sometimes overwhelming; we must infer judicial recognition of realities.[3] Moreover, the rolls themselves reveal judicial caution in self-defense cases and even attempts to trick defendants or to steer juries into an admission that would preclude a judgment of pardonable homicide.

The trial rolls indicate that the judges sometimes questioned the jurors closely, particularly when the jury's original statement left unclear whether the defendant had in fact been placed in a position from which he could escape only through physical retaliation. In a few such cases the jurors responded that the defendant might have turned tail and outrun his assailant, an assertion that condemned the defendant.[4] But usually jurors proved to be made of sterner stuff. In several cases from the early 1290s separate juries resisted what appears to have been a concerted effort to restrict the availability of pardons *de cursu* to those who truly deserved them under the law. Responding to judicial queries, the juries strengthened their original verdicts: the deceased "lay upon [the defendant's] stomach and held him tightly to the ground";[5] the defendant was "armed, but had drawn neither weapon," resorting instead to a broken branch;[6]

3. See below, section IV.

4. See e.g. *Le Livre des Assises et Pleas del'Corone en Temps du Roy Edward Le Tiers* (London, 1670), 43 Edw. 3, pl. 31 (1370). Hereafter cited as *Livre des Assises.*

5. C 260/7, no. 46A (1293). In this case, the jurors stated that Gregory le Waleis threw Thomas de Gloucester "to the ground, lay upon him, and drew his knife desiring to kill him. Thomas, perceiving this, and fearing likewise his own death, drew his knife and struck Gregory as the latter lay upon Thomas's stomach." The justices then asked the jury whether in fact Thomas might have escaped without killing Gregory, to which the jury responded, "No, because Gregory lay upon Thomas's stomach and held him tightly and firmly to the ground" ("*et ipsum strite et firmiter ad terram tenuit*"). Their reply having satisfied the court, the defendant was remanded to prison to await his pardon. The pardon is recorded in *C.P.R.,* Oct. ll, 1293, p. 40.

6. C 260/6, no. 6 (1292). The jurors were asked whether Gilbert had a sword or a knife and, if so, whether he had drawn either. When they replied that Gilbert was so armed, but had drawn neither weapon, the court, obviously doubtful as to the lethal nature of Gilbert's

the defendant could not have fled because the deceased was faster than he was.[7] Only in the second case did the bench refuse to accept the verdict the jury insisted upon. A second jury was called, which supported the first jury and ensured that the defendant would receive a royal pardon.

Although the rolls do not reveal it, it is possible that judges frequently badgered juries into returning verdicts of guilty. As Henry Summerson has demonstrated, we may not accept the trial rolls as evidence of all that transpired at the trial.[8] If my depiction of jury behavior in self-defense cases is accurate, then the rolls are patently deceiving guides to the real world of the medieval courtroom. There are, however, strong reasons for doubting that judges successfully steered juries toward capital verdicts. Relatively few defendants, as we have seen, received such verdicts, and too many verdicts of self-defense were registered for us to imagine a coercive bench. We must either assume that the bench was in sympathy with the jury in close cases or that it was powerless to halt a practice it opposed. The latter possibility cannot be rejected out of hand: clearly the bench opposed all forms of outright corruption, but the continuing protests against such practices suggest that they persisted despite official resistance.

The apparent weakness of the bench and of royal officials should come as no surprise. The institutional or procedural bars to establishment of jury corruption or nonadherence to legal rules in given cases—the very fact of a self-informing jury—reflected the limits to royal administration.

---

attack, asked the jurors once again whether Robert could have escaped without slaying Gilbert. The jurors reiterated their opinion that he could not have done so. This failed to satisfy the court, however, and only after a second jury had been impaneled and had supported the verdict of the original jury was the defendant awarded a special verdict. The enrollment indicates in a later hand that Gilbert was pardoned.

7. C 260/6, no. 16 (1292). The petty jury stated that Alan de la More killed John Tyrel in self-defense after a great chase. The two had argued until John ran home to fetch a sword. "Alan, seeing John approaching, and desiring to evade John's malicious intent, kept himself underneath the horse his father, Robert, was riding. Robert did all in his power to prevent John from striking Alan, but John chased Alan into a certain corner" where, as a last resort, Alan retaliated with a mortal blow. The court asked whether Alan could have fled before John returned from his house armed. The jury replied that the defendant could not have fled because John was faster than he (*"Johannes erat celorior predicto Alano"*). Compare C 260/23, no. 23 (1332), where the jurors testified that the defendant fled as fast as he could (*"velociori curru quo potuit"*), but his assailants were even fleeter and caught up with him (*"velociores demum ipsum . . . attinxerunt"*).

8. Summerson, "Plea Roll and Year Book." Summerson has shown that judges questioned juries at the eyre but that the plea rolls record jury statements as though made *sua sponte* and not in response to such questions. It does not appear, however, that the bench overturned acquittals; it is possible, however, that judicial attitudes led some juries to convict where otherwise they might not have done so. Whether the bench questioned jurors at gaol delivery (as opposed to the eyre) remains unclear. See above, Chapter 1, n. 58.

In the area of criminal law, the Crown was dependent upon the cooperation of society at large, and continued to be so, though in ever lessening degrees, until modern times. About the best officialdom could hope for was to convert its pervasive weakness into a moderate strength by associating itself with the popular impulses that the jury represented. This it did, though we cannot be sure it did so with any degree of self-consciousness. But it was, in any case, only one of several policies the Crown pursued. We must sort out the contradictory aspects of the royal administration of the criminal law before we can speculate as to why the Crown accepted not only the jury but prevailing jury practices as well.

## II

Medieval legislation reveals the preoccupation of England's rulers with serious crime. Homicide and theft were but parts of a larger problem of disorder that attended changes in late medieval society. The periodic demobilization of military forces unleashed unmanageable numbers of potential brigands. Plague and famine created dislocations that taxed the restraining tendencies of medieval social organization. Town life and wealth spawned antipathies for which there was no solvent, and assaults against both were not easily checked. It is difficult to overestimate the rudeness of conditions, the commonness of petty warfare, and the insecurity of life. As time went on conditions worsened, and the elaborate legislative schemes to halt violence became increasingly utopian and fruitless.

There remained of course a world of difference between rural settlements and the populous areas along the most frequented highways. But even peaceful rural villages were subject to occasional pillage by roving gangs and the henchmen of local political magnates. The late medieval rolls of the justices of the peace and the justices of gaol delivery evidence increasing amounts of organized criminal activity in all parts of England. Until a detailed analysis of late medieval crime is undertaken we shall not be able to speak with confidence about levels and locales of criminal activity.[9] Nevertheless, if legislation and the extant trials rolls are a guide to the perspective of the Crown and bench, we must conclude that officialdom perceived a land almost bereft of public order.[10] Governance

---

9. Hanawalt (*Crime and Conflict*) has produced such a work for the early fourteenth century. No similarly comprehensive study exists either for the late thirteenth century or for the century following the Black Death. For an important discussion of the role of arbitration as a brake on public disorder in the latter period see Edward Powell, "Arbitration and the Law in England in the Late Middle Ages," *Transactions of the Royal Historical Society*, 5th ser., vol. 33 (1983), pp. 49–67.

10. See Kaeuper, "Law and Order," pp. 734–37.

involved, it would seem, a constant struggle to gain the upper hand over a large criminal population.

To understand the degree to which the ruling elites focused their attention on the worst excesses of public disorder,[11] we must examine the history of the attempts to restrain the royal power to grant pardons of grace. We have seen that beginning in the 1290s English monarchs employed their pardon power to raise a military force and to obtain revenue.[12] This flow of pardons immunized large numbers of offenders from prosecution for all offenses committed before the date of the pardon, and many contemporaries apparently believed that the policy encouraged potential offenders, who might expect to secure pardons in the future. Parliamentary statutes set limits on the royal pardoning power, especially for serious homicides, those committed through ambush or other forms of premeditated attack, typically in the course of highway robbery or burglary.[13] The Crown acceded to passage of these statutes but continued to sell pardons to even the worst offenders. Whatever the success of the statutes, it is significant that the attack on royal pardons of grace was aimed not at all felonies in general but only at the most heinous kinds of offenses. The point requires some elaboration for not all historians have viewed the matter in this way.

The earliest statutes declared that the king might pardon only those who slew *se defendendo* or by accident, the traditional grounds for pardons *de cursu*. These statutes, therefore, appear to have endeavored to prohibit all pardons of grace, declaring that all felonious homicides lay beyond the scope of the royal power to extend mercy.[14] This, in itself, nearly defies explanation: surely contemporary conceptions of justice required greater latitude than the statutes allowed, and literal application

11. See McLane, "Royal Courts and the Problem of Disorder," p. 76.

12. See above, Chapter 1, text at nn. 88–90.

13. See above, Chapter 2, n. 134.

14. As early as 1309, Parliament petitioned the king about the frequent pardoning of thieves ("*larons*") who had been indicted for "*larcines, roberies, homicides*," and other felonies. Those responsible for the indictments, so the petition alleged, feared to remain in their communities; many refused to indict out of similar fear. The petition did not suggest any specific remedy, but the king replied that in the future he would grant pardons only to those found to have slain through misadventure, self-defense, or insanity. *Rotuli Parliamentorum,* 1:444b (1309). The Ordinances of 1311 carried out the royal response in more general language: "That no felon nor fugitive be from henceforth protected or defended from any manner of felony, by the King's charter of peace . . . unless in a case where the King can give grace according to his oath, and that by process of law and the custom of the realm." Quoted in Hurnard, *King's Pardon for Homicide,* pp. 323–24. The Statute of Northampton attempted to limit pardons to self-defense and misadventure, Stat. 2 Edw. 3, c. 2 (1328), and in 1336 a new statute ordered that the Statute of Northampton be observed, Stat. 10 Edw. 3, c. 2.

of the wording of these statutes plays havoc with the underlying theory of the king as fount of justice.[15] It would be a mistake, I believe, to read the early pardon statutes too literally. They may in fact have been speaking to extreme cases rather than to the large intermediate body of simple homicides, and they may have been assuming a distinction close to the one that the statute of 1390 made explicit. It is worth considering how this legislative perspective may have come about.

As we have seen, the law of self-defense required the defendant to prove that he had acted *in extremis*. Indeed, by the middle of the thirteenth century it was considered felonious for a person who was able to flee to strike and cause death, even if he had been provoked and was in substantial danger. Yet the early treatise writers, when they considered felonious homicide, dealt mainly with its core element, malice, in the sense of a deliberate, unprovoked attack.[16] They rarely considered the case where the deceased had been the assailant, and the defendant, acting without true malice but in unnecessary haste, had chosen retaliation rather than flight. It is unclear even that these writers discussed homicides committed in the course of a brawl freely joined, where one of the blows dealt produced an unforeseen fatal result. Given their definition of pardonable self-defense, had they been pressed to define the outer limits of excusable homicide they would have had to exclude such acts.[17] But

15. The king sometimes pardoned culpable slayers whose acts either bordered on self-defense or for other reasons were not considered especially heinous. See Hurnard, *King's Pardon for Homicide*, p. 244.

16. Bracton seems to consider an unlawful homicide as one committed "in premeditated assault and felony." Bracton, *De Legibus*, 2:438 (fol. 155). He describes felonious homicide "as where one in anger or hatred or for the sake of gain, deliberately and in premeditated assault, has killed another wickedly and feloniously and in breach of the king's peace." *Ibid.*, p. 341 (fol. 121). Bracton does not here consider the provoked slayer who responds merely to save himself without being *in extremis*. *Fleta*, written a generation after Bracton, refers to wilful homicide as one in which "a man, with corrupt intention, wickedly and feloniously slays anyone by a deliberate attack, in anger or hatred or for the sake of gain." *Fleta*, 2:60.

17. Bracton describes self-defense (by implication) as follows: "[I]f avoidable and he could escape without slaying, he will then be guilty of homicide." *De Legibus*, 2:340 (fol. 120b). Here, Bracton implies the strict rule of self-defense, but does not specifically refer to provoked slayings where the slayer might not have acted out of malice. Nor does he refer to such acts in his discussion of intentional homicide. See above, n. 16. In his discussion of self-defense, where the slaying was "unavoidable," Bracton states that the slayer acts "with sorrow of heart," 2:341 (fol. 121), and "without premeditated hatred," *ibid.*, p. 340 (fol. 120b). But what of the slayer who acts when it was avoidable, though "without premeditated hatred" and "with sorrow of heart"? Cf. *Fleta*, 2:60: "[I]f the necessity were avoidable, without slaying, a man is guilty of homicide, whereas, should the necessity be unavoidable, he will not be liable to the penalty of homicide, because he has not slain feloniously, but from fear and instinctively, to save himself when he could not otherwise avoid his own death."

their writings do not articulate a reason for treating these acts as capital felonies.[18] Thus the practice of focusing only on extreme cases had begun.

As concern about professional and secret homicide grew, the chasm between those acts singled out for special condemnation and those meriting pardons *de cursu* grew wider. The attention of both judges and legislators, like that of the treatise writers, may have been diverted from the intermediate category of simple homicide. Indeed, this might have been a result of the prevailing pattern of jury behavior, which, as we have seen, narrowed the courts' focus on homicide to the more extreme cases.

Yet another factor sheds light on the likely intent of the early-fourteenth-century pardon statutes: a parliamentary misconception regarding the granting of pardons *de cursu*. In the thirteenth century, kings personally oversaw the pardoning process. Under this procedure, a few technically undeserving slayers, in the interests of justice, had received pardons for self-defense after trial.[19] In the early fourteenth century, however, the pardoning procedure changed. Routine royal intercession ceased, and the chancellor was empowered to issue pardons *de cursu* in the king's name.[20] By virtue of this new procedure, pardons *de cursu* were issued only in those cases where there had been a judicial determination that the defendant had met the legal standard for self-defense. Thus, although the king retained the power to grant pardons for self-defense to slayers who had not met the formal rules of the law,[21] this power was

---

18. Bracton comes closest to explaining the rationale for the harsh rules of the law, but his discussion presumes the possibility of rational decision making. In discussing the capital liability of one who "thinking to strike a light blow, . . . has struck a heavy one and killed . . .," Bracton states, "For everyone ought to observe mean and measure in what he does." *De Legibus*, 2:438 (fol. 155b).

19. These included those whose acts bordered on, but did not fall within, the legal category of self-defense (Hurnard, *King's Pardon for Homicide*, pp. 239–43) and on occasion even brawlers (*ibid.*, p. 244).

20. A 1329 Year Book statement reflects the automatic nature of pardons: "Note that when a man is acquitted before the justices errant for the death of a man in self-defense ["*soy defendo*"], the process is such, that he shall have the writ of the Chief Justice, within which writ shall be contained the record of his acquittal to the Chancellor, who shall make him his writ of pardon without speaking to the king by course of law." Sir Anthony Fitzherbert, *La Graunde Abridgment* (London, 1565), "Corone," pl. 361. Cf. *ibid.*, pl. 295 (1330): "Scrope, C. J., and the other justices ordered the prisoner to remove the record into the Chancery; and the Chancellor made him a charter in such a case without speaking to the king." Cf. the Commons' petition to the king and the latter's reply in 1309. *Rotuli Parliamentorum*, 1:444b.

21. It is, of course, possible that the summary procedure for pardons *de cursu* reflected a new royal policy according to which the king conceded his power to pardon *except* in cases of accident or in those cases meeting the strict rules of self-defense. Having so reduced his options, he would have little reason to oversee the issuing of pardons *de cursu*. But it seems more reasonable to conclude that the king, in forfeiting the opportunity to pardon some offenders after trial, did so only as a by-product of his streamlining the royal administration

seldom if ever exercised. It was the rare case in which a defendant could convince the judges to carry forward his matter for personal royal consideration. The drafters of the early pardon statutes, however, may not have fully understood this;[22] the statutes may have been drafted under the incorrect assumption that such cases might still go forward after trial for royal consideration.

In sum, we cannot be certain that Parliament intended to deprive the Crown of its traditional power in cases long thought appropriate for royal mercy. By allowing pardons only in cases of accident and self-defense, Parliament may well have thought it was leaving intact the royal power not only to pardon *de cursu* according to the strict rules of the law, but also to pardon *de gratia* those simple homicides that the king, out of true mercy and by appropriate extension of the legal rules, desired to treat as if they met the formal requirements.

In any event, by the middle of the fourteenth century statutory preambles and legislative histories provide a clearer insight into the nature of the protest that Parliament had leveled against the Crown. While the statutes continued to distinguish between pardons *de cursu* and pardons *de gratia*, it appears that Parliament, seeking to combat what was perceived as a dangerous rise in professional crime,[23] was concerned mainly with those pardons *de gratia* obtained by the worst offenders. Notorious malefactors who committed homicide in the course of theft were quite possibly the main targets of the legislation.[24] Persons who had

---

of pardons *de cursu*. At the time he probably imagined that more suspects would then come to him before trial for a pardon *de gratia* in return for money or military service.

22. Yearbook recognition of the chancellor's summary powers with regard to pardons *de cursu* dates from the early fourteenth century, the period of the early pardon statutes, but Parliament may have overlooked this innovation.

23. There is no systematic study of the growth of professional crime that covers the entire course of the fourteenth century. My argument does not depend on the fact of increasing crime; it does depend on the contemporary belief in an increase in professional crime. We owe much of our evidence to parliamentary attention to the problem (see below, n. 24), which may reflect the perception of the higher classes rather than actual conditions. See Hanawalt, *Crime and Conflict*, pp. 235–37. The trial rolls from the later decades of the fourteenth century indicate frequent indictments of groups of offenders, especially in cases of theft, and indictments before justices of the peace also reflect a substantial amount of what seems to have been professional crime. See e.g. Putnam, ed., *Proceedings before Justices of the Peace*, pp. 212–39. Gangs seem to have operated openly and ubiquitously. See Hewitt, *Organization of War*, pp. 173–75; Bellamy, "The Coterel Gang: An Anatomy of a Band of Fourteenth-Century Criminals," *English Historical Review*, vol. 39, (1964), p. 698. For discussions of thirteenth-century crime, see R. H. Hilton, *A Medieval Society: The West Midlands at the End of the Thirteenth Century* (London, 1966), pp. 248–61; Pugh, "Reflections of a Medieval Criminologist," pp. 98–99; Given, *Society and Homicide*, passim.

24. The petition of 1309 had referred to the "too free pardoning of thieves [*larons*] who

acted on a sudden impulse or in the course of a common brawl were almost never mentioned, though they were probably responsible for most homicides. Parliament dealt, in short, with those acts that incurred public outrage and fear and seemed beyond the most generous limits of legitimate mercy.

During the later decades of the fourteenth century, parliamentary concern with the problem of professional homicide steadily increased. Possibly as a result of this concern, the terminology of royal commissions to justices of the peace came to define more fully particularly heinous homicide or "murder," as it once again had come to be called in official documents,[25] and thus to lend special importance to prosecution in such cases. The commission of 1380, for instance, which empowered justices of the peace to take indictments in cases of "murder," associated that term with ambushing and malice aforethought, or true planning.[26] And

had been indicted" for the crimes Parliament sought to prevent. *Rotuli Parliamentorum*, l:444b (1309). The statute of 1336 recited: "Whereas murderers, robbers, and other felons, be greatly encouraged to offend, by reason that Charters of pardon of manslaughters ["*homicides*"], robbery, felonies, and other trespasses against the peace, have been so lightly granted." Stat. 10 Edw. 3, c. 2. The statute of 1340 (Stat. 14 Edw. 3, c. 15), repeated earlier restrictions on pardons: "Charters have been granted without number to felons and manslayers ["*larons et homicides*"], to the evil example and fear of good people and lawful, whereby thieves, felons and offenders ["*larons et meffesours*"] be comforted to do their robberies and manslaughters ["*roberies et homicides*"] and the same do from day to day." In a petition of 1347, Parliament referred to malefactors without number who received pardons "to the great destruction of the people." *Rotuli Parliamentorum*, 2:171a. See also *Rotuli Parliamentorum*, 2:172a (1347). A similar petition of 1353 stated that the king, in response to "suggestions" which were less than truthful, had granted pardons to many notorious felons ("*larons*") and to common murderers, who were to fight overseas and who returned and plundered the countryside. *Rotuli Parliamentorum*, 2:253b. Kaye correctly notes that Parliament did not distinguish types of felonious homicide in these statutes and petitions. Kaye, "Early History," Part I, p. 378. It is possible that Parliament had in mind all felonious homicides; but it is unlikely that in its attempt to prevent the pardoning of really serious malefactors, Parliament proscribed pardons even to those of generally good reputation who, in a sudden quarrel, struck and slew another person.

25. For an excellent discussion of the use of "murder" as a term of art in justice of the peace indictments in the 1380s see Kaye, "Early History," Part I, pp. 383–89.

The term "murder" had not been commonly employed as a term of art for a particularly heinous homicide. But the concept of murder was reflected in the name given to the fine imposed on the local community for an unexplained homicide ("*murdrum*"). Many, but not all, such homicides had been committed in secret, the slayer taking his victim by surprise and making his escape without detection by third parties. See Plucknett, *Concise History*, pp. 444–45; Meekings, ed., *Wiltshire Eyre*, pp. 61–65; Hurnard, *King's Pardon for Homicide*, pp. 385–93. The *murdrum* fine was abolished in 1340 (Stat. 14 Edw. 3, stat. l, c. 4.) By that time, the term "murder" was once again coming to be identified in official documents with slaying itself. See e.g. John B. Post, "Some Limitations of the Medieval Peace Rolls," *Journal of the Society of Archivists*, vol. 4 (1973), pp. 633, 639.

26. "We have assigned you to inquire . . . into all thefts, notorious or open, and mayhems

from about that date, legislative demands for limitations on the royal pardoning power may have prompted the frequent insertion in pardons for "all felonies" clauses excepting "treason, murder, and rape."[27] In this context, "murder" was not employed as a catchall for felonious homicide but was a term of art.[28]

The statute of 1390 gave these legislative demands their fullest embodiment. Limits were imposed on the king's power to pardon homicides committed through murder, ambush, assault, or malice aforethought.[29] Pardons for these offenses were made quite expensive; they could be obtained only through a request making clear the nature of the killing; and to be effective they had expressly to cover these offenses. A trial was to be held to determine the nature of the slaying when a general pardon for homicide was presented to the court.[30]

Like its precursors, the statute of 1390 limited the king's pardon power only in cases of homicide. This supports the view taken here of the kind of homicide to which the legislation referred: if the king might not pardon any slayers save those who qualified for pardons *de cursu*, why might he pardon virtually all thieves? More likely, the king was allowed to pardon all slayers *and* thieves, save for the most vicious in either class, i.e., those who slew through stealth or in the course of an assault involving highway robbery or household burglary. For the most part, it was the professional criminal at whom the legislation was aimed. And we must suppose that officialdom not only sought to close the escape route of the royal pardon to such persons but that it also desired to see them brought to justice by the juries that tried them. It was these offenders who truly tested the system, not those lesser offenders who, with a little more time, money, or

and slayings of men through ambush or malice aforethought, and murders, and other felonies." *Rotuli Parliamentorum*, 3:84b. "Felonies," I believe, incorporated simple homicides. See Green, "Jury and the Law of Homicide," p. 468, n. 21 and accompanying text.

27. See e.g. *C.P.R.*, March 20, 1381, p. 610; May 7, 1381, p. 624; Dec. 12, 1385, p. 71; Jan. 8, 1386, p. 79; Jan. 16, 1386, p. 94; Feb. 27, 1386, p. 128.

28. See e.g. JUST 3/177, m.7/3 (1393), discussed in Green, "Jury and the Law of Homicide," p. 466, n. 197.

29. Stat. 13 Rich. 2, stat. 2, c. 1 (1390): "[T]hat no charter of pardon from henceforth shall be allowed before any justice for murder, or for the death of a man slain by await, assault, or malice prepensed, treason, or rape of a woman . . ." ("*[Q]e null chartre de pardon desore soit alowe devant quiconques Justices pur murdre mort de homme occys par agait assaut ou malice purpense treson ou rape de femme* . . ."). For a full discussion of the statute see Green, "Jury and the Law of Homicide," pp. 462–69.

30. 13 Rich. 2, stat. 2, c. 1 (1390). The section of the statute imposing heavy fines for pardons for the named offenses was repealed in 1392. See Green, "Jury and the Law of Homicide," pp. 469–70, n. 205.

foresight might, through a pardon of grace, legitimately have immunized themselves altogether against trial and the verdict of the country.[31]

# III

If the bench, reflecting the attitudes of the elites of English society, was concerned for the most part with the most serious offenders, so too were juries. We have seen that few perpetrators of casual homicide were hanged and that fully half of those alleged to have committed "murder" were sent to the gallows.[32] Doubtless the bench would have preferred an even higher rate of conviction for these latter defendants. They probably suspected that graft and fear accounted for many acquittals of professional thieves and slayers, persons who frequently moved about in gangs and who possessed the means to buy off or frighten their prospective jurors. Nonetheless, the judges must have recognized that most of the law-abiding populace shared a common point of view in this area. This community of interest regarding the most serious offenders may have conditioned the judicial response to jury leniency toward the least serious ones.

We are unable, however, to determine the extent to which the bench acquiesced in jury leniency in simple homicide and much nonprofessional theft. Before examining the factors that support the view that there was very substantial judicial acceptance of jury behavior, we must take note of a few developments regarding the law of pardonable homicide. These developments provide a more substantial context for understanding the impact of jury leniency than I have thus far set forth. The doctrinal changes we must trace are all the more significant because, in the main, jury behavior in simple homicide tended to prevent development of the substantive law.

First, I shall briefly outline the reasons for this process of doctrinal stultification. Then I shall discuss the changes that did occur and suggest that jury behavior conditioned the shape of the evolving law. This discussion sets forth the main body of evidence that reflects the judicial reaction to jury behavior. I shall argue that jury behavior to some extent slowed the development of a policy aimed at reducing serious crime, an ironic result of the dialectical process created by the combined adoptions of a general capital sanction for felony and a lay criminal trial jury. In the final section of this chapter I shall tentatively explore the reasons why the Crown retained the capital sanction for all grades of felony despite the problems it caused.

31. For further discussion of this theme see below, section IV.
32. See above, Chapter 2, text at nn. 16–21.

I

That juries manipulated the evidence in a large class of homicide cases can hardly have escaped the bench. Although the justices insisted that nothing less than dire necessity justified killing in self-defense, it is possible that they tolerated with some aplomb the juries' leniency in the face of the strict rules. Nevertheless, from the point of view of the bench, remand to gaol to await a pardon and the loss of goods probably seemed a small price to pay for those who had in fact committed capital felony. This fact, then, may have left the justices loath to undertake any extension of the formal law of self-defense. Rather, in every case in which self-defense was alleged, they pressed the jury on two questions: Had the defendant acted out of total desperation? Had he acted without malice?

The jury's inclination to shape the facts in the most positive way for many favored defendants appears to have significantly retarded development of the substantive criminal law. Doctrinal development in the common-law system depended heavily upon a flow of cases raising problems for which the law had no appropriate answer. This flow was choked off early and effectively by the forms and procedures of the criminal law. The absence of special pleading and the inability to raise questions of law by way of appeal from the courts' decisions were detrimental enough.[33] But jury behavior played an additional and key role: juries' efforts to foreclose the possibility of hanging led them to adopt a few existing and predictable patterns of response to cover a wide variety of situations. Had trial juries put forward in candid terms the details of homicides, as inquest juries often did before a coroner, the history of the law of homicide might have been different.

For example, research reveals no settled doctrine during this period regarding slaying in defense of one's kin, as opposed to the established right to defend oneself. Indeed, no discussion of the question by the bench can be found. It is difficult to believe that slaying in such circumstances was, in practice, a capital felony.[34] If it was lawful, why

---

33. See Milsom, *Historical Foundations*, pp. 415–17.

34. One late thirteenth-century treatise, in dealing with homicide that was not felonious, refers to a person "who slays a housebreaker, at least if he is defending himself or his household at the time." *Fleta*, 2:61. Compare F. M. Nichols, trans. and ed., *Britton* (London, 1865), vol. 1, p. 113:

> Or he may say, that although he committed the act, yet he did not do it by felony prepense, but by necessity, in defending himself, or his wife, or his house, or his family, or his land, or his body, from death; or that he killed the man in defense of our peace, or by some mischance, without any thought of felony; in all which cases, if proved, the appellees shall have judgment of acquittal.

Britton is here concerned only with defenses to an appeal. He does not suggest that all these defenses would result in an acquittal if the trial were pursuant to an indictment. Certainly,

does the legal process hide that from our view? One theory might have it that when a slaying had been in defense of kin, the defendant, after the formulistic "not guilty," entered a special plea stating the true facts, and the court accepted such a defense when it was corroborated by the jury. The clerk might then have enrolled the details, simply as a matter of form, in a manner consistent with the rules of defense of one's person. But that theory would have the clerks engaging in deliberate, uniform, and pointless falsification of the record. It is more reasonable to suppose that the defendant expressed his case in the strongest and safest possible terms, or that the jury did so on his behalf, and that the litany of deliberate but excusable homicide was always built upon the foundation of saving one's own life.[35] Defenders of kin (or of any other person for that matter) were reported as *self*-defenders. The concealment of the true facts was total, and the courts never had to grapple with the question of defense of another. The formulae of the law had, in the hands of the self-informing jury, indirectly stunted doctrinal growth.[36]

It is also probable that the conclusory character of jury verdicts inhibited the development of more subtle rules on the standards to be met by defendants claiming self-defense. If the judges had had to pass upon a wide variety of fact situations, ranging along a spectrum from murderous attack to genuine last resort, they might have developed a series of doctrinal principles and distinctions. The bench might have developed rules to deal with defendants who had come under attack and feared for their lives but had acted somewhat too hastily in retaliation; or, with those whose temper had gotten the better of them, whose malicious intent was of the moment and less than homicidal, but whose blow had been deadly. Instead, the courts were presented with only two types of homicide defendants: those said to have acted feloniously, with *malicia precogitata* and without evidence of mitigating circumstances, and those said to have

self-defense would not lead to acquittal in such circumstances. Nor, for that matter, is the passage clear evidence for the proposition that one who defended his kin was entitled *de cursu* to a pardon of the king's suit.

35. See above, Chapter 2, text at nn. 58–62.

36. In 1506 it was held that a servant might justifiably slay in defense of his master if his master were otherwise unable to escape, *Year Book* (Henry VII) (London, 1506), Mich., 21 Hen. 7, fol. 39, pl. 50, but the first clear reference to defense of kin that I have found dates approximately from the 1530s. Spelman noted that

> Fitzherbert showed an indictment [which alleged] that one Parker found a man between his wife's legs committing lechery, and he killed the man, and all the justices held this to be felony. But suppose a man means to ravish my wife against her will, and I kill him, it seems that I can do so in defence of my wife, just as in the case where he means to kill her.

J. H. Baker, trans. and ed., *The Reports of Sir John Spelman*, 2 vols., (London, 1977–78), vol. l, p. 72.

slain *in extremis*, in self-defense. Both judicial suspicion of the large latter group and the failure of the system to present "close cases" perpetuated the strict division between felonious and nonfelonious homicide.[37]

Although the development of the substantive law of pardonable homicide was thus limited, some significant legal developments did arise out of the judge-jury relationship. I shall refer to two of them here, one involving justifiable homicide—in this case, the slaying of thieves caught in the act—the other involving accidental homicide. Together these developments reflect both the conservative tendencies of the bench, for which jury behavior was at least in part responsible, and the area of agreement between bench and jury concerning particularly heinous social behavior.

**2**

The category of justifiable homicide, meriting acquittal rather than pardon and forfeiture, was extended in the fourteenth century to include the slayers of felons caught in the act of burglary, arson, or robbery. An examination of this development may suggest why those who acted in defense of property fared better under the evolving law than those who acted solely in defense of their person.

The line between justifiable and excusable homicide had long been unclear and prone to inconsistent judicial treatment.[38] From early times, execution upon a legal order was justifiable.[39] Slaying manifest felons[40]

---

37. The speculative nature of this section should be obvious. The direct evidence on judicial behavior that would provide the most satisfactory support for these conclusions is simply unavailable. My argument concerning jury behavior and judicial response is developed more fully below, subsection 4. The problem is discussed in the light of general developments in the law of nonfelonious homicide and the role that automatic forfeiture came to play in the fourteenth century.

38. See Hurnard, *King's Pardon for Homicide*, pp. 88–92.

39. See Bracton, *De Legibus*, 2:340 (fol. 120b).

40. These included "hand-having" thieves, notorious malefactors, and slayers attempting to escape from the "hue and cry" raised against them. For slayers of hand-having thieves, see e.g. J. Parker, ed., *A Calendar of the Lancashire Assize Rolls* [Manchester],1904), p. 87; Maitland, ed., *Pleas of Gloucester*, p. 23, pl. 89; W. Page, ed., *Three Early Assize Rolls for the County of Northumberland* (Durham, 1891), pp. 78–79, 80, 84 (hereafter cited as *Northumberland Assize Rolls*); A. J. Horwood, trans. and ed., *Year Books of the Reign of Edward the First*, (London, 1863), 30–31 Edw. 1, p. 512 (1302). For slayers of notorious malefactors, see e.g. JUST 1/734, m.22d/9 (1256); JUST 1/60, m.23/5 (1272) (keeper of the peace in Buckinghamshire slew a reputed malefactor who refused to give assurance that he would not harm the countryside and who sought, with drawn sword, to avoid arrest); KB 27/297, m.26d/l (1334); C 260/55, no. 58 (1343); C 145/21/36 (undated); G. Wrottesley, trans. and ed., "Plea Rolls of the Reign of Hen. III," in *Collections for a History of Staffordshire* (London, 1883), vol. 4, pp. 214–15; J. H. Wigmore, "Responsibility for Tortious Acts; Its History," *Harvard Law Review*, vol. 7 (1894), pp. 315, 323. For

and those formally outlawed,[41] if they resisted arrest, also came to be justified. Initially, this may have represented an attempt to harness the ancient custom of private retaliation—perhaps because it could not be entirely prevented—by legitimating it solely where the wrongdoer refused to submit to the judicial process.[42] As the judicial system and the test for refusal to submit to it developed,[43] these slayings came to be seen as being on behalf of the law (*pro lege*). While for a time some tension between the private and *pro lege* deed may have existed, we may suppose that the latter eventually won out.

By the thirteenth century, most localities were no longer allowed to execute captured outlaws and manifest felons without trial; that custom had become, by and large, frontier law.[44] Indeed, so profound was the impress of royal law that thirteenth- and early fourteenth-century judges sometimes insisted that the slayer of a resisting outlaw or manifest felon show that he had acted as a royal official or pursuant to an official order

slayers of would-be escapers from the hue and cry, see e.g. JUST 1/56, m.44d/1 (1249); *Northumberland Assize Rolls*, pp. 80, 84.

41. Bracton, *De Legibus*, 2:362 (fol. 128b) ("An outlaw also forfeits everything connected with the peace, for from the time he is outlawed he bears the wolf's head, so that he may be slain by anyone with impunity, especially if he resists or takes to flight so that his arrest is difficult").

42. As early as the seventh century, slayers of outlaws or of manifest felons who would not surrender to the "peace of the king" were protected by the law against retaliation by the kin of the slain. See Ine 33, in F. L. Attenborough, trans. and ed., *The Laws of the Earliest English Kings* (Cambridge, 1922), p. 47: "He who kills a thief shall be allowed to declare with an oath that he whom he killed was a thief trying to escape, and the kinsmen of the dead man shall swear an oath to carry on no vendetta against him. If, however, he keeps it secret, and it afterwards comes to light, then he shall pay for him." Ine's dooms date from about A.D. 694. H. G. Richardson and G. O. Sayles, *Law and Legislation from Aethelberht to Magna Carta* (Edinburgh, 1966), p. 13. For a later (tenth century) law to the same effect, see 2 Aethelstan 1.2, in Attenborough, ed., *Laws of the Earliest English Kings*, p. 127 ("If however, [the thief] tries to defend himself, or if he takes to flight, he shall not be spared"). Cf. Alfred 5 to Alfred 5.3, in *ibid.*, p. 67. Alfred employed the ecclesiastical "sanctuary" laws in his own legislation concerning "house protection," i.e., the protection of a suspect who remained in his home and voluntarily gave himself up to stand trial. See generally C. Riggs, *Criminal Asylum in Anglo-Saxon Law* (Gainesville, Fla., 1963), pp. 31–36.

43. Riggs describes the procedure that had come to replace the automatic prosecution of the feud. *Criminal Asylum*, pp. 41–42.

44. See e.g. *Northumberland Assize Rolls*, p. 70. In a case where a felon was slain, but not while in flight, local officials informed the court that it was the custom in Northumberland summarily to dispatch robbers taken with goods in hand. The late thirteenth-century law book *Britton*, (vol. 1, pp. 36–37), probably reflects the older rule rather than contemporary practice: "If any man be found killed, and another be found near him with the knife or other weapon in his hand all bloody, wherewith he killed him, the coroner shall be presently fetched, and in his presence the felon shall, upon the testimony of those who saw the felony done, be judged to death."

before he could be acquitted.[45] Other such slayers required royal pardons, usually for self-defense.[46] Here there was confusion. While it appears that it was lawful for anyone to slay an outlaw or manifest felon who resisted arrest, it was not uncommon for nonofficial slayers to be recorded, in addition, as having suffered attack and therefore slain to save their lives.[47] This, indeed, was the surest defense for one seeking to show that he could not otherwise have taken his victim, and it may have been an embellishment intended to allay judicial suspicion of nonofficial slayers. Yet the inclusion of details of self-defense, which ought to have strengthened the defendant's claim to an acquittal, may well have been responsible for the inconsistent judicial treatment of nonofficial slayers.[48] By the middle of the fourteenth century, however, the confusion was resolved. Most slayers of outlaws and manifest felons were acquitted; the courts required neither a pardon nor a theory of self-defense.[49]

45. See e.g. KB 27/343, m.2/4 (1346) (defendant commissioned by the sheriff of Norfolk was acquitted); JUST 3/139, m.27d/l (1356) (five men joined two constables in arresting a person who laid waste to goods and chattels of a resident of Norfolk; all were acquitted. The court ruled: "And because it seems to the court that what they did in this case, they did through the law ["*per legem*"] and through maintenance of the law, it is considered that the aforesaid seven ought to go quit"); JUST 3/135, m/16/2 (1343) (defendant and thirty-four others pursued and slew a person who had been indicted for several felonies. The court, after determining that the deceased had been indicted before his death and that the defendant had a commission based on that indictment, acquitted the defendant and his posse); A. Fitzherbert, *Graunde Abridgement*, "Corone," pl. 288 (1330); *Livre des Assises*, 22 Edw. 3, pl. 55 (1349).
46. See Hurnard, *King's Pardon for Homicide*, p. 90.
47. See e.g. JUST 1/65, m.47/15 (1286); JUST 3/43/l, m.14d/7 (1325).
48. See Hurnard, *King's Pardon for Homicide*, p. 91, suggesting that in the thirteenth century courts may occasionally have seized upon details of self-defense in cases of justifiable homicide and thought, somewhat irrationally, in terms of excusable homicide. Hurnard observes that courts more often acquitted where the alleged felon had been slain while resisting arrest than where he had been slain attempting to commit robbery, and she speculates "that it was all too easy for the courts to assimilate [the latter] cases to slaying in self-defense."
49. For example, in KB 27/297, m.26d/l (1334), a certain William, son of Ralph, was acquitted for the death of Adam Doughty, whom he had decapitated. According to the jury, Adam was a notorious robber who had feloniously burgled the house of Thomas, son of Jordan, in Lancashire. William tried to arrest Adam, but Adam stabbed William and fled. William pursued and slew Adam. The court specifically asked the jurors whether William could have taken Adam in any other way, to which they replied that he could not. There is no indication that the bench questioned the jury with regard to self-defense. In JUST 3/135, m.13d/3 (1344), the defendant, taking part with others responding to the hue and cry, shot a fleeing suspect with an arrow. The court ruled that the defendant had acted as an executor of the peace ("*ut executor pacis*") and acquitted him. In KB 27/528, Rex, m.xlvi/l (1393), according to the indictment, the defendant saw a stranger ("*extraneus*") leading away two horses belonging to others. He raised the hue and pursued the stranger and, in apprehending him, struck him on the neck with a sword so that he fell on the ground. Whereupon the

As we have seen, the class of manifest felons included the ancient "hand-having thief"—quite literally, a felon caught with the stolen goods. But it did not include one intercepted in an unlawful attempt to take goods or commit an assault. In the course of the fourteenth century, however, the courts began to acquit as justifiable slayers some of those who had acted to forestall an attempted felony, namely, those who had slain burglars or robbers. The self-defender, on the other hand, was subjected to the rigor of the law of self-defense for at least another two centuries. This uneven development requires explanation. Why the one change without the other?

While thirteenth-century records reveal occasional acquittals of defendants who slew those attempting burglary or robbery,[50] most such cases resulted in the granting of a pardon for actual, or alleged, self-defense.[51] As with the other early cases, embellishment by the defendant, repeated by jurors under oath, produced a sure result where judicial response to the bare truth was uncertain. The judges accepted the implications for legal theory of this factual grafting. Thirteenth-century treatises dealt with defense of property as an extension of self-defense.[52]

defendant beheaded the thief. The court considered the indictment "insufficient" and acquitted the defendant. For further examples see JUST 3/43/1, m.14d/7 (1325); JUST 3/137A, m.21/2 (1353); KB 27/519, Rex m.1/2 (1391).

50. See e.g. JUST 1/642, m.16/13 (1256) (*Northumberland Assize Rolls*, p. 94). Pollock and Maitland cite this case as an unusual one and assert that the defendant was fortunate (*History of English Law*, 2:478). A late thirteenth-century legal treatise refers to such slayings in somewhat ambiguous terms: "Anyone, however, who slays a thief by night is not held to be a homicide ["*non teneatur*"], and he who slays a housebreaker, at least if he is defending himself or his household at the time, slays justly ["*iuste interfecit*"], and in the same way he who slays another to save himself from death." (*Fleta*, 2:61). Fleta groups such acts with excusable slayings in self-defense, for which a pardon was required.

51. See e.g. Maitland, ed., *Pleas of Gloucester*, pl. 362 (1221); C 145/11/33 (1259); C 145/13/21 (1266); C 145/32/20 (1274); C 145/49/49 (1290); JUST 3/91, m.10d/10 (1293).

52. See e.g. Bracton, *De Legibus*, 2:408 (fol. 144b):

If anyone slays a night thief, he will do so with impunity only if he could not spare him without danger to himself; if he could it will be otherwise. For the life and death of men are in the hands of the king, (as in the case of a certain man . . . to whom the king granted a pardon for a death in such. circumstances). And so where one defends himself against hamsocn, which [the English call] the entering of a house in breach of the peace, and the intruder is slain, he will be free of liability if he who killed could defend himself in no other way.

(Footnotes omitted.) For Bracton, to be "free of liability" does not mean, in these circumstances, to be free of the need for a pardon: "[H]e who kills a thief, either a day thief or a night thief, is not liable, [i.e.,] if he could not otherwise escape danger; if he could he is liable. Nor is he liable who kills by misadventure." *Ibid.*, p. 438 (fol. 155). Bracton seems to equate cases of misadventure, where pardons were required, with cases of slaying a thief to "escape danger."

In the fourteenth century, however, the judges formulated a new doctrine giving the victim of housebreaking greater latitude in repulsing his assailant. The proposition was first stated laconically, as if an intonement of the hoary law: "It was presented that a man killed another in his own house *se defendendo*. It was asked whether the deceased came to rob him: for in such a case a man may kill another though it not be in self-defense."[53] Moreover, the court sanctioned outright acquittal in this case, thus bringing the defendant under the ancient rule applicable to slayers of manifest felons. In 1349 Justice Thorpe restated the rule more broadly: "And in many other cases a man may kill another without impeachment, as if thieves come to rob a man, or to burgle his house, he may safely kill them if he cannot take them."[54]

For a time, however, the courts were uncertain about the breadth of the rule. In 1357 Thorpe and his fellow justices were confronted with a defendant who had slain a burglar. The court ruled: "Because . . . what the defendant did he did in saving his own life in circumstances in which anyone ought to be able to do so lawfully, it is considered that he be quit."[55] This seems to indicate that, while a pardon was not necessary, the defendant had to show he acted in self-defense.

The hesitation of the bench to separate such cases from those of excusable homicide was reflected in another case. It seems to have been settled by 1353 that a man might slay someone who had entered upon his property with the intention of setting his house on fire.[56] Yet thirteen years later the justices of gaol delivery of Leicester Castle, Thomas de Ingleby and John Cavendish, showed indecision as to treatment of the defendant in *Neel's Case*:

> Reginald Walshman . . . came at night around midnight to the house of John Neel and called to John who lay there asleep in his bed to let him come in; he wanted to slay John in John's house; and John refused him entrance, so that Reginald began to break the doors and windows and he said he would burn the house and John's wife and everything within the house unless John permitted him to enter. And he intended to burn the house, and John for fear of his death and the burning and for salvation of his life and family got out of bed and went to the door; and Reginald was there with a rock which he threw at John's head, and John ducked and Reginald stood there with a knife drawn in order to

53. Fitzherbert, *Graunde Abridgement*, "*Corone*," pl. 305 (1330).
54. *Livre des Assises*, 22 Edw. 3, pl. 55 (1349). See Fitzherbert, *Graunde Abridgement*, "*Corone*," pl. 261 (1349); *Livre des Assises*, 26 Edw. 3, pl. 23 (1353).
55. JUST 3/139, m.29d/4 (1357).
56. *Livre des Assises*, 26 Edw. 3, pl. 23 (1353). See Robert Brooke, *La Graunde Abridgement* (London, 1576), "*Corone*," pl. 100; Fitzherbert, *Graunde Abridgement*, "*Corone*," pl. 192 (1353).

kill John and attacked him wanting to kill him, and John being naked
and believing that Reginald intended to burn his house and that
Reginald wanted to kill him, in saving his own life, stabbed Reginald
with a knife wherein Reginald was slain. And the jury say that John
could not otherwise have saved his own life.[57]

Neel was released in surety pending a gaol delivery seven months later,
when he was acquitted. The court had evidently first considered requiring
Neel to obtain a pardon, and it appears likely that the element of
self-defense was crucial to the judgment of acquittal.

Because the natural inclination of the jury was to embellish instances of
defense of property with details of defense of one's person, few cases
presented the courts with the critical test of pure defense of property. And
those cases that did come forward may have been perceived as ordinary
homicides with some embellishments concerning defense of home and
hearth. The mingling of defense of property with defense of person may
have resulted in judicial caution toward allegations of the former, and it
may have slowed the expansion of the category of justifiable homicide to
include defense of property. Nevertheless, that the court in the end
granted an acquittal in *Neel's Case* suggests that, whether or not
self-defense remained a necessary element, this expansion had been
accomplished. Moreover, by the last third of the fourteenth century
slayers of nocturnal housebreakers no longer appear among those pardoned for homicide *se defendendo*, though earlier such cases had been
abundant.[58]

Thorpe's 1349 ruling had pertained not only to housebreaking but also
to attempted robbery.[59] This position, or something very close to it, was
adopted by the whole court when Thorpe put the following case four
years later: "A man was indicted for homicide; it was found that the
deceased was a thief who assailed the defendant and pursued him closely
so that the defendant slew him. . . . [All] say that he will go quit."[60] Here,
too, it appears that some element of self-defense remained crucial to the
finding of justifiable homicide. The effect of this ruling is more difficult to
ascertain from the rolls than is the effect of the ruling concerning the
slaying of burglars. Again, the records of acquittals provide very few
details about the cases. Moreover, the absence of victims of attempted
robbery among those pardoned for self-defense is not helpful here. An
attack in the open had always been described as an assault with intent to

57. JUST 3.142, m.17d/l (1366).
58. See above, n. 51.
59. See above, n. 54 and accompanying text.
60. *Livre des Assises*, 26 Edw. 3, pl. 32 (1353).

slay, since this was a necessary allegation in self-defense. Other motives, such as robbery, had rarely been mentioned.

This part of Thorpe's ruling was nevertheless of considerable significance because, at least in theory, it broadened the scope of justifiable homicide to include slaying to prevent felony. The new rule concerning the slayers of housebreakers was perhaps less novel; the wrongdoer had already committed the ancient but nonfelonious breach of the peace known as *hamsocn*.[61]

The extension of justifiable homicide to include slayers of would-be burglars and robbers was very possibly a response to what was thought to be—and may in fact have been—an unprecedented contemporary rise in professional crime. Thorpe's ruling was not expanded, however, to include slayers of criminals who assaulted with intent to kill rather than to rob, not even to include slayers of would-be "murderers," as those who committed homicide through stealth were coming once again to be known. The failure to treat the slaying of a would-be murderer as justifiable homicide is particularly puzzling since by the end of the fourteenth century murderous assault was considered especially heinous. This is shown, as we have seen, by the 1390 statute greatly restricting the grant of pardons "of grace" to perpetrators of stealthy homicide.

The courts may have drawn this line between professional robbers and stealthy killers because the former were considered to be a threat to the entire community, while the latter were deemed a threat only to their intended victims. But it seems more likely that the judges were responding to the juries' practice of finding self-defense in many less serious, yet felonious and undesirable homicides. The bench must have realized that many homicides described as *se defendendo* had in fact been committed in the course of drunken brawls and similar rows. Against these, too, the law had to provide deterrence, and the procedure of pardon and forfeiture, which was a quasi-sanction, may have seemed an appropriate deterrent. The true self-defender, however, especially the one who had repulsed a murderous assault, might have deserved better; moreover, in his case even the logic of deterrence mandated acquittal. But how were the judges to identify the true self-defender? Jury testimony and the defendant's own story were so formulistic that discrimination among alleged self-defenders was an impossible task. Evidence as to the exact nature of the victim's alleged assault would have been difficult to obtain,

61. Bracton defines "hamsocn" as "the entering of a house in breach of the peace." Bracton, *De Legibus*, 2:408 (fol. 144b). See Pollock and Maitland, *History of English Law*, 2:454–58. In two early thirteenth-century cases [F. W. Maitland, trans. and ed., *Select Pleas Of The Crown* (London, 1888), pl. 60, 86], "hamsocn" (or "hamsoken") was complicated by theft.

as would have been the truth regarding the defendant's efforts to escape without dealing a mortal blow.

The theory of royal mercy that underlay the granting of pardons may also have had something to do with the retention of pardons in self-defense cases. Although by the fourteenth century pardons for self-defense and accidental homicide were granted *de cursu*, the vestiges of the earlier idea of special consideration survived at least in the formulae that were inscribed on charters of pardon.[62] Nevertheless, pardons for excusable homicide were retained as a matter of policy as well as of tradition. For, as we shall now see, while self-defenders required pardons in virtually every case, those who slew by accident did not. "Mercy" was required, it seems, only where suspicion of wrongdoing remained.

### 3

Throughout the thirteenth century the prevailing rule in cases of accidental homicide was that the slayer was required to obtain a royal pardon. The pardon issued as a matter of course upon a finding of unintentional homicide (misadventure). Even grossly negligent slayers were included within this class of excusable homicide.[63] By the late fourteenth century, however, the courts frequently granted an immediate acquittal for accidental homicide, no longer insisting that the slayer forfeit his chattels and secure a royal pardon. Though there is no clear evidence as to when and how the new policy was formulated, its widespread application is clear from the rolls.[64]

---

62. See e.g. C 66/230, m.21 ["Moved by mercy, we have pardoned . . ." ("*Nos pietate moti perdonavimus . . .*")]. The pardon still carried the proviso that the defendant "stand to right" ("*ita tamen quod stet recto in curia nostra*") should the kin of the slain wish to bring an appeal (literally, "should anyone wish to speak against him"). By the late thirteenth century, if not long before, the kin's right to appeal a pardoned slayer had lapsed. It is unlikely that it remained even in theory, though the form of the pardon was unchanged. Green, "Jury and the Law of Homicide," pp. 419–20, n. 22. Nevertheless, it is still barely possible that this ancient claim to private compensation against an excusable slayer accounted in part for the retention of the pardon requirement. One would still have to explain why a pardon was required rather than acquittal with an obligation to stand to right. The rule of automatic forfeiture suggests that pardoned slayers were disadvantaged for reasons other than the kin's right to appeal. Moreover, the expansion of the class of justifiable homicide was accomplished without concern for the rights of the deceased's kin. It led to acquittal of some who formerly required a pardon for self-defense. As we shall see, judicial policy changed with regard to accidental homicide with the same potential effect on the theoretical right of the kin to bring an appeal.

63. See generally Hurnard, *King's Pardon for Homicide*, pp. 98–108.

64. But see *Year Book* (Edward III), Hil., 44 Edw. 3, pl. 44 (1371); Fitzherbert, *Graunde Abridgement*, "*Corone,*" pl. 94 (1371) (judicial statements that acquittal is appropriate in accidental homicide cases). For a discussion of an unsuccessful attempt during the reign of

The majority of all homicide defendants delivered before the justices were acquitted outright. In most of these cases the clerk recorded on the trial roll only the homicide for which the defendant had been indicted, the date and place of the act, the jury's verdict of "not guilty" ("*non est culpabilis*"), and the court's judgment of acquittal. The evidence does not permit us even to estimate how many such cases were acquittals on verdicts amounting to misadventure. Occasionally, however, the clerk did record the facts of the case in more detail, and from this small body of hard evidence it is possible to discern a new departure in the courts' handling of accidental homicide. Judges now acquitted many defendants who had received a jury verdict of accidental homicide. There is additional support for this conclusion: late-fourteenth-century trial rolls contain few pardons for misadventures,[65] and coroners frequently neglected to record an indictment where the inquest jury found misadventure, as though they believed that the courts were not concerned with such cases.[66]

The gradual disappearance in the fourteenth century of the pardon requirement for accidental homicide may have been the natural outgrowth of an older distinction between homicides resulting from the slayer's act alone and homicides produced by intervening circumstances over which the slayer had no control. Thirteenth-century courts had already more or less systematically acquitted in some accidental homicide cases, for instance those involving carts and ploughs.[67] From one perspective, acquittals in these cases may be taken as a "rough-and-ready" approach to the problem of negligence. More often than not the victim, rather than the driver, had failed to use care.[68] In shooting accidents and other cases where the slayer was more likely to have been the negligent party, the pardon requirement was maintained. A second plausible explanation of the early resort to acquittals in driving cases is that, by and large, the slaying could be attributed to a nonhuman agent. The cart, plough, horses, or oxen, rather than the driver, might be perceived as the

---

Edward I (1272–1307) to reform the law in this direction, see Hurnard, *King's Pardon for Homicide*, p. 279.

65. E.g., the four rolls discussed in Green, "Jury and the Law of Homicide," p. 430, dating from the period 1351–85, contain many cases of self-defense but none ending in the defendant's remand to prison to await a pardon for accidental homicide.

66. See below, n. 96.

67. See Hurnard, *King's Pardon for Homicide*, pp. 101–4.

68. *Ibid.*, p. 102. See, however, George P. Fletcher, *Rethinking Criminal Law* (Boston, 1978), p. 359. Fletcher stresses "the important conceptual distinction between acquittal for no homicide and a judgment or pardon for an excused homicide." I agree that this was an important distinction, but I believe that in some cases the facts supporting a conclusion of "no homicide" were false and that the bench therefore sometimes required a pardon. See below, text at nn. 91–95.

responsible agent. There is an evident confusion between an embryonic concept of fault and the ancient theory governing homicide committed by a nonhuman agent, for which payment of a "deodand" was required.[69] The courts' stress on the driver's absence of intent, rather than upon his lack of negligence, is therefore revealing. Frequently, when a court had determined that the driver had not "intended" to strike the victim, it concluded that his horse or cart was to blame. The horse might as well have been riderless or the cart empty, for the courts treated such a case as no different from that of a death caused by a tree that had been blown down in a windstorm.[70]

Most of the late-fourteenth-century accidental homicide cases in which the defendant was acquitted involved situations where it was perceived that either the slain person himself or an intervening object had been the real cause of death. In this sense, these cases represented a logical extension of the earlier pattern of acquittals for accidental homicide.

Archery accidents were among the most common causes of unintentional slaying throughout the Middle Ages.[71] Target shooting, a favorite sport, continued to take its toll despite attempts to require strict safeguards.[72] Arrows went off course in several recorded instances, one, e.g., after striking a tree branch[73] and another after glancing off the ground.[74] The defendant in each of these cases was acquitted, though in the second only after the court took the matter under advisement.[75] Of the shooting-accident cases, these two are the closest in nature to the thirteenth-century acquittals. The defendant had set in motion the agent of death, but circumstances perceived to be beyond his control had

69. The deodand (literally, "to be given to God," but in fact given to the Crown) represented the value of the agent that caused the death. See Hunnisett, *Medieval Coroner*, pp. 32–34; Pollock and Maitland, *History of English Law*, 2:473–74.

70. See e.g. G. Fowler, trans., "Roll of the Justices in Eyre at Bedford, 1227," in *The Publications of the Bedfordshire Historical Record Society* (hereafter cited as *Bedford Eyre*), vol. 3 (Aspley Guise, 1916), p. 153 (cart); JUST 1/280, m.18d (1286) (cart); *London Coroners' Rolls*, Roll A, no. 30 (1301) (horse ran over deceased "against [the rider's] will").

71. Green, "Pardonable Homicide in Medieval England," pp. 77–82.

72. Jurors at a coroner's inquest, JUST 2/207, m.2d/1 (1397), described an accident resulting from the slain man's negligence in the course of an event subject to specific regulations at a well-marked area: "[I]t happened that . . . William Swayn negligently ["*necligenter*"] and in a disorderly way stood beyond the marker within the limits and bounds set up for the shooting match so that while William Swayn stood negligently in the said manner, William Stonehale shot him with one of his arrows." Cf. JUST 2/59, m.18/3 (1387), where the defendant had yelled a warning to someone who was crossing the shooting area.

73. JUST 3/167, m.72/1 (1384).

74. JUST 3/177, m.47d/2 (1391).

75. In this case, the court also ordered forfeiture of chattels. JUST 3/177, m.47d/2 (1391).

determined the outcome; on the other hand, in no way could it be said that the deceased had been responsible for his demise.[76]

Cases in which the deceased was said to have been at fault were not uncommon,[77] however, and in the late fourteenth century they began to play a significant role. A few shooting cases suggest that the deceased's behavior—contributory negligence, as it were—had become a matter of great concern. Indeed, it is in the context of the victim's action in these cases that the term negligence first gained prominence on the medieval criminal trial rolls. Only on the rarest occasion was that term associated with the slayer; his negligence was almost never at issue.[78] To the modern mind, it might seem strange that the law was more lenient toward those who had used lethal weapons in a negligent or even reckless manner[79] than toward those who had retaliated against murderous assaults.[80] But the paradox is easily explained. The court looked solely to the slayer's intent, and slaying without malice was not felonious. Thus, if it could be shown that the deceased had caused his own death in a manner the slayer could not have predicted, there was a strong presumption of nonmalicious

---

76. For an early example of acquittal in a shooting case, see JUST 1/1060, m.13d (1279), and the discussion in Hurnard, *King's Pardon for Homicide*, p. 279.

77. See above, text at n. 68.

78. In a 1416 case, JUST 2/170, m.1/2, a coroner recorded the following: "Geoffrey Angulluskey drove a cart . . . [and] through his negligence and inebriation the nearside wheel of the cart ran across the head of Julia who lay at the foot of the wall of her mother, Lucy, without any unusual motion of the cart or horses. . . . The value of the wheel is twelve pence; the said wheel killed Julia . . . and Geoffrey fled and he has no goods." The coroner assigned the negligence to the driver, the only such case I have found on any of the extant coroners' rolls, but he then treated the death as a misadventure due to other than a human agent. He blamed the death on the wheel, and assessed its value for purposes of the deodand. See above, n. 69. Geoffrey's goods were assessed presumably because he fled rather than remained and gave evidence. The coroner was subsequently amerced; an assize clerk later added: "The coroner is at fault for failing to mention who ought to respond." Most likely the assize clerk, like the coroner, treated the case as a misadventure due to other than a human agent, and the amercement was for failure to note who ought to respond for payment of the deodand. It is possible, although I believe very unlikely, that the clerk, noting the coroner's reference to the driver's "negligence," believed an indictment was merited and was assessing the coroner for failure to frame one.

79. See e.g. C 145/11/30 (1261) (defendant threw a knife at a cat but hit and killed his wife instead); C 145/85/18 (1320) (defendant threw a knife at a wall but hit and killed his wife instead).

80. Maitland remarks: "That a man who kills another in self-defence should require a pardon will seem to us even more monstrous than that pardons should be needed where there has been misadventure, for the 'misadventure' of this age covers many a blameworthy act." Pollock and Maitland, *History of English Law*, 2:483. In my view, however, the formal rules of self-defense took account of the fact that jury verdicts of self-defense concealed many blameworthy acts. While this does not account for the leniency toward negligence, it does help explain the relative severity of the self-defense rules.

homicide. It was to that end that the allegations in shooting cases leading to acquittals recited that the deceased had gotten in the way and been slain "by his own fault" (*"in defectu suo proprio"*),[81] or that the deceased had run into the target area through his own foolishness or negligence.[82]

The allegation that the deceased had been foolish, reckless, or at fault runs through the largest and, for legal theory, the most important class of cases identifiable as resulting in acquittal for misadventure. These are cases in which the defendant had the weapon causing death more or less under his control, but the deceased, it was said, ran or fell upon it. What came to be of critical importance were the attendant circumstances. Acquittals were gained easily in homicides caused by accidental contact with sheathed knives in games of football and wrestling.[83] More problematic were cases that fell between self-defense and accident, in which the deceased allegedly launched a deadly attack upon the defendant only to die "through his own fault," unintentionally plunging upon his intended victim's weapon.[84] In essence, these were cases in which self-defense had been transformed into accidental homicide.

Accidental death in the course of deadly assault, which appears occasionally on the early trial rolls,[85] became very common in the late fourteenth century.[86] By then, of course, a great deal more was at stake and much depended upon the characterization of the defendant's act. According to the policy initiated in the 1340s, the excusable slayer not only was required to obtain a pardon but lost his chattels whether or not he had fled.[87] By the later fourteenth century, however, if the excusable

---

81. See e.g. JUST 3/180, m.24d/8 (1393).

82. See e.g. JUST 2/207, m.2d/l (1397). But see JUST 3/185, m.8d/3 (1398), where similar allegations as to the deceased's behavior led to defendant's remand and pardon.

83. See e.g. JUST 1/1194, m.1/l (1272) (football); C 145/38/20 (1280) (football); JUST 3/167, m.30/l (1381) (football); *Bedford Eyre*, p. 1 (wrestling). Cf. C 144/27/31 (1287) (dancing).

84. Compare JUST 3/176, m.6/2 (1390); JUST 3/181, m.7d/l (1390); JUST 3/179, m.6/2 (1391); JUST 3/183, m.2/l (1395); JUST 3/179, m.49/l (1397); JUST 3/205, m.11d/7 (1427) (cases ending in acquittals); with JUST 3/179, m.31 (1387); JUST 3/179, m.28d/6 (1393); JUST 3/179, m.38d/3 (1394); JUST 3/180, m.46d/3 (1395); JUST 3/180, m.14/8 (1397) (defendants ordered to obtain pardons).

85. See e.g. C 260/2, no. 47 (1280); C 144/31/12 (1292); C 260/20, no. 16 (1309). See also Hurnard, *King's Pardon for Homicide*, pp. 95–96.

86. See above, n. 84 and cases cited therein.

87. See Hurnard, *King's Pardon for Homicide*, p. 147. See generally Pollock and Maitland, *History of English Law*, 2:481. It is not possible to determine the exact moment this new policy came into being. The first Year Book reference to a general rule of forfeiture is *Year Book* (Edward III), Hil., 21 Edw. 3, pl. 23 (1347). See also *Year Book* (Edward III), Mich., 44 Edw. 3, pl. 55 (1370); *Year Book* (Henry IV), Easter, 2 Hen. 4, pl. 6 (1400). Examination of the gaol delivery rolls yields very uncertain information. Clerks did not always record forfeitures, and, even before 1340, they often failed to note flight. Recording

slaying were accidental, the slayer stood an excellent chance of acquittal and retention of goods.[88] The court therefore was careful in these cases to determine—or at least to elicit a sworn assertion—that the defendant had drawn the knife or sword solely for the purpose of self-defense, that he had held it steady as a bar to further assault, and that the deceased had of his own motion plunged onto the defendant's weapon. The defendant, it was sometimes said, had not supplied any motion or force at all.[89] The tenor and form of the testimony bears a greater resemblance to that produced in the late-fourteenth-century shooting accidents than to that set forth in the thirteenth-century cases of deaths suffered by negligent assailants.[90]

Even with explicit, sworn statements from the jurors, the bench appears to have been cautious with allegations of death resulting from negligent assault. The acquittal rate when the jury brought back a finding of this kind seems to have lagged behind that for misadventures surrounded by other less suspicious circumstances.[91] Indeed, the fact that very few of these latter cases, such as deaths resulting from target shooting, appear on the rolls suggests that they led automatically to acquittal with relatively little testing of the evidence.

flight was unnecessary before forfeiture became general: where forfeiture was indicated there must have been flight. Afterward, since flight was no longer a prerequisite for seizure of goods, it was an equally purposeless point for the busy clerks to make. Hence, neither the failure to indicate forfeiture nor the indication of forfeiture without mention of flight necessarily indicates whether the automatic forfeiture rule was in effect. For gaol delivery rolls evidencing the haphazard application of the new rule, see JUST 3/129 (1336–46); JUST 3/131 (1337–55); JUST 3/134 (1341–51), *passim*. See below, n. 105 and accompanying text.

88.  But see JUST 3/177, m.47d/2 (1391), where the defendant was acquitted but forfeited his chattels.

89.  See e.g. JUST 3/137A, m.8/4 (135i) (after the deceased had struck the defendant and gravely wounded him, he ran after the defendant, who held a pitchfork between himself and his attacker; the deceased then "stupidly ran upon the pitchfork"); JUST 3/176, m.6/2 (1390) [the deceased had thrown the defendant into a ditch and had fallen accidentally on the latter's knife; the court asked whether the defendant had, out of any malice, held his knife upward toward the deceased ("*ex aliqua malicia sursum potuit cultellum suum versus . . .*")]; JUST 3/179, m.6d/2 (1391); JUST 2/60, m.13/2 (1394) (the defendant held a sword between himself and his assailant without moving it); JUST 3/179, m.3/1 (1389) (the jurors stated that the defendant had not moved his weapon but held it still; he nevertheless had to obtain a pardon for self-defense).

90.  See above, n. 85.

91.  Cf. cases cited above in n. 84 with cases cited above in n. 83. It is interesting to note that Thomas Cauteshangre, one of the coroners who responded to the new judicial policy of acquitting in accidental homicide cases by not framing indictments in many such cases, did continue to frame indictments in cases where the deceased was said to have run against a knife held up in self-defense. See e.g. JUST 2/155, m.9/3 (1382); JUST 2/155, m.10/3 (1383); JUST 2/155, m.11/5 (1385); JUST 2/155, m.16/1 (1389); JUST 2/155, m.21/3 (1392).

The more frequent enrollment of details in cases where "accidents" stemmed from fights suggests that the courts had some difficulty in determining liability in such cases. Perhaps the judges suspected that jurors had now found a convenient way to obtain acquittals for those who had perpetrated simple homicide: rather than portray them as self-defenders who struck the fatal blow, jurors could go one step further and turn them either into "accidental" slayers on whose weapons murderous assailants had, through their own fault, flung their bodies or into "nonslayers," the deceased having "slain himself."[92] Evidence of the bench's suspicion regarding such verdicts can be gleaned from the fact that many of these defendants who were not acquitted, but who were instead required to obtain a pardon, were pardoned for self-defense rather than for accident.[93] Judicial caution in the face of the new formula is understandable, yet at times appears extreme. One court, e.g., went so far as to discuss whether a pardon was required for a defendant who allegedly ran from his assailant and was spared when the latter slipped and fell upon his own knife.[94] Perhaps the cases involving assailants said to have fallen upon their own weapons had multiplied beyond all belief.[95]

92. For cases in which the formula "the defendant slew himself" ("*se ipsum interfecit*") appears, see e.g. JUST 3/179, m.4d/2 (1390); JUST 3/179, m.6/2 (1391). In a yearbook case [*Year Book* (Edward III), Mich., 44 Edw. 3, pl. 55 (1371)], Knivet, J., stated that had the defendant slain in self-defense, pardon and forfeiture would have been required; here they were not required because the deceased, in attacking the defendant, had fallen upon the defendant's knife and had thereby killed himself.

A sixteenth-century treatise groups this genre of case with suicide ("*felo de se*"). William Staunford, *Pleas of the Crown* (London, 1557), p. 20 (1557). At another point, however, Staunford treats such cases as though they turned upon the question whether the defendant had any recourse other than to draw his knife. *Ibid.*, p. 16a. The implication is that such homicides were perceived as accidents for which no blame attached to the defendant rather than as true suicides. Staunford distinguishes two fourteenth-century cases in an effort to explain why one required pardon and forfeiture while the other did not. A defendant who had held his knife in his hand as he lay on the ground had been acquitted while a defendant who had remained on his feet and held a pitchfork against his assailant's charge was pardoned. In both cases the deceased had plunged onto the weapon, but in the latter, Staunford asserts, the defendant had other means of escape. While fourteenth-century courts did not in fact adhere consistently to a distinction between defendants lying upon the ground and those on their feet, it is possible that in an attempt to weigh the credibility of the jury's testimony, the bench found the former cases more persuasive than the latter. It is also possible that the former cases more often led to acquittals because they were easier to assimilate to accidental homicides where parties engaged in sporting events had fallen upon one another.

93. See e.g. JUST 3/179, m.3/1 (1389); JUST 3/179, m.28d/6 (1393).

94. JUST 3/182, m.18/6 (1395). The defendant was eventually acquitted.

95. See e.g. JUST 3/179, m.27/2 (1388); JUST 3/179, m.27/3 (1388); JUST 3/179, m.4d/2 (1390).

This convergence of the self-defense and accident formulae came at a moment when the law of misadventure was in flux[96] and the complaints about professional crime were intense. The convergence offered an opportunity for carving out a species of justifiable self-defense leading to acquittal: only those who truly repulsed murderers would fit within the class; less worthy "self-defenders" would continue to move through the pardoning process, suffering forfeiture of goods and chattels. But the new category was based upon a fiction of accidental homicide that itself depended upon a tenuous distinction. It is impossible to determine how well it worked in relieving true self-defenders of the strictures of the law of excusable homicide, or even how long it persisted. The fifteenth-century rolls are too incomplete for us to judge.

It appears that within two centuries of its inception this trend toward acquittals in cases of misadventure was reversed. In the sixteenth and seventeenth centuries the rolls once again reflect a need for pardons in cases of accidental homicide. It is possible that one of the underlying reasons for judicial insistence upon pardons in misadventure was the invention and widespread distribution of firearms.[97] Whether the courts were seeking to deter negligence or to punish suspected malice is impossible to determine, but it appears that they returned to pre-fourteenth-century practice and refused to acquit defendants, whether or not the jury stated that the deceased had "slain himself."

## 4

The foregoing study of the late medieval law of nonfelonious homicide has centered on the effects of jury behavior on the development of the

---

96. The new judicial approach to accidental homicide also caused some coroners to be in doubt as to whether indictment was appropriate in cases of accidental homicide. The nature and extent of the confusion, however, are difficult to trace. When a human agent was involved, the coroner was supposed to record the suspect's name, the value of his goods, and, if he had not taken flight, in whose custody the suspect had been placed. Unfortunately, the extant coroners' rolls reveal very sloppy recording of the essential details so that it is often difficult to determine whether or not the coroner recorded an indictment. Failure to assess the suspect's goods and to note his present whereabouts does not necessarily mean there was no indictment. Each individual enrollment must be interpreted in the light of the entire roll. Some coroners marginated "*felonia*" beside their indictments, and omission of "*felonia*" only in cases of misadventure almost certainly indicates failure to indict. Failure to assess goods only in misadventures indicates that no human agent was being held responsible. On the basis of a thorough study of the extant rolls dating from 1350 to 1422, it is clear that treatment of misadventures was highly erratic, depending only in part on who was coroner; some coroners followed contradictory policies in identical cases. For a review of the extant evidence on this matter see Green, "Jury and the Law of Homicide," pp. 450–51, n. 149.

97. *Ibid.*, p. 495, n. 299.

substantive law. I have suggested that jury behavior in cases of simple homicide to some extent stifled legal development. Specifically, I have suggested that had there been a free flow of fact situations, judicial discussion of "close cases" might have resulted in the elaboration of the rules of self-defense and felony, singling out true self-defenders for better treatment (acquittal without forfeiture) and producing a class of felonious but noncapital homicide. But lacking direct evidence, it is difficult to prove that judges were in fact influenced by jury behavior. It is always possible, for instance, that judges were mechanically applying the rules of self-defense and that they would have continued to do so even if juries had acted in accordance with the formal rules of liability for homicide.

While there can be no empirical evidence about how courts would have structured the law had juries behaved differently, there are developments in the law of nonfelonious homicide that suggest some legal fluidity and a judicial capacity—perhaps after consultation with the Crown—to modify the traditional common-law rules. The courts singled out slayers of burglars and thieves as justifiable slayers, thus eliminating for them the requirements of pardon and forfeiture. And the courts developed the theory by which some accidental slayers were acquitted on the ground that they were not true slayers but merely instruments by which the victims, through negligence, caused their own deaths.

However, in related areas the courts demonstrated considerable reluctance to modify the substantive rules. The slaying of a would-be murderer was not included within the class of justifiable homicide, and, although acquittals were freely allowed in accidents resulting from target shooting, courts were cautious in acquitting for accidental homicides stemming from fights. The pattern of relative nondevelopment in areas where the courts were faced with facts that might suggest the appropriateness of acquittal is as important as the pattern of fluidity and growth. On the one hand, the law remained static just where one might expect it to: where the defendant had been involved in a fight for which he might have been at least in part responsible. On the other hand, the defendant in some of these cases was under unprovoked and deadly attack. He was resisting behavior that the law sought specifically to deter in much the same way as were those who slew robbers and burglars. Yet only the latter were deemed worthy of acquittal. One is driven to ask why self-defense, especially in cases of defense against murderous assault, resulted in the application of the full rigor of the law of excusable homicide. The answer, at least for the fourteenth century, cannot lie solely in the mechanical nature of judicial application of the law. By then some self-defenders and some perpetrators of accidental homicide were being acquitted; others were not.[98]

A second possible explanation for the courts' behavior might h
the Crown's need for additional revenue. As long as true self-defenders
required pardons, they suffered forfeiture as well. But considering their
likely numbers, acquittal of all true self-defenders would have cost the
Crown a relatively small sum, and acquittal only of those true self-
defenders who had slain would-be murderers would have involved a still
smaller cost.[99] If the Crown could afford to acquit many of those who had
slain accidentally and most of those who had slain robbers and burglars,
it could have afforded to acquit those who had slain murderers.

The most plausible explanation for the retention of the strict rules of
self-defense was the difficulty, given the pattern of jury verdicts, of
identifying true self-defenders. But if jury findings that the defendant had
slain an attempted murderer were suspect, why were findings that he had
slain a burglar or robber not equally open to doubt? Why did the courts
treat with caution verdicts to the effect that the defendant had slain
accidentally in the course of a fight (i.e., where the defendant had stood
motionless and his assailant had hurled himself upon the defendant's
knife), while apparently giving credence to verdicts of mischance at target
shootings?

98. For a recent, useful comment on this problem see Thomas Glyn Watkin, "Hamlet and
the Law of Homicide," *Law Quarterly Review*, vol. 100 (1984), pp. 286–87. Watkin, who
deals with this matter only in passing, suggests that the "mere attacker, who is not a robber,
has not at the time of his demise yet committed a felony so as to place himself outside the
law." The "medieval approach was from the standpoint of the victim not the killer." This
is an important point and may speak to the early development of the law. By the fourteenth
century its claim on the juristic mind was probably much attenuated. I am not convinced
that, by that late date, those who prowled the highways waiting to ambush and slay their
victims were thought of as truly different from those who came to rob someone in his home.
Moreover, Watkin's suggestion does not seem to explain the difference between the
treatment of accidental slayers and slayers in self-defense.

99. It is impossible to determine either the number of true self-defenders or the
percentage of them who slew would-be murderers. Of the 10 to 40 percent of defendants who
received verdicts of self-defense, many, perhaps most, had failed to comply with the strict
letter of the law. Of those who had complied, many had retreated from an attack launched
by a friend or neighbor after a heated argument and probably only a few from a truly
murderous assault. In any case, many defendants had no goods; others had goods but
disposed of them before trial. Moreover, the Crown could not depend on juries to assess the
full value of the defendant's goods in cases of true self-defense.

The Crown did stand to gain from forfeiture as it applied to *all* cases in which juries
rendered verdicts of self-defense. See Green, "Pardonable Homicide," pp. 189–90. Moreover, since most of those cases were in fact instances of felonious homicide, the rule of
forfeiture served important deterrent and punitive purposes. See below, text at n. 105. The
true self-defenders were, of course, victimized by this interaction of jury behavior and
judicial response (unless juries refused to state that the true self-defenders had goods).

The suggestion here is that juries did not—or that judges supposed juries did not—engage in total fabrication of the facts but built upon or modified some core of reality. To emphasize the defendant's absence of malice, juries were not beyond construing common fights as one-sided attacks. They assigned to the deceased responsibility for commencing the struggle, often alleging that he had harbored a grudge against the defendant or had taken him by surprise. Such descriptions may have been ritualistic assertions extended by the jury in its desire to promote the defendant's case. Similarly, the assertion that the defendant held his knife motionless against his attacker's reckless charge stretches the truth but a little further than the clearly acceptable assertion that the defendant actively fought back by striking one blow as he stood, gravely wounded, with his back to the wall.

But it would have been quite another thing for the jury to invent a shooting match or to place the parties in a field where they labored side by side with sharp-edged tools that might go astray. Converting slaying during a fight into slaying to prevent a burglary may have demanded more distortion than the jury was prepared to countenance. After all, in many cases the true facts would have been known to many individuals not sitting on the jury. Reducing complicated facts to particular forms that did "justice" might not have engendered popular disapproval; complete transformation of the facts might have. Moreover, although we cannot be certain about the nature of medieval trials, it is possible that in many cases the defendant told his story first and that the jury repeated, or built upon, his statement.[100] While the defendant doubtless sought to put the best possible face upon the basic fact that he had slain in the course of a fight, he may out of prudence have stopped short of attempting to achieve acquittal through a total invention.

The fact that the bench countenanced some change within the area of nonfelonious homicide, and that rational explanations are available for areas in which the court was reluctant to mandate change, does not, however, prove the proposition that, other things being equal, the bench would have been willing either to modify the outer limits of nonfelonious self-defense or to create an intermediate category of noncapital felonious homicide. Either of those changes would have meant shifting the line between life and death rather than between acquittal and pardon. It is at least possible that even had juries behaved differently, the legal definition of capital homicide would have remained unchanged—that if all perpetrators of felonious homicide had been convicted of that crime, they would all have been hanged.

100. See *ibid.*, p. 433 text at nn. 76–77.

Moreover, even if it is assumed arguendo that judicial confrontation of close cases might have resulted in the elaboration of the law of felonious homicide and self-defense, it must be conceded that such a development could have occurred without a body of close cases. Judges must have been aware that many homicides resulted from brawls that defendants had freely joined and that juries systematically concealed this aspect of the defendant's behavior. The judges could have redefined felonious homicide to secure justice, to induce different jury behavior, or both. Yet they did not do so. Systematic nullification of the formal rules of felonious homicide continued for perhaps two centuries or more.[101] Why did the Crown not seek to end such nullification by changing the formal rules? To answer this question we must consider once again the development of the administration of the criminal law.

## IV

By way of conclusion to Part I, we should attempt to bring together the main themes of these first chapters, to put the problem of the law-finding jury in perspective, and to speculate on the role that rule and sanction nullification played in the larger world of criminal justice. In doing so, however, we must not exaggerate the degree to which any single aspect of the administration of the criminal law was shaped by conscious choice.

The history of the English criminal trial jury has its origins in the twelfth-century transformation of the criminal law.[102] This transformation, which represented an evolutionary development about which we know very little, involved a shift from a more or less private to a more or less public criminal law and a shift from monetary composition between private parties to capital punishment at the hands of the Crown. In theory, neither development required the use of juries, grand or petty. In practice, Henry II, either through improvisation or through elaboration of an existing institution, resorted to presentment by a jury of laymen. It was a short step to the employment of the trial or petty jury, though had the church not opposed the use of the ordeal, that step might not have been taken. The Crown's recourse to the trial jury suggests an acceptance of deep-seated social attitudes, an awareness of profound administrative weakness, and a sure instinct about how to make things work. It is impossible to say how these elements were related causally, if indeed they

101. There is strong evidence of jury manipulation of facts for the period 1250–1430. The rolls for the period 1430–1550 are too sparse for analysis; thereafter, it appears that juries infrequently returned verdicts of self-defense. See *ibid.*, p. 493. While there is reason to believe the new pattern of jury verdicts began before 1550, the date of the change cannot be determined. See below, Chapter 4, text at n. 69.

102. See above, Chapter 1, section I.

were distinct. Probably we ought to understand them as different aspects of the same relationship between ideas and institutions.

The juries, both grand and petty, were bound to play a crucial role. They made possible the implementation (though only on a selective basis) of a royal and capital law of felony precisely because they were of the community rather than of officialdom. From the very outset there must have been a great deal of discretion in the functioning of presentment juries; certainly the trial jury, which reached decisions concerning life and death, made broad-based assessments of just deserts.

Unfortunately we know very little about the administration of the criminal law in the pre–trial-jury period. Specifically we do not know whether the jury behavior that we can ascertain was anticipated in earlier procedures. Until we know a great deal more about the assumptions the Crown and royal officials made concerning lay participation, we cannot really address the problem of the purpose of the jury. As a result, we can only describe how the system of criminal justice functioned and assess official response in the period for which we do have evidence, reconciling ourselves to the fact that for the most interesting questions we do not yet have answers.

Our primary observation has been that the trial jury mitigated much of the harshness of the new system of criminal justice. Given its institutional setting and powers, the trial jury was able to impose upon the new, formal royal process the traditional attitudes that had predominated in the criminal law during its earlier, private phase. This phenomenon is traceable in homicide, where one would expect it to occur with greatest frequency, but it doubtless affected all areas of crime to greater or lesser degree. The substantive law was harsher than social conditions and attitudes would allow. Moreover, juries were forced to make decisions about individuals partially on the basis of the reputation of those individuals in the community. Fact-finding involved an assessment of personal worth: Was the suspect the sort of person likely to have committed a certain act with malice? And almost inevitably trial jury verdicts came to be judgments about who ought to live and who ought to die, not merely determinations regarding who did what to whom and with what intent.[103]

The official response to jury law-finding is very difficult to reconstruct. We have seen that officials were likely to be most concerned with the bribing of juries, with extortionate practices, with intimidation by suspects and their associates. Moreover, the attention of officials was drawn to the most serious cases. Jury behavior in simple homicide and casual

103. See Pugh's remarks on this subject in "Reflections of a Medieval Criminologist," p. 98.

theft was to some extent concealed from view. Presentment of the innocent and lack of substantial evidence were all too common for judges to be certain that a given acquittal was not, strictly speaking, merited by the rules of the law. Finally, the bench must have been aware that juries were toughest on the worst offenders, that they made distinctions—both when they convicted and when they nullified either the rule or the sanction in the less serious cases—that corresponded to widely held attitudes.

Jury law-finding, then, was only one aspect of jury deviation from legal rules. It reflected disagreement with those rules but not necessarily a corruption of legitimate legal process. Although it also reflected the Crown's incapacity to achieve enforcement of the law, other aspects of jury behavior did so much more dramatically. Moreover, it was an aspect of jury behavior that the bench and Crown could accommodate, for it could be understood as an appropriate extension of mercy in individual cases.[104]

At the same time, jury nullification, particularly in homicide, involved some costs, for it slowed development of the law and induced the bench to deal too circumspectly with some cases meriting generous treatment. The true self-defender suffered most. Those true self-defenders who had slain in the course of resisting burglary or robbery were assured of full acquittal without the pardon requirement only after the middle of the fourteenth century. This seems especially ironic given the bench's concern with professional crime. Even in the very late fourteenth century, when officialdom was attempting to deal with those who committed homicide through ambush by removing eligibility for pardons of grace, slayers of such offenders still required pardons. Thus jury resistance to the full reach of the capital law of felony interfered, albeit indirectly, with the judicial attack on the truly pressing problems of the criminal law.

The law of sanctions and the criminal trial jury interacted to produce a substantial distortion in the legal process. In the law of homicide, a large and mainly false category of self-defense was employed as a catchall for less serious forms of homicide. Pretrial incarceration, the strains of standing trial, remand to await pardon, and the forfeiture of goods became the de facto sanctions for what a later age called "manslaughter." Acquittal was probably accorded some true self-defenders, though probably not most. The Crown maintained the substantive legal rules and the institutional structure despite this quite obvious distortion. It did so at the

---

104. See *ibid.*, p. 9, for the suggestion that in the late thirteenth century the bench showed compassion toward some "imprisoned or fined for appeals which failed," releasing them "for their poverty." This "compassion may have infected jurors."

risk of increasing difficulties in confronting serious crime. Why, we must ask, should this have been so? Why did the Crown not introduce a lesser offense corresponding to simple homicide, or casual theft, for which imprisonment and/or a fine would be the penalty, thereby singling out the worst offenders for capital punishment and the true self-defenders for pardon without forfeiture, and removing the aura of suspicion that attended slayers in self-defense against thieves and ambushers?

In one sense, of course, perpetrators of simple homicides who were alleged to be self-defenders *were* fined. At least after 1343, all of them were supposed to suffer forfeiture even though they received pardons. Indeed, the rule of automatic forfeiture, which penalized the true self-defenders as well, may have been a belated response to juries' handling of simple homicide.[105] In another sense, some thieves and some felonious

---

105. Maitland ascribes the new rule to royal desire for revenue generally:
> So far as we can see, the homicide who obtained a pardon on the score of misadventure or self-defence (unless he had fled on account of his deed), did not in Henry III.'s time incur that forfeiture of his chattels which was inflicted upon him in after days. But very often he had fled, and this, so it seems to us, may have enabled our ever needy kings to establish forfeiture as a general accompaniment of the "pardon of course." [*History of English Law*, 2:481].

I suspect, but cannot prove, that the bench was influenced by the frequent recourse of juries to a verdict of self-defense. The new rule of forfeiture also affected misadventure, but, as we have seen, judges began to acquit accidental slayers, except where they suspected misadventure verdicts concealed simple homicides.

There is, however, another explanation, which the bench itself gave as early as 1347. A Year Book entry of that year noted that the Statute of Gloucester, Stat. 6 Edw. 1, c. 9 (1278), authorized a pardon for cases of accident and self-defense but said nothing about saving the defendant his goods. *Year Book* (Edward III) Hil., 21 Edw. 3, fol. 17, pl. 23 (1347). In fact, the Statute of Gloucester dealt with procedures for the granting of writs of inquest into cases of homicide. See Hurnard, *King's Pardon for Homicide*, p. 281; Pollock and Maitland, *History of English Law*, 2:481. It therefore provided no occasion for dealing with the matter of forfeiture.

The same Year Book entry reveals an important misconception of the Statute of Marlborough, Stat. 52 Hen. 3, c. 26 (1267). That statute decreed that the *murdrum* fine (the fine imposed upon a hundred for an unexplained homicide) was not to be levied in cases of misadventure. The *murdrum* fine was abolished altogether in 1340, perhaps some decades after it had fallen into disuse. The bench in 1347 read the Statute of Marlborough to say that misadventure was no longer to be treated as "murder," in the substantive sense of felonious homicide. Due to this misreading, the judges concluded that pardons *de cursu* in accident and presumably self-defense cases were of relatively recent vintage (1267), and that the procedure in such cases had been developed soon after by the Statute of Gloucester (1278). Since neither statute dispensed with the rule of forfeiture, which applied in all cases of felonious homicide, the judges' conclusion that forfeiture applied to all of the "new" excusable homicides is understandable. For a discussion of these erroneous statutory constructions and subsequent commentary upon them, see Pollock and Maitland, *History of English Law*, 2:481–82.

slayers could avoid prosecution by paying a "fine"—the cost of a pardon of grace: money in normal times, forty days of service in time of war. Between these two provisions, many thieves and felonious slayers suffered a penalty even if they were not prosecuted or, in the case of the former, were prosecuted but avoided conviction through securing a verdict of self-defense.

There were advantages to the system as it worked in practice. The retention of a general capital sanction in felony meant that many slayers and thieves sought a pardon of grace from the Crown. Even those who had committed the less serious forms of these offenses may not have trusted their lives to juries and, instead, immunized themselves from prosecution. They turned themselves in, relieving central and local officials of some of the overwhelming burden under which they worked. Fewer suspects had to be taken, incarcerated, and tried. The threat of execution, in short, automatically acted as a dragnet.

Moreover, the pardon power gave the Crown considerable control over the destiny of many subjects. Recipients of pardons of grace were direct beneficiaries of royal largesse. Whether the Crown exacted military service or money, or nothing at all, the pardoned offender owed his life to the king.[106] This was also true, though in an attenuated form, if the offender stood trial. If he was acquitted or was granted a verdict of excusable homicide and a pardon *de cursu*, he stood as the beneficiary both of his peers and of the Crown. Of course, the open availability of pardons of grace may have increased jury leniency, and judicial toleration of jury leniency may have increased the number of offenders who put their lives on the country. This, in turn, must have diminished the numbers who sought refuge in the Crown. Indeed, as it operated in practice, the system probably tended to drive into Chancery seeking pardons of grace a disproportionately large number of the most serious offenders, i.e., those whom juries were far more likely to convict, and tended instead to encourage lesser offenders to stand trial. If so, this unintended result must have made enforcement of the statutes limiting the royal power to pardon all the more imperative. The advantages of the system were intimately connected with its disadvantages. If the pardon

While the judicial misreadings of earlier statutes are understandable, there remains the question of what occasioned judicial inquiry into the problem of forfeiture in excusable homicide. Maitland's suggestion regarding the need for revenue and my own related suggestion regarding jury behavior in cases that otherwise would clearly have led to forfeiture must remain tentative. In any case, my analysis of the effect of the rule once it had been propounded does not depend upon my suggestion regarding the motivation of the bench in 1347.

106. For discussion of this theme as it relates to the use of pardons and other forms of mitigation in the eighteenth century see below, Chapter 7.

power was a source of strength—and certainly it was—it was also productive of substantial weakness.

In any case, casual theft and everyday brawling (with the inevitable ensuing deaths) could not be ended altogether by formal legal rules. Indeed, from the perspective of the Crown and bench, a moderation of the law might only have made matters worse. The adoption of a lesser sanction for simple homicide and lesser forms of theft might have seemed to condone jury attitudes and thereby resulted in their amplification. Or it might have produced more convictions only at the expense of encouraging already endemic physical violence. In short, by adhering at least in theory to the strictest rules of criminal liability—by posing what might have been thought to be the greatest threat to the greatest number—the Crown might well have believed that its approach to homicide and theft represented at least a modest deterrent, one that also produced an important source of deference, money, and military service.

On balance, then, it is not surprising that the Crown and bench accommodated themselves to jury leniency. Serious offenders were the real enemy, and so long as juries were relatively harsh in dealing with them the Crown's incapacity to enforce the legal rules against less serious offenders was not fatal to the administration of the criminal law. The bribing and intimidation of jurors by professional criminals posed a far greater threat to the system. Moreover, although jury-based nullification in casual theft and simple homicide both slowed the development of substantive rules designed to deal with serious offenders and established a tradition of community participation that would sometime be difficult to control, it also served dramatically to advertise the merciful quality of royal justice.

# Part II          Transformations

# 4 The Transformation of Jury Trial in Early Modern England

The extensive powers of the medieval criminal trial jury resulted not from legal theory but from social and institutional circumstances. The jury helped the royal administration of criminal law to function, perhaps even alleviated tensions that might have brought it to a halt, by exercising its mediatory powers in two distinct but related ways. In individual cases, juries prevented the imposition of sanctions they deemed too harsh in light of the defendant's behavior, reputation, or the hardship he had already suffered. More generally, and as the result of its role in individual cases, the jury reflected the interests of the local community as opposed to those of central authorities. The Crown required the jury to play a role the royal bureaucracy was as yet unprepared to undertake—the gathering of evidence; this, in turn, enhanced the jury's power to render verdicts that both blunted royal power and made what power there was relatively palatable.

The stronger central institutions became, the less they required of juries, either as substitute bureaucrats or as political mediators. Indeed, the stronger the position of central government, the more it was bound to regard the jury as part of the problem rather than as a solution. By the Tudor period, jury-based nonenforcement of the rules of law seemed less often a political and social necessity and more often an affront to justice. The question remained: How far would the government go in its purification of the jury? Would an attack on embracery and similar perversions of justice suffice, or would the government attempt to remove the jury's power to reflect a different notion of justice on the merits of a given case than that embodied in formal rules?

Very little is as yet known about the institution of the trial jury in Tudor and Stuart England, about governmental policy toward juries, or about the vicissitudes of jury power. Much of what we do know we infer from the broader history of criminal law in the period. A virtual revolution was under way from the mid-fifteenth century, if not earlier, which had the effect of reducing the power of the trial jury and placed greater power in the hands of the bench. Although there is uncertainty about the reasons for this transformation in the criminal law, the institutional developments are unmistakable. The jury ceased during the later Middle Ages to be a (mainly) self-informing institution. Although the process by which this occurred and the corollary emergence of the prosecution are largely hidden from our view, the later stages of prosecutorial development in the second half of the sixteenth century are visible. Crown officials then took increasing responsibility for the initiation and prosecution of criminal cases and for the management of the trial itself. The effects of these changes upon the jury were substantial. For one thing, the government sometimes used great art in persuading juries of the defendant's guilt; perhaps more significantly, the jury lacked the means to manipulate the evidence, to suppress whatever might give the lie to the way it chose to view the facts. Moreover, perhaps as a result of these changes, the bench brought pressure to bear upon some juries that acquitted in the face of inculpatory evidence, binding them over to appear before Star Chamber or even fining and imprisoning them directly.

The government applied the most pressure—took the greatest pains to persuade—where its interest was greatest. In a succession of well-known state trials, mainly for treason, the Tudor and Stuart monarchs pressed their advantage to the fullest. Juries in these cases were probably chosen for their presumed loyalty and were discouraged from disappointing royal expectations. This is not to say that state trials invariably, or even often, ended in the sacrifice of the innocent but that the government tried to avoid the acquittal of the guilty through either mismanagement of the prosecution or an excess of mercy.

Yet there is reason to doubt that the state trials accurately reflect criminal procedure in the routine felony cases, which the Crown lacked both the interest and the capacity to manage. Although in particularly serious cases of homicide or theft the bench might take a special interest, pressing its view strongly upon the jury, in a far larger number of cases the bench actively questioned the defendant and revealed its point of view but left the jury to reach its own conclusion. To be sure, the mere fact of a prosecution—pretrial examinations available to be read in court, witnesses ready to testify for the Crown—must have made some difference. But in routine cases the jury's traditional role was never expressly repudiated. Though usually closely guided by the bench, the jury was allowed to weigh all the evidence in light of both the defendant's reputation and bearing and its own conception of his just deserts.

The direct and indirect changes in the administration of the criminal law in the late sixteenth and early seventeenth century produced a pattern of verdicts that differed from its medieval counterpart. The new pattern, which scholars are only now beginning to sketch out in detail, may usefully be summarized at this point. The overall percentage of convictions at assizes was strikingly higher than in the later Middle Ages. This was true both in homicide and in theft. The former offense came to be divided in the late sixteenth century into murder, which was capital, and manslaughter, which was not unless it was the second such offense. The conviction rates were relatively high for both. The crime of theft remained divided into burglary and robbery, for which conviction was very common, and grand larceny, for which conviction was far less common. Many of those indicted for grand larceny were, by virtue of the jury's undervaluation of the goods stolen or their own plea of guilty to a lesser offense, convicted of petty larceny, which was not capital, just as some of those indicted for murder were mercifully convicted of manslaughter. Convictions were high in those capital felonies that had long been viewed as particularly heinous and in those noncapital offenses that had come to serve as catchalls much as self-defense had served in earlier times. This series of changes in case outcomes resulted in part from the new divisions between capital and noncapital offenses and in part from the pressures that officials were able to bring to bear in the wake of changes in the administration of criminal law. Still other outcomes reflected age-old social attitudes that authorities were either unable or unwilling to resist. At some points, there was conflict between judge and jury; at others, authorities acquiesced in traditional jury practices, or even encouraged those practices.

The developments of the early modern period, then, mark only a partial revolution in criminal process. Moreover, the changes made for little difference in most cases, though they made for a dramatic difference in cases where the Crown or the bench used the new tools to the fullest. A new judge-jury relationship was emerging, but the old habits of thought and behavior survived, leaving the implications of the developing law obscured. How far the Crown had gone, in at least some cases, toward reversing the old, de facto order of things is evident from the attack launched on the judiciary during the Interregnum by those proclaiming the jury's right to find the law. This attack the Cromwellian regime disdainfully brushed aside; neither would the restored Stuart monarchy concede such a right to the jury. How well, on the other hand, the medieval ethic of the jury's right to find the facts according to its own conscience survived is evident in the judiciary's concession in 1671 of the principle of noncoercion. The rhetoric of the jury right, the law of noncoercion, and their fusion in some legal literature toward the end of the seventeenth century are the subjects of the two following chapters of this middle section. These chapters analyze the unofficial and official legal writings from the years 1640–89 that established the ideology of the jury right.

Before turning to these writers and their discussion of the history and role of the trial jury, we shall, in the present chapter, survey the evolution of criminal procedure in the sixteenth and early seventeenth centuries. This interpretive and necessarily selective overview is divided into four sections. The first deals with the major changes in the administration of the criminal law and how they came about. The second analyzes some effects of the new criminal procedure on the substantive criminal law. The third discusses the impact of these procedural and substantive developments on the trial and on the role of the jury. The final section examines the relationship between the problems of the administration of the criminal law generally and the bench's handling of individual cases, specifically the role that the bench found it convenient for juries to play. I suggest that although this period saw a significant shift in courtroom power from the jury to the judge, the jury continued in many routine cases to function in a manner that provided a credible basis for many of the arguments of later pro-jury writers.

# I

The most important changes in early modern criminal procedure were the decline of the self-informing jury and the development of the prosecution.[1] Which of these two developments came first is not known. The link between them is a problem of the greatest importance and may provide some hint regarding the origin of modern criminal procedure.

As we have seen, the medieval jury was presumed to know something of the events underlying the cases it heard.[2] Doubtless it often knew a very great deal—or at least some of its members did. Before the middle of the fourteenth century, petty jurors were sometimes among the presenters who promoted the case from the start. In the case of homicide, some who served on the inquest jury subsequently served on the petty jury or spoke of the case to those who did. We have seen also that the discourse between the judge and the defendant may have influenced the jury in some cases. But the job of the bench was far from easy, for aside from what the trial jury reported there was in the formulistic indictments little

---

1. I am grateful to Professor James S. Cockburn for allowing me to cite and comment upon a typescript version of his forthcoming book, the *Introduction* to his multi-volume edition of *Calendar of Assize Records: Home Circuit Indictments, Elizabeth I and James I* (London, 1975–82). I have incorporated chapter and subsection references to Professor Cockburn's forthcoming book (hereafter cited as Cockburn, *Introduction*) alongside references to his earlier works that convey similar information. Where his *Introduction* modifies his earlier work I have so noted. Though it deals only with the Home Circuit, Professor Cockburn's detailed study will, upon publication, stand as the most comprehensive account of procedure at late-sixteenth- and early-seventeenth-century assizes. My own (largely derivative) account of trial procedure, the text of which was completed before I had access to Professor Cockburn's *Introduction*, serves as a framework for my synthetic and interpretive essay on the impact of the major procedural changes. My commentary on the differences between Professor Cockburn's conclusions and my own is below, n. 179.

2. For discussion of details in this paragraph see above, Chapter I.

evidence about the crimes charged. A clever and steely defendant was not easily gotten round.

By the mid-sixteenth century the situation was very different. There were several sources of information to which the jurors were exposed after they had been sworn. Much of this information resulted from pretrial activity undertaken by the justices of the peace, in accordance with duties set forth in the Marian bail and committal statutes.[3] The information was also available for the use of assize clerks, clerks of the peace, and the bench.[4] In two steps, taken in two consecutive years, the traditional but intermittent investigatory activities of the justices were regularized and significantly elaborated. The Marian statutes mandated practices that for a century or more had served to inform grand jurors and that probably also established a public version of the facts that came to the attention of prospective trial jurors.

The first step in this process, and possibly the only step that the Crown intended at the outset, was the Marian bail statute of 1554, which tightened the procedure for the granting of bail. To remedy abuses that had frustrated the assize courts in their attempts to try suspected felons, the statute ordered that the justices granting bail examine the prisoner and "them that bring him" and send the results of the examination, in writing, to the judges at the next gaol delivery.[5] The assize courts would then be in a position to monitor bail procedure. They would, as Langbein states it,

3. Stat. 1 and 2 Philip and Mary, c. 13 (1554–55); Stat. 2 and 3 Philip and Mary, c. 10 (1555). See John H. Langbein, *Prosecuting Crime in the Renaissance* (Cambridge, Mass., 1974), Appendix A and Part I, "The Marian Statutes"; John H. Langbein, "The Origins of Public Prosecution at Common Law," *American Journal of Legal History*, vol. 17 (1973), pp. 315–24.

4. For an important discussion of the practice regarding use of depositions generated by the Marian statutes, see James S. Cockburn, "Trial by the Book? Fact and Theory in the Criminal Process, 1558–1625," in J. H. Baker, ed., *Legal Records and the Historian* (London, 1978), pp. 69 *et seq.* Cockburn argues that most of the "orchestration" at trial was done by the assize clerks. Justices were frequently not present; their indictments underwent some significant changes. In the present treatment, I assume that witnesses were in fact bound over and that some check on them—or prompting of them—was possible through the use of the examinations provided by the justices of the peace. See Cockburn, *Introduction*, ch. viii, sect. iii. Cockburn ("Trial by the Book?" p. 69) concedes the role of the justice of the peace down to the time of the trial. Orchestration at the trial by the assize clerks and bench is fully consistent with the views expressed here. See also Inner Temple Petyt MS 511/13, fol. 69. And see John H. Baker, "Criminal Courts and Procedure at Common Law," in James S. Cockburn, ed., *Crime in England, 1550–1800* (Princeton, N.J., 1977), p. 16, for a synthesis of the views of Langbein and Cockburn.

5. Langbein, *Prosecuting Crime*, pp. 10–ll; Langbein, "Origins of Public Prosecution," pp. 320–21. See also Langbein, *Prosecuting Crime*, p. 6, for discussion of an earlier (1487) attempt to deal with the problem of bailing by justices of the peace.

have a basis for reviewing the propriety of the bailment in any case in which the accused had turned fugitive and the issue now was whether to discipline the bailing JPs. But when the accused was going to be gaoled, not bailed, there was no danger that he might not appear to stand trial.[6]

In the latter case there was no requirement that the justices of the peace make an examination. The bail statute was not concerned with procedure at trials of those held without bail—the most serious cases—and had only indirect and unintended effect on trials of those who had been bailed. For this latter group, the depositions that had been produced to defend the bailment might then have been used in court, though there is nothing in the statute to suggest that either Crown or Parliament had this in mind. The bail statute appears, in short, to have dealt solely with the problem of bail.

Within a year, Parliament passed a second statute, the so-called committal statute, dealing with pretrial procedures conducted by the justices of the peace. This statute extended the examination and deposition procedures to cases in which suspects were held without bail. Moreover, it ordered the justices to bind over witnesses to appear at trial and to give evidence against the accused. The committal statute, it has been argued, "turned the pretrial investigation into a device for the production of prosecution evidence at trial in every case of felony in the realm."[7] The statute ensured the appearance, where it could be had, of a private prosecutor. In theory, a private prosecutor was necessary in every case; in practice, an official might play the role of prosecutor.[8] The prosecutor and any other witnesses who had been bound over gave their evidence in open court, where they might be prompted by, or examined in the light of, their pretrial depositions. Although the written depositions were not given under oath and thus were not binding as such, they were useful in coordinating and sustaining the case for the prosecution.[9] In many if not all felony trials, the jury witnessed a rigorous testing of the defendant's story. No longer could the defendant tell an elaborate tale and then reply to all skeptical queries with mere repetitions of his side of the case. The judge was now armed with evidence that he could use to challenge the accused's statements. More effectively than in the past, the

6. Langbein, "Origins of Public Prosecution," p. 321.
7. *Idem.*
8. *Ibid.*, pp. 317–18.
9. For an analysis of the assize clerks' treatment of pretrial evidence see James S. Cockburn, "Early-Modern Assize Records as Historical Evidence," *Journal of the Society of Archivists*, vol. 5 (1975), pp. 229–31. See Cockburn, *Introduction*, ch. viii, sect. iii.

bench could sum up the evidence, comment upon the defendant's story, and leave the jury in little doubt regarding its view of the case.[10]

These developments in criminal procedure have the deceptive look and feel of carefully planned Tudor governmental machinery. Until recently, the Marian statutes were regarded as an imitation of Continental criminal process, part of a program to make English criminal procedure more efficient and effective.[11] That view is no longer tenable. The procedure which the statutes mandated differed crucially from Continental procedure.[12] The all-important committal statute appears to have been something of an afterthought, drafted hastily and with the bail statute as its model,[13] and both the bail and committal statutes may only have made mandatory investigatory practices that were already common among the justices of the peace.[14] If the examination and binding over of witnesses did not begin with the Marian statutes, when and why did they begin? Were they nonetheless a tool of Tudor or pre-Tudor statecraft? There is as yet no answer to these questions, but we may consider some tentative hypotheses.

The role of the justice of the peace in the prosecution appears to have been a natural evolution that took place over a century or more.[15] We have seen that the justices were an active part of criminal administration from the middle of the fourteenth century.[16] Their duties ranged widely, from arresting persons suspected of the most trivial offenses and releasing them on recognizances for their good behavior, to trying felons at quarter sessions, and even to condemning convicted felons to death.[17] From these duties grew the justices' capacity as prosecutors. To their duty to arrest

10. For a contemporary account of a felony trial see Thomas Smith, *De Republica Anglorum*, Mary Dewar, ed. (Cambridge, 1982), pp. 110–16. [The original edition was published in 1583; the work was written in the period 1562–65 (*ibid.*, p. 1). I have left quotations from Smith in the original, as given by Dewar.] Smith must be used with care; on this point, however, his account is probably trustworthy. For a discussion of routine felony trials see below, section III.

11. Holdsworth, *History of English Law*, 4:528–29.

12. Langbein, *Prosecuting Crime*, Part I. See esp. pp. 21–33. The central difference was that the English deposition was not given under oath and was not an instrument of record.

13. *Ibid.*, pp. 61–62; Langbein, "Origins of Public Prosecution," p. 322.

14. Langbein, *Prosecuting Crime*, pp. 79–93.

15. Langbein, "Origins of Public Prosecution," pp. 319–20. Although my account leans heavily on Langbein's work, in this and the following several paragraphs I draw conclusions (by way of speculation) that Langbein does not draw and for which his work bears no responsibility. Professor Robert L. Woods, Jr., is presently completing an important study of the early Tudor justices of the peace which promises to expand our knowledge in this area substantially. I am grateful to Professor Woods for his comments on this section of this chapter.

16. See above, Chapter 1, text at nn. 84–86.

17. Putnam, *Proceedings before Justices of the Peace*, pp. xix–xxxv.

persons on suspicion was added the power to examine suspects and witnesses.[18] From keepers of the peace (with powers of arrest) to justices of the peace (with summary powers of conviction in minor offenses) was a dramatic step. To dislodge the local constables as law officers was one thing; to become a part of the English judiciary was quite another. What may have made this step possible was that the keepers' powers to hold or release suspected persons were so great that they inevitably involved investigation and judgment. The distinction between release on bond and release after summary conviction and payment of fine must at some point have become negligible, for the bond itself might be set in accordance with the quantum of evidence produced against the suspect and the seriousness of the act with which he had been charged.[19]

It was natural for the justices to examine suspects in cases in which they were bound to render judgment, whether technically a legal "judgment" or something closer to an administrative decision. It was also natural for them to examine in cases on which they or some other, higher judge would sit pursuant to a grand jury's accusation. Thus, having grown accustomed to examining those accused of disturbances of the peace, the justices may have treated in similar fashion those suspected of treason, theft, or homicide, whom they were to bind over pending the action of a grand jury. It is possible that such investigatory action was commenced primarily in order to secure an indictment rather than to gather evidence for the trial itself. Inevitably, information that led to an indictment would subsequently be held over for use at trial. Thus, during two centuries of English criminal administration largely hidden from our view there were three critical, and probably connected, developments: the justices of the peace began to investigate, perhaps even to act as prosecutors; the grand jury underwent its metamorphosis from active presenter to passive indictor; and the trial jury began to receive most of its evidence at the trial itself.

All of these developments represented a kind of internal institutional growth, but at least indirectly they were also responses to external pressures. The expansion of the duties of the justices of the peace was, as we have seen,[20] a governmental response to social and economic problems of the later Middle Ages. Some of those duties, including the power to examine, were fashioned specifically to deal with the criminal activity that such problems produced. In this sense, the transformation of the

---

18. Langbein, "Origins of Public Prosecution," p. 319.

19. See Harding, "The Origin and Early History of the Keeper of the Peace," pp. 102–9, for a fuller discussion. Harding stresses the keepers' role in receiving, and ultimately judging, complaints of trespass.

20. See above, Chapter 1, section III.

criminal process was partly the result of governmental action. It is difficult to show, however, that in other than this sense the justice of the peace as prosecutor was a creature of governmental conception or mandate.

The social changes that created the need for the justices may also have helped to shape their specific responsibilities. Both the jury of present-ment and the self-informing trial jury were by-products of the society whose decline the justices were supposed to halt. Those institutions presumed a stationary population; their capacities might be outstripped by more than modest levels of crime. The increase of serious crime, especially that perpetrated by roving gangs or by persons from afar, must have revealed the limitations of the two juries;[21] the at least partial default of these essentially local institutions left the population without the protection it required. A vacuum from "below" drew the justices in at the same time that the need to produce indicted and convictable persons before commissioners of oyer and terminer constituted pressures from "above." Moreover, the pressures from below were more direct and suggested the very nature of the remedy: the justices must see to it that juries were informed.

The origins of early modern trial practice are therefore more ancient and more complex than the most visible agents of change, the Marian bail and committal statutes, suggest. Nevertheless, the Tudors knew a useful institution when they saw one, and they were responsible for the crystallization of prosecutorial practice. For the transformation of trial procedure paralleled—perhaps touched—several interrelated develop-ments that are commonly associated with early Tudor government. Although these developments do not explain the emergence of the prosecution, or provide evidence of its pre-Marian stages, they help us to understand the nature of the terrain in which the justices came to function as quasi-prosecutors.

The early Tudors sought to ensure the stability of their monarchy through making existing institutions work as they were in theory sup-posed to work. They employed the Council and the court of Star Chamber to monitor the actions of royal officials and to root out the abuse of official institutions.[22] Tudor efforts to purify jury process follow this pattern.[23] By subjecting to investigation and judgment not only persons believed to have tampered with jurors but jurors themselves—in some cases entire juries—the Crown opened an important avenue to royal control of trial proceedings. For the moment, the object of Star Chamber interest was the

---

21. See above, Chapter 3, text at n. 9.
22. See J. A. Guy, *The Cardinal's Court* (Sussex, 1973), pp. 30–31, 52–53, 63–64.
23. *Ibid.*, pp. 61–63, 137.

true malefactor: the person who obviously abused the juror's oath to render a verdict according to conscience. Unlawful pressures and inducements were alleged and proved: obstruction of the law, not unlawful "law-finding," was the most common charge against jurors in the early sixteenth century.[24]

Throughout the fifteenth and early sixteenth centuries, Parliament sought in a more traditional manner to render juries impervious to the political pressures that local magnates might bring to bear on behalf of their retainers. A series of statutes continued and attempted better enforcement of property qualifications for prospective trial jurors.[25] To the extent these were enforced, they must have in the great majority of cases separated jurors and defendant both by class and by neighborhood and thus exacerbated the problems that social mobility and professional crime created for effective operation of the self-informing jury. The statutes effectively reduced the pool of eligible jurors, concentrating it within a class many of whose members did not desire to serve and found means to avoid doing so.[26] It is possible that this particular governmental strategy hastened the day when resort to whomever bailiffs could find on assize days regardless of station (the *tales de circumstantibus*) became, if not the rule, something more than the exception.[27]

Still, it would be wrong to conclude that the vitality of the concept of trial by the country was weakened to the point that the very existence of

24. See below, n. 149 and accompanying text for discussion of cases in Star Chamber. One early statute relating to the Welsh Marches [Stat. 26 Hen. 8, c. 4 (1534)] dealt with punishment for perjury. It mandated fines for verdicts against "good and pregnant evidence," but it seems to presume subornation of perjury or browbeating of jurors by friends or relatives of the accused: "[D]ivers murderers, friends and kinfolk to such offenders have . . . suborned [jurors] to acquit [offenders]." See also G. R. Elton, *Policy and Police: The Enforcement of the Reformation in the Age of Cromwell* (Cambridge, 1972), pp. 310 *et seq.* Elton's discussion leaves open the possibility that jurors were punished merely for being too merciful, but seems to indicate that true perjury was almost always at issue. Elton's analysis of jury decision making is perhaps the most interesting "inside" look in the literature.

25. For statutes relating to criminal trial jurors, see e.g. Stat. 2 Hen. 5, st. 2, c. 3 (1414): lands or tenements of an annual value of 40 shillings; Stat. 23 Hen. 8, c. 13 (1531): in trials of murder and felony in cities and towns, jurors shall have forty pounds (suspending freehold requirement to prevent constant challenges on basis of previous statutes and substituting total worth requirement). For a complete listing of statutes, 1225–1730, see James C. Oldham, "The Origins of the Special Jury," *University of Chicago Law Review*, vol. 50 (1983), Appendix, pp. 214–21.

26. James S. Cockburn, *A History of English Assizes* (Cambridge, 1972), p. 118. See Cockburn, *Introduction*, ch. vi, sect. i.

27. Cockburn, *History of English Assizes*, p. 118. See Cockburn, *Introduction*, ch. vi, sect. i. See Stats. 4 and 5 Philip and Mary, c. 7 (1557–58) and 14 Eliz., c. 9 (1572) for extensions of the use of the *tales* to criminal cases.

the institution was brought into question. Rather, the unquestioned right to trial by peers underlay the urgency of the reform measures; abolition was not a live issue. There were doubts in some circles about the effectiveness of the institution of the trial jury but not about the need for its continued use.[28] Early sixteenth-century judges were not unmindful that the jury shielded them from a role they had little desire to play.[29] A century and a half later even so powerful a figure as Sir Matthew Hale conceded that rendering verdicts on the facts was an awesome responsibility that the bench should not be anxious to shoulder.[30]

The sanctity of the trial jury was revealed in yet another way. Charges of subornation of jurors had been leveled at grand juries as well as at trial juries. With the development of the indictment process, control over the grand jury was greatly increased, for royal officials were no longer at the mercy of the hundredors' selective memories. In turn, increased royal control of indictment helped make possible the mid-sixteenth-century changes that increased judicial control over the trial jury.[31] But in the late fifteenth century control over indictment coincided with the moment of greatest threat of political decentralization, and the Crown's mastery of the indictment process depended upon its leverage over the powerful local figures who administered grand jury proceedings. Although the trial jury seemed to require men of greater substance, the grand jury might well—from the Crown's point of view—have benefited from an infusion of thinner blood. The government of Henry VII, drawing upon the momentum of its centralizing programs, attempted to avoid the grand jury altogether in noncapital, statutory offenses. The infamous statute of 1495,[32] as short-lived as its drafters, Empson and Dudley,[33] introduced

---

28. Baker, ed., *Reports of Sir John Spelman*, 2:*106–7*. (Italics indicate references to Baker's "Introduction.")

29. *Ibid.*, p. *43:* "The judges sought refuge from the evils of mankind and the agonies of decision by umpiring the ancient game strictly according to the rules, and by refusing to meddle with questions of fact." (Baker here seems mainly to refer to civil trials.) See also *ibid.*, p. *138:* "No doubt judges could exert influence on a jury, but the forms of charge and oath made plain that the ultimate responsibility for a conviction rested on the jurors' consciences. The judges' task was to see that the rules were observed, and they evidently performed that limited role with absolute propriety." See Sir Thomas More, *The Apology of Sir Thomas More, Knight* (London, 1930), p. 150. More wrote in 1533 that "I durst as well trust the truth of one judge as of two juries. But the judges be such wise men, that for the avoiding of obloquy they will not be put in the trust."

30. Sir Matthew Hale, *Historia Placitorum Coronae: The History of the Pleas of the Crown*, 2 vols. (London, 1778), vol. 2, p. 313.

31. See below, section III.

32. Stat. 11 Hen. 7, c. 3 (1495). [Repealed: Stat. 1 Hen. 8, c. 6 (1509)].

33. On Empson and Dudley see G. R. Elton, *England under the Tudors* (London, 1958), pp. 56–57; Kenneth Pickthorn, *Early Tudor Government: Henry VIII* (Cambridge, 1934), pp. 148–49. According to Pickthorn: "The main motive of repeal was certainly not a sense of

prosecution on informations into criminal procedure in noncapital cases. By its terms, however, it virtually conceded the requirement of an indictment jury in capital cases;[34] and by implication, the statute and the crisis it provoked recognized the requirement of a trial jury in all felonies. The experience strengthened the foundations of jury theory by drawing attention to the argument that the defendant's right to trial by peers involved not one, but two, decisions by the country.[35]

There were, of course, limits to the role that jury reform alone could play in the efforts to create a greater degree of social order. The prosecution and condemnation of serious offenders had long been hampered by the system of royal pardons;[36] secular court jurisdiction over felony suspects had, in the course of the fifteenth century, been substantially reduced due to expansion of the benefit of clergy;[37] and to a more limited but significant degree, the privilege of sanctuary[38] became a serious problem in the early sixteenth century. The early Tudors took steps to bring these impediments to order under control, though not to eliminate them entirely. The closest Henry VII and Henry VIII came to eliminating one of the ancient privileges was their handling of sanctuary, a subject we need not pursue here.[39] In the case of pardons of grace, the

outrage in a public mind saturated with jurisprudence, jealously tenacious of law above statute, but rather a determination of the propertied to be done with the exactions of Empson and Dudley'' (*ibid.*, p. 149).

34. ''Provided always that any such information extend not to treason, murder or felony, nor to any other offence wherefore any person shall lose life or member.''

35. The statute and the roles played by Empson and Dudley figure prominently in seventeenth- and eighteenth-century jury tracts. See e.g. below, Chapter 6, n. 116.

36. See above, Chapter 1, text at nn. 88–90.

37. See below, nn. 42–50 and accompanying text.

38. A felon who had escaped to a church or other designated holy place could remain there inviolate for forty days. If he confessed his felonies to a coroner within that time, he was allowed to abjure (swear he would leave) the realm. The coroner then assigned the abjuror a port and gave him a cross to carry as a sign of his abjuration. So long as the felon headed straight for the port, no one was permitted to harm him. See Hunnisett, *Medieval Coroner*, pp. 37–54. See generally N. Trenholme, *The Right of Sanctuary in England* (Columbia, Mo., 1903). For the Anglo-Saxon background of medieval sanctuary see Riggs, *Criminal Asylum in Anglo-Saxon Law*, pp. 31–36.

Although sanctuary was not abolished until 1624 (Stat. 21 Jas. 1, c. 28, §§ 6, 7), the Tudors set strict limits upon the institution. Abjurors were branded to ensure their identification [Stat. 21 Hen. 8, c. 2 (1529)], and the statute of 1530–31 did away with abjuration of the realm (Stat. 22 Hen. 8, c. 14, § 1). Now the felon in sanctuary was to choose, or be assigned to, one of a number of appointed sanctuaries in England. Thereafter, he could not leave that appointed sanctuary without pardon or special license. See R. F. Hunnisett, ''The Last Sussex Abjurations,'' in *Sussex Archaeological Collections*, vol. 102 (London, 1964), p. 39; I. D. Thornley, ''The Destruction of Sanctuary,'' in R. W. Seton-Watson, ed., *Tudor Studies Presented . . . to Alfred Frederick Pollard* (London, 1924), pp. 198–207.

39. See Eric W. Ives, ''Crime, Sanctuary, and Royal Authority under Henry VIII: The

Crown did not seek their elimination but sought intermittently to employ them in a manner that discouraged, rather than encouraged, heinous offenses by accepting legislation that revived the medieval proscriptions against the pardoning of particularly serious offenders.[40] Pardons *de cursu*, on the other hand, continued to flow copiously in cases of "self-defense"—until, that is, the reform of the privilege of clergy and the mid-century developments in the criminal jury trial combined to create a workable law of felonious but noncapital manslaughter.[41]

The institution of benefit of clergy took its basic form during the late-twelfth-century struggle between church and state, symbolized in the clash between Henry II and Thomas Becket.[42] The Crown conceded to the Church ultimate power to try and punish ordained clergy, but it ordered that a cleric first be tried in a royal court and, if convicted, that he then be delivered over to the bishop as guilty in the eyes of the secular law.[43] Access to benefit of clergy originally required that letters of ordination be formally presented to the trial court. By the late fifteenth century, however, mere literacy, and even feigned literacy, had come to suffice, so that even some of the worst lay offenders could avail themselves of the benefit.[44]

In 1489 the Crown sought to reduce the impact of benefit of clergy by prohibiting a layman from twice having recourse to it for homicide, rape, robbery, theft, "and all other mischievious deeds."[45] In order that the court might know who had already been once benefited, the offenders were ordered branded after first conviction. For "manslayer," the brand letter was "M";[46] for all other felonies, of which theft was by far the most common, "T." An offender other than an actual cleric may not have been

Exemplary Sufferings of the Savage Family," in Arnold et al., eds., *On the Laws and Customs of England*, ch. 10.

40. Statutes granting pardons were issued frequently, but typically they excluded serious homicide, burglary and robbery. See e.g. Stats. 1 Edw. 6, c. 15 (1547); Eliz. 1, c. 30 (1562–63); 13 Eliz. 1, c. 28 (1571); 27 Eliz. 1, c. 30 (1584–85); 3 Jas. I, c. 27 (1605–6). For references to cases in which defendants charged with homicide pleaded eligibility for such a pardon on grounds they had slain "on a sudden occasion," or the like, see below, n. 63.

41. This development is discussed at length in section II.

42. See G. Dalzell, *Benefit of Clergy in America* (Winston-Salem, N.C., 1955), pp. 9–42; Leona Gabel, *Benefit of Clergy in England in the Later Middle Ages* (Northampton, Mass., 1929); Pollock and Maitland, *History of English Law*, 1:441–57.

43. See e.g. JUST 3/127D, m.11d (1337): "And in order that it might be ascertained in what capacity [the prisoner] should be delivered, let the truth of the matter be inquired into by a jury."

44. Plucknett, *Concise History*, p. 440; Joel Samaha, *Law and Order in Historical Perspective* (New York, 1974), pp. 57–62; Stephen, *History of Criminal Law*, 1:459–64.

45. Stat. 4 Hen. 7, c. 13 (1488). See also Baker, ed., *Reports of Sir John Spelman*, 2:329.

46. "Murder" was at this time used as a catchall term embracing all felonious homicide. See Green, "The Jury and the English Law of Homicide," pp. 473–74.

turned over to the church; certainly he was not after 1576. If after conviction he successfully pleaded clergy, he was subjected to branding and, at the discretion of the court, up to a year's imprisonment.[47] This important curtailment of benefit of clergy was only the beginning. Soon thereafter, legislation excluded laymen from pleading clergy for petty treason, that most heinous of common law felonies.[48] Subsequently, in piecemeal fashion, most other serious offenses were similarly placed outside benefit of clergy for laymen.[49]

As we shall see, this regulation of the benefit of clergy bore rich fruit. Statutory recognition of clergy for virtually all "literate" male offenders[50] for the first commission of a lesser felony (including manslaughter and simple theft) removed much of the pressure from juries, at least in some cases. Where clergy was proscribed the pressure remained, but this cannot have been serious so long as the parliamentary approach to the gradation of punishment and the typical juror's concepts of liability continued to overlap. Where these were in conflict, the jury presumably sought to use its de facto power to put the defendant beyond the law. Until the jury's power to do so was substantially reduced, the system would, in cases of conflict, function much as before.

# II

The development of English criminal trial procedure was more evolutionary than sudden. We have seen that the Marian statutes dealt with practices that to some extent predated the 1550s; and it has been

47. 18 Eliz. 1, c. 7, § 2 (1576). See Cockburn, "Trial by the Book?" p. 76. See Cockburn, *Introduction*, ch. xi, sect. ii.

48. Stat. 12 Hen. 7, c. 7 (1496–97). See Green, "The Jury and the English Law of Homicide," p. 475, n. 223.

49. E.g. robbery or murder (used as term of art) in a church, on the king's highway or in the victim's house: Stat. 4 Hen. 8, c. 2, § 1 (1512) (statute only temporary); arson added to previous list: Stat. 23 Hen. 8, c. 1; buggery: Stat. 25 Hen. 8, c. 6 (1533–34); piracy: Stat. 27 Hen. 8, c. 4, § 3 (1535–36).

50. See Cockburn, "Trial by the Book?" p. 77: "Between 1559 and 1589 the assize files do not reveal a single instance in which clergy was denied because the claimant failed the reading test." Thereafter, such failures were noted; Cockburn suggests that the evidence "indicates the reemergence of benefit of clergy as a meaningful test of literacy," and that its reintroduction was connected with the "introduction of 'plea bargaining' at assizes." See Cockburn, *Introduction*, ch. xi, sect. ii. For an important discussion of the treatment of women at the Home Circuit assizes see *ibid.*, ch. xi, sects. ii, iii, and vi (table II). Women were not allowed benefit of clergy until 1693 (stat. 4 Wm. and Mary, c. 9). By virtue of a statute of 1623, however, they were allowed to claim the benefit in cases involving larceny of goods worth ten shillings or less (stat. 21 Jas. I, c. 6). Many women did claim pregnancy, a claim that was often false or that was made "true" through conception during imprisonment after conviction (technically, too late, but often allowed).

persuasively argued that the procedures outlined in the statutes represented an ideal that, in practice, did not become universal until long thereafter.[51] The line of development is flatter than focus on the statute book alone would suggest. Nonetheless, the Tudor and early Stuart period witnessed a sharp and important increase in the production of pretrial examinations and witness testimony for use in criminal trials. This is reflected in virtually every aspect of the system.[52] Though we know little about how such testimony was employed, who employed it, and on whose direction they did so, it is likely that the assize clerks wielded significant influence in the conduct of trials and that they were in some fairly direct fashion carrying out government policy.[53] But it is not altogether clear just what the government policy was or whether the changes that flowed from that policy were foreseen.

The shift from a trial dominated by the self-informing jury to a trial based mainly on evidence produced by the prosecution not only transformed the relationship between judge and jury but gave greater opportunity for judicial instruction and enhanced the growth of the substantive law. Open confrontation between the witnesses and the defendant must have produced far more candid testimony than the conclusory tales that juries had formerly recorded in their verdicts. Now close and difficult cases came inescapably to the attention of the bench. Complicated testimony of a sort not often heard before allowed the bench to refine and elaborate rough distinctions, and to apply and elaborate those already propounded in the Inns of Court. In this process the law of crimes took on its modern form.[54]

The paradigm example of substantive legal development is once again the law of homicide.[55] Of the two other principal concerns of the royal courts, treason and theft, little will be said. The law of treason was

51. Cynthia Herrup, "The Common Peace," doctoral dissertation (Northwestern Univ., 1982), ch. 5. See Cockburn, *Introduction*, ch. viii, sect. ii.

52. See Cockburn, "Trial by the Book?" *passim*, whose discussion assumes the existence of a substantial body of pretrial documents. See Cockburn, *Introduction*, ch. viii, sect. iii.

53. *Idem.*

54. Baker *(Reports of Sir John Spelman, 2:303)* has definitively shown that discussion of the substantive law had already begun at the Inns in the late fifteenth and early sixteenth centuries. Some of this discussion was prompted by cases wherein defendants based claims upon statutes dealing with clergy and pardons. My own discussion focuses on the application and further development of the emerging law in actual cases before the royal courts. I have on a previous occasion overstated the degree to which the post-1550 development was innovative rather than elaborative ("The Jury and the English Law of Homicide," pp. 491–92).

* 55. This discussion is a foreshortened version of my fuller account in Green, "The Jury and the English Law of Homicide," pp. 473–97.

elaborated in a series of statutes and applied in state trials that are now famous and have been described at length elsewhere.[56] There were notable developments in the law of theft, but they were either statutory and geared mainly to increasing the scope of capital theft by the preclusion of benefit of clergy for specified offenses,[57] or judicial and concerned largely with the definition of physical circumstances involved in such offenses as burglary and robbery.[58] Few of the changes in commonly tried cases of theft involved the theory of felonious intent and, as we shall see, it was this problem that lay at the heart of future tensions between judge and jury.

The development of the substantive law in homicide as in other crimes involved a dialectical process that centered on the judge-jury relationship but which was affected by much else, including, of course, the Tudor use of the benefit of clergy. The statutes defining eligibility for benefit of clergy, unlike the medieval statutes dealing with pardons of grace, succeeded in making a lasting impact on the substantive law of felonious homicide. Perhaps the most important difference between those two attempts to deal with professional or otherwise serious homicide was the stage of the judicial process at which the protection proscribed by the legislation was normally obtained. As we have seen, pardons of grace were obtained before trial, and, until 1390, they foreclosed prosecution. Thereafter, while courts were in theory required to test such pardons, they generally took at face value almost all pardons set before them and thus, by default, left administration of the statute of 1390 to the Crown.[59]

---

56. John Bellamy, *The Tudor Law of Treason* (London, 1979); G. R. Elton, *The Tudor Constitution: Documents and Commentary* (Cambridge, 1960), pp. 59–60, 80–81. For a study of the application of the law of treason during the Reformation, see G. R. Elton, *Policy and Police*, pp. 384–400.

57. See above, n. 49.

58. Baker, "Criminal Courts and Procedures," p. 41. For an example of the interplay out of which rules developed (though in this case not a new rule), see J. H. Baker, "Criminal Justice at Newgate 1616–1627: Some Manuscript Reports in the Harvard Law School," *Irish Jurist*, vol. 8, new ser. (1973), p. 313. In an indictment for theft [Harvard Law School (hereafter, H.L.S.) MS 112, p. 296], where a servant stole from his mistress and placed the stolen items in his own trunk (as the evidence showed), the jury, having left the bar, returned to ask advice of the court. Their concern was that it had not been shown that the trunk had been removed from the house. The Recorder told the jury that under the law the alleged deed was a felony, for the act of putting the goods in the trunk and afterward denying that he had done so indicated that the defendant had taken the goods with felonious intent. (The jury convicted the defendant and he was hanged.)

In the sixteenth century, the bench began to exclude from the categories of "luxuries," which could not be the subject of an indictment for theft, certain edible birds and animals, thus increasing the scope of the law of capital theft. See Baker, ed., *Reports of Sir John Spelman*, 2:318.

59. See Green, "The Jury and the English Law of Homicide," pp. 469–72.

Benefit of clergy operated in a different way. Although in the Middle Ages the benefit could be pleaded either at the outset of the trial or after an adverse verdict,[60] the trial was always held, a jury impaneled, and a verdict given. That remained the case as clergy expanded; indeed, with that expansion, it came to make no sense at all to turn over to Church courts most of those who benefited from "clergy."

Because many convicted defendants were likely to plead clergy,[61] and because clergy was not available for all offenses, the nature of the felonious homicide became an important jury question. For the first time, it would seem, juries had to be questioned closely concerning the specific nature of the defendant's felonious act.[62] For the first time, a jury verdict of "felony but not murder" might save the defendant's life, even though it would not spare him entirely from punishment.[63] The new statutory scheme regarding clergy presented an important opportunity for legal growth.

The combined effects of the clergy statutes and of the transformation of the trial itself were significant. Some of them are easily traceable in the reports and legal literature of the sixteenth and early seventeenth centuries; others are less well understood. One clear result of these changes was that the law of homicide as applied by the courts evolved within a matter of decades into one of the most complex areas of the substantive criminal law. For the purpose of determining eligibility for clergy, the general rule of *Salisbury's Case*,[64] which distinguished deliberate but sudden homicide from homicide through something approaching true

60. In the reign of Henry VI, it was established that the "clerk" had to be convicted before claiming the benefit. Stephen, *History of the Criminal Law*, 1:460. See Leona Gabel, *Benefit of Clergy*, p. 30.

61. See Cockburn, *History of English Assizes*, p. 129 (20 percent of all felony defendants for the period 1558–1714); see Cockburn, *Introduction*, ch. ix, sect. ii (46 percent of men, 1559–64); Samaha, *Law and Order in Historical Perspective*, p. 62 (28 percent of all felony defendants in Essex for the period 1558–1602). See Green, "The Jury and the English Law of Homicide," p. 493.

62. *Salisbury's Case* (1553) [Edmund Plowden, *Les Commentaries* (London, 1558), fol. 100] is the earliest recorded case that demonstrates this point. See below, n. 64 and accompanying text. There are no gaol delivery or criminal assize rolls for most of the fifteenth century or the first half of the sixteenth century.

63. See Baker, ed., *Reports of Sir John Spelman*, 2:305, n. 5, for two cases (1531, 1540) in which defendants, claiming eligibility for statutory pardons, pleaded that they had committed felonious homicide but not murder. Such cases may have required close questioning of the jury, but it is unlikely that there were a great many of them (as there were regarding benefit of clergy). Nevertheless, the development of the law of homicide resulted in part from the Tudor revival of the medieval statutes precluding pardons of grace in murder.

64. See above, n. 62. And see my discussion in Green, "The Jury and the English Law of Homicide," pp. 484–85 and accompanying notes.

premeditation, was further refined.[65] For example, of all the new doctrines which emerged from the bench in its treatment of complex cases, none was more difficult to apply than the rule of manslaughter committed in "hot blood," or "continuing fury."[66] Rules applicable to the slaying of officials—most important, the rule of implied malice, which made such slayings murder—also took a heavy toll of the once-streamlined law of intentional slaying.[67]

A second, less easily traceable result of the benefit of clergy statutes and the changes in trial procedure was their effect upon the treatment of defendants in homicide cases. Since assize records are primarily indictments with brief and sometimes ambiguous notations as to the outcome at the trial stage,[68] they do not provide much insight into jury behavior. Nevertheless, the pattern of late-sixteenth-century jury verdicts in homicide is revealing. Compared with the fourteenth century the conviction rate was high (50 percent or more as compared to 20–25 percent), but the percentage of defendants actually condemned remained about the same (20–25 percent) and the percentage of self-defense verdicts was significantly lower (3–8 percent as compared to 10–40 percent).[69] Thus it appears that juries, recognizing that benefit of clergy provided an alternative sanction for simple homicide, or, as it was now coming to be called, "manslaughter," felt free to convict in many cases they had formerly described falsely as acts of self-defense. The formal rules and the social response had come closer together. And we may speculate that more often than in the past recipients of pardons for self-defense were in fact true self-defenders. The extension of justifiable homicide by a statute of 1532 to cover slayers of would-be murderers[70] may have been facilitated by a lessening of the fear that manslaughterers would be acquitted along with true self-defenders. Indeed, although officially the medieval treatment of excusable homicide was not abolished until 1828,[71] there is evidence that judges frequently allowed self-defenders, whether they had slain murderers or not, to go quit without pardon or forfeiture as early as

65. J. M. Kaye, "The Early History of Murder and Manslaughter," pp. 590–92.
66. Green, "The Jury and the English Law of Homicide," p. 492, n. 286.
67. Kaye, "Early History of Murder and Manslaughter," pp. 591–92.
68. James S. Cockburn has edited the extant assize indictment files for the reigns of Elizabeth and James I. See his forthcoming introductory volume (Cockburn, *Introduction*) for his analysis of these records.
69. Green, "The Jury and the English Law of Homicide," p. 493. Not all of the "condemned" were in fact hanged. Some probably were pardoned or had their sentences commuted. See below, nn. 162–68 and accompanying text. See Cockburn, *Introduction*, ch. ix, sects. iii–vi.
70. Stat. 24 Hen. 8, c. 5 (1532). For a discussion of the intended scope of this statute, see Green, "The Jury and the English Law of Homicide," pp. 480–82 and nn. 245–48.
71. Stat. 9 Geo. 4, c. 31, § 10 (1828).

the sixteenth century.[72] This too may have reflected heightened confidence in jury verdicts.

The history of the judicial treatment of accidental homicide, on the other hand, appears to be more complex. It is difficult to chart the line of development in this area from the adoption, in the fourteenth century, of the rule of automatic forfeiture for excusable homicide to the abolition, in the nineteenth century, of both pardon and forfeiture. At the outset, we have seen, the judicial handling of accidental homicide was relatively lenient: the courts granted acquittals in a wide variety of cases that had formerly led to pardons for accidental homicide.[73] The theory most often employed to rationalize acquittal in these cases was that the deceased, through his own actions, had slain himself. Although this theory was repeated in the sixteenth century,[74] and might still have governed the outcome of some cases, it is clear from the notations of judgments on the late-sixteenth-century Chancery records that pardon procedures were followed in the majority of accidental homicide cases.[75]

The reasons for this strict treatment of accidental homicide are not altogether clear. The most dramatic aspect of the new approach was the insistence upon initiating the pardon procedure for deaths resulting from shooting accidents, both by bow and arrow and by firearms.[76] The latter

72. Very little is now known (or may ever be known) about judicial treatment of defendants for whom a jury returned a verdict of self-defense. Scholars have assumed that even before the statute of 1828 (Stat. 9 Geo. 4, c. 31, § 10), judges allowed juries to acquit such defendants, but the evidence these scholars have adduced is inconclusive. See Michael Foster, *Discourse on Homicide* (2nd ed., London, 1776), pp. 288–89; Pollock and Maitland, *History of English Law*, 2:481, n. 3; Stephen, *History of Criminal Law*, 3:76–77. See also Joseph Beale, "Retreat from a Murderous Assault," *Harvard Law Review*, vol. 16 (1903), pp. 573–76.

The evidence from the assize rolls is also unclear on this point. In the late sixteenth century there were still cases ending in verdicts of self-defense and, apparently, an order that the defendant obtain a pardon. See e.g. James S. Cockburn, ed., *Calendar of Assize Records: Sussex Indictments, Elizabeth I* (London, 1975), p. 319, no. 1639 (1596). In other self-defense cases there is no indication that a pardon was required. See e.g. *ibid.*, pp. 281–82, no. 1475 (1594); p. 333, no. 1714 (1597).

The strongest evidence for the proposition that self-defenders were not required to obtain pardons is the fact that Chancery class 260, which contains many post-1550 cases in which the pardon procedure was required for accidental homicide, contains practically none by that late date for homicide in self-defense.

73. See above, Chapter 3, text at nn. 64 *et seq.*

74. See William Staunford, *Les Plees del Coron* (London, 1557), p. 16a, commenting on a 1370 case (Y.B. Hil. 44 Edw. 3, pl. 94).

75. See Chancery classes 260 and 244, *passim*. The hundreds of cases where pardon procedure was followed for accidental homicide between 1550 and 1650 suggest that judges were infrequently allowing such defendants to go quit.

76. See e.g. C 260/166, no. 20 (1573); C 260/171, no. 46 (1583); C 260/173, no. 52 (1588); C 260/184, no. 131 (1631).

devices, of recent invention and currency, were responsible for close to 40 percent of the accidental homicides for which pardons *de cursu* were granted in the century 1550–1650.[77] The special dangers surrounding the use of firearms no doubt contributed to judicial conservatism in accidental homicide generally, and this concern might explain the insistence on pardons in cases of unintentional slayings through the use of more traditional weapons.

It is also possible that the flow of evidence now revealed more clearly than before the degree of negligence attributable to the defendant in accident cases. Juries, having lost most of their control over the production of evidence, might have found it more difficult to persuade the court that the deceased had been responsible for his own death. Indeed, jury verdicts of excusable accidental homicide might have been returned in cases that, according to the evidence produced at trial, appeared to the bench to fit within the emerging category of involuntary manslaughter.[78] Surely, in these cases, the bench might have deemed insistence upon the pardon requirement appropriate. In those (presumably) rare instances, on the other hand, where trial testimony was consistent with a special verdict that the deceased had slain himself in the course of an attack upon the defendant, the bench might have felt greater confidence in assimilating the cases with self-defense and allowing an acquittal.[79] If so, this was one more example of the effect of the new trial procedure on judicial treatment of excusable homicide. But this remains a matter of speculation.[80]

77. This estimate is based upon a study made for me by David Clark, formerly of the Public Record Office, of the post-1550 cases contained in Chancery classes 260 and 244.

78. This category was recognized as early as 1576. See Robert Brooke, *La Graunde Abridgment* (London, 1576), *"Corone,"* pl. 229. See Kaye, "Early History of Murder and Manslaughter," p. 593 for a discussion of Brooke's view. See also Baker, ed., *Reports of Sir John Spelman*, 2:*314*. Baker cites an early sixteenth-century reading that sets forth the distinction drawn by Brooke.

79. Such cases rarely appear among those accidental homicides for which pardons were granted.

80. The history of the jury and the law of homicide after 1550 remains shrouded in mystery. The subject requires a systematic analysis of the series of criminal assize records that begin in the 1550s.

I have suggested that the emergence of a large category of noncapital felonious homicide and the beginnings of modern trial procedure produced changes in the behavior of both bench and jury. My tentative thesis is that the conditions that had produced the earlier pattern of jury behavior and judicial response had been substantially removed. There were fewer verdicts of self-defense and probably there was greater judicial leniency in those cases that did occur. Factors other than the existence of a category of noncapital felony and the new trial procedure probably played an important role. But these factors, I believe, must be considered in relation to the formal law and trial procedure. Juries might have been comprised of persons less inclined to save defendants through verdicts of excusable homicide, but it may still be true that, absent the category of manslaughter, they would not

Certainly tension between judge and jury as to the border between manslaughter and excusable homicide was still common after the middle of the sixteenth century.[81]

The rough distinctions in the Tudor law of homicide reflected age-old attitudes regarding capital liability. The success of the new use of the benefit of clergy, the chief agent for introducing these distinctions into daily courtroom judgments, depended upon a means of monitoring the veracity of verdicts. Without such a means, there would have been no assurance that the new category would not suffer at the hands of jurors. The substitution of clergy for pardons *de cursu* would have availed the Crown and bench almost nothing. For although the law of homicide was being made to reflect social attitudes, its operation was also intended to set limits where particular juries might otherwise respond to "unwarranted" feelings of mercy or illegitimate forms of pressure.

Although the friction between law and social attitudes was greatly reduced, it was by no means eliminated. And, in time, as the law of murder and manslaughter was further refined, the potential for disagreement increased. The policy that led the bench to "imply malice" or to take a strict line with the negligent use of firearms must have had some connection with widespread social views. But the fit between judicial policy and a jury's sense of justice could not be perfect. The judicial concern with application of the law to set an example, for instance, might make the bench impatient with a jury's merciful desire, in a given case, to overlook the general reasons for concern with a certain sort of behavior.

have been willing to convict. Judges might have threatened and fined juries to force convictions, but it is hard to see how these measures could easily have been applied had trial procedures remained unchanged: as in earlier times, it would have been extremely difficult to separate the cases of honest verdicts from the cases of pure fabrication.

I introduced statistics (above, p. 122) on verdicts to suggest a relationship between the structure of formal legal categories and jury behavior, and to suggest that, taken at their broadest, characteristics of social attitudes toward homicide remained fairly constant throughout the period 1300–1600. I do not mean to suggest that these observations constitute an in-depth picture of the social history of the law of homicide in Elizabethan England. Further research can shed light on a number of important questions and provide significant refinement of the rough outline presented here. It is possible to determine the social status of defendants and jurors in homicide cases and to correlate that information with verdicts. It may be possible also to establish differences in the practices of justices of the peace and the bench. See e.g. Samaha's analysis of the extant Essex criminal records (*Law and Authority in Historical Perspective*). See also Joel Samaha, "Hanging for Felony: The Rule of Law in Elizabethan Colchester," *Historical Journal*, vol. 21 (1978), pp. 763–82; Herrup, "Common Peace," ch. 5; J. A. Sharpe, "Enforcing the Law in the Seventeenth-Century English Village," in V. A. C. Gatrell et al., eds., *Crime and the Law: The Social History of Crime in Western Europe since 1500* (London, 1980), ch. 4.

81. See below, Chapter 6, text at nn. 70–83.

The jury's most important factual inquiry, and the one that most often led to friction with the bench, involved its assessment of the defendant's intent. Of course, judge and jury sometimes disagreed on the matter of whether the defendant had struck a blow, shot a gun, or taken an object of value, but disagreement was far more likely to concern the defendant's motives. The factual issue of intent was complicated enough, but it was all the more so when juries brought to it powerful feelings about the defendant's personal worth and the justice of taking his life for the act he had committed. Although Tudor developments in criminal procedure did not eliminate the jury's field of play regarding these considerations, they may have substantially circumscribed jury discretion by making recourse to it visible to the bench. It is ironic, then, that the ambiguity of the merciful role of the jury was intensified.

Part of the ambiguity surrounding the trial jury resulted from the jury playing a different role in each of the three main kinds of cases it commonly faced. Its role in homicide cases was the most complex. The emergence of the distinction between culpable-but-sudden homicide and slaying through malice aforethought simultaneously reduced the number of cases involving judge-jury tension and built into the fact-finding process more room for the kind of discretion juries had always exercised. The flow of evidence provided some control, but in fact many cases lay so close to the legal line between capital and clergyable homicide that the bench had no grounds for second-guessing the jury.[82] Moreover, homicide had always involved a large number of cases of relatively little interest to authorities. Casual fights that resulted in death were always of less concern than were homicidal attacks in the course of robbery or arson. For centuries the law reflected an attempt to prevent the kind of brawling that might result in serious injury, but the administration of criminal justice reflected also the recognition that such a policy could have only a very limited impact. The transformation of the criminal process, to the extent that it was planned at all, was not effected in order to deal with such cases. Nor did it in fact have a determinative impact on the historic role of the jury in its resolution of those cases.

Theft, like homicide, was a routine felony. Much of it was casual, in the sense of opportunistic[83] rather than truly planned, and much of it was perpetrated by vagrants filching to sustain a mean existence rather than by gangs of professional thieves. Nevertheless, even much casual theft

---

82. The difference between capital homicide and *true* self-defense had of course been very clear. The new line between murder and manslaughter was blurred, as was that between manslaughter and true self-defense, for manslaughter covered the entire universe of cases that had not in reality fit within one of the two more ancient categories.

83. See e.g. J. S. Cockburn, "The Nature and Incidence of Crime in England 1559–1625," in Cockburn, ed., *Crime in England*, pp. 63–64.

was committed stealthily, and by outsiders, and if it was not specifically planned, it was nonetheless committed by persons ready to seize upon an unexpected opportunity. There was no element of provocation, at least not in the ordinary sense; one did not (typically, at least) steal to defend one's honor. If the petty thief was pitied it was because necessity had stripped him of any honor whatsoever.

The line between nonclergyable and clergyable theft was mechanical, but it perhaps corresponded roughly with a general view that trivial, nonviolent takings ought not to place the thief beyond redemption and that even some substantial nonviolent ones ought to be forgiven at least once.[84] The preclusion of clergy in robbery and burglary may have been popular, for many such cases involved gang attacks or truly professional crime; the conviction rates in these offenses were relatively high.[85] Of course, these lines could make but rough approximations. There may in general have been opposition to the literacy standard. In particular cases, a robber or burglar might seem to have more in common with an unlucky petty thief, and the fact that he took several pounds rather than several pence might reflect nothing more than the fortuity of his victim's wallet.

The jury's role in such cases was quite different from its role in homicide. Because there was in theft little question regarding intent, there was little opportunity to conceal a merciful verdict. Juries were forced to acquit the defendant, perhaps against substantial evidence that he was involved, i.e., to deny robbery or burglary when one or the other had in fact been proven, or to undervalue goods despite incontrovertible evidence of their real worth. The jury's role in theft was open to view, especially after the decline of the self-informing jury. Moreover, justices of the peace, assize clerks, and the bench probably took an active role in cases that fell within the statutes of preclusion, for these cases represented a kind of behavior that Parliament had singled out as especially threatening to the social order. Merciful verdicts were not unknown in theft; in fact they were very common. In the Elizabethan and Jacobean period many defendants indicted for grand larceny were, through open undervaluation of the goods that had been stolen,[86] found guilty of

---

84. The effect of the statutes regulating benefit of clergy was to make larceny of twelve pence or more capital for the second offense. Multiple offenses of larceny of less than twelve pence remained petty larcenies and noncapital.

85. Herrup, "Common Peace," pp. 267 et seq. See also Cynthia Herrup, "Law and Morality in Seventeenth-Century England," Past and Present (forthcoming, 1985), for an important discussion of mitigation and conviction in theft cases. I am grateful to Professor Herrup for allowing me to cite her unpublished manuscript.

86. See Cockburn, Introduction, ch. ix, sect. i. It should be noted that where a defendant's act was clergyable he might be indicted for petty larceny, or found by the jury to have committed petty larceny, in order that he might be whipped, a harsher punishment

noncapital petty larceny. But most of these merciful verdicts were strongly recommended by, or in any case undertaken with the leave of the bench, and they did not lead the bench to conclude that what the jury was doing was deciding difficult questions of law. There is some indication that a social theory of necessity was coming to play a quasi-legal role,[87] as simple homicide had done in the Middle Ages. By and large, however, to the extent that there was conflict between judge and jury in cases of theft, it was a matter of differing opinions on the appropriateness of extending mercy (in specific cases) to thieves who clearly fell within the new classes of capital theft.[88]

Treason cases became common in the sixteenth century, especially after the English Reformation. They were complex cases that raised legal and factual issues of nearly every kind. Treason, which was altogether nonclergyable, went through many changes in its definition, but at its core the crime included writing or speaking words signifying an intent to do the Crown serious harm.[89] It was not always easy to prove that a person had spoken certain words, and often their correct interpretation was not obvious without reference to the demeanor and inflection of the speaker.[90] Here, within factual issues involving both commission and intent, there was more than enough room for jury discretion, but acquittals in treason

than mere branding for a first offense. This practice was common in the late seventeenth century, until transportation was ordered for clergyable felony. At that point, verdicts of simple grand larceny increased and a harsh punishment (short of execution) was achieved. See below, Chapter 7, n. 30. I am grateful to John Beattie for this important point.

87. For evidence that some commentators thought necessity might even be a legal defense, see Baker, ed., *Reports of Sir John Spelman*, 2:*300, 323*. For discussion of necessity in theft cases, see Cockburn, "Nature and Incidence of Crime," pp. 60–61. The notion of necessity was reflected in the justifications stated for pardons (usually commutation) granted after conviction. It is possible that juries began to take such considerations into account (as though it was a form of mitigation at law) in reaching their verdicts. See below, Chapter 7, section III, for discussion of this kind of jury behavior in the eighteenth century.

88. But see Baker, "Criminal Justice at Newgate," p. 314, where the jury may have been attempting to reject the law (H.L.S. MS 112, p. 296). The defendant was indicted as an accessory to a burglary; it appeared on the evidence that he had received the principals and the goods but had not had knowledge of the breaking and entering. The jury convicted the principals of burglary and the accessory of mere felony (clergyable). The judge directed the jury "not to distinguish whether the party were accessory to the burglary or to the felony only," but one of the justices "was in doubt." The jury "were very much unsatisfied, yet they went and afterwards returned and found the accessory guilty of accessory to the burglary."

89. Bellamy (*Tudor Law of Treason*, pp. 31–33) argues that this had been the law since 1352 (Stat. 25 Edw. 3, stat. 5, c. 2), and that it is wrong to think that the 1536 statute (Stat. 28 Hen. 8, c. 10) originated the standard that required no overt act beyond words proving the intent.

90. *Ibid.*, p. 178.

were far fewer in number than in homicide and theft.[91] The Crown paid a great deal of attention to treason prosecutions, making certain that the evidence for conviction was very strong. On occasion, judges spared no effort to charge the jury with the importance of conviction and the inappropriateness of mercy.[92] There is some question concerning how far the Crown went to ensure that the jury would be sympathetic to its point of view, but it cannot be doubted that the Crown exerted pressure in some cases.

In summary, at the same time that advances in criminal procedure strengthened the position of the bench vis-à-vis the jury, developments in the substantive law reduced the area of conflict between the two institutions. Conflict remained, but in varying degrees, depending on the kind of case involved. Treason cases were few enough, and important enough, for the Crown to manage most of them in a way that avoided conflict. In theft, the new form of prosecution made it difficult for the jury to conceal merciful verdicts within findings of fact; if there were merciful verdicts, they were recognized as such—even encouraged—by the bench. Homicide presented far fewer instances of conflict than in the past because of changes both in substantive law and in procedure. But fact-finding was, if anything, more complex than ever, especially in cases close to the borders of the newly drawn legal categories. Here the jury continued to have some freedom of action, and, unlike the situation in theft, its freedom extended beyond the open granting of mercy to the concealed finding of law.

## III

The extent to which juries exercised discretion in routine cases, or were led to believe that they might legitimately do so, naturally depended on the manner in which judges oversaw trials, charged juries, and reacted to verdicts that displeased them. These are subjects about which all too little is known.[93] Trial records are somewhat fuller for the late sixteenth and early seventeenth centuries than for the Middle Ages, but they remain opaque on the point that most interests us, the judge's handling of the jury. Nor is there abundant material reflecting official views (bench,

91. See Elton, *Policy and Police*, p. 387. See also Bellamy, *Tudor Law of Treason*, p. 117.

92. Bellamy, *Tudor Law of Treason*, pp. 164–65.

93. See generally Cockburn, "Trial by the Book?" and Cockburn, *History of English Assizes*, pp. 120–24. See Cockburn, *Introduction*, ch. vi, sect. iv. The only comprehensive contemporary description of a routine case in the pre-Restoration period is Smith, *De Republica Anglorum*, ed. Dewar, pp. 110–16. Additional glimpses are provided by accounts in *State Trials* and in early seventeenth-century chapbooks. See Langbein, "Origins of Public Prosecution," pp. 324–34.

council, or Crown) of the jury's role. Enough of the official view remains for us to be certain that trial juries were thought to be fact finders and assessors of the credibility of those who testified at the trial, not law finders. But on the question of the limits of appropriate jury discretion, especially as regards the granting of merciful verdicts, the evidence is ambiguous. What does emerge, however, is the outline of the central paradox of the early modern history of the criminal trial jury. The development of controls over the jury, and their use in some cases (mainly the so-called state trials), produced a reaction in which it was asserted that the jury possessed a legitimate law-finding role. At the same time, judicial attempts to deal with the great press of routine cases led to a form of judicial dependence upon the jury. It began to appear that efficiency and at least a limited degree of jury discretion were natural allies. As a result, although the bench's position vis-à-vis the jury became stronger, the system of criminal law continued to function in a way that allowed for the inferences that proponents of jury law-finding desired to draw.

Although the Tudor transformation of criminal procedure appears to have redesigned the balance of power between judge and jury and between defendant and prosecution, it did not immediately result in a much more highly structured trial. Rather, a few substantial changes radiated new prosecutorial powers in ways that were sometimes dramatic, sometimes subtle. The extent to which these powers were used depended upon the government's interest in a given case or upon its concern with establishing an efficient process for a large class of cases. Because so little of the trial was formalized and so much of it proceeded according to the needs of the moment, it is difficult to speak of the "typical" trial. There were relatively few state trials, where governmental interest and power were most determinative; there were numerous routine felony trials, where the courtroom balance of power was more even; there were a myriad of trials that fell between these two extremes.

Most of the extant evidence regarding the management of the Tudor and early Stuart criminal prosecution comes from the collections of state trials, predominantly composed of treason cases. These trials were well known in their own day, both because of the personalities involved and because of the government's interest in publicizing the prosecutions of suspected traitors.[94] Most of the important treason trials were held in London, either before King's Bench or before justices of oyer and terminer,[95] and thus they were assured of a large and politically significant

---

94. Bellamy, *Tudor Law of Treason*, p. 137.
95. *Ibid.*, p. 133. For a decision to remove a case to London see Sir James Dyer, *Ascun Nouel Cases. Les Reports des divers select matters et Resolutions*, 3 vols. (London, 1794), vol. 3, p. 286b (Hil., 1570).

audience. But the point of the prosecution was not lost on the county where the offense was committed, for indictment proceedings continued to be held locally.[96] Those who knew anything at all about criminal trials must have been aware of the difference between proceedings at the great political trials and proceedings in more routine cases at the assizes. But the differences were largely of degree and may have been thought to reflect—as they almost certainly did—different levels of governmental interest in getting all of the facts before the jury. What was apparent was that the government had not taken political cases out of the hands of the jury, however much more pressure it in fact brought to bear upon jurors to render a verdict of guilty.

As we have seen, early modern criminal procedure was distinguished as much by the passive indictment jury as by the passive trial jury. The Crown could assert itself by handpicking the grand jury[97] or by overwhelming it with evidence. The latter strategy was usually successful and can hardly have been thought illegitimate. Most of the important state trials for treason followed upon reports to the Council, which then carried on an extensive investigation and forwarded the most promising cases to grand juries.[98] Indictment under these circumstances was nearly a foregone conclusion.[99] The resulting document was usually long and denunciatory, embodying the essentials of the Crown's case, and very likely drafted in part for its dramatic effect upon a hushed courtroom, as the defendant—perhaps a once-mighty subject—stood at the bar listening to the charges against him. It was in any case more elaborate and devastating in tone than the typical charge of homicide, theft, or other routine felony.

An overwhelming majority of defendants in most kinds of cases pleaded not guilty—in this there had been no change since the Middle Ages—even in response to the most detailed indictments, including those based upon examinations of the accused himself.[100] In some treason trials this meant

---

96. Bellamy, *Tudor Law of Treason*, p. 133.

97. British Library (hereafter, B.L.) MS Caligula B. i, fol. 319. According to Bellamy (*Tudor Law of Treason*, p. 128): "In the sixteenth century, when the government felt it to be necessary, it did not hesitate to appoint the [grand] jurors itself."

98. Bellamy, *Tudor Law of Treason*, pp. 125–27. Perhaps a quarter of the cases investigated in the period 1532–40 were dropped. See Elton, *Policy and Police*, pp. 386–88.

99. Statistics regarding specific kinds of cases are difficult to compile. Typically, bills not found were discarded. See Baker, "Criminal Courts and Procedure," pp. 19–20; Cockburn, "Trial by the Book?" p. 71. Elton's statistics (*Policy and Police*, p. 387) indicate that not more than 5 percent of treason cases put before grand juries resulted in an *ignoramus*. For common-run cases see Cockburn, *Introduction*, ch. v, sect. iv.

100. But see Cockburn, "Trial by the Book?" p. 73. Cockburn notes that there were, apparently, no confessions at assizes between 1558 and 1586, but that thereafter confessions

the repudiation of an alleged confession, with occasionally the implication that the confession had not been voluntary.[101] In all felony cases the court was supposed to ensure that defendants were fully aware of the implications of a guilty plea,[102] although by the end of the sixteenth century there is substantial evidence of a form of "plea bargaining" that produced confessions to reduced, noncapital charges.[103]

We have seen that the early Tudors continued the late medieval campaign to obtain twelve honest men, if not a jury downright solicitous of the Crown's interests. In the mid-1580s, the forty-shilling requirement was raised to four pounds, a figure that remained in force with minor exception until the late seventeenth century.[104] These efforts were often frustrated by nonattendance of the panel at the assizes. Thus the growing dependence upon the *tales*, and, ironically, the decline—rather than the upgrading—of the common-run felony trial jury.[105]

At state trials, however, this was rarely the case. Royal officials were generally too careful on such occasions, and failure to attend was less often braved by those called.[106] How far the government went in state trials to secure a friendly jury is still a matter of debate. Surely it defended itself against a jury inimical to its interests. There is some evidence of the "preparation" of jurors before the trial got under way, even an indication that Star Chamber played a role in pretrial rehearsals of the case for the

became common in theft, when there were experiments with "plea bargaining." See Cockburn, *Introduction*, ch. vi, sect. iii.

101. Bellamy, *Tudor Law of Treason*, p. 164.

102. Seventeenth-century sources reveal this. See e.g. Hale, *History of Pleas of the Crown*, p. 225: "[B]ut it is usual for the court, especially if it be not of clergy, to advise the party to plead [not guilty] and put himself upon his trial." See, however, Baker, "Criminal Justice at Newgate," p. 315, for a report of a case (H.L.S. MS 112, p. 297) in which one who had "confessed the indictment" and "afterward, being asked what he would say why judgment of death should not be given against him, answered that he was not guilty and that his former confession was out of ignorance and unadvised. But [the Recorder] cited the example of David with the Amalekite, *Samuel* 2, Cap. 1, that his blood must be upon his own head."

103. Cockburn, "Trial by the Book?" p. 73; See Cockburn, *Introduction*, ch. vi, sect. iii. Baker, "Criminal Courts and Procedure," p. 35.

104. Stat. 27 Eliz. 1, c. 6 (1584–85). For the late seventeenth and eighteenth centuries see below Chapter 7, n. 4 and accompanying text. For discussion of the impact of inflation on sixteenth-century juror-qualification requirements see Oldham, "Origins of the Special Jury," pp. 148–50. Oldham concludes that the real value of the property requirements was small, even after the statute of 1584–85.

105. Baker, ed., *Reports of Sir John Spelman*, 2:*107;* Cockburn, *History of English Assizes*, p. 118. See Cockburn, *Introduction*, ch. vi, sect. i; see also Oldham, "Origins of the Special Jury," pp. 146–47.

106. Bellamy, *Tudor Law of Treason*, p. 168. Jurors at state trials were frequently men of substance, both socially and economically. See Oldham, "Origins of the Special Jury," p. 154.

prosecution.[107] In general, however, the Crown seems to have relied upon the force of its case and upon the defendant's lack of opportunity to foresee the elements of the Crown's case rather than upon true jury packing. The government's efforts may as well have been aimed at countering the impact of local interests that might sway a jury to acquit; for it must have been the case that the classes from which the Crown sought to select trial jurors were subject to the very pressures of county politics that the elaborate ritual and presentation of monarchical sanctity were designed to erode.[108] In more routine cases, local sympathies rather than politics had to be overcome. But there were simply too many cases, too few willing jurors, and too little effective governmental machinery to ensure that even a "neutralized" jury would always be impaneled. It seems likely that the government achieved less through efforts at jury selection than it did through charging (and threatening) those selected.[109]

Just as one must be alert to the difference between state trials and common-run proceedings, one must also recognize that trials in London and other urban centers generally differed in important respects from trials in the provinces. This was especially true with regard to the relationship between jurors and defendants in cases of theft, which dominated the assize calendars. Smith, whose account is open to question on many points, probably was accurate in stating that in London defendants rarely knew the jurors, and vice versa, for they came from very different classes.[110] London assizes processed a virtual parade of lower-class robbers and pickpockets, many of them professional; even men of the *tales* must have been a cut above these rogues. In the counties, and especially in rural areas, the jurors far more frequently faced their neighbors or village ne'er-do-wells of whom they had long been aware, or with whose more fortunate relations they fraternized.[111]

---

107. Bellamy, *Tudor Law of Treason*, pp. 167–68.

108. *Ibid.*, p. 181. See Stat. 33 Hen. 8, c. 23 (1541), which empowered the Crown to hold treason trials upon commission of oyer and terminer in the shire of the Crown's choosing.

109. Cockburn, *History of English Assizes*, p. 123. See Cockburn, *Introduction*, ch. vi, sect. i. But see below, n. 179 and accompanying text for discussion of this problem. In my view, the bench exercised its power selectively. Cockburn himself notes ("Trial by the Book?" p. 73) that the court apparently manipulated the law to counteract jury leniency; if so, the bench could not always rely on its own powers of persuasion to obtain the verdict it preferred.

110. Smith, *De Republica Anglorum*, ed. Dewar, p. 113.

111. For a study of trial jury composition at early seventeenth-century quarter sessions and assizes see Herrup, "Common Peace," ch. 5. Herrup found that those (mainly quarter-session) jurors whom she could trace came from the lower end of the yeomanry, lower-middling persons of some property who were used to undertaking official responsibilities that the more wealthy, substantial freeholders were able to avoid. Herrup's conclusions accord roughly with those of Joel Samaha ("Hanging for Felony," p. 781): "The trial juries

Smith's point, however, was that defendants rarely challenged prospective jurors: neither knowing them nor being known by them, they had little reason to do so.[112] Whatever the truth of Smith's remarks about class differences, such differences as there might have been hardly suffice to explain the relative rarity of recourse to challenges in criminal cases over practically the entire early history of jury trial.[113] Traditionally, defendants had been entitled at common law to three dozen peremptory challenges.[114] This number had been reduced in the 1540s to twenty,[115] though it is difficult to imagine why anyone paid attention to the matter. In 1554, however, Throckmorton probably set a record by challenging as many as ten of his panel,[116] and in the following year Parliament increased the allowance in treason to the original thirty-six.[117] Perhaps these maneuverings were purely symbolic. The fact is that, by exercise of their challenge rights, defendants could have brought assizes to a standstill. Either they did not know this, or they were discouraged from such lawful sabotage.

Having been selected and sworn, jurors once again heard the indictment against the accused.[118] At state trials the impact of this recital upon the jurors (and those in attendance) was meant to be very great. In more routine cases, where jurors might hear up to a half dozen or more cases before reaching their verdicts,[119] the court supplied them with notations of the prisoners' names and the charges brought against them.[120] Except for the great state causes, most trials were very brief. From the jurors' perspective, trial was a contest in which accuser and accused exchanged

[in Colchester] were comprised of ordinary people in the town—petty tradesmen such as alehouse keepers and occasionally even day labourers.''

112. *Idem.* But see Cockburn, *Introduction*, ch. vi, sect. i, for exceptions.

113. The medieval trial records are unhelpful on this point. For the Elizabethan and Jacobean periods, see Cockburn, *History of English Assizes*, p. 120; see Cockburn, *Introduction*, ch. vi, sect. i; Herrup, ''Common Peace,'' p. 376, n. 2. Apparently, challenges were more common in the early sixteenth century in urban areas where defendants sought to remove those who *failed to meet* statutory property qualifications [see Stat. 23 Hen. 8, c. 13 (1531), which removed the freehold requirement and substituted a high (forty pounds) personal worth standard. Above, n. 25].

114. Baker, ''Criminal Courts and Procedure,'' p. 36. For contemporary discussion of challenge (in assize order books) see B.L. MS Harleian (hereafter cited as Harl.) 1603, fol.76v. and B.L. MS Lansdowne (hereafter cited as Lansd.) 569, fol. 9v.

115. Stat. 33 Hen. 8, c. 23 (1541–42).

116. Bellamy, *Tudor Law of Treason*, p. 140.

117. Stat. 1 and 2 Philip and Mary, c. 10 (1555).

118. B.L. MS Lansd. 569, fol. llv.

119. Cockburn, *History of English Assizes*, p. 119. See Cockburn, *Introduction*, ch. vi, sect. ii.

120. [T. W.], *Office of the Clerk of Assize* (London, 1676), p. 48; B.L. MS Lansd. 569, fol. llv. See Cockburn, *Introduction*, ch. vi, sect. ii.

their stories in a heated give-and-take. The accuser might be prompted by the bench, which had in hand a written record of the charges he had laid before the justices or, in pretrial sessions, before the assize clerks.[121] The accuser's statement was supposed to correspond closely with the actual indictment upon which it had been based, lest the indictment be quashed for variance. In fact, there were frequent variances in details, which were rarely challenged. Nonetheless, the jurors' impressions of the main elements of the case against most defendants must now have been distinct and convincing.[122] Other witnesses[123] for the Crown then spoke, perhaps prompted by the bench,[124] sometimes adding little to the prosecution case beyond emphasis and whatever force their reputation, demeanor, and number might have carried. It is not clear whether the jurors always heard the pretrial examination of the accused; where it supported the Crown's case they almost certainly did, but probably in other cases they did not.[125]

The case for the defense was put by the accused, for himself and by himself. No one interceded on his behalf to influence the impression he made upon the jurors. In rare cases, the accused had the assistance of counsel at the outset of the proceedings in order to make objections on matters of law as they arose from the indictment;[126] but at trial, upon indictment,[127] the accused was not allowed counsel, a rule that persisted in treason until 1696 and in all other capital cases until well into the eighteenth century.[128] We may never, at this remove, understand how contemporaries felt about the denial of counsel. Some apparently believed that the judge served as counsel to the defendant,[129] or that the government's case had to be so strong to convict that it would be beyond the power of legitimate legal advice to refute it.[130] Most may have worried that intervention by counsel would make it more difficult for the jury to

121. See above, text at nn. 8–9.

122. For discussion of Cockburn's contrary view (Cockburn, *Introduction*, ch. vii, sect. ii) see below, n. 179.

123. On witnesses see B.L. MS Harl. 1603, fols. 76v–77. See also Smith, *De Republica Anglorum*, ed. Dewar, pp. 113–14.

124. Baker, "Criminal Courts and Procedure," p. 38.

125. T. G. Barnes, ed., *Somerset Assize Orders, 1629–1640* (Frome, 1959), p. xviii. See Cockburn, *Introduction*, ch. viii, sect. ii.

126. Sir Edward Coke, *The Third Part of the Institutes of the Laws of England* (4th ed., London, 1669), p. 137.

127. The rule was different in appeals and misdemeanors, where counsel was allowed. Baker, "Criminal Courts and Procedure," p. 37.

128. Stat. 7 and 8 Wm. 3, c. 3 (1696) (treason). The extension of the right to counsel in felony [see Stat. 6 and 7 Wm. 4, c. 14 (1836)] was recognized in practice long before it was made statutory.

129. For a relatively late expression of this view see William Hawkins, *Pleas of the Crown*, 2 vols. (London, 1721), vol. 2, p. 400.

130. *Rex v. Thomas*, 2 Bulst. 147, 80 *Eng. Rep.* 1022 (1613), per Coke, C.J.

get at the truth,[131] and this appears to be the way that contemporaries rationalized a rule that was sometimes subjected to telling criticism.[132] Some of the criticism of the denial of counsel stemmed from the fact that counsel for the prosecution played a prominent role in state trials. There was a hollow ring to the bench's refusal to even the scales in such cases,[133] and the belief that the rule was intended to secure convictions may have carried over into attitudes toward the handling of routine cases where counsel rarely appeared for the Crown.

However much ammunition the Crown employed in a given case—the coaching of witnesses, the reading of examinations (including those few induced by torture), the use of counsel for questioning the defendant or for making dramatic, inflammatory speeches—from the jurors' perspective the defendant's answer remained the crux of the contest. The government may have therefore assumed that the truly innocent person could not be made to appear guilty, whereas the guilty might not reveal themselves without being subjected to the most searching interrogation. For the Crown forced the defendant to rebut evidence he had not seen beforehand[134] and to answer questions designed to throw him off balance. Moreover, the Crown employed sworn witnesses to aid private prosecutors, while only grudgingly allowing any witnesses, and never sworn ones, for the accused.[135] It appears that the Crown devised a proceeding wherein the accused was stripped of defenses that, from its perspective, only stood in the way of truth and aided the accused in the too-easy task

131. Staunford, *Les Plees del Coron*, fols. 151v–52; Ferdinando Pulton, *De Pace Regis et Regni* (London, 1609), pp. 184–85: "[P]eradventure, [the defendant's] conscience will prick him to utter the truth, or his countenance or gesture will show some tokens thereof, or by his simple speeches somewhat may be drawn from him to bolt out the verity of the cause." Cf. the earlier eighteenth-century rationale of Hawkins, *Pleas of the Crown*, 2:400: "This indeed many have complained of as very unreasonable, yet if it be considered, that generally every one of common understanding may as properly speak to a matter of fact, as if he were the best lawyer; and that it requires no manner of skill to make plain and honest defence, which in cases of this kind is always the best; the simplicity and innocence, artless and ingenuous behaviour of one whose conscience acquits him, having something in it more moving and convincing than the highest eloquence of persons speaking in a cause not their own . . . whereas on the other side, the very speech, gesture and countenance, and manner of defence of those who are guilty, when they speak for themselves, may often help to disclose the truth, which probably would not so well be discovered from the artificial defence of others speaking for them."

132. E.g. Robert Parsons, *The Jesuits Memorial for the Intended Reformation of England under their first Popish Prince* (London, 1690), p. 249.

133. Bellamy, *Tudor Law of Treason*, p. 142.

134. See Stephen, *History of Criminal Law*, 1:227–28, n. 239.

135. Baker, "Criminal Courts and Procedure," p. 38. Witnesses for the accused were not allowed to be sworn until 1696 in treason and 1702 in felony. Stats. 7 and 8 Wm. 3, c. 3, § 1; 1 Anne, st. 2, c. 9, § 3. See also B.L. MS Lansd. 569, fol. 11.

of fooling his countrymen or playing upon their compassionate tendencies. Smith's description of a routine felony case is famous: the accused and accusers stood in "altercation";[136] the judge asked questions, guided by examinations that the defendant would have ex tempore to explain away. All of the pressure was brought to bear on a single point: the jurors waited to hear the accused speak for himself.

It is easy to underestimate the importance of the oral and personal aspect of trial by jury. The proceedings I have described in summary fashion were weighted in the Crown's favor, but they did not do away with the centerpiece of the medieval trial: the defendant's unsworn testimony and tacit appeal to his countrymen. That remained inviolable. None of the pretrial examinations was of record; the defendant might repudiate any confession he had made; and every prosecution witness had to testify personally, regardless of the strength of his deposition.[137] The coordinated prosecution developed within the logic of the English trial by peers; it was not an attempt to undermine that form of trial. From the government's perspective, it redressed a severe imbalance that had resulted from the inability to challenge the defendant and thus turn the trial into a proper test. Juries typically had been inclined to hang only the nastiest offenders, and even these they sometimes acquitted out of fear, pity, or infirmities of evidence. The Crown had a long way to go if it was intent upon substantially broadening the field of offenders it could convict of capital charges, or significantly reducing the chances that an individual offender would mislead the jury. In state trials, where the stakes were especially high, each "mistaken" acquittal loomed very large. Precautions were called for, the more so because defendants were often clever, in league with others, and politically powerful enough to sway an insufficiently "neutralized" jury. Common-run felonies were handled differently. The prosecution could go only so far, given the press of time and the difficulty of securing detailed evidence. Far less was at stake, and jury leniency was to be expected, indeed, to a certain extent, tolerated. The odd case of unwise leniency, or plain obduracy, could be dealt with by stern treatment by the bench or even by procedures in Star Chamber.

At some point the judicial coercion of juries violated the sanctity of trial by peers, but it is not clear just where that point was. This problem has received more attention than careful sorting out. Although little will be offered here by way of firm conclusions, it is necessary to provide a background to the discussion in Chapter 6 of the debate over the legality

136. Smith, *De Republica Anglorum*, ed. Dewar, p. 114.
137. An exception was made where the deponent had died or fallen gravely ill before the trial. See Hale, *History of the Pleas of the Crown*, 2:284–85.

of threatening and punishing juries that was carried on in both lay and official literature of the mid-seventeenth century.

From medieval times the bench played a leading role in the questioning of defendants. Medieval juries had two overlapping and presumably complementary duties: to state what they knew and to render a verdict. They were not under a duty to know all the facts. They might, and often did, say they did not know the truth of the matter, but they were not to suppress what they did know or to avoid the opportunity to become better informed. At the trial the principal source of information, over and above what the jurors had already learned, was the defendant himself. The fact that the jury was "self-informing" in no way implied that their verdict was to be settled by the time they were sworn. Like the judge, they were sworn "to hear and to determine," and they were expected to put questions where they desired further information. Having consented to be tried by the country, the defendant could be examined by them, or by the judge on their behalf. If there were limits to the judge's role of informing the jury, they were imposed by his dependence upon the defendant and the jurors for evidence.

The transformation of the trial in the early modern period did not bring this judicial role to an end. Quite the opposite: it enhanced that role, and made it far easier to play. Even the appearance of counsel at the state trials was in service to the bench, which followed up the counsel's questions or the accused's replies to them with questions of its own. Of course, it was impossible for the bench to take so active a part in the trying of the accused without signaling to the jury its own view of the truth of the matter. This must have been all the more inevitable as the flow of candid evidence increased. Whether the practice of commenting upon the evidence followed from the fact that often the judge's views were at all events obvious, we cannot say. We do know, however, that the practice was common by the mid-sixteenth century, if not long before,[138] and it may have been thought a part of the judge's duty to help inform the jurors. Judicial impartiality did not require that the judge keep his opinions to himself but only that his comments be favorable to the defendant where that was appropriate. As we shall see, there developed a significant tradition of favorable comment on the evidence and on the desirability of a "partial," or saving, verdict.[139] The tradition of the active judge was integral to trial by peers, and it remained so long after "coercion" was ruled unlawful.

138. See Baker, ed., *Reports of Sir John Spelman*, 2:*141*. Baker asserts that the bench used this role with discretion.
139. See below, Chapter 7.

There was no real separation between the judge's comments upon the evidence and his charge to the jury. The charge might embody the most direct statement of the judge's point of view and must have been influential in many major trials. During the sixteenth and seventeenth centuries it does not appear that charges were elaborate in most routine cases: the law was typically straightforward and the judge rarely bothered to sum up his views of the facts.[140] Many cases must have resolved themselves into assessments of credibility that the bench either happily or for a lack of time or interest was willing to leave to the jury. The judge's charge always invoked the jurors' duty to God and their consciences,[141] and it was upon that admonition that the trial proper ended and the jury's resolution process began. About that process we know very little. It is not even clear whether juries typically retired from the bar to discuss cases or, as appears to have been the case at eighteenth-century Surrey assizes, simply huddled together in front of the bench.[142] Juries usually heard several or more cases before "retiring" to resolve them and, in the press of time, must have reached their verdicts quickly.[143] Having been guided by the bench, jurors probably knew how they would determine most cases even before they gathered for discussion. They probably also knew which cases remained unclear and had been left largely to their discretion, the judge having given only some indication of his view concerning the range of appropriate results.[144]

Where the bench believed that the jury had convicted the defendant against the evidence, it might reprieve the defendant and request that the Crown pardon him either freely or upon condition,[145] a practice that

140. Cockburn, *History of English Assizes*, p. 122. See Cockburn, *Introduction*, ch. viii, sect. iii. For what was probably a typical charge, see Smith, *De Republica Anglorum*, ed. Dewar, p. 114.

141. See Langbein, *Prosecuting Crime in the Renaissance*, p. 50. Langbein quotes a "charge" that seems to have been in its entirety: "Doe in it as God shall put in your hearts" [*The wonderful discoverie of Elizabeth Sawyer a witch . . . written by Henry Goodcole, Minister . . . and her continual Visiter in the Gaole of Newgate* (London, 1621)]. See also Smith, *De Republica Anglorum*, ed. Dewar, p. 114: "[D]oe that which God shall put in your mindes to the discharge of your consciences, and marke well what is saide."

142. There is some evidence that in this period the jury left the bar and sequestered itself. See STAC 5, A3, no. 30 ("in usual manner did sequester themselves"); Smith, *De Republica Anglorum*, ed. Dewar, p. 114. See however Cockburn, *Introduction*, ch. viii, sect. iv, who suggests that juries may have deliberated at the bar.

143. See Cockburn, *Introduction*, ch. vi, sect. ii.

144. But see Cockburn, *Introduction*, ch. viii, sect. iv, and ch. ix. Cockburn suggests that juries did not exercise much discretion; resolutions, he believes, were made speedily and largely ratified the views of the bench. For my comments on Cockburn's conclusions see below, n. 179.

145. See below, nn. 165–67 and accompanying text.

extended even to some state trials.[146] Most instances of judge-jury disagreement, however, involved perceived acquittals against the facts, and here the bench often confronted the jury head-on, using what pressure it could. Judicial coercion must be kept separate from the judge's unquestioned right to make his views known to the jury. Coercion involved threat of punishment for not finding as the judge deemed appropriate. At some point, even the physical discomfort involved in being held without refreshment or sleep by a judge who would not accept a verdict amounted to coercion, but it was, of course, its least serious form and the one most difficult to characterize as unlawful.[147] The judge might examine each juror individually in the hope of breaking his resolve,[148] but probing the jurors to make certain they were firm in their view and forcing them to consider further and to report again was a standard and accepted part of trials. Threatening to punish, and actually punishing, were of another sort of behavior—one that historians are only now beginning to explore in depth.

We have seen that the early Tudors took steps to punish bribery and extortion at all levels, including such behavior when it touched criminal trial juries. Star Chamber was active in these cases, and, no doubt, this was one part of the Court's business that made it popular. The use of examinations and witnesses for the prosecution made it easier to monitor such behavior, for the presumption of embracery or perjury was strong in cases where the verdict clearly flew in the face of the evidence. Did the Crown use the theory of true perjury as a makeweight in prosecutions of jurors who were not thought guilty of bribe taking or other "ministerial" wrongdoing but were thought nonetheless to have found against the evidence? Perhaps so. More likely, however, the Crown typically presumed that a finding against the evidence involved bribery or similar wrongdoing and punished the jury accordingly within accepted notions of its duty to enforce the law.

The surviving records of Star Chamber proceedings do not settle all questions regarding the theory upon which that institution punished juries. During the reigns of the first three Tudors, such prosecutions were common enough, but they appear to have been aimed mainly at ministerial wrongdoing.[149] Thereafter the quantity of Star Chamber prosecutions

146. See Elton, *Policy and Police*, p. 303.

147. It was a longstanding rule that jurors were not to eat or drink until they rendered their verdict. See e.g. B.L. MS Harl. 1603, fol. 77.

148. B.L. MS Add. 25228, fol. 41, pl.850 (1620).

149. See e.g. STAC 1, II, no. 121 (perjury); STAC 2, XXIII, no. 114 (perjury); STAC 2, XXIV, no. 199 (perjury). "Perjury" may in fact be the charge when the jurors were thought to have been too merciful. More likely, authorities believed the jurors had gone against their oaths knowingly and for an ill motive. STAC 3, VI, no. 69: the information charged that half

of jurors increased. Although in 1554 the entire common-law bench ruled that it could not on assize fine or imprison jurors,[150] its members occasionally continued to do so as well as to exercise its increasing power to monitor juries by binding them over to Star Chamber,[151] typically for finding "contrary to the evidence," a phrase that had become common by the later decades of the sixteenth century. In many such cases where juries were bound over to Star Chamber or were subsequently summoned to appear there, the informations aver that the jurors acted for personal gain or out of favoritism, or the interrogatories include questions concerning allegations of bribes.[152] A few of them may be interpreted to proceed

of the jury were "men corrupted," but this may mean only that they went against the evidence. See also above, n. 24 (regarding punishment for "perjury" of jurors in the Welsh Marches).

150. "Dalison's Reports," B.L. MS Harl. 5141a, fol. 27. The report states that the bench proscribed fining by courts presided over by justices of assize, justices of oyer and terminer, justices of the peace, or justices of gaol delivery. This accords with the view expressed by Hale in the 1660s, when he grudgingly admitted King's Bench's right to fine (or, at least, its immunity to collateral review) because it was a superior court. See below, Chapter 6, text at n. 38.

151. For juries bound over to Star Chamber see below, nn. 152–56. For juries fined (or threatened with fines) by assize judges see Cockburn, *History of English Assizes*, p. 123. See Cockburn, *Introduction*, ch. vi, sect. iv. See also Smith, *De Republica Anglorum*, ed. Dewar, p. 121. Smith remarked that juries sometimes "not onely be rebuked by the Judges, but also threatned of punishment, and many times commaunded to appeare in the starrechamber, or before the privie counsell for the matter. But this threatning, chaunceth oftener than the execution thereof, and the [jurors] answere with most gentle wordes, they did according to their consciences, and pray the Judges to be good to them, they did as they thought right, and as they accorded all, and so it passeth away for the most part." Smith may have understated the use of coercion in such cases. [Cockburn ("Trial by the Book?" p. 72) calls it a "pious disclaimer." But see his *Introduction*, ch. vi, sect. iv, for practice on the Home Circuit after the mid-1570s, and my comments below, n. 179. Herrup's study of early seventeenth-century East Sussex quarter sessions and assizes ("Common Peace"), however, suggests that judicially imposed fines were rare and that Star Chamber was employed primarily where there was suspicion of outright corruption.] Smith noted that he had "seene in [his] time" a jury "for pronouncing one not guiltie of treason contrarie to such evidence as was brought in were not onely imprisoned for a space, but an houge fine set upon their heads, which they were faine to pay." This seems to refer to the punishment of the jury in *Throckmorton's Case* (see *State Trials*, 1:901–2 and Bellamy, *Tudor Law of Treason*, pp. 172–73). Smith concluded: "But those doinges were even then of many accounted verie violent, and tyrannical, and contrarie to the libertie and custome of the realme of England. This cometh verie seldome in use, yet so much at a time the enquest may be corrupted, that the Prince may have cause with justice to punish them: For they are men, and subject to corruption and parcialitie, as others be."

152. E.g. STAC 4, VIII, no. 17. The interrogatories in this case follow a common form used even where, as here, the extant record of the information states only that the jurors found "against pregnant evidence." The questions put to the jurors were designed to determine: how the jurors came to serve; whether they had been chosen by the defendant or by his friends or relatives; whether they had received money; what evidence the jurors

solely upon the theory that the jury wrongly but with good intention took the law into its own hands, or extended mercy where doing so was inappropriate, but typically the charges were much stronger.[153] In most of the cases brought into Star Chamber the jurors actively defended themselves by asserting that they had evidence of their own[154] or that the evidence presented in court seemed to them to be inconclusive.[155] Occasionally some members of a jury claimed that they had been persuaded by their cojurors.[156] By and large the jurors deposed in Star Chamber asserted their right to assess the evidence as they saw it and denied having acted out of corrupt motives.

based their verdict upon. STAC 4, X, no. 31: one of the jurors disclosed after the trial that the other jurors had forced him to go along with an acquittal. He stated that two others had gone along on the belief that the remaining nine "be all bribed and have received money." These allegations led to the entire jury being bound over to Star Chamber. STAC 4, X, no. 32: strong suggestion that Star Chamber was investigating a charge of bribery; STAC 8, II, no. 42: the jurors denied corruption or hope of gain, as alleged; STAC 8, II, no. 46: corruption and subornation alleged in the information; STAC 5, A 34, no. 3: the jurors denied that they had been "laboured" or spoken to on the defendant's behalf.

153. E.g. STAC 4, III, no. 41; STAC 4, III, no. 43: some suggestion that the foreman overbore the others for a corrupt motive; STAC 4, VIII, no. 16: information alleges that the jury "most wilfully, falsely and untruly found . . . not guilty"; STAC 4, VIII, no. 16; STAC 4, X, no. 35; STAC 5, A 3, no. 30.

154. STAC 4, III, no. 41: the jurors were charged with neglect of duty to find according to "pregnant evidence" and for "little dreading the offense of perjury." Most of the jurors said that they were "near neighbors" of the parties and the witnesses and knew "the credit and estimation of every of the same deponents and witnesses, and also some of the said defendants, knowing more of themselves in that matter than was openly given in evidence." STAC 4, X, no. 35: one juror deposed that six of the others "said of their own knowledge they knew that [the defendant] was not at the felony and further said that their own knowledge was as good to them and better than any evidence" given in court. STAC 5, A 51, no. 6: jurors said that the chief witness for the Crown was known to most of them "to be of light behavior and small credit although he was not so known to the judges." See also STAC 5, A4, no. ll.

155. E.g. STAC 4, III, no. 41: the jurors said that "they did according to their oaths, consciences and the truth of the matter justly and truly give their verdict." They said that "all of the evidence given against [the defendant] was only matter of suspicion and presumption, not sufficient in the conscience of the [jurors]. . . . All which matters the said defendants are ready to aver and prove as this honorable court shall award, and [they] pray that they may be dismissed out of this honorable court without any further vexation or trouble." (No result noted.) STAC 5, A4, no. ll: jurors gave a very detailed answer reviewing the large body of testimony given against the defendant (for counterfeiting coin) and explaining why it seemed insufficient for a conviction. See also STAC 5, A 34, no. 3; STAC 5, A 51, no. 6; STAC 5, A 52, no. 34.

156. STAC 4, III, no. 43: Eleven of the jurors stated that the foreman was the only juror who could read and that he convinced them that there was no evidence against the defendant. The foreman said that he believed the defendant to be innocent and admitted to some persuading of the others. STAC 4, VIII, no. 17: Two jurors claimed that although they opposed the others' opinion that the defendant had acted in self-defense they finally gave in. They gave their verdict "against their minds." See also STAC 4, X, no. 35.

It would appear that as common as the binding over of juries to Star Chamber became, the theory upon which such treatment proceeded never entirely detached itself from the traditional notions of jury corruption over which, it was agreed, Star Chamber had jurisdiction.[157] Nearly all of the disputed verdicts were given in trials on indictments for what authorities deemed particularly egregious behavior. From their perspective, the jury was either corrupt, in the sense of acting for personal gain, or wilfully dishonest, in the sense of going against their true beliefs out of contempt for the law. It is significant, for example, that these cases did not raise the kind of issues raised by cases on the border between murder and manslaughter. These issues did emerge by the middle of the seventeenth century, by which time the common-law courts had inherited from Star Chamber the power to monitor verdicts and to fine and imprison jurors who acted wrongfully.[158] By then, surely, the courts no longer always required a theory of ministerial wrongdoing, and the true issue of coercion—as opposed to protecting against foul play—was squarely presented. As we shall see, coercion on such grounds was practiced, but also protested, and never entirely assimilated.

Whatever the theory was upon which jury verdicts were monitored and jurors punished, because of the presumption of ministerial wrongdoing that theory was broad enough to cover virtually any case wherein the bench believed the defendant ought to have been found guilty on the evidence. In practice, then, juries were sometimes "menaced" or even punished, and whether one thinks contemporaries viewed these constraints as prevention of perjury or as coercion of jurors' consciences, they were a part of the criminal process that presumably left its mark both upon the fate of defendants and on contemporaries' understanding of the role of the criminal trial jury.

157. See William Hudson, *A Treatise on the Court of Star Chamber*, in Francis Hargrave, ed., *Collectanea Juridica*, 2 vols. (London, 1791–92), vol. 2, p. 72. Hudson addresses the issue of perjury, which he does not define. He asserts that in the Tudor period "there was scarce one Term pretermitted but some grand inquest, or jury was fined for acquitting felons or murderers; in which case lay no attaint." Hudson gives several examples, some of which relate to grand juries, a coroner's inquest jury, persons lying in an affidavit or examination. Six appear to be trial juries: Throckmorton's jury and five others (including the one that acquitted one Hoody, who may be the same Hoody as in STAC 5, A 3, no. 30, above, n. 153). Hudson does not make clear the reasons for the fines. Perjury probably means a conscious lie under oath, and excludes merely foolish (or otherwise) opinions about the evidence. It might include "lying" in order to extend mercy in a case where the jury honestly believes mercy is appropriate, but possibly it was charged only where, on the bench's view of the evidence, the jury was acting out of fear, favoritism, or contempt for the law. See also R. Crompton, *Authoritie et Jurisdiction des Courts* (London, 1637), fol. 32b.
158. See below, Chapter 6, section II.

# IV

The increased duties and activity of the justices of the peace insured that the institution of indictment by true bill would supplant the more ancient system of presentment. The indictment procedure and the preparation necessary to it paved the way for the pretrial examinations and the production of witnesses that were central to early modern prosecutorial practice. In turn, systematic in-court presentation of evidence enhanced the powers of the trial judge, while it diminished the evidence-gathering role of the jury, and thus its powers. The new triangular relationship of prosecution, judge, and jury accompanied the development of substantive legal doctrine, a development that the Tudor adjustment of benefit of clergy helped greatly to stimulate; doctrinal refinement and gradation of offenses eased the tension between judge and jury, though tension remained and occasionally the bench used one technique or another to induce the outcome it desired. But trial by jury had by no means become trial by the bench: older traditions were maintained, depended upon, and further sanctified.

One important measure of the harshness of early modern criminal process is the rate of execution for treason, murder, and felony. Modern historians have recorded their shock at the numbers sent to the gallows, for by eighteenth-century standards, not to mention later ones, the numbers are high.[159] From the perspective of Elizabethan and Jacobean Englishmen, too, these figures may have seemed lamentably high,[160] though the execution scenes themselves were boisterous and revealed a fascination with morbidity that was fueled by the popular chapbooks of the day.[161] Nevertheless, although the numbers of men and women hanged may have been high in absolute terms relative to those executed in the Middle Ages, the percentage of those tried who were found guilty of capital crimes and condemned was no higher than it had been for the three preceding centuries, and the percentage of accuseds actually hanged was substantially lower.[162]

159. See Donald Veall, *The Popular Movement for Law Reform* (Oxford, 1970), p. 3. Veall quotes statistics from J. C. Jeaffreson, ed., *Middlesex County Records*, 4 vols. (London, 1886–92), vol. 2 (1887), p. xvii, and vol. 3 (1888), pp. xvii, xix, for executions in Middlesex, 1608–58.

160. See Coke, *Third Part of the Institutes*, p. 255.

161. See Langbein, "Origins of Public Prosecution," pp. 326–34.

162. Cockburn, *History of English Assizes*, pp. 128–31. Cockburn estimates that "only about ten *per cent* of those convicted were actually executed." He apparently is including many who were convicted of a noncapital offense by virtue of jury leniency as well as those convicted of a capital offense and subsequently favored by Crown or bench. His figure, then, does not include those indicted for a capital offense who were ultimately acquitted. The

Some of the means used to avoid carrying out sentences of death were in the hands of the bench or Crown. Here, too, the transformation of procedure played a role. The Crown now embarked on the large-scale posttrial system of pardon and commutation that was to dominate the administration of the criminal law well into the nineteenth century. To be sure, reasons of state—rewarding the turning of state evidence, obtaining fit and able military conscripts—accompanied the application of emerging penological ideas and the influences of post-Reformation religious thought.[163] But pretrial depositions as well as posttrial petitions rationalized selection of those to be saved. In this regard, the flow of evidence at trial was of particular importance where the bench reprieved offenders it believed had been convicted against the evidence.[164] Some of the of-

---

percentage of medieval accuseds hanged was 20–30. See above, Chapter 1, n. 79. See also Herrup, "Law and Morality in Seventeenth-Century England," nn. 1, 9.

163. The problem of postconviction mitigation of the law of sanctions in the eighteenth century is treated below, Chapter 7. The beginnings of this development have received relatively little attention in the literature on the history of the criminal law. See Cockburn, *History of English Assizes*, pp. 128–31; Cockburn, "Trial by the Book?" p. 75. See Cockburn, *Introduction*, ch. ix, sect. vi. Pardons granted at the request of justices of assize cited a variety of reasons for clemency. As a group, they are not markedly different in this respect from the many more such pardons granted in the eighteenth century. See e.g. C 66/1329, mm.25–26 (July 2, 1584): (infanticide) on the information of the Mayor and J. P. and on the plea of mercy from the jury; C 66/1256, m.32 (March 22, 1585): (clipping coin) in consideration of convict's confession of the crime, his informing against an accomplice, and the trivial extent of the offense; C 66/1388, m.27 (May 27, 1592): (housebreaking) a young man led astray by comrades, able to do good service, and his first offense; C 66/1426, mm.20–21 (July 14, 1594): (treasonable words) that she was pregnant at the time and in compassion for the frailty of her mind; C 66/1413, mm.11–12 (May 24, 1596): (burglary) truly sorry for his offenses, has revealed many criminals, some of whom have threatened him with death or robbed him of his goods; C 66/1591, m.22 (Nov. 14, 1602): (highway robbery) acted on the instigation of an accuser and also he is young and it is his first offense.

164. Smith provides insight into reprieve on grounds of an unsafe verdict (*De Republica Anglorum*, ed. Dewar, p. 120): "If the enquest of xii men do seeme to the Judges and the Justices to have gon too violently against the evidence given in matters criminall, either it is that upon slender evidence they have pronounced him gilty, whom the judges and most part of the Justices thinkes by the evidence not fullie prooved guiltie, or for some other cause, do thinke the person rather worthie to live than to die. The enquest is neverthelesse dismissed: but when the Judges should pronounce the sentence of death . . . he [*sic*] will differ it, which is called to reprive the prisoner (that is to say to send him againe to prison) and so declare the matter to the Prince, and obtaineth after a time for the prisoner his pardon: for as for provocation and appeale which is used so much in other countries, it hath no place in England, after sentence given by the xii."

The bench might also seize upon technical error in the indictment (so that the defendant might move to quash the indictment) where it believed the verdict unsafe or the punishment too harsh. See Baker, ed., *Reports of Sir John Spelman*, 2:301.

fenders who were reprieved were conscripted into the military,[165] transported overseas,[166] or unconditionally pardoned[167] after sentence had
been pronounced. More were never sentenced at all but were allowed
clergy despite their ineligibility or their failure to read, or were allowed
claim of pregnancy although they were not in fact pregnant, or had not
been at the time of their conviction.[168] In these latter cases, too, the
defendant's fate was in the hands of the bench, although it is possible that
the jury that convicted had reason to anticipate such merciful treatment.
Leaving aside all such instances of postconviction escape from the
gallows, the percentage of accuseds the jury had reason to believe it was
condemning to death was little if at all higher than in the Middle Ages. It
is, then, fair to ask whether very much had changed with regard to the
balance of power between judge and jury.

Indeed, there had been change. By redefining the scope of capital
felony, the Crown turned a significant percentage of the cases involving
concealed verdicts *against* the law into lawful verdicts of clergyable
felony or simple misdemeanor. These verdicts had the imprimatur of the
bench; juries in these cases were now finding fact in accordance with the
accepted view of their role. Moreover, in some cases where the jury left
to its own devices might have found a clergyable offense, the bench
induced, even directed, a verdict of capital felony. And probably in many
cases in which the defendant received merciful treatment, it was the
bench, not the jury, that made the decision to mitigate the law. This was
obviously so where reprieve or pardon followed conviction; it was
arguably so where the jury extended mercy on the recommendation of the
bench, a matter to which we shall turn in due course.

165. Cockburn, *History of English Assizes*, p. 129. See Cockburn, *Introduction*, ch. ix,
sect. vi.

166. *Ibid.*, p. 130. See M. S. Gretton, ed., *Oxfordshire Justices of the Peace in the
Seventeenth Century* (Oxford, 1934), pp. lxxxix–ci.

167. See class C 66 *passim*. See Cockburn, *Introduction*, ch. ix, sect. ii.

168. Cockburn, *History of English Assizes*, pp. 128–29. The bench might, on the other
hand, apply the literacy test strictly. See Baker, "Criminal Justice at Newgate," p. 315,
where the Recorder (H.L.S. MS 112, p. 297) doubted that a convicted felon who read
"distinctly and well" could in fact read. Believing the defendant had memorized the usual
lines, the Recorder assigned the defendant another passage. [The defendant read the new
passage with ease; the reporter "doubted whether (the defendant) ought to be put to read
again." Had the *"Quod legit ut clericus"* been entered on the record, the reporter stated,
"clearly . . . (the defendant) ought not then to have had another (passage) assigned him."]
On judicial treatment of convicted women who claimed pregnancy see Cockburn, *Introduction*, ch. xi, sect. iii. As Cockburn points out, the bench often exercised leniency in such
cases. According to Cockburn's figures [*ibid.*, ch. xi, sect. vi (table II)], about 15 percent of
indicted persons were female; about 40 percent of indicted females were convicted; of those,
about one third successfully claimed pregnancy. See also Herrup, "Common Peace," ch. 5,
for similar indictment and conviction figures.

In sum, the Tudor transformation of criminal procedure combined several interrelated factors that greatly increased judicial control over the exercise of discretion. In a sense, the Crown and bench had turned their weakness into a strength. Unable to impose rules of law greatly at variance with widespread social attitudes, authorities modified the substantive law, implicitly recognizing the power of those attitudes and dramatically reducing the field of disputed cases. Resolution of these cases was kept largely in governmental hands: making use of the tools of pretrial examinations and witnesses for the prosecution, the bench monitored verdicts, employed blunt threats, and, where necessary, called upon the support of Star Chamber process. Having secured convictions in apparent conformity to the rules of law, the bench made a show of its beneficence through relieving the rigors of these very rules in selected cases.

There were, of course, limits to the Tudor and early Stuart revolution in criminal trial procedure. Even in state trials, where acquittals were relatively rare,[169] some juries stood firm although the evidence against the accused was strong enough to produce a close case.[170] In routine felony trials juries held out more frequently in the face of pressure from the bench.[171] Jury finality regarding the facts put in evidence was by no means completely overthrown; not only did it remain a matter of daily practice but, given the narrowness of the government's most commonly stated rationale for the punishment of juries, it retained vitality at the level of legal theory.[172] Finally, and most important, the relative strength or weakness of the government was reflected in the scope of the cases it chose—or dared—to dispute.

For a variety of reasons, the government often chose to work with and not against juries in order to achieve its central aims. The administration of the criminal law had made important strides forward with regard to determining the outcome of significant cases, but those cases were still a very small percentage of the total number of criminal offenses. Much crime went unreported, or unprosecuted;[173] evidence in routine cases

169. See Elton, *Policy and Police*, p. 397; Bellamy, *Tudor Law of Treason*, pp. 169–72.
170. Bellamy, *Tudor Law of Treason*, p. 181.
171. Cockburn, "Trial by the Book?" p. 73 (by implication; see above, n. 109). Cockburn (*Introduction*, ch. vi, sect. iv) argues that after the mid-1570s the jury was very passive, as evidenced by, inter alia, the absence of Home Circuit bindings over to Star Chamber. See my comments below, n. 179.
172. See also below, n. 179.
173. Cockburn, "Nature and Incidence of Crime," pp. 50–51. Cockburn cites the "not implausible" estimate of a contemporary magistrate, Edward Hext, that 80 percent of all criminals evaded trial. See Cockburn, *Introduction*, ch. viii, sect. i. See also Bruce Lenman and Geoffrey Parker, "The State, the Community and the Criminal Law in Early Modern

often was hard to obtain; and only so many juries could be brought under control. The machinery of detection and prosecution simply failed to hold its own. Moreover, so many offenders had been statutorily precluded from pleading benefit of clergy that in property crimes especially the rules of law and social attitudes remained apart.[174] The number of cases in which jury and bench were bound to clash was once again on the rise. At the same time, by the late sixteenth century the continued increase in criminal activity had reached what authorities thought were crisis levels. This may have increased the interest of society in prosecution, conviction, and punishment, but only to a point: the severity of the law of sanctions and perhaps also a growing sense that much property crime was less the product of inherent evil than the result of the economic troubles of the day[175] undermined the effectiveness of law enforcement at all stages.

Then as now authorities lacked a coherent strategy for dealing with serious criminal behavior. Rather, they responded in several contradictory ways. On the one hand, authorities apparently experimented with a form of "plea bargaining," reducing charges from nonclergyable to clergyable (or to petty larceny) in return for guilty pleas. In so doing, the bench implicitly conceded that it could not ensure a guilty verdict at the capital level or even count on a given jury to convict of minor theft or of manslaughter rather than acquit the defendant altogether.[176] On the other hand, the bench urged—even coerced—juries to convict defendants in order to set an example. In still other cases, the bench encouraged juries to undervalue goods and convict the defendant of a clergyable offense,

Europe," in Gatrell et al., eds., *Crime and the Law: The Social History of Crime in Western Europe since 1500*, pp. 18–20.

174. Probably this was not so with regard to professional criminals or hardened rogues who committed highway robbery and burglary; it may have been so with regard to first offenders who committed these offenses "opportunistically." Inflation had driven many petty robbers into the ranks of the nonclergyable.

175. The problem of the relationship between jury behavior and attitudes toward the causes of crime is addressed below, Chapter 7, section III, with reference to the late seventeenth and eighteenth centuries. For the sixteenth and early seventeenth centuries the evidence is sparser and more difficult to assess. Some contemporaries seem to have equated crime and poverty, not always in a sympathetic fashion. Cockburn, "Nature and Incidence of Crime," pp. 60–61. Society as a whole may have adopted a more sympathetic view. Much remains to be done, perhaps county by county. See Herrup's pioneering work, "The Common Peace," ch. 6. Herrup assesses the relationships among religion, poverty, crime, and mercy in her study based upon early seventeenth-century East Sussex quarter sessions and assizes. See also T. C. Curtis and F. M. Hale, "English Thinking about Crime," in Louis A. Knafla, ed., *Crime and Criminal Justice in Europe and Canada* (Waterloo, Ontario, 1981), pp. 116–26. And see my comments below, Chapter 9, section III.

176. Cockburn (*Introduction*, ch. vi. sect. ii) suggests that "plea bargaining" was undertaken to avoid time-consuming jury trials.

either to avoid the possibility of a full acquittal against the evidence or, out of compassion, to do rough justice in cases where the punishment would otherwise have appeared disproportionate to the culpability of the offender. Inevitably, especially in close cases, the bench had either to fight with juries or to adopt their standards of justice and, having thus stamped most resolutions as in accordance with judicial will, to allow juries some leeway in reaching their verdict.[177] There was a cost in this: the failure to contest the verdicts of merely merciful juries, seen alongside the determined attempt to overturn verdicts authorities viewed as corrupt and truly damaging, must have reinforced society's sense that jury insistence upon the former kind of verdict was appropriate. The bench strove, of course, to retain its substantial degree of control over such discretion. By recommending merciful acquittals or partial verdicts, the bench attempted to maintain the notion that the discretion to mitigate the law lay with it and not with the jury. But not all could have been really deceived. It was in fact a shared power, and the age-old view that a shared power was integral to the very right to trial by peers survived the legal transformations of the sixteenth and early seventeenth centuries.[178]

Two important additional factors guaranteed the survival of the tradition of the jury's right to exercise discretion. The fact that the trial remained oral and personal reinforced the popular conception that the trial was as much an assessment of just deserts as it was a search for the truth in the case at hand. This was not, of course, the way in which authorities viewed the matter. The oral and personal trial was also consistent with the view that the jury was bound to find the facts and nothing else. It represented both the concession of a fundamental right to have the truth of accusations tested under the most grueling circumstances and the potentially contradictory notion that the accused could not be shielded by another personality from the heat of the contest. Nevertheless, so long as the sanction for felony remained so severe, and so long as it applied at least in theory to so large a field of cases, the very nature of the trial was bound to be seen as related to the concept of merciful verdicts.

Moreover, the development of the substantive law of homicide at once reduced the number of disputed cases and provided cover for jury discretion in some of those cases in which the jury was inclined to go its

177. I deal with this point more generally, below, Chapter 7, section IV.
178. Some contemporaries may have exaggerated the barbarousness of English law, because, as Baker points out (*Reports of Sir John Spelman*, 2:299, 300), of their understatement of the "extent to which sanctuary, abjuration, clergy and the jury system itself, saved lesser felons from the gallows." But it is likely that society at large, though it may have viewed the law of sanctions, and occasionally its application, as "barbarous," understood the extent of mitigation of the law in practice.

own way. The question of life or death more than ever depended upon a subtle assessment of intent, and that assessment had to be made retrospectively by way of inferences drawn from the defendant's present assertions and demeanor.

The survival of the right to grant merciful verdicts did not, in logic, imply the survival of the power to find the law. This power had never had a grounding in theory; the medieval jury's de facto power to find law had always been founded on the realities of process. The age of nearly unlimited jury control of evidence was passing; the age of the law and of the bench was commencing. The conflict between judicial and social concepts of liability remained, to be played out perhaps less often but far more visibly in the courtroom relationship between judge and jury. Whether the jury would return a verdict clearly at odds with the evidence set forth by the prosecution, in the face of judicial charge and threat of punishment, was now the question upon which control of the legal process depended. The right of the jury to do so had now to be invented and given a place in political and constitutional theory.[179]

179. How far the balance of power had in fact shifted from jury to judge—leaving aside, for a moment, the question of society's perception of the matter—remains unclear. Marshaling evidence regarding several related points of procedure, Cockburn (*Introduction*, ch. x) draws the inference that on the Home Circuit after the mid-1570s the jury was virtually a passive body. I do not find the arguments for such a view of the jury entirely persuasive even for the Home Circuit. (Cockburn concedes that his conclusion might not apply to other circuits.) I shall summarize and comment upon Cockburn's main points.

Cockburn notes that the increase in the number of indictments in the latter half of Elizabeth's reign led the bench to experiment with plea bargaining, thereby removing many cases from the jury. To speed up trial procedure and to reduce the total number of jurors required to hear cases, judges increased the number of cases that a single jury heard before retiring. Each case, Cockburn concludes, must have proceeded rapidly, given the number of cases tried in the few days during which the bench sat; the relatively inexperienced jurors (most sat at only one assize) cannot have found it easy to keep each case separate or to recall much more than the judge's opinion as to the appropriate outcome. Few cases (5–10 percent) resulted in partial verdicts, which suggests relatively little recourse to discretion on the part of the jury. After 1575, there is little evidence of judicial punishment of jurors, which again is suggestive of the degree to which the jury did as the bench bade it to do.

The overall trend seems clear, and in the main we are in accord on the point that the bench exercised very substantial control. Certainly this seems to have been the case at Home Circuit assizes. But judicial control had its limits; and even when it was dominant, it did not preclude some significant degree of jury-based mitigation. I have dealt in my own essay with some of the factors to which Cockburn points, but have not drawn from them the same inference with regard to the role of the jury.

I think it particularly important that redrafted indictments and plea bargains siphoned off a large number of cases in which the jury might otherwise have exercised discretion, though it seems to me that this suggests not only that judges sought to expedite process but also that they entertained doubts about their ability to obtain a capital conviction in such cases. At any rate, this hardly accounts for the great majority of cases; and Cockburn himself shows that much mitigation was postconviction, by virtue of judicial intervention. Thus not all cases where mercy was thought appropriate had been dealt with before they went to the jury. We cannot assume, therefore, that the jury did not have the opportunity to extend mercy; more likely (as Cockburn would agree), the jury substantially reduced the number of cases that the bench would otherwise have dealt with through posttrial reprieve and recommendation for pardon. The question remains, Did the jury do so solely on judicial mandate?

Multiple arraignments must have made it somewhat more difficult for jurors to keep individual cases in mind. But jurors would not have found it beyond them to recall the one or two (if that many) of the six or so defendants arraigned for whom they independently concluded that death was too harsh a sanction. As Cockburn establishes, ten to twenty cases per day meant that each case averaged no more than half an hour, and many cases took no more than fifteen or twenty minutes. But jurors (on Cockburn's evidence) did not deliberate after each case. Rather, they deliberated toward the end of a two-or-three-hour period of testimony. For all we know, many cases took a mere ten minutes and the total time for deliberation was that much longer. For the few "difficult" cases there may well have been ample time. It is premature to conclude that jurors, who typically sat only at one assize session, were too inexperienced to reach decisions on their own: they may well have sat previously at quarter sessions or on any of the many other kinds of juries of the day. Doubtless, service before royal judges was more awe-inspiring and induced an unusual degree of timidness. Cockburn's findings concerning frequent resort to mere bystanders and the apparent institution of professional jurors are in this regard of great importance. It is not clear, however, that these corruptions rendered jurors "passive" in all, or even most cases. Judicial attitudes probably deterred acquittals in egregious cases and ensured them where the offense was slight: as I have argued, changes in the law and the use of benefit of clergy had brought judge and jury closer together. But judicial attitudes had probably changed in other ways, too, perhaps also because of the press of business. We cannot be certain that the bench cared very deeply about the ultimate resolution of all those close cases that had not already been resolved through bargain. It is true that there were relatively few partial verdicts on the Home Circuit, but there were many acquittals. Why should not these stand as some evidence of jury-based discretion? Many acquittals followed a pattern that suggests that the quantum of evidence was not the sole determinant. It is, of course, possible that the bench told juries to acquit women or persons who stole one kind of object rather than another; more likely, however, juries were themselves inclined to do so, and where the offense did not seem particularly serious, or definitively proven, the bench did not attempt to dissuade them.

It is not even clear that in the more serious cases the bench always had its way. Cockburn (*Introduction*, ch. ix, sect. i) states that "forty two percent of those tried for non-clergyable highway robbery were acquitted." This was a relatively serious offense, and Cockburn cites the acquittal rates as dramatic evidence of the reluctance to send offenders to the gallows. But whose reluctance? Can all these acquittals really have been mandated by the bench? Moreover, there were cases, Cockburn states (*idem*), where, because "attempts to influence the jury were time consuming," judges "simply ignored the jury verdict and ordered the punishment of prisoners whose delinquency was, presumably, notorious or had been demonstrated to the judge's satisfaction by the evidence. Despite acquittal, such men might be whipped [or] imprisoned." This in itself suggests a certain degree of jury independence, and it reveals the effects on the bench of the all-important constraints of time. Juries in such cases might have been frustrated in their desire to acquit, but not in their desire to prevent execution. They might in fact have been well satisfied with the "compromise" punishments that were inflicted.

In some other, perhaps less serious cases, jury resolution probably went on as before, at least in the popular imagination. Surely the bench often recommended a specific verdict, but it was still the jury that actually rendered that verdict. In form, certainly, the jury undertook the exercise of discretion. Often it did so in substance as well, in a certain sense: i.e., if we ask, not merely whether the bench gave orders, but whether jurors thought of themselves as sharing in the decisions they were rendering. For even when judges were dominating juries, they were often using them to register verdicts that departed from the letter of the law and accorded with widely held social attitudes; and, from the point of view of the bench, so much the better if the jury genuinely favored the result. To be sure, Cockburn's important work suggests we must proceed with great caution. Nonetheless, I believe it remains a fair conclusion that, amid all the abuses, shortcuts, and cynicism, from the perspectives both of jurors and of the observing community, the exercise of jury-based discretion remained a part of the doing of justice, even at Home Circuit assizes. Surely this could have been the case on other circuits. As Cockburn points out (*Introduction*, ch. ix. sect. i), partial verdicts appear to have been common at London and Middlesex trials, and the struggle between bench and jury reflected in punishments at the bar or in Star Chamber continued in still other parts of England, long after Home Circuit justices had, for whatever reason, abandoned the practice of formally disciplining jurors.

# 5 Conscience and the True Law: The Ideology of Jury Law-Finding in the Interregnum

The government that tried and condemned Charles I in January, 1649, found later the same year that it was unable to have its way with John Lilburne. As leader of the Levellers, the most imposing of the groups that clashed with the Cromwellian regime, Lilburne appealed to his jurors, in a celebrated phrase, "as judges of law as well as fact."[1] When the jury acquitted him of treason, this claim to a "jury right"—a right of the jury to decide the law—brought the criminal trial jury for the first time into the forefront of English constitutional and political debate.[2]

The emergence of a theory of the jury's right to decide the law was not in any simple way a reaction to the transformation of criminal process in early modern England. On the one hand, much of what the radical reformers attacked predated the Tudor period; on the other, much of their program was inspired by the political crisis that accompanied the struggle against the Stuart monarchy.[3] Nevertheless, the Leveller attack on the judiciary in criminal cases was a response to the power and behavior of the bench, and that power and behavior were largely owing to new forms of criminal procedure.

1. See below, text at nn. 67–77. On the Levellers see e.g. H. N. Brailsford, *The Levellers and the English Revolution* (London, 1961); Joseph Frank, *The Levellers* (Cambridge, Mass., 1955); G. E. Aylmer, ed., *The Levellers in the English Revolution* (London, 1975), pp. 9–55. Aylmer reviews the history of the Levellers and discusses recent literature that points to important differences among the leaders of the movement. See also Robert B. Seaberg, "Remembering the Past: Historical Aspects of Leveller Political Thought," doctoral dissertation (Syracuse University, 1977). Seaberg takes issue with much recent writing on the main thrust of Leveller thought; see below, n. 32.

2. This obviously has relevance to debate in published works. The issue appears not to have been formulated as one regarding a right to "find law" until the late 1640s either in published writings or in discourse generally. If it was formulated earlier, it appears not to have attained widespread currency.

3. In one sense, the Leveller program was aimed at the Westminster bench as it had developed since the twelfth century. I suggest below (text at nn. 36–37) that the Levellers overstated the actual powers of the bench (and understated those of the jury) in the medieval period. In their minds, they were attacking usages that long predated the Tudor period. Not only were they attacking what they took to be ancient practices, but they were also contending with particularly virulent symptoms of what they believed to be the Norman disease that had manifested themselves in the Parliamentary struggle against Charles I.

At the same time, the radicals' insistence on a community-based system of criminal justice was not a claim to an entirely novel approach to the criminal law. For, as we have seen, even as the power of the bench increased, some substantial degree of reliance on the trial jury's discretion continued. And if the bench viewed such discretion as appropriate within fairly narrow limits, others might have inferred from actual practice that the jury was supposed to have considerable leeway in rendering verdicts according to its sense of justice. Of course, what the radicals most insisted upon the actual administration of justice did clearly deny them: truly local trials before a lay bench or before a weak official bench.[4] For the government, jury discretion was tolerable only within the context of a centrally administered, closely overseen, and highly managed system of criminal law. For at least some of the government's opponents the purpose of jury discretion—the essence of the historic right to trial by peers—was being frustrated by what had become the official approach to the administration of the criminal law.

What did Lilburne mean by the jury's right to decide "law as well as fact"? What was the source of his theory of trial by jury? How did that theory evolve during the Commonwealth? In the discussion that follows, I shall attempt to answer these questions through an analysis of Leveller political theory and the conception of English history on which it was based. The "jury right" was more than just another Leveller reform item: the supposed right lay at the very heart of Leveller political and social theory, and at least in its theoretical implications the right involved the gravest threat that the Levellers posed to the governments of the Interregnum. For Lilburne and for some of his followers, the coercion of jurors meant more than the deprivation of the defendant's right to trial by jury. Coercion of jurors also meant the loss by Englishmen of control over the law. Finality of the verdict of the country had long implied the sanctity of the community's judgment concerning the accused. Now it also came to stand for the sanctity of the community's judgment regarding the substance of the "true law."

The Levellers were only one of many groups that comprised the mid-seventeenth-century movement for reform of the law. There were many sides to that movement, nearly all of which, save for the debate over the criminal trial jury, have received significant scholarly attention. It may be useful to sketch the outlines of the entire movement and the Levellers' distinctive place within it against the background of the Civil War and its immediate aftermath, the Interregnum governments.[5]

4. See below, text at nn. 85 et seq., for discussion of such writers as John Jones and James Frese.
5. The most recent and comprehensive account of the movement for law reform is Donald

Even before the outbreak of the Civil War, the Long Parliament forced upon Charles I the abolition of the Courts of Star Chamber and High Commission.[6] Reform of the common-law judiciary included dismissal and punishment of those judges who, in Parliament's eyes, had rendered unconstitutional decisions; after the Civil War began in 1642, it also included attempts to subject the bench to parliamentary (as opposed to executive) control.[7] The legal reformers in Parliament moved against feudal tenures and the Courts of Wards and Liberties, and reflected broad agreement among the propertied as a whole on the need to undertake reform of some of the procedures that resulted in excessive costs and delays both in the common-law courts and in Chancery.

Divisions among groups demanding law reform were soon mirrored by divisions within the revolutionary movement. The Levellers were among the first to challenge the moderate goals of the parliamentary leadership during the Civil War. They were a mixture of soldiers from the ranks of the New Model Army that had been formed under the leadership of Oliver Cromwell in 1645, and civilians, who by the mid-1640s experienced disenchantment with the limited goals espoused by the leaders of the parliamentary cause.[8] The surrender of Charles I in 1646 and the commencement of negotiations between the king and Parliament for a reformed constitutional monarchy alienated the burgeoning Leveller movement and gave it a basis for opposition. In a profusion of tracts and broadsides, this embryonic opposition proclaimed its demands for reform of suffrage and for social and legal reform. The last entailed a trenchant attack on the common law, both private and public, and particularly on

Veall, *The Popular Movement for Law Reform* (Oxford, 1970). See also Stuart Prall, *The Agitation for Law Reform during the Puritan Revolution* (The Hague, 1966); Barbara Shapiro, "Law Reform in Seventeenth Century England," *American Journal of Legal History*, vol. 19 (1975), pp. 288–97; G. B. Nourse, "Law Reform under the Commonwealth and Protectorate," *Law Quarterly Review*, vol. 75 (1959), pp. 512–29; C. R. Niehaus, "The Issue of Law Reform in the Puritan Revolution," doctoral dissertation (Harvard Univ., 1957); Mary Cotterell, "Interregnum Law Reform: The Hale Commission of 1652," *English Historical Review*, vol. 83 (1968), pp. 689–704.

6. For the abolition of Star Chamber (and the conciliar courts of the Council of the Marches of Wales and the Council of the North) see Stat. 16 Chas. 1, c. 10 (1641); for the abolition of High Commission see Stat. 16 Chas. 1, c. 11 (1641).

7. See Shapiro, "Law Reform in Seventeenth Century England," and sources cited therein.

8. Mark A. Kishlansky, "The Army and the Levellers: The Roads to Putney," *Historical Journal*, vol. 22 (1979), pp. 795–824. Kishlansky downplays Leveller influence in the army before late 1647. Moreover, until 1647 the Levellers' disenchantment with Parliament had mostly to do with Presbyterian measures against the separatists and with their own "ill-treatment" at parliamentary hands. See below, text at nn. 9 *et seq.*, for discussion of the post-1647 Leveller movement.

the control over the common law manifested by the centralized bench at Westminster and the elitist legal profession.

Negotiations with the king were paralleled in late 1647 by discussions between Cromwell and the Army representatives of the radicals, many of whom were now openly known by the epithet of "Levellers."[9] The stalemate in the latter negotiations was followed by an outright conflict between the Army's establishment leadership and some radicals, but the escape of Charles and commencement of the second phase of the Civil War (1648) brought all opponents of the king closer together. Lilburne (who had been held in the Tower for his attacks on Parliament, then released in 1647 only to be sequestered once again the following year), Richard Overton, and William Walwyn were by now widely recognized as the leading Leveller publicists.[10] Rapprochement with Cromwell in 1648 halted neither Leveller diatribes against the Presbyterian-dominated Parliament (including demands for religious toleration) nor their proposals for "universal" male suffrage and a system of law accessible to the common man.

Purged by the Army, the rump of the Long Parliament proceeded to bring the captured king to trial and public execution. In February, 1649, a Commonwealth was established to bring order to the strife-torn country. Although the Levellers had taken part in the discussions that led to the purge and to the execution of Charles, they remained suspicious (to put it mildly) of the Rump's membership, especially after the readmission of the Conformists, and hostile to its reforms. These reforms included appointment of a High Court of Justice, which did not provide for trial by jury, and the passage of a series of Treason Acts.[11] Leveller disenchantment and published criticism of the new regime resulted in the arrest of Lilburne, Overton, Walwyn, and Thomas Prince. In May, the Army put down a small Leveller rising at Burton with force. By the autumn of 1649, when Lilburne was brought to trial, the movement had been largely destroyed.

Political and religious radicalism, though no longer perceived as a threat to the very existence of the regime, both pushed the Rump forward and intensified its determination to embrace only a very moderate reform program. It led, also, to the Rump's decision to afforce the activities of its own parliamentary law committee by the creation of an extraparliamentary law reform commission under the leadership of the respected barrister

9. For discussion of the "Putney debates" see e.g. Brailsford, *Levellers and the English Revolution*, ch. 13; Aylmer, ed., *Levellers in the English Revolution*, pp. 28–29, 32–33.

10. See sources cited above, n. 1. On Lilburne's career, arrests, protestations, etc., see Pauline Gregg, *Free-Born John: A Biography of John Lilburne* (London, 1961).

11. Veall, *Popular Movement for Reform*, p. 163; Aylmer, ed., *Levellers in the English Revolution*, pp. 45–46.

Sir Matthew Hale.[12] Although the Hale Commission functioned during the early 1650s to draw the steam out of the radical reform movement, it promoted a number of substantial, moderate reform measures.[13] Its failure to effect many of these, despite the dissolution in 1653 of the Rump, reflected the power of the prevailing legal establishment and the deep suspicion, prevalent even among moderates, of those groups, largely, by this time, religious radicals, most insistent upon purifying the common law and its institutions. The demonstrations surrounding Lilburne's trial in 1653 for returning to England without permission while under decree of banishment cannot have helped matters.[14]

From late 1653, Cromwell was Lord Protector by virtue of a new, written constitution.[15] For the next five years, until his death and brief succession by his son Richard, the movement for far-reaching law reform slipped into the background. Some changes in the legal system were effected by the essentially moderate government, changes that did not meet the demands of either the remnant of the Leveller movement or the religious radicals (The Fifth Monarchy Men). These reforms, as well as other moderate proposals for reforms that were debated but not enacted, touched private common law, the Court of Chancery, the system of land registration, and some aspects of the law of sanctions.[16] The record, by the end of the Protectorate and the Restoration in 1660 of Charles II, was one of intense and widespread interest in eliminating that part of the legal quagmire that inconvenienced the propertied classes, but little more. As we shall see, there were proposals regarding the jury. These, however, were in the direction of securing more trustworthy jurors, not of democratizing the institution or of shifting power to it and away from the bench. The jury reforms that the radical Levellers demanded were never seriously considered.

12. The definitive study of the Hale Commission is Cotterell, "Interregnum Law Reform." Many members of the committee that selected the Hale Commission members sat on the Parliamentary Law Committee. A majority of those selected either had been called to the bar or had at least studied at one of the Inns of Court. Cotterell (*ibid.*, p. 692) found that thirteen members of the Commission were not radicals but were "men of power, wealth and position, devoted to the pursuit of power and status, whose interest lay with a strong establishment. . . . They sought, not an overturning, but the reform continuity for which Cromwell stood." Five "radicals" sat on the Commission. Three of the twenty-one members cannot be assigned to either group (*ibid.*, p. 693).

13. *Ibid.*, pp. 695–704. See also Shapiro, "Law Reform in Seventeenth Century England," pp. 291–97.

14. For Lilburne's 1653 trial see below, section VI.

15. For discussion of the "Instrument of Government," see J. P. Kenyon, *The Stuart Constitution* (Cambridge, 1966), pp. 333–35; Godfrey Davies, *The Early Stuarts, 1603–1660* (Oxford, 1959), pp. 176–77.

16. See sources cited above, n. 13.

The term "Leveller"—it should be stressed at the outset—is employed largely as a term of convenience. The Levellers were not a unified group; those who called themselves Levellers, took part in Leveller demonstrations, or signed Leveller petitions stood for different positions on a variety of issues.[17] Even those usually referred to as leaders of the Levellers were by no means in agreement on all matters. Lilburne and Walwyn differed in their religious views. Overton and Walwyn have been considered "true Levellers," being more radical on social and economic issues than Lilburne, Prince, and John Wildman, the "constitutional Levellers."[18] As I shall indicate, there was no one Leveller theory regarding the criminal trial jury. Nonetheless, there may have been more agreement regarding that institution than any other. Political and social disagreements were probably more pronounced with regard to the civil jury, especially as it dealt with property issues, just as disagreements over the institution of property itself loomed large among Leveller leaders and their followers.[19]

The account I shall give of Leveller political and historical theory is generalized and obscures some differences among the leading Leveller writers, but, again, these differences did not necessarily affect Leveller views of the criminal trial jury. Most Levellers—indeed most Leveller leaders—did not think deeply about the history of the jury. Although their views about the jury were probably influenced by Lilburne's 1649 trial, they did not develop a systematic theory that explained why the jury ought to have the powers Lilburne claimed for it.

In what follows, I shall delineate the framework of ideas—political, legal, social, and religious—into which contemporary radical claims concerning the criminal trial jury seem to have fit. Though we cannot know how many caught up in the Leveller movement viewed the institution in any one way, we can attain a collective impression of the range of views they held. I shall also identify the strain of Interregnum radical (or law-finding) jury theory that was passed on to posterity. Here disagreement between Lilburne and other more radical Leveller leaders proved important. From the perspective of this book, it is the Leveller legacy that is of greatest interest. In this essay, however, it is the more radical, stillborn jury theory that receives greatest attention. In its light we may understand the distance between many of the Levellers and the Cromwellian regime; we may see how central the institution of the

17. For an excellent summary of the recent scholarship on Leveller factions and disagreements among Leveller leaders see Aylmer, ed., *Levellers in the English Revolution*, pp. 9–55.
18. Christopher Hill, *The World Turned Upside Down* (New York, 1972), pp. 86–120.
19. *Ibid.*, pp. 91–99.

criminal trial jury was to a truly revolutionary conception of society; and we may marvel both at the manipulation of contemporary historical learning and at how far that learning was from the actual history of the criminal trial jury.

There were three phases in the mid-seventeenth-century criminal trial jury debate. In the first phase, up to Lilburne's 1649 trial, "radical" law reformers combined an insistence on the right to indictment and trial by peers with specific demands for frequent, convenient, and local trials. Jurors were to be "of the neighborhood," for such persons were best informed regarding the circumstances of the felony and the credibility of the witnesses and principals. There was in this first period little, if any, public discussion of the jurors' knowledge of law; indeed, the early tracts assume the correctness of the "old decantatum": judges are to determine the law; jurors are to determine the fact.[20]

What Lilburne meant when he claimed in 1649 that his jurors were "judges of law as well as of fact" is not entirely clear. The writings occasioned by his 1649 trial, as the debate over the jury deepened, represent the second phase of the jury argument. John Jones, who seems to have shared many of the Levellers' ideas, gave meaning to Lilburne's aphorism in the course of his elaboration upon traditional Leveller historiography. His works set forth a far-reaching argument for total jury control over the law, an argument that may have been no more than a posthumous statement of Leveller theory a year after the Cromwellian regime had largely destroyed the Leveller movement.[21] Jones provided a rationale for taking nearly all power out of the hands of the bench. His defense of the jury right combined his own version of Leveller historical views with a radical Puritan argument concerning the right of the people to interpret the law as they would interpret Scripture, which he conceived to be the law's principal basis.

The final phase of the debate over the jury right began with the regime's second prosecution of Lilburne in 1653. Lilburne now enunciated a more precise theory of the jury right, one that appears to have taken its form from the specific circumstances of his prosecution. He claimed that the statute of banishment under which he was tried was not valid under English law. The jury had the right and duty, he argued, to judge a statute or an indictment in the light of English fundamental law, and to acquit the defendant if, despite a judicial charge to the contrary, the jury found that the statute was void. Moreover, Lilburne now asserted that the jury ought to acquit the defendant if it believed that the prescribed punishment was

20. See below, text at nn. 48–50.
21. For a discussion of the decline of the Leveller movement see Christopher Hill, *The Century of Revolution* (Edinburgh, 1961), pp. 134, 139, 169–70.

unconscionably severe in light of the acts proved to have been committed by the defendant. The jury should test the "legality" of the indictment and decide the fairness of the prescribed punishment. The elements of this new law-finding theory proved to be of great significance. They did not perish with the opposition to the Interregnum government but rather (as we shall see in Chapter 6) passed into the hands of the Quakers and subsequently became a staple of post-Restoration pro-jury argument.

# I

For seven years the jury debate smoldered in revolutionary and Commonwealth England. The debate began with Lilburne's 1646 tract, *The Just Man's Justification*, and ended with the last of Lilburne's trials in 1653. Ironically, the most intense discussion of the jury came in the wake of Lilburne's trial in September, 1649, when the Levellers were no longer a large and unified force. Only then did it become clear that, at least for some of the more significant writers, the jury issue represented one of the truly unifying themes of Interregnum radical political theory.

However, at the outset of the entire reform movement, which encompassed the activities of many different groups reflecting various political views, the role of the jury in the everyday criminal trial was not of great concern. For virtually all reformers, other demands respecting the criminal law took precedence over the jury: among them bail, speedy trials, reform of the law of sanctions, and prison reform.[22] These demands, which had their origin in early seventeenth-century reform agitation,[23] continued throughout the Interregnum to interest most reformers, including both moderates and those radicals who came to oppose the new Cromwellian regime. Moreover, against the backdrop of the entire law reform movement, reform of the criminal law was for most reformers only one of many issues, and it was concerned less with a vision of a new society than with mitigation of the necessary evils of the old society. In time, the criminal law might wither away; for the present, it ought not to be so repressive.

The modest aims of early Leveller thought regarding the jury are reflected in the third *Agreement of the People* (1649), which declared that "judgments of conviction of life, limb, liberty or estate" must not be achieved other than by "twelve sworn men of the neighborhood; to be

22. See e.g. Richard Overton, *Certain Articles for the good of the Commonwealth* (London, July 17, 1647), [British Library (hereafter, B.L.): E. 398(28)], reprinted in Aylmer, ed., *Levellers in the English Revolution*, pp. 82–87. See generally Veall, *Popular Movement for Law Reform*, chs. 5–7. Cotterell ("Interregnum Law Reform") provides the best account of the "moderate" reforms that were eventually taken up by the Hale Commission.

23. Shapiro, "Law Reform in Seventeenth Century England," pp. 281–88.

chosen in some free way by the people . . . and not picked and imposed, as hitherto in many places they have been."[24] This declaration brought together the three principal pre-1649 demands about the criminal trial jury: that all felony trials be jury trials, that the jury come from the neighborhood where the crime was committed, that the jury be selected by the people rather than by officials.

Speedy, cheap, and local trials met with the approbation of many early reform writers. Several tracts complained of the time-consuming and costly trips to Westminster, though it is true that these complaints were mainly directed at the hardships of civil pleas.[25] But the decentralization issue was not one-sided: critics countered that the hundreds could not produce a sufficient number of competent persons, either literates or men of reputation.[26] For the most part, consideration of convenience and capacity dominated the discussion concerning jury trials until, in late

24. *An Agreement of the Free People of England* (London, May 1, 1649), [B.L.: E. 571(10)], p. 6, § xxv, reprinted in William Haller and Godfrey Davies, eds., *The Leveller Tracts* (Gloucester, Mass., 1964), pp. 318–28. (This tract was probably authored by Lilburne, William Walwyn, Overton, and Thomas Prince.) In an earlier section of the *Agreement* the authors stated that in all capital cases other than treason "recompense shall be made to the parties damnified, as well out of the estate of the malefactor, as by loss of life, according to the conscience of his jury" (p. 6, § xxi).

The 1647 *Agreement of the People* (London, Nov. 3, 1647), [B.L.: E. 412 (21)], reprinted in Aylmer, ed., *Levellers in the English Revolution*, pp. 89–96, did not deal directly with the jury. The 1648 *Agreement of the People* (London, Dec. 10, 1648), [B.L.: E. 476(26)], provided that "judgment or conviction of life, liberty, or estate" should be "only by twelve sworn men of the neighborhood" (p. 14, § 9).

25. E.g. *To His Excellency Thomas Lord Fairfax: . . . The Humble Representation of the Desires of the Officers and Souldiers . . . for the County of Northumberland* (London, Dec. 5, 1648), [B.L.: E. 475(13)], p. 5; *The Declarations and Humble Representations of the Officers and Souldiers in Colonel Scroops [etc.] Regiment* (London, Dec. 7, 1648), [B.L.: E. 475(24)], p. 5; *A Petition presented by the Inhabitants of Newport-Paynell* (London, Dec. 26, 1648), [B.L.: 669 f. 13(63)]; *The Humble Petition and Representation of the Officers and Soldiers of the Garison of Portsmouth* (London, Jan. 18, 1649), [B.L.: 699 f. 13(73)]. See also Gerrard Winstanley, *More Light Shining in Buckinghamshire* (London, March 30, 1649), in G. Sabine, ed., *The Works of Gerrard Winstanley* (Ithaca, N. Y., 1941), p. 638: "[T]hat all trials be in every hundred by twelve men of the same neighborhood"; *The Remonstrance of (those Reproachfully called) the Levellers* (London, Sept. 21, 1649), [B.L.: E. 574(15)], p. 6.

26. E.g. *The Representative of Divers well-affected persons in and about the City of London* (London, Feb. 6, 1649), [B.L.: E. 541(16)], p. 1: "[I]t is impossible to find a competent number of jurors to try any criminal or civil matter within any Hundred in England . . . whereunto there shall not be put in a lawful challenge, that they are either kinsmen, friends, tenants, parties, or concerned in the matter"; William Ashurst, *Reasons against Agreement with . . . The Agreement of the People* (London, Dec. 26, 1648), [B.L.: E. 536(4)], p. 11: "And all this justice to be done, and lie in the breasts of twelve men in every hundred, who may be chosen of men that can neither write, read, nor have any estates." See also below, nn. 112–20 and accompanying text.

1649, Lilburne focused attention on the law-finding role of the criminal trial jury. Only then did discussion center on the history and purpose of the institution rather than on its formal attributes.

Nevertheless, from 1646 on, Lilburne was feeling his way toward the proposition he announced in the heat of his 1649 trial. *Just Man's Justification* had called for trials "in the County, or Hundred . . . without any appeal but to a Parliament." All causes civil and criminal should "monthly be judged by twelve men, of free and honest condition, chosen by themselves, with their grave or chief officer amongst them . . . ."[27] For Lilburne, local trials meant both freedom from the obfuscations of Westminster jurists and jury control over determination of guilt or innocence. Jurors were to "judge" cases, a term Lilburne did not explain; control over law, as separate from and in addition to control over fact, was at most an implicit assumption of this early tract. Lilburne criticized what he implied were typical aspects of the criminal trial—the formidable justices, whose rulings were both incomprehensible to the defendant and beyond challenge by him; the incompetent jury, selected from know-nothings of the city rabble and willing to follow the judge's lead.[28] Lilburne sought in his 1646 tract to return the trial to what he deemed its historic place in the local community. The tenor of the tract suggests that despite the routine nature of the demands in successive versions of the *Agreement of the People*, the criminal trial jury played a significant role in Leveller thought.[29]

The Leveller conception of the criminal trial jury was based upon a distinctive view of the history and nature of English law. How was it that the Levellers' legal theory could combine systematic criticism of the common law with a glorification of the jury system? To answer this question, it will be useful to set forth some elements of the Levellers' "Norman Yoke" theory of history, which was a reaction against the establishment historical view inherited in the late 1630s from Sir Edward Coke.

27. John Lilburne, *The Just Man's Justification* (London, June 10, 1646), [B.L.: E. 340(12)], p. 15.

28. Lilburne railed against the use of Latin ("and so without [the people's] understanding" [*ibid.*, pp. 11–12]), the inconvenience of the Westminster courts, and the coercive aspects of the Westminster bench (*ibid.*, p. 15).

29. See also John Lilburne, *The Copy of a Letter* (London, Aug. 9, 1645), [B.L.: E. 296(5)], p. 17, which may refer mainly to civil cases: "Oh for Justice! Justice betwixt a man and his neighbour, impartially, without respect of persons, which alone under God is the only cure of all England's maladies." Hill [*Puritanism and Revolution* (London, 1958), pp. 76–77] recognized the importance of the criminal-trial jury for Lilburne in the pre-1649 period.

Coke had found a basis both for growth of the common law and for resistance to Stuart divine right pretensions in the common law itself. The common law in its purest form was expressive of reason; through long and careful study of it one might grasp the reasoning process that allowed for determination of what was right. This formulation had proved convenient to the common lawyers for denying the king's claim to be able to interpret the law.[30]

Moreover, Coke's view was attractive to the parliamentarians who beheaded the king in the name of the law. For if the common law was as old as English society and had never been supplanted by monarchical force—in 1066 William had confirmed and assented to the liberties of the common law—then law preceded kingship. Thus kingship and prerogative were part of and must conform to the rules of the common law, and the assembly of the kingdom was responsible for defense of the fabric of the common law. While this view of the common law and common law reasoning supported an argument against a particular king and against a peculiarly royalist concept of the law, it did not constitute an argument against kingship, as the rulers of the interregnum period came increasingly to understand. Coke's proposition was an argument for the common law and for reform of that law on an incremental basis, as those professional lawyers and judges trained to understand the legal system saw fit. It rested on an ingrained trust in the common law. The Puritan Revolution did not, after 1649, move steadily to the left until a reaction set in. The revolution, at least with regard to the essential structures of the common law, *was* the reaction.[31]

The Norman Yoke view, on the other hand, cut against the most fundamental political and social conceptions of the Cromwellian ruling elite. The Leveller historical argument constituted an attack on feudalism and on what were alleged to be Norman feudal perversions of the "true" law. The attack focused on the Norman invasion, which cut feudal England off, historically, from its Anglo-Saxon past. The Leveller "myth" of Anglo-Saxon liberties argued that in that almost forgotten age all men were "free," held their land freely, met in free popular assemblies, declared the law, and judged one another in their free, local, and popular courts. These assumptions were employed both sincerely and polemically to buttress arguments against a social and political hierarchy

---

30. On Coke and the common-law tradition see e.g. J. G. A. Pocock, *The Ancient Constitution and the Feudal Law* (Cambridge, 1957), chs. 2–3; Christopher Hill, *Intellectual Origins of the English Revolution* (Oxford, 1965), ch. 5; Hill, *Puritanism and Revolution*, pp. 57–67.

31. See Hill, *Puritanism and Revolution*, pp. 57–67; Pocock, *The Ancient Constitution and the Feudal Law*, pp. 125–26. For discussion of the Parliamentarians' approach to law reform see below, n. 109 and accompanying text.

that not only placed power in the hands of the central government but also drastically limited representation in Parliament.[32]

The Levellers drew their political theory from history and Scripture.[33] They found in these sources the basis for a contractual form of civil polity, one that England's rulers had often breached but which had always been revived, and one that would once again be restored by a new "Agreement."[34] Their approach to Parliament reflected a deep ambivalence concerning the limits of valid delegation of authority. A people's representatives could not be deputized to pronounce law that conflicted with God's will. The remedy was either to reinstate the ancient tradition of local assemblies or to make Parliament more representative and to resist a Parliament that defied divine command.[35]

32. See e.g. Hill, *Puritanism and Revolution*, pp. 75–82; W. Schenk, *The Concern for Social Justice in the Puritan Revolution* (New York, 1968), pp. 78–79. See also Robert Seaberg, "The Norman Conquest and the Common Law: The Levellers and the Argument from Continuity," *Historical Journal*, vol. 24 (1981), pp. 791–806. Seaberg argues, against Hill (*idem.*), Pocock (*The Ancient Constitution and Feudal Law*, pp. 125–27), and Richard T. Vann ["The Free Anglo-Saxons: A Historical Myth," *Journal of the History of Ideas*, vol. 19 (1958), p. 268] that the Levellers did not reject the notion of historical continuity, though the one they adhered to differed from that adopted by Coke and his followers. Seaberg rightly stresses the overlay of Norman procedures that, from the Levellers' point of view, undermined the true substance of the common law. He argues that the Levellers believed that the "true substance" remained implicit in the law and that the Levellers did not retreat from a historically based theory of rights to one based on "natural right and reason" (Pocock, p. 126). Rather, they called for a reform of institutions and procedures that would save the historically identified "true" law. This essay is not the place to attempt a resolution of the on-going debate on Leveller political and social ideas. Suffice it to say that not all Levellers agreed on this issue, and that arguments from history and from "natural right and reason" lay side by side in Leveller (as well as in other contemporary) thought. My discussion of the Leveller perspectives on the institution of the criminal trial jury complements Seaberg's approach.

33. For the Levellers' reliance on history see above, n. 32. I argue that the Levellers drew upon Scripture (see below, text at nn. 105–7) with regard to the criminal law and the rights of Englishmen before the law. I believe that some of the Levellers tended to equate the Anglo-Saxon past with a society that lived according to Scripture. This was the social context they hoped to revive; at some level it had never entirely lapsed, though Norman rule had nearly destroyed it. Thus, although the Leveller claims do have a "natural rights" ring [see Quentin Skinner, "History and Ideology in the English Revolution," *Historical Journal*, vol. 8 (1965), p. 162; Perez Zagorin, *A History of Political Thought in the English Revolution* (London, 1954), pp. 27–29], they do not constitute a rejection of historically based rights. See below, n. 107.

34. Seaberg deals extensively with this important point: "Remembering the Past," pp. 49–64, 138–39, 211 ff., 279, 317, 337, 339, 341–42, 461–63. See also [Richard Overton?], *Regall Tyrannie Discovered* (London, Jan. 6, 1647), [B.L.: E. 370(12)], p. 42: "[T]he King receives his crown by contract and agreement."

35. See Aylmer's summary statement in Aylmer, ed., *The Levellers in the English Revolution*, p. 13.

The Leveller argument was an argument not only for political leveling but for legal leveling as well. Law, according to the Leveller view, was a form of divine command comprehensible and accessible to the common man. Legal procedures and institutions could—and since Norman times did—vitiate the substance of true law. Thus the Levellers joined those who criticized the use of Law French, complicated legal terminology, expensive writs, inconvenient delays, and the other obstacles to speedy and "equal" justice. Legal institutions were supposed to guarantee that equal justice prevailed, and no institution was more important in this regard than the criminal trial jury.

Although the Levellers shared the Cokeian view that the jury preceded the Conquest, they broke with that view on two fundamental issues. First, the Levellers asserted that the jury also preceded an organized judiciary.[36] Second, they argued that Norman feudal governance, far from embracing the jury, nearly destroyed it. According to the Levellers, the Normans and their successors had attempted to pervert and eliminate the jury, despite the fact that Magna Carta had confirmed its use and a succession of medieval monarchs had in turn confirmed Magna Carta.[37] Of the true history of the criminal trial jury, they, like Coke, knew very little. The fact that the criminal trial jury emerged *after* Magna Carta; that its original role was, at least in the main, to gather evidence; that the medieval jury had nevertheless been able to apply the law almost at will; that its de facto role had been greatly reduced only in the sixteenth century: all this would have come as a surprise to the Levellers. Not only would it have clashed with the Levellers' reading of history, it would have undermined an important element of their argument concerning the practical impact of Norman and Plantagenet rule on English liberties.

Although the Levellers identified the jury as one of the first elements of English social and political life, they said very little about the institution's historical role. They appear at first to have accepted the view that the jurors' task was to find fact; law was for the (preferably community-

36. E.g. [Richard Overton?], *A Remonstrance of Many Thousand Citizens* (London, July 7, 1646), in Don M. Wolfe, ed., *Leveller Manifestoes of the Puritan Revolution* (New York, 1944), p. 125; [Overton?], *Regall Tyrannie Discovered*, p. 16. Overton probably assumed that someone from the community served as judge. His main point was that the Normans created a centralized judiciary that was not responsive to community mores. By "organized judiciary," I refer to the Norman itinerant justices. Some Leveller writings are ambiguous even about the existence of a local judge and seem to treat the early jury as a group of law sayers.

See Seaberg, "The Norman Conquest and the Common Law," p. 801. Seaberg contrasts the views of the chroniclers Holinshed and Daniel ("who judged trial by jury as a Norman custom") to the view shared by both Coke and the Levellers.

37. [Richard Overton?], *Vox Plebis, or, The Peoples Outcry* (London, Nov. 19, 1646), [B.L.: E. 362(20)], pp. 6, 9–10.

based) judges to pronounce. But if the judges found the law ineptly or wrongfully, they ought to be removed and punished according to the example set by the Levellers' hero, King Alfred.[38] Before 1649, the Levellers did not go beyond this remedy to embrace a theory of jury intervention on behalf of the true law. Their predominant concern was to resist attempts to pack, influence, or overbear juries or to eliminate them altogether. The Levellers' glorification of the jury may have drawn them closer to the position that the jury, representing the people, ought to find the law directly rather than merely apply it in accordance with the instructions of the people's delegates and the delegates' chosen functionaries. But that position remained latent in the Levellers' political theory, in their understanding of institutional history, in their concept of the source and nature of law.

A modest form of law-finding was latent, too, in the Levellers' arguments for reform of the law of sanctions. The Levellers constantly invoked the notion of the "reason" and "equity" of the law.[39] In their view, a true or godly magistracy interpreted the law in the light of "conscience," thereby doing justice according to God's will.[40] And just as legal forms ought never to soil this process of doing justice, legal sanctions ought not to deviate from divine mandates concerning just deserts. Thus, the Levellers' (and others') attack on the death penalty in cases of theft was scripturally based; to take life for simple theft was contrary to equity and conscience, literally contrary to Scripture.[41] It may

38. For discussion of the role of Alfred see Seaberg, "Remembering the Past," pp. 43, 374. See also e.g. [Overton?], *Vox Plebis*, p. 6; John Lilburne, *An Impeachment of High Treason Against Oliver Cromwell* (London, Aug. 10, 1649), [B.L.: E. 568(20)], p. 6; James Frese, *A Second Why Not* (London, Sept. 3, 1649), [B.L.: 669 f. 14(72)], p. viii.

39. E.g. John Lilburne, *England's Birthright Justified* (London, Oct. 10, 1645) in William Haller, ed., *Tracts on Liberty in the Puritan Revolution, 1638–1647,* 3 vols. (New York, 1934), vol. 3, pp. 2, 32; William Walwyn, *England's Lamentable Slaverie* (London, Oct. ll, 1645), [B.L.: E 304(19)], p. 5; Richard Overton, *The Commoners' Complaint* (London, Feb. 10, 1646), in Haller, ed., *Tracts on Liberty*, 3:380; Richard Overton, *A Defiance against all Arbitrary Usurpations* (London, Sept. 9, 1646), [B.L.: E. 353(17)], p. 6; John Lilburne, *The People's Prerogative and Priviledges, asserted and vindicated* (London, Feb. 14, 1648), [B.L.: E. 427(4)], p. 41.

For a discussion of the Leveller concept of "equity," see J. C. Davis, "The Levellers and Christianity," in Brian Manning, ed., *Politics, Religion and the English Civil War* (London, 1973), pp. 227–34.

40. E.g. Richard Overton, *England's Miserie and Remedie* (London, Sept. 19, 1645), [B.L.: E. 302(5)], p. 3; Richard Overton, *An Appeal* (London, July 17, 1647), in Wolfe, ed., *Leveller Manifestoes*, p. 159.

41. Overton, *An Appeal*, p. 193: "That according to the law of God, and the old law of the land, matters of theft may not be punished with death"; William Cokayne, *The Foundations of Freedome, Vindicated: or, The Reasons of William Ashurst . . . Examined and discussed* (London, Feb. 17, 1650), [B.L.: E. 541(25)], p. 10; See Veall, *Popular*

be that the Levellers considered the role of the trial jury to be particularly important in such cases. Whether the jury acted on its own or at the behest of the bench, it applied the law according to "conscience" in order to ensure that the defendant would receive his just deserts. This may be what Lilburne had in mind when he referred to the ancient practice by which jurors would "judge" cases. Reform might be achieved by statute, but statute could go only so far: each case, each instance of finding fact, required its own verdict according to "conscience."[42]

In the years preceding Lilburne's 1649 trial, Leveller political thought emerged largely piecemeal in tracts that were responses to immediate political developments. Moreover, before 1649 the chief political threat to Leveller leaders (and specifically to Lilburne) came not from the common law bench but from Parliament.[43] Thus, alongside the reform movement's denunciations of Norman legal institutions and procedures, there developed an attack on the parliamentary exercise of criminal jurisdiction over commoners. It was in this context that Walwyn, Overton, and Lilburne charged that Parliament had adopted the tyrannical ways of the Stuarts. Parliament (or what remained of it) had become, they charged, an arbitrary lawmaking body rather than a representative of the people that defended God's law on the people's behalf. Instead of stripping away the hated Norman perversions of the true common law, Parliament employed them for its own ends. Vindication of the "equity, justice, and mercy" of the law had not been achieved and could not be unless subjects were allowed recourse to their traditional right to trial by peers before a truly law-abiding magistracy.

*Movement for Law Reform*, pp. 128–36, for a discussion of the movement to abolish capital punishment for theft.

42. Lilburne wrote, in 1653, that laws should be devised so that "as little as possible . . . should be left to the discretion, will or pleasure of the Administrator." *The Upright Mans Vindication* (London, Aug. 1, 1653), [B.L.: E. 708(22)], p. 14. As we shall see, however, this did not apply (as of that date) to Lilburne's views on the jury with respect to its taking notice of the probable sanction.

43. Lilburne, *The Copy of a Letter*, pp. 1–2. Lilburne had been arrested and imprisoned by the House of Commons in 1645. He sought specification of the cause of his imprisonment and asserted that he was entitled to "the lawful trial of his equals." Overton, *England's Miserie and Remedie*, pp. 1–6. Overton wrote on behalf of Lilburne, similarly castigating Parliament. Walwyn (*England's Lamentable Slaverie*, pp. 1–6) joined the chorus of criticism of Parliament's treatment of Lilburne in Oct., 1645. Lilburne's major tracts decrying his imprisonment in 1649 and continuing his claim to a right to trial by jury include: *The Legall Fundamentall Liberties* (lst ed., London, June 8, 1649), [B.L.: E. 560(14)]; *An Impeachment of High Treason; Strength out of Weaknesse* (London, Sept. 30, 1649), [B.L.: E. 575(18)]. See also Walwyn, *The Bloody Project* (London, Aug. 21, 1648), in Haller and Davies, eds., *Leveller Tracts*, pp. 135–46.

Lilburne's attacks on Parliament grew out of his arrest and imprisonment for allegedly libelous writings between 1646 and 1648.[44] During those years he attacked both the laws he was charged with breaking and the claims of the Lords and the Commons to jurisdiction to try him. Lilburne's most powerful pre-1649 tracts on the role of judge and jury date from early 1648, when he was seeking a writ of habeas corpus.[45] After the writ was refused Lilburne (and others on his behalf) criticized the courts for acceding to parliamentary despotism. When Lilburne was eventually brought before King's Bench and the court denied having power to release a person held by order of Parliament, Lilburne criticized and belittled the common law bench for its timidity.[46] None of Lilburne's writings during this period articulates a jury law-finding argument; their focus is the right to trial by peers and the alleged usurpation of legal authority by Parliament. The members of Parliament were neither his true judges nor his true jurors. Parliament, he claimed, had resolved law-finding and fact-finding into a single power and had taken that power upon itself.[47]

Lilburne at this early stage expressed a traditional view of the common-law judge-jury relationship. His aim was to deny the right of Parliament to try him; he asserted that Parliament had in notorious instances

arbitrarily and tyrannically summoned and convened men before them (for things decideable and determinable only at common law) without any due process of law, and have taken upon them, contrary to all law, justice, equity, and conscience, to be both informers, prosecutors, witnesses, parties, jury, and judges, and thereupon have passed most illegal, arbitrary, and tyrannical censures upon the free Commons of England . . . when as by the fundamental law of the land, no judge whatsoever, can be judge of matter of law and fact both, it being the proper right of the jury of twelve men, of a man's peers or equals to be judge of matter of fact, which must be proved by legal witnesses duly

44. Gregg, *Free-Born John*, pp. 135–249.

45. Lilburne's pleas for a writ of habeas corpus and for trial by common-law judge and jury include, e.g., *The Prisoners Plea for a Habeas Corpus* (London, April 4, 1648), [B.L.: 434(19)], p. 8 (Lilburne sought "justice without partiality, mercy, pity, or compassion"); *The Prisoners mournful cry, against the Judges of the Kings Bench* (London, May 9, 1648), [B.L.: E. 441(17)], p. 5 (Lilburne sought "the benefit of the law . . . that is all the favor, mercy, pity, and compassion he craves").

46. John Lilburne, *The Lawes Funeral* (London, May 15, 1648), [B.L.: E. 442(13)], pp. l, 26, *et seq*.

47. Lilburne, *People's Prerogative and Priviledges*, p. 41; Lilburne, *A Whip for the present House of Lords, or the Levellers Levelled* (London, Feb. 27, 1648), [B.L.: E. 431(l)], pp. 16–17; Lilburne, *A Plea, or Protest* (London, March 17, 1648), [B.L.: E. 432(18)], pp. 13–14; Lilburne, *The Lawes Funeral*, p. 7.

sworn, and not by the complainer, prosecutor, or party, and then the judge is only to be judge in matter of law.[48]

Lilburne's division of law and fact, and his assignment of the former to the judge, can be found also in the writings of Overton and, indirectly, John Wildman.[49] Wildman approvingly reprinted the petition to the House of Lords in February, 1648, of the conservative Parliamentarian John Maynard, who had met and befriended Lilburne in the Tower. Maynard argued that the "jury are sworn to find according to the evidence." They are "bound to indifferency and impartiality," for they may themselves be passed upon as defendants on another occasion. The jury are to be of the neighborhood, for

> the law presumes, that such may have either some cognizance of the fact, or of some circumstances thereof, or of the party accused, whose condition and manner of conversation is much to be regarded, for discovering his intention in any fact supposed to be treason or felony.

The matter of law, on the other hand, is entrusted to the judge "for preventing all errors, confederacies or partiality."[50]

During the spring of 1648 Lilburne continued to seek release from the Tower and a trial by judge and jury.[51] He never abandoned the conventional law-fact distinction, although at one point he characterized the jury "as it were the God Almighty" and the judge "as the minister or priest to pronounce and declare the sentence and judgment of the God Almighty."[52] When King's Bench refused to free him in May, Lilburne declared that the judges were "indeed and in truth mere ciphers."[53] They were "ciphers" because they deemed themselves powerless to overturn the unlawful acts of the House of Lords, "their superiors."[54] Lilburne would use the epithet "ciphers" to great and different effect in 1649, when

---

48. Lilburne, *People's Prerogative and Priviledges*, p. 41. See also Lilburne, *A Plea, or Protest*, pp. 13–14.

49. [Overton?], *Vox Plebis*, p. 18: "That which is of matter of fact, is to be tried, *per legalem judicium parium*, or a lawful trial of a man's peers: That which is of matter of law, is to be tried by the judges"; John Maynard, *The Humble Plea and Protest* (London, Feb. 14, 1648), reprinted in John Wildman, *The Lawes Subversion* (London, Mar. 6, 1648), [B.L.: E. 431(2)], p. 35: "The matter of fact is only intrusted to the jury, and the matter of law to the judge, for the preventing of all errors, confederacies or partiality."

50. Maynard, *Humble Plea*, pp. 34–35.

51. Lilburne, *A Plea, or Protest*, pp. 13–17.

52. *Ibid.*, p. 17 (margin).

53. Lilburne, *The Lawes Funeral*, p. 1.

54. *Idem.* Lilburne repeated this charge in the spring of 1649, in a letter to Lenthall, the speaker of the House of Commons, to whom Lilburne complained about his imprisonment on order of the Lords. By allowing the Lords to act as they did, the Commons made "ciphers of [themselves]" (*The Legall Fundamentall Liberties*, p. 13).

he was allowed trial at common law by judge and jury. Then, when the target was no longer a parliamentary tribunal, Lilburne found the bench *too* powerful, declared that judges *ought* to be "mere ciphers," and claimed that his jurors were judges both of law and of fact.[55]

Lilburne's 1649 charge that the judges were mere "ciphers" and that the jurors were true judges went to the heart of what the Levellers believed was the establishment fallacy. The allegation challenged the view that the government, rather than the community at large, was ultimately responsible for determining the law. It also brought the myth of the Anglo-Saxon popular (and law-deciding) jury into the courtroom and into political debate. The impact of Lilburne's aphorism upon the history of the English criminal trial jury was profound. But at the time of its introduction, it was merely an aphorism and one without a fully articulated historical basis.

# II

Lilburne was tried in October, 1649, at the Guildhall, before a commission of oyer and terminer on a charge of high treason.[56] The Rump Parliament had passed several statutes of high treason in the spring of that year, a period during which Lilburne was engaged in almost constant publication against a government he succinctly characterized in the title of perhaps his most famous pamphlet, *England's New Chains*.[57] The new Treason Acts extended the crime to include expressions of opinion.[58] The

---

55. See below, text at nn. 67–77.

56. *State Trials*, 4:1269–1470. This account of the trial is a reprint of *The Triall of Lieut. Collonel John Lilburne* [compiled by Clement Walker] (London, Oct., 1649), [B.L.: E. 584(9)]. Walker worked "under Lilburne's direction, from documents provided by him and a stenographic report of the trial" (Haller and Davis, eds., *Leveller Tracts*, p. 31). My account of the trial stresses Lilburne's invocation to his jury and his defense of his claim to the jury right, a subject to which other accounts (understandably) give little space. For other discussions of the trial see the splendid account in Brailsford, *Levellers and the English Revolution,* ch. 30; Gregg, *Free-Born John,* ch. 25; Frank, *The Levellers*, pp. 325–26, n. 105. The Commission included inter alia the Lord Mayor of London, the justices and barons of all the courts of common law, and Richard Keble, one of the keepers of the Great Seal (Brailsford, p. 528). As Aylmer remarks (*Levellers in the English Revolution*, p. 46), it is not clear why the authorities did not try Lilburne, without a jury, before the High Court of Justice. Perhaps they did not dare. The jury had been "impanneled by the sheriffs of London," presumably in the usual way. See John Jones, *Jurors Judges of Law and Fact* (London, Aug. 2, 1650), [B.L.: E. 1414(2)], p. 57. Lilburne challenged four of the original panel before his jury was fully selected (Brailsford, p. 592).

57. John Lilburne, *England's New Chains Discovered* (London, Feb. 26, 1649), in Haller and Davies, eds., *Leveller Tracts*, pp. 157–70 and *The Second Part of England's New Chains Discovered* (London, Mar. 24, 1649), in *ibid.*, pp. 172–89.

58. Veall, *Popular Movement for Law Reform*, p. 163.

accusation against Lilburne was that by his writings he "maliciously, advisedly, and traiterously did plot, contrive and endeavour to stir up, and to raise force" against the government, and that to this end he both denied the supreme authority of the House of Commons and asserted that the government was tyrannical, usurped, and unlawful.[59]

The trial is now famous and Lilburne's defense is well known. At the outset he denied both the authority of the trial commission and the legality of the proceedings, including the closing of the trial to the public.[60] He strongly asserted a right to counsel to assist him in making his way through trial formalities (that he claimed mystified him) including a statute as well as an indictment written in foreign tongues.[61] Lilburne's initial protestations produced a remarkable reply from Judge Jermin that revealed how similar were the antagonists' conceptions of the ultimate source of law, despite their differences on questions of the delegation of authority, the role of the judiciary, and, hence, the allocation of power in the courtroom:

> [B]ut you must know that the law of England is the law of God. . . . It is the law that hath been maintained by our ancestors, by the tried rules of reason, and the prime laws of nature; for it does not depend upon statutes, or written and declared words or lines. . . . Therefore I say again, the law of England is pure primitive reason. . . . A pure innocent hand does set forth a clear unspotted heart. . . . If you refuse to [hold up your hand] you do wilfully deprive yourself of the benefit of one of the main proceedings and customs of the laws of England.[62]

Although Lilburne had spoken (without elucidation) of a "pretended crime" as the basis of his accusation, his plea, when it was finally coaxed from him, revealed no objection to the Act of Treason, either to the procedure that occasioned its passage or to its substance. He pleaded: "That I am not guilty of any of the treasons in manner and form, as they

---

59. Gregg, *Free-Born John*, pp. 294–95. Gregg lists the pamphlets named in Lilburne's indictment: *An Impeachment of High Treason, A Salva Libertate, The Legall Fundamentall Liberties, Outcry of Apprentices, Hue and Cry.* According to an article in the weekly *Mercurius Elencticus* (London, Oct. 22–29, 1649), [B.L.: E. 575(38)] at p. 208, the grand jury foreman told the bench: "We have only found [Lilburne] guilty of writing some part of those books he is charged with in the indictment, but not of high treason: which so astonished the judges, that they looked as if they would have eaten the jury." This (allegedly) occurred in open court; Lilburne had asked that the grand jury that had indicted him appear and repeat its indictment. There is no mention of this incident in the *State Trials* account. A similar version of the incident is recounted in *The First Days Proceedings* (London, 1649), pp. 10–11.

60. *State Trials*, 4:1270–83. The doors to the courtroom were subsequently opened to the public.

61. *Ibid.*, pp. 1291–94.

62. *Ibid.*, pp. 1289–90.

are there laid down in that indictment." If Lilburne's formal plea was that
the Act was null and void, he gave no hint of it in the version of his plea
that he himself later recorded.[63]

In the trial the government first presented its evidence, introducing
witnesses to Lilburne's role in the "treasonous" publications and then
reading at length from some of them.[64] Lilburne's renewed request for
counsel was met with the assurance that the court itself would act as his
counsel when a matter of law arose. The bench was his protector; as
Keble put it, "[W]e are on our lives too as well as you."[65] Thus having
pleaded to the indictment, Lilburne raised two main arguments on the
merits: there was no proof that the writings were published after the
passage of the Treason Acts, an important factual issue; and the evidence
did not suffice for a conviction, because the government could not meet
the "requirement" of two witnesses or prove unlawful intent. The latter
argument mixed a question of law (on which the court ruled, against
Lilburne, that two witnesses were not required) and a question of fact,
sufficiency of the evidence of intent (on which, it is possible, the jury,
having set its own standard, based its acquittal of Lilburne).[66]

63. *Ibid.*, p. 1294. But see Diane Parkin-Speer, "John Lilburne: A Revolutionary
Interprets Statutes and Common Law Due Process," *Law and History Review*, vol. 1 (Fall,
1983), pp. 276–96. Parkin-Speer, whose article appeared while my book was in press, makes
an interesting case for reading Lilburne's assertions to the bench at his 1649 trial in light of
several claims made by Lilburne in *Legall Fundamentall Liberties*, published earlier that
year. The assertions themselves should not be assumed to be part of Lilburne's formal plea,
but they are integral to his overall defense. How many of them were made before his jury
is not clear; most were made to the bench before Lilburne's jury was selected and sworn.
But the assertions and the claims in *Legall Fundamentall Liberties* do indicate the direction
in which Lilburne's thought was moving. Parkin-Speer stresses Lilburne's view that the
special commission of oyer and terminer and, indeed, the continuation in power of the Rump
itself, were unlawful. Presumably, this would have made the Act under which Lilburne was
tried unlawful, though Parkin-Speer doesn't stress this point (perhaps because Lilburne
seems not to have stressed it). Parkin-Speer emphasizes Lilburne's view that "when an Act
of Parliament is against common right, or reason, or repugnant . . . the common law shall
control it, and adjudge this Act to be void" (*Legall Fundamentall Liberties*, p. 50). This
view, drawn (indirectly) from Coke's famous dictum in *Bonham's Case*, was applied to the
Act that continued the Rump in power. Parkin-Speer discusses Lilburne's view that, absent
a lawful Parliament or bench, the defendant was left to interpret the common law. This the
defendant could do given the nature and source of common law; Parkin-Speer relates
Lilburne's view in this regard to his "Protestant individualism," and I do not think her
approach here differs markedly from my own. My lengthy discussion of John Jones, below,
provides a link between this view of law and the Leveller appeal to the jury, a matter about
which Parkin-Speer has very little to say.
64. *State Trials*, 4:1320–73.
65. *Ibid.*, p. 1317.
66. *Ibid.*, pp. 1373–76, 1382–93. The jury's reason for acquitting Lilburne will never be
known. It is less likely that the jury nullified the Treason Acts on which the indictment was

Having been denied assistance of counsel in making his defense, Lilburne asked the court whether he might then speak to the jury on matters of law as well as fact:

> that I may speak in my own behalf unto the jury, my countrymen, upon whose consciences, integrity and honesty, my life, and the lives and liberties of the honest men of this nation, now lies; who are in law judges of law as well as fact, and you [i.e., the court] only the pronouncers of their sentence, will and mind . . .

> *Lord Keble*: Master Lilburne, quietly express yourself, and you do well; the jury are judges of matter of fact altogether, and Judge Coke says so: But I tell you the opinion of the Court, they are not judges of matter of law.

> *Lilburne*: The jury by law are not only judges of fact, but of law also: and you that call yourselves judges of the law, are no more but Norman intruders; and in deed and in truth, if the jury please, are no more but ciphers, to pronounce their verdict.[67]

It is difficult to find a source for this remarkable claim as it applied to the jury; it does not appear in the pre-1649 writings.[68] As it happened, it was Lilburne's adoption of the role of defense counsel that occasioned his invocation of the jury's right to judge matters of law. Had the court acceded to Lilburne's extraordinary claim to counsel, he might never have made his claim to a jury right, although he could have hoped to provoke a debate on the law between his own counsel and the government's attorney, a debate which the jury might then have resolved by its verdict, with or without the approval of the bench. Lilburne's jury-right claim was, in part, couched in the familiar terms of the Norman Yoke theory. His judges were but "Norman intruders," agents of the usurper William and his successors. But what was Lilburne's conception of the pre-Conquest trial? Were there local "judges," or did jurors fill the "judicial" role? In their writings Lilburne and the other Leveller leaders had left their view of the original role of the jury unclear; there is only

based than that it determined Lilburne did not "traiterously . . . plot" to stir up revolution. (In his defense, Lilburne did not spare the jury the details of his acts of patriotism during the Civil War.)

67. *Ibid.*, p. 1379. Note Keble's use of the word "ciphers" earlier in the proceedings (*ibid.*, p. 1314): "You [Lilburne] would make yourself judge in your own cause, which you are not, and so make ciphers of us."

68. Hill (*Puritanism and Revolution*, p. 77) notes that, on an earlier occasion, Henry Marten "told [his] jury to put their hats on in court, to demonstrate the fact that they were 'the Chief Judges in the Court,' and the judges inferior to them." But it is not clear that this meant judges of law; Marten may have been insisting upon the jurors' right to make untrammeled determinations of fact.

occasional indication that they believed that pre-Conquest jurors were "judges."[69]

We may learn something of the nature of Lilburne's theory of jury right from his ensuing colloquy with the bench. Lilburne turned the court's attention to his copy of Coke's *Commentarie upon Littleton*, which he had with him throughout the trial. The first page he quoted related to the assize of novel disseisin: "In this case the recognitors of the assize may say and render to the justices their verdict at large upon the whole matter."[70] This practice, Lilburne asserted, was common in "all actions of trespass or assault, where the jury do not only judge of the validity of the proof of the fact, but also the law, by assigning what damages they think just."[71] Moreover, he noted, Coke stated that verdicts might be general or special, and Littleton observed: "Also in such case, where the inquest may give their verdict at large, if they will take upon them the knowledge of the law, upon the matter they may give their verdict generally."[72] Coke, Lilburne stated, supported Littleton on this point. This, and only this, was the case that Lilburne put at his trial for his claim that jurors were judges of the law. His closing speech dealt with disputed questions of fact (the date of publications alleged to be his; the testimony of the witnesses; his intent), and assertions that his treatment, from the time of his arrest until the closing moments of his trial, prevented him from making a proper defense. Toward the end, he repeated his claim to the right of the jury to judge law as well as fact, again in the course of a protest against the absence of counsel.[73]

The bench thought little of Lilburne's jury-right assertions. They dismissed his contention without addressing themselves to it. Keble's reply to Lilburne's citations from Coke was blunt: "You have spent a little time, but you have done yourself no good; I thought you had understood the law better than I see you do."[74] According to the surviving record, the bench was content to let the matter drop, as Lilburne turned immediately to matters of fact and thereafter made only rhetorical reference to the jury right.

The court may have considered Lilburne's jury-right claim too insubstantial to require rebuttal. At most, Lilburne had pointed out that where there were "mixed" questions of law and fact, the jury was permitted to apply the law to the facts as it found them. It is difficult to believe that Lilburne was unaware that the civil jury to which Coke was

69. See above, n. 36 and accompanying text.
70. *State Trials*, 4:1381 (Coke, *Commentarie upon Littleton*, p. 366).
71. *Idem.*
72. *Idem* (Coke, *Commentarie upon Littleton*, p. 368).
73. *Ibid.*, pp. 1382–1401.
74. *Ibid.*, p. 1381.

referring was subject to attaint for mistaking the law. Surely nothing he read out suggested either that judges might not charge juries on the law or that juries might with impunity disregard judicial charges. Actually, Lilburne had disregarded Coke's contrary views in the very source from which he read to the court. At the end of Littleton's short statement on juries in cases of novel disseisin, from which Lilburne had drawn his first citation, Coke had appended his famous dictum: judges, not juries, are to respond to questions of law; juries, not judges, are to rule on questions of fact.[75] In counterpoint to Littleton's most general statement about jury verdicts, the last to be cited by Lilburne (and the one Lilburne appeared to find most helpful), Coke had immediately juxtaposed: "Although the jury, if they will take upon them (as Littleton here says) the knowledge of the law, may give a general verdict, yet it is dangerous for them so to do, for if they do mistake the law, they run into the danger of an attaint. . . ."[76] Lilburne had in fact read to the court from Coke's comment, but only so far as the words "general verdict"; on the matter of attaint, he had remained silent.

Lilburne's assertion regarding the jury right remained merely rhetorical, not surprisingly since there was no basis at English common law for the proposition that jurors were the only judges of law, and barely any that they might take their own knowledge of the law as their guide. Moreover, Lilburne did not distinguish civil and criminal cases. He found nothing in the law books that diminished the authority of the bench in the conduct of jury trials, though it was at least in part from his disrespect for judges that his inspiration regarding jurors was derived. He quoted out of context, in what the bench must have taken to be an outrageous fashion. Finally, Lilburne gave the jury little direction on those questions of law he apparently meant them to take upon themselves. He seems to have wanted the jury to find unlawful the entire proceeding, especially the standard refusal of counsel, and to acquit him on that account: Lilburne did not at this juncture specifically allege that the law on which he was indicted was void, due either to its substance or to the procedure attending its passage. He seems to have stood on his initial argument concerning the number of witnesses required in cases of treason, and he may have wanted to argue the law of intent. These were weak reeds, but perhaps they were among the issues of law on which his "countrymen" were to pass their judgment.[77]

And pass judgment they did. Lilburne's jury took less than an hour to find him not guilty. Brailsford has described the ensuing scene:

75. Coke, *Commentarie upon Littleton*, p. 366.
76. *Ibid.*, p. 368.
77. See above, nn. 63–66 and accompanying text.

The jury were then discharged, and through the cheering multitudes Major-General Skippon escorted the prisoner back to the Tower. The very soldiers who guarded him shouted for joy. . . . At the Fleet Bridge the people lit bonfires. . . . As the evening wore on, the church bells rang out and bonfires sprang up all over the City, while the people in their thousands shouted and drank and feasted in the streets.[78]

In honor of the jury a medal was soon struck bearing their names, Lilburne's portrait, and an inscription: "John Lilburne, saved by the power of the Lord and the integrity of his jury, who are judge of law as well as fact."[79] At least in London, events had given prominence to Lilburne's invocation to his jury, whatever the common man took its meaning to have been.

The weakness of Lilburne's jury-right claim must have been apparent to many contemporaries. Certainly it was apparent to lawyer Henry Parker, a proponent of moderate law reform, who launched a powerful attack on Lilburne in his tract, *A Letter of Due Censure*, published in the spring of 1650.[80] (Parker's tract took no account of the recently published *Judges Judged*, the first of John Jones's two tracts in defense of Lilburne. That tract and Jones's second one—a reply to Parker—will be considered together in the next section.) Parker made short work of Lilburne's "authorities":

All that is affirmed by Littleton and Coke is this, that in some cases the inquest may render a verdict at large upon the whole matter. . . . In the application of these authorities, you rush hastily upon three gross errors. For first you strain these authorities to all cases and questions of law, whether easy or uneasy whatsoever, and this cannot be done without manifest violence to the words of your authors. Secondly, you strain these authorities to all jurors whatsoever, whether they have knowledge of the law, or not. . . . Thirdly . . . you infer: therefore the judges are mere ciphers, therefore the judges have no right or power to deliver their judgments, therefore the determination of the judges is no way forcible or obliging. This is a *non sequitur*. For though the verdict be given in upon the whole matter, and so enclose law as well as fact, yet the binding force of the verdict, as to matter of law, may be derived from the sanction and ratification of the judges, not from the jurisdiction of the inquest. And it may well be supposed, that the jurors may err in matter of law, in which case the judges must alter the erroneous verdict by a contrary judgment.[81]

---

78. Brailsford, *Levellers and the English Revolution*, p. 602.
79. *Ibid.*, p. 603.
80. Henry Parker, *A Letter of Due Censure* (London, June 21, 1650), [B.L.: E. 603(14)].
81. *Ibid.*, pp. 23–24.

Parker excoriated Lilburne for belittling his judges and mocked him for setting up his jurors above the bench. Among the "common tradesmen, and husbandmen, such as ordinarily [are] empanelled, there is not one of a thousand that understands law in a point of any intricacy."[82] Lilburne, Parker retorted, had concluded that "judges, because they understand the law, are to be degraded."[83]

These were all points well taken. Lilburne appears foolish to have taken his stand on Coke, and the reliance on civil cases made his invocation of jurors' knowledge of law all too suspect. But Lilburne was headed in another direction. His claims were based not upon existing law or jury practice, but upon what he conceived to be his heritage, his birthright. They were claims upon "good law" and upon a tradition of resistance to longstanding adulterations of that law.[84] Although Lilburne did not elaborate the point, the jury right was a claim—an aphorism—based on the Levellers' political theory. If Lilburne's claim is viewed in the light of the Levellers' understanding of England before the Conquest, that claim gains considerably in force and content.

# III

Lilburne's aphorism was given specific meaning in the two most detailed and interesting of the Interregnum jury tracts, *The Judges Judged* and *Jurors Judges*, written in 1650 by John Jones.[85] These tracts were at once commentaries on Lilburne's 1649 trial and attacks on Coke's version of the history of the criminal trial jury. Jones's writings, which contained the most important discussion and analysis of trial by jury in England before the Restoration, built upon Leveller historical learning and politi-

---

82. *Ibid.*, p. 24.
83. *Ibid.*, p. 21.
84. See *The Second Part of the Triall of Lieut. Col. John Lilburn* (London, Dec. 1, 1649), [B.L.: E. 598(12)], written by Clement Walker with Lilburne's help (see Frank, *The Levellers*, p. 227). The author(s) claim that in the trial of Sir Nicholas Throckmorton ("Throg-Morton") in 1554 "the jury took upon themselves to be judges of law as well as fact, and against the will and minds of all the judges acquitted the prisoner, and at the Bar justified their verdict and would not revoke it. . . . Without doubt . . . Lilburne had seriously read over that notable trial of . . . Throgmorton, in whose very steps he treads, in making his application to the jury, as the absolute guardians and judges of his life, as he in Queen Mary's time did" (pp. 27–28). Lilburne had probably found the account of Throckmorton's trial in Holinshed. See Raphael Holinshed, *Chronicles of England, Scotland, and Ireland* (orig. published ca. 1579, 6 vols., London, 1808), vol. 4, pp. 31–55. In Holinshed's account, Throckmorton told the jury that the statutes applied in his case were not according to God's law (p. 54), but in his final statement to the jury he did not directly appeal to them as judges of law (p. 55).
85. John Jones, *Judges Judged Out of Their Own Mouthes* (London, May 6, 1650), [B.L.: E. 1414(1)]; *Jurors Judges of Law and Fact* (London, Aug. 2, 1650), [B.L.: E. 1414(2)].

cal theory. Although Jones was not, strictly speaking, a Leveller, his works reveal the radical implications of the Leveller position.[86]

In *Judges Judged*, Jones labored to demonstrate that the later medieval monarchs had overturned a system of local determination of pleas in which the original royal justices in eyre had played a crucial and popular part. This historiographical tour de force, based upon an intricate and novel argument, developed more systematically than any other contribution to the Norman Yoke tradition an attack on the Westminster judiciary in general and on Sir Edward Coke in particular.

> Are not all the people of England disseised of their freehold, liberties, franchises, and free customs, when they are deprived of that justice which they ought to have administered amongst them at home by virtue of the King's writs . . . directed to sheriffs of their own choice, in their own counties or stewards of hundreds, and courts baron, in their precincts, where the free-holders themselves are judges themselves, by ancient common-laws, and customs of England, before Magna Charta and by it declared, and confirmed unto them as aforesaid?[87]

The answer to this rhetorical question was obvious.

But how had the original system of justice lapsed? King's Bench, Jones argued, had imposed itself upon the system of popular justice. The critical turning point in the history of the judicial system, according to Jones, began with the failure of King's Bench to follow up on indictments before sheriffs and itinerant justices that had not led to trial and punishment before justices in eyre. The Statute *Articuli Super Cartas* (1300) sought to remedy this situation.[88] It provided, said Jones, for temporary commissions to royal justices, the later justices of trailbaston, who were empowered to act *on their own discretion* in pursuing indictments that had not been prosecuted. The result of this series of events was the undermining of the justices in eyre. This was doubly unfortunate. First, the justices in eyre had not been responsible for the original defects; the fault lay with King's Bench, which had failed to ensure the making of indictments. Moreover, Jones asserted, the justices in eyre had never been entrusted with discretion to decide whether fines or imprisonment

---

86. Veall (*Popular Movement for Law Reform*, p. 103) describes Jones as a pamphleteer "sympathetic to the Levellers." My discussion places Jones as a critic of contemporary lawyers and legal practices, whose historical account of the bench and jury has much in common with Leveller notions about the source of human rights, the delegation of authority, and the constraints on the power of delegates. In the main, I believe that on these issues Jones was elaborating on Leveller thought in a way that the leading Leveller writers (who admittedly did not themselves speak with a single voice) would have approved, at least as of 1649–50.

87. *Judges Judged*, p. 36.

88. Stat. 28 Edw. 1.

*

ought to be imposed. The grant of that power to royal justices in Westminster represented an unwelcome shift of power away from the local community. The final stage, regular and routine trial by royal justices of gaol delivery, destroyed whatever vestiges of the old, locally based system had persisted into the fourteenth century.[89]

Jones argued that, unlike King's Bench, the justices in eyre predated Magna Carta and were confirmed by that document.[90] Further, the justices were "chosen by the people,"[91] a conclusion Jones drew from Coke's assertion that "[o]fficers or ministers . . . for execution of justice . . . were . . . chosen in full and open county, by the freeholders . . .,"[92] which in reality referred to sheriffs, keepers of the peace, and coroners, but not, of course, to justices in eyre. Jones read Magna Carta's prescription "that all offenders ought to be amerced by their equals, according to the quantity of their trespass" to have given freemen the power, in county court, before sheriffs or justices of local choosing, to determine fines and sentences of imprisonment. Jones purported to have understood this system to have predated Magna Carta, and in its essentials to have predated Henry II. He berated Coke for failing to acknowledge the seniority of the justices in eyre to the more recent King's Bench, ascribing Coke's view to "spite and envy."

> And where, in this leaf, he would persuade the people to suspect justices in eyre of corruption and of monopolizing justice to wrong the people that chose them, can the people believe that these justices (who are to be chosen by them, and to be displaced by them, when and as often as they see cause) will, or can wrong them more than those chosen by the King and his servants, without their consent, unless they can believe that they may be persuaded to give their consent to wrong themselves?[93]

Finally, Jones argued that the Crown had duplicitously turned the Statute *Articuli* on its head. The statute's provision to supply justice "where no remedy was before," he asserted, had in fact been intended to give justices in eyre power to move against the king's servants in Westminster, who had failed to give force to the original system. The justices in eyre were supposed to remain an instrument of the people; their jurisdiction was to extend beyond enquiring into offenders against the laws—they were now to hear of the failure of royal justices to execute

---

89. *Ibid.*, pp. 75–82.
90. *Ibid.*, p. 79.
91. *Idem.*
92. *Idem*; Sir Edward Coke, *The Second Part of the Institutes of the Laws of England* (3rd ed., London, 1669), fol. 558.
93. *Judges Judged*, p. 80.

upon the people's indictments and assignments of punishment. Coke's interpretation of the statute had supported that of the Crown, which, Jones argued, turned the mandate of Parliament against the people's courts and judges, and instead concentrated all judicial power in the hands of royal servants, the justices of King's Bench—a concentration of power to which Coke was himself heir.[94]

Jones's use of historical evidence was, to say the least, amateurish and manipulative. He primarily depended upon Coke's flawed account, which he reworked to suit his own point of view. The immediate target of Jones's attack was the Commonwealth bench. Rather than reject the entire history of the royal judiciary, Jones sought to divorce the early period of the eyre system from its successor stages. In this lay his originality, a flight of fancy that led to ludicrous conclusions: the hated eyres, whose justices were the scourge of the countryside, appeared in Jones's account as popular visitations to local tribunals whose ancient and definitive powers continued unabated, before whom fines and amercements were imposed by "equals," as ordered by Magna Carta. Judicial history had been rewritten in a way that actually glorified one of its darker moments.[95]

Jones's version of legal history after the Conquest deemphasized the importance of the Conquest itself and thus did not depend so heavily as some other accounts on the sparse Anglo-Saxon evidence. Unlike Lilburne's or later versions, it conceded a role for royal justices, while accounting for their authority in such a way as to make them agents of the people. Nevertheless, this elaborate attack on Coke and on the Westminster bench shared a central objective with the Leveller writings of the late 1640s: the resurrection and strengthening of the imaginary "original" jury system at the expense of the bench. Jones's history of the judiciary was in fact a history of the jury system, and it promoted two of the most important aims of the radical reform movement, the decentralization of legal institutions and the conferral upon the jury of control over the law. Jones's tract distorted history in the service of a theory of a community-based system of law and legal administration.

In *Jurors Judges of Law and Fact* Jones turned his attention more directly to the question of the role of the jury.[96] This essay, published in August of 1650, filled in his historical account of the judiciary by

94. *Ibid.*, pp. 79–82.
95. See above, Chapter 1, text at n. 43, for a discussion of the judicial eyre.
96. See above, n. 85. In *Judges Judged*, Jones had written about the jurors as judges of fact: "Are not men's lives triable for matter of fact, and not of law (except treasons that reach to thoughts?) Are not jurors the judges of matters of fact? What great learning, or experience in law is requisite for a judge to pronounce the sentence of death, where the verdict has determined the life?" (p. 27).

describing (once again in details drawn largely from Coke) the powers of jurors who gave evidence before royal officials. The tract also set forth a theory of law that substantiated Leveller claims. The occasion for Jones's tract on jurors was the publication in June of Henry Parker's *A Letter of Due Censure*, which attacked Lilburne's arguments to the jury in his trial of the preceding year.[97] Jones replied to Parker:

> In the next place, where you say Mr. Lilburne promoted his twelve men to a new jurisdiction: I am sure, that is another lie of yours, for you may read in the Lord Coke's *Institutions* upon the thirty-fifth chapter of Magna Charta that county courts, courts baron, sheriff's tourns, and leets were in use before King Alfred's time; in all of which courts the jurors were the judges, and their then untraversable verdicts were the judgments in all causes; and sheriffs and stewards, who were the King's commissary judges in their tourns, and leets, . . . were and still are but the suitors' clerks in counties, hundreds and courts baron, to enter their judgments, and do execution thereupon by themselves and their bailiffs, as public servants, or ministers of common justice, to their jurors, and the rest of the Commonwealth.[98]

Jones's account of legal institutions in the period before King's Bench and its circuit justices took control of all felonies managed to jumble public and private courts, criminal trials and view of frankpledge, local and royal officials, and, indeed, prefeudal and feudal England. All judicial proceedings, Jones asserted, culminated in the "untraversable" verdicts of jurors, verdicts that were attended and later executed by royal officials.[99] That such officials had no power save that of execution and that such power involved no discretionary aspects was clear in Jones's mind. Indeed, these were propositions that flowed from the nature and sources of legal command:

> And what is dissenting, or not assenting to jurors' verdicts, but a denial, which is more than a failure of justice, for the speeding whereof they [i.e., the judges] may have no negative voice; for ordinary jurisdiction that was the Supreme One that gave the sovereign (which is superior to every singular person) to Kings (as now to the keepers of the liberties of England); there is still the superlative jurisdiction beyond all comparison, that can be inferior to no authorities, but God's that gave it to his people, to his children, not to be given by them to any above them in their generalities, but himself, from whom they have received, and to whom they must restore themselves and all that is theirs, but to be contrived, and substituted by them unto the worthiest

97. Parker, *A Letter of Due Censure*.
98. *Jurors Judges*, pp. 24–25.
99. *Idem*.

men amongst them, to be employed for and under them, as they might find most convenient for their worldly peace and subordinate government; to which end they deputed kings, as now the Parliament hath done keepers of the liberties of England, *reserving so much of their ancient ordinary jurisdiction to freemen, that none but such may be jurors, and none but such may be their judges for their lives, lands, and estates.* And therefore as the keepers of our liberties are subordinate to the Parliament, so are their commissaries to them, and both in their judgments, to the verdicts of the jurors, which [are] their true saying of the whole matter, as well for law, as fact.[100]

All that remained was the power, and duty, of execution, for which legal orders—writs *de procedendo ad judicium*, attachment, and compulsion to execute—were provided. The remedy of attaint was also available to the prosecution or the defendant, Jones announced, but it gained its force and effect only through the verdict (on law as well as fact) of a subsequent jury.[101]

It was this system of jury domination of the law, Jones argued, that later and unwarranted extensions of power to royal justices undermined. The original and total jurisdiction of jurors derived from God's grant of divine command to the people. All power was thereafter delegated by the people, through monarchs, their agents, to royal officials. Jurors were more "ancient" than such officials and retained full power over the law; as officialdom grew, embroiled itself in civil wars, and changed its form, "always the freemen judged their neighbors constantly."[102] Until, i.e., the destruction of justices in eyre by the Westminster bench. Thereafter the history of the judiciary was the history of the usurpation of a power implanted in the people by God. It was an account of a changing structure of officialdom, of centralization, and of waning local judicial institutions, that, by the seventeenth century, had produced a perversion of justice:

But how many true men have been hanged, and thieves saved by judges interposing, and obtruding their pestiferous pretended learning and experience in their laws between the weak consciences of ignorant jurors, and the truth? Which kind of jurors they make sheriffs return for such purposes, when they may have such returned as know the facts, and have sounder learning and experience in express law than themselves.[103]

---

100. *Ibid.*, pp. 32–35 (emphasis added).
101. *Ibid.*, pp. 35, 44.
102. *Ibid.*, p. 47. See also *ibid.*, pp. 49 *et seq.*, for Jones's challenge to Parker's assertion that "mechanics, bred up illiterately to handicrafts" were not capable of understanding the law.
103. *Judges Judged*, p. 27. Jones's (surprising) remark about thieves suggests that,

# IV

Jones's history ended where the jury debate had begun: the complaints about judicial packing and badgering of juries that arose just before the creation of the Commonwealth. Jones resorted to historical discussion in order to counter the view that Lilburne's defense was based upon a fictional jury right. According to Jones, the right to jury trial was ancient and had never wholly been taken away, though its true purpose had been undermined by the development of the judiciary. Not only was jury trial ancient, but through usage and through that compilation of good usage, Magna Carta, it had been confirmed as one of the liberties of Englishmen. It was, however, more than one of the fundamental liberties. The very existence of jury trial, and the scope of the jurors' power, rested ultimately on the source of law. God had granted to the people—to the community—knowledge of his law. Though the people had, in turn, delegated ministerial functions to officials, judicial responsibility had been retained by the community; the jurors declared and applied the law in judging their fellows. Judicial badgering usurped the people's right and duty not only to find fact but to decide the law. To the people, as the source of knowledge of the true law, fell the responsibility to interpret the law. In this theory lay the originality and power of Jones's version of radical jury ideology.

At first glance, Jones's concept of the source of law does not seem a radical departure from Interregnum political theory. Even the most fervent republicans, who accorded absolute power to parliamentary edict, would have agreed that statute represented an application of divinely inspired reason by delegates of the people. The striking feature of Jones's view, however, was its insistence that the power of ultimate declaration of the law had not been delegated—not, at least, that declaration of law to be made in the context of judgment by peers. Presumably such judgment would by its nature conform to the essence of statutory pronouncement, but the latter was a collateral lawmaking process, less fundamental and less pure precisely because it was the by-product of the delegation of authority to enact law on divine command.

Establishment political theory developed the notion of delegation much further than Jones (and perhaps the more radical Levellers) allowed. Prudence—divinely inspired reason, Commonwealth officials might have said—dictated that because the law was by nature complex, its interpretation was beyond the lay mind. Consistency, fairness, and adherence to legislative intent required the knowledgeable guidance of the judge. The

despite his strong reliance on Scripture, he was not among those who opposed the death penalty for theft—at least not in some kinds of cases.

people's legislative representatives had spoken in the framing of laws; what remained was the interpretation of those laws by trained legal minds. Jurors therefore had nothing to do with law; their province was solely the finding of fact.

In an attempt to defend Lilburne's claim regarding the right and duty of the trial jury, Jones drew upon ideas in Leveller writings of the late 1640s, making explicit for the first time the implications of those ideas. For most Levellers, as we have seen, the institution of the bench and its role in stating the law was a given. They shared Jones's view of the source and nature of law and seem to have gone well beyond the official notion of the jury's role in their discussion of verdicts according to conscience. But they had subsumed the jury's interpreting of legal mandate and its doing of discretionary justice within the fact-finding process.[104] Jones spoke for all the Levellers when he articulated the relationship between jury verdicts and ultimate justice but only for some in his denial of a law-declaring role for the bench. History and theory mandated for Jones a conclusion that logic supported but did not necessitate. In reality, we have seen, judge and jury shared the law-finding power that traditional legal theory gave exclusively to the bench. So long as the bench accepted even discretionary, merciful jury verdicts as though they were purely findings on fact, the fact-finding process remained relatively open-ended and the Leveller discussion of the role of conscience and just deserts could be understood as a commentary upon that process. Disagreement might arise concerning the considerations appropriate to the finding of fact, but disagreement need not take the form of a debate over the legitimacy of the traditional law/fact dichotomy.

Lilburne's trial and Jones's tracts, however, made it difficult to view Leveller thought as concerned only with fact-finding. They brought the latent law-finding tendencies of Leveller writings to the surface, thereby seemingly connecting Leveller political and social thought to a theory of the trial that threatened governmental control over law and legal proceedings. Through Jones's tracts we may better understand not only the implications of Lilburne's claims but also how far those claims and the tendencies of the pre-1650 radical law tracts, even those with a conventional view of institutional arrangements, must have suggested a revolution in the administration of criminal law.

At base, the most radical theory of jury trial clashed with the Cokeian view on the issues of delegation and the nature, if not the original source, of law. The Levellers insisted that law was not inherently complex; in criminal trials it was just a matter of right and wrong. Law came to the

---

104. See above, nn. 39–41 and accompanying text. See, however, James Frese, *A Second Why Not*, p. viii.

mind and conscience of the simplest man. The very nature of law presumed judgment by peers in accordance with standards comprehensible to the defendant. Jury trial was not to be formed in the image of enacted laws; rather, enacted laws were to conform to the logic and purpose of trial by jury. The more they did so, the more they would become simple and direct expressions of reason based on divine command.[105]

Simple, direct expressions of reason: such were the worldly embodiments of God's law. If only the common law might be reduced to that form. There was, of course, an available source for determination of right and wrong and of the punishment appropriate to specific wrongful acts: Jones and most of the Levellers were ready to advert to the Scriptures. But what constituted commission even of those wrongs? When was there malice in the heart? That mixed question of law and fact required interpretation, an application of reason to the facts and, thus, a judgment according to divine inspiration. In short, it was within the province of the jury. There had been a time, so the theory ran, when the jury functioned in its purest form, before the growth of a meddling judiciary, and while laws were yet in the language of the people and were pronounced publicly by the wisest in the hundred moot. Those were the days of the vindication of God's law, as that law was meant to be vindicated. Now the post-Reformation Church had once again been purified, stripped of its diverting ritual, its members brought close to God. The importance both of the relationship between man and God and of the ongoing process by which men achieved an understanding of the meaning of God's will had been affirmed: each person would read, comprehend, and interpret Scripture for himself. Thus could the common law now be purified, returned to its original form and meaning, made conformable to the essence of Scripture. Like the Anglo-Saxon "lawmen," the latter-day jurors would come to know and interpret the law. Judgment would be passed as the conscience directed.[106]

"Conscience," of course, embodied the community's sense of justice. Only the community could know the particular nature of the actor and his deed. Legal decentralization meant less expense and delay, greater freedom from judicial interposition; but it also meant community control and a resurrection of the true jury of neighbors. It meant as well vindication of the community's sense of justice as guided by its knowledge of the defendant and his act, and as guided by its understanding of law. Thus were the most radical legal minds radical purifiers. Their vision

---

105. Schenk, *Concern for Justice in the Puritan Revolution*, pp. 78–79.
106. See Hill, *Puritanism and Revolution*, p. 81, for discussion of the importance of the translation of the Bible into simple and direct language.

of the true English society imagined a pre-Conquest community of Puritan freemen, equal in the eyes of God, whose judgments they passed upon their peers gone astray.[107]

So read, the arguments of the radical Levellers augured a truly decentralized system of criminal law.[108] Not only would trials be local, but—as authorities especially might have perceived it—law itself would be local and no longer "common" in the original sense of that term. Moreover, the very purpose and nature of the legal system, as represented by the handful of most radical tracts, had little in common with the established understanding of that system. For the radicals, the criminal law was a matrix of community mores, to be imposed communally—neighbors judging neighbors. Shared experiences and context would guarantee fairness. This system was corrective, perhaps in a therapeutic sense, or retributive, as in the Old Testament tradition. The radical reformers were not primarily concerned with a national crime wave, with judicial administration, or with interpretation and enforcement of parliamentary statute. For them the criminal law was primarily a process of community self-identification and confirmation, and only second a system of rational self-defense.

## V

Both Cromwell and the radical Levellers began with the Scriptures; their legal theories shared the same ultimate premise. For Cromwell, however, the exigencies of governance revealed the divine origins of delegation of authority to the Godly Magistrate. The criminal trial jury was a tool devised and employed by the Magistrate. It informed him in the use of his wisdom but only in a most limited sense. It comes as no surprise that Interregnum law reform conceded the existence of juries but not much more. Between 1652 and 1655, during the period in which the Hale Commission was active and after the publication of nearly all of the radical Leveller pamphlets, the government entertained proposals regard-

107. This I take to be the implication of Jones's account of law, community, and jury trial. I am bringing together a body of radical Leveller ideas in a way that not even Jones did in order to suggest what must have underlain Jones's view of the jury. It also seems to me that Jones saw in the jury the true embodiment of historical continuity—or the institution that retained the potential for vindicating God's law, the true theory of delegation, and the revival of England's "pure" society. Although the rights of Englishmen could be understood as "natural rights," they could also be identified with the original English society. See above, nn. 32, 33.

108. Hill (*Puritanism and Revolution*, p. 81) states that the oft-repeated Leveller demand for trials in the county or hundred was "like the elevation of the jury over the judge . . . an appeal from the existing state power to surviving vestiges of the old communal institutions."

ing jury composition and challenges to jurors, with the end of making the jury a more reliable system of fact-finding.[109] The reforms were based on the assumption that the judges found the law and that the judges were themselves tightly controlled agents of a centralized system.

The law tracts of the early 1650s reveal the distance between the radical Leveller conception of the criminal trial jury and the perspective of moderate reform proponents. Though it was during this period that reform activity reached its height, it proceeded largely on establishment terms. The principal areas of reform interest included private law, equity, and court procedure. On the criminal side, the law of sanctions garnered most interest; and there was talk of gaol reform: even the most compla-cent men of affairs knew a scandal when they saw one.[110]

The question of jury reform centered more often on the civil than on the criminal trial jury. The tracts resonate with the traditional concerns of men of property. Even the Levellers—men of property themselves—[111] complained as much or more about the costs, delays, and inconveniences of private suits. Nevertheless, the criminal trial jury had come to symbolize the real testing point regarding lay participation in matters of government. The debate between Lilburne and Jones on the one hand, and Parker on the other, continued to reverberate even after the eclipse of the Leveller party.

Parker himself continued to criticize the Levellers' program of de-centralization. In a tract on the resolution of "Cases Testamentary" Parker advocated reforms that would reduce the "surplusage of testa-mentary business," but he opposed shifting the locus of litigation from Westminster to the provinces. Conceding that local litigation was "the old manner of jurisdiction, which was used in England long before the Norman Conquest," Parker asserted that England was no longer "a cantonized country" that "obeyed several petty princes." He attacked "that party which would cantonize us the second time" and thereby increase "quarrels and controversies." Parker's targets here were "il-literate judges, and unexpert counsellors" rather than jurors who were

---

109. The Commission's discussions of reform proposals are preserved in "Minutes of the Extra-Parliamentary Committee for regulating the law," B.L. MS Add. 35,863. Discussion of the jury (mostly civil) is at p. 41 (juror qualifications and methods of appointment), p. 65 (jurors to value land for payment of debt), pp. 77–81 (juries to be retained in probate cases). I am most grateful for the help of Professor Cotterell, who kindly furnished me with a guide to these and other parts of the "Minutes." She corroborated my own conclusion that the Commission was attempting to strengthen the jury system by raising qualifications with regard both to economic status and to literacy.

110. Veall, *Popular Movement for Law Reform*, Chapter 6.

111. *Ibid.*, p. 100.

not up to the task.[112] Other moderate reformers, however, did not spare the jury. Henry Robinson complained that "most commonly one or two active and nimble-pated men oversway all the rest . . . and too often for the worst." Moreover, they escaped punishment:

> If they give a corrupt or erroneous verdict, there cannot justly be any penalty inflicted on them, because they may pretend they did at first declare themselves unfit for such employment: that they undertook it unwillingly, but were compelled thereunto; and when they saw there was no avoiding it, they endeavored to proceed therein according to the uprightness of their own consciences; if they be thought to have done amiss, it was but what they could not remedy, and are heartily sorry for it.[113]

Robinson, whose main concern was with civil causes, preferred a county-based system with one judge for each hundred. The judge, who would not be elected by residents of the locale, so that he would not be "swayed with alliance," would decide cases without the use of a jury.[114] John March, who professed to respect the jury in civil and criminal cases as "the most exact and equal way of trial in the world," pleaded for reform of the rules of qualification.[115] He sought "twelve able understanding gentlemen . . . such as are known in their country to be men of competent worth for so great an employment [i.e., jury service]." This would preserve the institution of the jury as "the only judges of matters of fact." March resisted the notion that the jury ought to be closely directed by the judge. He acknowledged that juries were "weak and ignorant," but sincerely desired to see the institution strengthened. March believed jurors ought to "judge [fact] according to their own conscience"; they might ask the judge's advice but were not bound to do so, nor if they did ask were they "tied to follow it."[116] Only reform could save the virtues of the jury system, and that reform ought to deal with procedures for securing responsible (and respectable) jurors, not with the existing relationship between judge and jury. This was in fact the path of reform taken by the Hale Commission.[117]

112. Henry Parker, *Reformation in Courts, and Cases Testamentary* (London, Nov. 14, 1650), [B.L.: E. 616(5)], p. 7.
113. Henry Robinson, *Certain Considerations . . . to a more speedy, cheap and equall distribution of Justice* (London, Nov. 14, 1650), [B.L.: E. 616(2)], pp. 2–3.
114. *Ibid.*, p. 11.
115. John March, *Amicus Reipublicae. The Commonwealths Friend or An Exact and Speedie Course to Justice and Right* (London, May 19, 1651), [B.L.: E. 1360(1)], p. 100.
116. *Ibid.*, pp. 104, 103, 102, 103.
117. See "Several Draughts of Acts . . ." (London, July 12, 1653), in *A Collection of Scarce and Valuable Tracts (Somers' Tracts)*, 13 vols. (2nd ed., London, 1809–15), vol. 6 (1811), pp. 218–19, § xxx–xxxiii.

The voices of radical trial jury proponents were still audible during these years, but barely so. Stripped of a movement—even, for a time, of a prominent leader—and with no foothold within the moderate law reform camp that dominated the work of the Hale Commission (whose own place within the councils of government was tenuous), radical jury proponents were left to aim their arguments and epithets at a deaf political establishment. Walwyn's *Juries Justified,* the most significant jury tract to appear after the publication of Jones's writings and before Lilburne's 1653 trial, was a reply to Robinson's critique of the jury. Walwyn reiterated the Leveller historical position. Never one to accept all of Magna Carta uncritically, Walwyn distinguished its "superstitious" elements ("[that] are but as a French garb or clothing, which the Conqueror and his successors, by main strength, forced our forefathers to put on") from its "true English liberties" that had been "reduced into that excellent law . . . the Petition of Right, and wherein trials *per* juries is the principal."[118] Robinson was wrong, Walwyn asserted: there were "understanding fit men" in every hundred. Everything depended, of course, upon what one thought the nature of law and the jury's task ought to be. For Walwyn, the jury was to discern "right and wrong," what "an ordinary capacity (careful to keep a good conscience, and [one] that is tender of an oath) shall soon perceive the true state thereof; and be able to do right therein according to the evidence."[119]

Walwyn denied that one or two wrongheaded jurors could determine the outcome; the unanimity requirement prevented that. Moreover, he rebutted Robinson's charge that there was no penalty for a corrupt or erroneous verdict; the jury, he said, faced the possibility of an attaint.[120] Perhaps Walwyn, like Robinson, had civil causes mainly in mind, for a controlled tone pervades *Juries Justified.* The issue was the right of the local community to resolve its own "causes and controversies" between private parties rather than to resolve those between society and an alleged criminal offender.

Walwyn's renewal of the Norman Yoke theme was carried forward in early 1652 by several tracts. Their authors opposed the setting of a steep property qualification for jury service, which would "violate" the "fundamental constitution."[121] Causes were to be tried locally by people, to

118. William Walwyn, *Juries Justified: or, a Word of Correction to Mr. Henry Robinson* (London, Dec. 2, 1651), [B.L.: E. 618(9)], p. 5.
119. *Ibid.,* pp. 4, 9.
120. *Ibid.,* pp. 10–11.
121. *The Onely Right Rule for Regulating The Lawes and Liberties of the People of England* (London, Jan. 28, 1652), [B.L.: E. 684(33)], p. 6. This tract also asserted "that until the Norman Conquest, the Nation never knew or felt the charge, trouble, or intanglements of judges, lawyers, attorneys, solicitors, filors, and the rest" (p. 5). See also *To the Supreme*

whom, in the words of one writer, "the laws shall be read by the minister . . . four times a year."[122] In two of these tracts there was a distinctly religious tone reflecting the views of the radical religious reformers who had begun to figure more prominently than the remnant of the Leveller party.[123] And there was, too, a shift of focus from the role of the jury to the appropriate sanctions for serious offenses.[124] Here the last voices of the Leveller movement melded with those of many Interregnum reform proponents. It had long been common, and even respectable, to oppose the imposition of capital punishment for theft. One had only to separate the question of who would control the determination of punishment from the matter of what that punishment ought to be to gain an ear among even the moderate proponents of law reform.

The movement for reform of sanctions, which lasted until the closing years of the Interregnum, united those who believed that the criminal law ought to conform to scriptural command with those whose main concern was more practical—that, e.g., thieves, with little to lose, were more inclined to kill their victims so that they could not bear witness against them.[125] The movement produced the first great burst of English penological writing, which subsequently fed into Continental streams and re-emerged in England a century later.[126] The English writings were themselves influenced by the early New England experience, where the ideas they expressed had been put into practice three decades before. In that setting, the administration of the criminal law was dominated by godly magistrates; the criminal trial jury played as yet a less significant role than it did in the parent country.[127] The English experience, on the other hand,

Authority, the Parliament of the Common-Wealth of England (London, June 29, 1652), [B.L.: 699 f. 16(54)].

122. Articles of High-Treason . . . against One Hundred and fifty Judges, Lawyers, and Attornies (London, Feb. 21, 1652), [B.L.: E. 655(10)], p. 8. For the Levellers this did not mean the most common people. As has often been said, the Diggers viewed the jury, even the Leveller version of it, as an instrument of the propertied classes. See, e.g., Veall, Popular Movement for Law Reform, p. 156. I suspect, however, that Winstanley's political (as opposed to religious) objections to the jury had more to do with the civil than the criminal jury (save perhaps for criminal cases involving trespass to land).

123. Articles of High-Treason, p. 8. See also John Cook, Monarchy no Creature of Gods making (London, Feb. 26, 1652), [B.L.: E. 1238(l)]. Cook argued that law should be "that which the judicious and most learned men judge so to be, not the sense or judgment of any private man" (p. 34). See below, n. 125 and accompanying text. On religious radicalism and law reform see Shapiro, Law Reform in Seventeenth Century England, p. 290.

124. E.g. The Onely Right Rule, p. 9; Articles of High Treason, p. 8. See above, n. 41 and accompanying text.

125. For the movement to abolish the death penalty see Veall, Popular Movement for Law Reform, pp. 128–36.

126. See below, Chapter 7, section III.

127. See e.g. George L. Haskins, Law and Authority in Early Massachusetts (New York,

was doubtless influenced by the fact of juries and jury behavior. Reform writers rarely referred to actual practice, but it is difficult to believe that they were not seeking to legitimize attitudes given daily expression in the courts of law, where judge and jury shared the power of mitigation generally and in cases of theft especially.[128] Moreover, most reformers were proposing an alternative sanction that accorded with prevailing notions of justice: imprisonment at hard labor, rehabilitation, and, above all, restitution.[129]

Within this embryonic movement the contribution of the Levellers was distinctive. More than any other group, they connected the scriptural approach to sanctions with the role of the criminal trial jury.[130] We have seen that for many Levellers the apportioning of just deserts was integral to the fact-finding process.[131] After 1649 claims regarding the jury's duty to play this particular role melded with a broad-based assertion of the jury's right to find the law, a development that helped pave the way for Lilburne's 1653 defense. If the government would not reform the law of sanctions, or charge defendants at a level that accorded with justice, it was the jury's duty to intervene and to vindicate God's law on earth.

In some important respects, Lilburne's own position fell short of that of his most radical followers. Although his writings evidence a progression from his 1649 aphorism to a better defined position in 1653, they also suggest that he did not follow Jones in equating law with unmediated Scripture. Instead, he clung to the more traditional notion that English fundamental law was historically evolved but remained consistent with Scripture, and thus with a more traditional form of political and legal theory.[132] By 1653 the jury, for Lilburne, was the common political

1960), pp. 118 *et seq*. The jury played an important role in felony cases, but these constituted a relatively small percentage of the cases before early and mid-seventeenth century colonial courts.

128. See above, Chapter 4.

129. On prison reform, rehabilitation, and restitution, see Veall, *Popular Movement for Law Reform*, pp. 132–37, and works cited therein.

130. The "moderates" sought to rein in the jury; religious radicals sought to replace the common law with Scripture and frequently favored application of statute by a magistrate. See Shapiro, *Law Reform in Seventeenth Century England*, p. 290.

131. See above, nn. 39–41 and accompanying text.

132. I believe Parkin-Speer ("John Lilburne: a Revolutionary Interprets") would agree with this. See above, n. 63. See also Schenk, *Concern for Social Justice in the Puritan Revolution*, pp. 78–79. Schenk distinguishes the more radical Levellers from Lilburne with regard to the quest for equality, making a point similar to the one I have developed here: "The radical Levellers, inspired by beliefs derived from both books of the Scriptures and by various conceptions of a state of nature, envisaged a federation of small communities of neighbours, fairly equal in ownership and status, ruling themselves without the interference of professional magistrates or lawyers according to simple and well-known laws. This ideal . . . was not entirely absent from Lilburne's mind, but in his case it was obscured by his

denominator. That it was of the English people at large was as important as that it was of the local community. The people did not *ab initio* find the law; rather, they retained the ultimate authority to overturn a judicial ruling, indictment, or statute on the grounds that it did not accord with the substance or sanctions of the fundamental law. He had not yet in 1649 formulated the argument, with specific reference to the jury, in just that way. He would do so four years later in what ultimately proved the most important of his trials. Then, in the shadows of Leveller defeat, he formulated an argument less radical than that of Jones and other proponents of a purely scripturally based and jury-found law but one that was to outlive the Cromwellian period.[133]

# VI

Lilburne's 1649 trial suggested an expansion of the jury's function, thereby giving direction to Leveller and other early Interregnum political writings on law and legal institutions; his trial in 1653 produced a more enduring argument respecting the jury, one that survived among dissidents and reappeared a decade later in the aftermath of the Restoration. Lilburne returned to England in June of 1653 after two years of a perpetual banishment imposed upon him in 1651 by parliamentary statute.[134] According to the terms of the statute, by returning Lilburne subjected himself to arrest, trial (to determine whether it was the real John Lilburne who had returned), and, potentially, sentence of death.[135] By the time of his return, Cromwell had dissolved the Rump Parliament, and Lilburne, still a popular figure around whom political opposition to the regime might coalesce, evidently hoped that his statutory judgment would similarly be dissolved.[136] Lilburne believed the statute to be void, an unlawful attainder passed upon him ex parte and without trial on the grounds of his alleged slander (against the privileges of a member of Parliament) of Sir Arthur Haselrig and the Committee of Haberdashers' Hall.[137] It is ironic that the most feared political opponent of the

preoccupation with purely political reforms and the limitations of his desire for equality. Lilburne's chief aim, we might sum up, was equality before the law; that of his more radical friends, equality established by law."

133. For an interesting discussion of the mid-1650s jury debate, local politics, and jury selection see Stephen Roberts, "Jury Vetting in the Seventeenth Century," *History Today*, vol. 33 (Feb., 1982), pp. 25–29.

134. Gregg, *Free-Born John*, pp. 321–23.

135. *State Trials*, 5:408–9.

136. Gregg, *Free-Born John*, p. 320; Veall, *Popular Movement for Law Reform*, p. 165.

137. John Lilburne, *A Second Address directed to his Excellency the Lord Cromwell* (London, June 16, 1653), [B.L.: 669 f. 17(20)]: "Parliament in the said Act did not judge your petitioner an offender according to any law in being."; "[T]he said Act is a law made after

Cromwellian regime had been placed *in extremis* because of his remarks opposing the resolution of a case involving the sequestration as royalist property of a Lilburne family colliery.[138] The statutory judgment, the basis for the 1653 trial, proved to be crucial to the shaping both of Lilburne's defense and of his theory of the jury's right to decide questions of law. The development of this theory marked the third, and final, phase of the Interregnum jury debate.

Lilburne's defense and the surrounding pamphlet literature, which he publicized on his own behalf between the time of his return and arrest in mid-June and his acquittal in mid-August, dealt both with the allegedly unconstitutional nature of the statute of banishment and with the inequitable and, hence, unlawful sentence of death for a minor crime.[139] The defense was anticipated in a remarkable tract, *A Jury-man's Judgement upon the Case of Lieut. Col. John Lilburn*, which was written anonymously (but likely by Lilburne himself) and published within a week of Lilburne's arrest. By subtitle the tract purported to prove to "every jury-man's conscience" that he "may not, cannot, ought not find [Lilburne] guilty upon the Act of Parliament"; to do so would make a juror a murderer "by the law of England."[140]

Addressed to "my dear friends and loving countrymen," *A Jury-man's Judgement* warned that it was necessary to "consider things very well beforehand, and come substantially furnished and provided with sound and well-grounded consciences," lest one be called upon to serve and then to find himself, from "fear, hope or favor," a murderer.

> [E]xcept we are fully satisfied in our consciences, that [Lilburne] has committed . . . some crime, which in the known law of England and the very nature of the offence is felony, and justly deserves to die for it, with what conscience can any of us pronounce him guilty? . . . [N]o, the law of England has not placed trials by juries to stand between men

the fact is done."; "[Y]our petitioner was not tried with liberty of defense."; "[T]hat sentence is not proportionable to the offense."

138. Gregg, *Free-Born John*, pp. 305–11.

139. E.g. *Humble Petition of divers well-affected people including the Cities of London, Westminster . . .* (London, June 24, 1653), [B.L.: 669 f. 17(24)]; *To the Parliament of the Commonwealth of England. The Humble Petition of many grieved People . . .* (London, July 26, 1653), [B.L.: 669 f. 17(35)]; [John Lilburne], *Lieut. Col. John Lilburn's Plea in Law* (2nd ed., London, July 2, 1653), [B.L.: E. 703 (12)]; John Lilburne, *Malice detected* (London, July 15, 1653), [B.L.: E. 705(19)]; Lilburne, *The Exceptions of John Lilburne . . . To A Bill of Indictment* (London, July 16, 1653), [B.L.: E. 705(20)]; *Oyes, Oyes, Oyes* (London, July 30, 1653), [B.L.: E. 708(7)]; Lilburne, *The Upright Mans Vindication*. See Gregg, *Free-Born John*, p. 326, and Frank, *The Levellers*, pp. 233–34, for Lilburne's orchestration of the pamphlet and petition campaign.

140. *A Jury-man's Judgement upon the Case of Lieut. Col. John Lilburn* (London, June 22, 1653); [B.L.: E. 702(6)].

and death to so little purpose, as to pronounce men guilty without regard to the nature of the offence, or to what is to be inflicted thereupon.[141]

Moreover, jurymen must be "satisfied in [their] understandings of the Parliament's authority to make such an Act." The author denied that it was ever a felony under English law "to scandalize members of a committee" or "to break the unknown privileges of a Parliament."[142] Thus the Act of banishment was "null and void."[143] Moreover, the parliamentary judgment itself was "contrary to the standing laws of the nation" because it was a judgment of life and limb without trial by peers and without the due process entailed in such trials.[144] Had Lilburne had such a trial "the jury [would have] been bound by the law of England to have proportioned the punishment to the offense."[145] The tract exhorted its readers to consider that ultimately they too would be judged:

[F]or what shall it profit us, either to please the malice or opinions of men, for to lose our own souls, rather let it be our choice not to fear those that can kill these bodies of ours, but to fear him who is able to cast both our bodies and souls into hell fire. . . . [T]he justness of our proceedings is that which will bear us out in the great and terrible day of the Lord.

And let us all pray earnestly unto God, that he will be pleased to give us all eyes to see, and hearts to consider, how much the safety and happiness of us all depends upon our sticking close to the old and good laws of the land, and to lay to heart how much it concerns the good men of England, the jurymen, especially, who are to determine all causes, to be able to judge, and to distinguish between true and counterfeit laws.[146]

The proceedings against Lilburne at the Old Bailey began in mid-July (from the thirteenth to the sixteenth) and were carried over to mid-August (from the eleventh to the twentieth).[147] Lilburne refused to plead before seeing a copy of the indictment.[148] Here he won a great victory: a copy of the indictment and assistance of counsel were allowed him; indeed he was given time to enter written exceptions. In the course of arguing for these "rights," Lilburne established the framework of his defense, stating by way of "exceptions" several of his central claims. He questioned whether

141. *Ibid.*, pp. 1–2, 6.
142. *Ibid.*, pp. 2–3, 6.
143. *Ibid.*, p. 7.
144. *Idem.*: ". . . by twelve good men of his neighbourhood, giving also liberty of exception and challenge of five and thirty, without showing cause."
145. *Ibid.*, p. 8.
146. *Ibid.*, pp. 10, 12–13.
147. *State Trials*, 5:407–19, 419–44.
148. *Ibid.*, pp. 416–19.

the "Act for the Execution of a Judgment" was an act of a true parliament of England. Furthermore, he asserted that a judgment of the sort contained in the act could only follow "an indictment, presentment, or some information or accusation" for "some crime," and a trial at which the accused was present; otherwise it was void in law and any indictment for breach of a condition of the judgment was likewise void.[149] The exceptions did not, however, focus on the failure of the Act to state facts that amounted to capital felony under the English law. This charge Lilburne reserved for the jury stage of his trial, which came on, after a month's recess, in mid-August.

Lilburne's speeches to the court and jury in August of 1653 are not well preserved.[150] But it seems clear that the defendant termed the Act grounding his indictment "a lie and a falsehood, an Act that has no reason in it, no law for it."[151] He repeated his charge that no true parliament had passed the Act and that, in any case, the judgment it imposed could only be imposed by a jury following trial at common law. Lilburne then called upon his jury to decide law as well as fact, to acquit him on the ground that the Act, the judgment, and the ensuing indictment were all null and void under the true law of England.[152] It appears, also, that Lilburne reiterated the exhortation contained in the opening paragraph of a short tract, anonymously authored, which he circulated at the outset of the August session. *A Word to the Jury in the behalfe of John Lilburn*[153] blended the Old Testament flavor of the radical Puritan jury tracts with the forthright appeal to English law that had been sounded in *A Jury-man's Judgement*:

> You [i.e., the jury] are of the neighbour, and Christ shows in the 10th [chapter] of *Luke* that that person is a neighbour that does works of love and mercy; it would be an abominable cruelty if you should find him guilty upon that pretended Act of Parliament, in regard he was not legally accused or convicted of any crime or fact for which he was banished or that it could be made felony if he returned.[154]

149. *Ibid.*, pp. 419–41.
150. *Ibid.*, p. 443. The account in *State Trials*, written mainly by Lilburne, states that "[n]othing of these three last days [August 18–20] proceedings are printed." What we infer about Lilburne's speeches on these days comes from contemporary tracts, including those by Lilburne himself. See Gregg, *Free-Born John*, pp. 331–32 and 395, n. 31.
151. *Ibid.*, p. 443. See *Lieut. Colonel John Lilb. Tryed and Cast: Or, His Case and Craft discovered* (London, Nov. 22, 1653), [B.L.: E. 720(2)], p. 125. See also John Lilburne, *The Tryall of L. Col. John Lilburn at the Sessions House in the Old Baily* (London, Aug. 19, 1653), [B.L.: E. 711(9)], pp. 4–6.
152. Gregg, *Free-Born John*, p. 332; *State Trials*, 5:443–44.
153. *A Word to the Jury in the behalfe of John Lilburn* (London, Aug. ll, 1653), [B.L.: 669 f. 17(44)].
154. *Idem*.

The tract characterized the Act as a bylaw, "such as have been . . . made [by tyrants] to succour themselves in their tyranny." The Rump Parliament had set itself up as a supreme power despite the flow of petitions exhorting its members "to surrender their power to a new Representative equally chosen by the people." The tract spoke also to the "soldiery," which had been raised to aid the people against tyrants and which was now obliged to use its arms "against those that impose such illegal, cruel, and bloody commands."[155] The merciful neighbor was to judge statute in the light of good English law and, finding it the law of a tyrant, to oppose it. Thus had Parliament's act of banishment provided a basis for the merger of the jury-right claim and the long-standing argument against the very basis of the Rump's power. Whereas the 1649 trial had produced a remarkable attack upon the judiciary, that of 1653 resulted in an attack on Parliament. The theory of a jury right remained the same: original power lay in the people; trial by jury assured protection against the usurpation of that power, whether by King, Cromwell, or Parliament, at least where it threatened to result in judgment of life and limb or in forfeiture of estate.

A second anonymous tract, *More Light to Mr. John Lilburnes Jury*,[156] published during the course of the trial, began with Coke's passage on chapter 29 of Magna Carta and with the crimes of Empson and Dudley, who (like the present judges) executed "unlawful Acts of Parliament."[157] Again, Parliament had usurped the role of the jury: "For they judge him that are not by law his judges; that belonging only to juries. . . ."[158] Moreover, Parliament judged him without due process and for a fact

that was never before known, or declared by any law to be a crime, whereby Mr. Lilburne or any other could be warned from the same.

And the reason is evident, for if there should be no firm, standing and established unalterable law which Parliaments, juries and all people were bound to maintain, no man could be certain of anything.[159]

Thus it was more than a question of an unjust law; even conceding its justice, it had been applied to Lilburne after the fact, in a manner that he could not have foreseen.

If the jury convicted Lilburne, according to *More Light*, it would "give encouragement" to Parliament.[160] Not only would the jurors condemn

155. *Idem.*
156. *More Light to Mr. John Lilburnes Jury* (London, Aug. 16, 1653), [B.L.: E. 710(23)].
157. *Ibid.*, p. 3.
158. *Ibid.*, p. 4.
159. *Ibid.*, p. 5.
160. *Ibid.*, p. 6.

Lilburne, they would condemn everyone, including themselves. The jury was bound in conscience, therefore, "to try all laws made by Parliament, by the fundamental laws." They could not "expect the direction of judges and recorders in the case, who many of them lie under sore temptations of losing their honors and places of profit" to go against Parliament's will: "[B]ut since it is evident to every one of your consciences, that [Lilburne] is not charged with anything that in the true law of England is a felonious crime, nor has in the least deserved to die, you can do no less than pronounce him not guilty."[161] And this, on August 20, is what Lilburne's jury did. "John Lilburne," the jury said, "is not guilty of any crime worthy of death."[162]

That Lilburne's jury, or at least that several of its members, took themselves to be judges of law as well as fact is evidenced by statements made to the Council of State, which examined the jurors closely on August 23.[163] Some jurymen stated that they were dubious whether the John Lilburne who was tried was the same John Lilburne who was referred to in the Act, an obvious ploy.[164] It is clear from the examination that the bench, in its charge to the jury, had stated that the jurors were judges of fact only. One juror asserted that, notwithstanding the charge, "the jury were otherwise persuaded from what they heard out of the law books."[165] This may refer to the long speech Lilburne addressed to the jury toward the end of the trial. An account of what he said has been lost, but we can infer that Lilburne challenged the validity of the Act, raised questions regarding proof of his being *the* John Lilburne, and, citing "relevant" authorities, exhorted the jury to find the law void and the sentence unlawful in its relationship to the crime alleged.[166]

Lilburne's aphorism regarding the jury as judges of the law had been given new definition and effect. In one regard, though, the claim Lilburne made in 1653 was more limited than his earlier one. Lilburne did not as a general matter deny the authority of the bench; nor did he deny the right of the bench to instruct jurors on the law.[167] Rather he invoked the jury as a shield, adjuring them to reject "void" law and to act on behalf of the

161. *Ibid.*, pp. 6, 8.

162. Gregg, *Free-Born John*, p. 332; *State Trials*, 5:446. See Thurloe, *State Papers*, 1:442.

163. *State Trials*, 5:445–50. Lilburne was held in prison pending the results of the examination. See John Lilburne, *An Hue and Cry after the Fundamental Lawes and Liberties of England* (London, Sept. 26, 1653), [B.L.: E. 714(1)]. He was thereafter ordered to be held prisoner "for the peace of this nation." He remained a prisoner of State until his death in 1657. See Gregg, *Free-Born John*, pp. 333–34.

164. E.g. Juror Emanuel Hunt (*State Trials*, 5:447).

165. Juror Gilbert Gayne (*ibid.*, p. 450).

166. Lilburne, *Tryall of L. Col. John Lilburn*, pp. 4–6.

167. Lilburne, *The Afflicted Mans Outcry* (London, Aug. 19, 1653), [B.L.: E. 711(7*)], pp. 1–9.

people, whose powers of delegation of authority to true representatives had been wrongfully usurped. His judges were not "Norman intruders"; they were, in a sense, weak and dependent, mere extensions of an unlawful Parliament. Free elections and adherence to the fundamental law of England were the proper correctives, not political decentralization and adherence to local community mores.

As we have seen, Lilburne only hinted at the substance of his views on the jury at his 1649 trial. He invoked the Leveller version of English history without connecting it explicitly to his theory of jury right. Perhaps he had not worked through in his own mind the problem of the origins of the jury. Subsequently, the "logic" of his position was developed by John Jones and others, though it is not clear how far Lilburne agreed with them. In the event, the 1651 statute on which he was tried in the summer of 1653 inspired a different argument concerning the jury's duty. The Act, both in the procedures attending its passage and in its substance, was easier to characterize as in conflict with the common law. Lilburne's 1653 defense strategy revealed how vulnerable Cromwell's new government might be made to appear and resulted in a constitutional debate concerning the constituency of the Rump and the legal basis of its acts.

Moreover, the facts alleged to be criminal were less serious than those for which English law had in the past exacted the penalty of death. It was this aspect of the prosecution that came closest to reviving the concept of "neighbors doing justice to neighbors." The jury was an instrument of mercy, its verdict mandated just deserts. It was, therefore, of no small importance that the jury found Lilburne "not guilty of any crime worthy of death." Lilburne had effectively drawn upon this most ancient aspect of the jury's role. He thus united his call to the jurors to resist tyranny with the claims of the many Interregnum reform writers who opposed the imposition of capital punishment for theft.[168] As we shall see, this juxtaposition of ideas became a significant motif in eighteenth-century writing on the criminal trial jury.

For the moment, however, the most significant aspect of Lilburne's 1653 claim was his invocation of the jury's duty to examine the charges against the defendant and to reject them if it found that the facts cited did not amount to a crime under English law. The claim was particularly well suited to political cases, whether for crimes that were statutorily based or for ones that depended upon judicial construction, that brought the government into conflict with vocal opposition. Passed on to the next generation of jury proponents, this claim dominated the Restoration literature on the jury. In the mid-1650s the Quakers inherited both the soul

168. See above, n. 41.

of Lilburne, who converted to their cause two years after his acquittal,[169] and his new concept of the right and duty of the true English criminal trial jury.[170]

169. Gregg, *Free-Born John*, p. 344.

170. See below, Chapter 6. For a different example of the influence of Lilburne's trial tactics see Colonel Penruddock's "Directions for all my Fellow Prisoners, now to be tried for their Lives by a Special Commission of Oyer and Terminer" (1655), in *A Collection of Scarce and Valuable Tracts (Somers' Tracts)*, vol. 6 (London, 1811), pp. 325–29. Penruddock had taken part in an abortive Cavalier rising against Cromwell in 1655. "Directions" refers to Lilburne and his "several juries" (p. 329). Penruddock, who wrote the tract while awaiting his trial for treason, advises his codefendants to exercise their full right of challenge, to "say we conceive the indictment is not sufficient in law," to ask for counsel, etc. (p. 325). The defendants should put their "plea to the jury, and put it upon their consciences, that God has made them over judges between us and the judge. . . . If the jury seem fearful to clear us absolutely, tell them that it is safest for the jury to find a special verdict, which gives the point in law to all the judges whether or not it is treason . . . and [places] all the bloodshed upon the judges" (p. 263). Penruddock addressed his own jury in these terms (*State Trials*, 2:261) but he was found guilty and beheaded. The device of a special verdict, or a variation upon it wherein the jury returned a verdict of "guilty of [certain specific facts]" *without* asking the bench to apply the law, was frequently employed by the Quakers and by jurors in trials for seditious libel. See below, Chapters 6 and 8.

# 6     The Principle of Noncoercion: The Contest over the Role of the Jury in the Restoration

The principle of noncoercion of jurors was established in 1671 in *Bushel's Case*.[1] Chief Justice Vaughan's opinion is now famous: a judge may not punish or threaten to punish jurors for their verdict. Historians, however, have not always agreed about either the basis for, or the meaning of, Vaughan's opinion. What right did Vaughan intend to affirm? On which tradition of jury right did he draw? And which tradition did his opinion further? To answer these questions, we shall turn first to the background of *Bushel's Case*, then to Vaughan's opinion, and, finally, to the interpretation that some contemporaries put upon that opinion. We shall be tracing the development of the true law-finding, or nullifying, tradition. As we shall see, this tradition, to which Lilburne's 1653 trial had pointed the way, evolved almost accidentally out of different but related aspects of the administration of the criminal law. Its relationship to the older tradition of merciful application of the law in common-run felonies was complex. The two law-finding traditions developed partly in tandem, partly separately, each being pushed forward in a kind of chain reaction of events. Although the true law-finding view was a dissident position, it gained support on the eve of the Glorious Revolution from an important segment of the political establishment. After 1689 Englishmen were left to draw different conclusions about the legitimacy of the tradition, about its relationship to merciful application of the law in routine cases, and about its place in the evolving English constitution.

Section I of this chapter deals with the Quaker trials of the 1660s. Some Quakers argued for a jury law-finding power like that urged by Lilburne at his 1653 trial. While their arguments fell short of the most radical Leveller notion of law-finding, they went well beyond the conventional and, for the most part, accepted notion of jury-based application of law. Other writers, however, conceived of the jury verdicts in the Quaker cases simply as findings of fact. For them, judicial berating and fining of jurors was an invasion of what everyone agreed was a fundamental aspect of the trial jury's role. Their concern about the behavior of some members of the bench was complemented by the concern of some parliamentarians and lawyers about judicial badgering of jurors in common-run felonies. This

---

1. Vaughan 135, 124 *Eng. Rep.* 1006.

concern was manifested when the House of Commons censured Chief Justice Kelyng, whose rough treatment of juries—mainly in homicide cases—seemed to deny their traditional power of mitigation. I shall consider this problem in section II.

The most famous of the Restoration Quaker trials, the prosecution of William Penn and William Mead, produced a tract literature in which the various strands of jury argument that had been developing since Lilburne's day converged. In section III I shall examine the trial and the defendants' claims, both as to law-finding and fact-finding and as to the fining of jurors for their verdicts in criminal cases. Against that background section IV considers Chief Justice Vaughan's opinion in *Bushel's Case*. Vaughan, active in the parliamentary censure of Kelyng three years before, chose to view the case solely in terms of the jury's age-old right to find fact. He argued from that indisputable right to the conclusion that the judge was never in a position to say with certainty that a jury had found against either law or fact.

If Vaughan provided a lasting rationale for the jury's freedom from coercion, he did not lay to rest the debate over the jury. His opinion failed to confront the law-finding issues of the day and was thus vulnerable to appropriation by those who favored jury law-finding, especially by those who opposed the later Stuarts' treatment of defendants and juries in treason and sedition cases. The tracts and issues of the late 1680s are the subjects of the concluding section, V.

The principle of noncoercion by no means crippled the bench, nor even greatly affected the daily administration of the criminal law. Many institutional devices remained by which the bench could, if it chose, influence the verdict of all but an intransigent jury. In most routine cases, moreover, judge and jury agreed on standards of just application of the law. As we shall see in Part III, although the administration of the criminal law in the eighteenth century created even greater judicial dependence than before upon jury mitigation of the law of sanctions, the fact that the bench had lost the ultimate means of coercion scarcely affected the processing of routine felony cases. In political cases, however, where from the government's point of view something more was at stake, the principle of noncoercion represented a roadblock for authorities. The bench's approach to the allocation of judicial and jury duties in the law of seditious libel may have reflected the government's frustration with the principle of noncoercion. This problem, which is introduced in section V, is also properly the subject of Part III.

# I

*Bushel's Case* brought to an end the legal proceedings that began with the arrest and indictment of William Penn and William Mead.[2] In the course of his trial, Penn, a leading Quaker preacher, requested that the court read his indictment to the jury, so that the jurors might "measure the truth of the indictment";[3] almost certainly, Bushel, and the three other jurors who insisted that Penn had been guilty of "preaching only" and refused to convict him for unlawful assembly and disturbance of the peace, believed the indictment to be defective. They did not doubt the truth of the facts alleged; that Penn preached, that a crowd formed, and that a tumult resulted was certain. What these jurors doubted, however, was that those facts amounted to the commission of the crime of taking part in "an unlawful assembly" or of causing a "disturbance of the peace" by a person who peacefully preached religious doctrine. In acquitting Penn and in thereby implicitly rejecting the theory underlying the indictment, Penn's jurors were responding not only to Penn's entreaties but also to those of Quaker writers since the early 1660s. Thus, the refusal of Bushel and the others to accept the official legal theory underlying the indictment did not mark the emergence of a new theory of jury nullification. Indeed, by 1670 the argument that the petty jury had a duty to scrutinize both the law and the indictment upon which the prosecution was based had attained widespread currency.

Restoration persecution of the Quakers began with the 1662 Quaker Act[4] and reached its height in 1664, the year in which Parliament passed the Conventicles Act, which made most nonconformist religious meetings unlawful.[5] The Conventicles Act, part of the "Clarendon Code," played a significant role in the enforcement of Anglicanism during the first decade of the restored Stuart monarchy.[6] By the terms of the Act, which elaborated upon the Act of 1662, those convicted of meeting in groups of five or more persons under pretense of religion, but not according to the forms of the Anglican Church, were to be imprisoned for three months unless they paid a fine of five pounds. For conviction on a second offense the penalty was more onerous, and those convicted of the third offense would suffer seven years' transportation or a fine of 100 pounds.[7]

---

2. *State Trials*, 6:951 (1770). See below, sections III and IV.
3. *Ibid.*, col. 958.
4. Stat. 14 Chas. 2, c. 1 (1662). See George Clark, *The Later Stuarts* (2nd ed., Oxford, 1955), p. 22.
5. Stat. 16 Chas. 2, c. 4 (1664).
6. On the Clarendon Code see e.g. David Ogg, *England in the Reign of Charles II*, 2 vols. (2nd. ed., London, 1956), vol. 1, pp. 206–7.
7. Stat. 16 Chas. 2, c. 4, sects. 1–3, 5.

The Act to prevent and suppress seditious conventicles was literally interpreted by the Stuart bench. The Act's preamble declared that Parliament sought to suppress *seditious* conventicles, but the body of the Act proscribed meetings, "under pretence or colour of religion" without repeating the adjective "seditious." The bench concluded that the jury must convict if there was manifest proof that the defendant had taken part in what appeared to be such a meeting, unless the defendant showed either that the meeting was not under pretense of religion or that it was not nonconformist. Conviction did not require proof of seditious purpose. That, the bench ruled, was presumed by law.[8]

The trials of Quakers in 1664 under the Act occasioned the first major campaign in print since Lilburne's day regarding the powers of the criminal trial jury. A considerable number of Quaker tracts described the sect's travails before the law and exhorted prospective jurymen to apply the Conventicles Act "lawfully"—by which was meant to require proof of sedition.[9] The Quakers established an effective program of legal education within their own ranks and perhaps also persuaded many non-Quaker jurors to the Quaker view of the statute's meaning.[10] The Quakers' position, as it unfolded over the course of a year, mixed moderate and radical claims regarding the jury's role in the application of the Conventicles Act.

The most substantial analysis and discussion of the Conventicles Act was embodied in *The Jury-man charged*, which was published late in

8. See e.g. William Smith, *A True, Short, Impartial Relation of the Proceedings . . . August, 1664* (London, 1664), pp. 3–4.

9. E.g. *A Declaration of the Present Suffering* (London, 1664); *The Liberty of the Subject by Magna Charta; Or, Several weighty things to be considered* (London, 1664); *The Jury-man charged; or, A Letter to a Citizen of London* (London, 1664); William Smith, *Some Clear Truths* (London, 1664); William Smith, *The Innocency and Conscientiousness of the Quakers* (London, 1664); *The Cry of the Innocent and Oppressed for Justice: Or A brief Relation of the Late Proceedings . . . London . . . October 1664* (London, 1664); Smith, *A True, Short, Impartial Relation of the Proceedings . . . August, 1664*; William Smith, *A Second Relation from Hertford; containing the unjust proceedings . . . [October], 1664* (London, 1664); *Another Cry of the Innocent and Oppressed . . . or, A Second Relation of the unjust proceedings . . . London . . . December, 1664* (London, 1664); *Another Cry . . . or a Third Relation of the unjust proceedings . . . London . . . February [1665]* (London, 1665). Much of the discussion that follows is based upon an analysis of these tracts.

10. Most Quakers were convicted, but many jurors resisted finding the defendants guilty until pressed to do so by the bench. See below, n. 17. It is evident that some jurors did not believe Quakers ought to be punished for their worship, which they did not believe had been proved seditious (or even against the true liturgy). It is difficult to determine whether they believed the statute did not reach Quaker worship or believed that although it did, it ought not to be enforced. For cases in which Quakers were acquitted, see Alfred W. Braithwaite, "Early Friends' Experience with Juries," *Journal of the Friends' Historical Society*, vol. 50 (1962–64), pp. 217–27.

1664. The tract was in part a commentary upon proceedings at the Hertford summer assizes, perhaps the most significant episode in the Quaker trials under the 1664 Act. Like most of the Quaker tracts on the subject, *The Jury-man charged* argued that the Act had been incorrectly applied by the Stuart bench:

> [T]he intention of the Parliament is manifest from the title and preface of the Act: the title, *an Act to prevent and suppress seditious conventicles:* but what sedition in worshiping God erroneously? The preface, for remedy against seditious sectaries and other disloyal persons, who under pretence of tender consciences, do at their meetings contrive insurrections, etc. . . . .[11]

Thus, the author concluded, Parliament sought to punish those who only pretended to take part in religious exercise, but who in fact used their meetings to further their seditious ends. Echoing Lilburne's 1653 defense, the author asserted that the very nature of the punishment—banishment for seven years—indicated that this was what Parliament had in mind: "[F]ar be it from us to think so unworthily of an English Parliament" that it would impose a "horrid banishment" for religious practice according to an imagined "erroneous persuasion, . . . for in all just laws the penalty is not greater than the nature of the fault requires."[12]

Finally, the author of *The Jury-man charged* criticized the bench's attempt to make guilt or innocence turn mainly on the question of presence at a religious exercise "in other manner than is allowed by the liturgy or practice of the Church of England."[13] How were witnesses to know whether the exercise was allowed or not? The bench's interpretation supposed either that witnesses were authorities on matters of religion, or that witnesses would simply describe what they had seen and the bench would inform the jury whether these practices were allowed. The former notion was unrealistic; the latter course was totally unacceptable:

> But will this satisfie you sir? Can you take a passionate and testy judge's word as your infallible director in so many most difficult controversies as must in this case be decided? Will you pin your faith upon the judge's sleeve in matters of religion (of which perhaps he knows no more than he can find in the statute book)?[14]

Must not the conscientious juror, if the question resolves itself to this point, look to the Scripture rather than take his rule from the judge? The

---

11. *Jury-man charged*, p. 13.
12. *Ibid.*, pp. 12–13.
13. *Ibid.*, p. 7.
14. *Ibid.*, p. 9.

question at most of the hundreds of Quaker trials in the mid-1660s did not resolve itself into this point, at least not overtly. Nevertheless, the appeal to the jurors' understanding of the true religion, of the unity of sincere worship, was a constant theme in the tracts, as one defense against the strict judicial interpretation of the Act.

As *The Jury-man charged* suggests, there were two aspects of the judicial interpretation of the Conventicles Act that Quakers opposed both in their writings and at the trials: that proof of a meeting under color of religion and contrary to the allowed liturgy sufficed for conviction; and that proof of mere presence at a Quaker meeting cast upon the defendant the burden of proving either that the meeting had not been for religious worship, or that the worship had been according to the Anglican form. Typically at the trials, there was little testimony about what had transpired at an alleged meeting; since the meetings were held in silence, the witness could testify to the defendant's presence but little more. Their religious nature had to be inferred, and the bench frequently pressed witnesses in vain for evidence that the meeting involved prayers.[15] If the jury believed that the meeting was under color of religion, evidence that Anglican prayers had *not* been said aloud was held to be sufficient proof. As Orlando Bridgeman, who presided at the Hertford summer assizes, instructed the jury:

> [You] are not to expect a plain, punctual evidence . . . for [Quakers] may speak to one another though not by or with auricular sound, but by a cast of the eye, or a motion of the head or foot. . . . [I]f you find, or believe in your hearts that they were in the meeting, under colour of religion in their way, though they sat still only, and looked upon each other, seeing they cannot say what they did there: it was an unlawful meeting.[16]

Bridgeman's instructions became the model for most judges during the ensuing months, as proof of presence at a Quaker meeting came to suffice for conviction under the 1664 Act.

Juries, then, if they were not to follow the lead of the bench (although most of them did),[17] naturally took their lead from the defendant. On occasion defendants put to the task of showing that they had not been

---

15. E.g. *The Cry of the Innocent*, pp. 19 *et seq.*

16. Smith, *A True, Short, Impartial Relation*, p. 3.

17. E.g. *Another Cry . . . or a Third Relation*, p. 14: The jury first returned a verdict of "guilty of meeting," but subsequently, apparently under some pressure, changed their verdict to "guilty."; *Another Cry . . . or, A Second Relation*, p. 14: At first eleven of twelve were found guilty but doubt was expressed about the twelfth, then the twelfth was convicted. The trial accounts were written by Quakers and may overstate the juries' original reluctance to convict.

engaged in religious exercise remained silent, but many invited the inference that they had met to worship God.[18] If the defendant admitted presence but not worship, the jury might acquit on insufficiency of proof of contrary religious practices. If the defendant admitted presence and worship, but denied seditiousness, his jury—if it sought to avoid finding him guilty—found that there had been a meeting and worship, but that the defendant had not broken any "true law."[19]

Thus it was that the tracts implored jurors to reject the judge's view of the statute—to find law insofar as that involved finding the true meaning of the statute.[20] As this exhortation was repeated during the fall and winter of 1664–65, more and more defendants admitted to having been present at religious meetings—i.e., they took their stand on what they asserted was the "true law."[21] Frequently, Quaker appeals to jurors to find law as well as fact were only implicit: they were couched in the claim regarding the jurors' duty to apply what the tract writer took to be the true meaning of the statute.[22] Indeed, these writers appear to have conceived of the jurors' duty as one of mere fact-finding. Sometimes the writers challenged the judges' ruling that mere presence at a Quaker meeting sufficed for a guilty verdict, asking prospective jurors to find that worship had not been proved. Or they beseeched jurors to find that there had not been proof of seditious activity—again a finding of fact.[23] For a jury to find these facts, of course, it had first to reject the bench's ruling as to the question of what facts were to be found. But recognition of this level of law-finding often remained submerged. For instance, *Another Cry of the Innocent and Oppressed*, for the most part a description of the Old Bailey

18. E.g. Smith, *A Second Relation from Hertford*, pp. 1 *et seq.*; *Another Cry . . . or, A Second Relation*, p. 14 (first defendant remained silent; second defendant was not given an opportunity to answer; third defendant denied being at a "seditious meeting or conventicle"; fourth defendant asserted that "there is nothing proved that the meeting I was at, is unlawful"; fifth defendant: "I was at no unlawful meeting"; sixth defendant admitted meeting "amongst the dear children of the Lord").

19. Joseph Besse, *A Collection of the Sufferings of . . . Quakers, from . . . [1650 to 1689]*, 2 vols. (London, 1753), vol. 1, p. 401. The jury in the case Besse epitomizes brought in a verdict of "guilty of meeting, but not of fact." The jurors said there was no evidence concerning what was done at the meeting, but when asked whether they believed "in their consciences, that [the defendants] were there under colour and pretense of worship," two replied that they did, but the worship was "in truth." One of them said: "[I]f any man in the world worship God in the spirit, he doth not worship contrary to the liturgy." [Several jurors, presumably including these two were bound over to King's Bench "for their misdemeanor" (Besse's phrase).]

20. E.g. Smith, *A True, Short, Impartial Relation*, p. 8.

21. E.g. *Another Cry . . . or, a Second Relation*, p. 17.

22. *Jury-man charged* (subtitle: "Wherein is shewed the true meaning of the Statute . . ."); Smith, *A True, Short, Impartial Relation*, p. 8.

23. *Jury-man charged*, p. 13.

Quaker trials before Justices Robert Hyde and John Kelyng in December, 1664, appealed to jurymen "to consult the law itself, which declares what the fact is," and not to rely on the judge's statement of what the law declares the facts to be.[24] Nevertheless, *Another Cry* describes this aspect of the jurors' role as resulting from their duty as "sole and absolute judges of matter of fact."[25]

The furthest reaching articulation of the Quaker position was set forth in the closing pages of *Some Clear Truths*, a tract written by William Smith in the fall of 1664.[26] In the "Postscript to all Honest, Sober and Impartial Jurors," Smith asked his readers to consider, when hearing a case, "whether it be properly and truly law that [the defendant] is tried by"; and "whether the thing done be really an offense against the law."[27] Law was based, Smith said (echoing early Leveller writings), on "mercy, justice and equity."[28] An interpretation that does not meet this standard does not "unite with the body of the law," and thus such a law is void.[29] The Conventicles Act will "unite" only if it is interpreted to require evidence of true seditiousness; jurors who convict on less evidence would wrongfully condemn the defendant.[30] In asking prospective jurors to judge the law as stated by the bench in the light of general principles of justice, Smith went beyond *The Jury-man charged*, and beyond nearly all of the other significant tracts, which advised jurors to take the "intended meaning" of the Act not from general principles, as such, but from the wording of its preamble (which was particularly to be understood in the light of the recent history of armed insurrection). *Some Clear Truths* was one of the most radical of the Quaker writings, but in its very broad implications for jury law-finding and in its explicit invocation of the jury's duty generally to measure indictments against "true law," it remained an anomaly.

Thus, for the most part, the Quakers' appeal to jurors was narrow. The Quaker writers made no assertion regarding the general duty of juries to state the law for the community; certainly there is little indication that they conceived of the English criminal law as merely a modern edition of the Scriptures. While they implicitly carried forward Lilburne's appeal not to find the defendant guilty of what they believed to be "void law,"

---

24. *Another Cry . . . or, A Second Relation*, p. 19.
25. *Idem.*
26. Smith, *Some Clear Truths.*
27. *Ibid.*, p. ll.
28. *Ibid.*, p. 7.
29. *Ibid.*, p. 12. See also p. 8: "And it is very clear and plain, that if there be no wrong-doers, as the object of the law, that then the law in itself is silent, as having nothing to operate upon that offends it."
30. *Ibid.*, p. 12.

they assumed the validity of the statute in question in order to address instead the issue of its "true" meaning. Nonetheless, the Quakers believed that no juror in good conscience could convict a person who worshipped God according to the "true religion." For the "conscientious Quaker," no statute that proscribed this form of worship—should Parliament ever create such a statute—could be valid. For the authority that constituted the ultimate legal command imposed the ultimate claim upon a man's conscience.

Thus, by the time Penn's case came to trial, the groundwork for his appeal to the jury had been thoroughly prepared. Ultimately, Penn would draw upon the example of John Lilburne. Yet the image of that figure of earlier, more tumultuous times had been perpetuated, albeit in a slightly different form, by the Quaker writers of the mid-1660s. Their calls to jurors to consider the "true law," although couched as appeals to jurors' consciences, were modest in their implicit acceptance of traditional common-law guideposts. The force of the Quakers' exhortations, however, was heightened by the special context in which they were raised, for theirs was an argument mainly against persecution of peaceful spiritual activity. The circumstances that gave rise to Penn's prosecution were similar but at least one step removed. The charge against Penn was not that a certain form of religious preaching or meeting was unlawful per se but rather that his actions amounted, under the circumstances, to causing an unlawful assembly and a disturbance of the peace. In *Penn's Case* the question of what circumstances were in fact involved was as complex and doubtful as the question of whether such circumstances amounted, in law, to a disturbance of the peace. This additional factual matter complicated both the nature of Penn's claim and the bench's reaction to his acquittal. For, as we shall see, the issue of finality of verdict regarding fact was itself very unsettled.

# II

Though Penn's trial was the highpoint of the long line of Quaker prosecutions, it should also be viewed as an important sequel to the parliamentary censure of Lord Chief Justice John Kelyng for his menacing, fining, and imprisoning of jurors. That parliamentary incident, which will be reconstructed below in some detail, resulted in what many contemporaries must have taken to be sincere support for the principle of noncoercion of jurors. Indeed, it quite possibly sent shocks through the legal world in a way that the Quaker proceedings did not. The charges against Kelyng related to trials at the Old Bailey and on the Western Circuit between 1665 and 1667, proceedings involving both grand and trial juries, one prosecution for violation of the Conventicles Act and several others for homicide. The manner in which Kelyng treated jurors was probably an exaggeration of the practice rather than an exception to it.[31] We have seen that since the middle of the sixteenth century, if not earlier, judges had at times imposed their views upon petty jurors—and even fined and imprisoned them. However, the theory upon which the bench acted had never been clearly articulated, and until the Restoration the legality of coercion remained largely untested.

Though fining jurors did not begin with the Quaker cases of the early 1660s, the practice may have been accelerated by judicial reaction to jury recalcitrance in those cases. As we have seen, the Quakers found supporters among their jurors. Some juries, refusing to convict defendants prosecuted under the Conventicles Act, acquitted; others rendered something akin to a partial verdict ("guilty of attending a meeting") that took the form of a special verdict but, not being stipulated as such, threatened to bring the proceedings to a stalemate. During (and shortly after) Sir Robert Hyde's tenure as Chief Justice of King's Bench, at sessions presided over by him or by his fellow justices—Twisden, Bridgeman, or Kelyng—juries were frequently threatened, fined, and ordered to remain in prison until the fines had been paid.[32]

31. The assize records for the decade beginning with the Restoration reveal only two instances of judicial fining of jurors in common-run cases, both in the years just preceding Kelyng's conflicts with juries. In both cases Hyde fined jurors and bound them over until the next assize (Shrewsbury Assizes, July 25, 1662, Oxford Circuit Crown Book, ASSI 2/1, fols. 83v–84, 93v; Gloucester Assizes, March 31, 1663, Oxford Circuit Crown Book, ASSI 2/1, fols. 95v, 96v). In the first case (homicide), Hyde fined two jurors ten pounds apiece "in regard they were most obstinate and did mislead the rest," and the other jurors four pounds apiece. In the second case (burglary), Hyde fined all the jurors five pounds apiece. There are no details regarding the acquittal of the defendant charged with burglary. In the homicide case, the jury insisted on returning manslaughter se defendendo, despite the fact that, according to the report, the defendant "did pursue [the deceased] with his rapier drawn when the [deceased] ran from him and had no weapon but a stick in his hand and did endeavour as much as he could to fly from [the defendant]." The defendant was the deceased's master. It is impossible to tell whether the jury was acting "mercifully" or from some other motive, or how the court viewed the jury's motive. According to the report, the jury "did wilfully refuse to observe the directions of the court in point of law therein given to alter the [verdict]" and the jurors "did go positively against full evidence and the direction of the court in point of law."

The assize records are by no means a reliable guide to the frequency of the fining of jurors. Those several cases involving fines cited as precedent in 1665 and 1670 and those charged against Kelyng in Parliament do not appear on the assize records themselves.

32. See e.g. above, n. 19, and below, nn. 33–36. See also the contemporary accounts listed above, n. 9. My discussion of the fining issue in the several years before the proceedings against Kelyng in the Commons has benefited from access to the excellent and far more detailed account in Alexander Scherr, "The Genesis of *Bushell's Case*: John Vaughan and Legal Change," (unpublished paper, University of Michigan Law School, 1981), pp. 17–37.

In some quarters there were doubts about the legality of fining, especially when it was undertaken by an inferior court. Matthew Hale, Chief Baron of the Exchequer, shared those doubts about what he termed an "arbitrary practice." In his *History of the Pleas of the Crown* he expressed his views as of the mid-1660s: "I have seen arbitrary practice still go from one thing to another, the fine set upon grand inquests began, then they set fines upon the petit-juries for not finding according to the directions of the court." The practice, Hale thought, was both of recent origin and on the increase. Significantly, it was not confined to the highest courts, but it "was endeavored to bring the practice of the King's Bench into use before justices of gaol delivery and oyer and terminer."[33] It is not surprising, then, that in two such cases where fines were estreated into Exchequer, process was stayed "as being contrary to law."[34]

Fines set directly by King's Bench were less prone to attack. In several 1664 cases, including *Rex v. Selby* and *Leech's Case*, King's Bench ordered an information against the offending jurors and fined them substantial amounts.[35] Jurors who refused to pay the fines were imprisoned until they relented. There was no protection available from a sympathetic Exchequer, and contest by means of a writ of habeas corpus brought the jurors back before King's Bench. Thus, in *Wagstaffe's Case*, which resulted from a trial before Kelyng in the summer of 1665, after Hyde's death and before Kelyng rose to Chief Justice, King's Bench tested and upheld the legality of fining.[36] The decision, handed down after Kelyng became Chief Justice, set the stage for conflict within governing institutions over the question of coercion.

*Wagstaffe's Case* was typical of many Quaker prosecutions. It was clear that there had been a meeting, but there was no direct evidence that it had been held for religious purposes. Following common practice, Kelyng had instructed the jurors that evidence of a meeting sufficed and that it was for the defendants to prove that the meeting was not "under pretense" of non-Anglican worship. Perhaps out of frustration, he fined the recalcitrant jurors, not even bothering to order an information against

---

33. Sir Matthew Hale, *History of the Pleas of the Crown*, 2 vols. (London, 1800), vol. 2, p. 160. It appears that the bench had ruled in 1554 that judges could not fine on assize (but presumably could in King's Bench). See above, Chapter 4, n. 150 and accompanying text. See also Barnes, ed., *Somerset Assize Orders*, p. 32, for coercion of a coroner's jury.

34. Hale, *History of the Pleas of the Crown*, 2:312.

35. *Rex v. Selby*, 1 Keble 769, 83 *Eng. Rep.* 1223 (1664); *Leech's Case*, Sir T. Raym. 98, 83 *Eng. Rep.* 53 (1664). Braithwaite ("Early Friends' Experience with Juries," p. 223) accepts contemporary evidence that the jurors in *Leech's Case* were bound over but not fined.

36. *Rex v. Wagstaffe*, 1 Keble 934, 83 *Eng. Rep.* 1328; 1 Keble 938, 83 *Eng. Rep.* 1331; Sir T. Raym. 138, 83 *Eng. Rep.* 75; 1 Sid. 273, 82 *Eng. Rep.* 1101 (1665).

them.[37] The jurors turned first to Exchequer, certifying Kelyng's action as error and requesting that the fines be removed from the record. Even Hale concurred with his brethren that Exchequer could not review a sister court in such a case. Though he doubted the legality of the fine, Hale directed the petitioners to sue a habeas in King's Bench.[38]

The return to the jurors' writ asserted that the jurors had found *"contra directionem curiae in materia legis et contra plenam evidentiam,"*[39] the form of return that would be employed five years later in *Bushel's Case*. From what little is preserved in extant accounts, it appears that opposing counsel established a pattern of argument that was to figure importantly in the later case. Counsel for the Quakers asserted that the return failed to state a legal basis for the fine, by which was meant that the return did not (nor could not) restate the entire proceedings in a way that allowed for review of the trial court's conclusion that the jury had found against fact and law. Thus, counsel alleged, there could be no effective remedy against the imposition of such a fine. The power to fine inevitably left lower courts far too much discretion and must, ultimately, undermine the fact-finding role of the trial jury. Maynard, in reply, sidestepped this charge, focusing on the situation that would result if judges did not have the power to fine. He stated Kelyng's views as of the summer of 1665: because attaint did not lie in criminal cases, without the power to fine there would be a failure of justice. A new trial, he asserted, would not be appropriate. In the end, "[t]rust must be laid somewhere," and the law presumed that it must reside in the wisdom and discretion of the judges of King's Bench.[40]

The various reports suggest that all of the judges agreed on several rationales that both upheld the fines and provided some limits upon the fining power. In theory, these unanimously held views might be said to constitute the opinion of the court.[41] But in practice, Kelyng and Twisden were in command, and they were determined to apply the furthest reaching doctrine of the case. So far as they were concerned, there would be no distinction between "superior" courts that could fine and "inferior" ones that might not. Nor would an information be necessary: the fines might be applied directly. As Twisden had stated, "The judge is entrusted with the liberties of the people."[42] The bench would determine whether jurors went against the evidence, for jurors "are not judges of

---

37. 1 Sid. 273, 82 *Eng. Rep.* 1101; Hardres 409, 145 *Eng. Rep.* 522 (1665).
38. *Idem.*
39. 1 Sid. 273, 82 *Eng. Rep.* 1101 (1665).
40. 1 Keble 938, 83 *Eng. Rep.* 1331; 1 Sid. 273, 82 *Eng. Rep.* 1101.
41. See above, n. 36.
42. 83 *Eng. Rep.* 75 (1665).

fact so as to go clearly against it."[43] The precedents that were cited (or that can be found in Kelyng's reports or elsewhere) fall either in Elizabeth's reign or very recently in King's Bench itself.[44] They are surprisingly meager. Kelyng was persuaded by them, but apparently he was moved most by the practical effect of an absence of power to fine.

Kelyng was possibly emboldened by the decision in *Wagstaffe's Case*, for in 1666–67 he attempted openly to control grand and petty jury verdicts, not merely in Quaker cases, where jurors practiced what most observers took to be true nullification of the law, but also (perhaps fatefully) in homicide trials, where jurors sought to exercise what had long been treated as a quasi-legitimate form of discretion. It was Kelyng's handling of a Western Circuit grand jury, and in particular of one of its members, Sir Hugh Windham, that brought the charges against him in Parliament.[45] Contemporaries identified Windham with the "country party" and some of them seem to have regarded the attack on Kelyng as in large part politically inspired.[46] Nonetheless, Kelyng's behavior in several other cases was also at issue, and there appears to have been strong sentiment against his treatment of juries and in favor of a bill making menacing and fining illegal.[47]

Proceedings against Kelyng commenced October 16, 1667, when the Chief Justice "was complained of by some of the House for his severe and illegal fining and imprisoning juries, both the grand and petty juries, for their verdicts, and also for giving some worthy gentlemen that served uncivil and insolent language."[48] A committee was appointed to study the matter and to report back to the House.[49] According to John Milward, a

---

43. *Ibid.*, p. 1331.

44. See also below, n. 177 and accompanying text.

45. Cockburn, *English Assizes*, pp. 123–24, 166; Langbein, "The Criminal Trial before the Lawyers," *Chicago Law Review*, vol. 45 (1978), pp. 298–99 and nn. 106–8. See below, n. 57. For a recent review of what is known about Kelyng in the years leading up to his confrontation with Windham, see Eric Stockdale, "Sir John Kelyng, Chief Justice of the King's Bench, 1665–1671," *Bedfordshire Historical Record Society*, vol. 59 (1980), pp. 43–53.

46. Langbein ("Criminal Trial before the Lawyers," p. 299, n. 106) cites Roger North's attribution to his brother Francis of the view that "changing the law" to disallow fining "was popular" [Roger North, *The Life of the Right Honourable Francis North, Baron of Guilford, Lord Keeper of the Great Seal, under King Charles II and King James II* (London, 1742), pp. 66–67].

47. I draw this conclusion from the language of the resolution passed by the House of Commons (see below, text at n. 51) and from the language of the parliamentary diaries. This is not to deny that politics had a great deal to do with shaping attitudes; it is only to say that those attitudes may have come to be sincerely held by some both in and out of Parliament.

48. *The Diary of John Milward*, ed. Caroline Robbins (Cambridge, 1938), p. 88.

49. *Idem.*; *Journals of the House of Commons*, 9:4, cols. 1–2; J. Hatsell, *Precedents of Proceedings in the House of Commons*, 4 vols. (London, 1776–1818), vol. 4 (1796), p. 113.

member of Parliament who kept a diary of Commons proceedings, the disposition of the House in establishing the committee was "to the intent that a course may be taken that judges may not at their own wills and pleasures impose fines and imprison or affront either grand juries or petty juries for giving and adhering to the verdicts."[50] The committee set forth its charges before the House on December ll, and concluded with a resolution:

> That the proceedings of the Lord Chief Justice, in cases now reported, are innovations in the trial of men for their lives and liberties; and that he hath used an arbitrary and illegal power, which is of dangerous consequences to the lives and liberties of the people of England; and tends to the introducing of an arbitrary government.[51]

The charges themselves fell under several heads but are beyond precise reconstruction. Apparently, one case was a trial of Quakers at the Old Bailey from the summer of 1665. The case seems to have preceded *Wagstaffe's Case* by no more than a month and took largely the same form.[52] On trial for their third offense, the defendants said they had come together "[t]o seek God in the spirit." The jury refused to convict them, according to Milward's version of the committee report, "because they had no full proof that there was not any religious [Anglican] worship performed."[53] Kelyng, it was charged, told the jury that the evidence was manifest and sent the jury out again, virtually ordering them to find the defendants guilty. Because "the jury would not alter from their verdict," Kelyng "imprisoned and fined some of them one hundred marks a piece, which fine some of them paid."[54] The committee report stated that Sir William Wild, the Recorder of London, who sat with Kelyng, attempted "to delay the fine" and to give the jury another opportunity to change their minds, but Kelyng "answered that he would make them know themselves, and said they were peremptory saucy fellows."[55]

50. *Diary of John Milward*, pp. 88–89.
51. *Journals of the House of Commons*, 9:35, col. 2.
52. Hatsell (*Precedents of Proceedings*, p. 114) understandably suggested that the case was *Wagstaffe's Case*. Thomas Rudyard, who was convicted by a new jury shortly after Penn's jury was sequestered, wrote from Newgate in early 1671 that *Wagstaffe's Case* was at issue in the proceedings against Kelyng: "Appendix" to William Penn, *Truth Rescued from Imposture* (London, 1671), in William Penn, *A Collection of Works of William Penn*, 2 vols. (London, 1726), vol. l, pp. 511–20. This appears not to have been the case; the jurors in *Wagstaffe's Case* were all fined in the same amount, which was not true in the case at hand. See below, text at n. 156.
53. *Diary of John Milward*, p. 159.
54. *Ibid.*, pp. 159–60.
55. *Ibid.*, p. 160.

The other matters charged against Kelyng involved homicide cases. Clearly the most important was the incident that resulted in *Windham's Case*.[56] Sir Hugh had served on a Somerset grand jury that returned a finding of manslaughter—possibly of death *per infortunium*—which "did not agree with his Lordship's sense." When they refused to alter their finding, Kelyng fined the grand jurors "and told Sir Hugh that he was the head of a party." Windham replied that he was a member of Commons and claimed his privilege, whereupon, according to Milward, "The Chief Justice told him that he would make him know that he was now his servant and that he would make him stoop."[57] Two other cases involved petty juries that refused to find murder. In one, a master's helper had beaten a boy "about the head with a broomstaff" for doing careless work. Kelyng would not accept a verdict of manslaughter and threatened the jury with a fine. This produced the result he wanted: murder was found, the defendant was hanged, in spite of the recommendation of "gentlemen" of the county that he be spared.[58] Yet another petty jury responded to Kelyng's threats by modifying their finding of self-defense to a verdict of manslaughter.[59] There were also one or two other charges of insolent language and arbitrary rulings,[60] but the coercion of juries lay at the core of the charges. Kelyng was said to have so "discouraged" grand and petty jurors that they might refuse to "serve upon any future juries if he be judge at that circuit." His behavior, the charges concluded, endangered lives and liberties and tended "to the introducing of an arbitrary government."[61]

The Chief Justice was not without his supporters, several of whom spoke in his defense. They portrayed Kelyng as essentially honest and in the right (though perhaps indiscreet), and moved that the Chief Justice be allowed to defend himself at the Bar of the House of Commons.[62] The

---

56. *Rex v. Windham*, 2 Keble 180, 84 *Eng. Rep.* 113 (1667).

57. *Diary of John Milward*, pp. 162–63; See also Anchitell Grey, *Debates of the House of Commons From the Year 1667 to the Year 1694* (London, 1769), 1:62–63: "Sir Hugh Wyndham (who first complained to the House of this business) [Kelyng] reproached for being the head of a faction, for no other cause, than finding a bill according to his conscience. He drew the verdict and made the jury find it. Sir Hugh said, he was the King's servant and Member of Parliament (upon his reproaches). [Kelyng] told the grand jury they were his servants, and he would make the best in England stoop."

58. *Diary of John Milward*, pp. 160, 163; Grey, *Debates*, p. 63.

59. *Diary of John Milward*, p. 160.

60. R. Latham and W. Matthews, eds., *The Diary of Samuel Pepys*, 11 vols. (London, 1970–83), vol. 8 (1974), pp. 483–84; Hatsell, *Precedents of Proceedings*, pp. 113–14; Grey, *Debates*, p. 63.

61. *Diary of John Milward*, p. 163; Grey, *Debates*, p. 63; *Journals of the House of Commons*, 9:35, col. 2.

62. *Diary of John Milward*, p. 163: "Sir Thos. Higgins made an excellent speech in the

motion was accepted. Kelyng's speech on his own behalf two months later showed belated tact and careful planning. Though it failed by itself to stem the movement for a bill against the fining of jurors, it largely defused the attack against him.

Kelyng's most detailed reply was to the charge that he had fined a jury for refusing to convict several Quakers. The case in question appears at length in a manuscript of Kelyng's reports.[63] It was not included in the printed *Reports*, perhaps because it had received rough treatment at the hands of the Commons. In the Commons Kelyng claimed that the jury "pretended that they had not full evidence," and he described how he had questioned the jury on all of the facts that he considered dispositive. The jurors had admitted that the defendants were at the Bull and Mouth, a notorious Quaker meeting place, and that they were "worshipping of God." But there was no direct evidence "that they were there under pretence of religious worship in other manner than appointeth."[64] This was clearly a ruse, the same one employed time after time at Hertford, London, and other assizes.[65] Kelyng evidently did not explain to the House that he had charged the jury that the defendants were required in law to prove they were together for a lawful purpose. Nor did he state, as he did in his report, that he told the jury that the defendants' claim of privilege against self-incrimination was a "confession." But he did report that the defendants had said the Church of England was not a true church and that this, too, was before the jury.[66] Kelyng must have been confident about his ground: *Wagstaffe's Case* had upheld fining in just these circumstances, and Kelyng reminded the House that "it is resolved, by all the judges, that juries are fineable."[67] Surely the Commons was aware that the jury in the case at hand had taken part in a widespread campaign

defense of the Chief Justice. That although his passions might lead him a little out of the way sometimes, yet he was a very good and just judge, and had done nothing against the law." Grey, *Debates*, p. 64: "[Higgins] says, Lord Kelyng [is] a man of choler and passion—Right-handed faults his zeal for the laws, but no ill man of bribery or corruption." Others who spoke on Kelyng's behalf were Sir Humphrey Winch, Sir Anthony Jerby, and Thomas Street.

63. "Lord Chief Justice Kelyng's Reports," B.L. MS Hargrave (hereafter cited as Harg.) 103, fols. 34v–37.

64. *Ibid.*, fol. 35v.

65. See above, text at nn. 20–23.

66. B.L. MS Harg. 103, fol. 35: "I told [the defendants] that they being indicted for an unlawful meeting, the proof lay on their part to make it appear what they were doing, and so to excuse, which they refused to do"; fol. 36: "I told [the jury] that [the defendants] being asked what they were doing, they answered they were not bound to accuse themselves which is a kind of confession that they were there under pretense of religious worship." See *Diary of John Milward*, p. 166, for an account of Kelyng's "defense" of his behavior in this case.

67. Grey, *Debates*, p. 67.

to render an Act of Parliament (the Conventicles Act) ineffective.[68] Given their responses under close questioning, there could be no credible claim that the jurors had exculpatory knowledge of their own or that they did not believe the witnesses. There was no true disagreement on the facts proved but rather upon the question (always one for the bench) of what facts were required to be proved. In reaching its own answer to this question, the jury had taken the law into its own hands, or so it seemed to Kelyng. If this case involved wrongful judicial behavior, it was because threatening and fining were wrong as a matter of constitutional principle, and in all cases short of outright corruption, not simply because jurors might have knowledge of their own.[69]

Kelyng turned next to the several homicide cases, beginning with the fray that ended in a slaying the jurors found to have been self-defense. On his view of the facts, Kelyng thought the case either murder or manslaughter, for the defendant had either commenced the fight or responded to insult with a drawn sword before finding his life in danger and retreating. Evidently, Kelyng charged the jury on a point of law and fined them for their recalcitrance in returning self-defense. Kelyng apparently had no reservation about reporting this case in Commons. The jury, he thought, had clearly found against the facts, refusing to apply rules of the law of homicide that had been settled for centuries.[70]

---

68. According to Milward (*Diary*, p. 167) Kelyng told the Commons: "[I]f he had not thus far proceeded against the Quakers and the jurors he did assure himself that he had not proceeded justly according to the act of Parliament."

69. The jurors almost certainly did believe that they had knowledge of their own. From their perspective, the defendants were innocent unless they had engaged in seditious activity. They believed that Quaker worship, though outside the pale of the established Church, was not seditious; their knowledge of the Quakers, of their loyalty to England, and of their religious spirit was an important factor. Given the official interpretation of the Conventicles Act, this did not constitute relevant evidence. The bench could be certain that jurors did not have knowledge of their own that the defendants were engaged either in Anglican worship or in peaceful nonreligious activity.

70. *Diary of John Milward*, pp. 160, 167. According to the charge against Kelyng, "[T]here happened a fray in which one man was slain; it was proved that the man that killed him was set upon and so did it in his own defense." Kelyng described the case in Parliament as follows: "Two men fell out, had their swords drawn and were parted, and after a while fell to fighting again. One of them was slain, but because it was said that he that killed the other fled to the wall and afterward slew him therefore the jury would not find it murder." It appears that this was a typical case of generous application of the law of self-defense. It is difficult to see how Kelyng thought "murder" not only an appropriate but the preferred verdict, but it is easy to understand the view that a verdict of manslaughter, not self-defense, was called for: the slayer had engaged in the fight before retreating. Moreover, the evidence of retreat probably was given in pro forma fashion, according to a tradition of which Kelyng disapproved (but in which the bench had long acquiesced).

Kelyng's *Reports* evidence great attention to the substantive law of homicide and his insistence upon verdicts that were commanded by the law.[71] One ancient doctrine concerned the manner in which a master or his helper might punish an apprentice, the subject of another of the cases charged against him. In his defense to this charge in Commons, Kelyng first cited a particularly gruesome case (as though it had been charged against him in the Commons, though it had not) wherein "a smith struck his prentice with a bar of iron [and] broke his skull." The jury, Kelyng said, would not find murder until he threatened them. Subsequently, he stated, "the judges in Westminster Hall gave their opinion that it was murder," for one may not chastise with "any . . . weapon or instrument to kill them."[72] According to Kelyng's *Reports*, this case was tried in London, not on the Western Circuit, and the jury returned a special verdict, though it is possible they had been urged to do so.[73] The Westminster bench ruled in this case that the facts amounted to murder. It thus provided Kelyng with powerful precedent and, moreover, allowed him to parade his generosity of spirit, for, as he stated in the Commons, after the Westminster ruling the defendant (presumably with Kelyng's leave) was pardoned due to his good reputation.[74] Kelyng appears to have employed this case tactically in the Commons in order to buttress his defense on the charge of inducing a murder verdict in the case actually charged against him. Though in the case charged the "instrument" of chastisement was less lethal (a broomstick), the master's servant, Kelyng apparently said, "beat [the apprentice] about the head . . . until the blood gushed out of his nose, mouth and ears." Kelyng stated that he caused the jury to "bring it in murder," for which the defendant was hanged.[75]

Again, Kelyng viewed the initial verdicts in the case of the fray and in both of the master-servant cases as directly contrary to settled rules of law. In this he was correct, but possibly on weaker ground, for these cases could be assimilated to cases in which there was room for true disagreement on the facts. Unlike Quaker trials, these were not cases in which the bench was confronted with what could be read as systematic appeals for jury nullification. Admittedly, it is unlikely that a true dispute over either law or fact existed in cases that involved the line between murder and manslaughter, or in ones that involved the line between culpable homicide and self-defense. For example, in even the most

71. E.g. Kelyng 56, 58, 61–2, 84 *Eng. Rep.* 1080–83 (1666).
72. *Diary of John Milward*, pp. 167–68.
73. Kelyng 64–65, 84 *Eng. Rep.* 1084–85 (1666).
74. *Diary of John Milward*, p. 168: "But although this man was condemned yet because he was very well spoken of (and for) by his neighbors he procured his pardon from the king."
75. *Idem.*

egregious case, that of the smith who struck his apprentice with an iron bar, it is unlikely that the jury rejected the proposition that such chastisement might constitute murder; as for the facts, probably so much was proved. But there were other considerations, ones that applied as much or more to the defendant who used a broomstick to chastise. Had the defendant acted out of sudden anger? Did he intend to kill as opposed seriously to hurt the deceased? Was the defendant of good reputation? None of these factors altered the law: strictly speaking, only provocation on the part of the deceased could reduce the crime to manslaughter. Nonetheless, there was in practice room for play, especially where there was no evidence either of true premeditation or of slaying in the course of robbery or burglary. The concept of "deliberateness" could be viewed differently in different cases that fell within the genre of those charged, even, strictly speaking, "against the facts." This was part of the jury's traditional de facto role—the merciful application of law to facts. At times the bench acquiesced in the jury's exercise of such discretion, at times not. The problem for contemporaries was, What might a nonacquiescing bench do to a jury that applied the law to the facts in this way? Kelyng had no doubts, and some precedent; but there was precedent (in the form of practice) in the other direction as well.

Kelyng's handling of the Windham affair in Parliament shows him at his most tactful. He asserted that the grand jury brought in a bill of death *per infortunium* and that for this reason he had explained to them that they must return either *billa vera* or *ignoramus*: "[I]f they find the proofs to be slight or not material, then to find it *ignoramus*, and if it be sufficiently proved then to bring it in *billa vera*, and then to leave it to the trial of the court."[76] Kelyng told the grand jury, he now said, that it may not judge "of point of law," by which he meant that it must find only the fact of the killing by the accused and not the legal nature of the deed. Because the grand jury persisted in its verdict, Kelyng admonished them "better to consider of it that night," but they did not change their minds. It was for this behavior, Kelyng said, that he fined some of the grand jurors. He had offered to withdraw the fine "if they would submit." When the matter came to a hearing, "the judges with one consent said that I was in the right." Afterward he nonetheless—so he now asserted—"caused the clerk of the assize to remit their fines."[77]

Kelyng made no reference to his interchange with Windham, and he perhaps took more credit for the discharging of the fine than was his due.[78]

---

76. *Diary of John Milward*, p. 68.
77. *Ibid.*, p. 169.
78. For the alleged interchange with Wyndham, see above, n. 57. According to an anonymous report of the subsequent proceedings before King's Bench, the grand jurors

It appears that the grand jury returned a verdict of manslaughter, not of *per infortunium*, an unimportant slip on Kelyng's part.[79] Nonetheless, Kelyng was correct on the law and must have felt confident about his position so long as he could divert attention from his insults to Windham. Perhaps significantly, Kelyng made no reference to his more extreme view that in some cases of homicide the question of whether the slaying had been murder or manslaughter was not even for the trial jury. On this view, where the Crown produced evidence of deliberation and the defendant failed to show provocation, the trial jury would merely find the fact of the homicide; it was for the court to "imply" malice. If the jury in such a case found a degree of homicide less than murder, it would incur punishment. Indeed, in *Rex v. Hood*, Kelyng fined a petty jury on just those grounds.[80]

According to Milward, the House debated Kelyng's behavior for four hours or more before resolving that fining and imprisonment were illegal and that a bill should be drafted to that effect, but that there should be "no further prosecution or proceedings against the Chief Justice."[81] It is

were discharged without fine "because it was a mistake in their judgments rather than any obstinacy." (B.L. MS Harg. 339, fol. 2). Keble [2 Keble 180–81, 84 *Eng. Rep.* 113 (1667)] reported that the fine was not assessed "because they were gentlemen of repute in the country."

79. B.L. MS Harg. 339, fol. 2. The bill proffered to the grand jury stipulated "murder."

80. Kelyng 50–51, 84 *Eng. Rep.* 1077–78 (1666). It appears that Kelyng believed it was for the bench to determine whether the defendant had shown provocation: "[U]pon the evidence it appeared that [Hood] killed him without any provocation, and thereupon I directed the jury, that it was murder; for the law in that case intended malice; and I told them they were judges of the matter of fact, viz. whether Newen died by the hand of Hood; but whether it was murder or manslaughter, that was matter in law, in which they were to observe the direction of the Court." Kelyng fined the jurors forty shillings apiece. Hatsell (*Precedents of Proceedings*, p. 114) suggests that *Hood's Case* was among those charged against Kelyng. Probably he confused this case with the one involving the fray (see above, n. 70 and accompanying text). The more common (and the correct) practice was for the judge to charge the jury that absence of provocation implied malice; that whether there had been provocation was a question of fact for the jury to determine; that it was for the jury to apply the law (of implied malice) to the facts the jury found; that the jury was to state in its verdict whether the defendant was guilty of murder, manslaughter, homicide in self-defense, or was not guilty. This practice, of course, enabled the jury to conceal a rejection of the law of implied malice within its finding of fact, and it is this that Kelyng sought to prevent.

81. *Diary of John Milward*, p. 170: "Many did aggravate, others did extenuate [Kelyng's] failings." Pepys recorded: "Here I did also see their votes against my Lord Chief Justice Keeling, that his proceedings were illegal and that he was a contemner of Magna Charta, the great preserver of our lives, freedoms, and properties—and an introduction to arbitrary government—which is very high language, and of the same sound with that in the year 1640" (*Diary*, p. 577, under date: 12 Dec. 1667. Almost certainly this was the thirteenth of December). According to Grey (*Debates*, p. 67), Wyndham moved "that since the Chief Justice had forgot to answer the reproachful language he gave him, that the House would

impossible to determine the precise reason for the House's decision on the bill. Possibly it reflected concern about the Crown's use of the bench, and about the strongly royalist tendency of some of the judges, as well as fear that the bench might use its monitoring of judicial proceedings to fine or imprison its political enemies.[82] Perhaps largely political concerns that were readily translated into "constitutional" concerns fostered widespread doubts about the legality of fining and made acceptable the view that, whatever one might make of the precedents, fining was, pure and simple, unlawful. Had the main consideration been Kelyng's treatment of recalcitrant juries in prosecutions of Quakers, the result might have been very different, for most Parliamentarians believed that the Quakers posed a threat both to public order and to respect for statute law.[83] But most of the cases with which the House had had to grapple were homicides, where something less was at stake. Kelyng's behavior—because it touched the most routine area of the administration of the criminal law—may have been taken to suggest how far the Stuart bench was prepared to go to revise long-settled practices involving the criminal trial jury.

The bill to declare illegal the fining and imprisonment of jurors died in committee. It had received two readings before the House in mid-February, 1668, and among those who had spoken to the bill after its second reading was John Vaughan, who would three years later write the opinion in *Bushel's Case*. Vaughan appears to have adopted a middle position, arguing that prohibition of "menacing" ought to be dropped from the bill, "it being a word of too large extent." A judge ought to be able to "tell a corrupt jury of the danger of an attaint, in a case where they shall proceed wittingly against both their oaths and duties." What Vaughan meant by "corrupt" is unclear; nor can we know whether Vaughan, as of 1668, would have endorsed the fining (as well as the "menacing") of jurors had he believed an attaint was unavailing and that

likewise forget it, for he [Wyndham] did." See also, *Journals of the House of Commons*, 9:37, col. 2.

82. See A. F. Havighurst, "The Judiciary and Politics in the Reign of Charles II," *Law Quarterly Review*, vol. 66 (1950), pp. 62, 229. See also Jennifer Carter, "Law, Courts and Constitution," in J. R. Jones, ed., *The Restored Monarchy* (London, 1979), p. 86; J. P. Kenyon, *The Stuart Constitution* (Cambridge, 1966), p. 420.

83. For the background to the renewal in 1670 of the Conventicles Act see Douglas Lacey, *Dissent and Parliamentary Politics in England, 1661–1689* (New Brunswick, 1969), pp. 58–61; Grey, *Debates*, pp. 146, 174, 220–22, 226–28, 230, 245–47, 254, 263–64, 295, 300. Vaughan spoke against the bill "because it crosses the fundamental laws of the nation" (presumably because it did not provide jury trial in some contexts); Hansard, ed., *Parliamentary Debates*, iv:413, 421, 444–47; *Journals of the House of Commons*, 9:60–61, 66, 78, 87, 101–2, 104, 108–9, 111, 113, 123, 128, 129–31, 135–36, 147, 150, 154; *Journals of the House of Lords* 12:237, 260, 262, 305–6, 308–10; 312, 317–18, 320–21, 324–26, 333, 335–36, 338–40, 342, 349–50.

a "failure of justice" was thus possible.[84] The bill was then committed to the study of Vaughan and nearly three dozen others.[85] That committee was subsequently saddled with consideration of a bill regarding the procuring of able and sufficient jurors.[86] Debate resumed in the House in early April, 1668, reviving the Committee's activity concerning judicial treatment of jurors—new complaints, this time regarding Justice Tyrrell, were aired—but the bill never received a final reading.[87] Largely in response to concerns of London authorities about Quaker preaching, the question of continuing the Act to prevent and suppress seditious Conventicles seems to have taken precedence, and, perhaps significantly, there was substantial overlap between its members and those on the committee for the jury bill.[88] By the end of the year Vaughan had been appointed Chief Justice of Common Pleas, and complaints about treatment of jurors had diminished. Kelyng, who had formerly been so active, soon passed from the scene altogether.[89]

# III

The prosecution of William Penn and William Mead grew out of the continuing struggle between the Quakers and City of London authorities. Despite continued arrests and fines, Quaker leaders continued to preach at large and well-publicized meetings. London officials had ordered that traditional meeting places of the Friends be locked and guarded by soldiers, but this only forced preaching out onto the streets where crowds gathered and—as city authorities saw it—the public order was threat-

84. According to Milward (Diary, pp. 190–91), Vaughan concluded his comments with the observation "that there ought also care to be taken to prevent miscarriage of juries as well as the severity of judges."

85. Journals of the House of Commons, 9:51–53; Diary of John Milward, pp. 187, 190–91; Grey, Debates, p. 84.

86. Journals of the House of Commons, 9:65, 70–71. A total of fifteen more persons were added to the committee (idem).

87. Ibid., 9:74–75, 77, 83–84. See Diary of John Milward, p. 243, for the complaint "brought in against Judge Tyrell [for] forcing a jury to go out again upon a prisoner after he had been tried before Chief Justice Kelyng, and had been acquitted by the jury . . . Judge Tyrell being present at the trial" (April 3, 1668). On that day Milward himself was added to the Committee (Journals of the House of Commons, 9:74). See also B.L. MS Add, 38, 336, fol. 348, regarding activity in the House of Lords: "It was ordered that the Lord St. John have leave to bring in a bill for declaring the fining and imprisoning of jurors illegal. This bill was brought in but did not pass."

88. Journals of the House of Commons, 9:74, 84.

89. Kelyng died in May, 1671. He was still on the bench in 1670, but it appears from the printed Reports that he was not present after Trinity Term of that year. See E. Foss, The Judges of England, with sketches of their lives and notices connected with the Courts at Westminster, 1066–1864, 9 vols. (London, 1848–64), vol. 7 (1864), p. 139.

ened.[90] On August 14, 1670, Penn addressed an especially large crowd in Gracechurch Street. Shortly after he began to speak, constables forearmed with warrants signed by the Lord Mayor, Sir Samuel Starling, moved to arrest both him and his copreacher, Mead. According to the document addressed formally to the keeper of Newgate, Penn was arrested for "preaching seditiously and causing a great tumult of people . . . to be gathered together riotously and routously."[91] Despite the form of this warrant both men were charged under the recently renewed Conventicles Act[92] and might have obtained release sine die through payment of fines. But they refused and instead demanded jury trial, as the Act allowed. They thus remained in custody until the close of their five-day trial, which began September 1 at the quarter sessions held at the Old Bailey.[93]

Neither Penn nor Mead was indicted for attendance at a meeting in breach of the Conventicles Act. Rather, the government charged them with causing an unlawful assembly and a disturbance of the peace, charges that came close to an indictment for insurrection. The indictment alleged that the two men agreed that Penn would preach and that Penn "by abetment of . . . Mead . . . did preach and speak"; it also alleged that "by reason" of the defendants' actions "a great concourse and tumult of people in the street . . . a long time did remain and continue, in contempt of . . . the King, and of his law, to the great disturbance of his peace."[94] At their trial the prisoners were brought forward, a jury was sworn and the indictment read. Asked to plead, the defendants requested a copy of the indictment, but the bench informed them of standard practice: they must plead to the indictment before receiving a copy of it. After extracting promises that "no advantage may be taken against" them, both pleaded "not guilty in manner and form."[95]

The court recessed until September 3, when the Crown produced three witnesses against the defendants. The first, James Cook, stated that he had been sent for to disperse the meeting. He saw Penn speaking to the people but "could not hear what [Penn] said because of the noise." He could not approach Penn "for the crowd of people; upon which Capt.

90. Catherine Owens Peare, William Penn (Ann Arbor, 1956), pp. 107–8.

91. Arrest warrant, Historical Society of Pennsylvania, quoted in Peare, William Penn, p. 110.

92. Stat. 22 Chas. 2, c. 1 (1670).

93. Peare, William Penn, pp. 110–13.

94. State Trials, 6:954–55. This account was published originally by Penn and Mead as The People's Antient and Just Liberties (London, 1670). It contains several appendixes dealing with, inter alia, Magna Carta and the proceedings in Parliament against Chief Justice Kelyng.

95. Ibid., p. 955.

Mead came to me . . . and desired me to let [Penn] go on, for when he had done, he would bring Mr. Penn to me." A constable, Richard Read, corroborated Cook's testimony. Read "found a great crowd of people," "heard Mr. Penn preach to them,"[96] and "endeavored with my watchmen to get at Mr. Penn to pull him down, but . . . could not, the people kicking my watchmen and myself on the shins."[97] Read could hear neither Penn's nor Mead's conversation with Cook because of the "great noise." A witness named Whiting saw Penn but not Mead; he supposed Penn was speaking but could not hear him.[98]

Penn and Mead occasionally challenged the witnesses, but clearly they believed that any factual errors in the witnesses' testimony should prove irrelevant, for both defendants admitted with pride that they had assembled to preach and to pray.[99] Neither defendant believed that the Crown's evidence, even if true, amounted to the breaking of any law. To their demand that they be shown the law upon which the indictment was based, the Recorder (Howel) replied that the indictment was based "upon the common law" and that he could not "run up so many years, and over so many adjudged cases, which we call common law."[100] This drew Penn's famous retort: "[I]f [the law] be common, it should not be so hard to produce." Once again he returned to the indictment:

Shall I plead to an indictment that has no foundation in law? If it contain that law you say I have broken, why should you decline to produce that law, since it will be impossible for the jury to determine, or agree to bring in their verdict, who have not the law produced, by which they should measure the truth of the indictment, and the guilt, or contrary of my fact? . . . The question is not, whether I am guilty of this indictment, but whether this indictment be legal.[101]

96. *Ibid.*, p. 957.
97. Sir Samuel Starling, *An Answer to the Seditious and Scandalous Pamphlet, entitled, The Trial of W. Penn and W. Mead* (London, 1671), p. 15. This account, written by the Lord Mayor of London, who presided at the trial, contains this testimony. The "official" account, by Penn, does not. On this point, Starling's account seems credible.
98. *State Trials*, 6:957. The official account does not contain the name of this witness. Starling's account does (p. 16).
99. *Ibid.*, p. 958. Penn: "We confess ourselves to be so far from recanting, or declining to vindicate the assembling of ourselves to preach, pray, or worship the Eternal, Holy, Just God, that we declare to all the world, that we do believe it to be our indispensable duty." Starling (*An Answer to the Seditious and Scandalous Pamphlet*, p. 17) asserted that the witnesses' testimony and defendants' "confessions" sufficed for conviction.
100. *State Trials*, 6:958.
101. *Ibid.*, 6:958–59. Starling's account (p. 19) contains a paraphrase of this speech, referring to it as though it had been added post hoc and never spoken in court. Starling also records a comment of his own that he evidently made at about this point in the trial: "Now the Common Law is Common Right, or *Lex Rationis*, imprinted in every man's understanding" (p. 17).

Irritated by Penn's continued demands, the Recorder insisted that the defendants "speak to the indictment," i.e., that they speak to the evidence presented against them.

[Y]ou are now upon matter of fact, which fact you have heard proved against you; you are to answer it: If the fact be found against you, you may then speak to the matter of law, in arrest of judgment, and you shall be heard.[102]

Penn would have none of this. To make his "best defense" before the jury he must have the Crown's statement of the law. At this point the Recorder, supported by the mayor, ordered that Penn be removed to the bale dock; it was in response to that order that Penn appealed to his jury ("my sole judges") to consider whether he was being tried in accordance with the fundamental laws.[103] Mead soon followed Penn to the bale dock, having stated to the jury ("who are my judges") that his indictment was "a bundle of stuff, full of lies and falsehoods."[104] The Recorder then charged the jury that the indictment was for "preaching . . . and drawing a tumultuous company."[105] From the distant bale dock, the full court heard Penn's parting shot:

I appeal to the jury who are my judges, and this great assembly, whether the proceedings of the court are not most arbitrary, and void of all law, in offering to give the jury their charge in the absence of the prisoners. . . . [A]nd you of the jury, take notice, that I have not been heard, neither can you legally depart the court before I have been fully heard, having at last ten or twelve material points to offer, in order to invalidate their indictment.[106]

In considering their verdict, the jurors agreed that Penn had preached to an assembly of persons, but could agree to no more. They reported to the Court that eight jurors were prepared to return a "guilty" verdict; four were not. Displeased, the bench berated the four and sent the jury

102. Starling, *An Answer to the Seditious and Scandalous Pamphlet*, p. 18.
103. *State Trials*, 6:959.
104. *Ibid.*, p. 960. According to Penn and Mead's account, Mead also told the jury that a "riot" involved three or more meeting together "to beat a man, or to enter forcibly into another man's land, to cut down his grass, his wood, or break down his poles." Starling (p. 20) also records this speech and adds that the recorder replied: "[Y]es, and to do any other unlawful act." This has reference to the Conventicles Act, breach of which under these circumstances the Lord Mayor deemed constituted the holding of an unlawful assembly.
105. *State Trials*, 6:690.
106. *Ibid.*, p. 961; Starling, *An Answer to the Seditious and Scandalous Pamphlet*, p. 21. The first half of this speech is in both Penn and Mead's account and Starling's account; the second half is in only Penn and Mead's account.

away to reconsider its decision.[107] When the jury returned, the foreman reported that they had found Penn "guilty of speaking in Gracechurch Street," to which the Recorder replied that they "had as good say nothing." The mayor questioned the jury: "Was it not an unlawful assembly? You mean [Penn] was speaking to a tumult there?" But further questioning availed the bench nothing; the jury was not prepared to answer to the core of the indictment. Penn was guilty only of "speaking or preaching to an assembly"; Mead was not guilty. Bushel and the others who would not bring in a guilty verdict stood upon their "conscience," as Penn had exhorted them to do. It was, or so Penn contended, the juryman's "right."[108]

In the end the jury abandoned the device of a truncated verdict and rendered a definitive "not guilty."[109] The trial was over, and the indictment was overturned. The bench was left to assess fines: Penn and Mead for contempt, Bushel and the other jurors for their disobedient verdict. The bench, because it viewed the evidence as manifest, came down harshly on the jurors, fining them for finding contrary both to the evidence ("in matter of fact") and to the instructions ("in matter of law").[110]

Precisely how the jurors perceived the case against Penn is beyond reconstruction. Penn had insisted that the court produce the law on which the indictment was grounded so that jurors "might measure the truth of the indictment, and the guilt of the fact." The recalcitrant jurors may have acceded to the court's view of the law, that preaching to a large and tumultuous assembly in a manner that continued a disturbance of the peace was a high misdemeanor, but doubted whether there was sufficient evidence of a tumult and disturbance of the peace. More likely, however, they both doubted the tumult and believed that the Crown had, in any event, to prove an unlawful intent, especially where the law of criminal trespass was being applied to a man of God preaching His Word to those gathered to hear him.

For Penn the message of his acquittal was unmistakable: the jurors had made their own assessment of the law, or at least had rejected that put forth by the court. What was now awaited—and would surely come—was exoneration of the jurors, who, by assessing the law themselves, had rebuffed the tyranny of the judiciary and vindicated their own true

107. *State Trials*, 6:961; Starling, *An Answer to the Seditious and Scandalous Pamphlet*, p. 22.
108. *State Trials*, 6:961–65; Starling, *An Answer to the Seditious and Scandalous Pamphlet*, pp. 22–30.
109. *State Trials*. 6:966; Starling, *An Answer to the Seditious and Scandalous Pamphlet*, p. 30.
110. *State Trials*, 6:969; Starling, *An Answer to the Seditious and Scandalous Pamphlet*, pp. 30–31.

historical and moral purpose. In the meantime, Penn would spend much of his stay in prison publicizing his case in a series of tracts. These tracts, written by Penn and the Quaker Thomas Rudyard, who was convicted of obstructing justice by a jury sworn in to replace Penn's jury,[111] dealt both with the duties of jurors and with the (alleged) right of the bench to punish them. These tracts appeared between October, 1670 and March, 1671, the period that saw as well the early stages of the legal contest over the fining and imprisonment of Bushel and his cojurors. To what extent the legal and rhetorical campaigns influenced each other we shall probably never know—perhaps they proceeded independently of each other, drawing primarily on a common pool of ideas. As we shall see, the central thrust of Vaughan's opinion, handed down in the fall of 1671,[112] differed significantly both from earlier legal arguments and from those in the contemporary jury-tract literature.

In *An Appendix by way of Defense*, a tract he attached to his account of the trial, Penn articulated his defense more clearly than he had at the Old Bailey.[113] His position was analogous to the familiar Quaker argument that the jury must look behind the indictment to the law upon which it was based lest the bench and the officials who framed indictments significantly misinterpret the Conventicles Act. But Penn varied the argument slightly. The crucial point of reference for his jury was not statute but the common law regarding the requisites for unlawful assembly and disturbance of the peace. An unlawful assembly required at most either assembling to commit an act that would, if committed, constitute a riot, or refusing to disperse when part of the assembly was threatening to commit such an act; it might also be charged where a large number of persons met under circumstances that created fear of great harm by either those who met or those who witnessed the meeting.[114] It

---

111. See below, n. 126.

112. The exact date upon which Vaughan issued his opinion is not known. Bushel had sued out his writ in November, 1670. The arguments at bar ensued during the following months. See Clark, *The Later Stuarts*, p. 108 (giving 1671 as the year of the decision). Rudyard, in his "Appendix" to Penn's *Truth Rescued*, which was written in Feb.–March, 1671 (see below, n. 122), referred to the case as pending in Common Pleas.

113. *State Trials*, 6:970–1000.

114. William Hawkins, *A Treatise of the Pleas of the Crown*, 2 vols. (London, 1716), vol. 1, p. 158: "An unlawful Assembly, according to the common opinion, is a disturbance of the peace by persons barely assembling together, with an intention to do a thing, which if it were executed would make them rioters, but neither actually executing it, nor making a motion toward the execution of it; but this seems to be much too narrow a definition; for any meeting whatsoever of great numbers of people with such circumstances of terror, as cannot but endanger the public peace, and raise fears and jealousies among the King's subjects, seems properly to be called an unlawful assembly; as where great numbers, complaining of a common grievance, meet together, armed in a warlike manner, in order to consult together

is unclear whether London authorities counted any assembly in breach of the Conventicles Act as an unlawful assembly. Apparently, authorities believed that a tumult had resulted, or at least had been highly likely to occur. Such a tumult clearly constituted a disturbance of the peace and made the assembly unlawful.

According to Penn, the government had to prove that the defendants had met with an intent to do—or to plan—physical harm to person or property, the traditional sphere in which common law crimes were located. The intent to worship God in a manner and form contrary to statute was clearly not such a design: "[T]hat dissenters meet with no such intention, is manifest to the whole world, therefore their assemblies are not unlawful."[115] The authorities, Penn argued, had resorted to an evil stratagem. The prosecution had "forged" a "romance-indictment" that cited circumstances which did not, in law, amount to an unlawful assembly or disturbance of the peace, but which included those phrases. The hoped-for verdict would then attach to the entire indictment, so that on the basis of evidence of religious assembly only, the jury would have, in legal effect, found an unlawful assembly and disturbance of the peace. Moreover, according to Penn, the indictment had been framed in such a way as to induce a verdict of guilty. It was "swelled with malicious scaring phrases" to give the impression that the defendants were "the most dangerous persons." Precisely because there was so little evidence against them the government had introduced fictitious testimony into the indictment. In short, the indictment was intended to be self-proving.[116]

The jury, applauded the *Appendix*, had not been fooled. It refused to do more than to find those facts proven at trial and had stated its verdict accordingly, thus comprehending its role as judge not only of fact, but of the law upon which the indictment was based. The jury had responded to the defendants' exhortation not to return a verdict of guilty unless it believed that the facts proved amounted in law to the crime of unlawful assembly. Nor could the jury have done otherwise: "For as well the jury as prisoners, were denied to have any law produced, by which they might

concerning the most proper means for recovery of their interests; for no one can foresee what may be the event of such an assembly."

115. *State Trials*, 6:971–72. Although Penn denied there had been a "tumult," except, perhaps, in response to the "unlawful" acts of the officials who disrupted the lawful assembly, Penn apparently did not believe that the mere fact of a tumult sufficed to make the assembly (which met without the intent to cause such a tumult) unlawful. "In short, because to worship God can never be a crime, no meeting or assembly, designing to worship God, can be unlawful" (p. 971).

116. *Ibid.*, pp. 973–74. Penn made good use of the historical lore concerning Empson and Dudley in his denunciation of the authorities' approach to the indictment process (pp. 989 *et seq.*).

measure the truth of the indictment, and guilt of the fact."[117] Thus, had the bench "produced" the law, as the defendants had demanded, the jury would then have been duty-bound to determine whether the indictment and judicial charge conformed to the law regarding the facts required for the alleged offense. Presumably this determination would have been informed not only by their own understanding of the law but also by their consideration of the defendants' arguments against the bench's interpretation of law.

This, then, was Penn's conception of due process in trials by jury—so far as one can now reconstruct it. Penn's claim that his jurors were his "sole judges" was not a claim that the bench played no role at all; the bench was to "produce" the law and to charge juries upon it, and even to monitor indictments for just the sort of abuses of which Penn and Mead believed they had been made victims. The jury, one might suppose, would give the bench's charge due weight. It operated as a shield where necessary, and, for the Quakers, unusual events had created present necessities.

Penn and Mead's views, and their behavior at their trial, were fiercely attacked by Sir Samuel Starling, the Lord Mayor of London, in a tract written in part as a reply to the defendants' trial account and the *Appendix*.[118] Starling, who had presided at the trial, produced an account of the proceedings that differed little in detail from that of the defendants but one that—perhaps sincerely—misconceived the nature of the campaign on behalf of the jury. Starling characterized the defendants' behavior as insulting attempts to undermine the law, and the jury's "special" verdict as a nonverdict, an abuse of their duty. Starling never doubted that the jurors merited the fines imposed upon them for their outright nullification of the law: the Crown, he believed, had lawfully charged and definitively proved an unlawful assembly.

Addressing the Westminster bench, Starling devoted much of his tract to a denunciation of Penn's notion "[t]hat the jury were the proper judges both of law and fact."[119] Not surprisingly, he thought that Penn's historical "precedents," reproduced in the *Appendix*, falsely demonstrated the jury's right to find the law. However, he wrongly interpreted Penn's appeal to the jury as his "sole judges" as an entire renunciation of

117. *Ibid.*, p. 974.

118. Starling, *An Answer to the Seditious and Scandalous Pamphlet*.

119. *Ibid.*, p. 2: "Now Gentlemen of the long robe look to your selves, and your Westminster Hall: If these learned reformers of religion shall likewise reform your laws and methods of proceedings (as doubtless they design it) and make twelve jurymen, eleven of which it's possible can neither write nor read, to be the sole judges both of law and fact; farewell then to your great acquisitions, your Year Books then will be out of date, and an ouster will be put to your Books of Entries."

the powers of the bench, a "claim" he rebutted as absurd and dangerous. The Quakers, Starling asserted, would reduce the justices to "ciphers," a term he may have taken from Lilburne's well known 1649 appeal to his jury.[120] The defendants, he continued, misinterpreted Magna Carta's most famous chapter. "By lawful judgment of his peers, *or* by the law of the land" did not guarantee trial by peers who acted as judges. As it was in the "disjunctive," the Crown might employ the "law of the land," which must mean trial by *both* judge and jury ("peers"). Magna Carta was entirely consistent with that well known legal maxim: "[T]he judges respond to questions of law." In claiming trial solely by jurors, Starling concluded, the Quakers aimed at a special sort of jury, not that employed by the common law; they intended ultimately to "turn the judges and juries also out of Westminster Hall and set up a High Court of Justice of Saints."[121]

Starling's tract provoked a retort from Penn. *Truth Rescued from Imposture* was written during February and March of 1671, in Newgate, where London authorities had imprisoned Penn anew, this time for breach of the Five Mile Act.[122] Now forced to state more precisely his pro-jury position, Penn defended his view that jurors are judges of law as well as fact, pointing to the form of the traditional charge to the petty jury: "to deliver their verdict or opinion, whether [the defendant] be guilty in manner and form." Since the indictment "comprehends both law and fact," the jury is judge of both, to determine "whether the fact proved be obnoxious to the law."[123] But how does the jury achieve its understanding of the law? This question Penn now answered for the first time. The jurors need not take the law solely from the bench; otherwise, the bench might require a verdict of guilty for "the most lawful act imaginable, it being such as he cannot deny, and which is proved by evidences." While acknowledging that a jury might be so ignorant that "there may be a necessity to inform them of the law, by the better skill of the justices," Penn argued that even in such a case the law stood only as it is

understood, digested, and judiciously made the jury's, by their own free will and acceptance, upon their conviction of the truth of things reported by the bench: As a man may be educated in any religion; but to make it his proper religion, it is requisite that he believe and embrace

120. *Ibid.*, p. 3.
121. *Idem.*
122. Penn, *Truth Rescued* (see above, n. 52). For Penn's activities between September, 1670, and March, 1671, see Peare, *William Penn*, pp. 127–34. *Truth Rescued* appears to have been written in February, 1671; Thomas Rudyard added an "Appendix" in that month and Penn added a "Postscript" in March, 1671.
123. Penn, *Truth Rescued*, pp. 500, 504–5.

it judiciously, not implicitly.[124]

Penn thus conceded an important role to the bench, while marking out the limits of its power and articulating his conception of the process by which the jury "finds the law."

Penn's views found support in Thomas Rudyard's *Dialogue, in a Plain and Friendly Discourse between Student and Citizen*.[125] The tract referred to Penn and Mead's trial, the *Appendix*, and to the trial of Rudyard, Francis Moor, and several others, all of whom were convicted by a jury that replaced the jury that had tried Penn and Mead.[126] In *Dialogue*, a self-styled student of the common law explains the importance of jury duty, the nature of the juror's role, and the unlawfulness of the punishment of jurors for finding according to their conscience. Echoing Penn (and well-settled Quaker strategy), the Student advises the Citizen as juror to observe the indictment closely so as to determine whether the evidence offered proves the defendant guilty not only of the acts alleged in the indictment but also of the "manner" ("which they call law"), for "though a person be proved to be guilty of some fact or misdemeanor, yet if it be not also proved to be done in such manner and form as the party stands indicted, he is not guilty, and ought to be acquitted by you."[127] To the Citizen's query, "But is not there both law and fact in an indictment, as those against W.P. and W.M. and the rest of the Quakers last sessions? And how shall a jury deal in such cases?"[128] the Student replies that the jury may return a special verdict, finding the fact and asking the Court to apply the law.

Citizen: What's the reason then, that the Court will not accept of such

---

124. *Ibid.*, p. 502.

125. Thomas Rudyard, *An Appendix, by way of Dialogue, in a Plain and Friendly Discourse between a Student in the Laws and Liberties of England, and a true Citizen of London* (London, 1670). This tract was appended to *The Second Part of the Peoples Antient and Just Liberties* (London, 1670) that was itself part of an expanded edition of Penn's account of his trial. *The Second Part* recounted the trial of Thomas Rudyard.

126. *The Second Part of the Peoples Antient and Just Liberties Asserted.* This account was probably written by Penn and Rudyard. It states that after Penn's jury had been incarcerated, a new jury was called to try Rudyard (who had taken part with Penn and Mead in convoking the assembly in Gracechurch Street) and about a dozen others for obstructing the prosecution for sedition of Samuel Allinbridge. To obtain the new jury, the account alleges, the clerk "picked here and there such persons that were judged the most likely to answer the malicious ends and horrid designs of [the] Bench, calling not the jury-men in order and direct course, as is usual in all courts of justice, where right is impartially administered; and withal, bidding the prisoners to look upon the jurors, and before they were sworn to make their challenges" (p. 364).

127. *Dialogue, in a Plain and Friendly Discourse*, p. 396.

128. *Ibid.*, p. 397.

special verdicts, but frequently turn the jury back, till they bring in general?

Student: Because then they have your oaths as well for law as fact; and if the judgments be severe, it shall lie at your door.[129]

This was, of course, a far riskier tactic than that of a simple statement of the facts that had been found unaccompanied by a request to apply the law.[130] Because it left the bench the legal right to enter a verdict of guilty, however, it could prove much more embarrassing.

The Student goes on to charge, along the lines of Penn and Mead's *Appendix,* that the authorities systematically loaded down indictments with incriminating terms: verdicts of "guilty" on insufficient facts might then be applied to the entire indictment. Moreover, the "City Magistrates" had a "further artifice." They indict persons "by the common law, and waive intermeddling with any of the statutes in force against such misdemeanors, as they pretend the persons indicted are guilty of."[131] Thus, stated the author, in an obvious reference to Penn and Mead's case, the bench, when asked to produce the law on which the indictment is based, answers that it is *"Lex non scripta."*

> By this means the prisoner is incapacitated to make his defence, and the jury kept ignorant, whether the offence charged to be done by the prisoner be innocency or guilt. . . . [T]hey might have framed an indictment against a man for *(vi et armis)* eating meat at his own table. . . . Therefore it concerns you to have great care and regard to the charge you undertake; which is, well and truly to try, and true deliverance make, according to what is evidenced to your conscience.[132]

Conscience, then, required that jurors do one of two things: Either they ought to return a special verdict and thereby force the bench openly to wrench the law to its own ends, or taking it upon themselves to find the law, they ought to find the defendant "not guilty."

Of course there were cases—*Penn's Case* was one—where the bench would not tolerate either course of action, where the bench believed that such jury behavior seriously threatened the social order. For what officials took to be an outright and illegal nullification of the law, the jury

---

129. *Idem.*

130. In many Quaker cases, including Penn and Mead's trial, the jury merely stated the facts it had found, omitting any finding whatsoever on what it knew to be the crucial facts. Moreover, it did not request the bench to apply the law. For cases involving Quakers in which jurors rendered such verdicts see e.g. Besse, *A Collection of the Sufferings of . . . Quakers,* I: 48 (1663, Bristol), 634 (1683, Somersetshire), 730 (1684, Sussex). It is not clear how the bench ought in law to have treated such truncated verdicts.

131. *Dialogue, in a Plain and Friendly Discourse,* p. 399.

132. *Ibid.,* pp. 399–400.

would be fined and imprisoned until the fines were paid. Inevitably, the question of the legality of the fining and imprisonment of jurors for acquitting in criminal cases "against manifest evidence" was central to the tracts occasioned by the trial of Penn and Mead. In the *Appendix* and the *Dialogue*, Penn and Rudyard dealt at length with this question. The defendants had protested at their trial against the bench's treatment of their jury, particularly against the court's refusal to accept the jury's first several verdicts. Penn had asserted that judicial fining of jurors offended the principle, set forth in Magna Carta, that no free man should be amerced "but by the lawful judgment of his peers." Indeed, Penn had made judicial behavior toward the jury a principal basis of his final appeal to the jury that it should consider the entire course of the proceedings against him illegal.[133]

In the *Appendix*, Penn developed more fully the question of jury control, recounting both ancient and recent precedents relating to trial by jury. He claimed that jury fining was an innovation, that the Court did "most illegally, tyranically fine and imprison [the defendants] . . . notwithstanding the late just resentment of the House of Commons, in Judge Kelyng's Case, where they resolved, 'That the precedent and practice of fining, and imprisoning of juries for their verdicts, were illegal.'"[134] Rudyard's *Dialogue* likewise recounted recent events in its argument against the legality of fining jurors. It made effective use of the Kelyng incident and, after summarizing *Penn's Case,* described the "packing and enforcement" of the jury that convicted Rudyard, Moor, and the others tried before it. The imprisonment of Penn and Mead's jury, the *Dialogue* asserted, had been directly responsible for the new jury's obsequious behavior.[135]

Not all of the arguments in the *Dialogue* were historically based or reduced to mere aphorisms. Some of them went to the nature of the criminal trial, arguing—as Vaughan was to argue—from the logic of the trial to the unlawfulness of fining jurors. Rudyard devoted the opening passages of the *Dialogue* to the jury's duty to find the fact—and to the proposition that they were better equipped to do so than was the bench. The jury, the Student explained, is drawn from the vicinage "where the fact is supposed to be done or acted" because "it's always presumed that the neighborhood are best acquainted with the persons inhabiting, or the actions and facts. . . . They may know the witness on the one side, or the

133. *State Trials*, 6:961–69. Penn argued that the proceedings were "most arbitrary and void of all law" because the bench gave "the jury their charge in the absence of the prisoners" (p. 961). Subsequently, he protested against the threatening of the jury by the recorder (p. 965) and then the fining of the jurors for their verdict (pp. 968–69).

134. *Ibid.,* p. 984.

135. *Dialogue, in a Plain and Friendly Discourse,* pp. 400–2.

other, to be persons of no credit, or . . . they may know the party accused to be a man otherwise qualified or principled, than to do such an act."[136] The Citizen was quick to see the point: it would be "very hard" if the jury were fined, since it may be taking into account things it knows of its own. Moreover, continued the Student, one ought to prefer the "knowledge of twelve men, agreeing together" to the "single apprehension of any one person whatsoever."[137]

The *Dialogue* also confronted—as would Vaughan—the logic of concluding, in a particular case, that the jury had found "against the law." The Student, quoting Coke, explained that since "the law grows out of the root of the fact," if the jury does not find the fact, then the jury "cannot be said to find against the law, which is no other than a superstructure of fact." The Student conceded that if the jury openly find the fact and then find against the law, "the Court ought to give judgment according to law."[138] Finally, the *Dialogue* produced an unusual argument regarding the problem of appellate review. Because no writ of error lay in such a case, jurors would be "remediless of relief" if judges could fine them, and thus they would be "in worse condition than the criminals that are tried by them." If the bench moved by way of attaint, the first jury would have some safeguard, as "the truth or falsehood of a juror's verdict, in matters of fact, may be tried." But in a criminal case, "the jurors are concluded, by reason that whether they have found with or against their evidence, can never be tried." The *Dialogue* thus appears to assume that attaint lay only in civil cases, and it employed this assumption in its argument against the fining of jurors.[139]

Starling's reply to the *Appendix* had included a lengthy discourse on the subject of fining. First Starling cited a string of cases, only one earlier than 1660, in which juries had been fined for verdicts unacceptable to the courts. These cases, *Wagstaffe's Case* and *Leech's Case* among them, were the backbone of the pro-fining argument, and Starling concluded from them that "[t]he fining of jurors that find contrary to their evidence is no innovation, but always practised."[140] Like Rudyard, Starling concluded that attaint did not lie in criminal cases, but he drew from this fact a very different conclusion. Not surprisingly he couched his argument against attaint in legal rather than theoretical terms, for any philosophical argument against attaint of juries could also cut against their being fined.

136. *Ibid.*, pp. 391–92.
137. *Ibid.*, pp. 392, 394.
138. *Ibid.*, p. 394.
139. *Ibid.*, p. 393.
140. Starling, *An Answer to the Seditious and Scandalous Pamphlet,* pp. 32–33. Starling's statement that the jury in *Leech's Case* was fined (p. 33) was rebutted by Rudyard in his "Appendix" to *Truth Rescued* at p. 514.

Starling cited Coke and Fitzherbert for the proposition that "attaint lies [for] . . . false verdict . . . against the Plaintiff or Defendant . . . in a plea, real or personal, sued out by writ or bill," but not in a criminal case. "It is agreed by all sides, that an attaint lieth not in an indictment of treason, murder or felony; much less in an indictment of trespass, which . . . is far lesser offence than them aforementioned." He relied on Brooke for the maxim that "where the King is the sole party, attaint doth not lie." Finally, he cited statutes establishing the remedy of attaint in certain cases and argued from this that its nonexistence at common law must be inferred. The strength of the government's case lay in the fact that, without the power to fine, there would be no remedy for an acquittal against manifest evidence; instead there would be, pure and simple, a "failure of justice."[141] Thus Starling, like counsel for the Crown who were busily attempting to justify the imprisonment of Bushel, echoed Chief Justice Hyde's admonition in 1665 that "jurors ought to be fined if they . . . take bit in mouth and go headstrong against the court . . . seeing the attaint is now fruitless."[142]

*Truth Rescued from Imposture,* Penn's answer to Starling's tract, contains an appendix by Thomas Rudyard which takes issue with the claim implicit in the title of Starling's section on fining, "The Fining of That Jury, that Gave Two Different Verdicts Justified."[143] Although Starling abandoned the charge in the body of the work, the implication of perjury is important, for such behavior might have justified the fines imposed on Bushel and the other jurors. Rudyard sought to show that the verdict rejected by the court, "Guilty of speaking in Gracechurch Street," and the general verdict of "not guilty" were not contradictory. The jury had been forced to resolve its verdict one way or another; Starling, Rudyard charged, has "a very treacherous memory, which is an ill companion for a Liar."[144]

Rudyard agreed with Starling on the technical aspects of the attaint issue, but went on to make a broader claim that implicated fining as well. "[We] not only grant to him that no attaint lies against such jurors, but that it is horrid injustice and oppression to punish them by that, *or any other way.*"[145] In a gloss on Starling's bald statement that where the king

---

141. Starling, *An Answer to the Seditious and Scandalous Pamphlet,* pp. 31, 33–38. "As nature abhors a vacuum in the universe, so it is the honour of our law, that it will not suffer a failure of justice" (p. 31).

142. 1 Keble 864, 83 *Eng. Rep.* 1288 (1665).

143. Thomas Rudyard, "Appendix" (see above, nn. 52, 122).

144. *Ibid.*, p. 512.

145. Rudyard cited Horn's *Mirror* on judicial abuses of juries, and the parliamentary statutes on attaint, saying that if attaint lay in such a case, it would be clear from the statutes. *Ibid.*, p. 519 (emphasis added).

is the sole party, there is no remedy of attaint, Rudyard asserted that an element of corruption must be present before a verdict is punishable, because although the indictment is prosecuted in the name of the King, he is acting in the interests of the public. Cannot the public, Rudyard asked, be entrusted with their own protection and safety?[146] Thus did Rudyard attempt to avoid Starling's (and the Crown lawyers') conclusion regarding a "failure of Justice."

Continuing (more cogently) his attack on fining, Rudyard denied that there was any, except recent, precedent for fining, and cited the censure of Justice Kelyng as invalidating the post-Restoration cases cited by Starling. Following the line of argument he had established in the *Dialogue,* Rudyard asserted that the procedure used in fining denied jurors the "due process of the common law," in that the jurors were condemned without trial, with no possibility of review or appeal, and without the lawful judgment of their peers. Rudyard cited Coke on the common law of England, particularly on the maxim that *Lex intendit vicinum vicini facta scire,* and claimed that, according to Coke's *"ratio legis,"* the law would have "left all controversies to [the judges'] sole arbitrary determination" had judges been better equipped to hand down verdicts.[147] Two interests, Rudyard asserted, were represented by those who argued against fining: the freedom of jurors, and the freedom of the people of England. In the interests of these freedoms, all Englishmen on trial should be judged by "twelve honest men of the neighborhood," who are presumed to be more fit to hand down a verdict than a judge, both by their numbers, "since . . . twelve men may neither be so easily corrupted as one single person, nor their judgment of such fact . . . so likely to be erroneous" and because, being of the "neighborhood where the offence was committed," they may be expected to have a fuller understanding of the crime than the judge. In this way, "lives and liberties can be secured against the lusts of . . . petty prerogatives."[148]

Rudyard's arguments against the practice of jury fining seem less an extension of either the Quaker "law-finding" theory or the older notion of the merciful verdict than elaborations upon the much more modest theory that he set forth in the *Dialogue.*[149] This theory was more difficult for the bench to refute, for it emphasized the inscrutability of fact that resulted from the possibility that the jurors possessed personal knowledge. If Rudyard's true claim was that, because the jury was judge of both law and fact, it could not in any way be coerced or punished for its verdict, the

146. *Idem.*
147. *Ibid.,* pp. 513–17.
148. *Ibid.,* p. 516.
149. See above, n. 136 and accompanying text.

claim was well hidden by the arguments that focused mainly on the fact-finding aspect of the jury's role, its claims to superior knowledge. Rudyard constructed a defense behind which the jury might effectively act as independently of the bench as if they were judges both of fact and law, but his view was bound to be much more acceptable to the bench, for it largely avoided the overtones of insurrection which made the "law-finding" theory so unpalatable. In this respect, Rudyard's argument against fining suggested the strategy that Vaughan was to follow, but Rudyard's central argument, based on the proposition that jurors were still self-informed, was to become only one—and perhaps the less significant—element of the Chief Justice's famous opinion.

# IV

Two and a half months after the final, tense day of Penn and Mead's trial at the Old Bailey, Edward Bushel, who had been imprisoned in Newgate for refusing to pay his fine of forty marks, sued a writ of habeas corpus out of the Court of Common Pleas. He claimed that the fine had no basis in law and that he was, therefore, being held without lawful cause. Bushel's suit, in which three of his fellow jurors joined, brought to a head the recent political and legal ferment over the issue of fining jurors.[150] Five years had passed since *Wagstaffe's Case,* when most of the bench

150. T. Jones 14, 84 *Eng. Rep.* 1123 (1670). The three who joined Bushel were John Hammond, Charles Milson, and John Bailey, all "merchants and tradesmen" and citizens and freemen of London. The other eight jurors "paid their fines and were soon discharged." See *The Case of Edward Bushel [et al.] . . . stated and humbly presented to the Honourable House of Commons assembled in Parliament* (London, 1671?). This petition is in Lincoln's Inn Library, *Miscellaneous Pamphlets,* vol. 104 at p. 37. The petition refers to the successful resolution of the case, which occurred in late 1671, and states that the jurors were discouraged by counsel "to seek [further] remedy or satisfaction in the courts of Westminster." Hence the petition to Commons. Subsequently, Bushel and Hammond did attempt to sue the mayor and recorder who had presided at Penn and Mead's trial, but their suits were rejected. For *Bushel v. Starling* see 3 Keble 322, 84 *Eng. Rep.* 744 (1674): suit for false imprisonment fails because "no writ of error lies . . . but he must be delivered by certiorari or habeas corpus and no other ways." For *Bushel v. Howell* see 3 Keble 358, 84 *Eng. Rep.* 765 (1674): action upon the case fails because "this action will not lie against a judge." See also *Bushel's Case,* 1 Mod. 119, 86 *Eng. Rep.* 777 (1674). For *Hamond (sic) v. Howell* see 2 Mod. 218, 86 *Eng. Rep.* 1035 (1677): suit for false imprisonment fails because "it was an error in [the judges'] judgments for which no action will lie" *(ibid.,* p. 1037). The defendant may bring a certiorari; "the Barons of the Exchequer might refuse to issue process upon" an erroneous judgment *(idem).* "[T]he whole court were of opinion, that the bringing of this action was a greater offense than the fining of the plaintiff, and committing of him for non-payment; and that it was a bold attempt both against the Government and justice in general . . . though the defendant here acted erroneously, yet the contrary opinion carried great colour with it, because it might be supposed very inconvenient for the jury to have such liberty as to give what verdicts they please" *(ibid.,* pp. 1036–37).

had concluded that such fining was indeed legal. Now, in a more prominent case, the matter came again before the royal justices, this time before the Court of Common Pleas. In a decision that definitively overturned the ruling in *Wagstaffe's Case,* Chief Justice Vaughan finally laid the problem to rest.

It is not entirely clear why Bushel's counsel turned to Common Pleas rather than to the more appropriate forum, King's Bench. They may well have believed that he would receive a friendlier hearing from the court presided over by Vaughan, who had played a prominent (though ambiguous) role in the parliamentary proceedings involving Kelyng, than he would from Kelyng's former associates on King's Bench.[151] Ironically, Vaughan was opposed on jurisdictional grounds to granting the habeas corpus but was outvoted by his fellow justices.[152] In the event, it would be Vaughan who, in consultation with all the justices of the king's courts, wrote the opinion that addressed the merits of the case.

With a few significant exceptions, Vaughan's opinion followed the contours of the arguments made by Bushel's counsel and by Serjeants Ellis and Baldwin. Those arguments largely rehearsed the case earlier put, without success, on behalf of Wagstaffe: the return was too general; it failed to state the legal standards laid down by the bench and rejected by the jury as well as the facts that the jury had allegedly found against; even if one conceded the sufficiency of the return, one need not concede that it was demonstrable that the jurors had gone against the court. Some of the arguments that went beyond those made in *Wagstaffe's Case* paralleled those in the tract literature—just then appearing—that Penn and Mead's trial had generated: e.g., the juror might have knowledge of the "falsity" of evidence presented in court, and as a consequence, because law arises from fact *("ex facto jus oritur"),* one could not conclude that the jurors went against the law.[153]

There were, however, several new arguments. Judges as well as jurors, it was observed, might mistake the law; it would, therefore, be unreasonable to penalize the jury while the judges themselves were not subject to

---

151. Kelyng was still Chief Justice of King's Bench, but his illness kept him from taking part in judicial matters; technically, the other judges of King's Bench were current, not former, associates. Possibly counsel for Bushel believed that Kelyng still exerted influence over the bench; they might even have feared that the Chief Justice would feel his health returning when presented with the opportunity to rule personally on the habeas!

152. T. Jones 14, 84 *Eng. Rep.* 1123 (1670). According to Vaughan: "This court has no cognizance of crimes. . . . [The court may hear cases] between subject and subject, but in a criminal case the plea is between the King and his prisoner." See also Vaughan's view that Common Pleas was not the appropriate forum in a case a year later: *Anonymous,* Carter 222, 124 *Eng. Rep.* 928 (1671).

153. 1 Freeman 4–5, 89 *Eng. Rep.* 3–4 (1670); T. Jones 14–15, 84 *Eng. Rep.* 1124–25.

penalty for error. In any case, one ought to assume the good faith of
jurors, as one did judges, for jurors were "judges" of the fact. Jurors, it
was urged, have *"divisum imperium"* with the judge. One of Bushel's
counsel addressed this issue with a phrase that anticipated the most
original part of Vaughan's opinion: jurors, Broome asserted, "are to
satisfy their own consciences."[154]

These last arguments, which went to the heart of the question of the
jury's duty, left open the problem of the possible "failure of justice" that
had seemingly determined the outcome of *Wagstaffe's Case* and that
counsel for the Crown relied upon heavily in the present case. Bushel's
counsel seemed by and large to accept the possibility with equanimity; it
was a part of the system, perhaps no greater a threat than that of judicial
error. Serjeants Ellis and Baldwin, in favor of Bushel, argued that there
was a remedy: an attaint would lie, they said, a view ultimately rejected
by Vaughan. Because attaint lay in this kind of case, if Bushel and his
fellow jurors might also be fined they would be subject to a double
penalty. In making this point Ellis distinguished between capital cases,
where, *in favorem vitae*, attaint did not lie, and the case at hand, one of
mere misdemeanor.[155]

Nudigate and Baldwin argued, as Vaughan later would, that according
to the precedents fining was appropriate only for true jury misdemeanor
(in the sense of outright corruption). Baldwin's handling of the two major
precedents put by counsel for the Crown may not have been entirely
honest. *Wharton's Case,* he asserted, was never cited as precedent but
had been passed *sub silentio.* As for *Wagstaffe's Case,* it had probably
involved "some [true] misdemeanors," for the jurors, Baldwin wrongly
claimed, were fined in unequal amounts: ten were held to pay 100 marks;
two were fined only five marks. It is possible that Baldwin (and subsequently Vaughan) was confused by the report of the case (very similar to
Wagstaffe's) that had been charged against Kelyng in the House of
Commons. In that case, the report of which Vaughan's committee (and
now Baldwin) may have had in hand, Kelyng had indeed fined the jurors
different amounts. Kelyng's report, however, makes clear that those fines
were assessed simply for finding against the direction of the court. Only
a very hurried and careless review of the report would have left a reader
in doubt on that score. More than likely, Baldwin (and perhaps Vaughan)
honestly mistook the case for that of Wagstaffe and wittingly misread it to
suit his own end.[156]

154. 1 Freeman 3, 89 *Eng. Rep.* 3 (1670).
155. *Ibid.,* p. 4, 89 *Eng. Rep.* 5; T. Jones 15, 84 *Eng. Rep.* 1124.
156. 1 Freeman 2, 4–5, 89 *Eng. Rep.* 2, 4 (1670). For reference to, and discussion of,

For the Crown, Scroggs, Maynard, and Powis relied heavily upon *Wagstaffe's Case,* hardly going beyond it to meet those arguments for Bushel that might be deemed novel. Powis seems to have stressed the possibility of a "failure of justice," the point that had so exercised Kelyng and Twisden (and before them, Hyde). Maynard, presumably to the same end, insisted that an attaint did not lie on an indictment. But for the most part, the Crown's argument rested upon a defense of the generality of the return, the assertion that Bushel's appropriate remedy was a writ of error and the fact that the jury might have escaped their dilemma by returning a special verdict. Scroggs came closest to meeting the opposition's stress on the importance of maintaining some degree of jury independence. There was, he said, a danger both ways: the jury might be overawed, but then, too, the defendant might "lose all he has by the wilfulness of the jury and have no remedy."[157] This argument, which overlooked the possibility of a judicial reprieve, apparently was in reply to Broome's assertion that the power to fine would destroy the jury's independence of mind.[158] It was this issue that Vaughan was to make central in his opinion and for which he was to supply an as-yet-unstated rationale. In doing so, he would sidestep the main argument of the Crown and, without condoning law-finding—either true nullification or merciful discretion—take the case on behalf of the jurors a long step beyond the arguments both of counsel and of the tract writers.

Vaughan's opinion, holding for the Court of Common Pleas (and indeed for all the justices of England but one) that jurors may not be fined or imprisoned for their verdicts, is remarkable for how little it addressed the most volatile issues of the day. Vaughan's absolute conviction that jurors were judges only of fact and not of law, was left largely implicit, despite the fact that Penn and Mead had emphasized the issue of law-finding. The opinion contains no hint of the struggle between bench and jury that typified many Quaker prosecutions. It is an oddly and confusingly organized opinion whose central theme is difficult to discern.[159] Vaughan's contemporaries seem to have concluded that the decision turned on the argument that jurors might in any given case have knowledge of their own and thus could not be charged with finding either against evidence or against law.[160] A close reading of the case suggests

Kelyng's report of the case actually charged against him in Parliament, see above, nn. 63–64, 66, and accompanying text.

157. *Ibid.,* pp. 3, 5, 89 *Eng. Rep.* 3–5 (1670).

158. *Ibid.,* p. 3.

159. Vaughan 135, 124 *Eng. Rep.* 1006.

160. See below, text at nn. 213–32, for a discussion of tracts by John Hawles and Henry Care, who claimed that Vaughan endorsed jury law-finding, but who seem also to have

that there was more to it than that.

Vaughan divided his opinion into four principal sections: the sufficiency of the return to the writ of habeas corpus; reasons against fining; consideration of precedents regarding fining; and consideration of precedents regarding the power of Common Pleas to discharge, upon habeas, persons imprisoned by other courts. This last matter need not detain us beyond recitation of the argument that, Vaughan implied, convinced the Court of its power to discharge the imprisoned jurors:

> [W]hen a man is brought by habeas corpus to the Court, and upon return of it, it appears to the Court, that he was against the law imprisoned and detained, though there be no cause of privilege for him in this Court, he shall never be by the act of the Court remanded to his unlawful imprisonment, for then the Court should do an act of injustice in imprisoning him, *de novo*, against the law, whereas the great charter is, *quod nullus libet homo imprisonetur nisi per legem terrae.*[161]

Vaughan had opposed issuing the writ of habeas corpus, but having been outvoted by his brethren he was determined to see the case through to its conclusion.

Vaughan's arguments regarding the sufficiency of the return of the writ of habeas corpus dealt first with the allegation that the jury had found *"contra plenum et manifestam evidentiam"* and then with the allegation that the jury had found *"contra directionam curiae in materia legis."* On the question of finding against the evidence, Vaughan observed: "The Court hath no knowledge by this return, whether the evidence given were full and manifest, or doubtful, lame and dark, or indeed evidence at all material to the issue. . . ."[162] How far, then, ought one to credit the bare assertion of a court that the evidence given to the jury was full and manifest? Laying an important foundation stone for the arguments that were to follow, Vaughan firmly denied that the judgment of the bench was beyond inquiry. Though a judge's "ability, parts, fitness for his place, are not to be reflected on," a judge is not to be presumed "unerring in [his] place." No one with any interest by virtue of "the judgment, action, or authority exercised upon his person or fortunes . . . must submit . . . to the implied discretion and unerringness of his judge, without seeking such redress as the law allows him."[163] Vaughan referred to the frequent review and reversal of judicial judgments, whether of "inferior" or "superior" courts, and concluded, perhaps gratuitously, that "corrupt

based their views of Vaughan's fact-finding argument mainly on Vaughan's references to the jurors' possession of out-of-court evidence.

161. Vaughan 155, 124 *Eng. Rep.* 1016.
162. *Ibid.*, p. 137, 124 *Eng. Rep.* 1007.
163. *Ibid.*, p. 139, 124 *Eng. Rep.* 1008.

and dishonest judgments . . . have in all ages been complained of to the King in Star Chamber, or to the Parliament." He made reference to such instances down to the impeachment of the judges who ruled for the Crown in the *Case of Ship Money*.[164] Kelyng was not mentioned, perhaps because he was neither "corrupt" nor "dishonest." Perhaps (but not likely) he had not even come to Vaughan's mind.

Vaughan's opening sally overrode the distinction between "superior" and "inferior" courts, a distinction even Hale had conceded in his grudging admission that King's Bench might not be reviewed by a common-law court. In logic, Vaughan had established only that King's Bench was reviewable by Parliament; in effect, however, given his refusal to remand a person imprisoned "against the law," Vaughan had announced that once a habeas had issued, the power of review extended even to the Court of Common Pleas. Vaughan's second argument on the sufficiency of the return set forth a critical rule of law regarding "fineable fault" in jurors. Jurors, he asserted, may be fined only for finding against their own view of the evidence. That amounted to perjury, in effect to a true misdemeanor. The return was deficient for failing to state that the jury had so found. Vaughan found support for this proposition in Bracton and *Fleta*, but his own rationale is of greatest interest. People commonly disagreed, he observed, about evidence in many contexts. Barristers and judges deduced "contrary and opposite conclusions out of the same case. And is there any difference that two men should infer distinct conclusions from the same testimony?" By what logic, then, must "one of these merit fine and imprisonment, because he doth that which he cannot otherwise do, preserving his oath and integrity? And this often is the case of the judge and jury."[165] Vaughan had gone well beyond claiming that the return was insufficient. He had asserted that the bench could not fine a jury unless it could prove bad faith out of the mouths of the jurors themselves.

Vaughan made short work of the question of sufficiency of return regarding acquittal "against the direction of the court in matter of law." The allegation is meaningless, said Vaughan, unless it means that the judge, having taken upon himself knowledge of the fact, directed the jury on the law. But if the judge is to find the fact, why use a jury? Vaughan's premise was:

> Without a fact agreed, it is impossible for a judge, or any other, to know the law relating to that fact or direct concerning it, as to know an accident that hath no subject.

164. *Idem.*
165. *Ibid.,* pp.141–42, 124 *Eng. Rep.* 1009.

Hence it follows, that the judge in logic can never direct what the law is in any matter controverted, without first knowing the fact; and then it follows, that without his previous knowledge of the fact, the jury cannot in logic go against his direction in law, for he could not direct.[166]

Vaughan conceded that a judge might *nearly* know how the jury has found the fact before he directs them. In some "special trial," the judge might ask the jurors how they found a certain fact or "whether they find the matter of fact to be as such a witness, or witnesses have deposed." But even here the judge's direction ought to be "hypothetical, and upon supposition, and not positive, and upon coercion," for "until a jury have consummated their verdict . . . they have time still of deliberation." Regardless of their previous reply to the judge on matters of fact, "they may lawfully vary from it if they find cause."[167]

This last assertion, that the jury may "vary from" its answer if "they find cause," was the weakest link in Vaughan's chain of reasoning. He must have realized that in some cases the jury had revealed enough of its findings on fact for the bench to conclude that the jury knowingly was going against the evidence. Indeed, in what is clearly an earlier, tentative draft of his opinion, Vaughan had conceded that where the verdict contradicted the jury's announced findings, and the jury failed to correct itself, the verdict was to be "set aside and a new trial . . . directed."[168] Presumably, where in such a case the jury refused to "correct itself," it could be punished for perjury. Only subsequently—in the final (published) version of his opinion—did Vaughan alter his views crucially and further limit the scope of the judge's power to conclude that the jurors had committed perjury, asserting that, after they gave their in-court answers, but before they pronounced their verdict, the jurors (or any one of them) might have (honestly) changed their minds regarding the evidence.[169]

If Vaughan meant to suggest that jurors in such cases typically did change their minds on the evidence, he was being insincere. His opinion carries force only to the extent that it argues that a jury *might* have honestly reassessed the evidence and that the judge could never be certain it had not done so. Vaughan's opinion is least convincing regarding prosecutions under the Conventicles Act where the defendants admitted attending the meeting but failed to show that religious worship

166. *Ibid.*, p. 147, 124 *Eng. Rep.* 1012.
167. *Ibid.*, pp. 144–45, 124 *Eng. Rep.* 1010–11.
168. B.L. MS Lansd. 648.9, fol. 315v.
169. The new-trial remedy seems to have been a substitute for proceedings by way of attaint, the remedy Vaughan had assumed existed in such cases only three years earlier. See above, text preceding n. 84. If so, what Vaughan had meant by "corrupt" in his speech in the Commons in 1668 was not limited to verdicts resulting from bribes but included those in which the jury simply did not believe.

(against Anglican form) was not involved. Acquittals in such cases (as in later prosecutions for seditious libel) were clearly based on rejections of the bench's view of the law. In other cases, including several of the homicide cases that Kelyng addressed in Parliament and prosecutions for unlawful assembly (the offense charged in Penn and Mead's case), the possibility of honest reassessment was not automatically excludable. As we shall see, Vaughan's failure to distinguish between those kinds of cases made it possible for later writers to employ his language in their justification of acquittals in cases of seditious libel.

Vaughan's listing of reasons against fining includes significant additions to those he gave in his discussion of sufficiency of return. He began with a reference to the argument for which the opinion is famous, that the judge could not direct because "he can never know what evidence the jury have."[170] But before stating the reasons why the judge was in this position, Vaughan returned to the most original premise of his opinion: even were the jury to have no evidence other than that deposed in Court, "even then the Judge and jury might honestly differ in the result from the evidence, as well as two Judges may, which often happens."[171]

The more famous arguments, concerning out-of-court evidence, head a catchall list of points that appear to have been culled from arguments made at bar. On the whole, they were unoriginal and routinely made. Vaughan stated that jurors were supposed to have "sufficient knowledge" to try a case in which no evidence on either side was produced in court. Moreover, they might have "personal knowledge" that conflicted with what was deposed in court. Finally, the "jury may know the witnesses to be stigmatized and infamous." These curt observations were followed by reference to jurors having the view of premises ("to this evidence likewise the Judge is a stranger"), which affected civil but rarely criminal cases; mention of the dilemma posed by the possibility of attaint (though Vaughan no longer believed that attaint lay in criminal cases);[172] recapitulation of rules presupposing that juries were self-informed and impartial (the vicinage rule, rules of challenge, the freehold requirement, the view).[173] To what end, he summarized, once again moving back to the true basis for his opinion,

> must [juries] undergo the heavy punishment of the villanous judgment, if after all this they implicitly must give a verdict by the dictates and

170. Vaughan 147, 124 *Eng. Rep.* 1012.
171. *Idem.*
172. This argument, which does not appear in the manuscript draft of Vaughan's opinion, appears to have been added either carelessly or insincerely (as a makeweight).
173. *Idem.*

authority of another man, under pain of fines and imprisonment, when sworn to do it according to the best of their own knowledge:

A man cannot see by another's eye, nor hear by another's ear, no more can a man conclude or infer the thing to be resolved by another's understanding or reasoning; and though the verdict be right the jury give, yet they being not assured it is so from their own understanding, are foresworn, at least *in foro conscientiae*.[174]

Vaughan thus turned away from standard arguments derived from jury practices, some of which practices were becoming outmoded or pertained mainly to civil cases, to restate the fundamental, and original,[175] element of his discussion of the sufficiency of the return. Even if the judge had all of the evidence before him, judge and jury might disagree, and jury trial was premised on a preference for the jury's assessment of that evidence.

The remainder of this section of Vaughan's opinion reveals the extent of his reliance on civil cases. It is not surprising that Vaughan drew his examples from his own domain in Common Pleas. Most significantly, he insisted that jury independence in criminal cases should be as great as in civil cases, where judges could not fine. Nowhere in his opinion did Vaughan give space to Kelyng's and Twisden's concern about a "failure of justice." If in criminal cases there was liability neither to attaint nor to fine, presumably it was because the defendant, not the Crown, had more at stake.[176]

Vaughan's discussion of precedents follows, in the main, that of counsel at bar. He was fully prepared to sanction fining of a jury for accepting a bribe or for committing any other true ministerial breach—including, of course, giving a verdict *provably* against oath. Most of the precedents that others had cited, he asserted, either certainly or at least apparently fell into the class of legitimate impositions of fines. The two most prominent criminal cases commonly thought to be precedents for fining jurors who gave verdicts against the evidence were *Wharton's Case* and *Wagstaffe's Case*. Vaughan stated that even those cases might have involved true jury misdemeanor. Probably he allowed his reading of main trends to influence his view of particular cases.[177] In any event, at several

174. *Ibid.*, p. 148, 124 *Eng. Rep.* 1012–13.
175. The last twenty-seven words ("and though . . . *conscientiae*") do not even appear in Vaughan's tentative manuscript draft.
176. Vaughan 146, 124 *Eng. Rep.* 1011: "If [the judge] could not [fine the jury] in civil causes . . . he could not in criminal causes upon indictments . . . for the fault in both was the same, namely, finding against the evidence and direction of the Court, and by the common law; the reason being the same in both, the law is the same."
177. Vaughan appears to have followed Baldwin on these two precedents. See above, text at n. 156. Vaughan evidently preferred to think that the best report of *Wharton's Case* was Noy's, which suggested that the fine was imposed because "the judges conceived the

points he commented on the absence of clear evidence that courts had fined in accordance with the allegations in the return in *Bushel's Case*. There was, he said, no evidence that the common-law bench or Star Chamber had ever fined "only for (i.e., as the judge inferred) finding against the evidence"; in civil cases, there was no evidence of fining at common law before statutes of attaint, or thereafter, "until Popham's time," when the fines were not clearly other than for jury misdemeanor.[178]

Taken at face value, Vaughan's opinion rested ultimately on two propositions: the common law required trial by jury; in such trials, without the confession of the jurors themselves, it could never be *shown* that the jurors had gone against fact or, hence, that in applying the law the jurors had rejected judicial instructions on how the law ought to be applied. Further than this he did not go. Although jurors might "resolve both law and fact complicately," presumably they were supposed to follow instructions on the law. He cited no exception to the rule that jurors were to adhere to the facts they had found. The word "mercy" does not appear in his opinion.

Some of Vaughan's arguments based on the self-informing role of the jury ring false, for they hark back to much earlier times; but others do not. Jurors' knowledge of reputation was still sometimes an important evidentiary guide, both in criminal cases and in the civil trials from which Vaughan took his lead. The rule that jurors must go only by evidence produced in court had not yet been firmly settled in criminal cases, and certainly it was not considered wrong for a jury to *acquit* on outside evidence. But it remains unclear just how significant these arguments were for Vaughan. As he stated, even if the judge did know all the evidence, judge and jury might nevertheless disagree. The judge could not assume perjury; the jury was bound to swear to what it believed, however an outsider might have viewed the case, however wrong the jury might be. Moreover, objective truth was not easily obtained in such matters: Vaughan compared the assessment of witness testimony to the interpreta-

---

jury had been unlawfully dealt with" (Vaughan 153, 124 *Eng. Rep.* 1015); he said of *Wagstaffe's Case* that "by the record it is reasonable to think the jurors committed some fault besides going against their evidence, for they were unequally fined" (*idem*). Vaughan struck from his published opinion the view expressed in his manuscript draft (B.L. MS Lansd. 648.9, fol. 315v) that "[Bushel's] case has been grounded upon many particular cases which I think have been grossly mistaken, therefore it's fit to give it a plenary resolution at this time." Vaughan did not deal with *Leech's Case*. Braithwaite ("Early Friends' Experience with Juries," p. 223) conjectures that Vaughan's omission of *Leech's Case* confirms Rudyard's assertion ("Appendix" to *Truth Rescued*, p. 514) that the jurors in that case were not in fact fined (see above, nn. 35, 140).

178. Vaughan 152, 124 *Eng. Rep.* 1014; ibid., p. 146, 124 *Eng. Rep.* 1012.

tion of religious texts.[179] Finally, no matter how wrong the jurors were in their sincere belief, the law guaranteed resolution of guilt or innocence according to *their* "understanding." Although the king might pardon a defendant convicted against the fact, as it appeared to the judge, acquittal by the jury was final.

It is useful to compare Vaughan's opinion with an anonymous (and hitherto unnoticed) contemporary manuscript tract, or draft argument, "Reasons against the Fine and Commitment of the Jurors."[180] "Reasons," which appears to pre-date *Bushel's Case*, almost certainly was occasioned by the fining of jurors in a case involving the Quakers. It is unlikely that the case was *Wagstaffe* or the very similar one charged against Kelyng in the House of Commons, for here the jurors were imprisoned until all of the 100 mark per juror fines ("imposed jointly and severally") had been paid.[181] The arguments in "Reasons" bear close relationship to those made by Serjeant Ellis in *Wagstaffe's Case:* great emphasis is placed on the notion of a *"divisum imperium"* between judge and jury and on the fact that judges are not punished for their errors. But "Reasons" contains a religious motif all its own.[182] Though it takes the form of a lawyer's brief, it might have been a lay tract designed to make the strongest case for juror independence and for verdicts reached according to conscience without the barest suggestion that jurors ought to engage in law-finding.[183]

"Reasons" contained most of the arguments that Vaughan made in support of the jury's right to be free from coercion. Like Vaughan, the author of "Reasons" confines fineable wrongdoing to perjury and other true misdemeanors. "Reasons" implies that the precedents for fining were actually cases involving some jury misdemeanor, but it relies ultimately on the view that precedent ought not to be followed if it is

179. *Ibid.*, p. 141, 124 *Eng. Rep.* 1009.
180. B.L. MS Sloane 827, fols. 35–42v. To my knowledge, this manuscript has never before been discussed in print.
181. *Ibid.*, fol. 42.
182. *Ibid.*, fol. 36: "If not according to their consciences then they offend God and incur punishments both temporal and eternal"; fol. 38v: "[N]either is it superfluous to consider that this trial by a jury in criminal cases is said to be a trial by God and the country which seems to imply the absoluteness of it, so that the acquittal by the country is an acquittal by God and finding guilty by the country a finding guilty by God."
183. "Reasons" refers to the reign of Henry VIII as "perhaps . . . not beyond the memory of some men living" (fol. 40v). It also refers to the Petition of Right (1628) (fol. 35); a person born in the last year of Henry VIII's reign would have been eighty-one in 1628. The author probably means that some living persons have heard or read about the time of Henry VIII. Clearly, "Reasons" bears all the marks of the mid-to-late-1660s jury-right debates. In my view, it was the work of Ellis or of someone influenced by his arguments in *Wagstaffe's Case.*

"against reason and the principles of justice." The tract makes the increasingly commonplace arguments that jurors have knowledge of their own and that, as law arises from fact, the judge cannot direct on the law until the jurors have pronounced their verdict.[184]

"Reasons," like Vaughan's opinion, holds that attaint does not lie, but it confronts the possibility of a failure of justice, as Vaughan did not do. First, the author concedes that "the administration of the law must be entrusted somewhere and there must be a *ne plus ultra* in all controversies." This trust had been distributed between judge and jury, both of whom are on oath to do justice. There is little reason to think, the author continues, that acquittals will cause a great deal of harm. That "one or two juries in an age are mistaken" does not suggest that many more will be, for "persons of their conditions" have more at risk than "persons of greater rank" who "are perhaps better guarded."[185] Moreover, trial by jury assumes jury independence. Here the author compares civil (i.e., Roman and canon) law with common law. In the latter system, evidence is given viva voce and is not made part of a sworn record that remains for later examination. Testimony given at common law, "upon a sudden altogether," cannot be sifted in the same way, nor "so well observed or remembered, for *vox audita perit.*" It would be unreasonable "that men's lives, liberties and estates should be bound up in so narrow and dangerous a compass as the direction of a judge against evidence seeming so to him."[186] The author of "Reasons" thus supplied a more powerful version than did Vaughan of the argument for relying upon twelve men's memories. And it was not only a matter of accurate observation and recall. The reason for using a form of trial to which jury independence was integral was that "no man if he be condemned can blame the King or the nobles or the judges or men of power, the frequent objects of envy, but his own peers and so every man rests content and his government secured."[187]

Vaughan was content to take the jury as a given; it required no justification beyond the comment that one man's memory is less accurate than that of twelve men. It was enough to observe that the jury was on oath to give a verdict according to *its* understanding. The problem for Vaughan resided more in the realm of science than in the realm of politics. Because people drew different conclusions from the same evidence, one could not presume insincerity. It was a point that Ellis and his fellows had not seen and that escaped the author of "Reasons." But it was also a

---

184. *Ibid.*, fols. 40v, 38v, 40.
185. *Ibid.*, fol. 41.
186. *Ibid.*, fols. 38v–39.
187. *Ibid.*, fol. 39.

point that begged the question, Why depend so heavily upon laymen's "understanding"? Surely the answer could not be solely that they might have knowledge of their own, for they could (and often did) report that knowledge to the judge. As "Reasons" implied, the true answer to the question, Why a *"divisum imperium?"*—i.e., Why use a jury in the first place?—involved considerations of trust and politics which took account of the fact that the judiciary was in reality, or in common supposition, capable of exercising tyrannical powers. This was ground upon which Vaughan would not unnecessarily tread.

Vaughan broke relatively little new ground in his opinion. Where he did adduce novel arguments, he did so in a modest way. He denied that attaint would lie in a criminal case, but he took his lead from the lack of precedent rather than from the rights of Englishmen. He suggested that if fines were not imposed in civil cases, a fortiori they ought not to be in criminal cases. His language was softer than that of Hale.[188] If judge and jury disagreed on questions of fact, the jury prevailed, according to Vaughan, both because otherwise the institution would be a waste of time and because it was unreasonable to make jurors swear to what they did not believe. Preference for the jury's view was implicit in institutional arrangements; for Vaughan, historical usage ipso facto suggested correct practice.

Vaughan used extreme care to avoid any argument that smacked of the politics of the day. His legal precedents were similarly uncontroversial, drawn almost without exception from before the Interregnum and not tainted by any recent political maneuvering or misuse of power; indeed, he ignored the series of contemporary cases on which proponents of jury fining relied as precedent, save for the most important one, *Wagstaffe's Case.* Perhaps for this reason Vaughan did not rely on the proceedings relating to the censure of Justice Kelyng, although as a party to the proceedings he was certainly aware that many in Commons supported his stand on fining. Nor, in his discussion of attaint, did he seek support from Hyde, who had called attaint a "fruitless remedy."[189] Instead, without endorsing either side in the Quakers' struggle with authorities, or even acknowledging the turmoil, Vaughan attempted to settle this controversial question simply on the basis of "reason" and his own (perhaps idealized) view of the old common law.

188. Hale, *History of the Pleas of the Crown*, 2:311–12: "[I]t were impossible almost for any judge or jury to convict a jury upon such an account, because [it is] impossible that all the circumstances of the case, that might move the jury to acquit a prisoner, could be brought in evidence; this therefore seems to me to be but in *terrorem*."
189. See above, nn. 31–32.

It is difficult to tell from Vaughan's opinion the influence he expected it would have on the jury law-finding debate. The opinion seemingly took little notice of the real world: it was grounded in legal theory, and what followed from that theory was not his concern. If Vaughan had any thoughts about law-finding or the jury's right to apply law mercifully, he kept them to himself. Penn's entreaties, as well as those of the Quakers for nearly a decade, seem, in the light of Vaughan's opinion, wrongheaded and irrelevant, and to have had little or no effect on the outcome of *Bushel's Case*. And yet it is difficult to believe that Vaughan failed to realize that the fact-finding role as he depicted it would be used by the pro-jury elements to forward their cause. To Vaughan's mind, legal reasoning and precedent followed the Quaker pro-jury arguments up to but not including the point where they advocated jurors' control over the law. Pro-jury interpreters of *Bushel's Case*, however, did not stop where Vaughan did; instead, they glossed his opinion, employing it in their forthright arguments for jurors as judges of law.

## V

The ruling in *Bushel's Case* probably had little impact on proceedings in most routine felony trials. In the great majority of such cases bench and jury continued to function as before, in tandem and without open conflict.[190] In those few cases where the bench found itself impatient with a too merciful—or simply dishonest—jury, the judge employed mechanisms short of outright coercion that typically afforded the bench effective control.[191] True jury intransigence, though now protected by law, was probably very rare.

Political trials, such as those for treason, the unlicensed printing of news, and seditious libel, presented a different situation. Since authorities were more likely to take a strong interest, the risk of disagreement with a resolute jury was substantially greater. In these and similar cases the transition from the principle to the practice of noncoercion was probably slow.[192] The nearly two decades between *Bushel's Case* and the Glorious

190. See below, Chapter 7, sections I and II, for discussion of the typical felony trial in the late seventeenth and eighteenth centuries.
191. See below, Chapter 7, text at nn. 36–39.
192. Joseph Besse (*A Collection of the Sufferings of . . . Quakers, I*) claimed that the bench sometimes refused to accept acquittals in trials of Quakers [pp. 106 (1675, Cheshire), 110 (1683, Cheshire)]. When a jury that acquitted was ordered to go out again to reconsider, one juryman objected, whereupon Peniston Whaley, one of the justices, was enraged and said he hoped that the king would get rid of juries. He allegedly told another jury that "[i]f they did not agree, they should be kept there till they died" and they complied [p. 560 (1676, Nottinghamshire)].

Revolution were testing years for the bench and criminal juries, grand and petty. The complicated and oft-described political trials of the most tumultuous years, 1678–83 (the period of the Popish Plot and its aftermath) need not be retold in detail here.[193] Our immediate interest lies mainly in one aspect of the legacy of those years, the fate of Vaughan's opinion in the hands of a few publicists writing in 1680. For our purposes a brief background of the political trials of the period will suffice.

The Popish Plot was the invention of Titus Oates, who convinced a gullible court and a more gullible populace of Jesuit plans to kill the king, massacre Protestants, and engineer the succession of Charles's Catholic brother, James. As a result of ensuing arrests and prosecutions, between 1678 and 1681 some twenty people were either executed or died in prison.[194] In the first two years of the crisis, the virulently anti-Papist Chief Justice (King's Bench) Scroggs worked his relentless will on defendants and took a strong lead with juries, who were for the most part ready to follow. But as doubts about Oates (if not the Plot itself) set in, Scroggs scrupulously and skillfully exposed false accusations, incurring the wrath of anti-Papist mobs.[195] The Court, which had been thrown off balance by Oates's accusations and the resultant move in Parliament for exclusion of James from the order of succession, gradually recovered maneuvering room. Already in 1680, there were prosecutions of Protestant publicists whose anti-Papist attacks were alleged to blame the crisis on the Court's encouragement of Catholic hopes.[196] The following year only the resistance of Protestant London grand juries frustrated royal efforts to destroy Shaftesbury, the leader of the nascent Whig party.[197] The pendulum soon swung fully against the most outspoken of the pro-Exclusion Protestant Whig leaders. Stephen Colledge was convicted by an Oxfordshire jury on charges of treason in 1681; Edward Fitz-Harris was convicted and executed for treason later that year. The purge reached its height two years later in the wake of the discovery of the Rye House

193. On the Popish Plot and the prosecutions it inspired see e.g. John Miller, *Popery and Politics in England, 1660–1688* (Cambridge, 1973); John Kenyon, *The Popish Plot* (London, 1972); J. R. Jones, *The First Whigs. The Politics of the Exclusion Crisis, 1678–1683* (London, 1970), esp. ch. 2; John Pollock, *The Popish Plot: A Study in the History of the Reign of Charles II* (London, 1903). For the ensuing attack on the Whigs see e.g. Michael Landon, *The Triumph of the Lawyers. Their Role in English Politics, 1678–1689* (University, Ala., 1970), esp. ch. 5; G. W. Keeton, *Lord Chancellor Jeffreys and the Stuart Cause* (London, 1965), esp. ch. 10. See generally Clark, *Later Stuarts*, ch. 5.

194. Kenyon, *Popish Plot*, p. 205.

195. *Ibid.*, pp. 175–78; Clark, *Later Stuarts*, p. 94. See also the detailed study of Scrogg's behavior at the Wakeman trial, J. P. Kenyon, "The Acquittal of Sir George Wakeman: 18 July 1679," *Historical Journal*, vol. 14 (1971), pp. 693–708.

196. See below, text at nn. 207–8.

197. See below, n. 225 for recent discussions of the proceedings against Shaftesbury.

Plot to seize the king. Among the victims were Lord Russell and Algernon Sydney, though neither had in fact been part of the plot. Jeffreys's role in the anti-Whig prosecutions as an implacable foe of opposition to authorities, first as Crown counsel and then as Lord Chief Justice, is now famous.[198]

The bullying tactics of the Stuart bench during this period should not blind one to the fact that in many instances the prosecutions were popular. Local officials returned juries sympathetic to the Crown as often as they returned juries likely to engage in some resistance. Jury packing was common and practiced on all sides.[199] The changing winds of local or national politics determined whether such pretrial manipulation would favor or disadvantage the defendant. Defendants in such cases were not themselves strangers to tactics that might lawfully be employed in court to secure favorable or at least open-minded jurors: in some cases challenges were frequent. The bench played both ways the rule that jurors must be freeholders, sometimes challenging jurors as nonfreeholders, sometimes denying that the rule grounded a challenge for cause.[200] Some juries were harangued and berated by the prosecution or bench; others— where the bench was confident that the jurors could be trusted to convict the "guilty"—were told that they must determine the truth according to their own consciences.[201] Conscience might thus be invoked in the apparently magnanimous spirit of encouraging jury independence of mind. Yet again, invocation to "conscience" might reflect judicial doubts about the evidence for the Crown. In late 1679 Scroggs, standing against the tide of anti-Jesuit feeling, urged Wakeman's jury to regard the evidence, not public feelings: "Never care what the world says, follow your consciences."[202] The courageous jury found Wakeman not guilty.

For Scroggs, of course, the claim to conscience was a claim upon the jurors' honest assessment of fact. No hint of law-finding was intended. And like Vaughan, Scroggs recognized that factual assessment was not an

198. F. Keeton, *Lord Chancellor Jeffreys*, chs. 9–10.

199. *Ibid.*, p. 97; Ogg, *England in the Reign of Charles II*, 2:520. See Kenyon's comments on the composition of juries in the Popish Plot trials. "Acquittal of Sir George Wakeman," p. 702.

200. See Sir John Hawles, "Remarks on Fitz Harris's Trial," in *State Trials*, 8:435.

201. E.g. *Rex v. Green, Berry and Hill*, *State Trials*, 7:220. Scroggs made it clear that he believed the defendants were guilty and then told the jury: "So I leave it to your consideration upon the whole matter, whether the evidence of the fact does not satisfy your consciences, that these men are guilty. And I know you will do like honest men on both sides."

202. *State Trials*, 7:686. See also *Rex v. Langhorn*, *State Trials*, 7:484, where a doubtful Scroggs told the jury: "Follow your own consciences; do wisely; do honestly; and consider what is to be done." See Kenyon, "Acquittal of Sir George Wakeman," pp. 701–2.

infallible science.[203] The juror was sworn to say what he believed was true, not to achieve objective truth. Scroggs made this point in his charge to Henry Care's jury in 1680 in an effort to forestall a verdict of not guilty on grounds the evidence did not yield an absolute certainty of guilt.

You must take evidence in this case, as you do all year long, that is, in other cases, where you know so: for human frailty must be allowed; that is, you may be mistaken. For you do not swear, nor are you bound to swear here, that [Care] was the publisher of this book; but if you find him guilty, you only swear you believe it so. God help juries, if so be in matter of fact they should promise otherwise. They cannot swear to it.[204]

The uses to which the claim upon conscience might be put were many. Vaughan's language seems to reverberate in the *Reports* of Restoration political trials. It clearly reverberates—but to very different effect—in the jury tract literature of the day. John Hawles, whose *Englishman's Right* was published in 1680 and enjoyed wide readership, many successive reprints, and unending quotation, drew so heavily upon Vaughan's arguments as virtually to be a gloss upon the opinion.[205] Hawles set the tone for many pro-jury writers down to Fox's Libel Act. His characterization of Vaughan's opinion also became the accepted pro-jury view in America, though the influence of his tract there was insubstantial until *Zenger's Case* in 1735.[206]

Hawles's tract, as well as large portions of a book by Henry Care,[207] were occasioned by the spate of prosecutions for unlicensed printing of news, seditious libel, and treason during the first years of the Popish Plot. Although neither tract mentions the prosecutions in 1680 of Benjamin Harris and of Care himself, it seems likely that those trials, and what Hawles and Care took to be judicial rulings on the law of seditious libel

203. This is not to deny, however, that the Restoration bench approached fact-finding in a more "scientific" manner than had earlier jurists. It is only to say that the political cases (and the problem of coercion) of the period resulted in emphasis on the juror's "conscience" and understanding, and in assertions that the juror's sworn "belief" be respected whether or not it accorded with objective truth. Perhaps increasing confidence in the (relatively) "scientific" aspect of jury fact-finding made it easier to adopt such a stance. For an important discussion of contemporary notions about the science of fact-finding see Barbara J. Shapiro, *Probability and Certainty in Seventeenth-Century England* (Princeton, 1983). And see below, Chapter 7, text at nn. 15–17.

204. *State Trials*, 7:1128. (Alternatively spelled: Carr.)

205. John Hawles, *The Englishman's Right* (London, 1680).

206. Stanley N. Katz, ed., *A Brief Narrative of the Case and Trial of John Peter Zenger*, by James Alexander (Cambridge, Mass., 1963), pp. 15–16.

207. Henry Care, *English Liberties: or, the Free-Born Subject's Inheritance* (London, 1680).

(rather than the treason trials of alleged Catholic plotters), revived the claim to the jury's right to decide law.[208] The law of seditious libel was still taking shape during the first two decades of the Restoration. Its roots lay in Star Chamber practice,[209] and certain rules of law—e.g., that truth was no defense—might be expected to have been inherited and reaffirmed by the common law bench. But questions regarding the allocation of duties between judge and jury, concerning, i.e., what was law and what was fact, were less clearly questions to be answered by reference to Star Chamber practice. Whether a writing was seditious might fairly be claimed a matter of fact for the jury to decide; it might also be insisted that criminal intent should not be implied by the bench but should be determined instead by the jury. The settlement of the Stuart doctrine of seditious libel was not in any simple way a result of the ruling in *Bushel's Case*. It may be that the principal basis for the practice in seditious libel cases—that the jury was to find only whether the defendant "published" (wrote, printed, or published) the words in question whereas seditiousness and intent were matters of law for the bench—was the fact that a record of the allegedly offensive words existed, so that those words were, unlike all other criminal "acts," available for judicial inspection.[210] Nonetheless, it seems likely that the

208. *Rex v. Harris, State Trials*, 7:926–32; *Rex v. Care, Ibid.*, 1111–30. See Philip Hamburger, "The Origins of the Law of Seditious Libel" (ms. pp. 32–37), *Stanford Law Review* (forthcoming). All Hamburger pp. herein referred to are from ms. When published, Hamburger's study will importantly modify all earlier work on the pre-1730 law of seditious libel. Hamburger argues, inter alia, that Harris's prosecution was for "a strange combination of seditious libel and *Scandalum Magnatum*" (p. 32) and that Care's prosecution was, strictly speaking, for unlicensed printing (pp. 34–37). The defendants, states Hamburger, were charged with, among other things, publication of "seditious libels"; Hawles "professed to think" that such cases "were but poorly conducted common law seditious libel prosecutions." He complained, "with uncertain ingenuousness, that traditional powers of juries in libel trials were being abused" (p. 36, n. 73). Whether or not Hawles was "ingenuous," I believe his writings were taken seriously, especially as prosecutions that were clearly for seditious libel became common.

209. Holdsworth, *History of English Law*, 8:336–42, esp. 339. But note that Hamburger ("Origins of the Law of Seditious Libel," Part III) provides an important reassessment of the early development of seditious libel. Hamburger argues that Star Chamber was concerned not with seditious libel broadly defined but with that form of seditious libel that involved defamation of public officials.

210. See Holdsworth, *History of English Law*, 8:343; see also Thomas A. Green, "The Jury, Seditious Libel, and the Criminal Law," in Green and Richard H. Helmholz, *Juries, Libel, and Justice: The Role of English Juries in 17th–18th Century Trials for Libel and Slander* (Los Angeles, 1984). Hamburger ("Origins of the Law of Seditious Libel") has reassessed the applications of these doctrines in the period 1660–95. His work rests on only a few cases, partly because he has excluded those cases that he believes were in fact prosecutions for unlicensed printing. As to the issue of "libelousness," Hamburger concludes: "In the seventeenth century, the bench determined in practice whether a

tensions between judge and jury that the Quaker trials occasioned and that culminated in *Bushel's Case* affected the development of the law of seditious libel.

The Quakers' opposition to the Conventicles Act of 1664, and especially their assertion that jurors ought to determine the meaning of the Act, pushed the bench to declare that jurors were to determine only the question of whether the defendant had attended the alleged meeting. The bench would decide whether such attendance at the alleged meeting implied unlawful religious worship. (This was so, at least, if the defendants did not show that the purpose of the meeting was not religious or, if religious, not contrary to Anglican forms.) We have also seen that Chief Justice Kelyng attempted to reduce the jury's scope of fact-finding in homicide. Where murder was alleged, and no provocation was shown, the jury was to find whether the defendant intentionally slew the deceased; if so, the court would determine whether the act implied malice.[211] Thus judge-jury conflicts in the early 1660s led the bench to reserve to itself as questions of law matters that had traditionally been left to the jury as questions of fact.

*Bushel's Case* increased the importance of placing limitations upon the scope of fact-finding. It may have encouraged the bench to reserve to itself—where it could—the kinds of determinations within which jury law-finding or merciful verdicts might otherwise be concealed. As we shall see, only in seditious libel did the bench succeed in restricting the jury to largely stipulated facts and thus force a jury that did not want to convict to return a verdict that was flagrantly contrary to the evidence. Although some juries adopted a ruse analogous to that employed in Quaker prosecutions, and returned a verdict of "guilty of publishing

writing's content was defamatory or libelous." He implies that juries could have (though they rarely dared to do so) disagreed with the bench (pp. 53–54). As to intent, Hamburger states (pp. 55–60) that the bench followed the law of homicide, wherein murder was presumed unless the defendant produced evidence of provocation, accident, etc., in which case intent became a matter for the jury. In seditious libel, the defendant might similarly produce evidence that he lacked knowledge or malice. Hamburger concedes that the defendant's task was not easy: "In the 1680s, judges and Crown lawyers disparagingly referred to questions of knowledge and malice as mere formalities, in order to remove such issues from the control of the jury" (p. 59). Apparently, judicial treatment of the defendant's exculpatory evidence depended upon the judge's view of the publication—whether it was sufficiently or "insufficiently defamatory to imply malice." Even on Hamburger's analysis, then, in practice, in most seditious libel cases, libelousness and intent were implied or not by the bench, not by the jury. In homicide, it should be pointed out, defendants might claim provocation almost as a matter of course. They (or their witnesses) were not embarrassed by an act that lived on for judicial inspection. They might be countered by witnesses for the Crown, but the testimony of witnesses was always open to attack, and the question of credibility of all witnesses was conceded to be a jury question.

211. See above, n. 80 and accompanying text.

only," given the establishment of the principle of noncoercion, the Stuart doctrine of seditious libel was particularly advantageous to the Crown. The application of that doctrine in the prominent trials of 1680 thus provoked Hawles and others to come to the defense of the jury and, specifically, to "find" in the principle of noncoercion support for very far-reaching propositions about the right to find law as well as fact.

Hawles's *Englishman's Right* is cast as a dialogue between a barrister and a juryman. The barrister stresses the importance of the duty to serve on juries and instructs the juryman regarding his proper function. The juryman, for his part, asks all the "right questions." Whether Hawles was concerned with the increasing use of packed juries, the rate at which Englishmen avoided jury service, or the ignorance and timidity of jurors in the face of the Stuart bench, his message was the same: "[T]he office of a juryman is, conscientiously to judge his neighbour; and he needs no more law than is easily learnt to direct him therein."[212]

Hawles adopted virtually all of Vaughan's language. All discourses by the judge to the jury on the law "ought to be hypothetical, not coercive." The judge should so charge juries because "*ex facto jus oritur*, all matter of law arises out of matter of fact, so that until the fact is settled there is no room for law." Hawles also endorsed Vaughan's view of the impenetrability of the fact-resolving role of the jury. He followed Vaughan closely in saying that since the jurors were drawn from the neighborhood, they might be supposed to have knowledge of their own touching the facts of the situation and the credibility of witnesses. The jury's verdict, formed in good conscience, was determinative. The judges, said Hawles, "do often recapitulate and sum up the heads of the evidence; but the jurors are still to consider whether it be done truly, fully and impartially (for one man's memory may sooner fail than twelve's)."[213] In the end, Hawles repeated Vaughan's effective formulation, "A man cannot see by another's eye";[214] if judges and jury disagreed, so be it. Trial by jury was trial by peers, not by judges.

At a crucial point in the dialogue the juryman asks whether juries are restricted entirely to the finding of fact. Through the response of the barrister, Hawles developed the law-finding argument that was to be for more than a century the lodestar of many of the opponents of the seditious libel doctrine. Hawles implied that he had derived the argument from Vaughan, but in fact he simply attached it to one of Vaughan's most conventional statements. The jury, Hawles noted (quoting Vaughan), must deal with law "as it arises out of, or is complicated with, and

---

212. Hawles, *Englishman's Right*, p. 1.
213. *Ibid.*, p. 9.
214. *Ibid.*, p. 27.

influences the fact.''²¹⁵ Vaughan meant—but failed explicitly to state—that the jury must take the law from the bench and must apply it in the manner that the bench has ruled it should. Hawles drew an opposite inference which deserves close study. Hawles's barrister begins by conceding that matters of fact constitute the jury's "proper province" and "chief business." But this, he states, does not determine the matter:

> For to say, [the jury] are not at all to meddle with, or have respect to law in giving their verdicts, is not only a false position, and contradicted by every day's experience; but also a very dangerous and pernicious one, tending to defeat the principal end of the institution of juries, and so subtlely to undermine that which was too strong to be battered down.²¹⁶

The jury must "apply matter of fact and law together; and from their consideration of, and a right judgment upon both, bring forth their verdict." The barrister's examples, borrowed from Vaughan, are not startling: the general issue in trespass, breach of the peace, felony, and seditious libel. In homicide, e.g., the jury is free to return "murder, manslaughter, *per infortunium*, or *se defendendo*, as they see cause." Did this mean for Hawles, as it did for Vaughan, only that the jury must apply the law, as stated to them by the bench, or did "right judgment" mean something more?²¹⁷

Clearly Hawles meant more, but he could find no further support in Vaughan's opinion. Thus he turned to other sources. Apparently borrowing from a tract on Penn and Mead's case, Hawles has the barrister ask, "[T]o what end is it, that when any person is prosecuted upon any statute, the statute itself is usually read to the jurors, but only that they may judge, whether or not the matter be within that statute?"²¹⁸ This appears to go beyond Vaughan, but its full meaning remains ambiguous. Read in the light of Quaker prosecutions under the Conventicles Act, it seems to adopt a far-reaching position: the jury must not feel bound to "apply" the statute as interpreted by the bench. Then, perhaps taking his lead from an account of Lilburne's dispute with the bench in 1649, Hawles drew upon the passage from Littleton, stating "[t]hat if a jury will take upon them the knowledge of the law upon the matter, they may."²¹⁹ This, Hawles suggested, was conclusive. We have seen how weak a reed this passage was, and Hawles, a trained barrister, must also have known it proved less

215. *Ibid.*, p. 10.
216. *Ibid.*, pp. 10–11.
217. *Ibid.*, p. 11.
218. *Idem.*
219. *Idem.* For Lilburne's use of Littleton see *State Trials*, 4:1381 and above, Chapter 5, text at nn. 70–76.

than he asserted for it. But the position of juries in seditious libel cases seemed to him untenable; juries, he said, might be turned into "engine[s] of oppression."[220] Their right, and duty, to judge the law was self-evident.

Thus, the heart of Hawles's argument dealt not with the problem of judicial directions on the law but with the problem of defective indictments. Here it was that Hawles grafted the claims of Lilburne, Penn, and opponents of the seditious libel doctrine in his own day onto the opinion in *Bushel's Case*:

> And . . . it is false to say that the jury hath not power, or does not use frequently to apply the fact to the law; and thence taking their measures, judge of, and determine the crime or issue by their verdict.
>
> As juries have ever been vested with such power by law, so to exclude them from, or disseize them of the same, were utterly to defeat the end of their institution. For then if a person should be indicted for doing any common innocent act, if it be but clothed and disguised in the indictment with the name of treason, or some other high crime, and proved by witnesses to have been done by him, the jury, though satisfied in conscience, that the fact is not any such offence as it is called, yet because (according to this fond opinion) they have no power to judge of law and the fact charged is fully proved, they should at this rate be bound to find him guilty.[221]

Hence, the central point of the tract and the core of the juryman's right and duty was this: the jury, to render a guilty verdict, must be satisfied in conscience not only that the fact has been proved but also that the fact constitutes an offense under the law. There can be little doubt that Hawles held the same views regarding judicial charges. The argument was not new; Quaker writers had made it since the Restoration. Now, however, it was made with reference to indictments for treason and seditious libel, and it was clothed in and accorded the respectability of the words and (seemingly, though not really) the logic of the opinion in *Bushel's Case*.

Hawles's law-finding argument comes in the middle of his tract. It is followed by lengthy borrowings from Vaughan's arguments against the fining and imprisonment of jurors and is thus made to seem an integral part of Vaughan's opinion. The barrister comments that the recent appearance of Vaughan's *Reports* is an important event; all prospective jurymen ought to read it, along with Magna Carta, the Petition of Right, and other fundamental statements of Englishmen's rights. Jury trial, as defended by Vaughan and defined by Hawles, was central to those rights. As the barrister concludes (in what were in fact Lilburne's words):

---

220. Hawles, *Englishman's Right*, p. 12.
221. *Ibid.*, pp. ll–12.

[T]he law of England has not placed trials by juries to stand between men and death or destruction to so little purpose, as to pronounce men guilty without regard to the nature of the offence, or to what is to be inflicted thereupon.[222]

Hawles's gloss upon *Bushel's Case* was adopted by Henry Care, who published *English Liberties: or the Free Born Subject's Inheritance* shortly after his trial in 1680 for printing unlicensed (and seditious) news. Care lifted whole passages from Hawles, including Hawles's commentary on indictments. Elaborating on Hawles's argument, Care asserted that if the indictment put words of law wrongly in apposition to the facts

> it is an apparent trap at once to perjure ignorant juries, and render them so far from being of good use, as to be only tools of oppression, to ruin and murder their innocent neighbors with the greater formality: for though it be true, that matter of fact is the most common and proper objective of a jury's determination, and matter of law that of the judges, yet as law arises out of, and is complicated with fact it cannot but fall under the jury's consideration.[223]

Once again, Vaughan's words appear: No allegation "*contra materia legis*" will be heard, for "*ex facto jus oritur*"; law is "complicated with fact." These phrases, which had become code words for the pro-jury writers, were harnessed to the arguments developed by Hawles. For many, the meaning that Hawles and Care read into those words would quickly come to stand for the essence of the Englishman's right to trial by jury.[224]

The petty jury was only the final bastion of opposition to allegedly tyrannical prosecutions. Grand juries might (and sometimes did) refuse to return a true bill, whether the charge was homicide, theft, or a political crime.[225] In the years following *Bushel's Case*, the Crown fought a two-tiered struggle in some political cases, first to secure an indictment

---

222. *Ibid.*, pp. 38–39. See Lilburne, *Jury-man's Judgement* (1653), p. 6 (above, Chapter 5, text at n. 141).

223. Care, *English Liberties*, p. 259.

224. See e.g. *A Guide to Juries, setting forth their Antiquity, Power and Duty* (London, 1699; first published as *A Guide to English Juries*, London, 1682), pp. 17, 25; Lord John Somers, *The Security of Englishmen's Lives, or the Trust, Power and Duty of the Grand Jurys of England* (London, 1681), pp. 10–11.

225. For the grand jury in routine cases see Zachary Babington, *Advice to Grand Jurors in Cases of Blood* (London, 1680; orig. published 1677). The problem of grand jury "recalcitrance" in political cases has received a great deal of attention, esp. regarding *Shaftesbury's Case* and *Colledge's Case* in 1681. See e.g. Havighurst, "Judiciary and Politics," pp. 241–43; Helene E. Schwartz, "Demythologizing the Historic Role of the Grand Jury," *American Criminal Law Review*, vol. 10 (1972), pp. 712–21. See also K. H. D. Haley, *The First Earl of Shaftesbury* (Oxford, 1968), ch. 28.

and then to obtain a trial jury conviction. At either stage, Crown officials might be hard pressed to convince jurymen that the official characterization of an offense coincided with the law. Hawles's *The Grand-Jury-Man's Oath and Office Explained*, which appeared in the same year as *Englishman's Right*, argued that grand juries ought to return an *ignoramus* if they believed that the offense alleged was not a crime. The grand jury, according to Hawles, must look to facts, not to words of form inserted by zealous prosecutors:

> Here lies the knot, the pinch of the business, which rightly understood, would silence this controversy for ever. You must note therefore, that sometimes these words are only of course, or matter of form, raised by a just and reasonable implication of law; but sometimes they may be thrust in to raise a pretence or colour of crime, where there is really none.[226]

Hawles therefore asked the grand jury to distinguish two kinds of case. In one, the act charged is itself criminal, whether or not it is "malicious" or "seditious," etc. If the jury is satisfied that the act is criminal and that the person charged probably is guilty of the act, it must return a true bill. In the other case, however, the act is innocent or indifferent unless it is undertaken with a "malicious" or "seditious" intent. In this instance, the jury must be satisfied that the "words of form" are proved, or else it must reject the indictment. Since they judge fact, grand juries must find the facts which make an act criminal; they ought not to find noncriminal facts and then leave to the bench, under the rubric of law, the determination of criminality. If they do so, said Hawles, they might indict for treason one charged with "looking on the tombs at Westminster" or for high misdemeanor one charged with printing the Bible.[227]

For a grand jury to reject a bill because the act charged was neither criminal nor committed with criminal intent it had, of course, "to take upon [itself] the knowledge of the law."

> [Grand] jurors are to consider both law and fact or else they will never deliver just and lawful verdicts. To what purpose does the law provide, that jurors should be so well qualified as to estate, understanding and sufficiency, and so strictly sworn, but only to detect offenders and preserve the innocent from needless vexation and trouble? How far juries are judges of law as well as of fact is pretty well set forth in a small treatise lately published, entitled, *The Englishman's Right*.[228]

226. John Hawles, *The Grand-Jury-Man's Oath and Office Explained: and the Rights of English-Men Asserted* (London, 1680), pp. 16–17.

227. *Ibid.*, pp. 14–15.

228. *Ibid.*, pp. 13–14.

With this allusion, Hawles united his argument for a true shield at the grand jury stage with his claim that the trial jury possessed the power to decide law as well as fact, a strategy that Care and the author of *The Guide* also subsequently adopted.[229]

In the period we have reviewed, the pro-jury position became, in fact, several different positions. The tract writers moved easily from one argument to another, sometimes confusing them but always uniting all of them under the rubric of the Englishman's right to trial by jury.[230] At times the assertion that juries ought to decide law was inseparable from claims to control over fact. To understand the entire complex of pro-jury arguments, therefore, it is necessary to separate the various strands of jury theory and to view them in relation to earlier thinking.

The basis of the jury's power was, of course, the right to resolve issues of fact. Following Vaughan's logic, this implied the right to apply the law to the facts. Because "law arose from fact," unless the jury rendered a special verdict, no one other than the jurors had an opportunity to play this role. This concept of "application of law" was the most limited of the contemporary theories of law-deciding. It presumed, for many (certainly for Vaughan), jury adherence to the judicial interpretation of the law. The judge could do no more than put hypotheticals, but that was because he could not be sure of the fact. Once the jury found the fact and determined to which hypothetical it corresponded, application of the law could follow automatically.[231]

229. Care, *English Liberties*, p. 261; *A Guide to Juries*, pp. 59–62, 68. See also *Twenty-four Sober Queries Humbly Offered to be seriously considered by all juries in city and country* (London, 1680, printed for Benjamin Harris).

230. See e.g. John Somers, *The Security of Englishmen's Lives*, pp. 9–11. Somers's tract was occasioned by the proceedings against Shaftesbury. Somers drew upon Vaughan for the proposition that juries (grand and petty) "determine the law in all matters where issue is joined" (p. 10). For an analysis of the influence on Somers of Fortescue's *De Laudibus Regum Angliae* see Caroline A. J. Skeel, "The Influence of the Writings of Sir John Fortescue," *Transactions of the Royal Historical Society*, 3rd ser., vol. 10 (1916), pp. 77–114.

231. Some tract writers who were not explicit about the jury's right to render merciful verdicts, or who even opposed such verdicts, nonetheless described the jury's role in terms that may have seemed to leave room for such discretion. See [Giles Duncombe] *Tryals Per Pais: or the Law of England Concerning Juries by Nisi Prius, etc.*, By S. E. (2nd ed., rev., London, 1682). The first edition of this tract, signed S. E. [Samson Euer] contains little commentary on the scope of the criminal trial jury's power. In Duncombe's 1682 edition there is a commentary on *Bushel's Case* at pp. 441 *et seq.*: "[A]nd that question which has made such a noise, viz. whether a jury is fineable for going against their evidence in court, or the direction of the judge? I look upon that question, as dead and buried, since Bushel's case, in my Lord Vaughan's reports" (p. 443). Duncombe then accurately deals with Vaughan's opinion (pp. 444–45). He subsequently notes that juries may take the law unto themselves where law and fact are joined, but concludes (unlike Vaughan) that if they

Some, perhaps most, would have agreed that the jury's method of applying the law was not always required to be absolutely mechanical. Indeed, judges had long encouraged jury leniency in many cases involving homicide or minor theft, a practice that continued, perhaps even increased, after the Restoration. It became commonplace to assert that the jury ought to apply the law mercifully. Although in theory juries were to apply the law as it was stated for them, in practice they applied the law to conform to their own rough sense of justice. Only when, in a given case, the bench deemed jury leniency inappropriate was the issue of jury deviance raised. Vaughan's opinion in *Bushel's Case*, which Hawles and Care took to address Kelyng's behavior in homicide cases as well as the treatment of the jury in the case of Penn and Mead, thus strengthened the jury's hand. Among the tract writers this right of merciful application of the law became the most common "proof" of the jury's right to decide law and fact "complicately."

At the other extreme was the most pronounced form of law deciding: the right of the jury to determine whether the act with which a person was charged constituted a crime. Here, according to some tract writers, the jury's power and right were definitive. Neither the language of the indictment nor the judge's direction should divert the jury's attention from this duty. To pronounce guilt when one believed in conscience that no true crime had been charged was to commit "murder." This argument was also extended to grand juries where, in the light of the proceedings against Shaftesbury, it was absorbed into the historical myth of the grand jury as a shield against, rather than a sword of, the Crown. It merged also with the older attack on the use of informations. Right to jury was right to judgment by two lay bodies, mainly to provide a double check on fact but also to prevent prosecutions for activity that was not truly criminal.

As we have seen, the tract writers urged juries to assess the words used in indictments that made otherwise innocent acts criminal. Without evidence of criminal malice or seditiousness there should be neither indictment nor conviction. In the case of the petty jury, this argument is complex; the series of propositions (which were never spelled out as such) runs as follows. First, the jury was to decide law; i.e., it was to decide whether as a general matter the act charged was criminal. Second, the jury would decide fact; i.e., if the act was criminal, the jury would

mistake the law they run the danger of an attaint. Finally, Duncombe states that juries "determine the law in all matters where issue is joined and tried, but [not] where the verdict is special. . . . [I]n such cases, the judge cannot of himself answer, or determine one particle of the fact, but must leave it to the jury, with whom let it rest and continue forever, as the best kind of trial in the world for finding out the truth, and the greatest safety of the just prerogatives of the Crown, and the just liberties of the subject; and he who desires more for either of them is an enemy to both" (pp. 447–48).

determine whether the defendant had committed it. If (as the jury saw it) the act charged was criminal only when committed with a certain intent, the jury would determine whether the defendant had committed it with that intent. This second, fact-finding stage, of course, could involve a degree of law-finding. For, as stated above, in reaching its verdict the jury would apply to the facts it had found the law as stated by the bench, but in a manner dictated by considerations of mercy. So long as the bench approved of the (merciful) verdict, this last form of law-finding was assimilated to the mechanical application of the law as stated by the bench.

The Stuart bench conceded, at least in theory, that it could not coerce convictions. As of 1671, it conceded both in theory and in practice jury finality concerning fact and concerning the application of the law to fact—with one important proviso: that the jury apply the law *as stipulated by the bench*. It would not tolerate, as a general matter, jury determination of criminality; nor would the bench tolerate a "merciful" verdict if it thought that the verdict disguised a rejection of the law as stated by the bench. Instead, as we have seen, the bench retreated, where it could (and where it felt it imperative), to the device of reserving to itself certain "questions of law." And thus it was that in cases of seditious libel the bench hoped by severely restricting the scope and nature of the facts to be found to eliminate the jury's power to conceal law-finding within fact-finding.

It was at just this point, however, that the Stuart bench suffered a major setback, one that ensured that the Restoration legacy of the criminal trial jury would be complex, confusing, and even contradictory, and that the contest over the true meaning of Vaughan's opinion in *Bushel's Case* would continue into the eighteenth century. This setback occurred on the eve of the Glorious Revolution in the prosecution of the seven bishops who refused to read James II's second *Declaration of Indulgence*.[232] When the bishops petitioned the Crown, stating their reasons for refusing to read the *Declaration*, they were indicted for publishing a seditious libel. Their trial focused the growing opposition—an opposition that reached far into the political establishment—to James II's policies and religion, and to the behavior of the Stuart bench during the preceding decade.[233] At the trial the bench badly divided on the question of whether the bishops' petition was libelous and, hence, whether it implied mal-

---

232. Kenyon, *Stuart Constitution*, pp. 454–55; J. R. Jones, *Country and Court: England, 1658–1714* (Cambridge, Mass., 1979), pp. 238–40; Clark, *The Later Stuarts*, p. 126; Hill, *Century of Revolution*, pp. 198–99, 238–39.

233. *State Trials*, 12:183–434 (1688).

ice.[234] In the end the jury was left to decide the issues of intent and libelousness in the most highly charged political context possible. The subsequent acquittal of the bishops was greeted with great celebrations, and was taken to signal the victory of the jury as a bulwark of the constitution against executive and judicial tyranny. It perhaps rekindled memories of the appeals of the hapless Colledge and Fitz-Harris, seven years before, to their juries as judges "of law and fact."[235] Momentarily, at least, the Stuart regime had worked a fusion of the proponents of the radical law-finding position and much of the Whig establishment.

As we shall see, this final Restoration episode became a central event for eighteenth-century constitutional and legal theorists. But it was an event from which different persons could draw very different conclusions. It perhaps reinforced the almost universally held view that jury verdicts were final, but it in no way settled the question of the legitimacy of judicial steering of juries that might otherwise find against manifest evidence: most eighteenth-century observers believed that the jury had found the facts correctly. Nor did the *Seven Bishops' Case* settle the question of the doctrine of seditious libel. Virtually all commentators deemed that doctrine dangerous, even illegitimate, when exercised by a "dependent" bench, as, from the perspective afforded by the watershed of the Glorious Revolution and the Act of Settlement of 1701, the Stuart bench seemed to have been. But was the doctrine inherently wrong? Could not an independent judiciary be entrusted to apply it fairly?[236] For many the jury had proved itself a vital element during one stage in the development of the constitution. Jury intervention, they concluded, had been a crucial defense against tyranny; true it was that the jury might again play that role, should England ever suffer at the hands of a tyrannical Crown and bench, but such a retrograde development was (so they thought) unlikely ever to recur.

For others, however, the right to jury trial meant the right to a jury verdict on all the facts, including intent and seditiousness. A bench that withheld that right was per se tyrannical. If the post-1689 bench pronounced the law of seditious libel in its original form, the jury ought to reject that judicial pronouncement, for in such circumstances—and possibly in some others—the jury had the right to decide law as well as

234. For a discussion of the *Seven Bishops' Case*, see below, Chapter 8, text at nn. 8–10.
235. *Rex v. Colledge, State Trials*, 8:694; *Rex v. Fitzharris, State Trials*, 8:377.
236. Hamburger ("Origins of the Law of Seditious Libel," pp. 88 *et seq.*) has shown that the doctrine of seditious libel not only survived the Glorious Revolution but was thereafter substantially broadened (to include "seditious" criticism of the government, not merely of specific government officials; to include mere writing, whether or not publication was intended); moreover, the de facto control of the bench over the question of libelousness became de jure.

fact. The legacy of the Restoration was thus severalfold. Though, as we shall see, there emerged a settled division of authority between judge and jury in routine cases, that division remained unresolved and problematic in many political contests. Nor could these two kinds of cases remain entirely separate. The two traditions of jury law-finding that passed on into eighteenth-century thought and practice influenced each other in important ways. Most significantly, the merciful discretion that survived the Tudor transformation in criminal administration and that was safely left to juries in common-run felonies (though it clearly went beyond Vaughan's identification of "conscience" with a good-faith belief regarding fact) was bound to affect views regarding the legitimacy of true nullification in prosecutions for seditious libel.[237]

237. See below, Chapter 8.

# Part III    Resolutions

# 7    Jury Trial and Its Critics in the Eighteenth Century

Between *Bushel's Case* and the late eighteenth century the English criminal jury trial underwent little significant change. The first great watershed in the history of trial practice was the development in Tudor times of a formal prosecution; the second was the increasing recourse to counsel and the development of a true law of evidence in the late eighteenth and early nineteenth centuries. Perhaps the modern trial took shape only in the middle decades of the nineteenth century, the point at which our present story ends. But if one searches in vain for dramatic change in trial procedure, the eighteenth century does reveal developments both in the role of the criminal trial and the way in which contemporaries thought about the jury. These two developments were related, and it is mainly the history of that relationship that Part III addresses. There are many strands to the history of jury trial, 1689–1800, too many certainly to outline here. But the main ones can be set forth briefly.

The eighteenth century saw a consolidation and rationalization of the age-old practices that characterized the administration of the criminal law generally and the role of the trial jury in particular. Building on developments of the preceding century, authorities brought jury practices further under control even as they conceded the principle of the inviolability of the general verdict. Although jury trial itself changed little, the context of the trial altered significantly as authorities elaborated on the practical approach to penology that had emerged almost accidentally in the sixteenth and seventeenth centuries. The "selection" of offenders by Crown, bench, and jury for one or another level of punishment became a complex and, at times, an awe-inspiring ritual. Authorities were all the readier to share the power of mitigation with juries in a system in which most of the beneficiaries of mitigation suffered some substantial punishment.

As the jury's role in this evolving system of mitigation became formalized, and in a sense tamed, that role expanded accordingly; but the jury was now more than ever just one part of the system, and the scope of its role in practice depended increasingly upon surrounding institutions and procedures. So intrinsic was the jury to the officially sponsored process of mitigation that many contemporary observers were either

267

confused as to whether the judge or jury was in control or wrongly concluded that the latter was the dominant of the two. As we shall see, what contemporaries—especially those who wrote about the law or took an active part in political debate—thought about the jury was of great importance. We cannot always tell when they are exaggerating to make a point or are simply seeing what they want to see, but it would be wrong to dismiss their depiction of the jury as purely polemical. They provide evidence of the contemporary understanding of the role and power of the criminal trial jury.

Largely as a result of the reception of the Enlightenment tradition of penology, some jurists and publicists began to criticize (albeit, often in terms long employed in England) the prevailing administration of the criminal law. Their writings reveal certain distinctively English habits of thought that may have blunted the force of the reformers' message: English reformers attempted to combine criticism of what they perceived as ad hoc jury-based mitigation with endorsement of the long-standing constitutional role of the jury as a bulwark against tyranny.

Moreover, as we shall see in Chapter 8, about the same time that doubts arose concerning jury mitigation in common felonies, the jury emerged as central in the debate over the law of seditious libel. In this important noncapital, political offense the jury's role had been limited by legal construction, and this limitation was attacked by pro-jury writers as contrary to the English constitution and to the purpose of jury trial as a protector of fundamental liberties. Authorities who had accepted and encouraged jury-based mitigation in common-run felonies were hard pressed to explain limitations upon the jury in political cases. In 1792, the limitations were removed by a statute guaranteeing the general verdict in seditious libel cases, but stating little in express terms about how juries ought to employ the powers the general verdict conferred.

In the long run, the tradition of jury adherence to the letter of the law was a product of the mounting campaign for legal reform. That campaign, briefly surveyed by way of conclusion in Chapter 9, saw the repeal of many of the capital felony statutes and the development of notions of legal certainty and of theories of deterrence that undermined the arguments for jury-based mitigation. Not that such jury behavior came to a sudden and complete termination. It remained (and still remains), but was practiced far less frequently. When legal reform through a (perceived) democratic process dismantled much of the capital law of felony that had been created seven centuries before, jury deference to the letter of the law in criminal cases became standard practice for the first time in English history.

The eighteenth-century criminal trial has recently been described so thoroughly and so well that only a brisk and derivative summary will be necessary in this chapter.[1] Of course there were, as there had always been, many different kinds of crimes and, hence, many different contexts for criminal trials in the eighteenth century. We shall pay most attention to theft, by far the most common offense tried at the eighteenth-century assizes. Not only was theft common, but mitigation of the capital sanction for theft was both commonplace and the subject of commentary in trial accounts, pardon records, and the professional and lay literature of the day. Mitigation of the law of homicide continued, though it was less often commented upon. As we shall see in the following chapter, much of the attention to jury behavior in the diminishing number of homicide trials arose from the political offense of seditious libel, not out of routine felonies. Suffice it to say that we are here mainly concerned with extremely common and open mitigation of the law, practices which juries by and large did not hide from themselves, the bench, or society at large. These instances of mitigation were easily separated from cases in which there was substantial doubt about the level of offense that had been proved in court, for they were quite evidently simple rejections of the prescribed sanction.

We shall also leave aside such obvious instances of nullification (even where the facts were clear) as that practiced in prosecutions for rape and infanticide. These cases, though important, were relatively rare and had little visible impact upon widespread attitudes toward jury practices. However, the attitudes toward jury behavior that were shaped by trials for property crimes may have influenced social views toward such practices in other kinds of cases. In this sense, I am dealing very broadly with the phenomenon of jury intervention. But this suggestion remains tentative; the important differences among offenses, and among attitudes toward them, require much further study.

1. See generally Langbein, "Criminal Trial before the Lawyers" and "Shaping the Eighteenth-Century Criminal Trial: The View from the Ryder Sources," *Chicago Law Review*, vol. 50 (1983), pp. 1–136. Langbein's studies provide the most comprehensive and trenchant analyses in print of the relationship between criminal procedure, the law of evidence, and jury control. See also Baker, "Criminal Courts and Procedure"; Beattie, "Crime and the Courts in Surrey," in Cockburn, ed., *Crime in England*, pp. 164–74; and see Beattie's forthcoming book on the administration of the criminal law in the eighteenth century, *Crime and the Courts in England, 1660–1800* (Princeton, 1985). My own account draws heavily on Langbein, Baker, and Beattie. I have cited them for statements regarding procedural details that my own research on eighteenth-century trial accounts have borne out. I am grateful to Professor Beattie for allowing me to read, cite, and comment upon his forthcoming book. Citations (to manuscript chapters only) appear in the footnotes to this study. In the main, I have cited Professor Beattie's published articles. For an account of Restoration London and Middlesex criminal-trial resolutions see Valerie C. Edwards, "Criminal Equity in Restoration London and Middlesex" (paper presented at the Sixth British Legal History Conference, University of East Anglia, Norwich, July, 1983).

The phenomenon of jury-based mitigation that I discuss was of particular importance because of its visibility, especially to those who commented upon jury behavior. It framed the issue for later generations who depended upon the works of London reformers and polemicists. In the countryside there were, doubtless, other traditions. Jury repudiation of the law as it applied to poachers and the like was an important aspect of contemporary culture, as were attempts by the government to pack and influence juries before whom such offenders were brought to trial. Many common-run cases thus took on the form of "political" prosecutions, at least in the understanding of much of the population. The impact of these prosecutions on contemporary views regarding the jury is difficult to trace, though some historians have made important headway. Suffice it to say that the absence of these episodes from my account in part reflects the fact that the attitudes they engendered were infrequently assimilated into contemporary accounts of the jury and in part reflects the limitations of my study.

Section I of this chapter summarizes the changes in criminal administration that variously affected the continuing practice of jury-based intervention in felony cases. In section II, I elaborate upon the jury's role, but mainly upon the contemporary understanding of that role. Those topics are further discussed from a different angle in section III, which analyzes the criticism of selective enforcement by some reform-minded publicists in the latter half of the eighteenth century. Section IV puts the developments discussed in this essay in perspective and suggests the ways in which one might interpret both the acquiescence of authorities in the prevailing system of criminal administration and the mounting attack on that system.

# I

Trial procedure in the eighteenth century still bore a close resemblance to the model sketched in the sixteenth century by Thomas Smith. The most distinctive aspects of trial were the defendant's self-representation in full sight of the jury and the presentation of witness testimony largely ungoverned by rules of admissibility. The most dramatic moments of trial were those of relatively unmediated confrontation between the accuser, who still bore the expense and responsibility of setting forth the case for the prosecution, and the accused, who, until late in the century only occasionally had the advantage of counsel.[2] The judge remained in the

2. As late as 1771, William Eden could still say of the trial: "[T]he whole examination is rather in the nature of a discussion between the parties, than of a prosecution against an undefended, oppressed individual." *Principles of Penal Law* (London, 1771), p. 219. For

foreground, putting his own questions; he had no reservations about revealing his point of view. As in the past, the judge's directions to the jury were brief, but pointed and leading, if not coercive.[3] Also as in the past, the jurors, drawn mainly from the artisans, tradesmen, and small farmers who composed the lower-middling ranks of society, deliberated briefly and reached verdicts that largely accorded with the views of the bench.[4]

There were of course some changes which, although mostly minor, may have influenced the outcome of some cases. Thus, it appears the Crown set out its entire case through the private prosecutor and his witnesses before the defendant spoke, so that any argument between accused and accusers came relatively late in the trial.[5] Moreover, in the early eighteenth century the judge played an even more active role than before in questioning the defendant on the basis of evidence presented in open court. The bench also gave increasingly more complex instructions, as rudiments of the law of evidence took shape and as the increasing use of witnesses produced more evidence upon which to comment.[6] Finally,

development of rules of evidence see Beattie, *Crime and the Courts*, ch. 8. For discussion of the emergence of defense counsel in routine felony cases see *idem*; Langbein, "Criminal Trial before the Lawyers," pp. 307–14.

3. Langbein, "Criminal Trial before the Lawyers," p. 284.

4. Beattie (*Crime and the Courts*, ch. 8) analyzed the social and economic status of jurors at the Surrey assizes. I have drawn here upon his study, which is the only analysis of eighteenth-century jury composition I have seen. Other studies of this sort are now being undertaken; they are, I believe, unlikely to alter Beattie's conclusions significantly. Beattie's findings suggest that jury composition—which is not to say jury attitudes or the judge-jury relationship—had not substantially changed since the late seventeenth century. Beattie also argues, however (*idem*), that the jury qualification statute of 1730 (Stat. 3 Geo. 2, c. 25) was intended to insure a steadier flow of jurors from the lower-middling groups in society. Jury service became a more respectable activity (a response, perhaps, to the upgrading of the grand jury); the Crown relied on fewer, hence more experienced persons, individuals drawn from the higher ranks of the very large class of persons that remained the target of summons for trial jury service.

5. Baker, "Criminal Courts and Procedure," p. 38. Although the older form of altercation continued in some instances, the characterization here represents the main trend. This is reflected in the trial accounts known as The Old Bailey Sessions Papers (*O.B.S.P.*). For most of the eighteenth century, these accounts were formally entitled, *The Proceedings of the Sessions of the Peace, and Oyer and Terminer, for the City of London and the County of Middlesex*. Nearly complete runs of the *O.B.S.P.* are in the British Library and the Library of the Guildhall, London. Langbein, "Criminal Trial before the Lawyers," pp. 267–72, describes these trial accounts. Similar patterns are evidenced in the records of Surrey assizes for this period. See Beattie, *Crime and the Courts*, ch. 8. Practice in and near London may in some respects have differed from practice elsewhere, but it is likely that the changes I have noted fairly rapidly became general throughout England.

6. I base this statement on a review of the *O.B.S.P.* for the eighteenth and early nineteenth centuries. Langbein is now working on the rise of the law of evidence and its effects on trial procedure and on judge-jury relations.

juries in the late decades of the seventeenth century heard a large number of cases before retiring; thereafter, at least on some circuits, they deliberated after each case, and often they did not actually retire.[7]

Some of these developments may have made the jurors' task more difficult. Although the production of evidence was more organized, the separation of accusation and denial meant that testimony that went unanswered may have been either forgotten or given too much weight.[8] Then, too, the open "altercation" of an earlier day, while putting some defendants so much on the defensive that their nervousness counted too heavily against them, may have at least revealed telling emotions that now remained hidden. And though the increasing diffuseness of testimony may have been mitigated by the judge's commentary,[9] judges had for long commented upon the evidence; more witness testimony meant more commentary for the jury to digest. By the same token some jurors obviously had trouble keeping straight the complex array of defendants, evidence, rebuttals, and commentary put before them.[10] As a result the most experienced jurors, probably including the foreman, exercised significant influence over their fellow jurors in the brief discussion of each case.[11] But these differences in practice were subtle; there is no reason to believe that they initiated or reflected a new era in the history of trial by jury.[12]

If the eighteenth-century felony trial differed from that of two centuries before, it was because changes external to trial procedure had a palpable

7. Beattie, "Crime and the Courts in Surrey," p. 174. Beattie concluded that in Surrey juries "do not appear to have found it necessary to withdraw very often." See Beattie, *Crime and the Courts in England*, ch. 8.

8. For a description of standard trial practice see *The Complete Juryman: or, A Compendium of the Laws relating to Jurors* (London, 1752), p. 158. The prosecutors first examined the witnesses produced against the defendant, then the defendant cross-examined them; the defendant next examined his own witnesses and the prosecutors cross-examined them.

9. See M. Grosley, *A Tour to London; or, New Observations on England, and Its Inhabitants* (London, trans. 1772; orig. published 1765), p. 145. Grosley attended a trial in King's Bench. His account, which must be used with caution, states that the judge "summed up to the jury the whole charge, and the result of the depositions"; see also Francois de la Rochefoucauld, *A Frenchman in England, 1784* (1784; trans. and annot. by S. C. Roberts, London, 1933), p. 126.

10. Beattie found that in Surrey although the same jury heard a half dozen (or so) cases, verdicts were rendered after each case. *Crime and the Courts*, ch. 8.

11. Beattie (*idem*) states that typically one panel of about fifteen jurors handled all the cases at eighteenth century Surrey assizes. Several members of each dozen sworn to sit on a given case had served at a previous assize. One must consider, too, that jurors became "experienced" in the course of a single assize, after serving in many cases.

12. This view must remain tentative until the extant trial reports have been fully analyzed.

impact on the ways in which that procedure was employed and on the patterns of resolution that emerged from it. It is necessary to identify these changes before asking, in the following section, how the criminal trial jury functioned (and was thought to function) in practice.

Although the development of a formal law of evidence in criminal cases is difficult to discern before the late eighteenth century, judicial notions regarding both the nature of evidence and the appropriate standard for proof of guilt may have been changing in important ways over the course of the seventeenth century. It has been argued that seventeenth-century transformations in scientific theory affected juristic modes of thought, and these new conceptions are reflected not only in legal writings but also in judicial charges.[13] These developments paralleled or followed the decline of the self-informing jury. It was the practice of judicial summing up of the evidence proffered by witnesses that provided the opportunity for the bench to comment upon the degree of certainty or probability that jurors must accord certain elements of testimony before finding the defendant guilty. More often than not the bench mainly stressed the weight that it itself accorded testimony, but its reasoning in this regard often was revealed in judicial recommendations to the jury.[14]

We have seen that the Restoration bench sometimes invoked the principle of verdict according to conscience.[15] This principle took a variety of forms. It is hard to discern in it reference to a specific standard of proof, but clearly it carried the implications that jurors must act upon their own beliefs and that they must be fully satisfied that their beliefs were supported by the great weight of the testimony. Scroggs invoked the principle when he himself doubted the evidence; Hawles invoked it in the course of exhorting jurors to assess all the evidence, not just those elements or facts that the bench ruled appropriate for determination by the jury. These were special circumstances, of course, but they contrib-

---

13. Shapiro, *Probability and Certainty in Seventeenth-Century England*, ch. 5; see also Shapiro, "Theories of Knowledge and English Juries" (paper read at the American Historical Association Convention, Dec., 1984). I am grateful to Professor Shapiro for allowing me to cite her paper. Shapiro argues: "The traditional 'satisfied conscience' standard had initially been a rather vague notion employed because the jury was on oath. It became the vessel into which was poured the new learning about criteria for evaluating facts and testimony. 'Satisfied conscience' gradually became synonymous with rational belief" (p. 8). Shapiro identifies the new standard ("satisfied belief") with the "beyond reasonable doubt" standard (p. 12) that was frequently employed in the late eighteenth century; "[i]ts introduction caused no comment, precisely because it was consistent with notions of 'belief,' 'satisfied conscience,' and 'moral certainty' as employed in and out of the courtroom" since the seventeenth century (p. 13).

14. Beattie, *Crime and the Courts*, ch. 8.

15. See above, Chapter 6, text at nn. 201–4.

uted to a perspective on fact-finding that eighteenth-century concern with rules of evidence—hearsay and the like—greatly enhanced.

We cannot know the impact of these developments on jury fact-finding in routine cases. Probably they counted for something in important political cases, especially in the light of statutory reference to "credible" testimony in cases of treason.[16] But the concern among jurists with scientific assessment of evidence may have made itself felt more generally. Judges as well as juries had long been inclined to mitigate the law of sanctions in many capital cases. As we shall see, eighteenth-century legislation greatly increased the scope of offenses for which death was at least a potential sanction, thereby expanding the universe of cases subject to the process of selection of the worst offenders. Eighteenth-century commentators often remarked upon the tendency of the bench to advise jurors that conviction of capital felony required something close to absolute certainty of guilt.[17] An extremely high standard of proof (which was a very important source of the traditional presumption of innocence) was one—though only one—of the devices that were central to the regime of mitigation.

There were, then, several sources for the increasing concern with the standard of proof, the last-mentioned being the oldest and the most significant. Restoration advances in scientific theory can't be discounted, but they should be seen as having provided a more modern intellectual approach to longstanding practice. Their impact upon the emerging law of evidence is palpable, but it was nonetheless indirect, making itself felt via the catalysts of politics and, most important, the administration of a criminal law based upon mercy as well as terror.

From 1671, judges were precluded from actually coercing jurors to return a conviction. For a time some judges may have broken the spirit, if not the letter, of the ruling in *Bushel's Case*, but for the most part straightforward coercion disappeared from the English courts.[18] Strictly speaking, the ruling directly altered trial practice in only a negative sense—something only occasionally done, or even threatened, was no longer allowed. Indirectly, however, the constraints imposed by *Bushel's Case* may have altered practice by intensifying the bench's inclination to apply more subtle forms of influence at every point in the trial.[19]

Although the petty jury remained relatively uncontrolled, the grand jury did not. By the mid-eighteenth century it was finding true bills in 85

16. Shapiro, *Probability and Certainty in Seventeenth-Century England*, p. 190.
17. See below, nn. 58–59 and accompanying text.
18. See above, Chapter 6, section IV.
19. See Langbein, "Criminal Trial before the Lawyers," *passim*.

to 90 percent of all capital cases.[20] These figures no doubt reflected the development of the prosecution and especially of pretrial examinations.[21] The evidence that a case existed against the accused was usually too strong for the grand jury to return an *ignoramus*; the commotion over the packing of grand juries during the Restoration represented a momentary turnabout in highly charged political cases long after the grand jury had, from the Crown's point of view, come to be "reliable" in common-run felonies.[22] The benefit of the doubt went to the prosecution at the grand jury stage. Lay prosecutors possessed greater powers than before, once their complaints were moved before the justices. A sincere-sounding accusation was bound to go a long way. False accusations, whether malicious or merely mistaken, were now less effectively filtered.[23] Although the grand jury might undervalue goods in order to indict a suspect for only petty larceny, in general it is fair to say that if the community was going to play a significant role, increasingly it would have to play it at a later stage.

At the very moment that relatively pro forma grand jury proceedings were placing greater strain on postindictment institutions of mitigation, the scope of capital felony was expanding.[24] Most of the new laws concerned the taking or destruction of property;[25] many of them did little more than remove the right to benefit of clergy for offenses that had long before been capital at common law. The genesis of this legislation is little understood,[26] but some of its effects are well known. The capital statutes empowered property owners, small as well as large, to put at risk the lives of ever greater numbers of Englishmen. These laws may have increased

20. Beattie, "Crime and the Courts in Surrey," p. 163; Baker, "Criminal Courts and Procedure," p. 20. See Beattie, *Crime and the Courts*, ch. 7. Beattie found that Surrey grand juries (1660–1800) rejected ll.5 percent of capital property crime accusations and 15 percent of homicide accusations.

21. For an important study of developments in mid-eighteenth-century pretrial policing and prosecutorial practices see Langbein, "Shaping the Eighteenth Century Criminal Trial."

22. See above, Chapter 6, n. 225 and accompanying text. Beattie (*Crime and the Courts*, ch. 8) shows that this episode had the effect of upgrading the status of grand jurors.

23. Accusations made under oath had to go forward from the magistrate for grand jury consideration; by the mid-eighteenth century, magistrates exercised discretion regarding accusations not made under oath. See Beattie, *Crime and the Courts*, ch. 2.

24. This development has its roots in the sixteenth-century statutes limiting eligibility for benefit of clergy. See above, Chapter 4, text at nn. 42–50.

25. See e.g. E. P. Thompson, *Whigs and Hunters* (New York, 1975), for a study of one such act, *The Waltham Black Act* [Stat. 9 Geo. 1, c. 22 (1723)].

26. See John Styles, "Criminal Records," *Historical Journal*, vol. 20, (1977), p. 980; G. R. Elton, "Introduction: Crime and the Historian," in Cockburn, ed., *Crime in England*, pp. 4–5; John H. Langbein, "*Albion's* Fatal Flaws," *Past and Present*, no. 98 (1983), pp. 115–19. See also Beattie, *Crime and the Courts*, ch. 5.

the problems of enforcement by further burdening already overbusy courts and swelling the numbers of those who were ultimately punished at less than the prescribed level of sanction. Also, in a more subtle way, the new statutes occasionally influenced the criminal trial: judges were required to interpret the statutes, and this was sometimes reflected in the length and technicality of judicial charges. Frequently the bench sought to confine the statutes, so that narrow construction of the criminal law became a common form of mitigation.[27]

Even more pronounced was the rapid increase in the practice of undervaluation of stolen property. Medieval in origin, and common enough in Tudor-Stuart times, undervaluation became a major form of  resolution during the eighteenth century.[28] Its prominence resulted from the coincidence of the multiplication of capital statutes for property offenses, many of which precluded clergy except in cases of minor theft, and the creation of a new lesser sanction, transportation. Transportation had been in use episodically from around 1600, but not until the early eighteenth century was it statutorily prescribed for a wide range of offenses.[29] Very soon it became a catchall for most of those defendants who had committed capital theft but whom the Crown, bench, or jury desired to spare. In effect, transportation had come largely to replace clergy (in the form of branding and discharge), serving both as a prescribed sanction and as a safety valve where mercy was deemed appropriate.[30]

27. Douglas Hay, "Property, Authority and the Criminal Law," in D. Hay et al., eds., *Albion's Fatal Tree* (New York, 1975), p. 32; Leon Radzinowicz, *A History of Criminal Law and Its Administration from 1750*, 4 vols. (London, 1948–68), vol. 1, pp. 25–28, 83–91, 97–103.

28. See the figures in Beattie, "Crime and the Courts in Surrey," pp. 175–79. "Partial verdicts," where a verdict of guilty on the indictment as framed would have meant death unless bench or Crown interceded, involved characterizing the value of the goods stolen as less than twelve pence (petty larceny) or as more than twelve pence but less than whatever amount the relevant statute prescribed as the threshold for capital felony. (It might also involve characterizing the circumstances of the offense in such a way as, e.g., to convert a burglary into clergyable larceny). See also Jerome Hall, *Theft, Law and Society* (2nd ed., New York, 1952), pp. 139–41; Radzinowicz, *History of Criminal Law*, 1:94–97.

29. Stat. 4 Geo. 1. c. 11 (1718). The statute allowed the bench to sentence convicts to transportation for seven years in cases of clergyable felony and petty larceny. See Beattie, "Crime and the Courts," p. 158; Cockburn, *History of English Assizes*, p. 130; Langbein, *Torture and the Law of Proof* (Chicago, 1977), pp. 39–44, and works cited in accompanying notes. See also Beattie, *Crime and the Courts*, ch. 10, for an excellent account of the pre-1718 experiments with transportation and the legislative history of the statute. Beattie's work on the history of punishment, 1660–1800, constitutes a major step forward in the history of the administration of the criminal law.

30. Beattie (*Crime and the Courts*, ch. 10) points out that before transportation came into general use juries were urged to convict of petty larceny, for which the punishment was

By the middle decades of the eighteenth century the apparatus for sifting defendants tried on capital charges—a process that Beattie aptly characterizes as one of "selection"[31]—had become fairly complex. Some defendants were acquitted outright; others were convicted, condemned, and hanged because of the seriousness of their offenses and "as a terror to others."[32] Many capital defendants were saved by undervaluation or a "finding" of simple larceny instead of burglary (either on the jury's own action or because of judicial advice to the jury), and thus were convicted of an offense for which transportation or whipping were the prescribed sanctions. Still others, having been convicted of a capital offense, looked to the bench for relief. Of these, a very few were saved by appeal and retrial, or by a legal ruling, the verdict notwithstanding, by King's Bench or by the trial court itself.[33] Many more were granted judicial reprieves, thus securing time to petition the king for mercy in the form either of pardon on condition of transportation or of outright pardon. The bench played an important role regarding these posttrial petitions. At the close of every session the judges sent to the Council or Home Office letters containing the names of those they thought ought to be spared.[34]

whipping, rather than simple grand larceny, which was clergyable. Thus what appears to be greater mercy was in fact conviction of the lesser offense that carried the harsher punishment. After passage of the 1718 transportation statute, recourse to petty larceny declined and conviction for simple grand larceny became more common.

31. Beattie, "Crime and the Courts in Surrey," p. 171.

32. See e.g. SP 37/5, fols. 98v–99 (1766), Mr. Justice Perrott's letter to the Council recommending a convict not be saved: "I beg leave to certify that the law upon which this man was indicted had for its object the protection and security of the industrious poor who are obliged to labour for their bread abroad and are therefore daily liable to be stripped of all their honest labour has furnished them with and once stripped of that are little able to replace it. An act founded upon such principles I thought should not become a dead letter but that an example should be made as a terror to others and to give a very valuable part of his majesty's subjects that protection and security intended by the law." See also Bernard de Mandeville, *An Enquiry into the Causes of the Frequent Executions at Tyburn* (London, 1725), p. 36: "[I]t is not the death of those poor souls that is chiefly aimed at in executions, but the terror we would have it strike in others of the same loose principles"; Henry Fielding, *An Enquiry into the Causes of the late increase of Robbers, etc.* (London, 1751), p. 264: "The terror of the example is the only thing proposed, and one man is sacrificed to the preservation of thousands. . . . If therefore the terror of this example is removed (as it certainly is by frequent pardons) the design of the law is rendered totally ineffectual"; Sir Samuel Romilly, below, n. 120 and accompanying text.

33. Baker, "Criminal Courts and Procedure," pp. 45–48.

34. This was a continuation, and expansion, of a procedure that dates from at least the sixteenth century. In the eighteenth century, judges are mentioned frequently in State Papers (e.g. SP 36/113, fols. 5, 15, 78). After the mid-1780s, these circuit letters are grouped in the Home Office records (e.g. HO 6, 2/23; 4/23; 7/15; 12/58). For discussion of judicial requests for pardons see below, nn. 48–53 and accompanying text. For a detailed discussion of pardon procedure and practice see Beattie, *Crime and the Courts,* ch. 9.

Frequently the judges received requests from the Council or Home Office for supporting data, both in the cases that the judges had moved and in others moved by the defendant or by his employer, friends, or kin.[35] In many of these latter cases, the trial judge recommended against clemency, which presumably doomed the defendant.

The jury was only one of several sources of mitigation, and even then many of its merciful verdicts were encouraged—practically commanded—by the bench. But it was more active in this regard than it had been since medieval times, and much of the mitigation it practiced had taken on a kind of legitimacy it had not possessed before. There was now more law and more prosecution, and thus greater reliance on jury or postverdict determination of whether someone who had committed a nominally capital offense actually ought to hang. The trend was not new, but frequency of practice conditioned concepts of legitimacy, and these concepts in turn shaped society's understanding of the eighteenth-century criminal trial.

# II

Although there can be no doubt that the jury was one of many institutions of mitigation, it is difficult to determine the degree of independence jurors had, or believed they had, in reaching verdicts of a discretionary nature. Langbein has shown that long after *Bushel's Case* the bench retained a number of devices that assured it control over the jury. The bench commented on the evidence and embodied such commentary in instructions that sometimes read like recommendations.[36] The bench could withdraw a case before it went to the jury in order to allow time for the gathering of more and better evidence;[37] its sense of timing in this regard was relatively acute because there was now more frequent exchange between judge and jury, or between jury and trial participants, that revealed the jury's view of the case.[38] The jury might be made to disclose its reasons for finding for or against the defendant, and the judge could send the jury back for further discussion if he thought the reasons insufficiently grounded on the evidence presented.[39] Thus the bench

---

35. See e.g. SP 36/115, fol. 24; SP 36/116, fol. 105.

36. Langbein, "Criminal Trial before the Lawyers," pp. 284–87. See also H. Misson, *Memoirs and Observations in his Travels over England* (London, trans. 1719; written 1698), p. 328: "[O]ne of the judges makes a discourse upon all that has been said, recapitulates the discourses *pro* and *con*, weighs and considers all things, draws his conclusions, and declares to the jury, that conformably to the laws of the country they ought to bring it in so and so."

37. Langbein, "Criminal Trial before the Lawyers," pp. 287–89.

38. See *O.B.S.P., passim.*

39. Langbein, "Criminal Trial before the Lawyers," pp. 289–96. In a few early modern

possessed the means for achieving practical control of juries. Had judges employed those means frequently, the tradition of jury independence in common-run felonies would have diminished substantially. In fact, as Langbein would agree, only the first device—comment on the evidence, containing strong hints of the judge's view of the appropriate outcome— was a common feature of eighteenth-century criminal trials. To a significant degree, however, judicial comment allowed the bench to achieve the modest control it felt necessary and appropriate to exercise. For there was, in any case, little area of real disagreement between judge and jury over the outcome of most trials.

In light of the power that the bench possessed to control the jury, it is striking to consider the actual fate of defendants. Acquittal and conviction rates varied from decade to decade and from place to place, but Beattie's figures for Surrey, 1736–53, would seem a typical set of jury verdicts.[40] Beattie found that defendants charged with capital property crimes were treated, in roughly equal numbers, in one of three ways. One third were found guilty of the capital charge; one third were acquitted; and one third were convicted on a lesser, or "partial," charge, e.g., either petty larceny or simple (noncapital) grand larceny. Of those found guilty of the capital charge, only one half were hanged; the remainder were pardoned on condition of being transported. Of those granted partial verdicts, 85 percent were transported. The remainder were whipped or imprisoned, or were discharged after successfully claiming benefit of clergy. Thus, of the total tried for capital property offenses, some 15–20 percent were hanged, at least 40 percent were ordered to be transported, and perhaps 40 percent were not punished at all beyond pretrial incarceration and any posttrial stigma that might have attached.

If there was a trend across the entire period, it was toward fewer actual executions, fewer outright acquittals, and more transportations (followed later in the century by more terms of imprisonment at hard labor). The assumption that offenders ought to be punished and reformed became more general; the willingness to take life long remained constant, then

---

trials the judges accepted the jury's verdict of acquittal and urged a surviving kinsman to appeal the suspect. See Ernst, "Moribund Appeal of Death," pp. 177–80.

40. Beattie, "Crime and the Courts in Surrey," pp. 179–81. See also Beattie's *Crime and the Courts*, which contains far more complete statistical tables than those he has previously published. In his book, Beattie details the fluctuations and long-term changes in the patterns of resolutions. He links these to specific events, prevailing social perceptions of crime, and changes in attitudes toward treatment of human beings. Beattie also demonstrates that the figures varied substantially as between the "old" (more serious) capital offenses and the "new" (less serious ones). See Beattie, *Crime and the Courts*, ch. 9 and table 9.4. Langbein's figures for mid-century Old Bailey cases are similar ("*Albion's* Fatal Flaws," p. 106).

dramatically receded. Although in percentage terms no more individuals were executed in the early eighteenth century than in earlier times—the 20 percent figure remains the typical figure across the half-dozen centuries we have studied—the alternative sanction, transportation, was considerably more punishing than the alternative sanctions resorted to in the past, pardons and clergy.

The new regime of mitigation must be distinguished in yet another way from its predecessors. In the medieval period, property crimes at the capital level might be reported as petty larceny by the grand jury, pardoned before trial, or mitigated through acquittal by the trial jury.[41] It is difficult to determine what percentage of the many trial jury acquittals were in the nature of merciful verdicts. There is little indication that the medieval bench encouraged merciful acquittals; such verdicts remained hidden and, at most, tolerated. In the later Middle Ages, the grand jury was brought under greater control, but pretrial pardons were plentiful and benefit of clergy was extended to an ever larger number of persons, reducing the number of cases in which the jury's verdict was of great importance. The sixteenth-century statutes removing many property crimes from benefit of clergy brought the jury once again to the fore: the practice of undervaluing goods or of convicting the defendant of a form of theft that was still clergyable became far more common than it had been in the medieval period. The jury could preclude capital punishment without granting a full acquittal, though not entirely at will since the bench might still exercise its power to deny that the defendant was truly literate. As we have seen, the bench often encouraged jury undervaluations (and other forms of "partial" verdicts) and thus helped to initiate the practice that came to dominate jury trials by the eighteenth century.[42] Although this practice had increased in the late sixteenth and early seventeenth centuries, it was the statutory provision for transportation in many property offenses that made it standard form after 1718. The novelty, of course, lay in the creation of a largely jury-administered scheme of mitigation that was legitimated both by the complicity of the bench and by the reality of some substantial punishment for those who were its beneficiaries.

Within this evolving scheme of mitigation numerous factors induced acquittals and partial verdicts. Judicial recommendations to the jury often, though by no means always, were based on the quantum of evidence against the accused. The bench demanded that proof be virtually absolute before the jury convicted at a capital level.[43] Where such proof

41. See above, Chapter 2, section II.
42. See above, Chapter 4, text at n. 176.
43. See below, nn. 58–59 and accompanying text. Judges frequently reprieved defendants

was lacking the bench recommended a form of mitigation that was "principled," i.e., in accordance with the evidence that had been adduced, but its recommendations in this regard were virtually always also conditioned by prevailing notions regarding the seriousness of the offense or its assessment of the character of the defendant.[44] In many instances, neither judge nor jury was disposed to give full expression to a newly minted capital law.[45] In others, the law itself was not nullified, but a defendant who had stolen only marginally more than the threshold amount was treated in the same way as one who had stolen just a little less. The circumstances surrounding the defendant's act were also taken into account. Although the earliest statutes precluding clergy singled out accompanying circumstances that society had long considered especially heinous, many later ones did not; some of these latter statutes merely lowered the capital amount in offenses that did not involve physical threat or assault. In prosecutions under such statutes evidence regarding surrounding circumstances became critical—not for the purpose of exonerating the defendant entirely, but for treating him mercifully.

Almost inevitably many partial verdicts were the result of a combination of circumstantial considerations and considerations touching the defendant's background and character. Character witnesses played a complicated and significant role. At trial their purpose was to exonerate the defendant, to testify that he was of such good reputation that he could not be presumed to have committed the offense with which he was charged.[46] In their charges to juries, judges may have treated such testimony mainly in this regard, but witnesses served also to support the defendant's plea for mercy after conviction. Juries may have had difficulty keeping these different roles separate, and it is even possible that the behavior of the bench encouraged the jury to confuse them. Judges counseled partial verdicts on the basis of such testimony even when it was clear that the defendant had committed the act in question. Moreover, the bench did so not only where the offense was trivial but also in more serious cases where the witnesses testified that the defendant was of good

they believed ought not to have been convicted on the evidence. And see e.g. SP 36/113, fol. 121: because "the whole [case] depending upon one single witness," the judge recommended commutation to transportation for fourteen years (1751); SP 36/115, fol. 34: "because the evidence was not sufficient in law to convict him of the offence," the judge recommended transportation for fourteen years (1751); see also HO 47/5, no. 5: because of the "great doubt thrown on this case . . . perhaps [the defendants] should be transported to some place with a more favorable climate than their present destination of Africa" (1786). I am grateful to Elizabeth Clark for this last reference.

44. See Beattie, *Crime and the Courts*, ch. 9; Langbein, "Shaping the Eighteenth-Century Criminal Trial," pp. 26–30.

45. Beattie, "Crime and the Courts in Surrey," p. 172.

46. See Hay, "Property, Authority and the Criminal Law," p. 42.

character or had been in straitened circumstances or misled by others.[47] Although juries sometimes convicted with a recommendation for mercy,[48] the bench did not always attempt entirely to sever the question of guilt from the matter of appropriate sanction by first securing a conviction and then undertaking to exercise mercy judicially. In practice, the bench did not seek a monopoly over the practice of mitigation. Rather, it tolerated and implicitly legitimated the age-old jury practice of mitigation without always setting clear standards for the jury regarding the weight to be given to any of a number of considerations that paraded as evidence.[49] Assessment of guilt by the jury, as well as consideration of postsentence reprieve by the bench, was frequently made into a test, in the most general sense, of the defendant's just deserts.

The specific considerations upon which a given jury acted when it acquitted a defendant or rendered a partial verdict on other than strictly legally prescribed grounds are seldom revealed to the reader of extant trial accounts. Some conclusions about typical reasons for mitigation can of course be drawn. Mitigation was common, for instance, where the evidence was not "absolute," or where the defendant had stolen little more than the capital amount. (Some offenses were so systematically treated as though they were not capital that the interesting question is not, Why were most such offenders spared? but, Why were the very few unlucky ones singled out?) The details of mitigating circumstances and the constituents of "good character," however, often remain unclear. One is forced to extrapolate from letters and petitions in cases where the defendant had been condemned, but where judge, jury, or others urged

47. Beattie, "Crime and the Courts in Surrey," pp. 171–73. In his excellent synopsis Beattie does not focus on the jury's perspective and perhaps understates the degree to which jury acquittals and partial verdicts were impressionistic and based on a mixture of motives that not even the jurors themselves were pressed to sort out.

48. See e.g. SP 36/113, fol. 76 (1750): Mr. Justice Burnet's report to Council: "The jury found the prisoner guilty; but at the same time desired that I would represent him as an object of mercy upon condition of transportation"; SP 36/113, fol. 78: Michael Foster wrote: "The jury recommended [the convict] to mercy, and I reprieved him"; SP 36/116, fol. 150 (1751): "The jury after the business of the day was over came in a body to the bar and recommended the prisoner to mercy, out of regard to his youth."

49. The intermixing of different kinds of reasons for extending mercy at the postconviction stage is reflected in a letter to the Council from Mr. Newton Ikin, recommending mercy for a convict who foiled a conspiracy to murder his gaoler [evidently while waiting for a reprieve after being sentenced to hang]: "These facts may possibly have some weight if Mr. Perrott [Baron and Judge] which it is expected he will, should make an unfavorable report to his majesty, for he refused the sheriff the favor of a reprieve for [the defendant]. His sentence I find to be generally thought severe, as the burglary was not positively proved, and the felony he was convicted of was no more than a cotton handkerchief of a very small value." SP 37/5, fol. 88 (1766). (Perrott did recommend carrying out the sentence, apparently without knowing these additional details. See SP 37/5, fols. 98v–99).

commutation and/or pardon. It is necessary to proceed with caution, for matters thought relevant to postconviction clemency were not necessarily persuasive with juries charged with finding the truth (or the just resolution) in the first place.

Although most of the extant petitions for pardons and commutations date from the later eighteenth and early nineteenth centuries, they were abundant enough by the 1550s to indicate that the range of reasons for which pardons were granted remained fairly constant from the mid-sixteenth to the mid-nineteenth century.[50] Judges' letters in support of pardons often cite the petitions of the defendant's minister or substantial neighbors.[51] To have the support of respectable members of the community to which the convict would ultimately return must have counted for a great deal. It is not possible to determine how often the jurors had known the views of such persons at the time of their deliberation. Drawn from the county, though not necessarily from the hundred where the offense occurred, some jurors may have known of the defendant's reputation, and we must assume that juries took this kind of knowledge into account in at least some cases resulting in mitigated verdicts.[52]

From judges' letters it is apparent that in addition to the nature of the offense itself, good character and previous behavior, youthfulness, submissiveness upon arrest, and evident remorsefulness weighed heavily both with them and with juries.[53] The sentence that most beneficiaries of

50. See above, Chapter 4, n. 163 and accompanying text. This subject requires further study. Although the stated reasons for pardons remained relatively constant, social attitudes toward mercy must have changed over time. For a study of the Puritan ideas that informed much social thinking about the role of mercy see Herrup, "Common Peace," ch. 6. See also my comments below, Chapter 9.

51. E.g. SP 36/113, fol. 5 (1750): Thomas Birch, J., requested a free pardon for one convicted of stealing a calf, because of "favorable circumstances" at the trial and because he received a petition from the "minister, church wardens, overseers and principal inhabitants of the parish wherein he resided"; SP 36/113, fol. 15 (1750): Mr. Baron Legge seeks a free pardon for a defendant on whose behalf he "received a petition for principal inhabitants of the parish wherein she resided"; SP 36/116, fol. 32 (1750): Mr. William Noel, Chief Justice of Chester, sought commutation for a defendant for whom the prosecutor and many of the defendant's neighbors spoke; SP 36/116, fol. 306: Sir Martin Wright (judge of King's Bench) received a petition from "diverse of the better sort of the inhabitants of Drayton, in Shropshire" that the defendant "may dwell amongst her neighbours again."

52. See above, Chapter 6, section IV, for discussion of the role of out-of-court information. The argument for the jury's right to a noncoerced verdict was based in part on out-of-court knowledge of the defendant's reputation. Although those making the argument probably meant that this kind of knowledge was relevant to the question of guilt or innocence, we have seen that the trial process confused this question with the question of the appropriate punishment.

53. E.g. SP 36/113, fol. 9 (1750): youth "and other favourable circumstances," including stealing goods "of no considerable value," making no resistance, confessing immediately; HO 47/6, nos. 1 (1787): youth, and because prosecutor had recovered his sheep; 2 (1787):

jury-based mitigation received was transportation for seven years (in lieu of execution or transportation for fourteen years); substantial evidence of good character and of likelihood of reform must have seemed sufficient justification for one of the standard lesser sanctions. Perhaps it was the moderate quality of mitigation that led the bench to accept what was in any case inevitable, and to share openly its power of commutation with the jury. Whatever the reasons, the acceptance of shared powers of mitigation was of the greatest importance. It demonstrates that the criminal trial jury was still a social morality play over which officials exercised only a partial control. It also revealed that judge and jury, though they may have represented different social strata and different attitudes toward criminal behavior, generally acted in tandem, not one against the other.[54] In the administration of the law regarding common-

youth, inexperience, penitence; 3 (1787): good reason to believe the defendant was instigated to commit the offense by some of those persons admitted to testify against him; 5 (1787): appeared "to us" (six "freeholder-neighbors") to be sober and industrious, no earlier offences "we know of," has wife and three children "whom he has hitherto supported by his industry"; 10 (1787): good behavior during confinement, first offence; 11 (1787): good behavior, repentance; 20 (1787): first offence, employable; HO 47/15, no. 39 (1792): of former good reputation, husband a bad man who misused her. Hay, "Property, Authority and the Criminal Law," pp. 42–46, argues that judicial recommendations for mercy reflect class-based attitudes wherein "respectability" played a leading role. Hay has understated the role of other considerations, e.g., the problem of unsafe verdicts, reputation, repentance, etc. [On this point see Peter King, "Decision-Makers and Decision-Making in the English Criminal Law, 1750–1820," *Historical Journal,* vol. 27 (1984), pp. 25–58. King's article provides an excellent analysis of prosecution and pardon. On the whole, we are in agreement.] It is possible that judicial attitudes regarding all of these factors were characterized by condescension and that, whatever the stated rationale, judicial mercy was proffered to obtain the deference of the lower classes. That remains unclear. It cannot be assumed, however, that jury attitudes were the same as those of the bench, even where juries extended mercy on the recommendation of the bench. From their own perspective, however, defendants may have been led by the apparent agreement between judge and jury to the conclusion that the jurors' attitudes and motives were the same as those of the bench. It does indeed seem plausible, as I believe Hay would argue, that merciful verdicts reinforced the view among all participants (defendants, jurors, observers) that the administration of law (and law itself) was just. This almost certainly engendered a certain degree of deference to authorities, to one's social betters, and even to one's social equals where the latter had been part of the process that had resulted in merciful treatment. For further discussion of Hay's views as they pertain to the role of the jury see below, n. 156.

54. This is evidenced also by jury verdicts in cases where no partial verdict was possible (e.g., sheep stealing). The jury had either to convict of the capital offense or acquit altogether. In such cases, juries convicted with great frequency, probably knowing in many such cases that the bench was going to reprieve the defendant and recommend a pardon on condition of transportation. Beattie, *Crime and the Courts,* ch. 9. In some cases, however, the jury ignored judicial recommendations for mercy. The judge felt bound to honor their

run felonies, everything conspired to the creation of an integrated fact-finding, law-applying, and sentencing process.

Contemporary observers depicted the role of the criminal trial jury largely in the terms we have set forth. Professional and lay writers on the law and legal institutions well understood the importance of the element of mitigation in the administration of the criminal law. They were not, however, wholly in agreement either on the factors that most often led juries to mitigate or on the degree to which juries acted on their own rather than taking their lead from the bench. Moreover, some of them did not view the process of mitigation as a carefully managed "selection" but viewed it rather as an unruly flight from the horrors of the sentence to the gallows. For this reason, among others, many observers doubted that a system of jury-based mitigation was a virtue; indeed, as we shall see, beginning early in the eighteenth century there was increasing criticism of a system of criminal administration that depended heavily upon this aspect of the jury's role.

In most eighteenth-century descriptions of the routine felony trial the judge looms large. Even foreign observers, who were mainly curious about the role of the English jury, were impressed by the care that the bench took in questioning witnesses and the defendant, in taking notes on all testimony, and in summing up the evidence for the jury.[55] Contemporary accounts confirm the impression left by the *Old Bailey Sessions Papers* that the bench dominated proceedings, but they do not suggest that judges frequently brought pressure to bear on the jury. Rather, the judge reviewed the evidence thoroughly in open court, leaving little doubt of his own conclusions and making recommendations to the jury.[56] Observors thought that these recommendations carried great weight, partly because of the intrinsic authority of the bench and partly because of the reasonableness and thoroughness of judicial summations. Some contemporaries, especially foreign observers, who tended to idealize the English criminal trial, asserted that the jury remained free to reach its own conclusions, implying that the bench rarely questioned jurors closely or sent them back to reconsider their first verdict. But even they conceded that juries typically agreed with the bench. The routine felony trial in very nearly all accounts was characterized by a harmonious judge-jury rela-

verdict but reprieved the defendant and recommended him to the Crown for commutation. E.g. HO 47/6, no. 12 (1787).

55. Misson, *Memoirs and Observations,* p. 328; Grosley, *A Tour to London,* p. 145; de la Rochefoucauld, *A Frenchman in England,* pp. 124–26; J. H. Meister, *Letters Written During a Residence in England* (London, trans. 1799; orig. published 1789), pp. 36–37.

56. Misson, *Memoirs and Observations,* p. 328. See also above, n. 9 and accompanying text. For an important study of one (probably typical) judge's practice see Langbein, "Shaping the Eighteenth-Century Criminal Trial," pp. 26–30 and accompanying notes.

tionship. Neither the judge nor the jury was a nullity; both were active and central institutions despite the fact that the judge was the partner that led.[57]

We have seen that most defendants were either acquitted or awarded a partial verdict. Judicial leadership, it appears, involved frequent recommendations that the jury not convict the defendant of a capital offense. Although it is clear that judges and juries took the kind of offense committed into account, contemporary writers have surprisingly little to say about judicial treatment of different kinds of offenses. For lay writers especially, the most important factor in acquittals and partial verdicts was the very high threshold of proof that the court required for conviction of a capital offense.[58] The bench, it was asserted, seized upon every possible weakness in the testimony against the accused, even mere technicalities, to save the defendant's life.[59] The jury was urged to take the greatest care in assessing testimony where life was at stake, and, according to contemporaries, this is precisely what juries did. All parties to the system of justice, often including the complainant, strained to find some pretext on which to avoid the ultimate sanction of capital punishment.

It is ironic that many contemporaries counted close and impartial scrutiny by judge and jury as a hallmark of English justice, for there were as yet few formal rules of evidence. In much the same way, the frequent recourse to judicial reprieves hid the absence of a formal system of appeal.[60] The death penalty drove the bench and jury to find informal substitutes for what the legal system lacked and perhaps thus delayed the

57. Misson, *Memoirs and Observations,* p. 329: "[W]ithout being under the least restraint to keep to the conclusions of the judge that has harrangued them"; de la Rochefoucauld, *A Frenchman in England,* p. 126. But see Grosley, *A Tour to London,* p. 146, who concluded that the judge thinks he dominates and the jury thinks it does: "The juries, on the contrary, maintain that the whole procedure in all its branches is referred to them; that the judge assists merely that his presence may awe the witnesses and the prisoner with respect, and to assist the jury by his experience and knowledge of the law. This competition, and the rivalship which it occasions, rendering both judges and juries equally alert, put the law in the place of man."

58. William Paley, *Principles of Moral and Political Philosophy* (London, 1785), pp. 550–51. See also B. L. Muralt, *Letters describing the Characters and Customs of the English and French* (London, trans. 1726; written 1694, published 1725), p. 71. Muralt noted that some people were "condemned for small matters, and others are easily acquitted at the same time that seem to be much more guilty" (i.e., are suspected of a more serious offense). This, he said, was because the English "don't determine anything but on the clearest proofs, without any regard to probability."

59. F. Lacombe, *Observations sur Londres et ses Environs* (London, 1777), p. 69.

60. See *A Treatise on the Right of Juries* (London, 1771), p. 42: "The good sense and liberal feeling of the law . . . cannot be enough admired: It impowers juries to acquit absolutely, but reduces and softens their power to convict, by enabling the Crown in its mercy to withhold punishment."

development of formal institutions. As a result of the way things worked in practice, some observers underestimated the degree to which the framework of protections surrounding the defendant was manipulated in accordance with the defendant's offense, bearing, and background. English criminal justice was not mainly a matter of the application of abstract rules. The threshold of proof required for capital punishment was flexible, subject to being heightened in given instances.

It is possible that in many instances where the defendant's character or offense was the real reason for the extension of mercy, judge and jury rationalized the verdict in terms of the "weakness" of evidence adduced against the defendant, of the possibility that the testimony against him was inspired by hope of reward, or of a real or alleged departure by authorities from the formal requirements of the law.[61] Authorities may thus have hidden both from themselves as well as from some contemporaries the degree to which mercy resulted from abhorrence of the death penalty or from considerations of character or offense.[62] But these nonformal considerations were, in fact, both significant and noticed.[63] Moreover, they were understood as requiring a substantial degree of discretion on the part of the jury. Judicial recommendations were not seen as "directions"; even when the jury was following the lead of the bench it was seen as assimilating the judicial inclination to mitigate the rigors of the law to its own independent process of deliberation.

At one level this process of deliberation had been purged largely of out-of-court evidence: by the eighteenth century, if not earlier, it may have been deemed inappropriate for jurors to take such knowledge into account.[64] At another level, however, consideration of the defendant's reputation and character involved an assessment that might be thought of as community based. At the very moment that the jury was losing its right to be self-informing, authorities were continuing to acquiesce in the jury's right to apply standards that could be characterized as not entirely accessible to the bench. As we shall see, the persistence even in this truncated form of the tradition of the self-informing jury strengthened the

61. On the matter of technical defects in indictments see J. H. Baker, "The Refinement of English Criminal Jurisprudence, 1500–1848," in Knafla, ed., *Crime and Criminal Justice in Europe and Canada*, pp. 19–24.

62. Misson (*Memoirs and Observations*, p. 329) thought the judicial recommendations for commutation were based on whether the defendant was "more or less guilty."

63. English law reform writers were especially attentive to the role of these factors in the mitigation of the law. See below, section III.

64. Beattie (*Crime and the Courts*, ch. 8) notes that jurors at Surrey assizes sometimes had actual knowledge of events and were allowed to make use of it. See also Langbein, "Criminal Trial before the Lawyers," pp. 298–99, n. 105.

hand of jury proponents in the late-eighteenth-century debate over the law of seditious libel.

Although contemporaries understood that trial juries frequently intervened to save the defendant's life, their discussion of jury behavior reveals the complexity of the system of trial by jury and the varying conclusions that might be drawn regarding the way in which that system worked. Some writers viewed the jury as an appendage of the bench, but most saw it as far more independent. Most writers thought that jury verdicts were influenced mainly by the evidence, but many understood the importance of the offense, and the defendant's character and reputation. All of these considerations were influential, given the general resistance to convict at a capital level all but the worst offenders. Although most contemporaries understood this, they did not always take care to separate these factors. Even when juries did convict, they often did so with (perhaps because of) the knowledge that the defendant's life would or might be spared. Many contemporaries may have missed this point and thus failed to consider whether the jury in such cases doubted that it had the right to intervene or simply preferred to leave the ultimate decision to the bench.

The general impression that the lay and professional writings of the eighteenth century convey is that juries were willing to punish but not often to condemn men and women who came from walks of life that were different, but not totally removed from their own. Jurors may have identified with the perspective of authorities, but, as many contemporaries saw it, they often also identified with the defendant. Observers did not see jurors as constantly drawn in one direction or the other, perhaps because the bench was similarly disinclined to enforce the law to its fullest and at least appeared to adopt standards close to those of persons from the ranks from which jurors were drawn. Judge and jury, it was widely believed, shared both point of view and the age-old right and duty to mitigate the law.

# III

The practical approach to penology that we have described was the end product of a dialectical process set in motion centuries before. The trial jury's systematic nullification of the law of capital sanctions was gradually accommodated by authorities through doctrinal and institutional changes, some—though only some—of which were conscious responses to the relatively benign sort of jury-based intervention that we have been tracing in this chapter. As authorities tightened their control of juries in cases where they felt something substantial was at stake and developed a set of relatively severe noncapital sanctions for the general run of cases, they not only acquiesced in, but even encouraged, jury participation in the selection of offenders for one or another level of punishment.

The result of this historical development was a scheme of selective enforcement in which the jury played a significant role. Had juries, however, adhered from the outset to the rules of law, a system of selective enforcement might nonetheless have resulted. Given the needs of politics, the attack on capital punishment, and the recognition that the able-bodied could be put to good use, the English might have adopted a Crown-based Continental-style system of pardon and commutation. As it in fact evolved, the English system of penology, wherein the jury was an important participant, was more visible, more complex, and perhaps less consistent in its resolutions than its French or Italian counterparts. But it probably reflected the attitudes of a larger part of society and induced a more widespread belief that the entire system of criminal administration was just.

Whatever degree of public support the English scheme of selective enforcement enjoyed, it nonetheless met with significant criticism over the course of the eighteenth and early nineteenth centuries. The criticism intensified in the last decades of the century due largely to the influence of Cesare Beccaria's work, *On Crimes and Punishments*, first published in English in 1767.[65] The central principles of Beccaria's attack on Continental systems of criminal justice are too familiar to require detailed discussion. Popularizing the ideas of earlier and more original Continental writers,[66] Beccaria argued for moderate and proportional punishments that were both humane and capable of being systematically enforced. Certainty of punishment, he held, was the best deterrent to crime:[67] prospective offenders should not be encouraged to suppose they could escape punishment through the extension of mercy. Beccaria took an absolutist position, leaving virtually no room for the power of pardon.[68] Punishment, he believed, ought to be prompt[69] and ought to bear a rational relationship to the nature of the offense,[70] but in no case was it to be capital.[71] Though on this last point some Continental reformers

---

65. Cesare Beccaria, *Essay on Crimes and Punishments* (London, 1767). References hereafter are to the J. A. Farrar translation (London, 1880).

66. See e.g. Coleman Phillipson, *Three Criminal Law Reformers: Beccaria, Bentham, Romilly* (London, 1923), p. 84; Radzinowicz, *History of English Criminal Law*, 1:268–80, esp. nn. 36 and 42.

67. Beccaria, *Crimes and Punishments*, p. 168.

68. *Ibid.*, pp. 190–91.

69. *Ibid.*, p. 186.

70. *Ibid.*, pp. 213–14.

71. *Ibid.*, p. 169.

disagreed with Beccaria, his tract, generally speaking, fairly captured and transmitted their views to English shores.

Continental penological views of the late eighteenth century influenced but were not perfectly replicated in the emerging critique of the English system. For some English reformers, the Continental principles were especially attractive because of the open and seemingly ad hoc character of selective enforcement in their own country. At the same time, however, these reformers held a conception of justice to which some degree of jury discretion was integral. The English version of the new penology reveals just how complicated a role the jury had come to play in English legal and political culture. In what follows I shall examine the initial English reception of the new penology and suggest the ways in which longstanding English practices affected that reception. I shall also contrast the English reformers to the principal defenders of the status quo, who agreed with the reformers only in their criticism of prevailing jury practices, and in their view that whatever mitigation was to be practiced ought to be centered mainly in the Crown.

The reformers to whose work we shall pay greatest attention were not necessarily typical in their criticism of the jury. Their understanding of jury practices, and of the impact of those practices on the administration of the criminal law, rested mainly on their familiarity with the trials at urban assizes of a seemingly endless parade of suspected thieves and slayers.[72] They were influenced by their perception of a rising crime rate and a growing criminal class. Their view, in short, was a view from the center. The reformers' criticism was blunted, however, by their adherence to two positions that enjoyed wide social agreement. First, many reformers believed that the severity of the law of sanctions was a principal source of the problems afflicting the administration of the criminal law. Jury mitigation, they perceived, was an inevitable response to that severity; until sanctions were reformed mitigation would be both common and in accord with humane principles. It proved difficult for reformers to write about the prevailing system without giving support, pro tem, to some of the practices to which they were in fact opposed. Second, for most reformers there was an important conflict between their belief that jury mitigation played havoc with a rational system of criminal law and their faith in residual powers of nullification as a safeguard against

72. Hay ("Property, Authority and the Criminal Law," pp. 54–55) has pointed out that London "had a highly transient population, and a large body of disorderly and parasitic poor," and that "instruments of control there were weaker, in part because the class relationships that fostered deference were [weaker]. . . . Equally, judicial mercy in London was more often a bureaucratic lottery than a convincing expression of paternalism." This may help account for the reformers' criticism of what seemed to some of them a nearly random process of selection.

executive and judicial tyranny. (It is the exploration of these jury-related themes that distinguishes my treatment of the eighteenth-century reform tradition from that of earlier scholars, e.g., Sir Leon Radzinowicz.) As we shall see in this chapter and the one that follows, the contradictions inherent in both politics and the administration of criminal law in the eighteenth century were mirrored in the academic legal literature of the period.

The major reform writings and the responses to them may be aligned as follows. In the years around 1770, William Blackstone, William Eden, and Henry Dagge produced pioneering works on penal reform. All of these writers were influenced by Beccaria, whose concern had been with the law regarding common-run felonies. Though all three reflected some understanding of the constitutional-safeguard role of the jury, only Dagge clearly (and favorably) responded to the uproar over the jury in seditious libel cases and to the agitation of the Wilkites in the late 1760s. A decade later Manasseh Dawes, influenced by both Blackstone and the philosophical writings of Joseph Priestley that appeared in the late 1770s, added a variation on the Beccarian themes. Dawes argued for reform of the law of sanctions, urging that death be replaced by imprisonment at useful labor. He dwelled on the causes of criminal behavior, striking at points a modern note. Interestingly, his work showed no attention to the seditious libel crisis and to the defense of the jury in that context that he was to make two years later (1784) in the wake of the trial of the Dean of St. Asaph. In the mid-1780s William Paley and Martin Madan published very different defenses of the law of sanctions that criticized jury-based mitigation of the law in common-run felonies. Taken together, these two works challenged the early penal reform movement. The voice of the future, however, was heard in the first work of Samuel Romilly, who replied in 1786 to Madan's discourse. Romilly called for reform of the kind for which the adherents of Beccaria had called. Like most of the other reform writers, Romilly devoted nearly all his attention to the traditional felonies, and little to the problem of the jury in political cases, this despite the fact that just two years earlier Romilly had written a powerful defense of the role of the jury in seditious libel cases.

Although all of these writers—proponents and opponents of reform—opposed jury mitigation, at least at its contemporary levels, they nonetheless reflected widely divergent perspectives on the system of criminal law in general. Because these commentators on jury practices built upon one another, we shall examine them separately and chronologically, even at the risk of repetition on points where they were in substantial accord. Before turning to these seven important late-eighteenth-century legal writers, however, we must take account of Henry Fielding's two mid-century tracts. Fielding foreshadowed the later writers, especially in his ambivalence about the role of the criminal trial jury.

Fielding's 1751 *Enquiry* into the causes of what he perceived to be a recent increase in criminal activity attacked jury mitigation of "two excellent Acts of Parliament" regarding pilfering and like offenses.[73] By valuing goods at less than a shilling, the jury leaves the thief "ordinarily to be whipped," so that he returns immediately to his trade. As a result, "the jury are perjured, the public highly injured . . . that two miscreants [principal and accessory] may laugh at their prosecutors, and at the law."[74] Criminals thus "are ever lying in wait to destroy and ensnare the honest part of mankind, and to betray them by means of their own goodness." They take advantage of the "passion of love or benevolence," the "only human passion that is in itself simply and absolutely good."[75] Fielding preached against naivete, against what he took to be a misplaced generosity of spirit; he extolled the virtues of mercy in the abstract, but scorned the sudden accesses of compassion that blinded men to the real effects of merciful verdicts in criminal cases.[76]

The tone of the *Enquiry* is harsh and angry. It has the feel of a complaint from the front lines, penned by a magistrate attempting to deal with what he took to be a national crime wave. In only the narrowest sense was it a penal reform tract. Far from criticizing capital sanctions, Fielding insisted upon adherence to the rules of the system. Though Fielding's endorsement of the "terror of examples"[77] to deter would-be offenders seems to sanction some degree of selective enforcement, the principal argument of the *Enquiry* is that failure to prosecute and refusal to convict were both unlawful and unwise. To the extent that the tract foreshadowed later commentary on the jury, it bore a closer resemblance to Madan's call for rigorous enforcement of existing laws than to the writings of Beccaria's

73. Henry Fielding, *An Enquiry into the Causes of the Late Increase of Robbers* (London, 1751), p. 73. For a recent study of the contribution of Henry Fielding and his brother John to pretrial investigation see Langbein, "Shaping the Eighteenth-Century Criminal Trial," pp. 49 *et seq.* See also Pat Rogers, *Henry Fielding: A Biography* (New York, 1979), ch. 6.

74. Fielding, *An Enquiry*, p. 73.

75. *Ibid.*, pp. 106–8. Fielding refers here to too-merciful prosecutors, but he clearly means also to characterize too-merciful jurors.

76. See also Samuel Johnson, *The Rambler*, no. 114 (London, April, 20, 1751): "[I]t may be observed, that all but murderers have, at their last hour, the common sensations of mankind pleading in their favour" (p. 4). "This scheme of invigorating the laws by relaxation, and exploiting wickedness by lenity, is so remote from common practice, that I might reasonably fear to expose it to the public, could it be supported only by my own observations" (p. 7).

77. *Ibid.*, p. 120.

disciples or to Paley's defense of the regime of selective enforcement of the criminal law.

Fielding's 1753 *Proposal* was written in an altogether different vein.[78] It was an original reform tract, reminiscent of Interregnum reform writings, and a significant addition to the early eighteenth-century English literature that counseled use of the workhouse for persons convicted of petty theft.[79] Though limited in scope by its attention to petty theft, and to first offenders at that, Fielding's argument was informed by a series of insights that were shared by the later reformers. His central purpose was to argue for sentences to the workhouse, instead of gaol, for first offenders.[80] In the main, his tract was frankly utilitarian. Like mid-seventeenth-century reform writers, Fielding saw little purpose in simple and brutal incarceration. He portrayed the prospective defendant as one who awaits trial in the worst of circumstances, unable to support himself and his family, prey to the wretches of society.[81] Sentencing the convict to gaol only made matters worse. Fielding believed that the existing system produced hardened criminals and induced juries to acquit defendants who deserved some punishment and who required—to use a modern term—rehabilitation.

The themes of mercy, fairness, deterrence, and social utility were woven into a logical and compelling argument. The accused, Fielding observed, must await trial in gaol no matter how "trifling" his offense or how much he is an "object of mercy." "If he be acquitted on his trial, as he often is by the mercy of the jury, against clear and positive evidence, he is again turned loose among the community with all the disadvantages I have mentioned above." If he is convicted, whipped, and gaoled, so much the worse: "What must be the situation of this wretch I need not mention; such in truth it is, that his second theft is in reality less criminal than the first. This was perhaps choice; but that will be necessity."[82] Transportation of pilferers, made possible by a recent Act, offered little improvement:

78. Henry Fielding, *A Proposal for Making an Effectual Provision for the Poor* (London, 1753).

79. See above, Chapter 5, text at nn. 124–31, for a discussion of Interregnum law reform writing on penology. For early eighteenth century works that continued the seventeenth-century tradition see e.g. Thomas Coke, *Work-houses the best Charity, A Sermon, preached at the Cathedral Church of Worcester* (London, 1702); Sollom Emlyn, "Preface" to *A Complete Collection of State Trials*, 6 vols. (2nd ed., London, 1730), vol. 1, p. ix. Emlyn recommended "hard labour at home." For an excellent discussion of early eighteenth-century reform ideas regarding use of workhouses and the "reformation of manners," see Beattie, *Crime and the Courts*, ch. 10.

80. Fielding, *A Proposal*, p. 71.

81. *Idem.*

82. *Ibid.*, pp. 71–72.

[T]his, though probably it may be real mercy, has such an appearance of extreme severity, that few judges are willing to inflict such a punishment on such an offense. But if it should be in the interest of a wretch in these circumstances, to be banished from a country where he must steal or starve, it is scarce the interest of the public to lose every year a great number of such able hands. By the means I have proposed, it seems to me, that the offender will receive a punishment proportionable to his offence; he and his family may be preserved from utter ruin, and an able member, instead of being entirely lost to the public, will be rendered more useful to it than he was before.[83]

Fielding's prescription for reform was clear enough, but what were his views regarding mitigation in the unreformed present? Were judges and juries to apply the letter of the law to the "wretches" and "objects of mercy" who came before them? One might suppose that the Fielding who in 1751 opposed merciful verdicts in capital cases opposed them in noncapital cases of petty larceny in 1753. This is not necessarily so. Fielding might have believed that perpetrators of more serious offenses deserved the strongest possible punishment but that those who committed "trifling" ones deserved very little punishment at all. All one can say is that the *Proposal* reflects recognition that such verdicts were inevitable in "trifling" cases and that Fielding found it difficult to deny that they were just. Fielding's tracts signaled a revival of English penal reform writing. They carried forward Interregnum ideas, adding to them the insights of an experienced London magistrate. But they also revealed the tensions that characterized the late-eighteenth-century English reform tracts.

Blackstone's final volume of his *Commentaries on the Laws of England, Of Public Wrongs*, contained the first analysis of the administration of the criminal law written after the publication in England of Beccaria's influential work.[84] Blackstone admired the Continental reform tradition, and *Of Public Wrongs* attempts to assimilate that tradition to the common-law world, sometimes pretending that English institutions already conformed to the reformist ideal and sometimes justifying the obvious and seemingly important dissimilarities between them. Blackstone accepted Beccaria's principles of justice and deterrence based upon a law of sanctions that was humane and applied with certainty.[85] Blackstone also understood the role that English juries played in common-run felonies. He simultaneously acquiesced in a substantial amount of jury-based mitigation of the criminal law and counseled reforms that

83. *Ibid.*, p. 72.

84. William Blackstone, *Commentaries on the Laws of England*, 4 vols. (1765–69; reprinted, Chicago, 1979), vol. 4: *Of Public Wrongs*.

85. *Ibid.*, pp. 16–17.

would greatly lessen the need for such practices.[86]

The great bulk of jury mitigation practice involved the rendering of partial verdicts in offenses against property. Blackstone argued that undervaluation was largely a response to inflation, which had brought more and more goods within the scope of capital felony statutes. This was a kind of "pious perjury" that achieved justice by preventing unforeseen economic forces from condemning to death persons whom the legislature had not specifically said ought to be hanged.[87] Blackstone knew, however, that juries went beyond this form of mitigation, that they were merciful in a far wider range of cases; he was more cautious in his condonation of these practices, but it is clear that he believed they accorded with natural justice. Much of the law of capital sanctions was wrong as a matter of justice and policy; reform—in the form of repeal— was required, and until it came about one had both to understand and to accept the mitigating role of legal institutions.[88]

But as an advocate of reform Blackstone did not go so far as Beccaria, who argued that a rational law of sanctions would dissolve the necessity for a power of pardon. Blackstone believed that there would always be a need for that power; moreover, he inherited a view of monarchy from which the pardon power was inseparable. For Blackstone, the goal was partly to reduce the frequency with which pardons were granted, but mainly to centralize the pardon power in the Crown. Blackstone understood Beccaria's argument regarding deterrence, but seems not to have accepted the notion that *any* decrease in certainty of punishment, whatever its source, had to be paid for in decreased deterrence.

Blackstone focused on a distinctively English problem that Beccaria did not have to address: the dangers inherent in dispersed powers of mitigation.[89] For Beccaria, the villain was mitigation itself, not a particular institution of mitigation. While necessarily more complicated than that of the Continental reformer, Blackstone's argument was also internally contradictory. He sought to justify the English system even as he called for its reform. Thus he sought at times to argue that all power of mitigation was in fact centered in the Crown.[90] But he was well aware of the truth: political control, certainty of the law, consistency of treatment of offenders were all sacrificed under an English administration of law that

86. *Ibid.*, 18–19, 239, 354.
87. *Ibid.*, p. 239.
88. Thomas A. Green, "Introduction" to *ibid.*, pp. ix–xi.
89. *Ibid.*, pp. 18–19.
90. *Ibid.*, p. 390. Blackstone asserted that "the exclusion of pardons must necessarily introduce a very dangerous power in the judge or jury, that of construing the criminal law by the spirit instead of the letter." Blackstone knew that such practices were common despite the possibility of royal pardon. See above, n. 88.

corrected for its potential inhumanity through ad hoc and variously situated institutions of mitigation.

Blackstone understood that the problems besetting English criminal justice could be resolved only through fundamental change in the manner in which all the institutions of the criminal law functioned. Change could not come piecemeal; it would have to begin with the law of sanctions, but the effects of that change would have to radiate throughout the entire system. Until sanctions were reformed the jury would remain an institution of mitigation, playing a role akin to the one it had historically played in the English constitution of accommodating the rules of law to the Englishman's sense of natural justice. The jury was a guardian against inhumanity as well as against tyranny. As a corollary, whatever reforms were undertaken regarding sanctions for common-run felonies, the jury would have to retain the ultimate power in order to guard against episodes of legal abuse in more overtly political cases.[91] There were, of course, costs involved in the use of juries, but these Blackstone characterized as "inconveniences."[92] Better to educate Englishmen to serve as jurors in a system that required of them wisdom and some knowledge of the law, restraint but a sense of justice, than to eliminate the jury in order to avoid potential or even present abuses.

Blackstone shared his contemporaries' view that much criminal activity resulted from social conditions,[93] and he was prominent among the early proponents of prison reform who argued that current incarceration practices only made offenders more dangerous.[94] Characteristically, however, he shied away from the conclusion that poverty or exposure to vice and to evil companions stripped one of a truly free will. That conclusion (for which he provided no logical rebuttal) he regarded as dangerous to the public order. Poverty, he asserted, ought not to ground a defense of involuntarism or of necessity, especially in cases of theft of food or clothing, for property would then be rendered insecure by the alleged wants of others, "of which wants no man can possibly be an adequate judge, but the party himself who pleads them."[95] Blackstone resolved the problem by invoking the power of the Crown "to soften the

91. *Ibid.*, pp. 343–44: "[S]ince in times of difficulty and danger, more is to be apprehended from the violence and partiality of judges appointed by the Crown, in suits between the king and the subject, than in disputes between one individual and another. . . . So that the liberties of England cannot but subsist, so long as this *palladium* remains sacred and inviolate."

92. *Ibid.*, p. 344.

93. See Green, "Introduction" to Blackstone, *Commentaries*, 4: iv–v.

94. For Blackstone's contribution to the movement for imprisonment at hard labor see Beattie, *Crime and the Courts*, ch. 11.

95. Blackstone, *Commentaries*, 4:32.

law, and to extend mercy in cases of peculiar hardship."[96] But as he doubtless realized, in practice juries daily served to help resolve this very dilemma.

William Eden also recognized the complexity of the role of the criminal trial jury.[97] Like Beccaria, he focused clearly on the problem of deterrence, echoing the Italian's message through his borrowings from Blackstone's terminology. Eden's analysis of the property-crime problem that afflicted late-eighteenth-century England is a classic formulation of the Continental reform theory. The source of the problem was, he said, "national prosperity." "Sensibility sleeps in the lap of luxury; and the legislator is contented to secure his own selfish enjoyments, by subjecting his fellow citizens to the miseries of a dungeon, and the horrors of an ignominious death."[98] Increased wealth brought increased selfishness and increasingly harsh laws to protect that wealth; it magnified one aspect of human nature, but it did not transform human nature entirely: "Still however [the legislator] feels a tacit disapprobation of the laws, which he has enacted; and even, when injured, [he] hesitates to bring the offender to justice. He knows that the punishment is disproportionate to the offense."[99] Nor did it blind the propertied to reality: "[O]r at least, if humanity be obliterated by interest, [the legislator] foresees, that the punishment cannot be inflicted, without raising the indignation of society against the accuser." The result, then, follows Beccaria's diagnosis closely:

> The delinquent therefore is discharged without prosecution; he repeats the crime under the expectation of repeated mercy. . . . It is a property inseparable from harsh laws, that they are neither regular, nor expeditious in their execution; consequently, that they flatter the hope of impunity, and, equally injurious to the society and the criminal, tend to the fatal multiplication both of crimes and of punishments.[100]

Eden argued that the existing system of criminal law emerged fortuitously, for the anger that generated new capital legislation gave way to the natural instincts of compassion when it came time to apply the law to

96. *Idem.* Blackstone was at his most internally inconsistent on this issue. After asserting that a defense of necessity would be unmanageable and dangerous, Blackstone stated: "In this country especially, there would be a peculiar impropriety in admitting so dubious an excuse: for by our laws such sufficient provision is made for the poor by the power of the civil magistrate, that it is impossible that the most needy stranger should ever be reduced to the necessity of thieving to support nature." Subsequently, he pointed to the power of pardon, which he suggested gave relief in rare instances.

97. William Eden, *Principles of Penal Law* (London, 1771).

98. *Ibid.*, p. 266.

99. *Ibid.*, pp. 266–67.

100. *Ibid.*, p. 267.

individual suspects. As a result, the system of penology actually encouraged criminal behavior. There are hints of this in Blackstone, but Eden made the point with force. Thereafter, virtually all reform writers charged that mitigation, though preferable to mass executions, was partly responsible for the crisis in criminal law.

The role of the jury as a mitigator of the law raised a number of problems, and the more Eden pursued them the more he shifted his attention from the question of deterrence to other considerations of justice. First, he criticized the practice of basing capital felony on the monetary value of stolen goods. Since money was "in its nature . . . of fluctuating value," to base punishment of the offender on such value is to make "adjudication of the law . . . vague and uncertain."[101] Turning to the jury's role, Eden observed that "the impulses of benevolence are opposed to the obligations of religion": jurors were "taught to trifle with their oaths, and to call such trifling 'a kind of pious perjury.'"

> In fact, upon trials of larcenies so limited, it is commonly found to be the chief anxiety both of judges and of jurors, to reduce the crime below its real predicament, by reducing the conviction below the value affixed by law. Such an anxiety is the natural consequences of laws, which, by an absurd distinction, make a trivial difference between two sums the criterion of capital crime.[102]

Unlike Blackstone, who placed the emphasis on "pious" rather than on "perjury," Eden criticized the practice of mitigation for the confusion it produced in the minds of the mitigators. He, too, was concerned with a kind of incoherence, but not so much a legal or political as a moral incoherence.

Trifling with laws and lives: the business of sorting out those who deserved to hang from those who did not appeared very different to Eden than it did to many of his contemporaries. Nevertheless, Eden took a liberal view of jury fact-finding in some kinds of cases. He defended the jury's

> indisputable, unquestionable right to acquit the person accused, if, in their private opinions, they disbelieve the accusers; or if in their consciences, they think, however erroneously, that the fact partakes not of that degree, or species of criminality, with which it is charged in the indictment.[103]

The first instance mentioned—if the jurors "disbelieve the accusers"—is in line with all contemporary analysis and comes as no surprise. The

101. *Ibid.*, p. 268.
102. *Ibid.*, pp. 268–69.
103. *Ibid.*, p. 153.

second basis for acquittal is of greater interest. Eden's formulation is ambiguous. He might have meant: if the jurors find that the fact required by law was not committed; if so he stated no more than a commonplace. But more likely he meant: if the jurors decide that the fact the law considers criminal is not really criminal, for, he continued, jury trial is a nullity unless jurors may determine "the criminality or innocence of the intention, the legality or illegality of the fact."[104]

Eden was aware that the jury's power to go outside judicial instructions had long been the subject of debate, especially in the context of cases wherein the government had a political interest. He cited the relevant passages in Blackstone, Hale, and Foster, and concluded: "When wise and good men differ upon points of great constitutional importance," humbler folk like himself should await the outcome. But, he added (bringing the discussion back to his own central concern), it was

> a certain truth, that the political liberty of every individual bears a proportion to the security given by the laws to the innocency of his conduct; which security decreases, in proportion to the multiplication of penalties, the uncertainty of penal laws, and the irregularity of trials.[105]

Thus Eden remained ambiguous regarding the limits of fact-finding. He attempted to treat jury law-finding as appropriate only in exceptional cases and to minimize the conflict between traditional English jury law-finding theory and the overriding principles of the new penology. Certainty, he believed, was not only crucial to deterrence but was indispensable for justice. All members of society had a right to know what was criminal and to what degree it was so. To announce that certain crimes were capital but then to punish various commissions of them at different levels was to invite injustice. No one would be certain beforehand what his punishment would be; arbitrary decisions would abound. Eden apparently believed that reform of the penal laws would so reduce the need for jury mitigation that one might approve of occasional instances of jury-based intervention without endorsing principles that interfered with human liberty. Eden thus bridged Beccaria and Blackstone in a particularly effective way. And it would be to his *Principles of the Criminal Law* perhaps more than to the *Commentaries* that early nineteenth-century reformers would look for guidance.[106]

Nearly forgotten, on the other hand, was Henry Dagge, whose *Considerations on Criminal Law* was published in 1772, one year after Eden's

104. *Ibid.*, p. 154.
105. *Ibid.*, p. 158.
106. See below, Chapter 9, section I.

work and three after Blackstone's.[107] Reflecting the growing concern over the political role of juries, Dagge's book does not directly confront the problem of jury mitigation in common-run felonies. But Dagge was not unaware of the issue: he began by lauding Eden, who dwelled upon it, and he supported Eden's reform ideas. His main contribution was his strong support for the establishment of penal institutions that would inculcate moral virtues.[108] Dagge repeated Eden's—and through Eden, Beccaria's—argument that men will shrink from enforcing a strict law and that the end result will be an increase in crime and criminals. Legislators, he asserted, ought not to forget that "criminals are their fellow-creatures," the products of social inequality and degradation.[109] Laws ought to be aimed at improving man's lot, and so improving man, not at doing away with men led astray. But this social determinism theme, which had surfaced in Fielding's *Proposal,* remained largely buried in Dagge's work. Like Blackstone, Dagge entertained a vision of human behavior that differed perhaps from earlier more strictly moral approaches, but in the end he resisted the ideas that a later, more scientific age could not. Others, like Dawes, were to develop them further in the next few decades. For Dagge it was an important but subordinate argument: one ought to encourage compassion for the offender, who was often the product of his environment, and take account of that fact in the criminal law.

Dagge's work reveals the dilemma implicit in the work of other reform writers. Dagge did not criticize jury mitigation in common-run felonies, but his endorsement of Eden suggests that he saw the dangers in such practices. At the same time the thrust of Dagge's section on juries was a forceful statement favoring substantial jury law-finding powers.[110] Blackstone and Eden had recognized the virtues of the jury's power to nullify political prosecutions should there be a return to tyranny. Dagge made the point with far greater emphasis, drawing upon the history of civil society and English legal institutions to establish the advantages of the judgment of a jury of twelve common men over that of one man of the robe.[111] For him, the threat of intentional or unintentional judicial misreading of the law was the overriding concern: juries, he argued, must supply constant vigilance. As the seditious libel controversy heightened, the problems of jury mitigation, law reform, and the constitutional and legal balance of powers drew closer together. Dagge perhaps saw the

107. Henry Dagge, *Considerations on Criminal Law* (London, 1772).
108. *Ibid.,* p. xix.
109. *Ibid.,* p. xxvi.
110. *Ibid.,* pp. 123–36.
111. See below, Chapter 8, text at nn. 72–74.

larger constitutional issues more clearly than Blackstone or Eden, but he failed to explain how the jury would play a more modest role in one area while remaining the dominant constitutional safeguard in the other.

Dagge's concern with the social origins of criminal behavior reflected an insight that virtually all reformers shared.[112] At some level, the view that social conditions bred or at least encouraged criminal behavior was commonplace in the eighteenth century. Not a few of the petitions for pardons stressed the conditions that led the convict astray; if these notions were current among the secular and religious officials who drafted the petitions, they were no doubt current among those who, in their role as jurors, mitigated the severity of the law. Then as now, nearly all who held such views also believed that men freely willed their own actions. By and large the reformers shared this dualistic view of human behavior.[113]

Manasseh Dawes was among the more single-minded and eloquent of the deterministic reformers. In *An Essay on Crimes and Punishments*, published in 1782, Dawes castigated lawyers for their failure to understand the most basic principles of human behavior and heaped scorn upon the prevailing concepts of punishment.[114] Lawyers, wrote Dawes, "talk of the necessity of punishment, while they know little of the cause of those actions for which they would have it inflicted." "Criminals do not offend so much from choice, as from misery and want of sentiment."[115] Dawes adhered to "the principles of philosophical necessity," according to which:

> [A]ll actions are effects of some cause in the mind; and man being free, he has a self-determining power governed by consideration and judgment, which precede his volition, and direct it; all actions necessarily follow their causes, or volitions; and as they cannot be otherwise than they are, when committed, it ought to be, and is the duty of society to form the minds of individuals, so that they may detest what is constituted bad by law.[116]

112. E.g. Fielding, *A Proposal*, pp. 71–72. See also Jonas Hanway, *Distributive Justice and Mercy* (London, 1781), p. xii. Hanway favored true reform of convicts and thought that merciful acquittals were not helpful in this regard. He preferred reform of the law of sanctions and prison reform.

113. See Michael Ignatieff, *A Just Measure of Pain: The Penitentiary in the Industrial Revolution, 1750–1850* (New York, 1978), pp. 71–76. For further discussion of this matter see below, Chapter 9, section III.

114. Manasseh Dawes, *An Essay on Crimes and Punishments* (London, 1782).

115. *Ibid.*, pp. 2–3.

116. *Ibid.*, p. 40. See also *ibid.*, p. 155. "[The] principle of philosophical necessity . . . admits, that although the actions of men, when committed, cannot be otherwise than they are, yet . . . their future may." A possible effect of a certain act may be to punish the actor; this, in turn, may deter others who would otherwise have committed the same act.

Dawes contrasted the theory of "philosophical necessity" to "fatalism or predestination, which supposes all things come to pass in spite of man."[117] Man possesses a will, and his actions flow from that will, though that will is shaped by forces (ultimately by God) external to man. Although Dawes's theory of human freedom was murky,[118] his analysis of the cause of criminal behavior was clear enough:

> [C]riminals suffer eventually for the inevitable effects of certain causes which influence their moral conduct: let a gang of thieves, for example, teach an ignorant boy, that by certain methods of breaking a house, or personal robberies, he will succeed in his end, and be undiscovered, and he will listen to the instruction, and turn thief, in the hope of escaping detection, not being convicted if taken or tried; the mitigation of his sentence, the death of his prosecutor, a flaw in his indictment, or a pardon: the crime to him appears harmless; his study is to avoid the laws, which with him is the only iniquity.[119]

Dawes's program of reform involved moral instruction. But by implication it also countenanced reform of the administration of the criminal law. Although mercy was an appropriate response owing to the ultimate blamelessness of criminal offenders, it was also one of the conditions that engendered criminal behavior. In his own way, Dawes associated himself with the critique of the administration of criminal law that Blackstone, Eden, and Dagge set forth and that derived, ultimately, from the reception of Beccaria's work. And like the English writers who preceded him, Dawes argued that, pending reform either of human nature or of the law of sanctions, mercy—whatever its contributory costs—was appropriate.

---

117. *Idem.*

118. Dawes seems to have adopted a view of free will similar to that defended by Jonathan Edwards thirty years before in *A Careful and Strict Enquiry into the Modern Prevailing Notions of that Freedom of Will, which is supposed to be essential to Moral Agency, Virtue and Vice, Reward and Punishment, Praise and Blame* (Boston, 1754). But Dawes at times took a more sombre view: "[I]s it not a hardship to inflict a punishment for what must and will happen? or is it a justifiable effect of our living in society, that some of us should be cut off from it, because we cannot be otherwise than we are?" In his earlier work, *Philosophical Considerations* (London, 1780), Dawes asserted that "nature punishes us . . . by conferring the power of punishment upon us, at the moment of our creation, in the faculty of reflection. Thus man may be a free agent respecting himself, but not so in respect to the great author of nature. . . . If [man is] ignorant and bad, the cause may be traced in the faults of his education, productive of moral actions, injurious to himself and others. The future actions of one moral agent, may be made wise and virtuous, from an abhorrence of the perils attendant on the past actions of another." Thus the purpose and virtues of punishment (pp. 38–39). And again, in his *An Essay on Intellectual Liberty* (London, 1780), Dawes spoke of "the sacrifice of moral criminals, who became victims to laws for the welfare of society" (p. 10).

119. Dawes, *Essay on Crimes and Punishments,* p. 42.

Men of sense will compassionate all human and social offenders, lament their offences, and sigh over the unhappy cause of them;—they will look upon the wretched prisoner, perhaps half naked and starved, amputated or maimed, ill educated or destitute of taste, and grieve over his condition; regretting some hidden defect in the criminal constitution or civil government, and reluctantly give him up to a punishment, which vagrant liberty had prepared him for, against the inmost desire of his heart; they will not be contented that he has offended, but they will examine why; and tracing the cause, be disposed to forgive an effect, which it was impossible to avoid; and thus feeling the force and power of the mind, they will sparingly punish the man for what the mind only was deficient in producing.[120]

Unlike his predecessors, however, Dawes did not dwell on the question of which institution was the most appropriate mitigator. More philosopher than lawyer, Dawes commented on human nature and the responses to it of "men of sense," be they prosecutors, grand jurors, trial jurors, judges, or monarchs. His readers cannot have doubted that jurors, like the others who possessed the power to dispense mercy, were not only part of the problem but for the time being part of its solution.

William Paley's famous defense of the English system of criminal justice was no more supportive of jury-based mitigation than were the reformers' tracts.[121] Indeed, the jury was virtually the only aspect of the status quo that Paley criticized. Paley argued in favor of both capital statutes and very selective enforcement, but he believed that enforcement ought to be exclusively in the Crown.[122] Like Blackstone, Paley saw the dangers of dispersed powers of mitigation. The two differed on the reform issue: for Blackstone, the need for mercy ought to be reduced to a minimum; for Paley, the need for mercy was an important aspect of a just and rational criminal law.

Paley praised the English system as one that "assigns capital punishment to many kinds of offenses, but inflicts it only upon a few examples of each kind."[123] He rejected, however, the view of Eden that this system of penology was unpremeditated. The laws, Paley believed, were designed to be enforced selectively; the ends of deterrence and rational decision making dictated the form of penology that actually prevailed.

120. *Ibid.*, pp. 3–4.
121. Paley, *Principles of Moral and Political Philosophy* (1785). The substance of this work was drawn from lectures given at Cambridge at least as early as 1770. Paley may have been responding in part to Beccaria and Blackstone. See Radzinowicz, *History of English Criminal Law*, 1:248, n. 63. Beattie (*Crime and the Courts,* ch. 12) argues persuasively that Paley's work represents a response to the critics of the late 1760s and early 1770s rather than a response to the post-American Revolution crime wave of the mid-1780s.
122. Paley, *Principles of Moral and Political Philosophy,* p. 535.
123. *Ibid.*, p. 531.

The pardoning system saved nine of every ten who had been convicted. This was as it should be, for

> the selection of proper objects for capital punishment principally depends upon circumstances, which, however easy to perceive in each particular case, after the crime is committed, it is impossible to enumerate or define beforehand.[124]

Paley challenged every claim of the new penology. He agreed that English law "sweeps into the net every crime," and that, of those swept in, "a small proportion of each class are singled out." The law makes "examples," he said: "By this expedient few actually suffer death, whilst the dread and danger of it hang over the crimes of many."[125] Everything that Beccaria and his followers asserted was wrong with the English system Paley asserted was right. Everything, that is, save for jury discretion.

Juries, Paley asserted, were too cautious, gave too many too much benefit of the doubt:

> I apprehend much harm to have been done to the community, by the over-strained scrupulousness, or weak timidity of juries, which demands often such proof of a prisoner's guilt as the nature and secrecy of his crime scarce possibly admit of; and which holds it part of a safe conscience not to condemn any man, whilst there exists the minutest possibility of his innocence. Any story they may happen to have heard or read . . . is enough, in their minds, to found an acquittal upon. . . . [T]o reject such proof, from an insinuation of uncertainty that belongs to all human affairs . . . counteracts the case, and damps the activity of government: it holds out public encouragement to villany, by confessing the impossibility of bringing villains to justice; and that species of encouragement, which, as has been just now observed, the minds of such men are most apt to entertain and dwell upon.[126]

Paley understated the degree to which jurors were actually motivated by the character of the defendant or the nature of his act. In fact, jurors took into account the very considerations that Paley thought the Crown ought to take into account. Paley's real complaint was that jury-based mitigation resulted from consideration at the verdict stage of matters relevant to the question of the appropriate sentence. The jury, he believed, created the problem of inconsistent treatment of offenders: not only assessment of guilt but also degree of punishment depended in each case on the sympathies and inclinations of a new jury.

124. *Ibid.*, p. 532.
125. *Ibid.*, p. 533.
126. *Ibid.*, pp. 550–51.

Paley, however, agreed with the reformers on the end of punishment—
the prevention of crime. Indeed, he considered himself a reformer who
sought to make a good system work even more efficiently. Paley's stress
on prevention led him to conclude that severity of punishment ought to be
determined by difficulty of discovery and conviction, not by elusive
notions of the defendant's guilt. Crimes that were common, hard to
prevent, and equally difficult to prosecute ought to be very severely
punished—that the offender had taken a small amount surreptitiously,
rather than openly robbed his victim of a large sum, suggested he ought to
be punished more, not less, severely. Paley left questions of conscience
and guilt to God's judgment: man lacked the omniscience required to see
into the defendant's mind.[127] Small wonder that Paley had little patience
with jury discretion and instead took great pains to found his discretionary system on a regularized, formal, and consistent procedure of Crown-
based mitigation.
  If Paley shared with the anti-discretion reformers reservations about
the jury in common-run felony cases, he also shared with them strong
approbation of the jury's ultimate constitutional independence. Like
Dagge, Paley viewed the judge and jury as checks upon one another; the
judge instructs the jury, but the jury applies law to fact according to its
understanding.

> In proportion to the acknowledged excellency of this mode of trial,
> every deviation from it ought to be watched with vigilance, and
> adopted by the legislature with caution. Summary convictions before
> justices of the peace, especially for offenses against the game laws;
> courts of conscience; extending the jurisdiction of courts of equity;
> urging too far the distinction between questions of law and questions of
> fact, are all so many infringements upon this great charter of public
> safety.[128]

Paley appears to have seen the contradictions inherent in the different
roles that he thought the jury ought to be called upon to play. He may
even have understood that a jury with secured powers of nullification of
tyrannous laws was a jury that could not be controlled easily in common-
run cases. There were, however, some risks he believed worth running,
for in his view definitions of institutional roles could never be precise in
a just political system.
  The second major defense of the English law of crimes was embodied
in Martin Madan's *Thoughts on Executive Justice,* a tract that reflected
concern with the increase of crime in the mid-1780s and impatience with

127. *Ibid.,* pp. 527–31.
128. *Ibid.,* pp. 504–5.

the penal reform writers of the preceding decade.[129] Madan openly criticized the ethic of merciful verdicts, judgments, and sentences, and exhorted judges and juries to apply the law as it stood. It was "fashionable with many, to find great fault with the number or severity of" the criminal laws; for his part, however, he deemed that the country had been served well by them:

> I may say, that the legislature has from time to time been assiduous in meeting crimes, as they have arisen, with wholesome laws; but those, whose duty and office it is to administer the laws, have now, for many years, been preferring their own feelings as men, to the duty which they owe the public as magistrates.[130]

Madan likened judicial reprieves to the hated and abandoned suspending power exercised by the later Stuarts. The pardon power was in the Crown and was intended to be used judiciously, not wantonly. There were cases wherein the bench could reprieve: where it thought the jury was malicious, or the evidence insufficient, or where postconviction testimony warranted a reversal.[131] In most cases, however, the judge should invoke, not vitiate, the rigors of the law.

Madan's famous description of the judge doing his awesome duty bears repeating:

> [The judge] then, in the most pathetic terms, exhorts the unhappy convicts, to consider well how best to employ the little space that yet remains between that moment and the grave—he acquaints them with the certainty of speedy death, and consequently with the necessity of speedy repentance—and on this theme he may so deliver himself, as not only to melt the wretches at the bar into contrition, but the whole auditory into the deepest concern. Tears express their feelings—and many of the most thoughtless among them may, for the rest of their lives, be preserved from thinking lightly of the first steps to vice. . . . The dreadful sentence is now pronounced—every heart shakes with terror. The almost fainting criminals are taken from the bar—the crowd retires—each to his several home . . . the day of execution arrives—the wretches are led forth to suffer, and exhibit a spectacle . . . the whole country feels a lasting benefit.[132]

---

129. Martin Madan, *Thoughts on Executive Justice* (2nd ed., London, 1785; orig. published 1784). Madan's work was published a year before Paley's, but Paley's was probably conceived substantially earlier than it was published. See above, n. 121. For a pathbreaking analysis of the relationship between the reform tradition and the fluctuations in real (and perceived) rates of crime, 1750–1800, see Beattie, *Crime and the Courts*, chs. 11–12.

130. Madan, *Thoughts on Executive Justice*, p. 13.

131. *Ibid.*, p. 48.

132. *Ibid.*, pp. 28–30. For a remarkable insight into the "day of execution" and some

Equally imposing is Madan's description of what typically happens at trial, and how in his view the ends of justice are frustrated by misplaced sentiment:

> But perhaps [the defendant] happens to be young—it appears to be his first offense—he has, before the fact which is proved against him, had a good character—he was drawn in by others—was in liquor—or some other circumstances of the like kind strikes the minds of the jury; they forget their oath . . . and take upon themselves to acquit the prisoner, against all fact and truth. This I have so often seen, that I cannot forbear the mention of it. The judge, on this occasion, usually takes little further notice of the matter, than to congratulate the prisoner on his "narrow escape" and to tell him that "he has had a very merciful jury."[133]

Such juries, Madan concluded, found "according to their feelings, but against their oath."[134] And if they could falsely acquit they might also falsely convict—Madan did not repeat at this point that the bench might in the latter case reprieve the defendant and recommend that he receive a royal pardon.

Madan was not entirely opposed to reform of the law. He recognized that laws that were too severe—i.e., undermined the principle of deterrence—required revision.[135] The problem, of course, was to design an appropriate test of enforceability. Madan refused to accept the practices current among bench and jurors in his own day as the proper test. He sought instead to convince those who served in these institutions of their duty, but "duty" was an ambiguous concept. At what point did unwillingness to convict of a capital offense or carry out the sentence *not* conflict with duty? Why were not all statutes that were seldom enforced ipso facto in need of reform? Madan sought to avoid this problem by vesting mercy in the Crown. Judge and jury, he believed, were too close to the condemned, whose pitiful condition overwhelmed the imagination and left no room for the rational administration of justice. The novelty and power of Madan's approach lay in its royalism and its indifference to the balance of power between judge and jury, either in common-run or in political cases. Having disregarded the need for safeguards against a tyrannical bench, Madan was virtually the only writer of his time who did not advert to the dilemma posed by the jury's duty to preserve the fundamental liberties.

aspects of the "lasting benefit" that it confers see Peter Linebaugh, "The Ordinary of Newgate and His Account," in Cockburn, ed., *Crime in England*, pp. 246–69.

133. Madan, *Thoughts on Executive Justice*, pp. 137–38.

134. *Ibid.*, p. 138.

135. *Ibid.*, pp. 132–33.

Madan's tract provoked Samuel Romilly to write his first work on reform of sanctions, *Observations on . . . Thoughts on Executive Justice*, a tract that brought the reformist position back into clear focus.[136] According to Romilly, Madan's theory failed on a number of grounds, beginning with its avoidance of reality: prevention of crime could not "possibly be attained by the mere terror of punishment";[137] more executions would lead to fewer convictions. One might call for enforcement, but it could not be had, "for jurors would easily quiet their consciences upon a perjury which was the means of preventing murder."[138] Moreover, Madan's assumption that the legislature intended fuller enforcement was unproven and intuitively wrong:

And indeed it is hardly possible to doubt, that the parliament had the clemency of the crown in its contemplation, when it passed all those modern statutes, by which new felonies are created; for that the legislators of an enlightened age, and of a nation boastful of its humanity, should punish the slightest offences with death, is not to be accounted for, but upon the supposition, that those punishments are only held out as a terror, and never intended to be inflicted but in the most aggravated cases.[139]

Romilly was far from an admirer of this legislative policy, which perhaps thanks to Paley's defense of existing penology[140] he saw more clearly than had Blackstone or Eden. The law, he said, was supposed to be reasonable in order that it could be known. Clearly those most likely to commit offenses were among those least likely to know the laws for which they might lose their lives. Unless law accorded with justice and morality, one could not hold all men to know it: "[N]o authority, however great, will

---

136. *Observations on a Late Publication* [by Martin Madan], *intituled Thoughts on Executive Justice* [by Sir Samuel Romilly, but published anonymously] (London, 1786). Romilly stated in his memoirs that Lord Lansdowne, who was among those "dazzled" by Madan's book, recommended that he "write something on the same subject. This, of course, induced me to look into the book; but I was so much shocked by the folly and inhumanity of it, that instead of enforcing the same arguments, I sat down to refute them." Lansdowne, Romilly stated, "highly approved" the result, but the tract "had so little success with the public, that not more than a hundred copies were sold." Sir Samuel Romilly, *Memoirs of the Life of Sir Samuel Romilly*, 3 vols. (London, 1840), vol. 1, pp. 89–90.

137. *Ibid.*, p. 2.

138. *Ibid.*, pp. 89–90.

139. *Ibid.*, p. 82. See also Romilly, *Memoirs*, 1:370. Romilly asserted, in a letter to M. Dumont, that the Riot Act "was certainly never meant to be executed against all who should expose themselves to it; the only object was to hold out a terror; although it ought to have been foreseen that the circumstance of the law not being executed would prevent its inspiring terror." (Oct. 23, 1789).

140. *Observations on a Late Publication*, pp. 73–78.

ever be able to persuade mankind, that penal laws ought to constitute a science merely of memory, and not of reason."[141] Thus Romilly bitterly attacked Madan's attempt to dress his theory of enforcement in the garb of certainty to which Beccaria and his English adherents had appealed.[142] Romilly suggested that the rich, or society at large, bore some responsibility for the crimes of the poor. Perhaps punishment ought to fall on the better endowed in society; they, after all, were the "natural fathers and guardians" of the poor.[143] Not surprisingly, then, Romilly's condemnation of the law of sanctions was coupled with a plea for an expanded and enlightened use of incarceration to reform criminal offenders. He noted that Blackstone and Eden had drafted a "plan for the punishment of criminals" that was "wholly unobjectionable," characterizing it as "a kind of asylum to that very large description of offenders, who are rendered such by the defects of education, by pernicious connections, by indigence, or by despair."[144] Romilly also carried forward Fielding's utilitarian argument for such an institution:

> [W]hat it is that retards the execution of this excellent plan, it is not easy to conjecture; for, though the expense of erecting the penitentiary houses would be considerable, yet that is surely but a trifling object, compared with the benefit which, as it should seem, must necessarily result to the country from such an institution. And according to the calculations which have been made upon the subject, when the houses were once erected, the annual expense of maintaining them would be more than defrayed by the earnings of the convicts.[145]

Although it left little of Madan's tract unscathed, Romilly's argument held little support for the tradition of merciful jury verdicts. Such verdicts were inevitable, Romilly conceded, so long as the law of sanctions remained unreformed.[146] But with reform, jury mitigation would be largely unnecessary and generally unwise. Conviction would lead to a form of punishment that was both rational and humane. That was,

141. *Ibid.*, p. 38.
142. *Ibid.*, pp. 84–85.
143. *Ibid.*, p. 95.
144. *Ibid.*, pp. 59–60.
145. *Ibid.*, p. 61.
146. *Ibid.*, p. 90. Romilly's remarks were addressed to Madan's argument concerning full execution of the law. That, said Romilly, would lead juries to "take upon themselves to judge the policy and justice of the law." It would multiply the "evils which [Madan] so well discusses." I infer from this that Romilly agreed with Madan that, under existing circumstances, judges and juries mitigated the law. Romilly sought the opposite remedy from that for which Madan campaigned, and it seems a fair inference that Romilly believed jury mitigation was inevitable and just until reform came about. He characterized such mitigation as "perjury which was the means of preventing murder" (*idem*).

however, the argument of the future. For the time being the problem of the jury's role as a constitutional safeguard remained to be worked out. A systematic solution to the problem of the jury in common-run felonies might have received the attention it deserved had the problem of such cases not been entangled with the larger constitutional crises in which, even in the eyes of its severest critics, the jury also played an important and controversial role. This is clear in the writings of Romilly who, two years before publication of the critique of Madan, had himself contributed to the debate over seditious libel:

> Rigid, however, and I will add, tyrannical, as the law of libels is, nothing is to be dreaded from it while it is administered by the paternal hand of juries, who though they will never suffer it to be relaxed to the encouragement of defamation and licentiousness, will refrain and temper its harshness by their discretion and humanity.[147]

# IV

We are still far from understanding how the criminal trial jury operated in the eighteenth century. The process by which juries reached agreement, the degree to which jurors followed the lead of the bench, and the extent to which jurors actually believed they were acting autonomously, all remain beyond our ken. But the history of jury trial is in part the history of contemporaries' perceptions of the institution. We do know that many learned contemporaries believed that the jury was a powerful and at least semi-autonomous institution of mitigation. And more significantly, we can reasonably infer that most laymen believed that jury-based mitigation was a legitimate part of the administration of the criminal law. Authorities themselves seem to have encouraged this view of the jury. Even those jurists and lay publicists who questioned the wisdom of existing jury practices endorsed those practices so long as the prevailing law of sanctions remained intact. It remains, by way of conclusion, to reconsider how this view of the jury had come to be accepted and assimilated in a fashion that made it resistant to change.

From one perspective, the administration of the English criminal law, of which the jury was but one element, appears to have been a calculated and manipulated expression of the authority of what might be called the ruling classes.[148] This view helps one to understand what has seemed a

---

147. Sir Samuel Romilly, *A Fragment on the Constitutional Power and Duty of Juries upon Trials for Libels* (London, 1784), p. 3. Romilly comments upon the tract in his *Memoirs*, 1:86–87. I have used the copy of *Fragment* that is in Houghton Library, Harvard University.

148. See Hay, "Property, Authority and the Criminal Law." Hay does not argue that the

paradox in the criminal law of the eighteenth century: the multiplication of capital statutes alongside their fairly general nonenforcement. The argument holds that these statutes expressed the interests of the propertied classes and provided them with tools for protection of those interests. But it also recognizes the political and social difficulties that would have ensued from strict enforcement of the statutes and argues that the ruling elites had more to gain from only selective enforcement. These groups administered a program that combined terror with mercy. Nonenforcement was thus made to seem an aspect of justice and majesty, and it therefore also created a debt: England's rulers continued to reap a harvest of deference from those they ruled. In those cases in which the law was applied to the fullest, the thesis runs, there was attention to justification: enforcement was characterized by "circumspection" and "delicacy."[149]

How accurate a view of the administration of the criminal law does this perspective afford? Certainly some contemporaries analyzed the administration of the law in these terms;[150] for them this selective-enforcement theme became a rationalization for maintaining the status quo in the face of growing pressures for legal, and especially penal, reform. But their perspective was limited by their own social position; they perhaps failed to appreciate fully the point of view of those below them. No doubt the administration of the criminal law, and especially the practice of selective enforcement, emphasized the majesty of the law and engendered deference toward those who administered it. But these were incidents of a system that involved far more complex processes than solely the machination of a ruling class or classes.

As we have seen, the selective enforcement of the law of felony resulted from the circumstances of the origins of that law. The Crown had always had to struggle to make its legal mandate effective. It had frequently complained about nonenforcement, announcing its own weakness while pleading for obedience.[151] At the same time, English rulers had attempted to convert this weakness into strength through the use of pardons, benefit of clergy, and the pragmatic acceptance and even encouragement of merciful jury verdicts. If these devices underscored the beneficence and majesty of the law, they did not conceal from contem-

---

law was devised with these ends in mind or that all aspects of law enforcement were designed to take advantage of the class power inherent in the law. He is mainly concerned with the reasons for the reluctance of some of the ruling groups to reform the law.

149. *Idem.*

150. E.g. Paley, *Principles of Moral and Political Philosophy,* above, nn. 103 *et seq.* and accompanying text. See also above, n. 32 and contemporary writings cited therein. Some observers (e.g. Fielding) opposed pardons but favored the use of executions to strike terror. They were not clearly endorsing selective enforcement.

151. See above, Chapter 3.

poraries the fact that literal enforcement of capital felony laws lay beyond the power of the Crown. In practice, enforcement was a matter of an accommodation in which, at one stage or another, many parties played important roles.[152]

If some property owners failed to prosecute their thieving tenants in hopes of strengthening the bonds of affection that flowed upward, others looked the other way knowing that prosecution, if it succeeded, would destroy those bonds and increase the numbers of the unemployed and of professional thieves.[153] Still others may have doubted the success of prosecution altogether, for even propertied jurors could not be counted on to hang, or even to punish with severity, perpetrators of relatively minor offenses. We cannot be certain that grand juries would have followed the lead of prosecutors had capital punishment been resorted to with substantially greater frequency. For one thing, the testimony of witnesses might have been far harder to come by. Indeed, those suspected and captured in the first place were only a fraction of the total number who had broken a capital law, and that fraction might have been smaller still in a world of strict enforcement against all those taken and indicted.[154]

Mainly, of course, it was a matter of jury behavior that the Crown and bench had to accommodate. We have considered the circumstances that

152. This theme runs through much of the recent literature on the social history of the English criminal law in the seventeenth and eighteenth centuries. I have elsewhere suggested the importance of this approach to law enforcement—one often manifested in practices regarding enforcement at the county or more local level—for jury behavior (and officials' reactions toward that behavior) at the assizes. See my review of Cockburn, ed., *Crime in England*, in *American Journal of Legal History*, vol. 23 (1979), pp. 357–62. For relevant studies of criminal law enforcement see e.g. Samaha, "Hanging for Felony"; Herrup, "Common Peace"; J. A. Sharpe, "Crime and Delinquency in an Essex Parish 1600–1640," in Cockburn, ed., *Crime in England*, pp. 90–109; M. J. Ingram, "Communities and Courts: Law and Disorder in Early-Seventeenth-Century Wiltshire," in *ibid.*, pp. 110–34; Keith Wrightson, "Two Concepts of Order: Justices, Constables, and Jurymen in Seventeenth-Century England," in Brewer and Styles, eds., *An Ungovernable People*, pp. 21–46; T. C. Curtis, "Quarter Sessions Appearances and their Background: A Seventeenth-Century Regional Study," in *ibid.*, pp. 135–54; P. B. Munsche, "The Game Laws in Wiltshire 1750–1800," in *ibid.*, pp. 210–28; Cal Winslow, "Sussex Smugglers," in Hay et al., eds., *Albion's Fatal Tree*, pp. 119–66; John G. Rule, "Wrecking and Coastal Plunder," in *ibid.*, pp. 167–88; Douglas Hay, "Poaching and the Game Laws on Cannock Chase," in *ibid.*, pp. 189–253; Thompson, *Whigs and Hunters;* Timothy Curtis, "Explaining Crime in Early Modern England," in *Criminal Justice History*, vol. 1 (1980), pp. 117–37; Lenman and Parker, "The State, the Community and the Criminal Law in Early Modern Europe," in Gatrell et al., eds., *Crime and the Law*, pp. 11–48; Sharpe, "Enforcing the Law in the Seventeenth-Century English Village," in *ibid.*, pp. 97–119.

153. See Munsche, "The Game Laws in Wiltshire," pp. 222–23.

154. See generally Beattie, *Crime and the Courts.* Beattie's findings contain at least implicit support for the overall argument I am making.

made accommodation—with both loss of face and enhanced majesty—more attractive than literal enforcement through coercion of juries. There had always been a significant number of false accusations. Before the sixteenth century, authorities lacked the means to separate these from the cases involving trumped up verdicts. As the means of monitoring jury behavior developed, the bench employed its powers—usually, if not always, with success—to ensure the outcome of what it considered egregious cases. But pressures of time, the development of an enforceable, yet relatively severe lesser sanction (transportation), and the by-then powerful social expectations regarding both the role of the jury and the appropriate use of the gallows dissuaded legal officials from inducing capital verdicts much more often than they had in the past. Although by the eighteenth century the increase in property crimes and the sense of insecurity felt by the urban rich and rural propertied may have contributed to passage of legislation making more offenses capital, or making common-law mandates more explicit, there is little reason to believe that legislators imagined they were any more capable than their predecessors of strictly enforcing the law.

More than any other institution within the administration of criminal law, the trial jury reflected the limits of the power that authorities could bring to bear on those they ruled. Some juries could be effectively manipulated, or depended upon to deal harshly with property violations, but most jurors in most cases could be relied upon only insofar as authorities expected them to apply the law strictly in the cases that most of society itself thought especially serious. Authorities might derive benefit (in the form of respect for the law as well as outright deference) from jury-based intervention, perhaps the most prevalent form of selective enforcement, but the standards governing that process of selection were not theirs to set at will.

The choices were obvious. Law could be administered in summary fashion by a magistrate or according to the traditional mode of trial by judge and jury. Although Parliament increased the scope of offenses summarily triable by justices of the peace sitting without a jury,[155] jury trial was maintained in all felonies, as much for widely shared notions of justice as for narrowly conceived reasons of politics. Of those brought to trial only some—by virtue of background, reputation, attitude toward authority, or the nature of the offense itself—deserved to die. That decision did not have to be made—and perhaps ought not to be made—unilaterally by a judge. The judge might steer the process when it reached the trial stage, leading the jurors, who, given the standards the bench

155. Hay, "Property, Authority and the Criminal Law," p. 59; Baker, "Criminal Courts and Procedure," pp. 22, 24.

itself adopted, typically desired judicial leadership. The judge might comment upon the virtues of mercy and even, in some instances, go significantly beyond the jury in extending it. So far did the ruling elites adopt the posture of merciful law givers; so effectively did they make what may have been the best of a system in which enforcement was not commanded by the simple fiat of those elites, but depended upon and suited the views and interests of society generally.

From one perspective, the propertied classes created a network of laws they had no intention of fully enforcing; nonenforcement was itself a tool worth forging. From another, the law, at least at the capital level, was in fact "enforced," for the process of enforcement involved a multistage examination of the character and behavior of persons suspected of acts denominated felonies by common law or legislation. To state the law regarding capital offenses one had really to talk in terms of processes and resolutions. Not all felons deserved to be executed, but all (save for petty larcenists) were subject to a determination of whether they numbered among those who did. From this perspective, the law was not really mitigated, it was simply applied in the appropriate fashion. It was as though capital legislation read: persons who act in such a way are subject to death, transportation, imprisonment, or whipping, by determination of Crown, judge, and jury. The legal system as it was in fact devised, with its superabundant claims upon the lives of men, would have been intolerable had it not in practice accommodated the realities of contemporary social life, had it not reflected how far England's rulers, both in their brutality and their leniency, had adopted the standards and approaches to law enforcement of those they ruled.[156]

156. Hay ("Property, Authority and the Criminal Law," p. 61) asserts that "when we ask who controlled the criminal law, we see a familiar constellation: monarchy, aristocracy, gentry and, to a lesser extent, the great merchants. In numbers they were no more than 3 percent of the population." Hay says relatively little about juries. His argument is more plausible with respect to the summary powers of justices of the peace, the attitudes of members of Parliament, the disposition of those who administered the granting of royal pardons, and the language employed by judges when sentencing convicts to the gallows than it is with regard to either the behavior of trial jurors or the attitudes of the bench and the aristocracy generally toward that behavior. What Hay does say indicates he has mainly in mind juries in cases involving poaching and related offenses, where often landed jurors faced unpropertied defendants (See Langbein, "*Albion's* Fatal Flaws," pp. 107–08), though his remarks in "Poaching and the Game Laws in Cannock Chase" suggest that even in those cases jurors were not truly aligned with the propertied classes (pp. 189, 211). Hay might believe that those who "controlled the criminal law" controlled juries, or that juries typically sought to please (or at any rate not to displease) their social betters on the bench or in Parliament. [For an emphatic statement of this view see Peter Linebaugh, "(Marxist) Social History and (Conservative) Legal History: A Reply to Professor Langbein," unpublished paper (1984). I am grateful to Professor Linebaugh for allowing me to see his essay.] I have argued that while this was doubtless true in many cases, the standards that the

Maintaining the form of mitigation—of suspension of a blanket capital law—no doubt enhanced the authority and prestige of the ruling classes. It was a solution produced by history, both forced upon those classes and turned by them to their best advantage. But it was not without its costs. Sharing powers of mitigation meant defining jury trial in a certain way. Authorities first inherited and then enhanced an ethic of jury application of the law that they would not always find it easy to contain. The perpetuation of that ethic reflected the acquiescence of authorities in general social standards in common-run felony cases—so long, i.e., as those standards wore the stamp and ritual of official decision making—but it did not reflect a concurrence of opinion in other, more "political" cases. This, as we shall see, was to prove a critical problem in English governance. Moreover, there were other signs of unhappiness with the administration of a criminal law based upon dispersed powers of mitigation. There were some contemporaries who had begun to ask whether, after all, such an administration of law accorded with the best interests of society generally and of the propertied classes in particular.

The reform literature of the eighteenth century provides an important commentary upon the system. Read in conjunction with the trial descriptions of the more casual observers of the day, this literature suggests that many contemporaries viewed the criminal trial jury as relatively autonomous but not engaged in a struggle with the bench. But it also suggests that learned Englishmen exaggerated the degree of jury latitude that characterized everyday practice and underestimated the degree to which verdicts must have fit fairly settled and predictable patterns, patterns that mirrored not only the attitudes of the bench and of the common Englishmen who served as jurors but the expectations of most offenders.

---

small ruling elite adopted were themselves in part a reflection of the attitudes of a very large part of society. This was true both with regard to substantive standards and with regard to the matter of who was permitted to apply those standards. One of the most powerful techniques of rulership was to allow even relatively lower-class juries to sort out (within limits) cases according to their own sense of justice. With regard to the administration of the criminal law in the eighteenth century, the concept of "control" (as I believe Hay would agree) must allow for this dialectical interplay of attitudes. At some point, certainly with regard to the use of the criminal trial jury, one might want to replace the word "control" with the word "management"—the management of the administration of criminal justice in a fashion that redounded to the benefit of both managers and managed. Very possibly, the managers enhanced their control over the managed as a by-product of the managers' acquiescence in such a system of criminal law. I elaborate upon this point in Chapter 9. See "Introduction," in Brewer and Styles, eds., *An Ungovernable People*, p. 19. The editors make the related point that society at large had access to use or to challenge many aspects of the legal system; this fact helped to convince society of the existence of the rule of law and "helped humbler men to reach a grudging accommodation with the more egregious aspects of the criminal process." I have stressed direct access to the system of criminal law itself.

Both the reformers and their critics failed to appreciate the extent to which judge and jury conditioned each other's perspective and behavior within a legal culture that developed and applied its own informal rules of law in a relatively consistent fashion.

The reform literature also reveals several important contradictions inherent in prevailing attitudes toward crime, criminals, and the administration of the criminal law. First, as we have seen, contemporaries who favored reform of the law of capital sanctions and a concomitant reduction of the need for jury intervention tended to regard such intervention as both inevitable and just in the unreformed present. Their writings thus offered support to those seeking to justify jury-based intervention.

Moreover (and, ultimately, perhaps more important), many of the reform writers viewed criminal behavior as a product of social conditions, including among those conditions the existing administration of the criminal law. They coupled their support for reform of the law of sanctions with a call for rehabilitation. Reformers thus accepted one of the ideas implicit in contemporary social thought and in the prevailing system of commutation—the notion that much crime was socially caused—and, carrying that idea part way to its logical conclusion, they rejected both the manner in which the sentencing procedure was implemented and the principal form of treatment (transportation) of those offenders who were spared. But these writers also clung to a notion of free will and suggested by implication that it was for existing institutions to sort out the truly guilty from the great mass of relatively unfree offenders. Once again, in the decades preceding reform, the reformers provided a justification for age-old jury practices.

Finally, few reformers supposed that reform of sanctions would entirely remove the need for an ultimate right of jury intervention. Romilly had already written in defense of the jury in seditious libel cases when he turned his attention to the problem of sanctions in common-run felonies;[157] Dawes produced a similar tract on seditious libel two years after the publication of his *Essay on Crimes and Punishments*.[158] We shall see that Blackstone and others also—though in more moderate language— glorified the historical role of juries in political cases and suggested that the jury might again someday have to play a similar role. Though most of these later writers believed that the settlement of 1689 rendered unlikely a return to executive and judicial tyranny, they too offered a powerful argument for true nullification of the law to those contemporaries who thought such a turn of events had already come to pass. Perhaps as a

157. See above, n. 147 and accompanying text.
158. See below, Chapter 8, text at n. 58.

result, reform would come only after a political and legal crisis in which the virtues of an ultimate (though rarely resorted to) right of true jury law-finding were openly debated and widely accepted.

# 8     The Jury, Seditious Libel, and the Criminal Law

The seditious libel trials of the eighteenth century constitute an important chapter in the history of freedom of the press and the growth of democratic government. While much has been written about them and about the administration of the criminal law in eighteenth-century England, little has been said about the relationship between the libel prosecutions and the more pervasive and longstanding problems of the criminal law.[1] We have perhaps gone too far in positing—or simply assuming—a separation between political high misdemeanors and common-run felony cases such as homicide and theft. There were, however, points of contact between the two; most notably, the trial jury was employed in both. This conjunction raises the question of whether the use of the jury in the one kind of case influenced thinking about how it ought to be used in the other. I shall explore this subject in light of the tract literature of the seditious libel crisis. I hope thereby to elucidate the oft-repeated arguments concerning the jury's right to decide law as well as fact, and to characterize the kinds of knowledge that pro-jury writers thought jurors were to bring to their task. Finally, I shall set forth some tentative conclusions concerning the place of the seditious libel episode and its resolution in the history of the jury and the administration of criminal law.

At the time of the seditious libel crisis the two strands of jury law-finding theory that we have traced remained intact, one still active, the other largely historical. The tradition of merciful acquittals and partial

---

1. E.g. Holdsworth, *History of English Law*, 10:672–96. (Much of Holdsworth's account of the seditious libel law, its interpretation by Mansfield and others in the major trials, and Fox's Libel Act and its aftermath remains adequate. I sketch in the necessary details but do not replicate Holdsworth's lengthy account. I stress those details essential for my own purpose, which is to assess the manner in which those contemporaries who commented on the matter thought about the problem of the jury's role in seditious libel cases.) See also e.g. Leonard W. Levy, *Legacy of Suppression* (Cambridge, Mass., 1964), pp. 88–175; Frederick Seaton Siebert, *Freedom of the Press in England, 1447–1776* (Urbana, Ill., 1965), pp. 269–75, 380–92; H. M. Lubasz, "Public Opinion Comes of Age: Reform of the Libel Law in the Eighteenth Century," *History Today*, vol. 8 (1958), pp. 453–61; Robert Rea, *The English Press and Politics: 1760–1774* (Lincoln, Nebr., 1963); John Brewer, "The Wilkites and the Law, 1763–1774," in Brewer and Styles, eds., *An Ungovernable People* (New Brunswick, N.J., 1980), pp. 128–71; Patrick Devlin, *The Judge* (Oxford, 1981), pp. 119–26.

verdicts in common-run cases continued apace with something close to official acquiescence. Although true nullification of judicial instructions was not officially approved, some very respectable jurists not only lauded the nullifying behavior of juries in certain pre-1689 political cases, but, more significantly, could be read as suggesting that there might be occasions on which juries would once again be duty-bound to play that role.

The seditious libel tracts reflect the influence of these strands of thought in a variety of ways. Especially, they reveal both the extent to which the radical jury proponents were able to build upon the views of the more conventional, establishment writers and the importance of the interplay between notions of true nullification in political prosecutions and the tradition of merciful verdicts in common-run cases. After briefly describing the seditious libel controversy (section I) I shall examine these and other themes in the course of considering varying views of the constitutional role of the criminal trial jury (section II) and the tract writers' approach to finding law (section III), finding fact (section IV), and applying law to fact (section V). My conclusion (section VI) puts the seditious libel controversy into historical perspective regarding social, political, and constitutional aspects of the institution of trial by jury.

# I

The common law crime of seditious libel can be broadly characterized as the intentional publication of a writing that "scandalized" the government, i.e., tended to bring it into disesteem. Although indictments for seditious libel generally alleged that the accused had acted "falsely, seditiously, maliciously and factiously," the jury was to render what amounted to a special verdict in the form of a general verdict of "guilty" if it found that the accused intentionally published the writing and if it found that the writing bore the meaning alleged by the prosecution. The origins of the seditious libel doctrine lay in Star Chamber practice, but the doctrine was given final form early in the eighteenth century by Chief Justice Holt.[2] Significantly, the law did not recognize truth as a defense.[3] Moreover, as we have seen, it assigned to the court as matters of law two questions that had the appearance of questions of fact: whether the act was done with criminal intent, and whether the writing was seditious or defamatory. It was perhaps plausible to consider the latter question one of

2. Hamburger, "Origins of the Law of Seditious Libel," *passim*. See above, Chapter 6, nn. 208–10 and accompanying text, for discussion of seditious libel in the seventeenth century. On Holt's modification of that doctrine see Hamburger, *ibid.*, pp. 85–115.

3. Holdsworth, *History of English Law*, 8:336–42, esp., 339.

law because the nature of the crime typically meant that the entire record of the allegedly criminal act was embodied in a physical specimen that survived for judicial inspection. It was less plausible to cast the question of criminal intent as one of law to be inferred by the court. On both counts the doctrine was strongly resisted, from the Restoration trials of Care[4] and Harris[5] in 1680 and the great case of the *Seven Bishops*[6] on the eve of the Glorious Revolution down to the reform of the doctrine by means of Fox's Libel Act in 1792.[7]

We may note briefly the major phases of the seditious libel debate in the eighteenth century. From the perspective of nearly all the participants in that debate, the *Seven Bishops' Case* had taken on the garb of hallowed precedent. Most writers saw that great courtroom drama as an act by which the people paved the way for the constitutional settlement that followed the Glorious Revolution of 1688–89, wherein Englishmen consigned the law to its rightful place—the protective arms of an independent judiciary.[8] The case, which was tried in a highly charged political atmosphere, involved the prosecution of seven bishops who refused to read James II's *Declaration of Indulgence* in their churches. Because the bench divided on the question of whether the petition constituted a libel, that question was left, de facto, to the jury.[9] The acquittal of the bishops was taken to be both a rejection of James's pro-Catholic policies and a vindication, against the views of the bench, of the jury's right to determine the questions of intent and libelousness. The case became a precedent for opposition to tyranny, an act of last resort: jury nullification of the official doctrine of seditious libel, on which the bench had not *una voce* insisted, had saved the constitution. Yet for some, this did not require rejection of the Stuart doctrine of seditious libel. An independent and impartial bench could be trusted (or so the theory ran) to assign and

---

4. *State Trials*, 7:1111-30 (1680). (Alternatively spelled: Carr.)

5. *Ibid.*, pp. 926–32 (1680).

6. *Ibid.*, 12:183–434 (1688).

7. 32 Geo. 3, c. 60 (1792). Technically, criminal intent was not at issue in seditious libel. If the court found that the writing was seditious, it held that the defendant constructively intended the consequences of the act of publication. Fox's Act left the jury in a position where it could apply the judge's instructions on seditiousness; in the course of doing so, the jury was supposed to imply the requisite intent if it found the publication seditious. The jury was thus in a position to consider whether in fact there had been actual defaming intent— only in that sense had the issue been "left" to the jury—though to do so was to go against the instructions and, hence, against the Act. See below, text at nn. 62–64.

8. *Act of Settlement* (1701), in E. N. Williams, comp. and trans., *The Eighteenth Century Constitution* (Cambridge, 1965), p. 59: "[J]udges commissions be made *quamdiu se bene gesserint* and their salaries ascertained and established; but upon the address of both houses of parliament it may be lawful to remove them."

9. See above, Chapter 6, text at nn. 232–34.

determine all questions of law. Thus, in the century after the Glorious Revolution, much of the legal establishment both accepted the constitutional settlement and adhered to the essential elements of the Stuart law of libel.[10] For many others, however, the *Seven Bishops' Case* stood for more. It was a vindication of the integrity of the general verdict. For some this meant only that the traditional role of the trial jury, the finding of fact and the application to fact of the law as given by the bench, was preserved. Others, as we shall see, envisioned the general verdict as including not merely application of the law but also true law-finding.

From the outset the eighteenth-century debate concerning the seditious libel doctrine was couched largely in Restoration terms.[11] Chief Justice Raymond succinctly restated Holt's formulation of the Stuart doctrine in *Rex v. Franklin* in 1731, setting forth a division of judge-jury responsibilities that the courts would attempt to enforce until the passage of Fox's Libel Act.[12] His opinion, in turn, revived the Restoration defense of the criminal trial jury. Late in 1732, John Hawles's 1680 tract, *The Englishman's Right*, was reprinted for the first time. The new preface, signed by one J. K., warned of developments that threatened to destroy all that had been won in the Glorious Revolution and commended the tract "in which the original design, duty and power of jurors are so clearly

10. Mansfield, in *St. Asaph's Case* (*State Trials*, 21:1040) espoused the commonly held point of view as follows: "Jealousy of leaving the law to the Court, as in other cases, so in the case of libels, *is now, in the present state of things*, puerile rant and declamation. The judges are totally independent of the ministers that may happen to be, and of the King himself." (Emphasis added.) Mansfield took the view that the opponents of the official doctrine sought to make an exception of the law of libel: in that case alone the jury would find law as well as fact. A similar view can be found in an unpublished manuscript, "Sketch of an answer to a Pamphlet, entitled 'Letter concerning Libels, Warrants and Seizures of Papers,' " (B.L. MS Add. 35, 887, fols. 171 *et seq.*), probably written in 1765 in reply to the second edition of "Father of Candor's" famous work (see below, n. 117). As the present study makes clear, most pro-jury writers took the view that the jury was to find law as well as fact in libel, *as in other cases*. From their perspective, libel was currently an exception under the official doctrine, and ought not to be so.

11. Hamburger ("Origins of the Law of Seditious Libel," see above, Chapter 6, nn. 210, 238) argues that the doctrine was still loosely formulated at the time of the Harris and Care prosecutions (1680) and that it received its crystallization between 1696 and 1706, mainly at the hands of Chief Justice Holt. What I refer to as the "Stuart law of libel" is the set of doctrines that I believe were emerging in the period before the *Seven Bishops' Case* and that some Restoration tract writers understood (perhaps wrongly) to be the settled official doctrine. As Hamburger demonstrates, Holt's modification of these doctrines toward the end of the Stuart period was of great importance, but these changes concerned the definition of libel, not the allocation-of-powers question. Holt did not place greater restrictions on the jury's fact-finding responsibilities than the major Restoration critics of seditious libel assumed were already part of the law. The response to the *Seven Bishops' Case* must be understood, at least in part, in the light of the assumptions made by earlier critics.

12. *State Trials*, 17:625–76 (1731).

explained, that it will be sufficient to instruct all those, who shall, on these occasions, have the lives and properties of their fellow subjects in their hands."[13] In the tract itself Hawles argued that in all cases, including libel, juries were the true judges of law as well as of fact, not simply that in libel cases seditiousness and intent were matters of fact for the jury.[14] The reprinting of Hawles was closely followed by the publication in England of the report of *Zenger's Case* (1735). Defense counsel for the New York printer, Zenger, had drawn upon Hawles, and in England the combination of the tract and the trial (Zenger had been acquitted) now helped to launch a half-century-long attack on the law of libel and the abuse of trial by jury it allegedly involved.

After Franklin's trial the contest over the doctrine of seditious libel falls into three principal stages. In 1752, the Crown tried by special jury (frequently the practice in seditious libel cases) a bookseller named William Owen for the sale of a tract critical of the House of Commons.[15] Chief Justice Lee, on the urging of the solicitor general, William Murray (the future Lord Mansfield), charged the jury in accordance with Raymond's statement of the law. The jury, after hearing testimony regarding Owen's character and loyalty to the Crown and Camden's argument that the right to criticize Parliament was fundamental, acquitted the defendant. Underlying Camden's argument for the defense was the principle that, notwithstanding the bench's view of the law of seditious libel, the jury, unless it was convinced that the allegations of falsity and

13. Hawles, *Englishman's Right* (London, 1732), pp. iv–vii.

14. *Ibid.*, pp. 10–18.

15. *State Trials*, 18:1203–30 (1752). The special jury was employed in a wide range of civil and criminal cases, though not in felonies. Typically, in seditious libel prosecutions, special juries were drawn from a panel of persons of higher social and economic status than those on panels for ordinary juries. Their rank was by no means exalted. The jurors who tried Owen were described as follows: merchant, sugar-baker, linen-draper, draper, draper, grocer, hosier, grocer, oilman, merchant, merchant, grocer. No doubt authorities attempted to secure a jury that would defer to the bench on rulings of law, but authorities met with little success in seditious libel. Owen's jury was hardly alone in resisting strict application of the seditious libel doctrine. Contemporaries occasionally criticized the use of special juries in seditious libel cases, but surprisingly little attention was paid to the matter, perhaps because many defendants fared well at the hands of the middling sort who sat on special juries. Indeed, at least one defendant complained that summons for special jurors had not issued sufficiently early to ensure a full complement, with the result that talesmen had to be used to fill out nearly half of the jury. [John Miller, the publisher, tried in 1770. See *The Freeholder's Magazine* (London), vol. 2 (July, 1770), pp. 252 *et seq.*]. The *Freeholder's Magazine* (*ibid.*, p. 195) ended its report of Woodfall's trial with the comment that the jury (which found the defendant "guilty of printing and publishing only") was composed of seven special jurors and five "tales or common jurymen." For the background to the special jury see generally the excellent account in Oldham, "Origins of the Special Jury."

scandalous intent in the indictment had been proved, must acquit.[16]

Two anonymously authored, strongly pro-jury tracts followed immediately upon the prosecution of Owen. The tracts reflect the two quite different approaches that opponents of the seditious libel doctrine adopted over the course of the eighteenth century. *An Address to the Jurymen of London*[17] drew heavily upon Hawles, arguing that the jury must acquit if it is convinced that the facts charged in the indictment do not amount to a crime. Attached to the tract was a "Letter to be read to all Jurymen," signed: "Britannicus," which also drew upon the Restoration tracts and *Zenger's Case* and which asserted that the jury must be convinced of the "crime of the fact."[18] On the other hand, *The Doctrine of Libels and the Duty of Juries fairly Stated*[19] at once conceded that juries were judges of fact only and insisted that the jury must consider all the "circumstances," (e.g., truth, intent) involved.[20] The author thus seems to have adopted Camden's strategy, and, like Camden, made much of the analogy to the jury's fact-finding role in cases of homicide. Inflammatory rhetoric about "law-finding" had no place in this style of argument.

The second stage in the English government's use of seditious libel laws to silence criticism of its policies began in 1763 with the prosecution of John Wilkes for his famous No. 45 of *The North Briton*,[21] and climaxed in 1770 with the prosecution, on informations ex officio, of those who published and sold the "Junius" letter protesting the official policy on the American colonies. Mansfield, as Chief Justice of King's Bench, enunciated what had become the established law of seditious libel in the trials of the bookseller John Almon,[22] and the publishers Henry Woodfall[23] and

---

16. *State Trials*, 18:1227–28. "Then, gentlemen, to show you how necessary it is to prove the intention; if there is an indictment preferred against a man for an assault, with an intention to ravish; the intention must be proved, or else the jury cannot find him guilty. The same of an assault with an intention to kill, if the intention is not proved, he must be acquitted. If he kills, and the intention is not proved, that is, if it is not proved that he killed premeditatedly and of forethought, it is but manslaughter. Therefore in the case before us, if that part of the information is not proved, that he published maliciously, etc., you must acquit him."

17. *An Address to the Jurymen of London. By a Citizen* (2nd ed., London, 1755, orig. published 1752).

18. *Ibid.*, p. 22.

19. *The Doctrine of Libels and the Duties of Juries fairly Stated* (London, 1752).

20. *Ibid.*, pp. 14–15, 29–30.

21. *State Trials*, 19:982–1002, 1075–1138 (1763–70).

22. *Ibid.*, 20:803–68 (1770).

23. *Ibid.*, pp. 895–922 (1770). See also the account in *The Freeholder's Magazine*, vol. 2 (June, 1770), pp. 192 *et seq.*, esp. p. 195 .

John Miller.[24] Glynn, who defended all three, followed Camden's arguments in *Rex v. Owen*, at times verbatim. The Crown obtained a conviction in the case of Almon. The Woodfall jury, however, returned a verdict of "Guilty of printing and publishing only," which resulted in a judicial order for a new trial that was never held, and at the close of Miller's trial the jury returned a verdict of "not guilty" despite clear evidence of publication. These widely publicized "Junius" trials, together with Mansfield's consistent refusal to charge the jury that it should consider the question of criminal intent, provoked debate in Parliament over the seditious libel law. Glynn introduced the question of reform in the Commons;[25] Camden and Chatham supported him in the Lords.[26] They could not, however, agree on a new formulation. On the other side, opponents of an enquiry into the matter voiced their complete trust in the judges, including Mansfield. Solicitor General Thurlow may have spoken for many when he raised the specter of jury control over the law and of the dissolution of judicial authority.[27] Some twenty years would elapse before sufficient support could be mustered to pass a bill giving the jury the right to return a true general verdict in cases of seditious libel.

The period 1764–70 produced a spate of major seditious libel tracts. These tracts fall into two groups: the first in the wake of Wilkes's arrest and prosecution in the mid-1760s; the second around 1770, when the Wilkites and proponents of Almon furiously attacked Mansfield. The first series of tracts was composed of attacks on the official doctrine and replies to those attacks; it is not always possible to determine to which pro-jury tract a defender of the prevailing doctrine meant to reply. Possibly the earliest of the dissident tracts was Joseph Towers's *Enquiry into the Question, Whether Juries are, or not, Judges of Law as Well as of Fact*.[28] Like the writings of the preceding decade, *Enquiry* seems very dependent upon Hawles and recites as well from the *Guide to Juries* of 1682 "that all that the judges do is but advice."[29] Towers analogized to homicide, but he chose to characterize his description of the jury's role in such cases as determining law as well as fact. Perhaps the most important

---

24. *State Trials*, 20:869–96 (1770). See also *The Freeholder's Magazine*, vol. 2 (July, 1770), pp. 252 *et seq.*

25. *The Parliamentary History of England* (hereafter cited as *Parliamentary History*), ed. W. Cobbett (vols. 1–12) and T. C. Hansard (vols. 13–36) (London, 1806–20), vol. 16, cols. 1212–15. The ensuing debate in the Commons runs from col. 1215 to col. 1301. The issue had already arisen in the course of the debate over informations ex officio. See cols. 1124–90.

26. *Ibid.*, cols. 1302–6, 1312 *et seq.*

27. For Thurlow's speeches see *ibid.*, cols. 1146, 1290–93.

28. Joseph Towers, *An Enquiry into the Question, Whether Juries are, or not, Judges of Law as Well as of Fact; With a particular Reference to the Case of Libels* (London, 1764).

29. *Ibid.*, p. 54.

early pro-Administration tract was the *Letter from Candor to the Public Advertiser* (1764).[30] According to "Candor," there was nothing new about the prevailing doctrine: Mansfield applied the law largely as it had been applied by Jeffreys, a point that most critics of Mansfield were willing (even anxious) to concede.[31] In defending the law against the claims of the pro-jury writers, "Candor" recognized that there might be mitigating circumstances. But these, he said, were for consideration by the judge *after* the jury convicted, as it must do if it found that the defendant had published the alleged libel.[32] "Candor" understood how defendants were relieved from overly harsh sanctions in criminal cases generally, but he strongly denied that it was appropriate for the jury to undertake such mercy.

In reply to "Candor" came *An Enquiry into the Doctrine . . . concerning Libels, Warrants, and the Seizure of Papers* by "Father of Candor,"[33] and in counterpoint to "Father of Candor," the famous *Considerations on the Legality of General Warrants*, to which was added "A Postscript on a late pamphlet concerning juries, libels, etc."[34] "Father of Candor" characterized intent and seditiousness as questions of fact, thus matters for the jury, and proceeded to discuss how a jury ought to go about deciding whether a writing was libelous. "Father of Candor" suggested that, simply put, "plain truth and fact, and common sense" were at issue.[35] He thus opened up discussion of what was required of jurors and of the competence of the average jury, issues that loomed large in the debate over the next several decades. The "Postscript" to *Considerations* contained a particularly trenchant attack on the pro-jury position, one that referred to jurors as "illiterate" and "unused to legal ideas."[36] While conceding that jurors played a full role in homicide, the "Postscript" insisted that they merely found the facts and were bound to follow the judge's direction upon the law. If the jurors had any doubt about the law, they were to return a special verdict summarizing the facts they had found and to leave pronouncement of the general verdict to the

30. *A Letter from Candor to the Public Advertiser* (3rd. ed., London, 1770, orig. published 1764).
31. *Ibid.*, p. 5.
32. *Ibid.*, p. 18.
33. *An Enquiry into the Doctrine, Lately Propagated, concerning Libels, Warrants, and the Seizure of Papers . . . in a Letter to Mr. Almon from the Father of Candor* (London, 1764).
34. *Considerations on the Legality of General Warrants, and the propriety of a Parliamentary regulation of the same. To which is added "A Postscript on a late pamphlet concerning juries, libels, etc."* (2nd ed., London, 1765, orig. published 1765).
35. *Enquiry into the Doctrine*, p. ll.
36. "Postscript" to *Considerations*, pp. 42–43.

judge.[37] (This, according to the author of "Postscript," is what the jury ought to have done in the *Seven Bishops' Case*.)[38] In libel more than in other cases, the jury was likely "to be under the influence of popular passions,"[39] and thus ought to hold closely to finding fact.

"Postscript" to *Considerations* drew its own reply, *Postscript to the Letter, on Libels . . . In Answer to a Postscript in Defence of the Majority, and . . . Considerations . . .*,[40] which asserted that in libels it was particularly important that the jury play its historic role, for the Court in such cases was not likely to be impartial.[41] That role, the tract stated, was set forth by Lilburne at the end of his 1649 trial.[42] Thus, the tract suggested a far-reaching interpretation of law-finding, though it is not entirely clear that the author understood what Lilburne had been getting at. *Postscript . . . In Answer* charged that the author of the "Postscript" to *Considerations* took a view of the jury that was "much too lowly and contemptuous, owing I presume to his education on the Northern side of the Tweed, where very little use is made of them."[43]

The positions rehearsed in these and other tracts were repeated by proponents and critics of the prevailing doctrine in the heated political atmosphere of 1770.[44] Virtually all of the London papers carried news stories, editorial comments, book reviews, and letters to the editor dealing with the trials of Almon, Miller, and Woodfall, with important jury tracts and with the progress of the jury debate in the Commons.[45] Among the most interesting of the second series of tracts were those produced in 1770 by the Wilkites Robert Morris and George Rous. Morris's *Letter to Sir Robert Aston*[46] and Rous's *Letter to the Jurors of*

37. *Ibid.*, pp. 41, 44.
38. *Ibid.*, p. 45.
39. *Ibid.*, p. 47.
40. *A Postscript to the Letter, on Libels, Warrants, etc. In Answer to a Postscript in the Defence of the Majority, and another Pamphlet, entitled Considerations on the Legality of General Warrants* (2nd ed., London, 1765, orig. published 1765).
41. *Ibid.*, p. 24.
42. *Ibid.*, p. 19.
43. *Idem.*
44. For an excellent discussion of the political strife of this period and of the sources of the "radicalism" that forms a background to the major seditious libel trials see the works by John Brewer cited below, n. 50.
45. On the 1770 debates see e.g. *The Political Register* (London), vol. 8, no. 47 (Jan., 1771), pp. 31–36.
46. Robert Morris, *A Letter to Sir Richard Aston, . . . Containing a reply to his scandalous abuse [of R.M.]; and some thoughts on the modern doctrine of Libels* (London, 1770). This work was reviewed in *The Political Register*, vol. 8, no. 47 (Jan., 1771), p. 56. See the anonymous reply to Morris's tract, *A Letter to Robert Morris, Esq.* (London, 1771), reviewed in *The Political Register*, vol. 8, no. 49 (March, 1771), pp. 184–90.

*Great Britain*[47] dwelled at length upon the place of trial by jury in the English constitution. By now Hawles, though still quoted, played a less significant role, and Wilkite arguments concerning the susceptibility of the bench—especially of Mansfield—to bias in cases involving allegations of seditiousness came to the fore.

The agitation over the jury was, of course, only a small part of the political turmoil of the day. Wilkes's followers, middling men of some property who came largely from merchant communities of the country, focused on the criminal trial jury only fleetingly. Their main efforts concerned issues of more general significance: criticism of the government's foreign and domestic financial policies; impurities of the political process; private law, with its inequities for the small business-man; and the movement for speech and press, to which the jury debate was significantly but rather loosely attached. Nonetheless, the Wilkites were acutely aware of the importance of the jury as an element in the constitution[48] (especially as a necessary surrogate for what they viewed as a corrupt and unrepresentative parliament) and as an investigative as well as a protective body.[49] In this last capacity the jury, whose members were frequently drawn from their own social groups, was particularly crucial to their embattled movement, and they made certain that jurors in important political cases were apprised of their "rights." This campaign caused the administration to view the jury as all the more likely to act out of political bias.[50]

47. George Rous, *A Letter to the Jurors of Great Britain* (London, 1771), p. 50. This work was reviewed in *The Political Register*, vol. 8, no. 48 (Feb., 1771), p. 105.

48. See below, text at nn. 76 *et seq.*

49. See e.g. *The Political Register*, vol. 9, no. 50 (Sept., 1771), pp. 128–29. "Whatever twelve good men and true do in their consciences think to be against the peace . . . they are bound by their oath to present and to bring to justice. . . . [A] jury is sworn to do this, not only on information, but of their own knowledge" (editorial, p. 129).

50. On the Wilkite movement see Brewer, "The Wilkites and the Law," esp. pp. 153–64; John Brewer, "English Radicalism in the Age of George III," in J. G. A. Pocock, ed., *Three British Revolutions: 1641, 1688, 1776* (Princeton, 1980), pp. 323–67, esp. 342–54; John Brewer, "Commercialization and Politics," in Neil McKendrick, John Brewer, and J. H. Plumb, eds., *The Birth of a Consumer Society: The Commercialization of Eighteenth-Century England* (London, 1980), pp. 197–262. For a particularly trenchant attack on judicial browbeating of jurors see *The North Briton* (London), no. 64 (Sept. 3, 1768), p. 184. On jurors "true" duty see e.g. *The North Briton*, no. 168 (June 16, 1770), p. 426. Prospective jurors no doubt took note of the fact that London newspapers of Wilkite persuasion frequently printed the names of jurors. They could not expect to convict a defendant in a seditious libel case and remain anonymous. See e.g. *The Freeholder's Magazine*, vol. 2 (July, 1770), pp. 252–53. See Brewer, "Commercialization and Politics," p. 236. For a balanced letter (from "A Whig"), critical both of the government and of the tone and substance of Wilkite criticism (including the subversion of the judicial process by "jurors,

Throughout the entire period 1763–70 the jury debate remained several different debates. Some jury proponents opposed what was now called Mansfield's law/fact distinction in seditious libel, insisting instead that seditiousness and intent were matters of fact for the jury. In this, they drew support from the arguments of Glynn and Camden at the major trials. The more interesting debate, however, still concerned the jury's right to "find law," especially since the law-finding argument involved the confusing concession by jury proponents that the questions of intent and seditiousness were indeed "matter of law." Having accepted the bench's characterization, these publicists concluded that because these questions were of a sort that were traditionally in all other cases questions for the jury, the jury must therefore be a law-finding body.[51] This, in turn, intensified the squabble over the competence of jurors, who now had to be defended as law finders, a proposition that authorities, thrown on the defensive by the size and force of the Wilkite movement, regarded as both preposterous and dangerous.[52]

The third stage of the seditious libel controversy commenced with the trial in 1783 of William Shipley, Dean of St. Asaph.[53] Unquestionably, Shipley's case was the most important seditious libel prosecution since the *Seven Bishops' Case*. Shipley had published a tract by his brother-in-law, Sir William Jones, that allegedly incited to rebellion;[54] after the trial judge entered a conviction upon a verdict of "guilty of publishing only," a new trial was refused despite Thomas Erskine's ringing defense on Shipley's behalf. Yet after carrying the day on the law of libel, the bench set the conviction aside for a defect in the indictment.[55]

The tracts that followed upon *St. Asaph's Case* made use of Erskine's defense, some taking a narrow line and others going beyond Erskine's

men of rank, character and fortune"), see *The Political Register*, vol. 8, no. 49 (March, 1771), pp. 169–70.

51. E.g. Thomas Leach, *Considerations on the Matter of Libel. Suggested by Mr. Fox's Notice in Parliament of an intended motion on that subject* (London, 1791). See also the speeches by Mr. Cornwall and Mr. Dunning in the Commons in 1770. Hansard, ed., *Parliamentary History*, 16: cols. 1135, 1160.

52. See the speeches of attorney general De Grey and solicitor general Thurlow in the Commons in 1770. Hansard, ed., *Parliamentary History*, 16: cols. 1146, 1185–86.

53. *State Trials*, 21:874–1046 (1883–84). See Devlin, *The Judge*, pp. 119–31 for an interesting summary and commentary on this case.

54. William Jones, *Dialogue between a Scholar and a Peasant* (London, 1782), re-published by William Shipley as *A Dialogue between a Gentleman and a Farmer* (London, 1783).

55. *State Trials*, 21:1041–44. "The Court . . . [said] there were no averments to point the application of the paper as a libel on the king and his government." Willes, J., thought that "if the indictment had been properly drawn, it might have been supported." Mansfield, C. J., and Buller, J., did not give an opinion on that hypothetical (*ibid.*, p. 1044).

relatively controlled arguments to reiterate the vaguer law-finding claims that had now become a part of the tradition.[56] Joseph Towers's *Observations on the rights and duty of Juries in trials for Libels* revived Hawles's strong claims and based its endorsement of broad jury powers in part on the view that the bench could not be trusted to determine the proper limits of judicial power.[57] Perhaps the most ringing defense of the jury was Manasseh Dawes's *England's Alarm! On the Prevailing Doctrine of Libels*, which appeared in 1785. Dawes retreated to a historical perspective in making the case that juries had for so long been entrusted with plenary power to determine cases that it was no longer appropriate to claim they were incompetent to vindicate that duty.[58] Six years later Thomas Leach, who was himself trained in law, produced a still different defense of the jury, *Considerations on the Matter of Libel*.[59] Through juxtaposing the issues for determination in homicide and libel, Leach made the case for the jury and against the official doctrine in a way that must have put the proponents of Mansfield's position on the defensive.

Despite the outpouring of pro-jury writings, the debate was by no means entirely one-sided. Authorities drew the conclusion from years of jury resistance to the law of seditious libel that juries could not be trusted in such cases to return verdicts that accorded even loosely with the government's interpretation of facts. Juries, they believed with some justice, were open to political pressures; verdicts could, and sometimes did, depend upon the heat of the political passions of the day. The anonymously authored *An Examination into the rights and duties of Jurors* (1785), which was a response to Joseph Towers's law-finding tract, drove home the point against a position that had, to be sure, been carelessly overstated:

When we see this position, that juries are to judge all the criminality of a libel, as well as the truth of the fact of publication, supported, not by arguments drawn from the peculiarity of the case, which may require an exception to the general rule, but by general assertions, that jurors are complete and uncontrollable judges of the law in every instance, it

56. Levy, *Legacy of Suppression*, pp. 249 *et seq.*; Holdsworth, *History of English Law*, 10:688–96. See also *Rex v. Stockdale*, *State Trials*, 22:237–308, to which some tracts referred.

57. Joseph Towers, *Observations on the rights and duty of Juries, in trials for Libels* (London, 1784), pp. 5, 15–20, 29.

58. Manasseh Dawes, *England's Alarm! On the Prevailing Doctrine of Libels as laid down by the Earl of Mansfield* (London, 1785), pp. 8 *et seq.* For discussion of Dawes's writings urging reform of the law of sanctions in common-run cases see above, Chapter 7, text at nn. 114–20.

59. Leach, *Considerations on the Matter of Libel*.

is time for every honest man to oppose an innovation of the most dangerous tendency.[60]

Some of Mansfield's defenders responded to the law-finding argument in a more legalistic manner. For them, the argument for a narrow scope of fact proceeded along the lines of an argument for certainty of the law. John Bowles's tracts, written on the eve of passage of Fox's Libel Act, pressed that point effectively, at least at the level of debate.[61] They were among the most cogent writings of the half-century of debate, and they lent great rhetorical (if no practical political) force to Mansfield's opinion in *St. Asaph's Case*.

Mansfield had won the battle but he soon lost the war. The campaign against the seditious libel law culminated in 1792 with the passage of Fox's Libel Act. The Act did not explicitly convert the questions of intent or seditiousness into questions of fact but did state that in trials for seditious libel

[the] jury sworn to try the issues may give a general verdict of guilty or not guilty upon the whole matter put in issue . . . and shall not be required or directed . . . to find the defendant or defendants guilty, merely of the proof of the publication . . . and of the sense ascribed to the same.[62]

The "whole matter" included the question of criminal intent, which might or might not have to depend solely upon inferences drawn from the publication itself, and the question of whether the writing was seditious. The statute affirmed the jury's right to return a general verdict. It was clear that in doing so the jury would necessarily have the right—and duty—to apply the law regarding criminal intent and seditiousness as stated by the bench.[63] But in the Commons at least it was neither stated nor implied that the jury possessed any more right in libel than in other

---

60. *An Examination into the rights and duties of Jurors; with some strictures on the Law of Libels.* By a gentleman of the Inner Temple (London, 1785), p. 8.

61. E.g. John Bowles, *Considerations on the Respective Rights of Judge and Jury: particularly upon Trials for Libel, occasioned by an expected motion of the Right Hon. Charles James Fox* (London, 1791).

62. 32 Geo. 3, c. 60 (1792). For the debates on the form that the Act ought to take, see Hansard, ed., *Parliamentary History*, 29: cols. 551–602 (Commons), 726–42 (Lords), 1036–47 (Lords), 1293–1300 (Lords), 1361–71 (Opinions of the Judges), 1404–31 (Lords), 1534–38 (Lords). The Act began: "Whereas doubts have arisen whether . . . it be competent to the jury . . .; be it therefore declared and enacted . . ." Holdsworth (*History of English Law*, 10:690) accepts the view that the Act was couched in declaratory form in order to suggest that the courts had been mistaken in their view of the law.

63. The second section of the Act states that the judge shall "according to his discretion give . . . his opinion and directions to the jury on the matter in issue . . . in like manner as in other cases."

cases to reject the law as stated by the bench.[64] That the jury might do so in a concealed fashion was undoubtedly understood—and feared.

## II

The post-1750 discussion of the constitutional role of the criminal trial jury was pervaded by arguments that drew upon history. Virtually all commentators were convinced of the pre-Conquest origins of the jury. A few writers searched for its prototype in the classical world;[65] some traced the jury to the Goths;[66] most posited a Saxon origin, identifying the early

---

64. Erskine openly addressed the jury's right to reject the judge's instructions in the debate in 1791 in the Commons, stating that "[I]f a jury, in despite of law and evidence, were to acquit a felon, he was immediately discharged; such was the wisdom of the constitution in the interposition and augmentation of the powers of a jury, lest the Crown should bear too hard on the life of a subject; nor could a jury be amerced or imprisoned for their verdict." This was true in felony and, Erskine argued, ought to be true in libel. Hansard, ed., *Parliamentary History*, 29: col. 598. His remarks were not adverted to by others. Fox had spoken more ambiguously. He asserted that in all trials the judge could give his "opinion and advice." The bill, he said, would not prevent the judge from doing so in libel; it only "put the case of libels on a footing with all other cases." *Ibid.*, cols. 597–98. Pitt stated that juries were bound in libel (under the bill) as much as in other cases. *Ibid.*, cols. 601–2. In the Lords, Camden in 1791 came close to stating that the jury ought to have more leeway to decide the law in seditious libel than in other cases. His remarks can be read as in agreement with those of Erskine. *Ibid.*, cols. 728–32. Lansdowne thought libel was an anomaly: in libel "law and fact were but one thing. . . . [W]here, in God's name, could it be so safely entrusted as to twelve men, and how much better was it for the judge to be freed from such a critical duty, in all cases of libel, whether it were a public or a private libel." Nonetheless, the reporter recorded his next remarks as: "When judges confined themselves to their own province, to aid the jury by their advice, experience, and authority, without attempting to influence their decision, they should then have his best wishes." *Ibid.*, cols. 738–39. See also his remarks in 1792. *Ibid.*, cols. 1417–23. Presumably, in libel cases juries were to have more leeway than in other cases; i.e., they were not *bound* to follow the bench in any case, but the bench might exert greater influence in other cases. Stanhope took the strongest law-finding position, but he viewed the jury's power as unlimited in all criminal cases. *Ibid.*, col. 1409 (1792). Loughborough is reported to have said that "[e]xperience had convinced him, if the judge did his duty by explaining the law with care, juries would decide with perfect justice." *Ibid.*, col. 1296 (1792). The bill was silent on the matter. In the House of Lords, six opponents of the Act signed a protest against its passage, predicting "confusion and destruction." Hansard, ed., *Parliamentary History*, 29: cols. 1537–38. As it happened, juries proved relatively inclined to convict in seditious libel cases in the years following passage of the Libel Act. See below, n. 150 and accompanying text.

65. E.g. John Pettingal, *Enquiry into the use and practice of Juries among the Greeks and Romans; from whence the origin of the English jury may probably be deduced* (London, 1769), pp. iv–ix. See also Manasseh Dawes, *England's Alarm! On the Prevailing Doctrine of Libels*, p. 12.

66. E.g. *Historical sketches of civil liberty From Henry VII to the accession of the house of Stuart, with an account of the antiquity, use, and duty of juries* (London, 1788), pp. 96–97.

*laggamanni* as combining the roles of judge and jury.[67] For the most part, however, this fascination with the origins of the jury remained an antiquarian exercise.[68] It is true that eighteenth-century jury proponents thought that the jury's antiquity bolstered its place in the constitution, but no one disputed that the jury deserved some place. Exactly what place the jury ought to have was the question on which contemporaries disagreed. Here the eighteenth-century theorists had little in common with their mid-seventeenth-century forerunners. Few of the later writers contended, as had some Levellers, that historically the jury had preceded the judiciary or that the law flowed forth from the community through the jury. Whatever their perspective on the law-finding power of the jury, the eighteenth-century writers implicitly accepted the Lockeian view of the origins of civil society. They took for granted the quasi-balance of powers created by the settlement of 1689 and the dominant role of Parliament in the making of law. The jury, even in the view of most of those who favored jury law-finding, was supposed to guarantee that English law, whether common law or statutory law, was fairly stated and fairly applied.

For some eighteenth-century jury proponents the jury was not so much a part of the constitution as a symbol of the source of power that created civil government and the constitution itself. Henry Burtenshaw maintained that juries are not

> the creatures, even of the constitution, but coeval with it—with the constitution which declares all power to be in the people, and which has survived and remained unviolated through many revolutions of state government: they are themselves a government in miniature, and a symbol of that general democracy in which resides, and through which, under various modifications, is dispersed, all the functions of power, of justice and of policy.[69]

But even Burtenshaw recognized that laws were made in Parliament or "abroad, by [the people's] habits of life and usages," so that the jury, in his view, was to "interpret those laws when made."[70] Most commentators took an even more frankly instrumental view of the jury: the jury was

67. E.g. James Astry, *A General Charge to all Grand Juries . . . to which is prefixed a Discourse of the antiquity, power and duty of juries* (London, 1703), p. 4; John Fortescue-Aland, ed., *The Difference between an absolute and limited monarchy*, by John Fortescue (London, 1719), p. 56. See also Blackstone, *Commentaries*, 3:349–50.

68. But see *The Political Register*, vol. 9, no. 51 (Oct., 1771), pp. 191–92 ("On the Perversions of Law from its Constitutional Course") for a tract strongly reminiscent of Leveller historico-legal writings.

69. Henry Burtenshaw, *Letters to the Right Hon. The Earl of Mansfield* (London, 1781), p. viii.

70. *Ibid.*, p. 79.

a part of the constitution, established in order to fill a gap or to balance lay against official influence. Blackstone lent important support to this watchdog theory of the criminal trial jury. He cautioned against creation of more "convenient" procedures; the "delays, and little inconveniences in the forms of justice, are the price that all free nations must pay for their liberty in more substantial matters."[71] Despite ambiguity in its characterization of the jury's role, Blackstone's theory strongly implied that the jury remained a safeguard against some future recurrence of executive or judicial tyranny.

Blackstone's contemporary Henry Dagge traced the origins of civil society in terms familiar to eighteenth-century political theorists. He began with a discussion of man in his natural state and with a depiction of his resolution of disputes by private revenge; this period of continual strife, he asserted, gave way to government and, eventually, to the creation of distinctive elements of government: legislative, executive, and judicial. Even at this stage, "after the three powers were divided," difficulties remained:

> The judicial power being entrusted with the exposition of the law, and as it depended on their judgment whether the case or fact *sub lite*, was or was not within the description of the law, there was evidently a great latitude still left for the exercise of partiality or oppression.[72]

The "remedy," he concluded, was "the invention of juries."[73] Dagge assured his readers that it seldom happened that juries rejected the judge's instructions: "The opinion of the bench has generally its due weight."[74] For the most part, the jury was to find fact and no more, and the better the primary institutions of government worked the less the jury would be needed as a safeguard of the liberties those institutions were designed to protect. This view of the jury was adumbrated even by William Paley, who exhibited tolerance for a complex, sometimes unpredictable, legal process. In his view, there would and ought to be countervailing pressures, from which an equitable solution would emerge. The jury's role could not be given clearly defined limits; thus Paley cautioned against "urging too far the distinction between ques-

---

71. Blackstone, *Commentaries*, 4:344.

72. Dagge, *Considerations on Criminal Law*, pp. 123–24.

73. *Ibid.*, p. 125. See also "A Sketch of the British Constitution" in *The Court Miscellany, or Gentleman and Lady's New Magazine* (London) (June, 1768), pp. 315–18 and 361–63. This unsigned article, which gives the jury a prominent role in the constitution, seems to reflect Wilkite views, but it is careful to employ standard propositions in its creation of a powerful place for the jury.

74. Dagge, *Considerations on Criminal Law*, p. 135.

tions of law and questions of fact."[75]

None of these prominent academic legal writers directed his attention specifically to the debate resulting from trials for seditious libel. Indeed, none set out to write mainly about the jury. Rather each developed a distinctive approach to the legal system generally, fitting the jury into the larger scheme of things. None subscribed to a far-reaching theory of endemic jury law-deciding, but all believed—or strongly implied—that for the legal system to operate fairly, recourse to the jury-monitoring of judicial instructions on the law would sometimes be necessary. This conception of the jury was of course shared—and fruitfully used—by most writers who wrote in response to the government's doctrine of seditious libel. For these latter writers, however, the jury was not incidentally, but rather in the main, a safeguard against oppression.

Robert Morris, the Wilkite barrister and secretary of the Society for Supporters of the Bill of Rights, sounded a theme to which many of Mansfield's opponents rallied when he wrote: "The great province of a jury in criminal matters is to make true deliverance of the subject from false accusation, and especially from oppressive prosecutions of the Crown."[76] The jury, Glynn was quoted as stating at the trial in 1770 of the publisher John Miller, are "in times of danger the asylum of the people."[77] It was to protect "every subject of the state, from the abuse of executive power," wrote Thomas Leach, that the English constitution required "the unanimous suffrage of twelve of his equals."[78] Judges, who were still dependent upon the Crown for "pensions" and "places, which they hold at the mere pleasure of their minister,"[79] were not above "crafty distinctions and ensnaring eloquence"; they "throw dust in the eyes, and confound the sense of a well-meaning jury."[80] Such invective became a commonplace in the years between the Wilkes affair and the Dean of St. Asaph's trial.[81]

The encomiums of the more radical supporters of the jury typically began with generalities from Hale or Blackstone and went on to the limits

75. Paley, *Principles of Moral and Political Philosophy*, p. 505.

76. Robert Morris, *A Letter to Sir Richard Aston, . . . Containing a reply to his scandalous abuse [of R. M.]; and some thoughts on the modern doctrine of Libels* (London, 1770), p. 40.

77. Paraphrase of Glynn's speech in *Bingley's Journal* (London) (July 21, 1770), p. 3, col. 3. Glynn appears actually to have said (*State Trials*, 20:880): "For we all know, that in all times, the honest, intrepid, upright conduct of a jury must be the refuge of the people of this kingdom. . . . They must and will, in the natural course and evolution of things, flee again to the same asylum."

78. Leach, *Considerations on the Matter of Libel*, p. 9.

79. Morris, *Letter to . . . Aston*, p. 56.

80. *Bingley's Journal* (June 30, 1770), p. 1, col. 2.

81. See Brewer, "Wilkites and the Law," pp. 153–59.

of their authors' imaginations. Jury trial was, e.g., central to "the grand or principal law of this land, on which the justice of all the rest depend."[82] It was through the jury that subjects judged "when the fundamental laws are violated; when an attempt is made to subvert the constitution."[83] Even the charges that jurors lacked legal training, were just plain ignorant, or were subject to popular passions became occasions for praise, albeit at times with a defensive tone. Jurors, it was frequently said, did not lack the natural capacity for the role they were being asked to play. They have, wrote Manasseh Dawes, "generally a just sense of right or wrong."[84] "Juries have not a knowledge of the technical niceties of the law, as a profession," Capel Lofft conceded, "but the Constitution presumes them to understand it as a rule of civil rights in a general sense."[85] "Thanks be to God!" Anthony Highmore exclaimed, "there lives in mankind a sense of right and wrong that compels them to form the most impartial judgment they can."[86] All three of these writers were trained in law; all opposed one or another Crown policy; and all resented use of the libel laws to silence criticism.

To find law a general sense of civil rights and a sense of right and wrong were required, but not deep grounding in Scripture, custom, or the common law. For some, this was the irreducible core which law-finding theory had reached by the late eighteenth century.[87] So long as law-deciding was linked to "pious perjury" or to egregious cases where the jury was required to stand as a bulwark against judicial overreach, even the moderate, bench-oriented Blackstone could be put to some use. George Rous, yet another Wilkite barrister, quoted Blackstone's admonition to subjects that they learn the law; their lack of such learning, Blackstone had written, "has unavoidably thrown more power into the hands of the judges, to direct, control, and even reverse their verdicts, than perhaps the constitution intended."[88]

Some who supported the law-finding jury conceded that juries might make too much of their powers or misunderstand how they ought to be employed. Rous, e.g., wrote: "Jurors, like judges, may err through

---

82. "Letter to be Read by all Jurymen" (Signed: "Brittanicus"), printed with *An Address to the Jurymen of London*, p. 19.

83. Rous, *A Letter to the Jurors of Great Britain*, p. 50.

84. Manasseh Dawes, *England's Alarm!*, p. 8.

85. Capel Lofft, *An Essay on the Law of Libels* (London, 1785), p. 96.

86. Anthony Highmore, *Reflections on the distinction usually adopted in Criminal Prosecutions for Libel* (London, 1791), p. 33.

87. An editorial in *The Political Register*, vol. 9, no. 50 (Sept., 1771), p. 129, commented: "The wise institution of juries has contrived to make the conscience of every man a minister of the law to the utmost extent."

88. Rous, *Letter to the Jurors*, p. 10. See Blackstone, *Commentaries*, 1:8.

ignorance, or be misled by passion."[89] But the constitution wisely contained a remedy—where, i.e., a jury wrongly *convicted* the defendant. Drawing, as did many other tract writers, upon practice in common-run felonies, Rous asserted that "grace is always extended to the prisoner upon a proper representation from the judge. A refusal would be contrary to the duty of a sovereign, who swears, at his coronation, to execute justice in mercy."[90] In the case of seditious libel, however—at least before 1792—the government feared what it viewed as unwarranted acquittals, not unwarranted convictions. Those radical jury writers willing to face this problem manipulated the language of the moderates Dagge and Blackstone, characterizing truly unwarranted acquittals as a "lesser inconvenience"[91] and retreating to the well-worn maxim that it was better that many guilty went free than that one innocent man was convicted. However tolerable this maxim may have been in cases of manslaughter or petty theft, it was unlikely that authorities would be content to apply it to cases involving government critics.

# III

Only a minority of pro-jury writers who addressed the problem of seditious libel dealt openly and at length with true law-finding: the jury's right to reject an indictment, regardless of the judge's instructions, on the grounds that it failed to charge the defendant with a crime. Those who advanced this theory drew directly upon the late-seventeenth-century tracts by Hawles and Care, and the anonymous author of *A Guide to Juries*, all of whom had, in turn, drawn upon claims made by Lilburne and Penn. Perhaps the strongest version of this argument was the statement of the printer and bookseller Joseph Towers:

> It cannot be supposed . . . that any jury should be arbitrarily directed to bring any man in guilty, when they are not convinced in their own minds, whether the action the accused person is charged with be a crime or not . . . not only whether he has been guilty of the action alleged against him, but whether he has been guilty of a crime.[92]

89. Rous, *Letter to the Jurors*, p. 60.
90. *Ibid.*, p. 61.
91. Dagge, *Considerations on Criminal Law*, p. 135. See Blackstone, *Commentaries*, 4:344: [T]he "delays, and little inconveniences in the forms of justice, are the price that all free nations must pay for their liberty in more substantial matters."
92. Joseph Towers, *An Enquiry into the Question, Whether Juries are, or are not, Judges of Law, as well as of Fact; With a particular Reference to the case of Libels* (London, 1764), p. 52.

The most offensive aspect of the seditious libel doctrine—so far as pro-jury writers were concerned—was that truth was not a defense; moreover, the prosecution did not have to convince a jury that a libel in fact brought the government into disrepute or created a threat to public order, even though indictments for seditious libel alleged that the defendant had published certain statements "seditiously" and "factiously." Thus one writer, who reproduced some ten pages of Hawles's famous tract, concluded in his own terms:

> From all which it is evident, that however heinous a fact may be represented by hard work and artful innuendoes in an indictment or information, the jury may with impunity, and ought in conscience to bring in the general verdict, not guilty, not only when they think the fact has not been proved by sufficient witnesses, but also when they think the fact is not such a heinous fact as is charged in the indictment or information.[93]

Another writer made the point in his comments upon the Penn-Mead trial of a century earlier:

> [A]s the jury were not convinced, that the fact, with which Penn and Mead were charged was in itself a crime, they were unwilling to condemn them; though, attending to the matter of fact only, they could not avoid it, because the fact was fully proved. . . . [I]t is plain, the jury had respect, in their last verdict, entirely to the matter of law. For as they were convinced, that Penn and Mead had not been guilty of any criminal or illegal action, they could not honestly and conscientiously do any thing but acquit them.[94]

In their arguments for true law-finding powers, jury proponents looked for support to the rules of criminal procedure and to the nature of the substantive criminal law. Most of the arguments devolving from procedure touched upon the supposed theoretical liability of the jury to an attaint. Although this ancient procedure had probably never been applied in criminal cases,[95] most eighteenth-century jury proponents referred only to its "disuse," drawing the conclusion (perhaps from Restoration tracts)

---

93. *Address to the Jurymen of London*, p. 16. See also *The North Briton*, no. 168 (June 16, 1770), p. 426 (Letter from "Cato"); *The Freeholder's Magazine*, vol. 1 (Jan., 1770), p. 236 (anonymous tract, asserting that the jury, which applies law to fact, acquits where someone is indicted for "fact that is no crime"); *The Political Register*, vol. 9, no. 51 (Oct., 1771), p. 189 ("On the Perversions of Law from its Constitutional Course," asserting, "The judges may advise, and if their arguments convince a jury, the jury is conscience bound to find as they advise; but it is the finding of the jury which is the determination and interpetation of the law").

94. *Bingley's Journal* (June 23, 1770), p. 2, col. 1.

95. See above, Chapter 6, section IV.

that attaint, like the fining of jurors, had once been but was no longer permitted by English law. The original law of attaint, they asserted, must have assumed the right of juries to decide law as well as fact, for attaint had applied only in those cases where the jury had found "bad" law.[96] *A Treatise on the Right of Juries* (1771) carried this analysis one step further: the fact that since *Bushel's Case* the law had supplied no certain means of controlling jury verdicts in the case of an acquittal proved not only that the jury had the power but also that it had the right to find law.[97] Even Justice Willes, who voted with the majority in *St. Asaph's Case*, found this argument persuasive.[98] His views were rephrased on the eve of Parliament's consideration of the Libel Act by Thomas Leach, a barrister and police magistrate, who wrote:

> In the institutions of civil government, power and right, are, and must be, convertible terms. Civil power, and civil right, are the mere creatures of the law and know no other limits, than the law imposes upon them. The law speaks the language of prohibition, not of admonition. What it permits to be done, uncensured, and confirms, when it is done, it has delegated the power to do, and the exercise of that power, is of right.[99]

Similarly, jury writers argued that the theory of the special verdict presumed that juries had a valid law-finding role. A jury could render a special verdict in a case if it doubted the validity of a certain application of the law to the facts.[100] If the jury had no such doubts, it was therefore said, the jury might find law as well as fact.[101] This argument, however, established nothing more than that juries applied law to fact. The law might still be said to have been taken from the bench, a point that many tract writers well understood.[102] Finally, many writers cited the practice of defense counsel in seditious libel cases for the proposition that juries

96. *A Treatise on the Right of Juries* (London, 1771), pp. 16, 25, 39.

97. *Ibid.*, pp. 15–16.

98. 4 Douglas 171, 99 *Eng. Rep.* 824–25: "Where a civil power of this sort has been exercised without control, it presumes, nay, by continual usage, it *gives* the right."

99. Leach, *Considerations on the Matter of Libel*, p. 8. See also Charles, Earl Stanhope, *The Rights of Juries defended, and the objections to Mr. Fox's Libel Bill refuted* (London, 1792), pp. 98–99. Fox himself made this argument in introducing his bill in 1791. See Hansard, ed., *Parliamentary History*, 29: cols. 564–65.

100. Blackstone, *Commentaries*, 4:354.

101. Morris, *Letter to . . . Aston*, p. 48: "[W]here they are certain [of the "operation of law"], they may and ought to take the determination upon themselves. The power juries most undoubtedly have, of determining, upon the general issue, both the fact and the law which arises out of that fact." Rous, *Letter to the Jurors*, p. 9; Dagge, *Considerations on Criminal Law*, p. 131.

102. See e.g. Romilly, *Fragment on the Constitutional Power and Duty of Juries upon Trials for Libels*, p. 8.

had the right to consider questions of law. The bench frequently allowed counsel to argue points of law to the jury, or even to question the validity of the official doctrine of seditious libel in their summations.[103]

Yet arguments that relied upon the nature of criminal procedure and trial practice were entirely too fragile to support a far-reaching claim to jury law-finding. The attaint issue was dead (indeed, it had never been a live consideration in criminal cases); the existence of special verdicts, it could be countered, proved only that in some cases the jury had doubts concerning a very restricted "law-applying" role. As for the leeway allowed counsel in their summations, such judicial leniency was hardly a sound foundation for the construction of a matter of jury right. Few laymen sufficiently understood criminal procedure to appreciate what were, in any case, tepid rejoinders to Mansfield's dissertations on the ever growing body of precedent.

Of greater importance, though equally limited in logic, were arguments based upon the nature of the substantive criminal law, not only in political cases but in common-run cases as well. The criminal law, it was stated, was "within reach of the plainest understanding."[104] Such claims, it is true, were only a pale reminder of mid-seventeenth-century assertions concerning the relationship between criminal law and the Scriptures; nor was it the point that the common man could know the law merely by examining his heart. But the criminal law *was* knowable. The entire system of criminal justice assumed as much:

> To say the truth, one could hardly imagine a more extravagant absurdity, than to hold, that a criminal shall not remove the imputation of guilt by pleading ignorance of the law; and yet, that a jury who try him have no capacities to judge of that law.[105]

The logical conclusion of the argument that only the bench and bar possessed the ability to understand the law, it was said, was that "we may daily transgress without being wilfully guilty."[106] The robber, the sneak thief, the slayer: they knew the law as it applied to them. The point was frequently repeated, always with a certain tone of astonishment: if the jury was not to decide law because men of their station lacked the necessary understanding, then the rationale for the official doctrine of seditious libel was inconsistent with the common understanding of *mens*

103. *London Evening Post* (London) (June 21, 1770), p. 3, col. 3; Stanhope, *Rights of Juries defended*, pp. 128 *et seq.*

104. *Treatise on the Right of Juries*, p. 15.

105. *Idem.* See also Loughborough's remarks to the same effect in the Lords. Hansard, ed., *Parliamentary History*, 29: cols. 1297 (1792).

106. *The Gazetteer and New Daily Advertiser* (London) (Dec. 6, 1784), p. 2, col. 2.

*rea.*[107] The analogy to common-run cases—to the common suspect, the "daily transgressor"—lent force to the point, but at the same time the line of argument here involved did not ground a true law-finding theory. To say that the jury possessed the ability to apply the law was not to say that the law they were to apply was to be "found" by them rather than to be set forth by the bench.

# IV

For many commentators the issues of freedom of the press and, more generally, of the subject's right to criticize the government were more important than the jury question. The jury was significant not as an end in itself but as a safeguard against what were seen as the government's self-interested and abusive prosecutions.

Arguments asserting that the jury was the protector of liberty were made both by those who conceived of the jury primarily as a fact-finder and by those who adhered to one or another variant of law-finding theory. Distrust of the government did not commit one to any particular conception of the jury. Yet the doctrine of seditious libel posed a special sort of problem. By drastically reducing the scope for factual determinations, the doctrine placed the defendant's fate almost wholly in official hands.[108] To assert the jury's right to play its traditional fact-finding role required an attack on the libel doctrine itself. Hence, all appeals to the jury necessarily contained an express or implied demand that the jury reject the bench's instructions regarding the allocation of duties between judge and jury. Only a few writers bothered to focus on the problem—it seemed to go without saying. Of the pro-jury writers, Joseph Towers most effectively united the themes of distrust of government and the jury's right to decide the allocation-of-duties question raised by the seditious libel doctrine:

> It would, perhaps, be as unreasonable, that kings should be suffered themselves to determine the bounds of their own prerogative, as that judges should be permitted finally to decide, when the point in contest

107. Joseph Towers, *Observations on the rights and duty of Juries, in trials for Libels* (London, 1784), p. 42. But see the anonymously authored reply to Towers, *An Examination into the rights and duties of Jurors; with some strictures on the Law of Libels.* (By a Gentleman of the Inner Temple) (London, 1785). The author admitted that the promulgation of comprehensible laws was a necessary reform project. But in the meantime: "The end of the laws is obedience: but who will obey them farther than it shall please himself, if every man be allowed to plead an ignorance, almost impossible to be disproved?" (p. 61).

108. *A Second Postscript to a Late Pamphlet, entitled A Letter to Mr. Almon, in Matter of Libel. By the Author of that letter* (London, 1770), p. 15.

is, what is the extent of their own jurisdiction, and what is the extent of that of juries.[109]

Thus, much, if not most, of the literature proclaiming the jury's right to find law as well as fact was concerned with the problem of the allocation of duties between judge and jury. Though many tract writers seem not to have realized it, this conceptualization of the problem hid important disagreements on the law itself. For many writers assigned as facts for the jury matters that the bench did not consider at all relevant. Nonetheless, for many opponents of the official doctrine the claim regarding jury law-finding was simply an exhortation to jurors that they insist that certain questions were matters of fact rather than matters of law. Once the jury had claimed the questions for its own it would merely find the fact, in seditious libel as in other cases.

In the years following *Rex v. Franklin*[110] the assertion that seditiousness was purely a question of fact became quite common. Pro-jury writers argued that, at one level, the question of the seditiousness of the writing could be reduced to the question, Had the writing "scandalized" the government? But what test should the jury apply when making this assessment? The proponents of free speech and press and of the trial jury insisted that mere evidence of negative criticism was not sufficient, that a writing was not criminal unless, at the very least, measurable harm was its probable result.[111] Some characterized the test as more complex still. Robert Morris thought it should be "[t]he purport of expressions, the tendency to sedition, the infamy, the reproach of language"; that, he said, "can never so well be decided as by the common class of mortals to whom the publication is made. Who [is] more interested than juries (for juries are composed of the people) to preserve the peace and order of the state? . . . Juries are a tribunal ever changing as the times; they judge of men's writings and actions by what they see and feel."[112] The decider of fact, George Rous asserted, sounding a theme dear to the hearts of all Wilkites, "must enter into common life . . . must attend to the politics of the day . . . must imbibe the sentiments of the people. . . . Juries taken by lot . . . are peculiarly the proper judges in cases of libel."[113] The

109. Towers, *Observations on the rights and duty of Juries*, p. 29. In his reply to Towers, the author of *An Examination into the rights and duties of Jurors* asserted: "Where else shall we seek the boundaries, by which authority of different courts is restrained, but in the solemn adjudication of the superior courts of justice?" (p. 69).

110. See above, n. 12.

111. Highmore, *Reflections on the distinction usually adopted*, pp. 8 *et seq*. See also the letter from "B. L." in *The Freeholder's Magazine*, vol. 2 (June, 1770), p. 203: "tendency to subvert . . . liberty."

112. Morris, *A Letter to . . . Aston*, pp. 42–43.

113. Rous, *Letter to the Jurors*, p. 51.

determination that must be made, wrote Joseph Towers, required practically no knowledge of the law; the allegedly seditious publications were "generally addressed to men of all professions, and such of them as can be understood only by lawyers, are not very likely to produce tumults or insurrections."[114] Highmore developed the same theme: if one argues that a libel is dangerous because it might arouse the common people, then one assumes that the people understand the writing and therefore must be qualified to be jurors, to determine whether a writing is, in fact, likely to arouse. "No man ever wrote, or read, sedition, but he knew that it was so: and this, without a little more knowledge of the law than is amply sufficient to answer all the purposes of his civil capacity as a citizen."[115] Here, where pro-jury writers referred specifically to the kind of fact-finding they believed relevant to the matter of seditious libel, they frequently drew attention to the jury's traditional assessment of the element of provocation in cases of homicide.[116] It is possible that some pro-jury tract writers, in their attempts to portray seditiousness as a question of fact (as in other cases), were induced to concede more than they otherwise might have. They were led to define seditiousness in terms of a writing's tendency to arouse people, especially that class of common people from which jurors were typically drawn. Some writers seem at times to have turned their attention from the question of the truth or of the intrinsic value of the criticism, matters that were less easily portrayed as facts within the competence of the average jury.[117]

At yet a second level, most writers insisted that proof of scandal did not suffice to establish true seditiousness. There had also to be a finding of intent to scandalize—true criminal intent—indeed, true malice.[118] This,

114. Towers, *Observations on the rights and duty of Juries*, p. 33.
115. Highmore, *Reflections on the distinction usually adopted*, p. 35.
116. See below, text at n. 126.
117. It is possible that most writers thought that three separate tests ought to be applied: the writing must be false; it must have a tendency to "arouse"; the defendant must have intended that the writing "arouse." Indeed, a fourth test may be implied: the defendant must have known that the writing was false. Few authors approached these questions systematically; the highly polemical characters of the tracts leaves the impression that their authors would have required any or all of these tests, although they sometimes addressed one of them as though it were the "true" test. For an excellent discussion of "Father of Candor's" near rejection of the "bad tendency" test see Levy, *Legacy of Suppression*, pp. 149–54. "Father of Candor" [*An Enquiry into the Doctrine, Lately Propagated, concerning Libels, Warrants and the Seizure of Papers . . . in a Letter to Mr. Almon from the Father of Candor* (London, 1764)] implied that true harm or injury ought to be required. This position went beyond that taken by other writers, but it seems that (to the extent "Father of Candor" actually espoused it) it did not include statements that were "wilfully false" (pp. 48, 160). This tract has been reprinted (New York: Da Capo Press, 1970).
118. E.g. *Another Letter to Mr. Almon, in matter of Libel* (London, 1770), p. 31. The author states that the jury ought to acquit if the defendant acted "without any wicked

too, was at times portrayed as a matter of pure fact-finding in terms with which we are now familiar. What words were intended to mean, said Morris, was a factual, hence a jury question.[119] Though establishing that meaning, as Francis Maseres argued, required the jury to draw inferences from facts, those inferences were "secondary" facts, which required "common sense, not technical learning."[120] Juries were especially qualified in cases of libel since they knew "street talk"[121] and could draw the proper inferences. As another writer put it: a "jury of common coffeehouse politicians in London" was best qualified to determine the fact of whether words were meant to be scandalous.[122]

In most tracts, however, the discussion of criminal intent moved well beyond the immediate issue of seditious libel. Here, more than at any other point, writers looked to the role of juries in common-run felonies. Traditionally, juries assessed guilt or innocence largely on the basis of the intent with which an act had been committed. It was within this assessment that the jury, consciously or otherwise, had always applied its own standards of justice, weighing intent and conduct (and perhaps reputation) against the prescribed sanction. By ruling that criminal intent would be inferred by the bench from the writing itself, the bench threatened the more modest but ancient law-finding tradition and, hence, the values that the right to jury trial had long epitomized.

The pro-jury writers' failure to maintain consistently the idea—ought one say, the tactical stance?—that the question of intent could be reduced to a purely factual matter is reflected in their constant analogizing to the jury's role in homicide cases. In homicide cases, as many tract writers pointed out, the bench drew the jury's attention to the differences among malice aforethought, sudden deliberateness, unintentional homicide, and intentional but justifiable homicide, and thereupon left the matter to the jury.[123] The homicide analogy was in fact cited to prove that juries had the

---

intent." He analogizes this to a finding that a defendant in homicide slew "without malice," and then continues: "[I]f the jury are convinced, that although [the defendant] wrote or printed and published it, he did so without any traitorous, seditious, scandalous, or malicious intent, they ought to find him . . . not guilty." (*idem*). See also *A Dialogue between a Country Farmer and a Juryman* (London, 1770), p. 8.

119. Morris, *Letter to . . . Aston*, p. 42.

120. Francis Maseres, *An Enquiry into the extent of the power of juries on trials of indictments or informations* (2nd ed., London, 1785; orig. published 1776), pp. 30–31.

121. *Idem*.

122. *Another Letter to Mr. Almon*, p. 48.

123. E.g. *The Doctrine of Libels and the Duty of Juries fairly stated* (London, 1752), pp. 14–15; *Another Letter to Mr. Almon*, p. 31; Towers, *Observations on the rights and duty of Juries*, p. 21. Standard treatment of the jury's role in homicide encouraged this understanding. See e.g. *Readings upon the Statute Law, by a Gentleman of the Middle Temple*

right to apply law to the facts. It was this traditional law-applying role that the bench was attempting to remove in seditious libel cases, or so many pro-jury writers charged.[124] Thomas Leach, extrapolating from homicide to "all other cases of crime"—by which he meant seditious libel—declared:

> On indictment for murder, the jury decide, not only that the person, charged to have been murdered, did die, in consequence of the act of the defendant, and that such act resulted from a design to kill; which are matters of fact: But they also decide, whether from the particular circumstances, attending the homicide, it is to be ranked in that class, which the law justifies or excuses; or whether from the degree of criminal intention in the defendant it comes within the legal definition of the crime of manslaughter; or amounts to murder, which, if the intention of the libeller be matter of law, are evidently also matters of law.[125]

For Leach, as for so many others across the half-century of active debate, the homicide analogy provided the basic model. Did the defendant strike (did he publish); did the blow cause death (did the writing scandalize); were the blow and death (or the scandal) intended and, if so, was there true malice or was the act justified or excusable? There was bound to be occasional disagreement between judge and jury on what constituted one or another degree of malice, on the limits of justification and excuse, or on their application to a given case. That was often true in homicide and it was certain to be true in seditious libel. The centuries-long tradition of allowing the jury leeway in its application of the law of homicide appears to have colored assumptions about the appropriate judge-jury role in seditious libel. And just as disagreements between judge and jury on the law of homicide were conceptualized as disagreements merely about application of law to fact, so were such disagreements conceptualized by many opponents of the official doctrine of seditious libel.

It is not surprising pro-jury writers drew primarily upon common practices in cases of homicide, a shrinking category,[126] rather than upon such practices in prosecutions for theft, which accounted for most of the business of the assize courts. In the case of theft, mitigation operated

(London, 1725), pp. 97, 102; Giles Jacob, *The Student's Companion: or, The Reason of the Law of England* (London, 1725), p. 106.

124. E.g. *Doctrine of Libels,* pp. 14–15; Romilly, *Fragment on the Constitutional Power and Duty of Juries,* pp. 6 *et seq.*

125. Leach, *Considerations on the Matter of Libel,* p. 7.

126. See Lawrence Stone, "Interpersonal Violence in English Society 1300–1980," *Past and Present* (1983), pp. 22–33; Langbein, "Shaping the Eighteenth-Century Criminal Trial," pp. 44–46.

typically as an open means of commuting the death sentence for many defendants who had clearly committed the act with which they had been charged. Although it was also employed where the evidence was doubtful, we have seen that in this context the concept of "safe" evidence was itself a function of the desire to use execution only sparingly. The thief's behavior was viewed as premeditated and insidious, virtually always as reprehensible, rarely as excusable. It is true that in most cases, especially where there had not been physical violence, the act itself was deemed by many as not meriting capital punishment. Moreover the thief's behavior was often seen as in part the product of social conditions; it was hoped that the thief might be reformed. But the thief's behavior was viewed nonetheless as intrinsically evil.

Homicide presented a more complex problem. The taking of a life had always been viewed as a particularly serious matter. But the defendant's intent could be very evil or fully justified, or something in between. It might be (and often was) excusable under the law. In many cases, verdicts of self defense, accident, or manslaughter served to mitigate the law of sanctions in favor of defendants whose acts (like those perpetrated by thieves) were nonetheless viewed socially as evil. But in other cases, such verdicts reflected a very different social response. The behavior of the true self-defender was fully accepted. And like the true self-defender, the true "public defender" deserved at least vindication, if not approbation.

The homicide analogy was also attractive because the process of the jury's resolution was often hidden from view, perhaps from the conscious understanding of the jurors themselves. It was a process around which myths might grow. Eighteenth-century commentators could suppose that jurors in homicide trials were engaged mainly in a subtle assessment of the defendant's intent at the time he committed the homicide in question. To the observer, the jurors' consideration of the defendant's reputation and character might be assimilated to their determination of the defendant's intent. This consideration need not be understood as the largely separate matter that all contemporaries knew it was in theft cases, where more often than not it influenced the jury only in its "sentencing" role.

Finally, opponents of the official doctrine of seditious libel were greatly influenced by Hawles, who had cited the jury's right to decide among the various kinds of homicide verdicts as evidence of their right to decide law as well as fact. Through Hawles eighteenth-century writers—perhaps without realizing it—reached back to the parliamentary censure of Chief Justice Kelyng and, ultimately, to de facto practices of medieval juries. The daily practice in cases involving theft conditioned attitudes regarding the role of mercy and the right of the jury to share assessment of just deserts. But it was the jury's role in homicide cases that allowed the strongest, most attractive, and best documented argument for the jury's right to "apply" the law within the "factual" assessment of whether the defendant had acted with a truly criminal intent.

# V

The claim that the jury's inalienable role was that which it played daily in routine felonies—the application of the law that had been set forth by the bench—lay close to the core of the attack on the law of seditious libel. The true law-finding issues of the debate—the jury's capacity to comprehend the law sufficiently to determine whether the judge had chosen apt precedents or had interpreted the relevant common law or statutes correctly—would continue to attract great attention, but the more routine discussion of whether the jury had the right merely to apply the law in seditious libel "as in other cases" was perhaps an equally important aspect of the debate. When the jury writers addressed this most basic level of law-finding they revealed something of their conception of the nature and purpose of the jury trial in all criminal cases.

We have seen that in practice the criminal trial had always been person—as well as act—oriented. Assessment of the defendant's character had traditionally affected the jury's view of his just deserts.[127] Character and credibility of course bore on the question of whether the defendant had committed the act alleged in the indictment, and in that sense the jury found the fact that it was charged to find. This observation was contained in *The Doctrine of Libels and the Duty of Juries fairly stated*, published in 1752:

> [I]f from the character of the person libelled they think they have reason to believe, that he has been guilty of those facts, and that from the character of the person accused of libelling they have reason to believe [the defendant] would not have charged any man with such facts unless he had known him to be guilty, they ought to bring their verdict Not Guilty. . . . This is a latitude which every jury ought to take, and a latitude which will be of great importance for every man to endeavor to preserve a good character in his neighborhood.[128]

---

127. See Beattie, "Crime and the Courts," pp. 173–74, 179, for a discussion of the impact of reputation and character on verdicts in the eighteenth century. These considerations were influential also at the reprieve and pardoning stages. See above, Chapter 7, nn. 50–54 and accompanying text. It is likely that judicial and royal attitudes influenced those of trial jurors, and vice versa. Indeed, this dialectical pattern of influence was probably present from the beginning of trial by jury.

128. *Doctrine of Libels*, p. 10.

This "latitude" was implicit in every jury trial. Thus George Stanhope in his sermon entitled *The Duty of Juries*, which was delivered in 1701 at the Lent Assizes, conceded that in close cases

> [w]e may allow some abatements for a criminal action alleged against a person unblameable for the main, and impute it to ignorance, or sudden transport or passion, or misadventure, rather than to malice and wicked design; which abatements cannot fairly be allowed to those abandoned wretches, who are scandalous for mischievious dispositions and a profligate conversation.[129]

The problem was how to delineate between appropriate and inappropriate "abatements." That depended upon the sufficiency of the proof offered at trial, of which juries were without dispute the final judges. The official doctrine of seditious libel avoided this assessment entirely. The only facts left to the jury were so fully proved as to be virtually undeniable, and there was in any case nothing to balance against them, since intent was "implied" as a matter of law. What the opponents of the official law were demanding was the return to the jury, as a question of fact, or of application of law to fact, of the complicated, intensely social question of criminal intent.

The seditious libel literature often assigned to the jury an even more open-ended role than the above discussion of criminal intent suggests. Fundamentally, according to jury writers, whether in prosecutions for seditious libel, homicide, theft, or any other criminal offense, the defense of the general verdict amounted to the defense of the defendant's right to a "merciful" judgment by peers. And "mercy" might be appropriate even in cases where the defendant was guilty under the law. The core of the power to decide "law as well as fact" was the jury's right to nullify the law in particular cases without rejecting it as a general matter.

That the English criminal law was a "merciful" law was a cliche in the eighteenth-century literature.[130] The identification of the jury with mercy operated on two levels. Most writers, referring to the fact-finding process, asserted that, as Towers put it: "Where the matter is doubtful, in criminal prosecutions, an acquittal is always most consonant to the spirit of the

---

129. George Stanhope, *The Duty of Juries* (London, 1701), p. 12. Stanhope added: "But still . . . these are but probabilities and presumptions and must come in their proper place. For where they are admitted to overbalance credible and full peremptory proof, there we offend against the Text (i.e., Levit. XIX, 15) and have respect of persons in judgment" (*idem*).

130. E.g. *An Inquiry into the Doctrine Lately Propagated, concerning Attachments of Contempt* (London, 1769), pp. 40–41; *Treatise on the Right of Juries*, p. 42; Paley, *Principles of Moral and Political Philosophy*, p. 522.

law of England."[131] Hinting at a yet broader role for the granting of mercy, Highmore observed: "[T]he jury know that by their verdict alone, and not by the knowledge of law in the judge, the prisoner at the Bar must be acquitted or suffer death."[132] As in the capital felonies of murder or theft, he implied, so in the noncapital high misdemeanor of seditious libel. Morris drew an analogy to the royal power of pardon: "Like the king in the extension of mercy [the jury] make so noble a use of their power when their consciences permit them to acquit."[133] The anonymous author of *A Treatise on the Right of Juries* (1771) introduced his discussion of seditious libel with a conventional encomium of the merciful quality of the law in common felony cases:

> Mercy is the characteristic and leading feature of an English jury. They are apt now and then to err upon the favourable side: but let us consult the gentle spirit of our law, and we shall find it would rather dispense with the punishment of a hundred guilty persons, than permit a single innocent man to suffer. If on the other hand the jury should happen to be vindictive, the King's pardon interferes, to counteract them. The good sense and liberal feelings of the law in this well tempered regulation cannot be enough admired: It impowers juries to acquit absolutely, but reduces and softens their power to convict by enabling the Crown in its mercy to withhold punishment.[134]

In his *Address to the People of Scotland*, William Smellie described this commonplace but significant aspect of the jury's application of mercy. Commenting upon the statutory extension of jury trial to Scotland, and borrowing the terminology of the English seditious libel debate, he asserted:

> If, therefore, the power of judging of the law as well as the fact, were annihilated, the very intention of the legislature would be defeated; because the courts, and not the jury, would then be the sole judges. Intention is the essence of crimes. The facts [charged] may be distinctly proved. But, if from particular circumstances, the jury are convinced in their own minds, that the [defendant] either had no intention to commit a crime, or that the crime is not of so heinous a nature as to merit the punishment concluded for in the indictment, in all cases of this kind, the jury have not only a right, but they are bound,

---

131. Towers, *Observations on the rights and duty of Juries*, pp. 109–10. See also Romilly, *Fragment on the Constitutional Power and Duty of Juries*, p. 3.

132. Highmore, *Reflections on the distinction usually adopted*, p. 26.

133. Morris, *Letter to . . . Aston*, p. 40. Morris and other Wilkites opposed the widespread use of discretion in the courts, seeing it as a device by which authorities extended or withdrew the subjects' rights almost at will. They appear to have made an exception of the jury. See Brewer, "Wilkites and the Law," pp. 160–61.

134. *Treatise on the Right of Juries*, p. 42.

by the spirit of their oaths, and by the laws of God and man, to find the [defendant] Not Guilty of the crime. . . . They consider the nature of the crime, and the punishment that ought or ought not to be inflicted. In *all* such cases, the jury must necessarily determine both the law and the fact.[135]

Finding law as well as fact, applying law to fact, or rendering a "merciful verdict," amounted to assessing the nature of both the defendant's intent and his act in the light of the punishment that would follow upon his conviction. The jury might approve of the defendant's behavior, as in some political cases, or might disapprove of it but deem the prescribed punishment too severe, as in some common-run felonies. Very different underlying motives, to be sure, but nonetheless, at least within the confines of some jury tracts, the fusion of jury theories was complete.[136]

# VI

Fox's Libel Act marked a triumph for those whose concept of the English constitution was grounded in history. It vindicated the historic role of the jury as the last line of defense against executive tyranny. Although precedent could be found for treating seditious libel as an anomaly, the prior official doctrine nonetheless seemed to many a dangerous departure from deeply held assumptions about English governance. At one level Parliament's concern was with the law. Fox's Act was couched as a declaration of the common law, resting not on precedent but on general principles of that law.[137] Parliament looked first to the law regarding criminal trials generally. That law was assumed to govern; exceptions would be tolerated only where that law itself provided compelling reasons for them. Parliament's solution to the seditious libel problem was also the result both of politics and of the nearly irresistible force of broad constitutional principles. The pressures for the expansion

135. William Smellie, *An Address to the People of Scotland on the Nature, Powers and Privileges of Juries* (Edinburgh, 1815; orig. published 1784), pp. 13–15.

136. But see Maseres, *An Enquiry into the extent of the power of juries*. Maseres argued that consideration of the seriousness of an offense found by the jury was a matter for the court: "For if it shall be made to appear by just and legal reasonings at the bar, that the writing and publishing the paper in question, though it was done deliberately, and has the tendency ascribed to it in the information [as found by the jury], yet it is not an offense of such great and public consequence as to have been an object of legal punishment, it will be the duty of the court to forebear giving judgment. . . . But this . . . is a matter which judges only have a right to determine, either upon a motion made before them on behalf of the defendant in arrest of judgment, or of their own accord" (p. 34).

137. See above, n. 62 and accompanying text.

of rights of speech and press were enormous.[138] Those rights might still be limited (few questioned punishing truly seditious writings), but they could not be reined in through what appeared to society at large to be a drastic revision of the historically vindicated balance of power between judge and jury. Retreat to the technical high ground of "questions of law" served only further to expose the government to attack by the opposition. In manipulating the balance of authority at trial, the government was seen to be manipulating one of the institutions through which it had historically ruled and on which it rested its claim to legitimacy. Having administered the law largely with the aid of the jury (one is tempted to conclude), the Crown and courts found they could not now govern mainly through the bench.[139]

To appreciate the way in which the government was captured by its own administrative history, we must recognize how little England's rulers controlled the circumstances that made law-finding, or discretionary fact-finding, a dominant element in the administration of the criminal law. For the most part, prosecution for felony proceeded in accordance with the attitudes of society at large. The alliance between authority and mercy-granting juries reflected a mixture of wise policy, acquiescence in the inevitable, and shared assumptions about justice.[140] We have seen that we must be cautious about extending the argument that authorities manipulated the selective enforcement of the criminal law in order to secure the deference of those they ruled to the problem of the use of the criminal trial jury.[141] If we focus too narrowly on the administration of the criminal law in the eighteenth century, we obscure the question of the roots of the system of mitigation. These practices were historically the

138. Holdsworth, *History of English Law*, 10:672–74. Holdsworth took the view that the judges were right in their statement of the law, but that "it was clear that the law as laid down by the judges was quite out of harmony with the practical ideas and public opinion of the time" (p. 674). Levy (*Legacy of Suppression*, pp. 249–52) briefly discusses the tract campaign that preceded the passage of Fox's Libel Act. I discuss some aspects of the debates concerning the Act above, n. 64. Much remains to be said concerning those debates and the political views and interests of those in Parliament. Relatively few members of the Commons and the Lords spoke on the bill. Their views cannot be taken as the views of all, or even most, members. A true legislative history of the Act is badly needed; its results might lead to reconsideration of my analysis of the meanings of law- and fact-finding in the extraparliamentary debate concerning seditious libel in the period 1732–92.

139. This conclusion is necessarily tentative. I have stated the point broadly, and mean it to say as much, but it may be that it applies mainly to the disparity between the treatment of routine cases on the one hand and seditious libel on the other and that contemporaries viewed that disparity as an isolated phenomenon.

140. See above, Chapter 7, section IV.

141. Hay ("Property, Authority and the Criminal Law") makes the argument with respect to Parliament's refusal to reform the law of sanctions. He makes little reference to the role of the jury. For discussion of Hay's views on the jury see above, Chapter 7, n. 156.

by-product of the criminal law in theft and homicide cases where complainant, defendant, and jury had frequently been (and often still were), relatively speaking, members of the same class.[142] The Crown and the bench and their attendant officials had an interest in overseeing the maintenance of order, but frequently they played the role of referees who lacked the resources, time, or stake in the outcome to prevent the jury from reaching a verdict according to its own sense of justice. Moreover, these practices, which long predated the eighteenth century, reflected social attitudes that were not easily managed or always willingly tolerated. This is not to say that authorities failed to capitalize on these sources of potential weakness, consciously or otherwise. It is to say that to the extent authorities reaped the benefits of governing through merciful justice, the interaction of rulers and ruled was complex and two-sided. In important ways, authorities prevailed at the behest of those they sought to rule.

Our study of the seditious libel debate suggests that in yet another, related respect we must modify our understanding of the political and social implications of eighteenth-century law enforcement. The two strands of theory regarding the jury's rightful role could not forever remain separate. Jury law-finding in political cases could not be kept distinct from jury resolution in common-run felonies. In the popular mind at least, the strength and reach of the arguments against the seditious libel doctrine were almost certainly influenced by the nature of jury practice in common-run cases. Might it be that the same authorities who allowed juries to share the powers of mitigation in common-run cases found themselves by virtue of that policy on the defensive in prosecutions for seditious libel? If so, we must recognize that authorities sometimes reaped not deference but a bitter harvest largely of their own making. The irony is less striking than might at first appear: the policy of sharing powers of mitigation was, as we have seen, little more than acquiescence in practices authorities could not have eliminated easily. Having (over the

---

142. See Beattie, *Crime and the Courts*, chs. 5, 6; Langbein, "*Albion's* Fatal Flaws," p. 107. But see Douglas Hay, "War, Dearth, and Theft in the Eighteenth Century," *Past and Present*, no. 95 (1982), p. 154, n. 100. There is need for more research on this matter. My essential point is that, whatever the status difference between suspects and their accusers (and jurors), the status difference between accusers (and jurors) and the bench was frequently far greater. Moreover, accusers and accused were sometimes from the same locale, nearly always from the same county; judges oversaw resolution of local disputes to which they were themselves outsiders, both geographically and socially. This was probably as much or even more the case in earlier centuries. So long as jurors typically took their lead from the bench, the bench countenanced substantial leeway in less serious cases. And even when jurors took their lead from the bench, they were responding to judicial attitudes that were themselves in part the reflection of long-held and widely shared community standards.

centuries) converted great weaknesses into moderate strength, England's rulers found that that strength had, after all, its natural limits.[143]

It has been wisely observed that English authorities came to accept as binding certain concepts of due process in which they had cloaked their exercise of pure power.[144] Something akin to this phenomenon seems to have been at work in Parliament's resolution of the seditious libel crisis. The Libel Act debates reflected a consensus on one principle only, that the criminal trial jury should have a right to return a general verdict on all facts in issue. That principle was recognized as having long constitutional standing. To deny it (or seem to deny it) in trials for seditious libel was not only to offend that principle but to risk political fire for offending it precisely in those circumstances that suggested the worst sort of motives.[145]

Many in Parliament as of 1770 were persuaded by Mansfield's defense of the official doctrine of seditious libel.[146] Precedent and the uniqueness of seditious libel seemed to ground an exception to the general rule.[147] What, then, doomed the exception? Constitutionalism and politics are rarely separable. Parliament responded to both without being able to isolate either. The principle of a right to a general verdict in all cases had come to be identified socially with the prevailing theories regarding the purposes of the criminal trial jury. The principle was accepted by some

143. I have made this argument in the present essay with regard to the administration of criminal law in the eighteenth century. I believe that it applies as well to earlier periods. Judges in the medieval period may have sensed that their relaxed treatment of juries in most cases made it difficult for them to control juries in those few cases in which they took a real interest. The early modern bench may have analyzed the resistance to fining jurors in similar terms. The phenomena I am describing were present from the outset of the jury-trial experience. The contest over the doctrine of seditious libel was of special importance because it involved widespread political debate and revealed the limits of authority during the very period in which authority was (ostensibly) coming to have relatively substantial control over the administration of criminal law. I shall return to this point in the conclusion to this book (Chapter 9).

144. Thompson, *Whigs and Hunters*, pp. 258–69. "And the rulers were, in serious senses, whether willingly or unwillingly, the prisoners of their own rhetoric; they played the games of power according to rules which suited them, but they could not break those rules or the whole game would be thrown away." See also Hay, "Property, Authority and the Criminal Law," pp. 32 *et seq.*; "Introduction," in Brewer and Styles, eds., *An Ungovernable People*, p. 20: "[T]he imprimatur of the law conferred only limited power on those who were its beneficiaries. Both the *modus operandi* of the law and the ideology that lay behind it served to constrain authority and to limit those who tried to manipulate the legal process."

145. For references to the Libel Act debates see above, n. 64.

146. See above, n. 25.

147. But see the speech of Sir Thomas Townshend, who refused to make an exception in the case of libel. Hansard, ed., *Parliamentary History*, 16: cols. 1162–63. "He whom nature or education has not qualified for determining the guilt of a libel, is unqualified to sit as judge in cases of life and death" (col. 1162).

because they believed its rejection would appear (wrongly) to be a rejection of more general principles that all in fact accepted. It was accepted by others who would themselves have viewed a rejection in that way. At base in seditious libel was the historic role of the jury as a safeguard against tyranny. So long as that issue could be kept from being entangled with others, the sides might be clearly drawn; much would depend upon whether one viewed the settlement of 1689 as having rendered the safeguard unnecessary. But it could not be kept separate. So long as there were many in society who distrusted the role of authorities in seditious libel cases, the settlement would never be solely a matter of institutional framework as such. It would of course be a matter of the movement for free speech and of the liberties of subjects generally. No doubt that is how most members of Parliament saw the issue. But it would also be a matter of how society regarded the practice of institutions, of the very real importance of de facto powers, such as those of the jury in common-run felony cases. The idea that discretionary lay fact-finding was central to the administration of justice had taken on a life of its own, and no part of that administration could be shielded from it. Authorities could not, as it were, "bifurcate" the practice of trial by jury. The same judges who tolerated, or even encouraged, mitigated verdicts in homicide or theft could not easily explain why juries ought to play so limited a role in seditious libel. Notions of consistency and coherence were integral to the late eighteenth-century conception of justice. Nothing could gainsay them, not even the attendant risk of more subtle forms of inconsistency and incoherence—i.e., inconsistent jury verdicts—as the price of seditious libel law reform.[148]

---

148. Mansfield in *St. Asaph's Case* (*State Trials*, 21:1040) stressed the problem of inconsistent verdicts: "To be free, is to live under a government by law. . . . Miserable is the condition of individuals, dangerous is the condition of the state, if there is no certain law, or, which is the same thing, no certain administration of the law to protect individuals, or to guard the state. . . . In opposition to this, what is contended for? That the law shall be in every particular cause what any twelve men . . . shall be inclined to think, liable to no review, and subject to no control. . . . Under such an administration of law, no man could tell, no counsel could advise, whether a paper was or was not punishable." See also John Bowles, *Considerations on the Respective Rights of Judge and Jury: particularly upon Trials for Libel, occasioned by an expected motion of the Right Hon. Charles-James Fox* (London, 1791), p. 4: "It would be next to impossible that their [i.e., the jurors'] decision should accord with any uniform and fixed principles. The consequence would be, the prevalence of confusion and uncertainty in all legal proceedings where intervention of a jury takes place. A total loss of freedom must of course ensue; for the essence of freedom consists in the certainty of law." These considerations surfaced in Parliament both in 1770 [e.g. Hansard, ed., *Parliamentary History*, 16: col. 1146 (Thurlow); col. 1186 (De Grey)] and 1792 [e.g. *ibid.*, 29: col. 1297 (The Lord Chancellor)].

The recognition of the right of the criminal trial jury to return a general verdict resolved one immediate political problem, but it contributed little to the resolution of some other longstanding problems of the criminal law. One of the important side effects of the seditious libel controversy was its intensification of the prevailing social conceptions of the criminal trial jury. The magnification of those conceptions and their translation to the sphere of political misdemeanors may have affected the administration of the law generally and delayed the movement for reform of the law of sanctions.[149]

It is possible, of course, that the seditious libel problem and its resolution only temporarily delayed and then ultimately accelerated the movement for reform of the law of sanctions. The penal reformers' argument against jury law-finding—i.e., against merciful fact-finding in common-run cases—lost some of its appeal when the integrity of the jury system seemed to be threatened in political misdemeanors. Resistance to the bench involved a glorification of jury independence; criticism of juries on all fronts may have become unfashionable. But in the years following passage of the Libel Act, juries, as is well known, convicted more often than they had before in cases of seditious libel.[150] The general verdict allowed the tenor of the times to take its toll, and perhaps reminded observers of the volatility of jury attitudes. In those years, the warnings of Mansfield, John Bowles, and others might have seemed well taken:[151] the defendant's security was at risk; no one could be certain how juries would "apply" the law. One obvious solution to the problem of the jury that convicted against the law was a fuller right of appeal.[152] But for the

149. This is, of course, a matter of speculation. Doubtless, many factors delayed the impact of the criticisms of the late-eighteenth-century reformers. See below, Chapter 9, section I.

150. Holdsworth, *History of English Law*, 10:693. Levy, *Legacy of Suppression*, pp. 252–54. Both Holdsworth and Levy rely heavily on Stephen's account of the aftermath of the Act. See Stephen, *History of the Criminal Law of England*, 2:362–63. See also May, *Constitutional History*, 2:34 *et seq.*

151. See above, n. 148.

152. The Act itself (32 Geo. 3, c. 60, sect. IV) provided "[t]hat in case the jury shall find the defendant or defendants guilty, it shall or may be lawful for the said defendant or defendants to move in arrest of judgment, on such grounds and in such manner as by law he or they might have done before the passing of this act." See Holdsworth, *History of English Law*, 10:691–92. Holdsworth takes a view of the act that is perhaps too sanguine. He correctly stated that the question for the court was "whether the prosecution has satisfied the onus of proving that [the writing] is libellous." Whether "the settlement made by Fox's Act [was] very favourable to the accused" rests to some extent on one's view of the legal standards (including the relevance of truth) then existing that the court were always ready to apply and that juries might or might not apply depending upon the political climate. It rests also as a practical matter, on the way in which trial courts typically assessed the prosecution's case in seditious libel cases. Until a thorough study has been made of the

time being, the uncertainty of the law produced by the general verdict in seditious libel cases may have made it easier for penal reformers to resume criticizing jury discretion in common-run cases. The solution there was not to do away with the general verdict—that matter had been placed beyond reach—but rather to achieve certainty of law and punishment through the unmitigated imposition of humane and moderate sanctions.

The constitutionalization of the general verdict perhaps raised the stakes for the penal reformers. Having reidentified the jury as the quintessential democratic institution in English society, Parliament would have to demonstrate definitively what eighteenth-century reform proponents had only suggested: that the prevailing practice of jury-based mitigation in routine felonies had grown to such proportions that it was making a mockery of the law. Nothing less would suffice before Parliament could reduce the jury's role in common-run cases. Changes in jury trial would follow, rather than precede, changes in English attitudes toward the entire problem of the administration of the criminal law.[153]

treatment by the post-1792 bench of motions in arrest of judgment—in the light of the evidence proffered at trial by prosecution and defense in seditious libel cases—our own judgment must be reserved.

153. See below, Chapter 9.

# 9

# Epilogue and Conclusion

This concluding chapter falls into two principal parts, an epilogue and a summary, to each of which I have devoted two sections. In section I, I shall deal briefly and selectively with the background to the Victorian reform of the law of sanctions. I shall stress those developments that reveal the nature of the near impasse that confronted the English in the administration of criminal justice by the early nineteenth century.

From the perspective I have chosen, the movement for reform of sanctions appears to have involved, inter alia, a widespread rejection of traditional assumptions about the virtues of jury-based intervention and, indeed, about the entire longstanding system of mitigation. Although the precise reasons for this transformation in contemporary thought remain elusive, the sea change it reflected seems, as I shall suggest in section II, a most natural denouement to the centuries-long process I have been describing. In section III, I discuss the themes of the book at length and identify some important questions that my work raises but which I am as yet unable to answer; I also allude to problems that fall within the subject of this book but which I do not treat in any of the essays that I have brought together. In the final section, I recapitulate my central arguments in a more direct fashion.

## I

The movement for reform of the law of sanctions gained momentum in the early decades of the nineteenth century and bore fruit by the early years of Victoria's reign. Between 1830 and 1840, Parliament removed the capital sanction from many of the less serious offenses. Capital punishment was retained for those offenses for which, as it happened, juries had from earliest times been relatively willing to convict offenders; it was no longer the nominal punishment for those offenses for which the jury had long served as one of the principal institutions of mitigation. Reform of sanctions thus brought to an end a long phase in the history of the English criminal trial jury. Jury-based mitigation of sanctions would continue, but at a greatly reduced level. In the popular mind, and in reality, the jury would usually adhere to the letter of the law.

The widely observed role of the jury as mitigator of the law of sanctions figured prominently in several aspects of the early-nineteenth-century movement for law reform. This is the final stage in the English debate over the trial jury that I shall discuss. My discussion will be brief, for the movement for reform has been thoroughly chronicled, and my own purposes are limited.[1] For the most part, my observations are retrospective, offered by way of conclusion.

The movement for reform of sanctions had its roots in the mid-seventeenth-century movement for law reform.[2] But it was the statutory manipulation of benefit of clergy in the early eighteenth century that represented the first important step in the direction of reform. We have seen that the resulting practical penology of the period both built upon longstanding mitigation practice and accommodated the notion that the threat of death was a necessary deterrent.[3] Capital punishment would be imposed in only a handful of cases, but those cases would be identified as the residue of a winnowing process. The offender would be kept in doubt as to his fate for as long as it was deemed necessary and appropriate. Reform was shaped—and limited—by the perceived need for an element of terror in eighteenth-century penology.

Contemporaries sometimes explained the need to maintain the death sanction as the price for not maintaining a large and professional police force.[4] Resistance to abandoning the legacy of a makeshift local and amateur constabulary prevailed not only among the county-based justices of the peace and their allies but also among the urban working class. Fears that a national police force would spawn both political centralization and oppression by the employer class intensified toward the end of the eighteenth century.[5] Proponents of a police system succeeded in 1792 in

---

1. For a comprehensive statement of the reform movement see Beattie, *Crime and the Courts*, chs. 12–13. Beattie's masterful "Conclusion" (ch. 13) stresses the long-term preparation for the early nineteenth-century reforms and the speed with which reform was finally effected. I treat the developments involved sketchily and only in relation to the issue of the trial jury. See also Radzinowicz, *History of English Criminal Law*, vol. 1; W. R. Cornish, "Criminal Justice and Punishment," in Cornish et al., eds., *Crime and Law in Nineteenth Century Britain* (Irish University Press, 1978), pp. 7–65; and Douglas Hay's astute summary essay, "Crime and Justice in Eighteenth- and Nineteenth-Century England," in Norval Morris and Michael Tonry, eds., *Crime and Justice: An Annual Review of Research*, vol. 2 (Chicago, 1980), pp. 45–84.

2. See above, Chapter 5, section V.

3. See above, Chapter 7.

4. Langbein, "*Albion's* Fatal Flaws," pp. 115–16; David Philips, "'A New Engine of Power and Authority': The Institutionalization of Law-Enforcement in England 1780–1830," in Gatrell et al., eds., *Crime and the Law*, pp. 155–89. See also Beattie, *Crime and the Courts*, ch. 2.

5. Philips, "'A New Engine of Power and Authority,'" pp. 171–74.

passing an act for a stipendiary magistracy,[6] but not until 1829 did they secure legislation establishing the basis for a truly professional force.[7] In the intervening years the movements for reform of sanctions and for establishment of a professional police system dovetailed. The proponents of each reform fought against the common rationalization of the prevailing scheme of criminal administration: a police system would invite tyranny; in its absence, order depended upon the threat of the gallows; the decision regarding the gallows ought to be intrinsic to the prosecution of each individual offender.

In theory, the selection of offenders for capital punishment on a case-by-case basis need not have involved the criminal trial jury more than for the initial determination of whether the suspect was guilty. Once the jury had found the defendant guilty the matter of sentencing could have been left to the bench and the Crown. We have seen that most eighteenth-century criminal law reformers, as well as apologists for the prevailing system of criminal law, favored centering the entire mitigation process (to the extent that it was to exist) in the Crown. We have also seen, however, that most reformers viewed such a resolution of existing problems as unrealistic. They recognized that, in practice, the jury would not always find the defendant guilty and leave his fate to higher authorities. For the most part, reformers agreed that until the law of sanctions had been altered, juries would inevitably (and justifiably) play a substantial role.[8]

The system was even more complicated than most commentators indicated. In many cases the jury did in fact leave the decision on sentencing to the bench and Crown. But that was within the context of a system in which the jury possessed a great deal of power, should it wish to use it, and in which the jury's deference to the bench and the bench's deference to the jury were mutual. Moreover, in many cases involving jury-based mitigation the jury took its lead from the bench; again, the jury's willingness to do so must be understood in light of the fact that when the jury wanted to go its own way, it had the power to do so. Commentators may not have well understood the dynamics of the system, but their essential insight was correct: so long as the law of sanctions remained harsh, an entirely official system of mitigation of that law could not easily come into being.

Law reformers in the early nineteenth century accepted the jury's role within the existing system as a given. Like the eighteenth-century reformers, their principal objective was certainty of the law. Thus they

---

6. Stat. 32 Geo. 3, c. 53.
7. Stat. 10 Geo. 4, c. 44.
8. See above, Chapter 7, section III.

argued for reform of the law of sanctions so that mitigation would not often be required. They did not, however, fall back on the argument that mitigation might continue so long as it was solely in the hands of the Crown. Romilly, in his famous speech in Parliament in 1810, framed the issue in terms that others were to follow.[9] The jury, Romilly argued, had been placed in the impossible position of having to choose in each case between imposing a sanction that it believed to be far too cruel in the hope that the Crown would mitigate it and committing an act of perjury.[10] Not only did such perjury undermine the system of deterrence, but it also bred disrespect for the law. The reformers chose not to see the jury as part of a quasi-legitimate sentencing process, nor to view the oath as imposing responsibility to do justice in accordance with the terms in which juries had traditionally acted. Thus by the early nineteenth century the jury's longstanding tradition of merciful application of the law had come to be described as a kind of jury lawlessness. Far from blaming the jury for undertaking this lawless role, however, reformers sympathized with them in their plight, and portrayed themselves as friends of the jury who would save it from the "dilemma" that it faced daily.[11]

In his 1810 speech Romilly developed a theme that he had introduced decades before. Romilly had originally accepted Paley's description of the system of criminal law, asserting, in his reply to Madan, that Parliament had not intended that the law be enforced literally.[12] He had both accepted the notion that Parliament intended the law to be enforced selectively and, true to the principles of the new penology, attacked such a system. By 1810 Romilly had come to believe that, even if Parliament had not intended that the law be enforced literally, there were no clear principles behind the process of selection. On the basis of statistical research, he concluded that patterns of enforcement were always changing and were determined by the mood and inclinations of jury, judge, and Crown.[13] Romilly now argued, moreover, that the system led in practice to decisions by the judge that ought to have been made, if at all, by the jury. He observed that in many cases where the jury convicted the

9. Sir Samuel Romilly, *Observations on the Criminal Law of England* (London, 1810) (this tract contains the substance of Romilly's speech in Parliament).

10. *Ibid.*, pp. 22–23.

11. See below, n. 22 and accompanying text.

12. See above, Chapter 7, text at n. 139.

13. Romilly, *Observations on the Criminal Law*, pp. 16 *et seq.* At one point Romilly stated: "In this uncertain administration of justice, not only different judges act upon different principles, but the same judge, under the same circumstances, acts differently at different times" (p. 19). Several years earlier, Romilly had concluded that many capital felonies were the result of changes in the value of money, a severity that resulted from "no intention of the legislature, but altogether from accidental circumstances." Romilly, *Memoirs*, 2:230 (letter to M. Dumont, Aug. 25, 1807).

defendant, the bench subsequently reprieved him so that a pardon might be sought from the Crown. In these cases, Romilly argued, the bench based its decision upon facts which it itself had found.[14] Here again Romilly opened up a line of argument that others were to pursue. In the years that followed, the prevailing system of criminal administration was portrayed as totally unpredictable.[15] According to critics, the jury was left to guess what the bench might do in a given case, while the bench made its own assumptions about the grounds of the jury's decision. The result of the prevailing system of criminal justice, it was asserted, was that it actually produced crime.[16] In drawing this conclusion, reformers were perhaps fooled by the fact that there were more prosecutions in the early nineteenth century than in the recent past, an increase that probably reflected better enforcement rather than more crime.

Romilly's followers characterized the position of the jury in even more ironic terms. Sir William Grant, Master of the Rolls, argued that the jury was forced to adopt a kind of discretion that the jury was never intended to have.[17] Although this was true if one looks to the earliest period of the criminal trial jury, it hardly did justice to the long history of official acquiescence in jury mitigation of the law. Grant went on to criticize the exercise of discretion in a conventional manner. The law of sanctions, he argued, forced jurors to violate their consciences.[18] He played on the famous phrase, "pious perjury": like many of Blackstone's successors, Grant took the term "perjury" very seriously. He suggested that juries did not trust others to use discretion and so took it upon themselves; indeed, he noted, judges encouraged juries to do so. Grant seems not to have supposed that this kind of judicial steering of juries produced a fairly predictable scheme of resolutions. Rather he saw it only as contributing to the jury's dilemma.[19]

The dilemma of the criminal trial jury was often alluded to by early nineteenth-century law reformers in their argument for reform of the law

14. *Ibid.*, pp. 26–27.

15. See e.g. Lord Brougham's review of Romilly's published speech in *The Edinburgh Review*, vol. 19 (Edinburgh, 1811), pp. 396–97; John William Polidori, "On the Punishment of Death," in *The Pamphleteer*, vol. 8, no. 15 (London, 1816), p. 294.

16. E.g. *A Brief Address to the People of England on the Criminal Law* (London, 1827), p. 10.

17. Sir William Grant: speech in Parliament, 1811. Hansard, ed., *Parliamentary History*, vol. 19, App., cols. lxvi–lxvii.

18. *Ibid.*, p. 13.

19. *Idem*: "Ought laws to be so framed that there must be a continual struggle in the minds of your jurymen? . . . [Jurors] can not be unmindful of the lenity of the judges; but notwithstanding this, they are unwilling to risk anything: they will not trust to another the use of a discretion which they have the power and disposition to exercise themselves." See also Romilly, *Memoirs*, 2:230 (letter to Dumont, Aug. 25, 1807).

of sanctions. In 1819, and again in the 1830s and 1840s, parliamentary committees produced reports on the criminal law which portrayed prosecutors and jurors in the most sympathetic fashion. They had been left, it was asserted, to implement a system that was essentially unworkable, unfair, and counterproductive.[20] Parliamentary deliberations may have been influenced by the testimony of victims of crime, especially artisans and other men of small commerce, who had come to see the role of the jury in the same way that reformers saw it. Prospective victims petitioned Parliament for reform of the law of sanctions, asking that the death sentence be removed from offenses against their property so that offenders would be more likely to suffer some substantial punishment and the law would be more likely to deter criminal behavior.[21] Grand jurors and trial jurors also joined the clamor for reform. They too petitioned Parliament, urging reform that would save jurors from the dilemma that it now seemed nearly everyone agreed was their awful fate.[22]

The movements for reform of the police system and for reform of the law of sanctions coincided with the movement for reform of prisons.[23] Transportation to the American colonies had ended abruptly with the movement for independence, and for a time the English had experimented with incarceration of convicts in the famous "hulks" on the Thames.[24] Transportation to New South Wales began in the late eighteenth century, but by then the movement for incarceration and rehabilitation of convicts in English penitentiaries was already well under way. Some of the literature of this movement, the roots of which reach back into the seventeenth century, featured descriptions of life in English prisons where, it was claimed, conditions were brutal and virtually calculated to produce a large and hardened criminal class.[25]

One of the themes of the prison reform literature dealt with the effect on the criminal class of the prevailing system of sanctions. Prisoners were portrayed as fully aware that participants at every stage in the criminal process sought to prevent imposition of the harsh sanctions provided for by law. In 1831, Edward Wakefield, who had spent time in Newgate,

20. See e.g. "Report from the Select Committee on Criminal Laws," July 8, 1819, in *Parliamentary Papers*, (585), vol. 8 (1819), pp. 3 *et seq.*; "Second Report from His Majesty's Commissioners on Criminal Law," June 9, 1836, in *Parliamentary Papers*, vol. 36 (1836), pp. 183 *et seq.*

21. See e.g. "The Petition of the Master Calico Printers in the Vicinity of London" (Feb. 27, 1811), reprinted in Radzinowicz, *History of English Criminal Law*, l: App. 4, p. 727.

22. See "The London Jurors' Petition" (Sept. 6, 1831), reprinted in *ibid.*, pp. 731–32.

23. The literature on the subject of prison reform is vast. For excellent recent accounts see Michael Ignatieff, *A Just Measure of Pain: The Penitentiary in the Industrial Revolution, 1750–1850* (London, 1978); Beattie, *Crime and the Courts*, chs. 10–12.

24. Ignatieff, *Just Measure of Pain*, pp. 80–81.

25. See e.g. Hanway, *Distributive Justice and Mercy*, pp. 28 *et seq.*

described a world in which there was remarkably little fear of the law.[26] Suspects knew, Wakefield claimed, how to play on the sympathies of prosecutors; it was common knowledge, apparently, that a prosecutor who wanted neither to put a suspect's life in jeopardy nor to forfeit his own recognizance could be convinced to go through "the form of [his] part in the prosecution, taking care to shape [his] evidence in favor of the accused."[27] Suspects also knew, Wakefield alleged, that judges and jurors

> constantly nullify the law, by saving from capital convictions, one whom they believe to be capitally guilty. This occurs so frequently, and is so fully brought to the knowledge of the public, in the reports of trials at every Old Bailey sessions, and at every country assize, that I am unwilling to dwell on it at any length.[28]

Wakefield described mock trials held by the prisoners in Newgate in which the prisoners took the parts of judge, jury, and witnesses, and the prisoner at the bar: "On these occasions the prisoners show a remarkable knowledge of the temper of judges and juries, being in the habit of acquitting many prisoners whom they knew to be guilty."[29]

The parliamentary committees on reform of the criminal law had a virtual field day with this kind of material. At the very moment that the nation was establishing a professional police force, it was—or so it seemed—continuing to indulge a system of prosecution, trial, and sentencing that bred disrespect for the law and the notion among the criminals themselves that, having been made the subject of mitigation, they could continue to breach the law with impunity. Doubtless the select committees that issued reports in 1819 and in 1836 interviewed persons who said what the committee members wanted to hear: the evidence that the committees compiled was remarkably one-sided. The testimony of suspects and convicts was nevertheless of some real importance. To the assertion that juries were faced with an awful dilemma was added the charge that juries were mocked by the very persons whose lives they spared. Apparently, capital sanctions failed to produce the terror they had been intended to produce, and the administration of the criminal law was undermining any real possibility of true rehabilitation. Far from inculcating religious values, the system was making a mockery of them. The jury was not, of course, the only participant in this ill-begotten system of criminal justice. But it was a participant whose behavior was difficult to modify. A developing police force could be depended upon to take over

---

26. Edward Gibbon Wakefield, *Facts Relating to the Punishment of Death in the Metropolis* (London, 1831).
27. *Ibid.*, p. 58.
28. *Ibid.*, p. 61.
29. *Ibid.*, p. 62.

the role of defaulting or half-hearted prosecutors, and the bench and other officers of the Crown might respond to Parliament's concerns. But the jury could be reached only through reform of the law of sanctions itself. Not all members of Parliament were in agreement that there ought to be reform. There were those who interpreted statistics showing more numerous convictions for property crimes after the first, limited reduction of capital sanctions as indicating an increase in the number of those crimes rather than as a greater willingness on the part of jurors to comply with the letter of the law once the death penalty was no longer an issue. In the end, however, such doubters were unable to resist the tide of reform. By 1840 Parliament had added large-scale reform of the law of sanctions to reform of policing and incarceration.[30]

Reform of the law of sanctions had an immediate impact on jury behavior in many trials for felony. Parliament had largely removed the need for massive and daily jury-based intervention on behalf of criminal defendants. This development coincided also with the gradual transformation of the trial itself from a kind of morality play in which the defendant spoke on his behalf in full sight of the jury to a more impersonal and more highly structured trial in which the defendant was represented by counsel and where rules of admissibility governed the presentation of the evidence to the jury. A new world of criminal justice was being ushered in; the old one had surely drawn to a close when, in the light of widely held views, it seemed plausible to say that, after all, the jury had never been intended to be a discretionary body.

# II

Jury-based intervention did not end in the middle of the nineteenth century. It remains a pervasive and vital aspect of the (so-called) fact-finding process even in lesser felonies, where life is not at stake. In that setting, however, it has not always been noticed. Perhaps jurors themselves are, typically, unaware of the degree to which discretion creeps into the fact-finding process. It was the sanction of death that made jury law-finding in routine cases an important and recognized aspect of English culture. Jury mitigation of the law soon passed from public consciousness, save for episodic reappearances in what society has taken to be special circumstances. Late nineteenth- and early twentieth-century historians made relatively little of the fact that a tradition of jury intervention in common-run felonies had for centuries been central to the administration of the criminal law. Until recently, historians have por-

---

30. For a listing of capital statutes as of 1839 see Radzinowicz, *History of English Criminal Law*, 1:733–34.

trayed jury law-finding mainly as a matter of resistance to authorities in political cases, and they have viewed those cases in isolation from the general run of jury trials. They have viewed jury nullification the way they have viewed monarchical depositions: as sudden outbursts, undertaken in extreme circumstances, and seemingly lacking a basis in daily practices and attitudes.

It seems fitting that the foundation for the abolition of open and massive jury intervention was laid in the course of the debate over reform of the English police system. In earliest times the jury had played an evidence-gathering role, making up for the Crown's lack of policing and prosecutorial capacity. Subsequently that role was played by justices of the peace, constables, and the other minor officials that composed England's protopolice force. The limits of that meager force were widely recognized. Although authorities came to possess the capacity to gather evidence in cases that were scheduled for trial, they remained largely reactive, lacking the strength and numbers to prevent criminal activity. Partly for that reason, capital sanctions were maintained. The maintenance of those sanctions in turn made continuation of jury intervention inevitable. The development of the prosecution was a gradual process. Only very slowly did authorities achieve the capacity to control the jury, and even when they had done so there were reasons for allowing the jury to share the power of mitigation. The transformation of criminal procedure in the early modern period thus eventuated in a system of trial wherein juries that no longer controlled the production of evidence nevertheless frequently and openly rendered verdicts against the evidence produced in court. The struggle for control of the law was by that time very complex. The jury was coming to be a quasi-arm of the bench even as it remained an extension of society. At one level, procedural developments touching the jury reflected the fact that the criminal process was becoming increasingly formal; at another level, the jury remained a mediating institution that served multiple interests.

It is difficult to determine precisely how this two-sided relationship between authority and the jury began. I have characterized the jury as possessing the greatest degree of power during the medieval period. But it must be remembered that in those times the Crown and bench were relatively weak, so that the advantage they stood to gain from an alliance with men of substance in the local community was correspondingly great. Moreover, even if before the sixteenth century the bench could not have prevented jurors from behaving as they did, authorities may nonetheless have benefited from that behavior and felt little inclination to prevent it. I have suggested that, in the main, legislative and judicial devices for controlling the jury were not created in order to deal with jury-based intervention that took the relatively benign form of merciful verdicts in run-of-the-mill cases. Authorities did not seek to end that aspect of the jury's role; rather they sought to manage it, to set clear limits to its operation, and to create the means whereby they could monitor verdicts for what they considered true abuses.

By the eighteenth century authorities had gained so much control over the practice of jury-based mitigation that it had become an integral aspect of the official sentencing procedure. In form, of course, the jury continued to determine only the question of guilt or innocence, and it was in part the fiction so frequently involved in this aspect of its role that was bringing jury-based intervention into disrepute. By then, too, it had become clear just how powerful the jury could be. Its place in the constitution had been marked out in the constitutional and political crises of the seventeenth century and again in the late eighteenth century during the debate over the law of seditious libel. The constitutional role of the jury combined with the long-standing ethic of jury-based intervention in routine cases to produce a formidable political and legal ideology. Yet at a deeper level, an increasingly widespread concern for clarity, certainty, and predictability of the law—a concern shared by both proponents and opponents of reform—was feeding into the stream of opposition to jury-based discretion.

Reform of the libel law took the wind out of the sails of the movement for the right of the jury to find law (though not out of the tradition of resistance to unpopular political prosecutions, as the acquittals of, inter alia, Hardy, Tooke, Thelwall, and Hone demonstrate). Although the claim to that right was reasserted during the next decade, by and large conferral of the power to render a general verdict altered the nature of discourse concerning the jury. Jury discretion in seditious libel could now be concealed within the fact-finding process, as it had long been concealed in treason. Arguments might arise over the definition of the law, but they would be resolved by legislative decree or judicial elaboration of existing standards. True jury nullification (as distinct from discretionary, merciful verdicts) would continue episodically. But so long as such verdicts remained concealed or, if open, ad hoc and unaccompanied by a general claim to a right to find law, they could be—and down to our own day have been—accepted as anomalies and as one of the costs of the jury system. Ultimately, the reform of the law of sanctions had a similar impact on the tradition of merciful verdicts in routine felonies: by the later nineteenth century, jury discretion had largely been hidden from view. Moreover, the period of intense reform activity and criticism on all sides of the jury's supposed "dilemma" had conditioned much of society to think in terms of the jury's responsibility to adhere to the rule of law.

It is impossible to ascribe the demise of discretionary fact-finding (or law-finding) to a single cause. Reform of the law of sanctions was, of course, crucial, but that reform came about only after the assumptions that underlay the preexisting system were somehow no longer tenable. We have seen that the reform of the police system played a significant, albeit indirect and catalytic role, as did the movement for reform of English prisons. The emphases in the new penology on humanity and on the certainty of the law were also significant: what began as a claim that certainty was required for reasons of deterrence ended as a claim that certainty was necessary for fairness to the defendant. Rationality regarding penology was closely related to rationality regarding the nature of the trial itself. The sequencing of the trial in the early eighteenth century may have resulted from developments in the law of evidence, including the rules regarding the burden of going forward and the burden of proof. But the law of evidence developed more rapidly in the nineteenth century when Englishmen were no longer satisfied with a cumbersome system of posttrial reprieve and royal pardon on grounds of an unsafe verdict. It is possible that the law of evidence developed only after changes had been effected in policing, in sanctions, and in the structure of jury trial, but jurisprudence probably led as much as it followed. One might speculate that the increasing recourse to counsel by defendants was crucial for the development of the law of evidence, a development that probably predated the acceptance of other reform demands. In the end, however, although we can roughly date the close of the centuries-long phase of jury trial history that we have traced, we can as yet do little more. We await an informed analysis of the manner in which the end of that phase came about; the much-needed history of the rise of the modern trial has yet to be written.

# III

The movement for reform of the law of sanctions prepared the way for the modern view regarding the role of the criminal trial jury. The traditional view eroded suddenly, reflecting its fragility and inducing us to forget how long it had endured and how deeply it had been embedded in the English culture. We would do well, therefore, to end our study of the interplay of institutions, ideas, and behavior with a lengthy retrospective. I should state at the outset that I have sought in these chapters not only to answer some difficult questions but also to raise others for which I have found no satisfactory answer. I shall in the course of my summation review some of the unresolved problems that I have identified. This review will, I hope, make clear the limits of the present work, and thereby help to set a research agenda for those who share my particular interest and approach to the social and intellectual history of the criminal law and the criminal trial jury.

1

I have discussed the origin and early development of the criminal trial jury against the background of what I have called the Angevin transformation in the criminal law. That transformation—the gradual absorption into royal jurisdiction of virtually all felonies—prepared the way for a near-universal capital sanction. Why did the Crown embark on such a harsh sanctions policy? To what extent did authorities expect compliance? From one point of view, the capital sanction merely represented a return to an older and more primitive approach to the criminal law. The Anglo-Saxon system of relatively moderate punishment (i.e., monetary composition) had developed as a result of the Crown's interest, and perhaps that of society generally, in stemming the more ancient practice of the feud. We must not forget that for those few most serious offenses over which the Crown even in Anglo-Saxon times exercised exclusive jurisdiction, punishment was typically capital. One might conjecture that so long as the Crown had a monopoly on punishment, that punishment would be very severe.

On yet another view, the Angevins and their successors sought to make the strongest possible statement against criminal activity, but believed that enforcement ought to take account of both the circumstances in which offenses had been committed and the reputation of the offender. Roger Groot has shown that, at least in practice, the presentment jury undertook a good deal of selection among offenders. The presentment jury first named all those who were accused and then named those whom they truly suspected. The evidence does not allow for the conclusion that the presenters exercised discretion and stated that they did not suspect some persons whom they in fact suspected but chose mercifully (or on any other grounds) to exonerate. I have suggested, however, that we should not be surprised to discover that the presentment jury did operate on this basis. As I have tried to show, the trial jury did play such a role and played it in an expansive fashion. One must consider the adoption of the trial jury (and even the adoption of the harsh law of sanctions) in light of earlier experience with jury-like institutions. It is possible that, by the 1220s, the Crown assumed that trial juries would behave just about as they did. Certainly it is possible that the tension between authorities and juries that I have depicted in the medieval period reflected no more than disagreement about the *degree* of discretion that ought to be exercised.

Those who view the eighteenth-century system of criminal administration as one in which authorities made active and calculated use of selective enforcement might see in the twelfth-century transformation of the criminal law an early form of this approach to governance. Such an argument, it seems to me, would be difficult—though perhaps not impossible—to sustain. Except in homicide, royal pardons were fairly unusual before the end of the thirteenth century; most selective enforcement was in the hands of the jury before that time. It is possible to argue that the jury was itself an extension of the Crown, at least in the earliest period, when the trial jury was often merely a subset of the presenting jury. On this view the Crown struck an alliance with the most established free men of the local communities, placing in their hands the power of life and death over the populace on the countryside. By the end of the thirteenth century (the argument might run) the Crown was attempting to play a more prominent role in the granting of mercy: hence the increasing flow of royal pardons of grace. It would stretch the point too far to say that royal complaints about jury-based nonenforcement of the law were really aimed at shoring up the royal purchase on the power to dispense merciful judgments. There remains, nonetheless, fertile ground for investigation. Surely the Crown engendered deference through its use of the pardon, whether or not one views royal policy as involving conscious manipulation of the law in order to engender it.

My own view, as the essays in Part I of this volume suggest, is that the Crown's participation in the process of selective enforcement came about largely by way of accident, and that that policy was only one of many contradictory policies authorities pursued. It is difficult to explain the rise of universal capital sanctions in terms of a desire to achieve the deference of society through merciful nonenforcement of the law. We still know too little about penological theory in the twelfth and thirteenth centuries, especially about Continental practices and their influence within English ruling circles. There is need for research on the development of capital sanctions, on Continental influences, and on their melding with the administration of the criminal law in England.

I have suggested that authorities were well aware that juries manipulated the evidence in order to give effect to their views regarding just deserts and that the Crown and bench were unable to prevent juries from playing this role. But I have also suggested that authorities were not particularly ill-disposed toward this form of jury behavior. Other problems must have seemed more important, and there may not have been a great deal of distance between lay and official views regarding the appropriate sanction in most of the routine cases in which jurors exercised discretion. It is even possible that from fairly early on the Crown actively encouraged juries to play the role that I have described. Although judicial encouragement of jury mitigation of sanctions does not become visible to us until the sixteenth century, there is no reason to believe that this tradition began so late. The development of the prosecution and of means to control the jury made judicial participation in merciful verdicts in "appropriate cases" more affordable, but the Crown and bench had probably long before not only acquiesced in social standards but upon occasion encouraged them. It is true that one would expect to find some indication of this attitude in Bracton, *Placita Corone*, or in other law books of the thirteenth and fourteenth centuries. But the fact that one does not is hardly conclusive. To say the least, the last word has not been written on the role of medieval institutions in the granting of mercy. It is no longer so fashionable as it once was to focus on the machinery of the criminal law or on theories of kingship and justice in the Middle Ages. Attention has shifted to the sociology of crime, surely an important subject. Somehow bridges must be created among all these fields. The bridge I have attempted to create through an analysis of the judges' shaping of the law of homicide is no more than a beginning.

## 2

Crucial to the developments I have traced is the origin of the investigative activities of the justices of the peace and the place of those activities in the transformation of criminal procedure in the late fifteenth and sixteenth centuries. Although the developments involved were not undertaken in a conscious attempt to reduce trial jury discretion, they contributed indirectly to that end. Thus it was in this period that authorities largely brought the trial jury under their control. I have argued that the form of control that emerged allowed for a substantial degree of jury discretion. Although judges frequently steered juries not only to convict but also to acquit or to render a partial verdict, they did so in a way that preserved to some extent the reality and to a large extent the psychology of trial jury independence. This last proposition is, of course, the most difficult to prove. The leading authority on criminal procedure and jury trial in the sixteenth and early seventeenth centuries believes that juries exercised very little independence even in the assessment of questions of fact. In James Cockburn's view, juries knew what result the bench thought appropriate and gave their verdicts accordingly, so that, in effect, what appears to be jury independence was in reality fairly automatic jury ratification of judicially mandated mitigation. I have outlined the difficulties involved in this reading of the evidence relating to criminal assizes. Beyond the realm of this study, there is also evidence, effectively marshaled by Cynthia Herrup, that in the late sixteenth and early seventeenth centuries juries exercised very substantial discretion at quarter sessions, particularly in relatively minor cases, either on their own or by leave (but not solely on the order) of the bench. Although we must be cautious about generalizing from jury behavior where life was not at stake to jury behavior in capital offenses, it is difficult to imagine that society did not develop expectations about jury practice on the basis of the very common use of the jury in relatively minor cases.

I have dwelled at length on changes in substantive law and the law of sanctions that I believe reflected attempts to accommodate long-standing social attitudes. Although these changes reduced the need for jury discretion, they recognized the implicit or "silent" power of the Tudor-Stuart jury; i.e., as the law (and especially its judicial application) was brought into closer conformity with deep-seated and long-manifested social attitudes about just deserts, and so long as the bench recognized the limits that those attitudes established, the new instruments of control could develop and be applied with relatively little tension. These changes in legal rules and sanctions recognized also the realities of pretrial stages where the community as well as royal officials played a role in sorting out potential defendants. Research (now underway) that embraces the administration of the criminal law at all levels, and that analyzes that administration in terms of prevailing social and religious attitudes toward crime and criminals, will, I believe, support my view of a complex and two-sided judge-jury relationship. I suspect, however, that it will also lay bare, in a way I have not, the influence of local politics and the contest among central and local authorities for control over jury selection and over jury resolution of many kinds of cases. Jury independence from royal officials may often have reflected jury dependence upon local ones.

It remains likely that in the sixteenth and seventeenth centuries criminal assize juries behaved largely as they did in the following century. That is, juries were frequently influenced by the bench, and usually resolved cases in a way the bench approved of, but in many cases were left by the bench to determine the matter on their own. And even where the bench revealed its view of how a case ought to be resolved, it left the jury in a position whereby it might resolve the case as though it were resolving it for itself. Juries both followed the bench—i.e., took their view of the case largely from the bench—and believed they were making their own assessment both as to fact and as to the appropriate sentence. From the perspective of the jury, the judge's view was simply one very important consideration that ought to be taken into account. That, at least, is the way many contemporaries viewed the process in the eighteenth century, when the tools for steering the jury were just as strong, if not stronger. It is unlikely that in the earlier period jurors (and the denizens of England's local communities who observed them) thought juries played a less significant role.

Mid-seventeenth-century writings on the jury are an important source of evidence about contemporary perceptions of the institution and its behavior. As we have seen, this evidence, too, is ambiguous. Some evidence for the existence of the most basic form of jury independence resides in the tracts attacking the jury as composed of know-nothings and asserting that there were not enough qualified persons to serve. Had jurors simply ratified explicit judicial mandates, the deficiencies of jurors would have been less obvious and seemed less important. But this does not prove that jurors went beyond the finding of fact; it may prove no more than that some contemporaries doubted jurors' capacity to make accurate factual assessments independently.

The Interregnum tracts that argued for greater jury power pose even more difficult problems. These radical jury tracts clearly reflect the view that, at least in political cases, the bench steered juries far too strongly. But what of trials in more routine felonies? For the most part, the tracts place the true law-finding jury deep in the historical past; it cannot be found—one infers from the tracts—at the contemporary assize or quarter-session proceedings. But the tract writers equated true law-finding with a degree and form of jury power that we are certain did not exist in the sixteenth and seventeenth centuries. The tracts simply do not speak directly to the question of whether juries in routine cases exercised some more modest degree of discretion.

It is by no means clear why radical jury proponents were inattentive to the jury practices I have traced. Were they unfamiliar with the handling of criminal cases at assizes and quarter-sessions? Or should we conclude that juries did not exercise even the modest kind of discretion in routine cases that I have labored to show that they did exercise? My tentative view is that these writers probably were aware of contemporary practices but that, from their perspective, those practices were barely worth discussion. For what authorities saw as nearly too much jury autonomy, radical jury writers viewed as far too little. How had this come about?

I have suggested that the early modern bench steered juries, that jury discretion was to a large degree undertaken with judicial leave or encouragement, and that the local community largely accepted this judicial role. For the most part, the community believed it was doing justice as much on its own terms as was appropriate. Those relatively few political dissidents who strenuously opposed the common-law bench—as the radical jury writers certainly did—perhaps viewed the modest degree of jury-based discretion that characterized routine felony trials as a mere remnant of what they supposed was a once fully manifested, God-given duty. In their view, that duty had become a peripheral, judicially manipulated power; no longer was it the very essence of the trial jury's right. The tract writers thus reflected the existence of an ongoing tradition in a curious way. Contemporary jury discretion gave them a clue to the jury's "true" role even while it appeared to them to have been nearly destroyed by the bench.

1600's

   It is also significant that mid-seventeenth-century jury proponents
sometimes failed to distinguish between civil and criminal trial juries.
Like the Wilkites of the following century, the Levellers were concerned
with private law as much—if not more—than with criminal law. Both
groups sought a simpler, more accessible system of law to govern their
acquisition, transfer, and protection of property. But the Levellers sought
more than a reduction of both the mysterious forms of the common law
and the discretionary powers of the common-law bench; they looked to
the local community to judge cases, whether crimes, civil trespasses, or
disputes over property rights or contracts. Lilburne's invocation of
Littleton is of interest not only because the Leveller misread his chief
source for the proposition that the jury possessed the right to find law.
The jury that Lilburne (wrongly) claimed Littleton endowed with law-
finding power was a civil jury. Jurors in private-law disputes no doubt
continued to exercise discretion in their fact-finding role, and this
probably shaped their behavior when the same persons sat in criminal
cases. But because of the formal separation of law and fact in civil cases,
the civil jury had long before surrendered much of the power still retained
by the criminal trial jury. How this separation had come about is beyond
the scope of the present study. The influence of civil-jury practice upon
criminal-trial-jury behavior, and the attitudes of contemporaries toward
the civil jury, are, however, matters that do touch my own concerns,
though I have left them for others to pursue. Lilburne, it seems to me,
reflected an outmoded school of thought in his reference to the civil jury's
law-finding power. By his day, the claim of the criminal trial jury's
"right" to find the law mercifully, or to nullify judicial pronouncements
upon the law, was based largely upon the fact that it was the Crown that
brought (or stood behind) the prosecution. It was a tradition that gained
its force from the threat of capital punishment, its justification from the
defendant's "choice" to put himself upon the country, and its eventual
spread to noncapital, high misdemeanors from the fact that the alleged
"victim"—political authority—was, in one of its manifestations, the
bench that presided over the trial and charged the jury to do justice.

   The background to *Bushel's Case* reveals, we have seen, the tension
between judge and jury that sometimes accompanied the tradition of
generally accepted de facto jury independence. In several homicide cases
Chief Justice Kelyng challenged a kind of jury behavior that, from all one
can determine, was not atypical. Although it is possible that the jurors
whose verdicts he coerced had in fact been guilty of corruption, Kelyng's
critics did not assume that was the case. Their response suggests that jury
fact-finding was sancrosanct even when it appeared on the facts that the
jurors had indulged in a substantial degree of discretionary decision
making. Vaughan's opinion can best be understood against a background

of criminal proceedings in which judge and jury typically were in agreement not only on the facts but also on the merits of merciful discretion. The jury's right to an untrammeled general verdict could be vindicated precisely because there were few cases where judge and jury were likely to clash. I have suggested that the most important idea in Vaughan's opinion was not his statement that the jurors might have knowledge of their own but rather that the jury might see things in their own way. It is not clear what Vaughan meant by the term "conscience," but surely whether or not he was sincere Vaughan was pointing to some element in contemporary social thought. Vaughan's opinion suggests once more that the notion that the jury had an ultimate right to go its own way in its assessment of fact was not foreign to the period.

But Vaughan's opinion raises as many questions as it answers. Why did Vaughan not allude to the most relevant aspect of the background to *Bushel's Case*? Why was he silent about the line of cases involving Quakers in which juries had, from the standpoint of authorities, threatened the public order by making a mockery of the law and bringing courtroom proceedings to a virtual standstill? And why did not Vaughan lay down a rule (as he might have) that placed some limits upon the jury's power to frustrate both the bench and the law? Vaughan's draft opinion leaves the impression that he had at first intended to set some limits to jury deviation from the facts adduced in court. Subsequently he altered his opinion, providing what must have seemed to contemporaries a lame excuse: a jury, after it had been questioned by a judge, might somehow have changed its mind (in the direction of innocence) in the intervening time. Vaughan might have ruled that a jury that rendered a verdict totally in the face of the evidence presented in court (as it seemed to the bench) but could not explain why it had done so had gone beyond legal limits. For reasons that are difficult to uncover, Vaughan seems ultimately to have responded almost viscerally to a deep-seated notion concerning the sanctity of the juror's conscience. It is probably true that Vaughan and his judicial brethren could afford to do so since there were relatively few cases in which jury discretion born of "conscience" might lead to real conflict with the bench. But that is only to affirm rather than to deny the existence of the concept of verdict according to conscience.

### 3

Thanks to recent research, we now know a great deal about crime and criminal prosecution in the eighteenth century. John Langbein has shown, for instance, how cut and dried the trial process could be. Because, however, that process was employed for "selection" of offenders for one or another level of punishment (as Langbein and John Beattie have demonstrated), the trial inevitably took on several related but not always consistent social meanings. It is not surprising, for instance, that to many contemporaries the trial appeared to be open-ended and even arbitrary. Nor is it surprising that contemporaries disagreed about whether the judge or the jury was in control. There are, moreover, matters about which we cannot as yet be certain. How, e.g., did most of the populace view the trial? Did they identify the criminal trial jury as an extension of society or as an arm of authority? Did they regard jury verdicts as arbitrary, or did they possess a settled understanding of the kinds of offenders and offenses that were singled out for the various levels of available sanctions? Did they perceive the jury as a bulwark of liberty, or did they see jurors as pliant and venal (as some literary sources depicted them), as simply actors in a grand farce?

I have suggested that we must be cautious about assimilating jury trial to those institutions and procedures by which eighteenth-century authorities manipulated the affections of society at large. Although I am not certain that any institution or procedure ought to be viewed mainly in that way, some of them were handled in a manner that greatly strengthened the hand of authorities. However we characterize the intent of Crown and bench in these instances, we must distinguish the jury from other institutions on the basis of the effect its use had both on governance and on the relationship among the political and social orders of the eighteenth century. It is of course true that the criminal trial jury offered an important opportunity for cooptation of the middling and lower ranks of lay society. Authorities' use of the jury—and the apparent esteem in which the jury was held by the contemporary establishment—doubtless contributed to the stability of their rule. Through the jury, England's rulers extended the "beneficence" of the law to virtually all social orders. Judicial endorsement of jury verdicts was bound to enhance the position of authorities, whose mandates were implemented by an institution that many people probably viewed as reflecting the standards of society at large.

It is also true, however, that the jury's usefulness to authority depended upon the reality of the jury's independence both historically and in terms of contemporary decision making. The relationship between authorities and the institution of the jury was symbiotic. Authorities took their standards at least in part from juries; through the jury, authorities achieved more substantial enforcement of those standards than they might otherwise have achieved. Might one, then, postulate the existence of a "ruling class" that comprised the orders that served as judges, jurors, and prosecutors (many of whom were too poor to serve as jurors but sufficiently well-endowed to be the chief prey of thieves)? On such a view, upper, middling, and lower-middling orders created an alliance in order to govern, according to their own shared standards, the lowest orders—perhaps fully a third—of society. To a significant degree, this is an appropriate characterization of what actually occurred. But jurors commonly took their own standards from a variety of sources, and it seems likely that they saw the world through the eyes of frightened defendants even as they saw it through those of their own more insulated social betters with whom they presumptuously identified and whom they often sought to please. Jurors mediated by bringing rulers and ruled closer together. The standards that they accepted were for both practical and truly substantive reasons that much more acceptable to those above and below them. The power exercised by eighteenth-century authorities was very great, but the substance of the justice they provided, merciful as well as merciless, through their (unavoidable) use of juries reflected the interests of much of society. To put it slightly differently: authorities' power to determine the content of this substantive justice—to establish the terms upon which substantive rules would be applied—was severely limited, and no institution reflected this limitation more dramatically than the criminal trial jury.

This limitation was reflected not only in institutional realities and in widespread social expectations regarding the administration of justice; it was reflected also in influential contemporary discourses on the English constitution and on the lessons of history. Although truly radical Interregnum thought was never assimilated by later jury proponents, the nullification theory espoused by Lilburne (as of 1653), Penn, Hawles, and those who opposed the later Stuarts' manipulation of grand and petty juries achieved more than surface respectability. Having rested their legitimacy in part upon their defense of the historical constitution, the Whig government could not unilaterally determine the meaning of the post-1688 settlement. Eighteenth-century authorities might claim that, although the jury was still in use, it was no longer required as a bulwark against tyranny, but that claim was open to rebuttal by the political opposition. As I have argued, the longstanding ethic of jury discretion and the more episodic tradition of true jury nullification fused both in practice and in theory; they are not entirely separate even in the pages of so strong an ally of the prevailing political order as Blackstone.

## 4

I have devoted little space to the motives that underlay the mitigation of the law. This is of course an enormous subject, for motives varied from time to time and place to place. They varied, too, depending upon the background, character, age, and gender of the defendant (or the victim); upon the persons responsible in given cases for mitigating the law; and upon the stage of the prosecution at which those persons undertook to do so. By and large, I have treated the subject only very generally. I have focused instead on the way the English thought about the practice of jury-based mitigation, and I have left to the many scholars now at work on the history of criminal law the tasks of analyzing and characterizing geographical, temporal, and other variations in the behavior of juries (including the important differences between the treatment of men and women) and of assessing that behavior in the light of the history of the many other stages in the enforcement of the criminal law. A truly comprehensive history of jury-based mitigation of the formal law awaits the results of these forthcoming studies. I should conclude this section, however, with some brief observations on the matter of motives—that is, the attitudes that led society to mitigate the law—and on the relationship between that important subject and my own study of the criminal trial jury.

Students of Tudor and early Stuart England have pointed to the fit between, on the one hand, a system of criminal justice that announced legal imperatives in definitive terms but provided abundant opportunities for bestowing mercy and, on the other, a religious ethic that portrayed all men as sinners, as subject to temptation and transgression, but proffered opportunities for redemption to all but the worst of the fallen. Legal and religious systems of maintaining order and saving souls, they have asserted, in reality constituted a single system. Not only did society at large see the matter in this fashion, but authorities also explained it in these terms. Professor Herrup has developed this argument with particular force, characterizing Elizabethan and Jacobean enforcement of the criminal law as part of a religion-based process of rehabilitation, or moral regeneration. This seems to me, in fact, a plausible way of understanding the practical application of legal rules across the entire period, 1200–1800.

My own study of the history of the criminal trial jury points to some contours of the evolution of this worldview that, in some dimension, is with us still. The tendency to assimilate the law to prevailing religious notions is undoubtedly age-old. Religious and secular norms were not viewed as separate in the Middle Ages. Post-Reformation Puritanism intensified belief in the omnipresence of sin and the capacity for moral regeneration, but it did not mark a new departure in the identification of serious criminal offenses with breaches of divine command. The royal pardon had always carried with it—or was supposed to carry with it—the imprimatur of Godly Mercy; the refusal to forgive an offender, and the ritual of execution, were imbued with the notion that the offender was in the eyes of God beyond earthly redemption.

It may be that from the outset of the common-law period it was assumed that a variety of institutions, the jury included, would apply the law in a merciful fashion. We simply do not know how far authorities countenanced such behavior. At the very least, if authorities did believe that prosecutors, grand jurors, and trial jurors should conform to the formal rules of law, they also believed that the Crown should apply those rules in accordance with the standards of divine justice. I have suggested that society's reluctance to adhere to formal rules was far greater than authorities had at the outset assumed it would be. Indeed, society's disposition was apparently more merciful than that of the Crown, for early on the Crown left itself relatively few opportunities to intercede to prevent executions. Social (including religious) attitudes that were themselves in part—but only in part—engendered by secular and religious authorities combined with the relative lack of royal institutions of mitigation to produce a powerful degree of community intercession.

We have seen that authorities reacted to widespread social intercession in a variety of ways. In some of its manifestations that reaction must be viewed as an attempt to monopolize and to limit the exercise of mitigation. To the extent that they were unable to do so, and especially with regard to those instances where they viewed the extension of mercy as both inevitable and just, authorities came to understand the system of criminal administration in terms that both accommodated the divine aspect of secular justice and accorded with the realities of practice. This is, then, how I would interpret the perspective of authorities by the Tudor period. Authorities had by that period made sense for themselves and for others of the practices over which they were coming to exert greater, though still far from total control. Their assimilation (to a substantial degree) of society's definition of the role and purpose of legal institutions had already taken place and so constituted one of the limiting factors that prevented them from willing, or attempting, a more complete form of control. Within the context of prevailing legal and religious norms, norms to which authorities gave significant degrees of definition and shape, authorities sought both to control and to share the power of mitigation. They were influenced in their views regarding both the appropriateness of mitigation and the institutions that ought to bestow it by the kinds of cases with which they were confronted and by the realities of the still-early stage in the evolution toward relatively greater royal control that the system of criminal administration had reached.

The evolution toward royal control (I have suggested) is difficult to trace precisely because control came to involve manipulation of lay institutions, including the jury, even while the power of pronouncing the resolution of cases was left in lay hands. Thus it is difficult for us—as indeed it was for contemporaries—to determine whether the late seventeenth- and early eighteenth-century criminal trial jury was a relatively independent mitigator or a relatively dependent one. Authorities and society at large probably viewed the institution differently in this regard; it is possible that when authorities and jury proponents clashed it was as much because of social *assumptions* about what juries did, and were supposed to do, as because of what, at least in most cases, juries in fact did.

By the dawn of the modern era the understanding of the purpose of the institution of the jury may have altered in yet another significant way. New ways of thinking about human behavior had slowly emerged, mainly changing, but also weakening, the grip of religion upon society's understanding of the operation of the criminal law. As before, the law served to control and to rehabilitate, but the concept of rehabilitation was being transformed by the increasing emphasis upon the social origins of criminal behavior. Jurors sometimes took such notions into account in their decisions about the fate of offenders. For their part, authorities interpreted the jury's role as co-mitigator in terms of jurors' inclination to "use" the law to sort out the blameworthy at least partly in terms of the constraints under which offenders had acted and the likelihood that the new sanctions of transportation and hard labor would reform them. This more secular perspective on the causes of criminality and the prospects for reform was intimately joined with the more traditional religious conception of sin and redemption. Few contemporaries thought about them as truly separate interpretations of human behavior. But the implications of the new perspective should not be minimized, for that view contained a threat to the most crucial assumption that underlay the system of criminal law.

By the eighteenth century, if not long before, some contemporaries had come to hold two potentially contradictory views concerning human behavior: offenders were the product of social circumstances; offenders acted freely and should be held criminally responsible for their acts. The prevailing system of administration of the criminal law highlighted this contradiction. The maintenance of the death penalty alongside an open search for reasons not to apply it focused attention on, among other things, the degree of constraint under which a given offender had acted. Authorities, and apparently much of English society, accepted the fact that such constraints were very powerful. The pardon process itself, and certainly the reasons for which many pardons were granted, testified to this understanding of the nature of much human behavior.

Critics of the prevailing system made their own use of the same insight: the death penalty was unjust in many cases because the criminal was a mere product of his background—his upbringing, associates, and needs. At the same time, it was assumed that there was a realm within which people acted freely. Few writers attempted to draw a line between the act for which one was responsible and the act for which one was not. It was as though most critics assumed that, with reform of the law of sanctions, the problem of constraint would melt away. They seem to have shared an almost universal view that the disparity between the nature of the offense and the level of the proposed punishment determined the relevance of evidence bearing on the defendant's freedom to have done otherwise than he did. But this was neither a new phenomenon nor one that died with the reforms of the nineteenth century. Perhaps we will come closer to understanding this aspect of eighteenth-century English mentality when we consider the way in which the same contradiction prevails in our own assumptions and language regarding criminal justice.

It is conventional to say that we believe that nearly all offenders—indeed nearly all persons—are mainly free, and thus mainly responsible for their acts, save for the few "insane" who, we agree, bear no responsibility at all. Some, we believe, are more free than others, and it is the degree of freedom or nonfreedom that we, like those before us, take into account. The sanction of death is reserved, on this view, for those whose acts are, as it seems to us, both extremely serious and at least substantially free. That is a modern view, but it is useful to keep it in mind as one studies the history of criminal law from medieval to modern times.

# IV

The foregoing essays explore various aspects of the history of verdict "according to conscience," stressing the relationships among them. These relationships are often difficult to establish, for the various motives they reflect were not always separate in the minds of jurors, officials, or contemporary observors.

I have given considerable attention to the idea of the jury as a bulwark against tyranny, an idea that, from the seventeenth century until recently, has loomed large in historical scholarship. But I have attempted to demonstrate that this traditional view does not capture what was behaviorally the most significant aspect of the jury's place in medieval and early modern English culture. Pride of place must be reserved for the jury's role as a mitigator of capital sanctions in felony trials. This aspect of jury history, which bears a complicated relationship to the political role of the jury, is itself a multifaceted phenomenon.

We can best understand jury mitigation by focusing on jurors' attitudes regarding the appropriateness of punishment for specific defendants who had acted in particular ways. The most prevalent attitude was, in its most general form, a belief that the defendant did not deserve as harsh a punishment as the law provided. Such a belief is, of course, consistent with any number of specific attitudes toward the defendant or his behavior. For example, the defendant's peers may view his act as lawful, or they may view it as unlawful but not so serious as to merit the prescribed sanction. The latter, by far the more common view, may reflect either the view that the defendant has suffered enough or the view that, although the defendant has not suffered enough, the prescribed sanction would make him suffer too much. Either stance may spring from the common feeling that defendants deserve mercy if they repent of their behavior and/or if their behavior was in some significant degree the product of forces beyond their control.

In studying the effects of these aspects of jury behavior, I have developed several main themes. First, I have sought to show that the jury's role as mitigator was a by-product of institutional arrangements that were themselves (albeit indirectly) the result of the tensions between legal rules and social norms occasioned by the Angevin revolution. To a certain extent, the political implications of those tensions would in any case have made it difficult for authorities to develop an administration of the criminal law that was managed entirely by officials and so contributed to the need for a jury-like institution. But the existing weaknesses in English bureaucratic and policing capacities perhaps counted even more heavily: simply put, lay cooperation was required at every stage in the legal process. Once the institution of the jury came into being, both jury-based intervention and a struggle to limit its reach were virtually inevitable.

Second, the history of legal doctrine was itself affected by the interaction of legal and social tensions with the institutional arrangements embedded in the administration of the criminal law. The law of homicide and the rules of forfeiture and of statutory benefit of clergy reflected responses to social realities. Tensions were muted not by head-on collisions between judge and jury but by the manipulation of categories, by the creation of alternative punishments, and by the powerful ethos inherent in the ritual and substance of the royal pardon. The evolution of the substantive criminal law cannot be understood apart from social processes; yet the relationship between the doctrine of the criminal law and other social processes was so complicated that we may never be able to sort out fully the strands of that relationship.

Third, the ideology of jury mitigation (the more modest law-finding tradition) was relatively stable even though the specific motives that underlay mitigation were ever-changing. The community's attitudes toward criminal offenders were in part a product of transient notions regarding appropriate behavior, but they were also a product of more enduring relationships between individuals and society. Those attitudes were, moreover, in part a product of the very fact of jury participation. Institutional realities created or reinforced social norms and expectations. Man was not simply to be judged but, apparently, to be judged by his fellowmen. He might be the subject of divine mercy, but divine mercy was to be granted not only through God's vicar, the king, but also through all of God's subjects, the community as represented by the jury. Secular and religious authorities might help define the concept of mercy in cases in which juries participated, but so, too, did both episodic movements and longstanding traditions within the community at large. Verdicts that were at one level routine, even cynical, repudiations of the capital law and that registered instead approval of a harsh, lesser sanction were conceptualized (or at least rationalized) by participants and by both lay and learned observers in terms of the prevailing understanding of merciful verdicts according to conscience.

Fourth, the more radical tradition of the jury as judges of law as well as fact underwent important changes between the time of Lilburne's first trial and passage of Fox's Libel Act. It was a tradition born of, and influenced by, English constitutional and political conflict. The criminal trial jury came to represent the community in the face of (allegedly) tyrannical or otherwise illegitimate authority, and as concepts of political legitimacy changed, so too did the radical conception of the jury's law-finding role: from the true and sole judges to monitors of a legitimate but potentially abusive bench. Appeals to history played an especially important role in this tradition: the Levellers invoked an equalitarian Anglo-Saxon past; Hawles drew upon the "persecutions" of Lilburne and Penn; many Hanoverian critics of seditious libel doctrine took their stand upon the nullifying juries of the Restoration. The relationship between the radical tradition and the jury's role as mitigator in more routine cases was complex. We are still far from understanding the influence of jury-based mitigation on Leveller thought. Vaughan's defense of uncoerced fact-finding was open to misappropriation by political dissidents who probably cared little about the fate of common-run thieves. Even among those who shared eighteenth-century reformers' opposition to what appeared to be an ad hoc system of justice, the daily role of the jury in helping to resolve routine cases could be turned to advantage. As the two traditions drew closer together, at least in some corners of contemporary political rhetoric, the more radical view was restated in terms that invoked the purposes and values implicit in the more commonplace and officially assimilated view—making control of the latter all the more significant to all concerned.

Fifth, the struggle to define the terms on which mercy was to be granted, or to define the limits of appropriate jury behavior in common-run cases, was integral to the entire administration of the criminal law. Authorities might manipulate some stages of that administration with what seems like almost a free hand. If we focus on the shaping of indictments by officials, on their handling of royal pardons or mitigatory legislation, on the judge's role when passing sentence, or on the words and demeanor of royal officials at executions, we are likely to stress the degree to which the criminal law—and especially selective enforcement of that law—was an instrument of royal power. If we focus on the jury, the matter is more ambiguous. Although juries might be packed, harangued, threatened, and even, before 1670, coerced, there were always practical limits to the control authorities might exert. Moreover, acquiescence in jury intervention in some kinds of cases weakened attempts to control them in others. In the institution of the jury, one sees most clearly the dialectical aspect of the administration of the criminal law. Official attitudes, not only as they expressed themselves in judge-jury relations, but also as they were revealed in legislation, in judicial development of the law, and in the entire field of royal administration of both mercy and unforgivingness, reflected an assimilation of community attitudes. This fact does not vitiate the power of the concepts of class conflict and domination. It does suggest an approach—by no means a novel one—to the application of those concepts, one that might help us to understand a particular complex of forces at work in the English past. At least with respect to the use of the criminal trial jury, the phenomenon of domination might best be understood in terms of the widespread, community-based attitudes that officialdom assimilated, in part reshaped, and then imposed as though they were largely of its own creation.

Sixth, the English system of criminal administration that I have described involved substantial costs, only some of which were recognized by contemporaries. It involved a form of jury behavior that distorted and perhaps delayed development of the criminal law. By providing an opportunity for jurors to select from among those whom the law had doomed those whom the community would save, and those whom it would not, it gave vent to, and legitimated, not only merciful attitudes but also (we can be certain) the meanest sort of prejudices. As a result of the system, some judicial attempts to prevent juries from exercising mercy in common-run felonies were perhaps wrongly thought to reflect a taste for the gallows rather than principled opposition to jury law-finding and the belief that all mitigation ought to be left to Crown and bench. Though the problem of uncertainty of the law was ultimately recognized (and then perhaps even exaggerated by contemporaries), for long the perceived advantages of the approach to penology that the system accidentally produced delayed legal reform. Indeed, it delayed reform until jury trial had come to be viewed (in some quarters) as an open farce, risking the result that all jury discretion might come to be viewed as unlawful or unwise.

Finally, the roots of mitigation are embedded not only in religious norms, intracommunity relationships, legal mandates, and political realities; they are embedded also in the particular and enduring human response, in given cases, to excuse persons who have acted as those who sit in judgment of them might have acted, or with respect to whom (though the reason may not be clear) anger has subsided. The truly evil who deserve to die do so because—as it seems to jurors and other judges—the wrongs they have done are "unforgivable," which is to say, beyond earthly redemption. However, the perception of what is unforgivable is colored by personal and status relationships to the accused and the degree to which those who judge him are able to get beneath his skin, or, if they stand back, how much they come to understand his apparently criminal act as the product of forces over which he had little, if any, control.

It is difficult to trace the impact that notions of constraints on human behavior had on both official and lay participation in the administration of the criminal law. By the late eighteenth century, however, the trial had evolved to a large degree into a sentencing process in which the element of social determinism undoubtedly played a significant, if sub rosa, role. At the same time, determination of guilt or innocence had become so confused with the issue of the appropriate sentence that the entire proceeding was subjected to scorching criticism. The reform of the law of sanctions in the nineteenth century lessened the pressure on juries to find a basis for partial or entire exculpation in evidence suggesting that the defendant's behavior was to a significant degree beyond his control. Thus, the reforms, undertaken in order to produce certainty and, thereby, to deter criminal behavior, had the additional virtue of safeguarding the notion (ought one say: fiction?) that wrongdoers typically act with sufficient free will as to justify their conviction. As I plan to demonstrate in future studies on the jury, the concept of will, and the criminal law, one of the most significant characteristics of modern Anglo-American jurisprudence has been its tendency to separate the two determinations that the centuries-long evolution of English criminal administration had forced together. First the post-1850 jury would determine whether the defendant was guilty, in the sense of having "voluntarily" committed an unlawful act; then the defendant would be sentenced, often (by virtue of later reforms) in the light of a presentencing report in which he appeared as the plaything of social forces. This institutional solution to the ambivalence about the nature of human behavior that has increasingly afflicted modern culture has, for better or worse, served the purposes not only of those who rule us but of all of us as we rule each other and ourselves.

# Index of Persons and Places

# Index of Subjects